Handbook of bereavement

Handbook of bereavement

Theory, research, and intervention

Edited by
MARGARET S. STROEBE
University of Utrecht
WOLFGANG STROEBE
University of Utrecht
ROBERT O. HANSSON
University of Tulsa

CAMBRIDGE
UNIVERSITY PRESS

PUBLISHED BY THE PRESS SYNDICATE OF THE UNIVERSITY OF CAMBRIDGE
The Pitt Building, Trumpington Street, Cambridge, United Kingdom

CAMBRIDGE UNIVERSITY PRESS
The Edinburgh Building, Cambridge CB2 2RU, UK   http://www.cup.cam.ac.uk
40 West 20th Street, New York, NY 10011-4211, USA   http://www.cup.org
10 Stamford Road, Oakleigh, Melbourne 3166, Australia

First published 1993
Reprinted 1994, 1995, 1997, 1999

Printed in the United States of America

Typeset in Baskerville

A catalogue record for this book is available from the British Library

Library of Congress Cataloguing-in-Publication Data is available

ISBN 0-521-39315-9 hardback
ISBN 0-521-44853-0 paperback

Contents

Contributors

James R. Averill
Department of Psychology
University of Massachusetts
Amherst, Massachusetts

Maria L. Boccia
Department of Psychiatry
University of Colorado Health Sciences
    Center
Denver, Colorado

Bruce N. Carpenter
Department of Psychology
University of Tulsa
Tulsa, Oklahoma

Michael S. Caserta
Gerontology Center
University of Utah
Salt Lake City, Utah

Paul T. Costa, Jr.
National Institute on Aging
Baltimore, Maryland

Laura Dean
School of Public Health
Columbia University
New York, New York

Margaret F. Dimond
College of Nursing
University of Washington
Seattle, Washington

Seymour Epstein
Department of Psychology
University of Massachusetts
Amherst, Massachusetts

Sharon K. Fairchild
Department of Psychology
University of Tulsa
Tulsa, Oklahoma

Norman Farberow
Los Angeles Suicide Prevention Center
University of Southern California
Los Angeles, California

Andrew Futterman
Holy Cross College
Worcester, Massachusetts

Dolores Gallagher-Thompson
School of Medicine
Stanford University
Palo Alto, California

Marlene Galusha
Department of Psychology
University of Tulsa
Tulsa, Oklahoma

Robert O. Hansson
Department of Psychology
University of Tulsa
Tulsa, Oklahoma

Michael Irwin
School of Medicine
University of California
San Diego, California

Selby Jacobs
Department of Psychiatry
Yale University School of Medicine
New Haven, Connecticut

Hanna Kaminer
Faculty of Medicine
Israel Institute of Technology
Haifa, Israel

Ronald C. Kessler
Department of Sociology
University of Michigan
Ann Arbor, Michigan

Kathleen Kim
Department of Psychiatry
Yale University School of Medicine
New Haven, Connecticut

Mark L. Laudenslager
University of Colorado Health Sciences
    Center
Department of Psychiatry
Denver, Colorado

Peretz Lavie
Faculty of Medicine
Israel Institute of Technology
Haifa, Israel

Morton A. Lieberman
Department of Psychiatry
University of California
San Francisco, California

Helena Znaniecka Lopata
Department of Sociology and
    Anthropology
Loyola University
Chicago, Illinois

Dale A. Lund
Gerontology Center
University of Utah
Salt Lake City, Utah

John L. Martin (deceased)

Nada Martinek
Department of Psychiatry
University of Queensland
Brisbane, Australia

Robert R. McCrae
National Institute on Aging
Baltimore, Maryland

Warwick Middleton
Department of Psychiatry
University of Queensland
Brisbane, Australia

Vivienne Misso
Department of Psychiatry
University of Queensland
Brisbane, Australia

Elma P. Nunley
ACCT Counseling Center
Odessa, Texas

Colin Murray Parkes
The London Hospital Medical College
University of London
London, England

James Peterson
Professor Emeritus
University of Southern California
Los Angeles, California

Jennifer Pike
California School of Professional
    Psychology
San Diego, California

Beverley Raphael
Department of Psychiatry
University of Queensland
Brisbane, Australia

Martin L. Reite
Department of Psychiatry
University of Colorado Health Sciences
    Center
Denver, Colorado

Jacqueline H. Remondet
Department of Psychology
University of Tulsa
Tulsa, Oklahoma

Paul C. Rosenblatt
Family Social Science
University of Minnesota
St. Paul, Minnesota

Simon Shimshon Rubin
Department of Psychology
University of Haifa
Haifa, Israel

Catherine M. Sanders
Private Practice in Clinical Psychology
Charlotte, North Carolina

Stephen R. Shuchter
Outpatient Psychiatric Services
University of California
San Diego, California

Roxane Cohen Silver
Program in Social Ecology
University of California
Irvine, California

Phyllis R. Silverman
Department of Psychiatry
Massachusetts General Hospital and
    Harvard Medical School
Boston, Massachusetts

Margaret S. Stroebe
Department of Psychology
University of Utrecht
Utrecht, The Netherlands

Wolfgang Stroebe
Department of Psychology
University of Utrecht
Utrecht, The Netherlands

Stanley K. Stylianos
Central Toronto Youth Services
Toronto, Canada

Larry W. Thompson
School of Medicine
Stanford University
Palo Alto, California

Mary L. S. Vachon
Clarke Institute of Psychiatry
Toronto, Canada

Robert S. Weiss
Work and Family Research Unit
University of Massachusetts
Boston, Massachusetts

J. William Worden
Department of Psychiatry
Massachusetts General Hospital and
    Harvard Medical School
Boston, Massachusetts

Camille B. Wortman
Department of Psychology
State University of New York
Stony Brook, New York

Sidney Zisook
Outpatient Psychiatric Services
University of California
San Diego, California

Preface

Until fairly recently, researchers interested in the topic of bereavement tended to be scattered throughout the world, having little contact with one another and not much knowledge of each other's work. This was to some extent true of the editors of the current volume, until a conference meeting in the early 1980s led to the discussion of joint interests and the beginning of a collaboration that has continued without pause ever since. The main objective of our collaboration has been to work toward a synthesis of scientific evidence on the impact of bereavement. Out of this interest came a special issue of the *Journal of Social Issues*, "Bereavement and Widowhood," in 1988, to which an international, interdisciplinary group of bereavement researchers contributed.

Due to the constraints of a journal, the scope of the issue had to be limited. Thus, it seemed a natural extension of this work to produce a more comprehensive volume that would provide readers with an up-to-date account of knowledge about bereavement's impact and effects and the possibilities for social or policy intervention and treatment: The *Handbook of Bereavement* is the result of this endeavor. Well over half of the chapters were newly commissioned. Leading researchers from many different disciplines and many countries, including Australia, Canada, Israel, the United Kingdom, and the United States, were invited to contribute. It was very gratifying that, as for the journal issue, the response was overwhelmingly positive, such that all of the chapters are by "first-choice" authors. Of the original collection of papers, practically all have been substantially revised, extended, and updated.

In compiling such a volume, we owe thanks to many people, but we are particularly indebted to the authors. We have received unprecedented cooperation from each of them on this project. Some produced their chapters under difficult circumstances; all responded positively to our demanding editorial requests. It has been a delight to work with them, and we are grateful for all we have learned from them. A significant part of the enjoyment in compiling this volume has been the exchange of ideas through correspondence with the authors and the establishment of contact with them, which we hope will continue.

There would have been no *Handbook* without the early support and encouragement of George Levinger and the editorial board and advisers of the *Journal of Social Issues*, who gave such enthusiastic approval to our original proposal for a special issue and provided insightful feedback throughout its production. We are greatly indebted to him and to his successor as editor, Stuart Oskamp. We also thank the Society for the Psychological Study of Social Issues (SPSSI), publisher of the *Journal of Social Issues*, which gave permission for publication of the *Handbook* with Cambridge University Press. As editors, we are happy to support the goals of the society by producing this volume for them.

Each of the editors also has colleagues, friends, and family members to whom he or she alone is indebted. For the Stroebes, this is above all our daughter Katherine, to whom – for our part – we dedicate this book. Life is hard for children when both parents are involved in an all-engrossing project. Katherine showed great maturity in dealing with us and in understanding our reasons for editing this book. We are deeply grateful to her. Robert Hansson dedicates his efforts on this volume to the memory of his parents, Olafur and Ruby Hansson, and thanks Kathleen and Julie Hansson for their support and encouragement during the project.

After this volume went to press, we learned of the death of our author Dr. John Martin on January 17th, 1992. We are deeply saddened by this news, and wish to extend our dedication in remembrance of him.

PART I

Introduction

1

Bereavement research and theory: An introduction to the *Handbook*

MARGARET S. STROEBE,
WOLFGANG STROEBE, AND
ROBERT O. HANSSON

The loss of a loved one is a tragedy unequalled by any other for most bereaved people. It is an experience that occurs some time or other in nearly everyone's life, and many suffer losses long before they reach old age, when such events occur with increasing frequency. According to statistics for the year 1985, more than 2 million people can be expected to die in a single year in the United States alone. Of these, more than 16,000 are children between the ages of 1 and 14, and as many as 38,000 are young people between the ages of 15 and 24 (U.S. Department of Health & Human Services, 1985). Such statistics also show alarming infant mortality rates, more than 40,000 babies dying before they reach the age of 1 year. For each of these deaths, bereaved persons are left behind – parents, spouses, children, siblings, and friends – all of whom are at high risk of detrimental effects on their mental and physical health.

If one looks beyond such statistics to consider world events, concern for the bereaved becomes hugely magnified. Natural disasters and human conflicts have devastated families in many nations during recent years. Frequently under such circumstances, grief over the death of a loved one is compounded by related tragedies, as when one person alone survives the loss of an entire family, when personal injury adds to suffering, when the violent or brutal death of a loved one has been witnessed, or when homes and livelihoods are also lost through the circumstances of war or other disaster. Survivors of such terrible losses are particularly vulnerable to long-term adverse effects and are in special need of care and support.

Because of the intensity of the loss experience, the large number of people it affects, and the systematic variations with which its consequences are distributed across populations, bereavement has far-reaching implications. It is a concern that extends beyond the boundaries of clinical interest, the domain from which much of the early research drew its impetus. It affects at some point every family and raises logistic and policy issues for the health and social service agencies of every community.

In our view, bereavement is an issue that needs to be understood from a

3

sound base of theoretically oriented and empirically derived knowledge and not purely on subjective, descriptive accounts. Parkes, in chapter 6 of this volume, expresses the necessity for such a frame of reference most succinctly:

It is not enough for us to stay close and to open our hearts to another person's suffering; valuable though this sympathy may sometimes be, we must have some way of stepping aside from the maze of emotion and sensation if we are to make sense of it.

Thus, one of our major objectives in compiling the *Handbook of Bereavement* has been to provide an up-to-date review of scientific knowledge about bereavement: to assess the state of understanding of the grief process, to review and evaluate theories that provide explanations for its phenomena, to detail its effects and outcomes, and to examine the efficacy of various types of intervention.

Researchers in a variety of disciplines – anthropology, epidemiology, sociology, psychology, medicine – have contributed to this endeavor, as the multidisciplinary contributions illustrate. For example, with regard to health consequences, public health and epidemiological studies have identified illness and mortality consequences and predictors of differential outcome of bereavement. Clinicians and therapists have learned a great deal about the phenomenology of grief, predictors of abnormal grieving and poor outcome, and the effectiveness of intervention programs. Physiological theory and research have concentrated on the identification of mechanisms by which loss may affect the immune system, lead to changes in the endocrine, autonomic nervous, and cardiovascular systems, and account for increased vulnerability to external agents.

As for social and economic consequences, such as social status changes, network alterations, or financial implications, psychological theories and research have considered issues of coping with loss, the potentially adaptive functions of grief for the social group, the parallels and differences between different types of loss (e.g., parent vs. spouse, widowhood vs. divorce), and the problematic processes of support and care giving. Sociologists have explored the impact of widowhood on access to social roles, construction of new identities, and a host of further issues. Gerontology has contributed to the area through its study of coping with life events in old age (e.g., identifying changing needs and coping resources in old age, and acknowledging age-related interactions among health, independence, and adjustment).

In our view, the study of bereavement will progress from a synthesis of this wide variety of disciplines, and our aim has been to take a step in this direction. In the words of the late Henri Tajfel:

All of us in our various disciplines . . . are dealing with a common knot of problems seen from different perspectives, and it would be futile to claim a monopoly of some kind of a "basic truth" or conceptual priority for any one of these perspectives. (1981, p. 224)

Elsewhere (M. Stroebe, Stroebe, & Hansson, 1988), we have traced the historical development of theory, empirical research, and methodology in the field. The study of bereavement is, as we noted, a comparatively young discipline, and early research was often issue-generated rather than theory-generated. We identified historical changes in the kinds of research questions that have been topical in bereavement research and gave an overview of the major empirical findings and the conceptual developments that followed over the years.

In the present introduction we provide a brief overview of the scope of current, multidisciplinary research in the bereavement area as represented by the diverse chapters in this volume. We outline individual contributions, highlighting their main arguments and results. First, though, it will be useful to distinguish among three terms, as has now become fairly common practice in the field: *Bereavement* is the objective situation of having lost someone significant; *grief* is the emotional response to one's loss; and *mourning* denotes the actions and manner of expressing grief, which often reflect the mourning practices of one's culture.

The phenomenology and measurement of grief

What is grief? What are its symptoms, and what course does it normally run over time? How does one measure an emotional reaction to loss? How can one distinguish normal or uncomplicated grief from abnormal or pathological grief? These are questions that are central to the three chapters in part II. These chapters represent a development from the clinical descriptions of the phenomenology of grief that dominated earlier research to systematic attempts to describe patterns of common symptoms and address complex issues concerning the time phases of grief, its nature, and intensity.

Writing on the course of normal grief (chapter 2), Shuchter and Zisook draw on years of research collaboration. They discuss questions concerning patterns of symptomatology, the controversial issue of "stages" of grief and recovery, and the broad range of changes in cognitive and behavioral processes, as well as such aspects as interpersonal relationships during the course of grief. Central to their conception is the view that grief is a highly individualized process, that there are many and varied ways people grieve, that even one individual's grief varies from moment to moment. Too frequently in the past, accounts of grief have been overly simplistic. To describe adequately the phenomenology and natural history of normal bereavement, Shuchter and Zisook argue the need for a multidimensional approach, one that incorporates overlapping dimensions, including affective states, coping strategies, and the continued relationship with the deceased.

Like Shuchter and Zisook, in chapter 3 Middleton, Raphael, Martinek, and Misso endorse the need for a multidimensional framework for conceptualizing pathological forms of bereavement. At a time when, as these authors note, we are still struggling to validate and operationalize the construct of normal grief, conceptualizing pathological grief appears even more problematic. How do we define "pathological," "abnormal," "chronic," "unresolved," "absent," or "complicated" grief? Can we distinguish clearly between "normal" and "abnormal" grieving, or between problematic grief and such other clinical disorders as depression, anxiety disorders, or post-traumatic stress disorders? What do we know of the impact of cultural norms on pathological grief reactions?

Middleton and his colleagues grapple with the issues of validation and operationatization of the construct pathological grief, examining the most influential theoretical formulations (psychoanalytic and attachment theories) to have addressed pathological grief. Consideration is also given to a very neglected issue, namely, the relationship between pathological grief and personality disorders. An important distinction emerges from their discussion: If it is the case that bereavement accentuates preexisting pathology rather than that pathology is specific to grief, then, as they argue, "In many instances it may be more valid to view grief as a risk factor for such disorders than to view such disorders as manifestations of pathological grief."

Although Middleton et al. argue the case for more extensive use of clinical diagnosis as opposed to rating scales (e.g., to diagnose personality disorders in bereaved persons), much reliance is placed on psychometric measurement of bereavement phenomena. In view of the rapid growth in the number of instruments designed to assess various aspects of individuals' responses to bereavement, it is surprising that no comprehensive review and discussion of measurement issues has yet appeared in the literature. In chapter 4, Hansson, Carpenter, and Fairchild not only review psychometric instruments designed to measure the nature and intensity of the grief experience but also those assessing broader coping and health variables. Key issues of validity and reliability are discussed.

Current theories of grief, mourning, and bereavement

One might ask why we need theories on the phenomenon of grief, when to feel sad and depressed on losing a loved person seems so self-evident.

However, as the chapters in part II amply show, grief is not only a very complex syndrome but also one with diverse consequences. How, for example, can one understand the constant interplay among feelings of disbelief, hope, and despair that trouble the bereaved, or the alternation between affective responses of numbness, despair, and anger? Why do the bereaved search for the lost one, feel convinced of his or her presence, when they know that he or she is no longer living? Why do some bereaved persons cope with loss relatively well and others remain devastated for years?

Theoretical formulations should not only help us to understand certain counterintuitive reactions and complex symptomatology. They should also provide explanations of individual differences in mental and physical health outcomes. Most importantly, they should allow one to develop strategies of care and therapy to ameliorate distress and help toward the prevention of pathology. To date, there is no theory that fulfills all of these expectations. In fact, empirical research on bereavement typically has not been guided by an integrative theory base. In our view, it is essential for research to be theory-guided, and wherever possible theoretical underpinnings are stressed, not just in part III but throughout the chapters in this volume.

Although there is no broadly applicable, integrative theory of bereavement, two different general types of theory, which have grown out of different traditions and interests of researchers (W. Stroebe & Stroebe, 1987), can be identified from the literature. The earlier of these theoretical contributions emerged from the psychoanalytic tradition, the most influential being those of Freud (1917a), Lindemann (1944), and, more recently, Bowlby (e.g., 1980/1981). Such theories, which can be classified as depression models of grief (W. Stroebe & Stroebe, 1987), analyze grief as an emotional reaction and help greatly in understanding emotional symptomatology in response to loss. Complementary to these are stress theories (cf. Lazarus & Folkman, 1984). Applied specifically to bereavement (W. Stroebe & Stroebe, 1987), stress models of grief consider bereavement a stressful life event and offer an explanation for the physical health consequences of bereavement, which is not a focal concern of the depression models. One of the major proponents of this line of theorizing in recent years has been Horowitz (e.g., 1976/1986).

Rather than detailing such well-known, classic contributions (descriptions can be found in W. Stroebe & Stroebe, 1987; they are discussed briefly in Middleton et al.'s chapter 3, on pathological grief, and in M. Stroebe & Stroebe's review of the mortality of bereavement, chapter 12), in the third part of this volume we focus on contemporary theoretical perspectives from diverse disciplines, all of which contribute to the understanding of bereavement. It will become evident that these analyses provide very different insights into the grief process, not necessarily because they conflict but because of the level of analysis and perspective from which they examine bereavement.

Thus, Averill and Nunley (chapter 5) apply a social-constructionist approach to the emotion of grief, exploring two alternative conceptions of grief: as an emotion and as a disease. They relate the syndrome of grief to broader social systems, particularly to the health care system. They explore the implications of the continuing tendency to incorporate grief into the health care system, where the primary goal is to alleviate suffering. The isolation of grief as a problem to be treated under the medical model could diminish the role of other social systems as a source of meaning and support for the bereaved. It becomes evident from Averill and Nunley's analysis how culturally dependent our conceptualization of grief is: It is by no means universal or necessary to define it as an emotion.

By contrast, in chapter 6, Parkes outlines his concept of psychosocial transitions that he has developed over the years to explain adaptation to life changes such as bereavement. Parkes's model enables comparative analysis of different losses, his own empirical work having focused on loss of a spouse, loss of a limb, and loss of a home. It has far-reaching implications not only for the identification of high-risk persons but also for defining the role of others, including health professionals, in reducing risk. In an important extension of his original model, in this volume Parkes proposes how members of all the health care professions might become more directly involved as agents of change.

In a contribution that nicely complements the cognitively oriented paper by Parkes, Rosenblatt (chapter 7) argues that to understand grief, we must know how it is affected by the social context in which it occurs (e.g., family, personal relationships, culture, and ethnicity). Family systems theory and symbolic interactionism provide a conceptual backdrop against which to view the dynamics and implications of the social context. A central theme in Rosenblatt's work involves the potential consequences on a diverse population (like that in the United States) when communities and formal support systems fail to be sensitive to ethnic differences in grief and mourning customs and rituals. Such misunderstanding can result, for example, in intolerance and reduced access to, or diminished benefit from, formal support and health care systems among minority populations. Rosenblatt also highlights and illustrates cross-cultural differences in grief reactions, a theme for which his work is well known (e.g., Rosenblatt, Walsh, & Jackson, 1976).

The final chapter in part III (chapter 8) is by a newcomer to the field. We invited Seymour Epstein, a major figure in personality psychology, to apply his own theoretical approach, Cognitive-experiential self-theory (CEST), to the area of bereavement. CEST is a general theory of personality according to which people construct implicit theories of reality that reside within an experiential conceptual system that operates by principles different from those operating within their rational conceptual system. Implicit theories of reality strive to fulfill four basic functions. These functions, and the implicit belief dimensions associated with them, both influence and are influenced by bereavement. In contrast to psychoanalysis, CEST considers sensitivities and compulsions, not unconscious conflict, as the main source of maladaptive reactions. The construct of constructive thinking, a broad coping variable with specific components, is associated with the efficacy of a person's implicit theory of reality and can account for some anomalous findings on coping with bereavement.

Physiological changes following bereavement

Bereavement does not operate on one's bodily system in the same way as some alien bacteria do. Nevertheless, it is associated with a variety of mental and physical health consequences. What, then, are the biological links between grief and increased risk of morbidity and mortality among the bereaved? How can bereavement, which, after all, is an event external to the organism, affect bodily systems to cause ill health and even death? Clearly, if we can answer these questions, we go a long way toward finding intervention strategies to affect the biological system, modulate the risk of illness, and provide relief for those who suffer most.

The last decade has seen a number of breakthroughs in our understanding of physiological changes following bereavement. Physiological theory and research have concentrated on the identification of mechanisms by which loss may affect the immune system, lead to changes in the endocrine, autonomic nervous, and cardiovascular systems, and account for increased vulnerability to external agents. Only very recently, for example, have specific physiological changes been identified in the immune system following separations.

The contributors of the three chapters in part IV have been foremost among researchers in this area. All review their program of research, giving detailed accounts of the physiological mechanisms and biological systems, including discussions of the relevance of immune measures to changes in health, to enable those unfamiliar with such work to understand their results.

In chapter 9, Laudenslager, Boccia, and Reite review studies of the biological correlates of loss in nonhuman primates. A main objective is to present some of the recent observations from their own research group concerning social support models and the potential role of temperament in determining response to maternal loss in nonhuman primates. They present striking evidence from their animal studies that maternal separation influences immune regulation and that such early experience may have consequences observable in adult life. They identify certain intrinsic and extrinsic variables predicting immunologic outcome following the stress experience. Their research represents a major development toward the establishment of a relationship between markers of immune status and disease risk, the identification of high-risk individuals, and the long-term impact of early experience on health in the adult.

Chapter 10, by Kim and Jacobs, covers research on neuroendocrine changes following bereavement, the emphasis here being on psychiatric morbidity. The authors include detailed consideration of the results of neuroendocrine findings in depression and anxiety disorders, both of which have been found to complicate bereavement. As they note, neuroendocrine abnormalities in these disorders provide suggestions for associations between neuroendocrine changes and complicated bereavement. Finally, they suggest a paradigm of abnormal adrenocortical activity applicable to bereavement, which goes some way toward understanding the interaction between the neuroendocrine system and bereavement stress. It is important to note that Kim and Jacobs's identification of depression and anxiety disorders as precursors of complicated bereavement suggests a predisposing risk factor for poor mental outcome: A propensity to clinical depression and/or anxiety disorders may lead to complicated bereavement rather than the usually assumed causal sequence that bereavement leads to clinical depression and anxiety disorders.

In the final chapter in this part, Irwin and Pike (chapter 11) give an overview of research that demonstrates the relationship between bereavement and changes in immune parameters, particularly natural killer cell activity. They present their own empirical data documenting how depressive symptoms might relate to these immunologic changes in bereavement. They limit the breadth of their review to loss in humans, thus complementing chapter 9, by Laudenslager, Boccia, and Reite, on nonhuman primates. Their work suggests that individual psychological responses such as depressive symptomatology may mediate changes in physiological systems and affect immune function.

The psychological, social, and health impacts of conjugal bereavement

For a number of reasons, the stressful and disruptive nature of bereavement has most frequently been documented for widow(er)hood, the topic to which the whole of part V is devoted (although it should be noted that comparisons are frequently drawn with other types of loss). Conjugal bereavement is one of the most widely experienced stressful life events. More than 50% of all women 65 years and over and 12% of all men that age have become widowed (U.S. Bureau of the Census, 1984). Furthermore, the conjugal grief reaction can be particularly devastating because, as the chapters in part V underscore, the bereaved are often required to deal with the simultaneous disruption of their financial security, social status, and primary support networks. Not surprisingly, as the reports clearly document, marital bereavement is associated with deterioration in mental and physical health and with an excess in mortality from natural as well as violent causes.

In this part, we provide an overview of the multiple reactions and consequences of conjugal bereavement. We have tried to strike a balance among review articles (Sanders; M. Stroebe & Stroebe), large-scale statistical studies (McCrae & Costa), and small to moderate-sized comparative studies of longitudinal design (Gallagher-Thompson, Futterman, Farberow, Thompson, & Peterson; Lund, Caserta, & Dimond; W. Stroebe & Stroebe). The general goals of all the research reviewed here, despite a diversity in disciplinary backgrounds, have been to examine the process of adaptation and adjustment to the loss of a spouse, to examine risk factors (i.e., predictors that are associated with good or bad outcome), and to identify, where possible, potential strategies of intervention.

Although many of the authors are clinicians and draw heavily on personal, professional experience, it will become evident that no chapter comprises purely clinical descriptions of the grief experience. This reflects a major editorial bias: In our view, such subjective accounts are subject to the critical shortcoming that they are open to whatever interpretation the author wishes to make. Throughout the chapters included here, close attention has been paid to rigorous design and methodology. Paramount among these concerns are issues of representativeness of the samples (have we, for example, omitted from an empirical investigation those who are most distressed or physically affected by bereavement?), the need for non-bereaved control groups to identify main effects rather than interactions (for example, if widows are more distressed than widowers, this could reflect the excess in depression rates of females in general, as compared with males), and the validity and reliability of the measures used to assess grief reactions in all their complexity. (For a detailed consideration of methodological issues in bereavement research, see W. Stroebe & Stroebe, 1987.)

Part V begins with M. Stroebe and Stroebe's review of the impact of bereavement with the most dire of consequences: the death of the bereaved spouse. Examination of studies subsequent to a review a decade ago (M. Stroebe, Stroebe, Gergen, & Gergen, 1981) revealed fascinating new clues to the puzzle of why some bereaved themselves die. In the light of this evidence Stroebe and Stroebe were able to examine theoretical explanations of this "loss effect" that was not previously possible. It is surprising that no connection has ever been made between depression models of loss and the mortality of the bereaved. One possible reason may be because, as noted earlier, depression models have largely been used in explanations of emotional reactions, whereas the physical health consequences have been the province of stress models. In chapter 12 the explanatory power of both types of model is considered. It should be noted that these models can also be applied in explanation of the lesser mental and physical health consequences, as described in subsequent chapters in this section.

The following two chapters, by McCrae and Costa (chapter 13) and W. Stroebe and Stroebe (chapter 14), contrast greatly, not only in design but also in their results. McCrae and Costa draw on data from the follow-up investigation of a large-scale survey to examine some long-term consequences of widowhood. These authors argue provocatively for long-term "resilience" of widowed persons. They hold that after the period of intense grief is over comes a return to a "baseline" level of well-being, comparable with that of nonbereaved individuals. The data reported by W. Stroebe and Stroebe qualify the conclusions about psychological resilience. The results from their longitudinal study of widows and widowers also indicate that the majority of bereaved recover over a 2-year period. However, high-risk subgroups of individuals were identified who do not seem to adjust well to bereavement.

W. Stroebe and Stroebe's study shares a number of design features with the following two contributions, by Gallagher-Thompson, Futterman, Farberow, Thompson, and Peterson (chapter 15) and by Lund, Caserta, and Dimond (chapter 16), that distinguish them from much preceding research. All have prospective, longitudinal designs, beginning investigation soon after bereavement and following up over subsequent months and years. All include nonbereaved control subjects, carefully matched with the bereaved on sociodemographic variables. All address complex issues of sample bias, for example, selection into the studies and dropout over the duration of investigation.

Unlike the W. Stroebe and Stroebe study, though, the work by Gallagher-Thompson and colleagues and by Lund and colleagues specifically focus on older widowed persons. Both projects were designed in response to the concern of the National Institute on Aging to acquire systematic, empirically based knowledge about bereavement in older populations. Each project sets unique questions, examines different subgroups, and uses diverse measures. In combination, these empirical papers provide a sense of the representativeness of research results and of the multiple dimensions that bereavement reactions entail.

The identification of risk factors for poor bereavement outcome has been an important focus of recent research and has implications for both the prevention of and recovery from intense grief. Sanders, in chapter 17, provides a comprehensive and critical review of this literature, distinguishing among four general risk categories: biographical/demographic factors, individual factors, mode of death, and circumstances following the loss. She includes, where data are available, studies on types of loss other than conjugal bereavement. She also notes important methodological shortcomings in this research.

Grief reactions to different types of loss

It is generally accepted by lay people and professionals alike that certain bereavements are apt to be associated with more overwhelming reactions and severe adjustment problems than others. The loss of a young child, for example, is assumed by both researchers and clinicians to be particularly hard to bear. Key questions concern patterns of similarity and differences in grief reactions to various types of loss, the identification of variables that cause differential reactions, and the establishment of areas of particular difficulty in grief reactions to specific losses.

In part VI, we extend consideration of the bereavement experience to losses other than conjugal loss, selecting ones for which the survivors are particularly vulnerable to poor outcome. The part begins with a theoretical chapter by Weiss. In chapter 18, Weiss extends Bowlby's attachment theory to adult grief, arguing that loss should result in grief only for relationships that are in major respects identical to the attachment relationships that bond children to their parents. He develops the provocative thesis that there are only four relational bonds that have the characteristics of such relationships in adults. He then explores reactions to different types of loss and recovery from loss from this theoretical viewpoint. A particularly interesting new theme in this chapter focuses on the interplay of cognitive and emotional reactions (as people adapt but never really recover). These observations, in addition to fleshing out our notions regarding the nature of recovery, also address the product of recovery and the potential for immense individual diversity.

The title statement of Rubin's contribution (chapter 19), "The Death of a Child Is Forever," poignantly underlines the conclusion that the author reached from his extensive study of reactions of parents who have suffered the loss of a child, ranging from very young babies who died from sudden infant death syndrome to adult sons lost in the wars of Israel. As Rubin found, parents of deceased children maintain very close ties with their child – even after 13 years of bereavement – remaining preoccupied with their child and highly invested in the lost relationship, often to the detriment of relationships with surviving members of the family. Rubin developed the Two-Track Model of Bereavement to further understanding of the phenomena he observed, one that gives central place to the parent–child relationship and to biopsychosocial functioning during the stress of bereavement. Within this framework, he explores the "multiple meanings" that children hold for their parents.

It becomes clear that research on bereavement has in the past too narrowly focused on symptomatology and psychopathology, that much can be learned from exploring these broader dimensions of bereavement. Although for the most part the bereaved parents functioned well, their loss remained dominant and preoccupation strong in their lives. Thus, like many authors in earlier chapters, Rubin argues for a multidimensional approach to bereavement.

The death of a young parent, at a time when children are not yet raised and when family members are closely involved with one another, is a tragedy that evokes much sympathy and concern. Debate continues in the literature whether early parental loss leads to later problems, ranging from depression to antisocial personality disorders (cf. W. Stroebe & Stroebe, 1987). Silverman and Worden (chapter 20) report on their new longitudinal study, the child bereavement study. Rather than studying adults who had lost a parent in childhood or studying children already referred for therapy, these investigators looked at how a random sample of children were coping with the recent death of a parent. Questions were asked not just of the parents but of the children themselves, so that these different views on the child's adjustment could be compared, thus providing a family perspective.

The study pinpointed a number of unique concerns in childhood loss. For example, children were sometimes very frightened that the deceased parent could be "watching them." Also, like Rubin, Silverman and Worden emphasize the importance of retaining a connection with the deceased parent, which, rather than reflecting the pathology that labeling it "preoccupation with the deceased" implies, was a comfort to the children. Their conclusions are more optimistic than those of much previous research: Children were not overwhelmed by their loss or beset with serious psychological problems. Thus, they argue, researchers should depart from the language of "sickness" in describing grief and turn to a model of grief as a normative life-cycle event.

Bereavement following a death from AIDS is among the most harrowing of grief experiences. Martin and Dean have worked with the urban, gay, male community of New York City, which has been so affected by the AIDS epidemic, collecting data for the Longitudinal AIDS Impact Project, an ongoing study at the Columbia University AIDS Research Unit. In chapter 21, they document the circumstances surrounding AIDS-related bereavement within this community and the effects that these losses may be expected to have on those who survive. Certain characteristics of the illness make this bereavement both similar and dissimilar to that caused by other illnesses. That bereavements are likely to be both multiple (many losses occurring for any one individual in brief time periods) and chronic (the experiences are unremitting over time), that the survivor may himself be at risk of AIDS, that the terminal illness is long-drawn-out and extremely harsh for both sufferers and caretakers to bear, that it can be deeply stigmatizing for both the sick person and those close to him, that those who suffer are relatively young – these and other features combine to complicate bereavement reactions. The picture that emerges is one of a strongly affected community of people, one that is deeply in need of bereavement support.

Like those bereaved from AIDS deaths, survivors of the Holocaust are likely to have had multiple bereavements. They, too, feared for their own lives under particularly traumatic circumstances. But, just as there are some parallels, so are there unique features to Holocaust survivors' experiences and to the issues that concern researchers in this area. Kaminer and Lavie, in chapter 22, describe the extreme conditions and circumstances of Holocaust survivors that still, almost 50 years on, have a deep impact on many aspects of their lives.

In order to study survivors' long-term adaptation and coping, Kaminer and Lavie focused on sleep and dreams, comparing difficulties and disturbances among well-adjusted versus less adjusted survivors. One of the most fascinating results of this study was that the higher the intrusion of Holocaust-related memories and complaints and distress in everyday life, the more disturbed was the sleep and the higher the dream recall. They argue that the massive repression of dream content in the well-adjusted is an adaptive mechanism. This sheds new light on the unresolved issue of treatment approaches to traumatized survivors: Assisting them to repress the terrors of the past may have a highly adaptive value.

Coping, counseling, and therapy

Bereavement researchers have become very aware in recent years of the variety of ways through which grieving persons cope with their grief, so much so that any one person may respond to different losses in very different ways and even have very different support requirements at different points in time. Reflecting this diversity, support techniques range from the casual to the highly structured. Most bereaved persons cope with their grief with the help of family, friends, and neighborhood supports. Some seek aid from mutual help organizations; others need the support of grief counseling, that is, facilitation with "uncomplicated, or normal, grief to a healthy completion of the tasks of grieving within a reasonable time frame" (Worden, 1982/1991, p. 35), and a small minority require grief therapy, "those specialized techniques . . . which are used to help people with abnormal or complicated reactions" (Worden, 1982/1991, p. 35). The papers in part VII cover two main interests: ways that people cope with loss and the effectiveness of the various types of support, counseling, and therapy.

In chapter 23, Wortman, Silver, and Kessler address how people cope. The major goal of their research, extending over many years and including the study of different types of loss, has been to clarify the processes whereby people come to terms with sudden, irrevocable changes in their lives and to understand mechanisms through which such events can affect subsequent health and functioning. In the researchers' view, their empirical results failed to confirm, and even contradicted, assumptions that would be derived from previous theories, as well as common understanding of how people cope with loss. Therefore, they developed an explanatory concept to understand these findings and for predicting poor outcome that focuses on people's worldviews, that is, their beliefs, assumptions, or expectations about self, others, and the world that provide meaning. Such assumptions may become shattered by a traumatic bereavement causing intense distress. Wortman and her colleagues elaborate this account in their chapter, relating it to their empirical results, including those from their ongoing large-scale, representative, prospective studies of bereaved samples.

Like Wortman and her colleagues, Hansson, Remondet, and Galusha also provide a cognitive analysis of bereavement phenomena (chapter 24). Hansson et al., however, concentrate their interest on problems specific to older bereaved persons. Also, unlike the vast majority of research programs, they extend investigation beyond the period of intense grief. How do elderly widowed people cope and adjust over subsequent years of widowhood? Such a question becomes increasingly important to answer in view of the fact that life expectancy has increased in recent decades, with widowed persons having much of their lives still before them. Hansson et al. provide an analysis within a life-span perspective, exploring the status and experience of widowhood after intensive grieving has passed. Their longer term perspective on one's "career of widowhood" examines the question of how old age and widowhood interact to affect personal control, coping, and well-being. An important implication of this work is that providing widows with a career orientation will facilitate their recovery and well-being. This career perspective incorporates bodies of research from two other fields, life-span developmental psychology and occupational–vocational psychology.

A more sociological perspective on adjustment to widowhood, but one that also studies adaptation after the period of heavy grief and mourning is over, is provided by Lopata (chapter 25). Lopata's extensive work, not only with urban American widows but with widowed women in different countries of the world as well, has studied the support systems, social roles, life-styles, and self-concepts of the widowed over various points in time. Lopata shows how widowhood changes one's support system, and she details the resources, including social support, that can be of help in reorganizing one's life. Of particular interest are the insights from her examination of cultural differences in the experience of widowhood. She demonstrates important ways in which our assumptions regarding social support systems appear culture-bound. These insights, especially the contrasts in less developed/industrialized societies, help explain the dilemma faced by elderly, urban American widows, whose very traditional social and psychological support needs may not be served by a society that has quickly changed around them.

Social support following the loss of a loved person has been suggested as one of the key factors buffering the bereaved from the detrimental effects of loss. Stylianos and Vachon's critical review of the literature on social support (chapter 26) is therefore timely. They identify those support efforts that appear to help and those that do not, considering both informal and formal interventions for the bereaved in light of their changing support needs over time. Important is their emphasis on the "goodness of fit" between the donor, the recipient, and the particular circumstances, clearly a determinant of how much efforts to help the bereaved actually succeed. Also important is their consideration of the interplay of personality and social support. It seems reasonable to assume that some persons profit more than others from any sort of aid (certain individuals, not necessarily to their benefit, choose to cope alone), some will be very much easier for those around them to support than others, and some will put much more strain on those trying to help than will others. Thus, the identification of personality variables as mediating factors in supporting the bereaved is a central concern.

Lieberman provides a review of self-help programs for bereaved persons in chapter 27. The number of such groups has vastly increased since the early 1980s, and it is timely to consider their efficacy, compared with other techniques of support for the bereaved. Self-help interventions fulfill a critical function in that they supplement professional services and have the potential advantage of bypassing bureaucracy and avoiding the costs of formal therapy. Lieberman gives coverage, for the first time, to the theory behind these groups, to the conceptual distinctions between these and other helping efforts, to the factors that influence their relevance to different bereavement populations (parental loss of a child, a spouse), and to a rigorous examination of the effectiveness of such programs in ameliorating suffering among bereaved persons. Lieberman found support for the importance of self-help groups among the maritally bereaved, although research to date has been less clear for bereaved parents. That more is not known is due in part to the problems of conducting methodologically sound research on the efficacy of such groups. It is ethically unacceptable to assign bereaved individuals randomly to help versus nonhelp conditions, to include those who are unwilling to participate in such investigations, or to follow up dropouts to compare their health and well-being with those of participants.

The final chapter in this part (chapter 28), by Raphael, Middleton, Martinek, and Misso, extends the overview of intervention techniques to counseling and therapy. They outline more formal methods for assessment and planning of care for the bereaved, arguing that it is important to derive therapeutic assessments from research findings on the variables that constitute high risk and indicating how this should proceed. They describe specific techniques of counseling and therapy that may be helpful, as well as deal with broader issues concerning interactions with the bereaved – for example, helping communities to understand their roles in supporting those at risk. This contribution presents a rare comparison of techniques of intervention with the bereaved, giving an assessment of the applicability of various approaches.

Raphael and her colleagues extend the scope of their previous work on counseling (Raphael & Nunn, 1988) to consider therapeutic techniques for various forms of pathological grief and complementary therapeutic intervention for those suffering psychiatric disorders in association with bereavement. There may, for example, be a need to treat, counsel, or work through phenomena associated with post-traumatic stress disorders before a person bereaved through horrific loss may be able to grieve. Raphael et al. emphasize the importance of recognizing the vast range of individual responses and the need for the counselor or therapist to take these into account, developing and negotiating a "therapeutic contract" with the individual client and employing individually based assessments and treatment programs. Despite their recognition of the need for improvements in the provision of intervention, these authors conclude that there is much supportive evidence that bereavement counseling and therapy are effective.

Conclusions

Perusal of the chapters in the *Handbook* will show that much has been learned in recent years about many different aspects of bereavement. To take just a couple of examples, there has been a tremendous increase in our knowledge about the physiological mechanisms likely to mediate changes in health and well-being or about the specific consequences of (and interventions for) particularly traumatic losses. However, there are still a number of major controversies and differences of opinion among researchers –

concerning the efficacy of grief work in coping with bereavement, or with regard to the extent of resilience to bereavement, for example.

In the final chapter of the book, we, as editors, consider the state of knowledge, pinpoint areas of disagreement (giving our own views on these), highlight social policy implications, and suggest directions for future research.

PART II

The phenomenology and measurement of grief

2

The course of normal grief

STEPHEN R. SHUCHTER AND
SIDNEY ZISOOK

Writing an essay on the course of normal grief is more difficult than
immediately meets the eye. Grief is a natural phenomenon that occurs after
the loss of a loved one. If grief is normal, what, then, is "normal" grief? In
our experience, grief is such an individualized process – one that varies
from person to person and moment to moment and encompasses simultaneously so many facets of the bereaved's being – that attempts to limit its
scope or demarcate its boundaries by arbitrarily defining normal grief are
bound to fail. With this in mind, the rest of this chapter should be read not
so much as prescriptive of how the normal course of grief should run but,
rather, descriptive of the many and varied ways people grieve the death of a
significant other.

We begin with a brief review of the stages of grief, its expected duration,
and definitions and purported determinants of grief's resolution. Following
a discussion of the limitations of the approach, we outline a multidimensional approach to understanding the phenomena and course of
grief and supplement the discussion with data from our own work on the
multidimensional assessment of widowhood.

The stages of grief

In a similar manner to Kubler-Ross's conceptualization of staging death
and dying (1969), many investigators of the process of grief and bereavement have proposed stages of normal grief (Bowlby, 1980/1981; Glick,
Weiss, & Parkes, 1974; Pollock, 1987). The reader should be cautioned
against taking any such staging too literally. Grief is not a linear process
with concrete boundaries but, rather, a composite of overlapping, fluid
phases that vary from person to person. Therefore, stages are meant to be
general guidelines only and do not prescribe where an individual "ought"
to be in the grieving process. In our own staging of the grief process, we
previously have postulated at least three partly overlapping phases: (1) an
initial period of shock, disbelief, and denial; (2) an intermediate acute
mourning period of acute somatic and emotional discomfort and social

withdrawal; and (3) a culminating period of restitution (DeVaul, Zisook, & Faschingbauer, 1979).

The first phase, shock, may last from hours to weeks and is characterized by varying degrees of disbelief and denial. Feeling numb and paralyzed, the bereaved cannot believe that the death is real. Mourning rites and the gathering of family and friends facilitate passage through this stage. Bowlby's staging of the grief process separated this stage into two distinct periods: an initial reaction of numbness and disbelief followed by affects of pining, yearning, and protest (Bowlby, 1980/1981).

A second phase, acute mourning, begins when the death is acknowledged cognitively and emotionally. This stage includes intense feeling states generally occurring in periodic waves of intense emotional and often somatic discomfort. This distress is often accompanied by social withdrawal and a painful preoccupation with the deceased. Frequently, various aspects of identification with the deceased occur during this phase, as the entire thought content and affect of the bereaved person become bound up with the dead relative, spouse, or friend. Often, the mourners transiently adopt the mannerisms, habits, and even somatic symptoms of the deceased.

The acute mourning phase may last for several months before gradually being replaced by the return of a feeling of well-being with the ability to go on living. In this restitution phase, the bereaved recognize what the loss meant to them, that they have grieved, and now begin to shift attention to the world around them. Memories are, and loneliness may be, a part of that world, but the deceased, with their ills and problems, are not. The hallmark of the restitution stage is the ability of the bereaved to recognize that they have grieved and now can return to work, reexperience pleasure, and seek the companionship and love of others.

The duration of grief

There is little agreement regarding the time course of normal grief and bereavement. In general, the expected time course for what would be accepted as "normal" has increased through the years. For example, early investigators suggested a period of weeks to months (Engel, 1961; Lindemann, 1944). However, Paula Clayton and her colleagues found that up to 17% of all widows were still clinically depressed 13 months following the death of a loved one, with symptoms of crying spells, weight loss, and insomnia common (Bornstein, Clayton, Halikas, Maurice, & Robins, 1973). Similarly, in studying a group of London widows 13 months after bereavement, Colin Murray Parkes and colleagues found that only a minority of widows could look at the past with pleasure or to the future with optimism; contrarily, most widows described themselves as sad, poorly adjusted, depressed, often thinking of their deceased husband. having clear visual memories of them, and still grieving a great deal of the time (Parkes, 1971b). Thus, Parkes concluded that the process of grieving was still going strong after 13 months and that the question of how long grief lasts was still unanswered.

Our own findings have been similar to those of Marcia Kraft Goin, who suggested that not only do many people maintain a "timeless" emotional involvement with the deceased but this attachment often represents a healthy adaptation to the loss of a loved one (Goin, Burgoyne, & Goin, 1979). We have found several features of grief, particularly those related to attachment behaviors, to continue several years after the loss (Zisook, Shuchter, & Lyons, 1987). Thus, it seems that some aspects of grief work may never end for a significant proportion of otherwise normal bereaved individuals.

Resolving grief

Complicated grief reactions – atypical (Parkes, 1972), morbid (Lindemann, 1944), pathological (Raphael, 1975; Volkan, 1972), absent (Deutsch, 1937), abnormal (Hackett, 1974), neurotic (Wahl, 1970), "depression of widowhood" (Clayton, Halikas, & Maurice, 1972), "grief related facsimile illness" (Zisook & DeVaul, 1977), or unresolved grief (Zisook & DeVaul, 1985) – have been described. Often, these syndromes refer to either absent, delayed, intensified, or prolonged aspects of "uncomplicated bereavement." (See Middleton, Raphael, Martinek, & Misso's chapter on pathological grief reactions, this volume.) We have conceptualized such syndromes as nonresolution of the grief process, or unresolved grief, and have postulated a relationship between unresolved grief and a few relatively specific clinical syndromes, such as depression, chronic illness behavior, or "grief related facsimile illness" (Zisook & DeVaul, 1985). Unresolved grief may be more likely to occur when the relationship between the bereaved and the deceased was very close, dependent, conflicted, or ambivalent; social support is lacking; there is a past history of depression; current life events interfere with grieving; the death was sudden and unanticipated; the bereaved is in poor physical health; or when the survivor has suffered substantial financial losses. (See Sanders's chapter on risk factors in bereavement outcome, this volume.)

Although much data substantiate the clinical validity of unresolved grief, we have found it to be a somewhat overly simplistic concept. Most, if not all, bereaved individuals never totally resolve their grief, and significant aspects of the bereavement process may go on for years after the loss, even in otherwise normal patients. For some, identification syndromes continue. Others may continue to feel the presence of the deceased or have daily visions of him or her. Still others may feel pain, anger, and guilt for years after the death. Anniversary reactions may go on indefinitely. One person may no longer be depressed or preoccupied with thoughts of the deceased but may suffer ill health as a result of the loss. Another person may have good emotional and psychiatric health but never be able to or wish to remarry. Thus, we feel a more meaningful measure of normal grief would require a multidimensional assessment of a number of aspects of the grieving process.

Multidimensional assessment of grief

As our work in this area has evolved (Shuchter, 1986; Shuchter & Zisook, 1986), we have increasingly focused on a multidimensional approach to the grief experiences of newly bereaved spouses as they occur initially and over time. We have made assumptions of the face validity of these dimensions. What the relationship of these factors may be to other measures of outcome has yet to be determined. The remainder of this chapter describes six relatively independent dimensions of grief as experienced by 350 widows and widowers participating in an ongoing longitudinal study. In this study, widows and widowers were identified through death certificates at the San Diego County Department of Health and were contacted by letter inviting them to participate. Two months after the deaths of their spouses, subjects were given a structured interview and completed a widowhood questionnaire that included demographic information, psychodiagnostic data, specific grief-related questions, health measures, and self-report measures of psychopathology. Follow-up questionnaires were completed by participants at 7 and 13 months (to be completed also at 19 and 25 months).

A total of 350 widows and widowers entered the study – 250 (71%) women and 100 (29%) men. A full description of the population is available elsewhere (Zisook, Mulvihill, & Shuchter, 1990). For a group of demographically matched married controls ($N = 41$ men; $N = 85$ women), data were obtained at one point in time and not obtained for items that had specific reference to the death of a spouse. In the following discussion we will use selected data from this study to illustrate frequency trends of the various dimensions that will be described.

Dimension I. Emotional and cognitive responses to the death of a spouse

Shock. Confronted by the death of a spouse, most men and women experience some form of initial shock, that is, a period of time during which the impact of their loss has not registered. The quality of this experience may vary from states of relative numbness or emotional constriction

Table 2.1. *Emotional and cognitive responses to the death of a spouse*

	% Endorsing each item as positive			
	At 2 months	At 7 months	At 13 months	Married controls
Protective responses				
Numbness	12	6	4	—[a]
It's hard to believe	70	61	49	—
Emotional pain of grief/loss				
Cry whenever I think of him/her	30	29	20	—
I can't talk about spouse without crying	61	59	53	—
Yearning for spouse	77	70	58	—
Anger				
Anger at myself	11	10	7	—
Anger at spouse's physician	17	12	10	—
Envious of others	8	15	13	—
Guilt				
Guilt	12	12	8	0
Responsible for spouse's death	4	5	2	—
Anxiety and fearfulness				
Fearful	14	11	10	1
Nervous when left alone	9	8	7	1
Fearful of death	8	10	11	3
Overwhelmed				
I experience more demands than I can handle	4	6	5	—
Out of control	4	6	5	—
Helpless	22	21	18	6
Mental disorganization				
Trouble concentrating	20	21	14	2
Difficulty making decisions	17	22	18	4
Idea that something is wrong with my mind	5	5	6	1
Loneliness				
Loneliness	59	51	39	2
Lonely even with people	37	28	23	3
Relief	28	10	10	—
Apathy				
Feeling no interest	18	18	15	2

[a] No data.

and detachment to unreal, dissociated, dreamlike states to states of often surprisingly normal thinking and feeling. These may continue for minutes, hours, days, or weeks and, in short-lived forms, for months prior to the emergence of the emotional pangs, the anguish we call grief.

Pain of grief. These are exquisitely painful, often total-body experiences of autonomic explosion: a wrenching of the gut, chest pain, lightheadedness, weakness, the rapid welling up of tears, and uncontrollable crying that frequently accompany this state. These responses can erupt suddenly and unexpectedly, particularly in the first days and weeks, and usually in response to some reminder of the person's loss. These reminders can be from a thousand sources – from any of one's senses, from a lifetime of memories, and from the most innocuous-seeming situations. For some, everything is a reminder of their loss, and their pain remains more or less continuous at first. As time passes, the frequency and intensity of such pain subside, though often ready to reemerge in response to reminders of the loss.

Sense of loss. Closely associated with the emotional pain, and often a major trigger of it, is the survivor's growing awareness of the emotional fact of death, the sense that one has lost something essential that cannot be retrieved. The tearing and wrenching of attachment bonds create not only painful open wounds at the surface of the survivor but defects in the innermost fabric. The missing, longing, yearning, pining, and searching are both for the dead and the living. Myriad losses are experienced: losses of intimacy, companionship, parts of the self, roles, security, styles of living, a sense of meaning, visions of the future.

Anger. Anger is a commonly, though not universally, experienced emotion after loss. It is certainly a normal enough response to any experience of suffering. The forms that such anger takes and the objects of this anger can be quite diverse; it is an emotion seeking an outlet. It can be felt as anger, hatred, resentment, envy, or a sense of unfairness, and it can be directed at the deceased, family or friends, God, physicians, or oneself.

Guilt. The bereaved experience guilt in three major forms: (1) survivor guilt ("Why him and not me?"); (2) guilt related to responsibility for the death or suffering of the spouse; and (3) guilt over "betrayal" of the spouse. The most intense and lasting form of guilt is that associated with the perception that the survivor may have contributed to the spouse's death or suffering, whether by commission – improper feeding, deprivation of affection or support – or omission – not preventing his or her smoking, not changing life-styles, not pushing physicians hard enough to detect a disorder.

Regrets. Regardless of how many things one can anticipate and provide for, and regardless of how well or completely or lovingly a couple may have lived their lives together, when a spouse dies there are always regrets. The ultimate regret is that the spouse could not have continued to live, healthy and happily. Beyond that, the surviving spouse is likely to dwell on missed opportunities to do or say something that might have enhanced their lives or helped with suffering or completed some unfinished business. To the extent that death followed a prolonged illness and was expected, some couples are able to attend to such issues and mitigate against future regrets.

Anxiety and fearfulness. With the disruption of attachment bonds, there emerge intense forms of insecurity, feelings of anxiety, and the fearfulness when such anxiety attaches to specific concerns in the real world. The bereaved experience frequent anxiety, often in the form of free-floating waves or time-limited panic states.

Intrusive images. The events that occur in proximity to the death of one's spouse often remain riveted in the mind of the survivor, as though a series of photographs or videotapes were taken with all of the detail and color of the experience. The imprinting of these scenes speaks to the immense meaning of the events. Survivors are often astonished by the clarity of detail. The images are more likely to emerge when the person's mind is not actively engaged, particularly when home alone or before going to sleep. At times these images may be scenes of illness, accompanied by the changes in the dying person's appearance. These can be particularly devastating, as such often distorted or grotesque images may supplant other images and memories of more pleasant times.

Mental disorganization. During the early state of numbness or shock, the survivor's mental processes are usually quite clear, organized, and precise. The person may feel that his or her thinking is actually better than normal. As emotional breakthrough occurs, several facets of disorganization may appear: varying degrees of distractibility, poor concentration, confusion, forgetfulness, and lack of clarity and coherence. These states occur most often in the early weeks of bereavement but may persist for months.

Feeling overwhelmed. The cumulative effect of such numerous upheavals in the mental and emotional lives of the bereaved often leads to their sense of being overwhelmed, out of control, helpless, and powerless. The prospect of facing the myriad tasks of daily living and survival, battered by recurrent pain, limited in one's cognitive capacities, and alone can be perceived as a set of unmanageable forces with which men and women who may have always considered themselves to be quite strong emotionally feel unable to cope.

Relief. Accompanying these profound emotional and cognitive disruptions may be a sense of relief, especially for those whose spouses have suffered through a prolonged illness. The survivor has often experienced an even greater period of turmoil associated with the diagnosis and deteriorating clinical course of cancer, heart disease, or other. The relief is felt for the deceased, who is now freed from physical pain and the humiliation of witnessing his or her own deterioration, disfigurement, or personality change. The relief is felt by the survivors for themselves, their personal suffering in caring for their loved ones: the intense physical demands and the heightened empathic resonance with their dying mate's pain and lost dignity.

Loneliness. Following the death of one's spouse, the reality of being alone and the intensity of one's loneliness emerge and, over time, become a powerful force. The loneliness is both specific for the spouse who has died – accompanied by the yearning and pangs of grief – but also general for the companionship role that increasingly the spouse may have played. Often, this loneliness becomes more severe, or even initially manifests itself, *after* the first several months of bereavement.

Positive feelings. Widowhood is often portrayed as the death knell to happiness, now and forever, and certainly there are many men and women who in the early stages of their bereavement believe this must be true. At first, it may seem that all joy has been taken out of life. In reality, however, most widowed people are capable of and do experience a variety of positive feelings even through the most difficult periods. Grief does not necessarily consume a person's whole existence, though for some it may. People have the capacity to operate on multiple levels: at times immersed in grief and at times thinking, feeling, and interacting "normally." In the right circumstances the bereaved can feel joy, peace, or happiness as oases amidst their sorrows.

Dimension II. Coping with emotional pain

The human thrust toward homeostasis places the bereaved in an enormous conflict between very powerful and opposing forces. Faced with intense emotional anguish, a primary task is to shut off such pain. On the other hand, the disruptive changes that are the psychological and material reality of the survivor demand attention. Facing reality initiates pain, which, in turn, sets off a variety of mechanisms to mitigate against it. Throughout the grieving process, adaptation operates in highly idiosyncratic ways to allow the survivor to face reality while simultaneously protecting against too great an onslaught of affect. If the bereaved are fortunate, they will be able to

Table 2.2. *Coping*

	% Endorsing each item as positive			
	At 2 months	At 7 months	At 13 months	Married controls
Acceptance and disbelief				
I can't accept the death	21	18	12	—[a]
It's hard to believe	70	61	49	—
Emotional control				
I push my feelings away	48	45	47	—
I never let myself feel badly about my spouse's death	22	21	24	—
Rationalization				
I have been thinking my spouse's death was for the better	55	41	34	—
Faith				
There is an important reason why everything happens	74	71	72	70
Prayer has helped me with my feelings	72	66	67	—
I am comforted my spouse is in heaven	82	76	73	—
My faith in God has been shaken	18	20	19	10
There's great meaning in my religion	71	68	67	68
Avoidance				
I avoid looking at pictures or belongings	16	14	14	—
Visiting the cemetery is too painful	17	26	16	—
Being busy/active distraction				
I've been so busy I haven't had time to grieve	26	26	30	—
Involvement with others				
I've become involved in trying to help others	54	62	59	—
Expression and exposure				
I talk with people a lot about my loss	44	43	38	—
I express my feelings whenever possible	69	61	60	—
Crying spells	70	66	55	11
I spend a lot of time thinking about him/her	78	68	60	—
Indulgence				
(see Table 4: alcohol, cigarettes, medication)				

[a] No data.

regulate, or "dose," the amount of feeling they can bear and divert the rest, using defensive operations of the most mature as well as of the most regressive nature. (See Table 2.2.)

Numbness and disbelief. These were described earlier as affective/cognitive states that operate to protect the individual from the immediate impact of his or her loss. Their inclusion here simply underscores the recognition of such a state as a significant force within the bereaved's defensive operations.

Emotional control. Suppression is a rather high-level defense that enables the bereaved to defer grief to moments in time of greater convenience, greater support, privacy, or other psychological preparation. The person may be aware of being "on the edge" but chooses to, and has the capacity to, control these feelings in order to function at a job, protect others from their grief, or avoid the embarrassment of giving in to their feelings.

Altered perspectives. The distinctly human capacities for thinking, reasoning, and reinterpreting experience become powerful means of coping with the emotional pain of grief. *Intellectualization* enables the bereaved to step back from their immediate experience to observe the process in which they are engaged and to discuss at some greater distance what they observe, and it protects them from the potentially more devastating feelings that lurk about. *Rationalization* is a very prevalent and effective mechanism that allows the survivor to transform an awful truth into a better or more acceptable one, dampening the pain of the former. The most common themes seen in the bereaved are "The deceased is better off," following prolonged illness and suffering; "Things could be worse," especially in view of potentially prolonged suffering; "We were lucky to have what we had," which refocuses on past happiness; and, usually later in time, "I'm better off now," in relation to positive changes that have evolved in the bereaved. *Humor* accomplishes both some distancing from emotional sequelae and the transformation of tragedy to the comic or absurd while not totally avoiding the reality that faces the survivor. It also has a greater tendency to engage and entertain observers than to upset or push them away.

Faith. One of the most frequently used and effective means of coping with death has been through the survivors' faith – their belief in God. Faith facilitates the acceptance of the death as part of a plan, as God's will. Religious beliefs can provide the survivor with the sense that there is someone to help them cope with their suffering as well as to support them in facing the difficult tasks ahead. There is often some reassurance that the deceased will be provided for in the hereafter, and that, in many religions, the two will be reunited in heaven. The bereaved person is not alone: God is present to share the grief. Organized faith also provides comfort and support through the church and its congregation.

Avoidance and exposure. Avoidance is a quickly learned response as the survivor perceives that a given stimulus serves as a trigger to set off painful feelings of loss. Avoidant responses can generalize to the point where any reminder of the dead spouse becomes seen as a threat and all such exposures are avoided. Because of the ubiquitous nature of both real and symbolically established triggers, some bereaved find themselves trapped in a world of continuous threats and may severely limit their contact with the people, belongings, music, places, and other things with whose contact the bereaved are tortured.

Activity. One very effective and adaptive coping mechanism is in keeping busy, particularly involvement in useful activity. The bereaved utilize paid work, school, housework, hobbies, volunteer work: all activities in which they can invest themselves, focus their energies, and actively distract themselves from their grief. Such efforts provide a respite from suffering, sanctioned by its usefulness.

Involvement with others. Involvement provides an opportunity to step into someone else's shoes temporarily, again refocusing the survivor away from his or her internal experience. It is also a means of obtaining support, either directly or indirectly, from contact with others.

Passive distraction. Bereavement is a period when many people find themselves more "involved" with their radios and televisions than at any other times in their lives. These media can have the capacity to take people's minds off their sorrow even when they may not have the ability to pay much attention to what's being broadcast. These media have the further advantages of providing both human voices and shapes, helping the bereaved stave off a sense of isolation and loneliness.

Expression. Common sense suggests that the direct verbal and emotional expression of inner experiences is a highly adaptive means of coping with the painful aspects of grief. Most survivors experience some sense of relief through direct catharsis.

Indulgence. During bereavement, powerful, deeply felt cravings for nurturance or security can be transformed into needs for food, alcohol, tobacco, or sex. It is also a time when the sanctions against such "sinful" behavior may be overridden by either a strong sense of entitlement relating to the loss or by fatalistic or apathetic responses. What we see are changes in behavior initiated by such a loss.

Dimension III. The continuing relationship with the dead spouse

The fundamental dilemma facing the bereaved in their attempts to cope with their loss is that reality demands that they make an adaptation to life without their spouse, and yet powerful internal forces demand that they maintain this attachment, that they retrieve what has been lost. The empirical reality is that people *do not* relinquish their ties to the deceased, withdraw their cathexes, or "let them go." What occurs for survivors is a transformation from what had been a relationship operating on several levels of actual, symbolic, internalized, and imagined relatedness to one in which the actual ("living and breathing") relationship has been lost, but the other forms remain or may even develop in more elaborate forms. (See Table 2.3.)

Location. Most survivors experience their dead spouse as continuing to have an existence either in a spiritual form, usually in heaven, or with some lingering material elements located at the site of their burial if in a cemetery or where their ashes have been scattered.

Continuing contact. During the early weeks and months, the survivor is driven by such intense need that there is an intermittent sense of anticipation that the deceased will suddenly appear. There is searching through crowds, and sounds are responded to as the approach by their spouse. Hallucinatory experiences are commonplace, most often in the form of sensing the presence of the dead spouse. However, these can occur as auditory or visual hallucinations as well as haptic (touching) experiences of the spouse. The bereaved can feel their spouse hovering, watching out for them and protecting them. There is frequent communication with the deceased, as survivors discuss the events of the day, ask for advice, or reprimand the dead for their betrayal and abandonment. It should be pointed out that all of these "unusual" experiences occur in the context of normal reality testing.

Symbolic representations. Symbolic representations of the deceased are usually experienced in a highly ambivalent manner, both as painful reminders of the deceased and as valued sources of continued contact, items that are at times unbearable to see but cannot be disposed of because of their emotional connection. The person's clothing, a well-manicured garden, writings, wedding rings, the couple's bed – all may become powerful sources of both pain and comfort.

Living legacies. These are not symbols but living "extensions" of the personality, ideas, appearance, and other features of the deceased that are

Table 2.3. *The continuing relationship with the dead spouse*

	% Endorsing each item as positive			
	At 2 months	At 7 months	At 13 months	Married controls
Location				
Comforted that spouse is in heaven	39	38	33	—[a]
Continuing contact with the deceased				
Searching and waiting				
Look for spouse in crowd	20	22	14	—
Sense of spouse's presence				
Feel spouse is with me at times	71	67	63	—
Feel my spouse watches out for me	61	48	47	—
Communication with the deceased				
Talk with spouse regularly	39	37	34	—
Talk with spouse's picture	42	40	33	—
Symbolic representations				
Keep one of his/her belongings near me	48	49	41	—
Living legacies				
Identification				
I seem to be more like my spouse	39	38	33	—
I find myself doing things like my spouse	55	54	49	—
I've had physical symptoms like my spouse	7	10	10	—
Active perpetuation				
I'm interested in carrying out his/her wishes	80	71	65	—
Memories				
I purposely expose myself to reminders	35	36	33	—
I spend time looking at old pictures	29	30	22	—
Dreams				
I see my spouse in dreams	35	42	39	—

[a] No data.

borrowed and incorporated into the life of the survivor. Identification with the deceased through ideas, traits, and tastes creates continuity. Genetic features seen in offspring may develop a premium quality. Active decisions to carry on the works or traditions of the deceased through individual efforts or memorial donations may also play an important role in perpetuation of the relationship.

Rituals. Every culture evolves its unique beliefs, customs, and behaviors that attend to the deceased: disposing of the body, incorporation into religious ceremonies, prescribed acts of mourning, and official remembrances. In American culture, the funeral is the public acknowledgment and display: It presents the reality and finality, countering the effects of denial; it garners support for survivors; it pays tribute and initiates memorialization. Other ceremonies are initiated through visitation with its continued show of support, confrontation with reality, and stimulation of memories. The remains are usually in a cemetery, which becomes a potentially very painful and sometimes eventually comforting place. Where cremation occurs, ceremonies associated with scattering of the ashes become a unique means of expressing aspects of the relationship. All subsequent holidays, birthdays, and anniversaries become intensified foci for the relationship, at times exacerbating powerful grief experiences that may seem as fresh as the original experience. Over time these are usually attenuated but almost always present in some form.

Memories. As time passes, memories become the most powerful means of continuing the relationship with the deceased. As with all of these connecting links, they are bittersweet. They provide comfort in bringing the spouse back to life and stimulate pain as a reminder of what is lost. Memories are often selective, tending to idealize the deceased or their relationship in the earlier stages of grief and often taking months or longer to recapture an accurate perception of the person and their lives together. There are also distortions of memory, which can be affected by prolonged illness or deterioration where the "shadow" of illness may block out earlier memories and the bereaved remains captive of these later memories for many months.

Dreams. Among the more "mundane" and transparent dreams one sees in clinical practice are those of the bereaved, most frequently taking the form of matter-of-fact scenes in which the deceased is alive, fulfilling their ultimate wish. Survivors' dreams often explain why the deceased has been away, or may occur in a series of leave-takings or separations. Regardless of the particular forms of such dreams, they are inevitably disturbing when, upon waking, the dreamer's reality reappears.

Dimension IV. Changes in functioning

Health. The impact of bereavement on health status is profound and extends beyond psychological to physical health as well. Our research subjects had been generally healthy people. Table 2.4 reflects the influence of bereavement over time on general perceptions of health and specific psychiatric symptoms of depression and anxiety, as well as manifestations of increased alcohol, tobacco, and medication use.

Social and work function. Many factors are likely to contribute to changes in social and work function. While the earliest period of bereave-

Table 2.4. *Changes in functioning*

	% Endorsing each item as positive			
	At 2 months	At 7 months	At 13 months	Married controls
Health				
Physical-medical health				
Poor–fair	28	25	23	11
Good–excellent	72	76	78	89
Psychiatric health				
Depression – DSM III criteria for major depression				
Downhearted, sad, blue	29	25	16	3
More irritable than usual	11	43	45	28
Feeling no interest in things	18	18	15	2
I eat as much as usual	51	55	62	63
Trouble falling asleep	30	24	19	4
Trouble sleeping through the night	43	41	30	15
Tense or keyed up	27	21	15	—
Feeling worthless	8	11	5	0
Trouble concentrating	20	21	14	2
Difficulty making decisions	17	22	18	4
Feeling hopeless about future	14	14	10	2
Thoughts of ending life	2	3	3	0
Anxiety symptoms				
Spells of terror or panic	5	4	4	0
So restless you couldn't keep still	13	10	8	1
Alcohol				
Increased frequency of alcohol consumption	18	25	30	—[a]
Increased quantity	8	39	34	—
Cigarettes				
Increased use	39	41	40	—
Medications				
Over-the-counter sleep/nerves	8	6	7	2
Anxiolytics	23	12	10	4
Neuroleptics	3	4	3	—
Antidepressants	8	8	8	2
Sedatives	8	5	4	6
Counseling/therapy	18	20	18	—
Social functions				
Social days/month	8	9	9	11
Work functioning/adjustment				
Make more mistakes than usual	10	12	11	1
Dissatisfaction	30	36	28	10

[a] No data.

ment will usually increase the social interactions of the survivor as a result of the influx of social supports, visitation, and ritual tasks, there are many people whose grief results in varying degrees of social inhibition, withdrawal, and isolation. Such responses, or tendencies, may serve primitive needs to preserve and protect emotional resources, but at the same time they cut off some potential sources of support.

Numerous changes in role functioning may be precipitated by the death of a spouse, especially where there has been a segregation of these roles between the couple. (See Table 2.4.) There are more likely to be disruptive role-related changes where there are dependent children or when the survivor has had narrow, often stereotypical, gender-related roles in a long-standing "traditional" marriage. Work performance is at highest risk for those survivors who experience periods of cognitive disorganization and very intense, intrusive grief. The confusion, anxiety, distractibility, and memory disturbances can interfere significantly with the person's capacity to perform a task. Later in the course of grief, where clinical depression evolves, the depression may reproduce many of these same disorganizing phenomena, as well as impaired motivation, diminished energy, and disinterest in tasks. Such apathy will contribute further to functional deterioration.

Dimension V. Changes in relationships

The death of a spouse invariably alters the dynamics of most relationships. There may be changes in the needs experienced in the relationship, the levels of closeness or support, or the nature of the roles or meanings. Some relationships may end while others begin, but all are affected. (See Table 2.5.)

Family. The most complex changes occur within the family. Where there are dependent children in the home, the surviving parent must cope with both their children's and their own grief while maintaining a functional home even as the structure of the family and its members' roles change. Single parenting changes the sources of gratification and discipline. Where there are grown children, there may be conflicts in the expectations of the children and surviving parent over issues of emotional support, finances, decision making, and future directions. The survivor may have to contend with the grief of his or her own parents or in-laws: their efforts to enlist their own support, confer advice, or offer help. There is an opportunity for achieving greater intimacy, repairing old wounds, and sharing grief or, conversely, for exacerbating conflict and disruption.

A common source of disruption can be the intolerance of the survivor's family for the survivor's continuing grief. There is often a lack of apprecia-

Table 2.5. *Changes in relationships*

	% Endorsing each item as positive			
	At 2 months	At 7 months	At 13 months	Married controls
Children[a]				
Better (than before death)	56	56	50	—[b]
Worse	3	6	8	—
Very supportive	71	60	57	—
Unsupportive	3	6	6	—
Parents[a]				
Better	26	26	27	—
Worse	7	12	10	—
Very supportive	42	33	25	—
Unsupportive	7	7	8	
In-laws[a]				
Better	35	29	26	—
Worse	8	10	14	—
Very supportive	49	34	34	—
Unsupportive	8	11	13	—
Siblings[a]				
Better	38	43	37	—
Worse	2	5	6	—
Very supportive	56	47	43	—
Unsupportive	4	5	8	—
Friends[a]				
Better	43	37	42	—
Worse	2	4	5	—
Very supportive	62	49	46	—
Unsupportive	2	5	5	—
Dating				
I'm not sure how a single person acts these days	71	68	65	—
It's difficult to think about dating	71	62	52	—
I feel guilty about dating	32	35	25	—
Romantic relationships				
I'm fearful of getting romantic with another person	40	55	44	—
I'm only interested in developing friendships	80	75	67	—
I will be able to love someone else	48	52	59	—
I'm involved in a new romantic relationship	6	21	26	—
No one else will ever take the place of spouse	84	82	77	—
Remarriage				
I have positive thoughts about remarriage	27	43	43	—
Sexuality				
I have less than usual interest in sex	42	44	36	—
General relationships				
New relationships have been hard to develop	49	57	57	—
I believe I must be strong for the sake of others	66	61	54	—
My feelings are easily hurt	14	14	12	0
I feel that people are unfriendly	2	4	4	0
Very self-conscious with others	8	7	6	0

[a] Categories collapsed:
 "Better" = "much better" and "somewhat better."
 "Worse" = "much worse" and "somewhat worse."
 "Same as before" not included.
 "Unsupportive" = "somewhat unsupportive" and "very unsupportive."
 "Somewhat supportive" and "same as before" not included.
[b] No data.

tion for the extent in time or intensity of this experience. The family member may be struggling with his or her own grief and utilizing greater degrees of denial and avoidance than would allow the person to be more receptive to the widow's or widower's pain. This lack of empathy can disrupt any relationship.

Friends. Friends are often a major source of support of the bereaved, especially where their empathy and sympathy are available and freely given and where they are sensitive to and accepting of the enormous fluctuations in feelings, moods, and needs of the survivor. Friends can share the pain and allow its free expression. Problems can occur where the bereaved are reluctant to "inflict" their own suffering on those whom they care about or when friends do, in fact, have difficulties in tolerating intense grief. The limits of empathy are real and may be seen typically among friends whose identification with the bereaved makes them too vulnerable to such exposure (e.g., those who have a spouse who is ill). Some of the more enduring and supportive friendships evolve with those people whose life experiences resonate with the survivor's loss and pain, usually those who have grieved themselves and feel a greater acceptance of and comfort in this state. At times, friends or family members may feel threatened by the intensity of the survivor's neediness. This may translate into avoidance based on fears of being "swallowed up" by such needs or on projections that transform such needs into a sexual threat.

Romance. For many, the threat of reinvolvement on a romantic basis is unacceptable and rejected on many levels based on continued devotion to their spouse, societal sanctions, or fears of recurrent loss, as well as preferences for their single state. Where such interest reawakens, the bereaved then find themselves having to contend not only with all of the pleasures and problems of developing such a relationship but also with the continuing impact of their loss and its place within the new relationship. They will face the culture shock and awkwardness of new situations, some feelings of disloyalty to their dead spouse, the inevitable comparisons, and, where remarriage occurs, the complicated adjustments to often-competing loyalties and blended families. Even where successful marriages occur, grief does not end but becomes incorporated into this new relationship.

Dimension VI. Changes in identity

It should not be surprising that persons living through what is likely to be the most profoundly disruptive experience in their life are subject to dramatic changes in the ways in which they perceive themselves and the world around them. (See Table 2.6.) The first fundamental change is that of being

Table 2.6. *Changes in identity*

	% Endorsing each item as positive			
	At 2 months	At 7 months	At 13 months	Married controls
Self-perceptions				
Feel self-sufficient	79	77	75	87
Feel more sensitive	79	81	81	—
Feel useful and needed	67	58	63	86
A piece of me is missing	87	85	78	—
I am a better person for this experience	42	42	50	—
Self-esteem				
I feel good about myself	83	77	79	91
Unlovable	11	19	16	11
Worthless	8	11	5	0
Embarrassed about being widowed	5	8	4	—
Feel inferior to others	3	6	5	2
I continue to surprise myself by new tasks I have mastered	55	62	64	68
Philosophy/worldview				
My life has great richness	87	83	87	95
My life is pretty full	69	56	60	90
I try to get the most out of every day	88	85	88	92
Direction/purpose				
Feel hopeful about the future	63	53	60	72
I don't know where my life is headed	59	60	61	19
I look forward to tomorrow	78	79	83	92
I enjoy the freedom of being on my own	36	47	53	—
I like making decisions just for me	52	50	63	67
Feeling hopeless about the future	14	14	10	2
Overall adjustment (self-rated)				
Poor	8	4	5	—
Fair	31	31	25	—
Good	44	53	55	—
Excellent	18	11	15	—

a single person instead of being part of a couple. Regardless of the degrees of autonomy and independence within a marriage, there is an orientation toward the other person in most considerations and decisions. The survivor is often faced with a period of reorientation toward "selfishness," which is disquieting.

During the earliest phases of grief, there may be a period of intense regression as the survivor feels on the verge of being overwhelmed by the constant bombardment of anguish, images, confusion, and disorientation.

Self-perceptions emerge of helplessness, inadequacy, incapacity – childlike states that are experienced as all-enveloping and eternal. Such negative self-perceptions dovetail with the loss of esteem resulting from changes in social status, financial security, or the loving and positive "mirroring" functions of the spouse.

As time goes on and the survivor "survives" – that is, learns of his or her capacity to tolerate the grief, carry on tasks, and discover new ways of dealing with the world – new feelings and self-images may emerge. Often, there is an evolving sense of strength, autonomy and independence, assertiveness, and maturity as a result of mastering their trials and tribulations. Survivors see themselves as becoming more compassionate, more patient, and more balanced and flexible as people.

Frequently, there is a parallel evolution of belief systems reflecting changes in perceptions of how the world works. The tragedy that survivors experienced precipitates philosophical shifts toward existential and fatalistic orientations. Timelessness yields to a sense of limited time and the reality of death. Personal views of control and invincibility turn toward greater flexibility and vulnerability. There may be a greater tendency toward humanitarianism, a softening of the work ethic, strengthening of a family ethic, the appearance of hedonism where there had been restraint. With time and continued survival and growth, the bereaved may have the opportunity and capacity to transform their tragedy into new directions: careers, relationships, and personal evolution. Some creative elements are experienced by a majority of the bereaved. On the other hand, there are a small minority whose consumption by their grief remains relatively fixed for years.

Gender

As mentioned earlier, several factors may alter or affect the bereaved's responses to the deaths of their loved ones, and one of them may be gender. For example, men may differ from women in their grief experiences. To illustrate some of the ways widows' and widowers' grief responses may vary, we have selected a few items from each dimension of grief to explore these differences at 13 months. As can be seen from Table 2.7, there seem to be some striking gender differences on many individual items. Some may reflect general gender differences (e.g., females have higher physical health debility rates than males), whereas others are grief-specific reactions. For example, women feel a greater degree of helplessness and tend more to experience their dead spouses in a protective role. Men show less acceptance of the death, become involved sooner in romantic relationships, express themselves less, and drink more.

Table 2.7. *Gender differences at 13 months' bereavement*

	Male (%)	Female (%)
Affects		
I cry when I think about spouse	22	19
Yearning for spouse	56	59
Feeling helpless	5	22
Feeling lonely	33	41
Coping		
Can't accept the death	18	10
Push my feelings away	39	50
Too busy to grieve	33	29
Express feelings whenever possible	47	66
Continued relationship		
I feel he/she is with me at times	55	66
I feel he/she is watching out for me	33	52
Keep belongings near me	39	43
Function		
Health poor/fair in past month	16	25
Changes in alcohol consumption	+1.6[a]	−.8[a]
Relationships		
Friends very supportive	38	49
Involved in new romantic relationship	45	19
Identity		
Feel self-sufficient	80	74
More sensitive to life	84	80
Hopeful about the future	33	42
Overall adjustment to widowhood (good/excellent)	64	72

[a] Drinks/day.

Summary

A prototypical life stress event, bereavement is associated with immense turmoil and stress and may, at times, lead to substantial psychological and/ or medical morbidity. Grief's duration may be prolonged, at times even indefinite, and its intensity varies over time, from person to person, and from culture to culture. It cannot be understood from a static or linear perspective; rather, a full appreciation of the grieving process requires attention to its diverse, multidimensional perpectives. These include affective and cognitive states, coping strategies, the continuing relationship with the deceased, changes in functioning, changes in relationships, and alterations in identity. Although painful and sometimes destructive, grief often promotes growth and development and may bring out hidden resources and strength.

3

Pathological grief reactions

WARWICK MIDDLETON,
BEVERLEY RAPHAEL, NADA MARTINEK,
AND VIVIENNE MISSO

In many areas of medicine it is difficult to distinguish normal and abnormal, nonpathological and pathological, or health and disease. The study of bereavement shares this difficulty. This chapter focuses on major theoretical perspectives that might aid in defining or understanding pathological grief. A historical overview is provided, and questions are raised regarding the overlap between grief and defined disorder. In particular, discussion focuses on the problem that research to date has not clearly identified areas of psychopathology that are grief-specific. This reflects in part a lack of operationalized criteria for pathological grief.

Defining pathological grief

The field is still struggling to validate and operationalize the construct of "normal" grief (cf. Shuchter & Zisook, this volume). When the focus is then extended to include a range of "abnormal" forms of grief, the difficulties are compounded. Where grief for a particular individual, in a particular culture, appears to deviate from the expected course in such a way that it is associated with excessive or prolonged psychological or physical morbidity, it may be labeled as pathological. Such classification may be descriptive or it may imply a theoretical construct. Furthermore, often it is not clear as to whether the term *grief* is intended to pertain simply to the affective reaction to loss, as a commonly accepted meaning, or to refer to all aspects of the bereavement reaction and a range of other states.

Unfortunately, the multiplicity of such terms, many of which lack definition, adds confusion. At another level, their proliferation reflects not only the lack of a widely accepted alternative but also a reluctance to use an existing term that is not well defined. A modest sampling of the literature in the area demonstrates the difficulties with definition, with the following terms denoting some variation from normal grief: absent (Deutsch, 1937), abnormal (Pasnau, Fawney, & Fawney, 1987), complicated (Sanders, 1989), distorted (Brown & Stoudemire, 1983), morbid (Sireling, Cohen, & Marks, 1988), maladaptive (Reeves & Boersma, 1990), truncated (Widdison

44

& Salisbury, 1990), atypical (Jacobs & Douglas, 1979), intensified and prolonged (Lieberman & Jacobs, 1987), unresolved (Zisook & DeVaul, 1985), neurotic (Wahl, 1970), and dysfunctional (Rynearson, 1987).

Theoretical formulations

Many theoretical frameworks have addressed the question of pathological grief. The two most influential perspectives, psychoanalytic and attachment theories, are examined in the following sections.

Psychoanalytic theories

A major focus of Freud's own self-analysis was the loss of his father. Loss, and the internalization of lost objects, have since remained cornerstones of psychoanalytic theory. In 1917, Freud, noting similarities between mourning (i.e., "normal" grief) and melancholia (i.e., "pathological" grief), focused also on their distinguishing features. He identified four features of normal mourning: profoundly painful dejection, loss of capacity to adopt new love objects, inhibition of activity or turning away from activity not connected with thoughts of the loved person, and loss of interest in the outside world insofar as it does not recall the deceased. Initially, Freud (1917b) differentiated mourning from depression. Normal mourning was considered not to involve ambivalent feelings about the deceased nor a significant disturbance of self-esteem. The loss of the ambivalently loved object was thus associated with melancholia, which occurred in response to the internalization of that object. Normal mourning was seen as a process by which the bereaved progressively withdrew the libido invested in the lost object in preparation for reinvesting it in a new object.

Freud (1917b) raised issues that we are still grappling with today, when he suggested that "melancholia instead of a state of grief develops in some people, whom we consequently suspect of a morbid pathological disposition" (p. 153). He later expanded on the theme of premorbid factors, noting that "where there is a disposition to obsessional neurosis the conflict of ambivalence casts a pathological shade on the grief, forcing it to express itself in the form of self-reproaches, to the effect that the mourner himself is to blame for the loss of the loved one, i.e. desired it" (p. 161).

In 1924, Abraham suggested that internalization was not confined to melancholia but could also be a feature of normal mourning, a position consistent with Freud's (1923) further development of the concept of superego functioning. Abraham (1924) also suggested that both low self-esteem and ambivalence were present in both conditions, though in normal mourning the ambivalence was such that positive feelings far outweighed negative ones. Hostility toward the self, identified by Freud and Abraham as pathogenic, has also been described in normal grief reactions (Parkes, 1972/1987; Horowitz, 1976/1986).

In 1937, Deutsch drew attention to the controversial phenomenon of "absent grief." She argued that unmanifested grief would ultimately be expressed in an alternative form, for example, as unexplained periodic depressions. Her explanation, based on defense mechanisms, held that "if the ego should be too weak to undertake the elaborate function of mourning" (p. 14), two possible courses were open. The first of these was infantile regression expressed as anxiety, and the second, mobilization of ego defenses, which in their most extreme expression lead to omission of affect. Lindemann (1944) later noted that the delay in expression of grief may sometimes last years or that grieving may be precipitated by a subsequent loss.

Another important psychoanalytic construct applied to grief was Klein's (1940) concept of the depressive position, an infantile developmental stage associated with the infant's ability to recognize and relate to a whole object. Satisfactory negotiation of this stage, and the establishment of a good internal object, were to provide protection against subsequent depression in the event of loss. In Klein's view, persons who suffered pathological grief had never successfully overcome the infantile depressive position or established a good object relationship that would allow them to feel secure within their inner world. Vaillant (1988) made a similar claim, when he asserted: "We forget that it is failure to internalise those whom we have loved, and not their loss, that impedes, adult development" (p. 149).

Lindemann, a psychoanalyst, provided an important reference point for conceptualizing normal and morbid forms of grief (1944). He sought to define the symptomatology of acute (normal) grief from a psychosomatic perspective. It must be noted that his research subjects, however, from whom he derived his descriptions, were not representative of the population at large. They included "(1) psychoneurotic patients who lost a relative during the course of treatment, (2) relatives of patients who died in the hospital, (3) bereaved disaster victims (Coconut Grove Fire) and their close relatives, (4) relatives of members of the armed forces" (p. 141). Thus, one of the four groups was composed of subjects already suffering from a "psychoneurotic" disorder, and at least two of the other groups had lost relatives in a sudden and violent manner. In some cases subjects were present during the disaster that had claimed the life of a relative. How many of the subjects suffered with what today would be described as post-traumatic stress is unknown.

These observations raise the important question of to what extent pathology was preexistent or reflected post-traumatic stress rather than being a manifestation of bereavement. Lindemann relied heavily on analytic concepts in characterizing normal and morbid forms of grief. In doing so, he adopted a fairly narrow view regarding normality. For example, observing that some bereaved began manifesting behavioral traits characteristic of the deceased, he suggested that this bordered on "pathological reactions."

Lindemann defined morbid grief reactions as "distortions of normal grief." For example, one subject who had sustained multiple losses and serious personal injury experienced a brief delay in the outward manifestations of grief. Lindemann labeled this a morbid grief reaction, but referred to no subjects so affected who grieved more "normally." It remains unclear, therefore, whether Lindemann regarded a delay in manifestations of grief as inevitably morbid. In addition to chronically delayed grief, Lindemann described a number of other "distorted grief reactions." Nine different reactions were identified, ranging from psychosomatic illness, progressive social isolation, and furious hostility against specific persons to agitated depression and self-punitive behavior.

Some of Lindemann's classifications have not retained their status as pathological forms of grief in more recent formulations. They were important, however, because they integrated multiple parameters in describing "morbid grief," for example, duration, intensity of particular symptoms, physical and psychiatric illness, and changes in social functioning. Another enduring aspect of Lindemann's work was his reinforcement of the Freudian concept "grief work." On the assumptions that expressing affect is helpful and that it is important to relinquish bonds to the deceased, Lindemann, and many subsequent clinicians, have used techniques aimed at the facilitation of grief work in treating patients with "morbid" or "pathological" forms of grief. Subsequent writers have expanded Lindemann's relatively narrow concept of normal grief, with the recognition that even features of normal grief can be present for many years following loss. Lindemann believed that the duration of normal grief depended on the bereaved person's grief work, defined as the "emancipation from the bondage of the deceased, readjustment to the environment . . . and the formation of new relationships" (p. 143).

The influence of psychoanalytic theory has remained strong, not only on contemporary classifications of pathological forms of grief but also as the conceptual basis of counseling and therapy programs. (See Raphael, Middleton, Martinek, & Misso, this volume.)

Attachment theory

Noting similarities between infants separated from their mothers and adults facing bereavement, Bowlby integrated analytic and ethological concepts in the development of attachment theory (Bowlby, 1969, 1973, 1980/1981). Because attachment behavior had been observed in many species, grief was conceptualized as an extension of a general response to separation. The concept of an attachment instinct explained why distress was so universal in response to separation from an attachment object. The theory initially emphasized the role of the adult providing for and protecting the dependent child. However, it was extended to include the maintenance of a mutually reinforcing relationship with a particular adult. Grief was thus seen as a form of separation anxiety in adulthood in response to the disruption of an attachment bond.

Bowlby (1982) also concluded that mourning in mentally healthy adults lasts longer than had often been suggested, and found that several responses widely regarded as pathological were in fact common in healthy mourning. These included anger directed at third parties, the self, and sometimes at the lost person; disbelief that the loss had occurred; and a tendency, often unconscious, to search for the lost person in the hope of reunion.

Attachment theory also linked the manifestations of pathological grief to the subject's childhood experiences and to the pattern of parental attachment behavior. Individuals who had experienced "pathogenic parenting" were considered especially vulnerable. Bowlby described three forms of disordered attachment (1973): Adults whose childhoods were characterized by *anxious attachment* to parents were considered likely to have insecure attachments to marital partners and to be overly dependent. By contrast, the *compulsive self-reliant* individual was one who in childhood had been reluctant to accept care and was insistent on doing everything by him- or herself. The *compulsive caregiver* was an individual who had always, as a child, taken the role of giver rather than receiver. Following a major loss, the anxiously attached person would be expected to exhibit chronic grief, whereas the compulsive self-reliant individual would likely deny the loss and experience delayed onset of grief. Bowlby was less certain about the relationship between compulsive care giving and pathological grief, though he suggested that such people may also be prone to chronic grief (1980/1981).

Parkes (1965) in particular applied an attachment model to his observations on the course of grief. His model spoke of denial and numbing, followed by searching for the lost object, anger and guilt (protest), and finally mitigation and defense. In 1965, he identified three principal forms of pathological grief: *chronic grief*, denoting an indefinite prolongation of grief with exaggeration of symptoms; *inhibited grief*, in which most symptoms of normal grief were absent; and *delayed grief*, in which the painful emotions were avoided for a time at least. At this stage, in response to loss, the attachment phenomena were seen as pathological patterns in this way. Later, he and other workers related grief outcome to attachment styles in relationships.

Current conceptualizations

The psychoanalytic/psychodynamic and attachment models have continued to dominate present-day conceptualizations and to define research frameworks. A survey was carried out of "experts" who were identified in the scientific and clinical literature or through attendance at a major international meeting on grief and bereavement. Most of these respondents ($N = 76$) had long-term (>10 years) clinical or research involvement. They were surveyed on a range of issues, including the theoretical constructs that most influenced their work and their views on pathological grief. Given a range of models, 75.7% nominated attachment theory and 65.7% nominated psychodynamic theory in the top three models found to be most useful conceptually. Sociological, cognitive, behavioral, and ethological constructs were all at a significantly lower level (Middleton, Moylan, Burnett, & Martinek, 1991).

Increasingly, these and other workers have recognized that some criteria must be developed by which there are common understandings of what is meant by normal and pathological grief, whatever theoretical construct is used. This is also reflected in research attempts to measure and quantify the phenomena of grief and bereavement. Such measures range from the Texas Grief Inventory (Zisook, DeVaul, & Click, 1982) to the scales for numbness, separation anxiety, and depression of Jacobs et al. (1987b) to specific measures of bereavement phenomena (See Hansson, Carpenter, & Fairchild, this volume). Subscales have also been developed for pathological grief, such as Zisook and DeVaul's (1985) unresolved grief scale. Nevertheless, important key concepts still have to be delineated. The following are some of those issues.

Pathological versus normal grief

A thorough review of contemporary literature shows that there are still no adequate definitions of what is normal or pathological, either in attachment or psychodynamic frameworks. Any definition of what is pathological might be made on purely statistical grounds – for instance, outside 1.5 to 2 standard deviations from the norm, if there is a normal distribution of phenomena. Pathology might be defined by excessive intensity or too little intensity, excessive duration or too little duration, and so forth. This might incorporate descriptions such as those of Parkes (1965) referring to inhibited grief or intensified or prolonged grief (Lieberman & Jacobs, 1987).

Definition might also be made in terms of the processes that have been suggested in different staging or conceptual models of bereavement response.

Thus, grief may be seen as pathological when the processes of resolving the loss do not occur, as in the concept of unresolved grief (Zisook & DeVaul, 1985) or distorted grief (Raphael, 1975), or where delayed grief patterns predominate.

Pathological grief might also relate to the presence of different phenomena that would then be seen as pathognomic of this, as opposed to normal grief. For instance, earlier descriptions suggested that somatic symptoms reflecting identification with the deceased's last illness might be pathological (Lindemann, 1944). Such distinctions – that is, the presence or absence of particular phenomena – have proved relatively unhelpful in defining criteria for pathological grief. Many studies in fact suggest that such phenomena are frequent and not necessarily connected with other indications of pathology, such as disruption of function.

Some manifestations of bereavement may last for a prolonged period without indicating pathology. Zisook et al. (1982) reported on a sample of bereaved persons who, 10 years after the loss, still reported thinking often of their lost persons, dreaming about them, missing them, and responding to reminders of them by distress or crying. Thus, both the duration and presence of such phenomena over time are not clearly defined as pathology by any operational definition, although such a picture may well represent pathological grief.

A further aspect would relate to functional impairment. Most bereavements do not result in major, or at least prolonged, disruption of functioning, in extended absence from work, or an expressed need for psychiatric assistance. Most would agree that grief is not a disease, per se, even taking Engel's (1961) challenging conceptualizations to their ultimate argument. Diagnostic classifications have also failed to make this distinction adequately, doing so only in terms of "uncomplicated bereavement" (DSM III-R) as opposed to "adjustment disorders" and other potential psychiatric consequences.

Views of those who have researched this field are wide ranging. For instance, there are simple conclusions, such as those of Zisook et al. (1982) who define unresolved grief ultimately in terms of the response to a single item on the Texas Grief Inventory – namely, the person's perception he or she has "gotten over" the loss. Horowitz, Wilner, Marmar, and Krupnick (1980) see pathological grief as an intensification of the post-traumatic processes in which they view grief, with special emphasis on the "activation of negative latent self images" (a more psychodynamic model but extended from Freud's views by Horowitz's own conceptualizations) (Horowitz et al., 1980). Jacobs (1987a), working with an attachment model, has measured and defined the phenomena of bereavement as "numbness and denial," "separation anxiety," and "depressive phenomena." His views of the pathology of bereavement (Raphael & Jacobs, personal communication,

1991) suggest that he sees the hallmark of grief as the separation anxiety dimension and that pathology may be reflected in the absence of this or in its extreme intensification.

Our own research is currently attempting to define further the phenomena of normal bereavement in a community-based sample and then utilize agreed-upon diagnostic criteria to identify the frequency and correlates of pathological bereavement (Middleton et al., 1991). To this end, and following systematic review of the literature, it seems reasonable to identify the hallmarks as an intensification or inhibition of the phenomena of normal bereavement or as a delay or prolongation of the processes of normal grieving (W. Stroebe & Stroebe, 1987). The subtypologies of pathological bereavement follow from this, and possible definitions for these entities are suggested in the following discussion.

Subtypes of pathological grief or bereavement

As indicated, many different subtypes have been suggested, ranging from absent (Deutsch, 1937) to inhibited and delayed (Parkes, 1965) to distorted (Lindemann, 1944) to unresolved (Zisook & Lyons, 1991) to the more recent unexpected grief syndrome, ambivalent grief syndrome, and chronic grief (Parkes & Weiss, 1983).

In an attempt to judge the current meanings and common ground of such descriptions, our study (Middleton et al., 1991) asked researchers, clinicians, and other identified experts whether they considered six such syndromes of pathology to occur and if so what their characteristics and distinguishing features were. The six entities, drawn from the literature, were absent grief, delayed grief, inhibited grief, chronic grief, distorted grief, and unresolved grief. There was considerable agreement among the 76 respondents to this segment about delayed grief (76.6% believed it to occur and only 3.9% suggested it did not, the remainder being uncertain), chronic grief (74% believed it to occur), and, to a lesser degree, absent grief (64.9%). People were less certain about unresolved grief (57.1%) and inhibited grief (53.2%) and quite unsure about distorted grief (36.4% believed it occurred, but 23.4% didn't know and 29.9% didn't answer). Detailed descriptions offered by the respondents highlighted the following features.

Delayed grief was suggested as typical but just delayed, although the period of delay noted ranged from weeks to years. Parkes's (1965) original suggestion was that grief should be considered delayed if it took longer than 2 weeks after the bereavement to appear. *Absent* grief was defined by the inhibition or absence of the typical expression of grief, denial of feelings about the loss, no external signs of grieving, and continuing to act as though nothing had happened. This fits with Deutsch's (1937) original descriptions, although it does not provide clear links to its subsequent appearance as pathology.

Chronic grief was described as prolonged, unending, and unchanging, as being associated with depression, guilt and self-reproach, marked sadness, withdrawal, prolonged preoccupation with the person who had died, and prolonged and unending distress. *Unresolved* grief was seen to overlap substantially with chronic grief. *Inhibited* grief was described as the bereaved being unable to talk fully about, acknowledge or express the loss, or express feelings about it; an inability to cry; social or cultural or "learned" restraints on the expression of grief; or limited or partial grief response. It was seen as overlapping substantially with delayed and absent grief.

As there are no currently agreed-upon definitions derived scientifically from research studies (although these are currently in progress [Middleton et al., 1991; Byrne & Raphael, 1991]), it is useful to consider some interim diagnostic criteria involving the described features. Such criteria may help researchers and clinicians use common and shared accepted meanings for these terms and thus allow the development of a base of knowledge. As work extends using such criteria, they may be modified by future data, as are the DSM III, III-R, and now IV categorizations.

Pathological grief and related disorders

Whether grief appears as a syndrome, for instance, depression, or whether pathological patterns of bereavement as described earlier are correlated with psychiatric syndromes, such as depression, needs further elucidation. This is the more so because measures often have not separated specific phenomena of bereavement from other phenomena, such as depression, anxiety and post-traumatic stress disorder, and somatic complaints. Depression will be considered first, as it represents many of the difficulties, as well as current developments.

Depression. Depression and grief have been closely associated in the literature. DSM III-R states that "a full depressive syndrome frequently is a normal reaction to such a loss, with feelings of depression and such associated symptoms as poor appetite, weight loss, and insomnia" (p. 208). Many attempts to measure bereavement phenomena have utilized depression scales (e.g., Jacobs uses the CESD Depression Scale) or have examined bereavement reactions in terms of depressive syndromes. Furthermore, little attempt has been made to differentiate the phenomena, even when depression and bereavement are measured separately, as many of the items overlap, for example, sad and blue feelings, loss of interest, or sleep and appetite disturbance.

Clayton, Halikas, and Maurice (1972) have studied the bereaved on a depression model and found that 42% of a community sample met criteria for depression at 1 month after the loss and 16% at 1 year, with 11% being depressed for an entire year. Clayton (1990) identified what she considers to be significant differences between typical depression and the depression experienced by the bereaved. She identifies retardation as rare in bereavement and states that it should be considered pathological if present. Additionally, while hallucinations may be present, she claims that delusions have never been recorded. Other symptoms rare in bereavement but frequent in those with severe depression include hopelessness, worthlessness, and a loss of interest in friends.

Zisook's group suggests that initially depressive phenomena occur frequently but diminish over time. They also suggest that there is a relationship between unresolved grief and depression (Zisook, 1987). Robinson and Fleming (1989) selectively reviewed this field and suggest that cognitive patterns are the chief differentiating element, with persistent distorted and negative perceptions of the self, life, and the future being relatively rare in uncomplicated bereavement. W. Stroebe and Stroebe (1987; see also this volume chapter 14) report that 42% of widowed as compared to 10% of a matched group of married people at 6 months suffered some depression. They see clinical depression as one form or outcome of pathological grief and feel that timing, intensity, and duration of depressive-type phenomenology may ultimately determine whether or not depressive illness is diagnosed after loss.

Jacobs, Hansen, Berkman, Kasl, and Ostfeld (1989) found a high rate of depression at 6 months (32% of bereaved spouses) and at 1 year (27%). Widows were more likely to be affected than widowers, with most of the depressions lasting considerably longer than 1 month, and anxiety, restlessness and psychomotor retardation being prominent. Melancholia occurred occasionally, and more intense grief was associated with depression. There was considerable overlap with anxiety disorders. Such high levels of depression would be a cause for concern and for major intervention programs if one could be assured that the depressive disorder has really been adequately differentiated from the bereavement reaction. Current studies are addressing this issue (Byrne & Raphael, 1991).

Low self-esteem has also been suggested as differentiating depression and grief, from the time of Freud's original dissection of mourning and melancholia. This also relates to such findings as those of Robinson and Fleming (1989) (negative cognitions of self) and Horowitz et al. (1980) (negative latent self-images). The etiology of such depression in bereavement was linked in Freudian theory to unresolved ambivalence in the relationship with the lost object. Earlier studies (Raphael, 1978) highlighted how this might contribute to depressive phenomena in bereaved widows, and, more recently, Parkes's ambivalent grief syndrome reflects a similar pathogenic mechanism (Parkes & Weiss, 1983).

In sum, depressive disorders may best be differentiated from normal bereavement reactions by the presence in those with depressive symptoms of negative views of the self and the world, including low self-esteem and hopelessness, by suicidal ruminations and fantasies of reunion with the lost person, retardation or anxiety and restlessness, ruminative and pre-occupying guilt, and profound depressive mood.

Anxiety disorders. Anxiety disorders in the bereaved had been little studied until recently. Anxiety measures have not been as widely used in the assessment of bereaved people as have been depression measures. The concept of separation anxiety as part of bereavement phenomenology has only recently been operationalized (Jacobs et al., 1987b). Jacobs's 12-item scale for separation anxiety attempts to quantify this and includes such usual anxiety items as feeling tense, nervous, and fidgety, with attachment items (e.g., longing for one's spouse). His specific investigation of anxiety disorders during bereavement (Jacobs et al., 1990) found that 44% of bereaved spouses reported at least one type of anxiety disorder during the first year after bereavement, particularly generalized anxiety disorder and panic disorder. Here, too, there was considerable overlap with major depression. Again, such high levels are of concern, and the realities of anxiety phenomena in bereaved people need to be better understood.

Another recent study, of elderly (more than 65 years old) widowed men suggests much lower rates of anxiety disorders (Byrne & Raphael, 1991).

Both the Jacobs and the Byrne-Raphael studies used standardized diagnostic measures, but the appropriateness and validity of standard diagnoses and diagnostic processes postbereavement clearly need to be further understood. The suggestion by W. Stroebe and Stroebe (1987) that many phenomena of depression may occur but may or may not reach levels required for diagnosis is also likely to be relevant here. Nevertheless, it is clear that the possibility of anxiety disorders should be considered when assessing the bereaved and appropriate treatment implemented when disorders clearly are of such severity and distress as to reach diagnostic criteria levels and to create dysfunction.

Post-traumatic stress disorder (PTSD). Just as conceptualizations have often equated bereavement to a reactive depression, so too has bereavement been seen as an example of a post-traumatic stress syndrome (Horowitz, 1976/1986), the trauma being the loss. It is useful, however, to consider more closely the phenomena of post-traumatic and bereavement reactions, for there is much to suggest that these phenomena are different, that one or the other may predominate, or both may occur together as in particularly "traumatic" bereavements.

Studies carried out before the development of the diagnosis of PTSD, such as that of Raphael and Maddison (1976), suggested that bereavement problems were likely to arise in association with "traumatic circumstances" of the death, which might lead to a "traumatic neurosis," which blocked or interfered with the bereaved's capacity to grieve. Similar observations appeared in disaster-related bereavement situations, where, for instance, Lindy, Green, Grace, & Titchener (1983) suggested that in psychotherapy dealing with bereaved disaster victims following a nightclub fire there was a need to work through the effects of the trauma before the individual could grieve.

Rynearson (1981, 1984, 1987) described reactions to severely traumatic losses, such as suicide, homicide, and other forms of "unnatural dying." People bereaved by homicide experienced intrusive, vivid, repetitive images of the death. These unbidden images interfered with the bereaved's cognitive processing. Nightmares, heightened arousal, hypervigilance, and avoidance also occurred. Rynearson concluded that PTSD partly described and subsumed these observed phenomena.

Sudden, unexpected, violent, and untimely deaths have been shown to increase the risk of unfavorable outcome (Raphael, 1977, 1983). In particular, Lundin (1984) showed that those who suffered sudden unexpected deaths reported significantly higher degrees of unresolved loss (as measured by the 34-item version of the Texas Grief Inventory). It is not clear if PTSD phenomena were present or caused this complication, however. Other studies of outcome, such as those of Lehman, Wortman, & Williams (1987), who assessed bereaved survivors who had lost a family member in a motor-vehicle accident, also showed ongoing difficulty resolving such losses, as well as high levels of symptomatology, especially anxiety.

Disaster research contributes further in attempting to separate out the pathogenic effects of traumatic encounter with death and loss. Weisaeth (1983), in a study of a paint factory explosion, showed a dose-response effect between the level of exposure to a traumatic threat to life and the development of post-traumatic stress reactions and disorder. Other studies (Shore, Tatum, & Vollmer, 1986) indicated the effects of loss in relation to depression and other morbidity, also with dose-response effects, but not the specific effects of grief as opposed to trauma reaction.

The study that has contributed most to separating out these two issues is that of Pynoos and Nader (1990). They and their group developed two separate measures: a Grief Reaction Inventory (9 items) and a PTSD Reaction Index (16 items). In a study of the reactions of children following a sniper attack at school, the researchers were able to show that severity of exposure to threat correlated with post-traumatic stress symptomatology levels, and closeness of relationship to children who had died, with grief phenomena levels. Sometimes each group of phenomena was separate, but at other times there was interplay between the two. They also found that relieving traumatic anxiety takes psychological priority over mourning.

More recently, Schut et al. (1991) examined a population of 128 bereaved spouses specifically for the occurrence of PTSD, and attempted also to assess what circumstances of death could be regarded as risks for developing PTSD in the first 2 years of bereavement. They found rates ranged from 20% to 31% and that 9% met PTSD criteria at every stage throughout the 2-year data collection period. In examining the circumstances surrounding the death they found that while duration of illness did not count, perceptions that the death was unanticipated or that there had not been a satisfactory opportunity to make farewells were correlated with higher risk of developing PTSD.

These findings extend the earlier work (Raphael, 1977, 1983; Parkes & Weiss, 1983) on the effects of traumatic, especially sudden, circumstances of death and suggest that the development of a post-traumatic stress reaction or even disorder may be a consequence, complicating the outcome and interfering with the resolution of such losses.

PTSD-complicated bereavement is likely to be differentiated by the intrusive phenomena that often reflect the scene of the death or other traumatic images, affects of anxiety, hyperarousal, nightmares, and other ongoing reexperiencing or avoidant phenomena. The preoccupations of a bereaved person who is not suffering a traumatic stress effect are more likely to be filled with yearning for the lost person and later sadness and nostalgia.

Somatic symptoms and disorders. Although Lindemann's original description of acute grief spoke of "waves of somatic distress," sighing, breathing, and so forth, the actual correlation between bereavement as a stressor and the development of somatic symptoms and/or disorder remains complex and poorly researched. Transient somatic symptoms reflecting the deceased's last illness, for instance, chest pains after a loved one has died from a heart attack, are believed to represent some form of identification. Nevertheless, as Parkes's original study (1964b) of the "broken-heart" effects of bereavement indicated, there may also be an association with increased cardiac mortality. Increased somatic symptoms of tiredness, backaches, and fatigue have been described, as has increased health care utilization (Maddison & Viola, 1968). No clear relationships have been shown with the development of specific disorder, although increased vulnerability to a wide range of health problems, from cancer to alcohol abuse, has been presented. Whether neuroendocrine effects or effects on immune functioning (Bartrop, Luckhurst, Lazarus, Kiloh, & Penny, 1977) are responsible has not yet been established, notwithstanding the results of some sophisticated recent studies (see part IV this volume). Changed patterns of health behavior, the somatic effects of depression, as well as a range of biologically based pathogenic processes, have all been suggested. Yet to date there are no definitive findings about specific physiological roles and mechanisms.

Clinically, one must conclude that bereaved people may present a range of somatic complaints or problems. As in any situation, the possible biopsychosocial bases of such phenomena for this particular individual need to be thoroughly assessed, taking into account not only the bereavement but also the individual and his or her background.

Pathological grief as a reflection of personality disorder

Though many risk factors have been suggested as leading to pathological outcomes of bereavement, they have rarely been linked directly to the pathological syndromes (except for Parkes & Weiss's, 1983, unanticipated grief syndrome, conflicted grief syndrome, and so forth). An area of particular significance, however, and one not well understood, is the possible relationship of personality to bereavement and personality disorder to bereavement pathologies. Sanders (1989) drew attention to increased risk of pathological bereavement outcome associated with personalities that were characterized by feelings of inadequacy, inferiority, and insecurity. Vachon et al. (1982b) indicated that people who were apprehensive, worried, and highly anxious were more at risk, and Parkes and Weiss (1983) described people who were insecure, anxious, and fearful as being more vulnerable. Perceived supportiveness of the social network has been widely studied and consistently found to correlate with outcome (Raphael, 1983), and this may indeed be a reflection of personality styles and competence or incompetence.

More importantly, however, the conceptualizations of attachment theory emphasize the patterns of early attachment – anxious ambivalent attachment, avoidant attachment (insecure attachments), and secure attachment – and how these may influence reactions to loss. Personality development is clearly influenced by the formation of such attachments, and the patterns of adult attachment have been shown to reflect similar attachment themes (Feeney & Noller, 1990; Shaver & Hazan, 1987). A recent review (Ainsworth & Eichberg, 1991) delineates the complex way in which unresolved loss can influence attachment themes and responses to further loss. The effects of attachment quality as an organizer of emotional and behavioral responses, and thus, perhaps, personality styles, have been studied longitudinally, showing the persistence of these early attachment themes (Grossman & Grossman, 1991).

It could be suggested that those individuals described by Bowlby (1973) as having childhoods characterized by anxious attachment to parents could be seen as demonstrating the sorts of features DSM III-R (1987) uses to describe "dependent personality disorder." Two diagnostic criteria for this disorder are feeling "devastated or helpless when close relationships end" and being "frequently preoccupied with fears of being abandoned."

Bowlby (1980/1981) singled out anxious, insecure, compulsive care givers and ambivalent persons as being most prone to pathological grief, whereas Parkes (1985) described the "grief-prone personality" as one characterized by excessive grief and depression, intense clinging behavior, or inordinate pining for the deceased spouse. It seems logical to suppose that those who relate poorly to the living are probably going to relate poorly to the dead. Where the relationship prior to death was beset with problems, it seems likely that the predisposition to relationship difficulties will continue in some form after loss.

Where personality is mentioned in the bereavement literature, it is frequently in a generalized way that does not equate easily with a widely used classification system. Such mention is typically related to ratings on a personality instrument that does not allow actual personality disorder diagnoses to be made. Surprisingly, evidence that should suggest the possible presence of personality disorder usually is not approached from this perspective.

Clayton (1982) estimated that 4% to 6% of cases of grief were pathological. Such percentages will vary considerably, depending on the definition used. Nevertheless, it is surprising that it was not until 1984 that research focused specifically on personality disorder as a pathogenic factor in bereavement (Alarcon, 1984). Alarcon noted that the impact of personality on the experience of grief is surprisingly neglected in the literature, and hypothesized that "in the absence of major affective disorder, 'complicated' bereavement is primarily a reflection of a personality disorder" (p. 46).

Given the relevance of psychodynamic and attachment theory concepts to theories of abnormal personality, as well as the frequent reference in the bereavement literature to character types or traits, it is surprising that no studies have been conducted to address Alarcon's hypothesis. Yet most bereavement theories predict personality-related differences in reactions to loss (W. Stroebe & Stroebe, 1987). If Alarcon's assertion is true, the term "pathological grief" could be a misnomer: Rather than the pathology being specific to the grief, the grief would be accentuating preexisting pathology.

The validity of the concept of pathological grief

The inherent difficulties in achieving consensual operational criteria for defining pathological grief are somewhat analogous to those in the study of neurosis. The term *neurosis* is widely used, and yet, as those who framed DSM III (1980) concluded, there was no consensus as to how to define it, with some using the term descriptively and others using it to define a specific etiologic process.

Pathological grief is not represented in official diagnostic manuals. Nor is it an established clinical entity. Even in the symptomatology thought to represent pathological grief, there is considerable overlap with other, more operationally defined syndromes, such as depression, anxiety, or post-traumatic stress disorder. It also would seem likely that personality disorder is underdiagnosed in patients labeled as having pathological grief. Although the term implies that the pathology pertains to the grief, the existence of other syndromes, either coexisting or precipitated by grief, makes it difficult to establish content validity for the syndrome.

Where a person has an existing illness or predisposition to illness, and following loss has a worsening of the condition (or, in the case of episodic conditions, a recurrence), it may not be valid to rename such a response pathological grief. In many instances it may be more valid to view grief as a risk factor for such disorders than to view such disorders as manifestations of pathological grief. An example would be a person with affective disorder who has an episode of major depression following a loss. It would seem more valid to describe that person as having major depression than a form of pathological grief. The literature struggles with this issue. For example, Jacobs and Kim (1990) describe symptoms of depression and anxiety as being part of pathological grief, at the same time separating out depression, anxiety disorder, and pathological grief as representing complications of grief. Acknowledging overlap among these selected syndromes, it was estimated that between 25% and 33% of acutely bereaved spouses suffered some "complication of grief" during the first year.

Such figures are at odds with Clayton's (1982) view that 4% to 6% of grief is pathological or Zisook and DeVaul's (1985) figure of 17% unresolved. In a way this comes back to the concept of whether grief is a disease or if it causes pathology, and if so what are the processes. If, indeed, all grief were so pathogenic, the outcomes for society would surely be more problematic than current realities would suggest.

The validity of the concept must also be considered in terms of cultural norms. Although it is evident that grief is ubiquitous in the face of the loss of significant relationships, the cultural nature of the relationships, their bonds, and meaning will influence the pattern of response to loss. Similarly, cultural prescriptions about grieving, its meaning, its duration, and affect expression will all be relevant (see Rosenblatt, this volume). These problems have been difficult enough in studying normal bereavement, let alone how pathological grief may be defined in different societies.

These themes are also relevant at a microsociety level. Different individuals and groups within any society or culture will have mores defining the importance of relationships, the reactions to loss, and the expression of such reactions when they occur. This is very clear in the different patterns and intensity of response for men and women in Western society. More intense grief has been demonstrated for women in several studies following the death of a child. Whether this more intense (and usually more prolonged) grief is pathological would certainly be open to question.

Conclusions

Defining pathological grief is complex, given diverse theoretical constructs, multiple variables influencing the manifestations of grief, and the many parameters that can be used to measure aspects of bereavement outcome. It is therefore understandable that key variables such as premorbid personality or culture have not yet been adequately accounted for.

It seems unlikely that pathological grief will become a unitary concept. Instead, future research will likely adopt a multidimensional framework in conceptualizing what may appear to be similar consequences, or pathologies, but which derive from very different sources and develop along very different paths. By way of example, the association between personality structure and pathological grief may be one of the approaches. Such issues need to be researched to determine whether the "pathology" relates to the loss or whether it is but a manifestation of previously demonstrated disorder or adjustment/personality problems.

Depending on the circumstances of the loss, many variables are associated with outcome. To date, however, no study has managed the daunting task of controlling for all major variables (such as preexisting disorders, culturally determined mourning practices, or post-traumatic stress disorder). Hence, we are still asking whether pathological grief is largely akin to clinical depression, whether it is primarily a reflection of personality disorder, or whether there is a large cultural bias inherent in the concept.

Grief is being viewed increasingly as a complex and evolving process, requiring the use of a multidimensional model. It has become clear that two individuals may score similarly on a given grief measure, but by very different routes. Even apparent similarities may be deceptive, as illustrated in the following possible scenario: A woman who loses her husband and children in a violent accident has similar manifestations of chronic grief/ depression and social withdrawal to a woman with a dependent personality disorder who has lost an ambivalently loved mother. Broadly the pattern of grieving and social isolation for these two women may be similar to that of a third woman, a widow, from a culture where the prolonged outward expression of grief is expected and where the formation of new relationships is taboo. High scores on a grief measure in the former two cases would likely be valid/accurate assessments of pathology, whereas such an interpretation would be less warranted in the last case. However, this whole issue is really more complex than such simple formulations might imply.

Further research into pathological grief would be enhanced by limiting the proliferation of descriptive or otherwise undefined terms. Research into the dimensions of pathological grief should, at the very least, account for preexisting character pathology, culturally determined mourning practices, anxiety/depression, post-traumatic stress disorder, and somatic responses. More use will have to be made of clinical diagnosis as opposed to rating scales in areas where they are not a very satisfactory tool, for example, in diagnosing personality disorder, or with most current measures of the phenomena of bereavement.

Finally, as in all areas of human response, the question of what is normal or abnormal and pathological must reflect accepted conceptual themes for that society and its social systems. Grief is no exception.

4

Measurement issues in bereavement

ROBERT O. HANSSON, BRUCE N. CARPENTER,
AND SHARON K. FAIRCHILD

To date there is no common strategy for assessing the psychological reaction to bereavement. Widely differing measurement approaches reflect the complex nature of the phenomenon, as well as the diversity of purpose among researchers and practitioners. The essential question is how to measure grief in any meaningful sense. The emotional reaction to the loss of a loved one is particularly complex in that it tends to involve cognitive, affective, behavioral, physiological, and social symptoms (cf. W. Stroebe & Stroebe, 1987). Moreover, each of these can be assessed at several levels. The physiology alone might be assessed as part of the symptomatology (experience) of grief itself, such as hypoarousal or gastrointestinal problems; as disruption in related systems, such as immunologic or endocrine markers (Irwin & Pike, this volume; Laudenslager, Boccia, & Reite, this volume; Kim & Jacobs, this volume); or as consequences of grief, such as long-term epidemiological outcomes (McCrae & Costa, this volume). Similarly, assessment might proceed from particular perspectives, such as stress and coping.

In addition, grieving is thought to progress through somewhat overlapping stages of resolution (cf. Weiss, this volume; Shuchter & Zisook, this volume), and given symptoms may be present at several stages, although more characteristic of some stages than others. Thus, any given clinical picture should probably be viewed within its temporal context. Validation strategies for a grief instrument, therefore, often include an assessment of whether the nature and intensity of symptoms vary as expected over time. However, the assessment of an instrument's test–retest reliability becomes problematic if symptom levels are expected to change over time.

Other issues may further confound the assessment of grief. For example, the nature and functions of grief appear to reflect vast individual and cultural differences (Rosenblatt, this volume). Also, many of the symptoms central to the grief experience are also markers for other, more general psychological constructs, such as stress or depression, or are widely associated with such factors as aging, loss of social support, dispositional loneliness, and so on, raising concerns about discriminant validity. In clinical settings, however, distinguishing grief reactions from similar constructs may only be important when there are treatment implications.

Clearly, then, research and clinical assessments related to grief and recovery will need to be multidimensional and tailored to the research questions or client populations involved. Within that context, we have three goals in this chapter. In the first section we review recent instruments that focus primarily on the nature and intensity of one's grief experience. In the second section we review broader measurement strategies that typically extend the scope of assessment to include related health and coping variables. Finally, we will discuss a variety of contextual (and potentially confounding) factors that should be considered when formulating a measurement strategy for bereavement and recovery. The reader will note also that the focus here is primarily on psychometric approaches to measurement in bereavement. For the role of the clinical interview in exploring the nature of the lost relationship, the meaning of the loss, the presence of concurrent stressors, the client's personal and social coping resources, and the like, see Raphael, Middleton, Martinek, and Misso, chapter 28, this volume.

Grief instruments

A small number of instruments have emerged that may be useful in research and clinical efforts pertaining to grief. However, these instruments vary considerably in scope, in their specificity to grief (as compared to loss or stress generally), and in their relative emphasis on affective, cognitive, physiological, behavioral, or attitudinal disruption. They also differ widely in the rigor of their theoretical underpinnings, in level of conceptual and psychometric development, in their intended purpose (e.g., for initial health screening vs. more detailed diagnosis), in the populations for which they have been validated, and in their appropriateness and ease of use in research or clinical settings (Gabriel & Kirschling, 1989; Jacobs, 1987a). Moreover, very little has been done by way of comparing the various measures empirically (Jacobs, 1987a).

Measures of grief are, for the most part, designed to characterize symptomatology rather than the grieving process or adaptive behaviors. As a consequence, most assessment has focused on negative emotional states and the social–behavioral reactions that accompany such states. Thus, guilt, anger, anxiety, and depression are frequently measured characteristics, as are withdrawal, health problems, rumination, loneliness, and poor self-care.

Because grief is a relatively private experience, most researchers have opted for self-report measures, usually of a questionnaire or interview format. The type of item, however, varies widely along a dimension from global, traitlike items to behavior- and situation-specific items. (Although grief is technically a state, the long duration for most persons also makes it traitlike; thus, both types of items can be useful.) The scales are most often rationally developed, based on the researcher's concept of what might be important to assess, without a strong theory to tie together the constructs. There are relatively few empirically derived scales, and psychometric examination is usually modest.

Multifaceted measures

An early grief instrument, developed for the Harvard bereavement study, suggested the broad range of constructs that might be useful in clinical assessment (cf. Parkes & Weiss, 1983). In this research a multidimensional inventory focused on status of recovery with regard to level of functioning, movement toward solution, acceptance of the loss, socializing, attitude toward the future, health, anxiety/depression, guilt/rage, self-evaluation, and resilience. Since then, a number of similarly multidimensional instruments for which greater psychometric information is available have been developed. The Grief Experience Inventory (Sanders, Mauger, & Strong, 1985) and the Texas Revised Inventory of Grief (Faschingbauer, Zisook, and DeVaul, 1987) are among the most comprehensive of these instruments.

The Grief Experience Inventory (GEI) contains 135 items. On the assumption that grief must be viewed as a multidimensional experience, the GEI provides a profile of grief reactions across nine dimensions: despair, anger/hostility, guilt, social isolation, loss of control, rumination, depersonalization, somatization, and death anxiety. Alpha coefficients of internal consistency for these subscales range from .52 (for the six-item guilt scale) to .81 (for the 20-item somatization scale). Validation studies with the GEI demonstrated modest correlations between specific GEI subscales and related scales derived from the MMPI and discrimination between bereavement status groups.

The Texas Revised Inventory of Grief (TRIG) contains two subscales. The first subscale (eight items) concerns feelings and actions at the time of the death, for example, the extent to which the death affected one's emotions, activities, and relationships. The second subscale (13 items) focuses on present feelings (continuing emotional distress, lack of acceptance, rumination, painful memories). Thus, it may be possible to use the instrument to assess adjustment to date, to measure change over time, and to develop clinical norms against which to compare individual cases. One concern regarding the first subscale, however, is its retrospective nature and the potential for memory of past emotional states to be influenced by current state. Some evidence for construct validity has been provided by criterion group analyses and by findings that the intensity of present feelings varies as expected over time, that is, worsening over the first year and then gradual improvement. Coefficient alphas for the two scales are .77 and .86, respectively, suggesting a moderate level of reliability typical of relatively short scales.

Related measures

A variety of other instruments may also be of use to researchers and practitioners. For example, the 15-item Impact of Event Scale (IES; Horowitz, Wilner, & Alvarez, 1979) focuses on two major responses to any traumatic life event: the intrusion of thoughts, images, and feelings about the past event and attempts to avoid such feelings and cognitions. Validity evidence for the scale includes its ability to discriminate between bereavement status populations and its sensitivity to change over time (Horowitz et al., 1979; Zilberg, Weiss, & Horowitz, 1982).

Another useful approach combines the elements of existing measures to assess aspects of grief within a particular theoretical framework. Guided by attachment theory, Jacobs and co-workers constructed a 38-item scale to assess numbness and disbelief, separation anxiety, and depression (Jacobs, Kasl, Ostfeld, Berkman, & Charpentier, 1986; Jacobs et al., 1987a,b). The 20-item Center for Epidemiologic Studies Depression Scale (CES-D) (Radloff, 1977) formed the depression content of this combined measure. All three components discriminated between bereaved and nonbereaved groups, and the intensity of separation anxiety and depression was found to be stronger at that point in time of the bereavement consistent with theoretical prediction.

Finally, the seven-item Grief Resolution Index (Remondet & Hansson, 1987) may be a useful screening instrument with respect to prolonged bereavement-related distress. Items focus on acceptance, closure, and social reintegration. Scores are related to a range of long-term measures of emotional and social adjustment and to ratings of health status.

Summary

A variety of measures focus on the central features of the grief experience. They appear to have adequate reliability, but evidence is still modest regarding item coverage and choice of subscale constructs. Although they appear to be somewhat similar in symptoms assessed, the measures differ considerably as to whether they assess the symptoms as part of a single construct or as multiple constructs. Thus, the picture of internal validity is somewhat confusing. Initial external validity evidence is encouraging, but modest in scope.

Broader measurement strategies

The previous section focused on instruments with which to assess the psychological experience of grief. However, research and clinical assessments in bereavement typically involve also a wide variety of extant scales (with demonstrated reliability and validity) that measure prominent features of grief, such as depression scales. In addition, they often incorporate measures to assess allied features that would not themselves necessarily be viewed as symptoms of grief, such as disrupted work behavior, health, and family relations. To illustrate the range of measures available for bereavement assessments, we describe in this section measures used in recent longitudinal bereavement studies.

One such project is the University of Southern California study (Gallagher, Breckenridge, Thompson, & Peterson, 1983b; Gallagher-Thompson, Futterman, Farberow, Thompson, & Peterson, this volume). This project has addressed a variety of longitudinal questions using a comprehensive assessment battery, including the Texas Revised Inventory of Grief (TRIG), the Beck Depression Inventory (Beck, 1967), self-ratings of mental health, and the Brief Symptom Inventory (BSI; Derogatis, 1977a). The BSI contains 53 items that focus on nine dimensions of psychopathology (somatization, obsessive–compulsive, interpersonal sensitivity, depression, anxiety, hostility, phobic anxiety, paranoid ideation, and psychoticism). TRIG scores were most predictive of bereavement group status, although groups also differed significantly on depression, total scores on the BSI, and self-ratings.

Similarly, the University of Utah longitudinal bereavement study has developed a comprehensive strategy for assessment (Lund, Caserta, & Dimond, 1986a; Lund, 1989a; Lund, Caserta, & Dimond, this volume). Two widely used instruments, the Self-Rating Depression Scale (Zung, 1965) and the Life Satisfaction Index-A (Neugarten, Havighurst, & Tobin, 1961), provide a baseline for emotional well-being. In addition, 26 bereavement-related feelings and 16 bereavement-related behaviors (from the earlier Harvard bereavement study) are assessed. Five global grief subscales have been derived from the 42 items (emotional shock, psychological strength/coping, anger/guilt/confusion, helplessness/avoidance, and grief resolution behaviors). A consistent pattern of improvement was evident across these measures during the first 2 years of bereavement, although there continued to be evidence of loneliness, adjustment difficulties, and grief resolution behavior at 2 years. The battery of measures used in this study has also been useful in assessing the roles of social support and individual competencies or coping abilities in eventual adjustment to bereavement (Lund, 1989a).

The San Diego longitudinal study (Zisook, Shuchter, & Lyons, 1987;

Shuchter & Zisook, this volume) conducted similar assessments of general emotional well-being across a 4-year period. However, this study also assessed a surviving spouse's functioning more broadly, focusing on work, social, sexual, and illness experiences, health habits (including consumption of alcohol, tobacco, and medications), and renewed interest in dating and marital relationships. Affective disruption and renewed functioning across the four years of this study generally followed consistent and improving patterns.

In contrast, a goal of the Tübingen longitudinal study of bereavement (M. Stroebe & Stroebe, 1991; W. Stroebe & Stroebe, chapter 14, this volume) has been to investigate more closely risk factors for poor bereavement outcome. Thus, in addition to such psychological outcome measures as depression and adjustment to the loss, this study includes detailed analyses of matched nonbereaved control groups, measures of forewarning of the loss, perceptions of control, social support, and involvement in emotional grief work. Interview protocols also provide an indicator of coping style, for example, control of emotionality, self-disclosure with respect to the loss, seeking distraction, and avoidance of reminders.

Finally, numerous studies (including a number represented in the present volume) have also assessed physical health symptoms using somatic complaint checklists, ratings of illness experience, ratings of ability to perform the activities of daily living (ADL), self-ratings of overall health, and the like (cf. Kane & Kane, 1981). To the extent that scores on such indices of physical health can be separated statistically from scores on emotional disruption and depression accompanying bereavement (which also often include somatic components), they can be quite useful (W. Stroebe & Stroebe, 1987).

Contemporary issues in bereavement measurement

Although the types of instruments and measurement strategies described have proven useful in attempts to understand bereavement, a number of issues remain problematic. Their resolution could substantially contribute to conceptual and clinical progress in the field.

Measurement of process

Most psychometric work has emphasized "snapshot" assessments of health and psychological status rather than ongoing process (although a number of investigators have also assessed changing patterns of symptom configurations relative to theoretical predictions over time, e.g., Zisook et al., 1987; Jacobs et al., 1987a,b). However, there also exist a rich body of theory regarding adaptational process and behavior and a wealth of clinical descriptions concerning intellectual acceptance, emotional acceptance, identity change, and so on (cf. Parkes & Weiss, 1983). It would seem useful at this point to begin to refine theory-guided measures of expected progress with respect to such adaptational processes in order to include specified criteria for resolution of process.

Theoretical concerns

Measurement strategies might also shed light on the theoretical controversies in the field, one example being if we should try to measure constructs other than "recovery to baseline." Silverman (1988a) and Weiss (this volume), for example, have argued that bereaved persons never really recover, that they are forever changed in certain ways. Weiss concludes that perhaps what we should be measuring is adaptation, accommodation, or degree of damage. This is consistent with other research on coping (cf. Lazarus & Folkman, 1984), which suggests that major stressors have long-lasting and cumulative effects, encouraging us to view coping as the process of combating the problem rather than good outcome. This perspective, then, views bereavement as a coping process, as well as a reaction to loss and change.

Overlapping constructs

We noted earlier that many of the symptoms associated with the grief experience may also be markers for stress, depression, aging, loneliness, and so forth. To the extent that grief assessment relies on such constructs, the possibility increases that other factors are influencing outcomes. For example, although grieving persons might experience depression as a consequence of their losses, factors quite apart from bereavement, such as the depression that many people experience with age-related illness or disability, might elevate depression scores for some. As yet, we cannot say that grief-specific instruments measure anything beyond these related states, although it appears likely, given the finding in some studies of their relatively greater ability compared to measures assessing broad symptomatology, to distinguish between bereaved and nonbereaved groups. If so, such direct measures may be found to separate out better grief from confounding states.

Competency and functional status

Bereavement measurement approaches have, for the most part, focused on the presence and intensity of symptoms (mental, physical, social disruption, etc.), on the resolution of symptoms over time, and on comparisons with norms among nonbereaved groups. However, we have seen that the experience of such symptoms is highly complex and characterized by vast individual differences. Therefore, assessment of the personal and situational contexts in which bereavement occurs may be critical to treatment decisions. In particular, practitioners might want to include in their assessments a variety of measures more directly related to the kinds of care or treatment decisions they will be making.

Current work in gerontological assessment provides a useful model. The elderly also tend to experience complex symptoms associated with multiple, simultaneous diagnoses (cf. Hansson, Remondet, & Galusha, this volume). For example, to an increasing degree their overall well-being also reflects an interaction of physical, mental, and social factors, thus requiring multidimensional assessments. In response, practitioners dealing with the elderly have found it helpful to include in their assessments measures of competency and functional status. Thus, measures focus on the person's continuing (or changing) ability to function independently (at work, socially, in terms of the physical activities of daily living, etc.) regardless of the configuration of medical symptoms he or she is experiencing at the time. (See Kane & Kane, 1981, and Gallagher, Thompson, & Levy, 1980, for excellent reviews of this literature.)

The burgeoning literature on stress and coping also makes a strong case for emphasizing personal and other situational factors in one's reaction to stressors (e.g., Lazarus & Folkman, 1984; Carpenter, in press). An overemphasis on bereavement, per se, or an implied assumption that the only salient factor is one's bereavement status oversimplifies the grieving person's situation to a dramatic degree. Coping research reminds us that personality, other stressors, health status, cognitive schemas, and social support status all contribute to outcomes resulting from stress. For proper evaluation and remediation, our measurement approaches, then, ought to assess the personal and environmental contexts in which grief occurs.

A very few bereavement researchers have begun to incorporate competency or functional measures into their work. For example, Zisook et al. (1987) assessed earned income and noted self-reports of ability to work, enjoy sex, and the like. McCrae and Costa (this volume) assessed functioning with respect to physical activities of daily living. Kitson and Roach (1989) incorporated self-reports of social functioning, defined as level of functioning in one's role responsibilities in housework, cooking, working, activities with children, and so on.

Practitioners, however, are particularly concerned about identifying appropriate interventions and their likelihood of success. Broad-based assessment would likely be helpful in achieving this goal. Evaluation should focus, therefore, on adaptive features and would emphasize two classes of characteristics: capacities and tendencies. Evaluation of capacities tells us what the individual is capable of doing, so that treatment does not place unrealistic expectations on the client. In contrast, assessment of tendencies, by clarifying what one is inclined to do, warns the practitioner of maladaptive predilections and the most likely points of intervention.

Older client issues

Because widowhood is likely to occur in one's later years, bereavement assessment strategies should typically be sensitive to a variety of other concerns surrounding the assessment of older adults (Kane & Kane, 1981; Gallagher et al., 1980). For example, test procedures may be less reliable or valid among older clients who are unfamiliar with the content of specific tests or with tests generally or who experience test-evaluation anxiety, fatigue, or lack of motivation. It is especially important to assess subjects' coping resources (e.g., income and social support networks) and level of competence relative to the environment in which they will be expected to live. Measures of other recently experienced stressful life events, of the presence of significant health problems, and of cognitive functioning should aid in this endeavor. It is important also to incorporate into the assessment markers or predictors of the level of external services the individual is likely to require.

Temporal concerns

A number of interesting questions relate to the length of time over which bereaved persons should be assessed. Most persons show substantial recovery on mental and physical health measures within approximately a 2-year period (cf. Lund, Caserta, & Dimond, 1986a; W. Stroebe & Stroebe, chapter 14, this volume; Thompson, Gallagher, Cover, Gilewski & Peterson, 1989; Zisook et al., 1987). Yet, for some individuals, adjustment may take considerably longer, perhaps due to predisposing health or dispositional factors or to lasting changes in financial or social status resulting from the loss of a spouse.

As research clarifies the factors that place one at risk for prolonged bereavement, we may be able to target in advance those requiring long-term assessment. In the meantime, assessments should be highly sensitive to individual differences in the course of adjustment. It should be of concern that most bereavement studies first recruit subjects after the death of their loved one, and thus do not have access to pre-event measures on such individual difference variables. The role of personality, for example, has been shown widely and consistently to influence coping and well-being in longitudinal studies of aging (McCrae & Costa, 1984; McCrae & Costa, this volume). One interesting project that includes a particularly comprehensive focus on predictors of adaptation to widowhood is now underway, however. As a part of a longitudinal, multidisciplinary study of functioning in older adults, the MacArthur Battery is scheduled to provide prewidowhood assessments of experienced stress, marital relations, social support, personality, and mental and physical health. Follow-up assessments will span a 5-year period (Kahn, House, & Wortman, 1989).

Another question concerns measures that should show predictable improvement over time and those that should not. For example, many of the studies described here assessed a broad array of psychological variables. Some of these – for example, depression, fear, helplessness, and cognitive distortion – might be expected to subside over the normal course of bereavement. But other variables might be less likely to vary predictably over time because they more closely reflect stable individual differences in dispositional vulnerability, personality or coping style (cf. McCrae & Costa, 1984).

Simplifying assessments

Recent efforts to simplify the assessment of mental health among bereaved and nonbereaved adults have focused on the search for an underlying factor structure in the kinds of measures we have been discussing. For example, Zautra, Guarnaccia, and Reich (1988) assessed a sample of older adults (comparing bereaved, disabled, and controls) using three comprehensive inventories: the Mental Health Inventory (MHI; Veit & Ware, 1983), the PERI Demoralization Composite (Dohrenwend, Shrout, Egri, & Mendelsohn, 1980), and Bradburn's (1969) Positive Affect Scale. These scales in combination yielded 10 interpretable factors of mental health (anxiety, depression, suicidal ideation, two measures of positive affect, emotional ties, anxiety/dread, poor self-esteem, confused thinking, and helplessness/hopelessness).

Confirmatory factor analyses suggested the presence of two, negatively correlated factors (psychological distress and psychological well-being). Indices loading on the distress factor were anxiety/dread, helplessness/ hopelessness, confused thinking, anxiety, suicidal ideation, and depression. Indices loading on the well-being factor were poor self-esteem, emotional ties, both measures of positive affect, and depression (depression loaded on both factors). This factor structure appeared generally similar across the three groups of older adults, leading the authors to conclude that these instruments might be used for mental health assessments of a wide range of stressed and nonstressed older persons (including the recently bereaved). The authors noted, however, that the factor structure differed somewhat from that found using samples of younger adults.

The factor structure observed by Zautra et al. was similar to that found by Remondet and Hansson (1987), who assessed older widows on a range of instruments focused more directly on the bereavement experience. In that study, measures of current adjustment included self-esteem, depression, loneliness, anxiety, perceived success in handling the various tasks of adjusting to widowhood, and perceived success in resolving grief. Using a variety of additional instruments, respondents also reported on their psychological state immediately after becoming a widow. These measures focused on feelings of being prepared to deal with the logistic and emotional changes in their lives, desperation, fear, and confidence in their ability to survive the ordeal. A factor analysis of scores on these measures also produced two underlying factors, labeled emotional disruption and positive adjustment. The measures of fear, despair, depression, anxiety, loneliness, and poor self-esteem loaded on the emotional disruption factor. Self-reports of current health and satisfaction with family relationships also loaded, negatively, on this factor. The measures of perceived preparedness, resolution of grief, expectations for survival, and eventual adjustment to widowhood loaded on the positive adjustment factor.

These factor analyses suggest ways, then, in which bereavement assessments might be simplified. This would appear to be an important direction for future psychometric efforts in this area of highly complex symptomatology.

Cross-cultural issues

We noted earlier that cultures vary considerably in the meanings assigned to loss and in the nature of grief and its expression. Such fundamental differences increase the complexity through which we must view the grief response, and they may confound its assessment. These contextual issues play an important role in theoretical discussions of the nature of grief (e.g., Averill, 1968; Osterweis, Solomon, & Green, 1984; Rosenblatt, this volume; W. Stroebe & Stroebe, 1987), but they are not typically reflected in strategies for assessment. Psychometric efforts to redress this imbalance and to assess the validity generalization of instruments across cultures could prove rewarding.

Assessment instruments, to be useful across cultures, must be sensitive to cross-cultural variability, tapping a sufficient array of phenomena to highlight the individual experience of grief; in the absence of such variability, cultural boundaries for particular measures should be specified. Published reports need to indicate clearly the degree of individual variability rather than simply emphasizing mean values; and we must not too readily generalize findings to other populations or apply group findings to the individual. Cross-cultural comparisons are needed to clarify the cultural influences and establish the central features.

Family systems assessments

A final issue concerns the focus of bereavement assessment. Clearly, the person/spouse most immediately affected is an appropriate assessment target, but understanding the impact on the family system might be equally valuable for several reasons: (1) The death of the loved one necessarily alters the family system, placing additional demands on the bereaved, which will vary across systems; (2) changes in the system will take time to reach equilibrium, leaving the bereaved in an indeterminate state for some period of time; and (3) the remaining support system may also be bereaved and, consequently, poorly prepared to provide needed support. Rosenblatt (this volume) argues that our understanding of grief should include its implications for the family system, its rules and coping resources, and its ability to support the most immediately bereaved member, as well as its ability to continue to meet its own needs given the loss of an integral and contributing member.

Gerontological, clinical, and family researchers (among others) have long been interested in this broader, family systems perspective, and have incorporated it into their assessments. Extending this perspective to assessment strategies for bereavement would seem equally useful, and clinical interviews do often incorporate this broader focus (cf. Raphael, Middleton, Martinek, & Misso, this volume).

Unfortunately, family systems research has produced relatively few psychometrically sound instruments that might be applied to bereavement. One approach might be to use measures that characterize the family and work environment, such as the Family Environment Scale (Moos & Moos, 1986). A number of techniques for social network analysis might also be adapted to detect disruption or change in the structure, composition, stability, or support potential of bereaved family networks (cf. Acock & Hurlbert, 1990). In addition, a wide range of self-report instruments are now available to assess the state of intergenerational support, family cohesiveness, or caregiver strain in a family system (cf. Kane & Kane, 1981; Kosberg, Cairl, & Keller, 1990).

Practitioners may also find it useful to develop a historical account of a family's structure, patterns of relating, and mutual support. One method for accomplishing this is the genogram, an interview approach to mapping systematically the family tree across several generations, noting historical patterns of relational functioning, stability, dependency, abuse, resource allocation and sharing, coping with traumatic life events, problems with substances, jobs, the law, and so on (McGoldrick & Gerson, 1985). It should be emphasized, however, that while self-report measures of family experience may be vulnerable to distorting perceptual processes, genogram and social network analyses may be further confounded by factual inaccuracies associated with reliance on selected participant-informants within the network.

Conclusions

A number of points should be emphasized from the preceding discussion. There is currently no standard approach to bereavement assessment, a reflection in part of the complexity of the phenomena under study as well as the diversity of purpose among researchers and practitioners. A number of grief measures have been developed that have sufficient psychometric work to encourage further study. However, assessments are often multidimensional and commonly extend beyond the initial grief reaction to issues of coping, resources, risk factors, and recovery.

A wide range of issues still need to be addressed. We should be assessing the important components of grief process, in addition to symptoms and outcomes. Researchers should also address the remaining discriminant-validity questions surrounding their instruments, minimizing their overlap with more general measures of emotionality, mood state, and health problems. It would also aid practitioners to incorporate into assessments a greater emphasis on competency and functioning, regardless of the particular symptoms currently being experienced by the bereaved individual. Given the age demographics of bereavement experience, assessments would also benefit from a greater sensitivity to issues surrounding the psychological measurement of older adults. Finally, two contextual themes are worthy of further consideration: Bereavement assessments should in many cases extend beyond the most immediately affected individual to the family system, and efforts should be made to assess the validity generalization of instruments across cultures.

PART III

Current theories of grief, mourning, and bereavement

5

Grief as an emotion and as a disease: A social-constructionist perspective

JAMES R. AVERILL AND ELMA P. NUNLEY

The third edition of *The Handbook of Social Psychology* (Lindzey & Aronson, 1985) contains no references to grief. Rodin (1985), in her contribution to the *Handbook*, does discuss briefly some of the consequences of bereavement. However, her discussion focuses on the deterioration in health that sometimes follows the loss of social support in general; grief as an emotion is not mentioned. This lack of reference to grief in volumes that presumably represent the state of the art might suggest that grief poses no issues of relevance to social psychology, either theoretically or practically. But such a suggestion has little plausibility. On the theoretical level, grief raises fundamental issues regarding the ties that bind people together and hence that make society possible in the first place. On the practical level, grief places a heavy burden on society, in the form of funeral and mourning rites, care for the bereaved, and so forth.

The neglect of grief by psychologists is by no means universal. During 1985, the same year that *The Handbook of Social Psychology* was published, 98 articles and books were listed under the heading of grief in *Psychological Abstracts*. This compares with 27 listings in 1975, 42 in 1980, and 107 in 1990. Most of this burgeoning literature has to do with the clinical aspects of grief. Grief is not only a state of intense personal anguish; it is also associated with increased risk for a wide variety of psychological and somatic disorders. Indeed, the suggestion has been made that grief itself is like a disease (Engel, 1961). We will examine that suggestion later in this chapter. For now, suffice it to note that grief is increasingly being recognized as a problem to be treated within the health care system. This trend raises a number of important issues. For example, what changes, if any, must be made in the health care system to accommodate a phenomenon such as grief? And how might the nature, experience, and expression of grief change as it is incorporated into the health care system? We touch on both of these questions in this chapter. Our primary purpose, however, is to

Preparation of this paper was supported, in part, by a grant (MH 40131) to James R. Averill from the National Institute of Mental Health.

77

explicate the nature of grief as an emotion, using the alternative conception of grief as a disease to illustrate the relation of emotional syndromes to social systems.

The chapter is divided into two main parts. In the first part we present a general model for the analysis of emotion based on biological, social, and psychological systems of behavior, and we outline a conception of grief as a social (emotional) role. In the second part we examine medical models of disease, noting some of the similarities and differences between conceptions of emotion and disease; and we speculate briefly on some of the implications of treating grief within the health care system.

Grief as an emotion

Ours is a social-contructionist view of emotion (Averill, 1980, 1991; Averill & Nunley, 1992). Such a view rests on certain assumptions. First, emotions are complex syndromes or subsystems of behavior, no single element of which is necessary for the whole. Second, the way a person construes events is an aspect of the emotional syndrome; and, moreover, such construals are determined, in part, by culturally based beliefs and values. Third, the expression of emotion is also a function of culturally based beliefs and values. Fourth, there is no essential core (e.g., innate affect program) that is completely independent of the beliefs and values that shape other aspects of an emotional syndrome. Fifth, emotional syndromes serve to reinforce the beliefs and values by which they are constituted. These assumptions do not deny the importance of biological and psychological determinants of emotional syndromes, as will be illustrated with respect to grief.

The syndrome of grief

There is not space to describe in detail the complex set of responses that characterize grief (for details, see Averill, 1979; Bowlby, 1980/1981; Lindemann, 1944; Osterweis, Solomon, & Green, 1984, Parkes & Weiss, 1983; Rosenblatt, 1983). However, for the sake of clarity in subsequent discussion, it is helpful to distinguish among four general types of reactions:

> *Shock* – a dazed sense of unreality, as might accompany any traumatic event
> *Protest* – active attempts to maintain contact with the deceased (if only symbolically)
> *Despair* – disorganization of behavior, often with a sense of helplessness and depression, as the bereaved accommodates to the reality of the loss
> *Reorganization* – the establishment of new object relations

These types of reactions form a rough temporal sequence, and hence, they are sometimes referred to as stages of grief. However, the word stage may connote a rigid or fixed boundary; in actuality, considerable overlap exists among the stages, and reactions of each type can be observed at any time following, or even in anticipation of, bereavement. The point that needs emphasis is that grief is a complex phenomenon, too complex to admit to any simple analysis. For example, the active searching for the lost object, characteristic of the second (protest) stage of grief, may require a different kind of explanation than do the somatic disturbances (e.g., loss of appetite) observed during the third (despair) stage.

Recognizing the risk of oversimplification, we will sketch in broad outline some of the origins and functions of grief as an organized whole. We begin by outlining a systems approach to the analysis of emotion (Averill, 1990; 1992). We then relate grief to systems of behavior defined in terms of biological, social, and psychological principles of organization.

Systems of behavior

A system comprises a set of interrelated components, such that changes in one subset of components induce changes in other subsets, and these changes in turn feed back on the former. Systems of behavior are like other kinds of systems, except by definition they comprise interrelated responses (i.e., what organisms do). Behavioral systems can be analyzed in terms of both levels and principles of organization (see Averill, 1990). Levels of organization refer to the hierarchical arrangement of components into subsystems, systems, and suprasystems of increasing complexity. Principles of organization refer to the ties that bind the various components into a coherent whole at whatever level of organization.

Level of organization. Efficiency of operation is achieved when systems are organized in a hierarchical fashion. For our purposes, it is sufficient to recognize four levels of organization, as depicted in Figure 5.1. The lowest level consists of component processes or elements (which actually can be quite complex systems in their own right). This is the level at which the various manifestations, or "symptoms," of grief (somatic complaints, mourning rituals, intrusive thoughts, etc.) are located. At the next level, these component processes are organized into a coherent emotional syndrome or subsystem of behavior. An emotional syndrome can, in turn, be related to even broader systems of behavior, the nature of which will be explained shortly. Finally, at the highest level of organization, we have the inclusive unit. This is the most encompassing (supra) system that can be treated within a given frame of reference (i.e., without invoking different principles of organization).

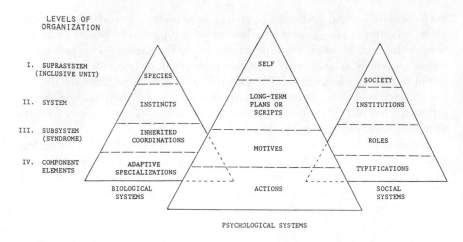

Figure 5.1. Systems of behavior defined in terms of levels and principles (biological, psychological, and social) of organization. (From Averill, 1990)

Principles of organization. Three kinds of principles may be distinguished – biological, social, and psychological – and these define three system hierarchies (see Figure 5.1). Biological principles are represented by information encoded in the genes; social principles are the rules and resources embodied in symbols and other cultural artifacts; and psychological principles are encoded in cognitive schemas (knowledge structures; cf. Mandler, 1984).

Relations among system hierarchies. The system hierarchies depicted in Figure 5.1 are abstract, theoretical constructs. With the possible exception of some rudimentary adaptive specializations in lower organisms (e.g., fixed action patterns), no actual behavior is a direct product of biological principles. Similarly, no actual behavior is due to social principles alone, although certain ritual practices come close. A response determined exclusively by psychological principles is also difficult to envision. Such a response would be idiosyncratic to the individual and hence impossible to describe in general terms; in actuality, not even the most eccentric response (e.g., an hysterical conversion reaction) is completely devoid of biological and social influences.

Stated somewhat differently, any complex human behavior (including emotional syndromes) can be explained in terms of biological, social, and psychological systems. No one type of system is more basic or fundamental than the others. This does not mean, however, that each type of system has exactly the same status in the explanation of behavior. For example, biological systems are temporally prior to social systems (in the course of human evolution), and the latter are temporally prior to psychological systems (each individual being born into a preestablished social order). In a temporal sense, then, biological systems are primary. On the other hand, biological and social systems can exert their influence only through the individual's psychological makeup, and hence psychological systems are primary in the sense of being "closest" to actual behavior. (This is why the psychological hierarchy is placed in the foreground of Figure 5.1.)

There is also a sense in which social systems can be considered primary. To the extent that a behavioral syndrome is common to a group of individuals, it must be organized (in part) by biological and/or social principles. But, as already noted, no complex human behavior is a direct result of biological principles. The final product is always shaped, added to, and given meaning within a social order. This fact, more than any other, lies at the heart of a social-constructionist view of emotion.

Emotions as subsystems of behavior. In Figure 5.1 we have located emotional syndromes at an intermediate level of organization, that is, as subsystems of behavior. In the biological hierarchy, this would be equivalent to what Dewey (1895) referred to as "teleological coordinations," but which might better be called in modern terminology "inherited coordinations," that is, genetically organized patterns of response. In the social hierarchy, emotions can be conceived of as social roles (as will be discussed in detail shortly); and in the psychological hierarchy, emotions are a variety of motive. (These terms – inherited coordinations, social roles, and motives – are not entirely adequate, for each has connotations beyond what we wish to imply. Nevertheless, we prefer to use familiar terms rather than to coin new ones.)

Because emotional syndromes are situated at an intermediate level of organization, analysis can proceed in two directions. The first, or "analytic," approach breaks the syndrome down into component processes. The second, or "holistic," approach proceeds in the opposite direction; that is, it relates emotional syndromes to systems of behavior at higher levels of organization. Our approach is primarily holistic. In the remainder of this section we will sketch in broad outline how the syndrome of grief has meaning (functional significance) in relation to broader systems of behavior defined in terms of biological, social, and psychological principles of organization; and we will examine in some detail the nature of grief as a social role (for additional details on the functions of grief, see Averill, 1979; Averill & Wisocki, 1981).

Grief as related to biological systems

As illustrated in Figure 5.1, the most inclusive unit in the biological hierarchy is the species. At the next (lower) level of complexity is what we have called biological systems *simpliciter*. These correspond to broad adaptive patterns that, in the older literature, were often referred to as basic instincts (aggression, harm avoidance, reproduction, and the like). Grief is related (subsidiary) to attachment as a biological system (Bowlby, 1980/1981) or, more accurately, to the disruption of attachment bonds.

Human beings are a social species, and as such, a social form of existence is necessary for survival. One way to ensure group cohesion is by making separation from the group, or from specific members of the group, a source of severe anguish and thus a condition to be avoided. This fact helps account for some of the responses manifested during the protest stage of grief, where attempts (actual and symbolic) to recover the lost object are common. When the loss is irreparable (as in death), reunion is, of course, not possible. Protest eventually gives way to withdrawal, apathy, loss of appetite, and other reactions common during the despair stage of grief. It is as though grief must run its biological course, to the distress and even physical detriment of the bereaved.

Grief as related to social systems

The most inclusive unit in the social hierarchy is the society (see Figure 5.1). Societies are, in turn, divided into various social systems, which (like their biological analog) are defined primarily in terms of the functions they subserve within the society as a whole (Luhmann, 1982). Some examples of social systems (and their related functions) are education (socialization), health care (prevention and treatment of disease), politics (collective decision making), and religion (meaning and value articulation). Social systems are, in turn, constituted by social roles. Emotional syndromes, to the extent that they are also determined by social principles of organization, can be conceived of as a kind of social role.

Separation and death have implications for the survival of societies as well as for human beings as a species. Therefore, it is not surprising that most societies have developed rather elaborate roles for the bereaved to enact. These roles (e.g., as reflected in mourning practices) are typically related to religious and political systems. They reinforce the fabric of society by assisting surviving members of the group to assign meaning to the loss, renew alliances, and realign commitments.

Because of their importance, mourning practices are not simply quaint customs that can be ignored at will. On the contrary, they are duties imposed by the group, often at considerable cost to the bereaved (cf.

Durkheim, 1915). However, the well-socialized individual who has internalized the relevant norms and customs of society will experience mourning not as something forced from without (i.e., a duty imposed by the group) but as something coming from within (i.e., a genuine emotional reaction). The fact that a response is based on social custom as opposed to species (genetic) endowment does not make it any less emotional from a subjective point of view.

Grief as related to psychological systems

Finally, let us consider briefly the hierarchy of psychological systems depicted in Figure 5.1. The most inclusive unit in this case is the self. At the next lower level of complexity, that is, psychological systems *simpliciter*, we have the long-term plans, or "life scripts," of the individual. As described earlier, biological systems are the result of biological evolution, and social systems are the result of social evolution; therefore, it might be assumed that psychological systems are the result of individual development or learning. But that is only partly true. Psychological systems are organized according to both biological and social principles, as these are transformed and elaborated upon during the idiosyncratic history of the individual.

Grief can be related to psychological systems in two ways. First, some symptoms of grief are undoubtedly due to an interrelated set of factors that have been variously attributed to the extinction (through a loss of reinforcement) of well-established behavior patterns, to the disruption of cognitive structures, and/or to the loss of feedback and social support formerly provided by the deceased. Second, grief has its own rewards (secondary gains) and its purposeful aspects. In fact, people have been known to feign grief in the absence of actual bereavement, showing apparently genuine anguish, depression, and even self-destructive behavior (Snowdon, Solomons, & Druce, 1978). Full-blown episodes of hysterical grief are, of course, rare. But how many persons who have actually suffered bereavement cultivate their grief for public show (to demonstrate the genuineness of their prior commitment to the deceased) and for the personal rewards it might bring (aid and succor from others)? The answer is probably most persons, at least to a limited extent.

Grief as an emotional role

With these remarks as background, let's examine some of the ways in which grief is, and is not, a social construction. For this purpose, we need to expand upon the notion of an emotional role (Averill, 1980, 1991; Sarbin, 1989). As described earlier, roles are units of analysis within the social hierarchy of behavior (see Figure 5.1). In a broader sense, however, the role concept cuts across the biological, social, and psychological levels of analysis. Human beings are not blank slates upon which society can write just any script, but neither does biology dictate the script. Most social roles – certainly, most emotional roles – are the products of a dialectic between biological and social evolution, as further conditioned during individual development.

An emotional role, like any other social role, can be analyzed in terms of privileges, restrictions, obligations, and entry requirements. Let us apply this kind of analysis to grief.

Privileges. While in an emotional role, a person may engage in behavior that would be discouraged under ordinary circumstances. The specific behavior allowed or excused varies, depending on the emotion. Among the privileges of grief are the public display of feelings that might otherwise be hidden (e.g., remorse, animosity). More importantly, grief exempts a person from the obligations of other social roles. Following bereavement, the individual is not expected to work, entertain, or care for others in the same manner as before. On the contrary, the bereaved individual has the right to expect care, nurturance, and assistance from others.

Restrictions. There are limits to what a person can do when emotional and "get away with it." Emotional responses should be appropriate to the situation: not too mild or too strong, too short or too prolonged, or too idiosyncratic. For example, if a bereaved wife begins dating too soon after the death of her husband, the genuineness of her grief and/or her adequacy as a wife may be questioned. Conversely, excessive grieving is also frowned upon. The person who grieves too intensely or too long may be regarded as hysterical or "affected."

Obligations. Whereas there are some things a person cannot do (restrictions) while emotional, there are other things that must be done (obligations). In all societies, for example, the bereaved are expected to perform certain mourning practices. These obligations can be neglected only at considerable risk; the individual who fails to comply with societal expectations following bereavement is often subject to severe sanction. In some societies, the obligations are only temporary; the bereaved is expected to abandon the grief role shortly after the funeral and to resume customary social obligations (as the biblical custom of a widow marrying her deceased husband's brother – Deuteronomy 25:5, 6). In other societies, the grief role shades into a more permanent social role, often lasting a lifetime (e.g., as widow or widower).

Entry requirements. Most, though not all, social roles have entry requirements; that is, they can be occupied only by persons of a certain age, sex, training, and/or social position. The same is true of emotional roles. Thus, in many traditional societies the way grief is expressed may be stipulated according to the age or sex of the bereaved, as well as to the nature of the relationship of the bereaved to the deceased – spouse, parent, child, cousin, and so forth. In contemporary Western societies, entry into the grief role is more open-ended as are the privileges, restrictions, and obligations associated with the role. However, one entry requirement that remains has to do with the nature of the loss. Our society is not structured to allow for grieving on certain occasions. For example, a person who has lost a spouse by divorce is not afforded the same emotional rights as a person who has lost a spouse by death. Also, grieflike responses are often experienced when children leave home (the empty nest syndrome), but this increasingly common problem is given little social recognition or support (Nunley, 1986).

Grief as a disease

Much more could be said about the nature of emotional roles, but we wish to turn now to another possible conception of grief – that is, grief as a disease rather than as an emotion. The importance of this conception is twofold. First, by serving as a foil for argument, an analysis of grief as a disease may help to clarify further the dynamics of grief as an emotion. Second, as grief increasingly becomes a concern for health care professionals, it will necessarily accrue some of the connotations of a disease. Some potential ramifications of this trend will be examined briefly.

A conception of grief as a disease is not as implausible as it might at first seem. As Levy (1984) has pointed out, grief is not universally treated within an emotional framework. The Tahitians, for example, classify responses to the loss of a friend or loved one not as signs of emotion but, rather, as symptoms of illness or fatigue. But we do not have to look to other cultures for examples. Grief is also compatible with contemporary medical models of disease: It is a debilitating condition, accompanied by pain, anguish, and increased morbidity; it is associated with a consistent etiology (real, threatened, or even fantasied object loss); and "it fulfills all the criteria of a discrete syndrome, with relatively predictable symptomatology and course" (Engel, 1961, p. 18).

Historically, too, emotions of all kinds – not just grief – have sometimes been regarded as diseases of the mind (e.g., by the Stoics, Kant). In part, this reflects a value judgment by those who view emotions as disruptive of ordered (rational) thought. But it also stems from the fact that both emotions and diseases are conceived of as something a person "suffers," as opposed to something a person does. To use a somewhat antiquated terminology, emotions are passions, not actions. The term *passion* stems from the Latin *pati, passio* (to suffer, suffering). *Pati* is, in turn, related to the Greek *pathos*. Diseases were also regarded as a kind of *pathos*. Hence, from the same root as "passion," we also get "pathology" and "patient."

Finally, on a more theoretical level, an analysis similar to the one we applied earlier to emotional syndromes can also be applied to diseases. That is, any particular disease can be analyzed in terms of biological, social, and psychological systems of behavior (or principles of organization). For some conditions (e.g., cancer), the biological may predominate; for other conditions (e.g., alcoholism), the social may predominate; and for still other conditions (e.g., hysterical conversion reactions), the psychological may be of primary importance.

In view of these considerations, a conception of grief as a disease does not seem at all implausible. In fact, one of the main reasons we raise this possibility is to pose the question: What is it about grief that leads us to classify it as an emotion rather than as a disease? In addressing this issue, Osterweis et al. (1984, chapter 2) list three reasons why grief is not, or should not, be classified as a disease: First, society does not consider grieving individuals to be sick; second, "normal" grieving can be distinguished from clinical depression; and third, the American Psychiatric Association's Diagnostic and Statistical Manual (DSM III-R) does not treat "uncomplicated bereavement" as pathological. Obviously, these three reasons beg the question.

Some of the main criteria for distinguishing emotional from nonemotional phenomena have been discussed in detail elsewhere (Averill, 1991). For our purposes here it suffices to note that, from a social-constructionist perspective, the nature and significance of emotional syndromes depend in fundamental ways on the broader social systems of which they are constituent parts. As an emotion, grief interdigitates with different social systems than do disease syndromes. Specifically, grief is part of the moral order (e.g., as defined by political and religious systems). By contrast, disease syndromes fall within the domain of the health care system.

To the extent that a social-constructionist view of emotion is valid, and to the extent that grief becomes incorporated into the health care system, either of two events is likely: Grief will increasingly lose its normality and become like other diseases, or the concept of disease will be expanded to include the social–moral domain. As we will discuss, advocates of a more holistic approach to medicine have argued for the second of these alternatives. We believe, however, that the first alternative is the more likely (but not necessarily the more desirable) outcome of current trends. In order to make clear the basis for this judgment, we must examine more closely the current medical model of disease.

The medical model

Actually, there is not one, but a variety of medical models. In its generic sense, the term *medical* refers to the preservation and restoration of health, whether practiced by a physician, a psychologist, or a tribal medicine man. Within this broad domain, our concern is with what we will call the scientific medical model, that is, a model based on modern science. But even here, distinctions can be made, depending on what is taken as the base science. The dominant biomedical model takes physiology and molecular biology as base sciences. By contrast, a psychomedical model can be delineated that takes psychology as the base science, at least for the treatment of psychopathology. We can even distinguish a sociomedical model, in which diseases are viewed as social constructions (cf. Mishler, 1981), thus making sociology the base science.

Engel (1977) has argued cogently for an expanded biopsychosocial medical model. Although such an expansion is certainly feasible and desirable in some respects, we doubt that it can ever be made to encompass an emotion such as grief without essentially altering the nature of the emotion. Our skepticism rests on three main points: (1) the common scientific orientation of the base disciplines, (2) vested professional interests, and (3) broader social–legal concerns. We will examine each of these grounds briefly, limiting (for the sake of simplicity) discussion to biological and psychological versions of the medical model.

Scientific orientation. As noted, the biomedical model relies on physiology and molecular biology for its scientific underpinning, whereas the psychomedical model adopts psychology as the base science. This is primarily a difference in content. In terms of orientation or attitude, the two models are more similar than dissimilar. Both adhere to the standards embodied in the scientific method; both tend to adopt an analytic as opposed to a holistic approach (as these approaches are described in an earlier section); and both tend to ignore the moral dimension of behavior (i.e., the person is not responsible or accountable for being sick). It is because of these similarities in orientation that we may speak generically of a scientific medical model that has both biomedical and psychomedical versions.

Professional interests. Medicine and psychology have similar, though often competing, professional concerns that help reinforce a scientific medical model. The delivery of health care is a major industry, involving hospitals, pharmaceutical companies, diagnostic laboratories, and so forth, as well as physicians and other professionals. This industry draws some of its rationale from the biomedical model and hence has a vested interest in the maintenance of that model (Engel, 1977). Similarly, psychologists have a vested interest in maintaining and extending their own version of the medical model. Psychology is a profession as well as a science, and like any other profession, it has guild interests to protect. One indication of this is the perennial controversy over certification, which assumes the existence of an objective (i.e., scientifically based) body of knowledge and associated practices of demonstrated effectiveness.

Social–legal concerns. Dominance of the biomedical model among physicians is fostered by broader social factors, as well as by scientific and professional concerns. To a certain extent, modern medicine is a victim of its own success, as the public has come to expect more than can sometimes be delivered. The result is reflected in the number of malpractice suits. Protection against suits forces physicians to adhere to conservative practices, for example, to follow well-accepted diagnostic and treatment procedures, such as those dictated by the biomedical model. Likewise, as psychologists assume responsibility for the prevention and treatment of an ever widening range of disorders, they also become potentially liable for failure (Szasz, 1986). The adoption of a psychomedical model provides some measure of security as psychological services are extended into new domains.

Some implications of incorporating grief into the health care system

For the above reasons – scientific attitudes, professional interests, and social–legal concerns – we are not optimistic that the medical model can, or should, be expanded to encompass such phenomena as grief. It is central to the medical model (whatever its scientific base) that disease states be divorced from moral concerns. This sets certain limits on the extent to which a health care system based on a scientific medical model can incorporate problems of living (including grief) without running the risk of "medicalizing" broad areas of society.

Without going into detail, some of the potential risks that arise when the medical model is extended to new domains can be seen in the controversies that surround the insanity defense, where otherwise legally culpable behavior is attributed to mental disease. Similar issues arise, albeit in much less dramatic form, when alcoholism, gambling, and other such conditions are treated as diseases. Or consider the vicissitudes in attitudes surrounding homosexuality, which at one time was considered a moral failing, at another time as a form of psychopathology, and now simply as a matter of personal preference.

Obviously, the classification of a condition as a disease has ramifications, both for the individual presumably "suffering" from the disease and for society at large. And what might those ramifications be with respect to grief? We will not attempt to speculate in detail, although two possibilities deserve brief mention because of their theoretical as well as practical relevance.

First, throughout this chapter, we have emphasized that emotions are constituted, in part, by the social systems to which they are related. It follows that the nature of grief itself may change as it is incorporated into the health care system. Needless to say, the objective of treating grief within the health care system is to alleviate suffering among the bereaved. But, in addition to the good that may be achieved by such a move, we should also be aware of possible negative consequences. Disease is a result, in part, of a disorganization or disregulation of function (Schwartz, 1979). The social norms and practices that help constitute grief as an emotion lend meaning and coherence to reactions following bereavement. A conception of grief as a disease will eliminate some of that meaning and coherence; and, as a consequence, bereavement reactions may become even more disregulated than they already are. And with the further disregulation of behavior, the pathological sequelae of bereavement may actually increase rather than decrease. Lest this seem like idle speculation, it might be noted that people who engage in traditional mourning practices tend to recover from bereavement faster than those who forgo such "formalities" (Pine et al. 1976).

The second point we would make is an extension of the first. If the nature of grief changes as it is incorporated into the health care system, this may create a rippling effect, as compensating changes occur in other social institutions to which grief is related. One example will suffice to illustrate the point. The family is a central unit in almost any society; hence, what affects the family may have wide-ranging ramifications. Rosenblatt (this volume) has discussed in some detail the importance of grieving to the integrity of the family unit and the ways that grief differs among families as a function of ethnic and cultural background. He further suggests that some "quality control" may be desirable because of the tendency of presumed grief experts (both researchers and health care practitioners) to ignore such differences.

We agree with Rosenblatt's concern. However, we must ask: quality control by whom? We believe the issue is not so much one of insufficient quality, but of the kind of social systems in which grief is to be conceptualized and "treated." Within a health care system based on a scientific medical model, many reactions that are accepted and even encouraged within a different (e.g., familial, religious) social context may be dismissed as superstitious at best and pathological at worst. Thus, to the extent that grief and mourning practices help reinforce traditional subgroup values and beliefs, one likely result of incorporating grief into the health care system is a weakening of support for such group differences and, hence, a further homogenization of society. Going further, as grief is often taken as a sign of love, it is not too far-fetched to suggest that a redefinition of grief may even occasion a reconceptualization of intimate relationships.

In short, a dialectical relation exists between emotional syndromes and the social systems of which they are a part. Changes in the way grief is treated will inevitably feed back on the social institutions that once gave it meaning, with effects that are difficult to foresee.

Concluding observations

We have been treating the conceptions of grief as an emotion and grief as a disease as though they were two, mutually exclusive alternatives – an obvious oversimplification. There are conditions, of which pregnancy and childbirth are prime examples, that are treated primarily within the health care system but that are not conceptualized as diseases. And, in fact, it has been suggested (e.g., Osterweis et al., 1984, chapter 2) that pregnancy might provide a good model for the treatment of grief by health care professionals. There are, however, limitations to this suggestion. The medical treatment of pregnancy focuses almost exclusively on physiological processes. The emotional aspects of pregnancy have only recently been given attention within the health care system, and then not without difficulty, as is evidenced by the growing popularity of midwives and natural childbirth.

But be that as it may. Our major purpose for drawing a sharp distinction between the concepts of grief as an emotion and grief as a disease has not been to argue for or against either alternative (for each has its advantages and limitations), nor to suggest that these are the only alternatives. Our purpose, rather, has been more theoretical and didactic. The contrast between grief as an emotion and grief as a disease serves to highlight the importance of considering emotions in relation to social as well as biological and psychological systems of behavior. When considering human emotions, a holistic framework must be developed that allows for understanding at different levels of functioning.

6

Bereavement as a psychosocial transition: Processes of adaptation to change

COLIN MURRAY PARKES

People are fascinating because of their individuality; no two problems are alike because no two people are alike. This tempts some people to reject theories of human behavior. There are none that can be expected to predict or explain more than part of a person, and it seems mechanistic to attempt to force people into preconceived models. Yet we must have some frame of reference if we are to be of use to those who cannot cope with life's vicissitudes. It is not enough for us to stay close and to open our hearts to another person's suffering; valuable though this sympathy may sometimes be, we must have some way of stepping aside from the maze of emotion and sensation if we are to make sense of it.

One might say that our central nervous system has been designed to enable us to do just that. Human beings, to a greater extent than other species, have the capacity to organize the most complex impressions into internal models of the world, which enable us to recognize and understand the world that we experience and to predict the outcome of our own and others' behavior. Psychological theories are one way of doing this, and the measure of their success is their usefulness.

This article describes a theory that the writer has found useful in explaining certain aspects of the human reaction to loss. Other theories are useful in explaining other aspects; these include theories about the nature of attachments, anxiety, family dynamics, and the psychophysiology of stress. Each of these adds something to our understanding of loss, and *they do not conflict* with each other. Aspects of most of these are considered elsewhere. The theory that follows is simple in essence but complex and wide ranging in its implications. It is not possible, in the space available here, to give more than an outline of its scope, inevitably condensed and shorn of detail.

Reactions to life events

Bereavement by death is a major psychological trauma and usually takes place in the presence of members of the caring professions; consequently, it

91

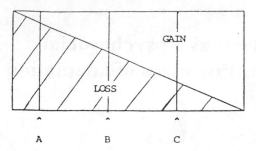

Figure 6.1. Gain and loss components of life changes.

has been much studied. In fact, one sometimes gets the impression that grief and mourning (the public face of grief) are confined to this type of loss, but there are some bereavements that are not a cause for grief and many griefs that have causes other than bereavement by death.

What, then, defines a loss? How can we distinguish grief from the other emotions that arise in the face of life events? Why is it that some life events menace our sanity while others are an unmitigated blessing? These questions are more easily asked than answered.

Grief is essentially an emotion that draws us toward something or someone that is missing. It arises from awareness of a discrepancy between the world that is and the world that "should be." This raises a problem for researchers because, though it is not difficult to discover the world that is, the world that should be is an internal construct; hence each person's experience of grief is individual and unique. Two women who have lost husbands are not the same. One may miss her husband greatly, while the other's grief may arise less from her wish to have her husband back (for she never did like him as a person) than from loss of the status and power that she achieved in marrying an important man. Clearly, grief is not a unitary phenomenon.

The situation is further complicated by the fact that there are many life-change events that bring about both loss and gain. The death of a loved person might be represented by a line at point A in Figure 6.1. Here the main component is one of loss, but the honest person will admit there are certain consequences of the death that add something wanted. Point B is more ambiguous, for here loss and gain may balance out, as in the case of the bride's mother who is told, "You are not losing a daughter, but gaining a son." A line at point C might represent the birth of a first baby. Here the gain element predominates, but most people would admit there are also losses (of parents' jobs, freedom, etc.) that cloud the celebration. In many life-change situations it is not at all clear what is being gained and what lost; attributions of loss or gain can only be made with hindsight, and the mixed feelings to which the event gives rise may prove perplexing.

That it is hard to classify particular life events into the categories of "losses" and "gains" suggests we should seek an alternative. One possibility is to focus on life-change events, but this too has its difficulties since life is constantly changing and many changes proceed smoothly, without unduly disturbing those who undergo them. In fact, the human tendency to seek out and explore novel situations and stimuli suggests we are well adapted to meet most of the environmental changes that impinge upon us, and we may even take pleasure in visiting new places, acquiring new possessions, and testing our mettle.

Psychosocial transitions

Studies of the life events that commonly precede the onset of mental illness (Brown & Harris, 1978; Caplan, 1961; Rahe, 1979) suggest the most dangerous life-change events are those that (1) require people to undertake a major revision of their assumptions about the world, (2) are lasting in their implications rather than transient, and (3) take place over a relatively short period of time so there is little opportunity for preparation. These three criteria are the defining characteristics for events that can be termed *psychosocial transitions* (*PSTs*) and that provide us with boundaries for a reasonably discrete area of study (Parkes, 1971a). They exclude events that may threaten but do not result in any lasting change (e.g., exposure to terrifying situations over short periods of time) because these seem essentially different in their psychological implications. Insofar as these events cause psychiatric problems (such as anxiety reactions or post-traumatic neuroses), these are likely to be different from the disorders associated with PSTs. The criteria also exclude gradual changes, such as those associated with maturation, unless these are associated with more rapid changes that "bring home" implications of the more gradual change. Thus the physical changes associated with sexual maturation do not constitute a PST, but they may bring about rapid attachments or disappointments that are PSTs.

One other characteristic of those life-change events that commonly predict illness is a tendency to be evaluated in a negative way. This criterion, while predictive in practice, has been excluded from the definition of PST because, as we have seen, it tends to be made with hindsight. It is tautologous to claim that negative or stressful events are causes of mental distress when it is the mental distress that has caused us to define the event as stressful! Furthermore, there are many events initially greeted as positive, such as having a baby, being promoted at work, or marrying the mate of one's dreams, that may subsequently tax our adaptive capacity to the limit.

The assumptive world

The internal world that must change in the course of a PST consists of all those expectations and assumptions invalidated by the change in our life space (i.e., the part of the world that impinges upon us – Lewin, 1935). These expectations constitute part of an organized schema or "assumptive world," which contains everything that we assume to be true on the basis of our previous experience. It is this internal model of the world that we are constantly matching against incoming sensory data in order to orient ourselves, recognize what is happening, and plan our behavior accordingly.

Waking in the morning, we can put on the light, get out of bed, and walk to the bathroom because we have an assumptive world that includes assumptions about the presence and layout of the doors, windows, light switches, and rooms in our home, and assumptions about the parts of the body that we must use in turning the light on, getting out of bed, walking across the floor, and so on. If as a result of some life event we lose a limb, go blind, lose our memory, move to a new house, or have the electricity cut off, we must revise our assumptive world in order to cope with the numerous discrepancies that arise.

The death of a spouse invalidates assumptions that penetrate many aspects of life, from the moment of rising to going to sleep in an empty bed. Habits of action (setting the table for two) and thought ("I must ask my husband about that") must be revised if the survivor is to live as a widow.

The pain of change

Such changes are easier said than done, for not only does a major PST require us to revise a great number of assumptions about the world, but most of these assumptions have become habits of thought and behavior that are now virtually automatic. The amputee knows very well that he has lost a limb, but this knowledge does not prevent him from leaping out of bed in the morning and sprawling on the floor because he has tried to stand on a leg that is not there. Likewise, the blind person "looks" toward a sudden noise, and the widow "hears" her husband's key in the lock. Each is operating on a set of assumptions that have become habitual over many years. Grief following bereavement by death is aggravated if the person lost is the person to whom one would turn in times of trouble. Faced with the biggest trouble she has ever had, the widow repeatedly finds herself turning toward a person who is not there.

These examples begin to explain why PSTs are so painful and take so much time and energy. For a long time it is necessary to take care in everything we think, say, or do; nothing can be taken for granted any more. The familiar world suddenly seems to have become unfamiliar, habits of thought and behavior let us down, and we lose confidence in our own internal world.

Freud (1917b) called the process of reviewing the internal world after bereavement "the work of mourning," and in many ways each PST is a job of work that must be done if a person is to adapt to the requirements of the real world. But the mind that is doing the reviewing is also the object that is being reviewed. A person is literally lost in his or her own grief, and the more disorganized one's thinking the more difficult it is to step aside from the disorganization and to see clearly what is lost and what remains.

Since we rely on having an accurate assumptive world to keep us safe, people who have lost confidence in their world model feel very unsafe. And because anxiety and fear cloud our judgment and impair concentration and memory, our attempts to make sense of what has happened are likely to be fitful, poorly directed, and inadequate.

Coping and defense

Of course, people are not completely helpless when the level of anxiety becomes disorganizing. We have a variety of coping mechanisms that usually reduce the level of tension or at least prevent it from rising any higher. Hence, people in transition often withdraw from the challenges of the outside world, shut themselves up at home, and restrict their social contacts to a small group of trusted people. They may avoid situations and chains of thought that will bring home the discrepancies between inside and outside worlds; they may fill their lives with distracting activities, or deny the full reality of what has happened. The complete range of psychological defense mechanisms can be called into play to protect someone from too painful a realization of a loss. These defenses will often succeed in preventing anxiety from becoming disorganizing, but they are also likely to delay the relearning process.

Taking stock

The magnitude of a PST is such that it includes simultaneous dysfunctions in several areas of functioning. Thus, the loss of a spouse may produce any or all of the following: loss of sexual partner, loss of protection from danger, loss of reassurance of worth, loss of job, loss of companionship, loss of income, loss of recreational partner, loss of status, loss of expectations, loss of self-confidence, loss of a home, loss of a parent for one's children, and many other losses. It may also produce relief from responsibilities, entitlement to the care of others, sympathy from others and an increase in tenderness (or at least inhibition of hostility and competition), attributions of heroism, financial gains, and freedom to realize potentialities that have been inhibited. These latter consequences, too, involve change in the life space and require that assumptions be modified, but because they also serve to assist those modifications (e.g., by providing time and opportunity for introspection and by keeping people safe from threat during that time), they are more likely to facilitate than to impair the transition.

PSTs thus emerge as a complex interweaving of psychological and social processes, whose implications are far from clear to the person who undergoes them and even less clear to the would-be helper. Only in the most general terms can anyone else be said to "understand," but this does not mean we cannot help. By asking those who are in transition to help us understand, by talking about their situation, we help them take stock, review, and relearn their assumptive world.

Resistance to change

Although minor changes are often embraced, major changes are more usually resisted. Resistance to change is seen as an obstacle by planners, but it is not always so irrational or so harmful as it seems. We can bring to the appraisal of new situations only the assumptions that arise out of old situations. Our old model of the world may be imperfect, but it is the best we have, and if we abandon it we have nothing left. Our first effort, in the face of change, must therefore be to interpret the change in the light of our old assumptions. To throw over old models of the world the moment they appear discrepant with the new is dangerous and often unnecessary. Closer scrutiny will sometimes reveal that our initial appraisal of the situation was incorrect and that the discrepancy was more apparent than real. Thus, a person who is told by a doctor that he has a terminal illness may be wise to ask for a second opinion before preparing himself to die.

Refusing to accept change also gives us time to begin rehearsing in our minds the implications of the change, should it come about. Thus, the patient who refuses surgery may need time to talk through its implications with his doctor and his family before changing his mind. While he does this, he is preparing a new model of the world, which will help ensure that the transition proceeds smoothly when, eventually, it comes about.

On the other hand, there may come a time when it is more dangerous to resist change than to accept it. Because the person in transition has no models of thought and behavior to meet the new situation, he or she will feel helpless and in danger. Three things are needed: emotional support, protection through the period of helplessness, and assistance in discovering new models of the world appropriate to the emergent situation. The first two of these may need to be provided before the person can begin to feel safe enough to accept the third. Thus, people whose sight has failed often refuse to learn blind skills until they have been supported in their helplessness and reached a point where they feel safe enough to accept the help of guide dogs, white canes, and all the other means by which blind people can rebuild their model of the world.

Terminal illness

Elizabeth Kubler-Ross's (1969) "phases of dying" – denial, bargaining, anger, despair, resignation, and acceptance – bear a close resemblance to Bowlby's "phases of grief" (numbness, pining, disorganization/despair, and reorganization; Bowlby & Parkes, 1970), and the link between dying and grieving was made by Kubler-Ross's former professor of psychiatry, C. Knight Aldritch (1963) in a paper titled "The Dying Patient's Grief." The consistency and even the occurrence of these "phases" have been questioned, and it would certainly be unwise to set them up as norms through which each dying patient should be expected to pass. But to those who work with late-stage cancer patients, they are very familiar even if they do not always occur in the sequence and manner that Kubler-Ross described. What these phases seem to reflect is a tendency for seriously ill patients to move from a state of relative ignorance of, and reluctance to accept, the facts of their illness toward awareness and acceptance. Along the way they may try to strike bargains ("If I accept surgery, then I shall live to see my grandchild born"), express anger ("It's not fair"), or despair ("I give up"). These kinds of phenomena are also commonly found in amputees and other disabled people, and they are best viewed as typical components of a PST. However, cancer patients undergo not one but a number of PSTs in the course of long and varied illnesses. Their psychological reactions are correspondingly unpredictable.

Cancer often takes a stepwise course as each new crop of symptoms appears and is treated. Each step is likely to involve some loss – of employment, mobility, strength, good looks, and so on – and each confronts the patient with a need to give up one set of assumptions about the world and to develop another. Lacking any clear basis for planning, most patients tend to be as optimistic about their future as they dare, and this optimism is fostered by their doctors and nurses, who prefer to "look on the bright side." Consequently, they are often unaware of the full implications of those cancers that will end fatally.

Even if they are informed and aware of the likely ending, it is rare for them to feel prepared for an outcome that, for most of us, is a step into the dark. None of the great religions is really clear as to what lies beyond life, and there are no training courses for the afterlife. It follows that the transition from life to death must be made without rehearsal and without any of the provisional models that, however inadequate, we bring with us to other situations.

Strange to say, this ignorance seems to mitigate anxiety, and most patients claim to be more afraid of dying than of being dead. Dying is envisaged as a projection of everything bad about illness. As the illness gets worse the symptoms will get worse, and "death agonies" are assumed to be an ultimate horror. The fact that, given a decent quality of care, it should be possible for medical attendants to relieve the physical distress of the dying makes it all the more important for them to relieve mental distress by communicating that fact (Parkes, 1978).

Preventive intervention

Many of the problems arising in the course of a PST can be mitigated if those who are at risk receive appropriate counseling and support. To plan this effectively, a sound knowledge of risk factors and methods of intervention is needed.

Determinants of outcome

Studies of a variety of types of transition and of the variation of response to each of these not only throw light on the nature and dynamics of PSTs but also enable us to identify people and situations that involve special risk. The identification of risk is, of course, an important step toward prevention of ill health, and studies of bereavement by death suggest that those most vulnerable to this type of loss can be recognized before or at the time of bereavement, and that members of this group will benefit from counseling. The wide range of empirical studies contributing to our knowledge of vulnerability in the face of a range of PSTs include the circumstances of the life-change event (e.g., anticipation, massive or multiple changes, brutal or violent events), the personality and previous experience of the bereaved person (e.g., self-confidence, success or failure of resolutions of earlier PSTs), and factors impinging after the event (e.g., social supports, opportunities for new roles and status). These studies are treated in more detail elsewhere (Parkes, 1990). They indicate that the outcome of a PST is related to the magnitude of the PST, the extent to which it has been correctly anticipated, and the supports and opportunities available. Such findings enable us to make predictions regarding the probable outcome of many PSTs.

Prediction of outcome is also improved from observation of the initial reaction to the event. Thus, severe and lasting distress, as well as excessive denial or delay in reacting emotionally, may presage later problems.

Intervention

Knowledge of risk factors is of value when planning intervention. If antici-pation is important, then any activity that helps people to prepare them-selves for an event is likely to reduce the risk. Similarly, those who cope by avoiding may need help in facing up to a transition, while those who are overwhelmed may need permission to escape for a while by taking a holiday or by the judicious use of psychotropic medication. But these expedients only provide a temporary solution, and we must also guard against the misuse of medication, be it alcohol or other tranquilizers. People of low self-esteem or dependent personality may need forms of help that build on their strengths and wean them from undue reliance on others, including the providers of health care.

Up to the present time, the only settings where these principles have been widely adopted are hospices and bereavement services. Although neither hospices nor bereavement services are universally successful in relieving the suffering of those they serve, there are a number of well-conducted studies indicating that the right help given to the right people at the right time can reduce physical and mental symptoms and improve the quality of life before and after bereavement (Mor, 1987; Parkes, 1981; Raphael, 1977).

If this is so, then we have to ask ourselves whether similar interventions might help people through the other major PSTs of their lives. Since doctors, priests, nurses, and social workers are likely to be in contact at such times and may be the only caregivers to whom these people will turn for help, it follows that they should develop the knowledge base needed and organize their services in an appropriate way. Whether we like it or not, we are agents of change, midwives at the birth of new identities.

What, then, are the essential resources for this new midwifery, and how can they be provided within the constraints of a shrinking economy? The resources are, of course, properly trained people with the necessary time and skills. To some extent these are the same people who have always cared for the sick. Psychosocial medicine has been around for a long time, but it used to be called "tender loving care." It relied on the communication skills and life experiences of the caregivers and was none the worse for that. However, it frequently seems to get displaced by other, "more important" priorities.

Yet the whole history of medicine tells us that prevention is more economical than cure. If, in fact, preparing someone for major surgery reduces the chances of postoperative complications and, as some studies have shown, gets people out of the hospital sooner (Egbert, Battit, Welch, & Bartlett, 1964), then it is likely to be an economical use of our time. Hospices are no more expensive than the service that they replace (Mor,

1987), and even the provision of support during the transition of leaving prison has been shown to save money by reducing the chances of recidivism (Shaw, 1974; Sinclair, Shaw, & Troop, 1974).

Furthermore, much of the support that people need at times of transition can and should be given by volunteers. Volunteers who have been carefully selected and trained to act as counselors, or whose own experience of the transition in question provides them with inside knowledge (although it is important to ensure that they have come through it and are not trying vicariously to solve their own problems), are often the best people to help others in transition. Not only are they less expensive, but they are often seen as less threatening because they are not "experts," and they have the one thing that professionals often lack – time to listen. These volunteers can be organized in specialized counseling services (e.g., ostomy associations or bereavement services), or they can take a wider frame of reference and offer counsel to anyone in crisis or distress (e.g., Samaritans, good neighbor schemes). These services will be much more effective if they are backed by and integrated with the services provided by members of the caring professions. This enables the professionals to discover their true value, facilitates referrals, and ensures that the volunteers receive the expert help that they need in training counselors and dealing with individuals whose problems require professional skills.

Social workers and other primary caregivers in the community are in a good position to identify people in transition, to assess their vulnerability, and where necessary, to provide the support needed or refer them to those who can. They should receive proper training in this field of study. Hospital and other institutional staff may also have important roles to play if they are involved in the diagnosis or care of people with life-threatening or chronic diseases.

Support for the supporters

Because transitions of one sort or another affect us all, we cannot come close to people who are facing them without, to some degree, sharing their feelings. We too suffer their losses and frustrations, and it is only by "hanging in" and seeing them come through to a new life that we will be rewarded for the pains we share. But not everybody who seeks our help will come through, and sometimes their pain sparks off pain in us that we thought we had forgotten, reminding us too vividly of our own losses. At such times we too need the help and understanding of a counselor. If it is all right for our clients to grieve, it should also be acceptable for us to express the sorrow and frustration to which our work gives rise. Any caring team must, therefore, take account of the need for support to the supporters, for in the end the only difference between carer and cared-for is in the roles assigned to us.

Conclusion

Societies have always had their elders, doctors, shamans, priests, and counselors. Most of these have a dual role – to provide wise counsel and to perform rituals. The rituals mark the rites of passage (Van Gennep, 1909). They identify people in transition, induct them into a temporary status (as "client," "mourner," "initiate," "patient," etc.), and then, after sufficient time has elapsed, mark the end of the transition to a new identity (as "widow," "adult," "disabled person," etc.). The rites performed by doctors include the provision of sickness certificates, prescriptions, and a range of other procedures (some of them bloody) through which patients pass on the way to their new life.

The success of scientific medicine in finding cures for many diseases has distracted many members of the caring professions from their traditional responsibility to care for people in transition. As a result, medicine and its allied professions find themselves faced with the need to change, to face a psychosocial transition of their own, whose implications penetrate all aspects of our work. We can expect similar difficulties in revising our models of the world, like those experienced by the bereaved, the disabled, and the dying when faced with irreversible changes in their lives. Social workers and counselors are likely to find it less difficult than medical personnel to make use of a theory of transition because much of their existing work is carried out from a similar viewpoint. Consequently, they may need to take the lead in educating doctors, nurses, and other health care workers. It is hoped that the theory presented here will facilitate this transition.

7

Grief: The social context of private feelings

PAUL C. ROSENBLATT

Grief is shaped by the social context in which it occurs (Averill, 1968). Two theories that provide a useful perspective in this connection are symbolic interaction theory (e.g., Berger & Kellner, 1964; Cochran & Claspell, 1987; Lofland, 1985; Marris, 1974; Rosenblatt & Wright, 1984) and family systems theory (e.g., Berkowitz, 1977; Krell & Rabkin, 1979; Rosenblatt, 1983, chapter 10). These two theories complement each other, illuminate the complexity and challenges bereaved people face in coming to terms with a loss, and demonstrate why the social context of grief is so important. Symbolic interaction theory emphasizes the social nature of reality and suggests how a significant loss might be viewed as a loss of reality. It also helps us understand how others are important in defining, feeling, and coming to terms with a loss. Family systems theory emphasizes how family rules and patterns shape loss experiences and how a significant loss affects and is played out in a system of family relationships.

In this chapter symbolic interaction theory and family systems theory are briefly outlined as they apply to bereavement. Then both theories are used to develop a perspective on social relationships in grieving and support, on social prescriptions for the bereaved, and on the limits of social knowledge of grief.

Defining a loss

The loss of definitional context

From the viewpoint of symbolic interaction theory, part of the social context for understanding, organizing, validating, and defining feeling, action, values, and priorities is removed when a significant person is lost. Thus, when people feel sad, angry, disorganized, empty, depressed, or anything else that might be labeled "grief," one source of those feelings is the loss of social context. Such feelings can occur even for losses that are desired (e.g., the end of a difficult marital relationship). Thus, grief may

102

reflect not only the loss itself but also the loss of the foundation for dealing with the loss.

Losing any person who has been important in defining self and situation provides a character to grief. It adds the qualities of searching for meaning, uncertainty about one's self and about what to make of what has happened, disorganization, confusion, and lack of confidence.

The loss of a social interaction basis for defining events, feelings, and meanings will compel people to search for alternative bases for defining situation and self. It may lead them to religion, popularized writings on loss, physicians and psychologists, or people who have had a similar experience. The definitional processes involve social activities that could be called "constructionist" (Berger & Kellner, 1964; Gergen, 1985) or "negotiational" (Swann, 1987).

Possessions may take on new significance to a person who has had a significant loss. People use photo albums, mementos, household furnishings, and other possessions to define their place in the world and their relationship to each other (Csikszentmihalyi & Rochberg-Halton, 1981; Rosenblatt, de Mik, Anderson, & Johnson, 1985, pp. 94–95, 146–148). When a relationship that helped in defining oneself and one's world has been lost, people may turn to things – both as reminders of the definitions that were maintained in relationship with the person now lost and in a search for new meanings that take the loss into account. The importance of possessions to bereaved people helps explain why concerns about inheritance of the property of the deceased can be the source of intense family conflict (Titus, Rosenblatt, & Anderson, 1979). The hints of meaning contained in the provisions of a will, and the meanings inherent in the pieces of an estate one might acquire, can define feelings, reality, the person who has been lost, one's relationship with that person, and one's place in the family. Similarly, possessions can become a locus of meaning during a divorce. Divorcing people may battle about objects in part because the objects are important as a source of meaning for the self and one's life situation now that the marital relationship is no longer a trustworthy or comfortable source of meaning.

Cultural definitions of loss and grief

Across the diversity of human cultures, there are striking similarities in grieving. Across cultures, most people seem to grieve the loss of someone close (Rosenblatt et al., 1976, chapter 1). In virtually all cultures, many people will feel that a person who has died continues in some way beyond death (Rosenblatt et al., 1976, chapter 3). Nonetheless, cultures differ widely in defining death and in defining what is an appropriate expression of grief.

Culture is such a crucial part of the context of bereavement that it is often impossible to separate an individual's grief from culturally required mourning. For example, in cultures with a belief system that says "do not grieve because grief will cause the ghost of the deceased to take you away" or "do not grieve because the deceased has gone to a better life," it is difficult to assess accurately what seems to be muted grief. It is difficult to distinguish where the rules that mute grief leave off and "real" grief begins. Similarly, when the rules say "cry" and people are crying, it is difficult to say whether the crying is genuine, deeply felt, and likely to occur in the absence of the cultural demands for crying. Presumably, what people do in grieving feels real to them, and their expressions of grief in accord with cultural rules validate the rules and become part of the context of grief for others.

Because there is such a wide range of culturally appropriate expression of grief across cultures, it seems important to conceptualize grief as a substantial range of responses, each of which authentically expresses feelings of loss when supported by a legitimating cultural context. For example, the grief of the Kaluli of New Guinea blends sadness with anger and an indignant feeling that compensation is due (Schieffelin, 1985). In Iran, grief includes an element of duty and of righteous anger at being victimized, coupled with a feeling of identification with the kin of religious martyrs (Good, Good, & Moradi, 1985).

A sensitivity to such cultural differences should help prevent ethnocentric assumptions that one's own culture or experience necessarily provides a valid baseline for understanding the grief of somebody from a different cultural background. For example, cultures differ markedly in rules about the openness, intensity, and control of anger and aggression in bereavement (Rosenblatt et al., 1976, chapter 3). In some cultures, ritual specialists and cultural belief systems effectively suppress or limit the anger of bereavement. In other cultures, the regulation of anger in bereavement is accomplished by isolating the bereaved for a substantial period of time or by marking the appearance of the bereaved as a warning to others. In the rare cultures that seem not to regulate the angry dispositions of bereavement, a death may lead to internecine violence and further deaths. Cultures thus differ widely in permission to feel anger in bereavement and in the expression of anger in bereavement. Thus, assuming that angry forms of grief are transitory or unimportant because they are not common in one's own culture leaves one ill-prepared to understand the grief of people from other cultural or ethnic groups.

Ethnic differences in defining loss and grief

The United States is culturally diverse. What is ethnically "normal" for one individual or family may be deviant for another. Yet American popular culture may suggest that ethnic differences do not extend beyond food preferences and holiday celebrations. Thus, Americans may not be prepared to appreciate how people differ in their grieving. This can lead to intolerance for the way somebody from another ethnic group grieves and to a blocking of emotional support for that person. For example, WASP (White Anglo-Saxon Protestant) Americans tend to "psychologize" their emotional pain, and people in many other ethnic groups tend to somatize theirs (Kleinman & Kleinman, 1985). People in the WASP culture, therefore, may find it difficult to support non–WASP-like grief.

Ethnic differences in grieving also may be a source of difficulty in close relationships between people whose cultural backgrounds differ. The differences may not be perceived until a significant loss makes them salient. Unfortunately, grieving individuals may lack the focus, energy, or flexibility to deal easily with relationship issues. Moreover, if the loss is the first significant loss experienced in the relationship, dealing with it in concert may be even more difficult. A first significant loss is often difficult because one is facing mortality for the first time (Rosenblatt, 1983, pp. 117–123). A first significant loss in a relationship may be difficult because it may only be then that one enacts the pattern of grief and emotional control peculiar to one's culture. Thus, in a couple's first grief experience, cultural differences may make one person's grieving seem bizarre to the other, who in turn may not know how to respond appropriately by the standards of the other or may not be willing to do so. If the grief is shared, it may make each less available to help support the other as they struggle with their grief and with the problem of working out rules and understandings for grieving in the relationship (Berkowitz, 1977).

In contrast, individuals who attempt to assimilate another culture's norms for bereavement, for example, ethnic Americans attempting to assimilate the WASP American norms that include self-control and suffering in silence (McGoldrick & Rohrbaugh, 1987), may experience guilt and depression and, ultimately, may not effectively come to terms with a loss (Moitoza, 1982). Researchers and mental health practitioners who assume a stable cultural grounding for a bereaved person may misunderstand the grief of somebody who has been moving from one culture to another or who is grounded in more than one culture. Yet many people may be in transit between cultures or grounded in more than one at the time of a loss and may struggle to find an appropriate cultural footing for their grief. They may also be multicultural in the sense of feeling and expressing their grief in a way that fits no single culture. This blending may seem genuine and appropriate to them, but it may confuse others who are not similarly multicultural and thus inhibit support.

Grief in family systems

Family systems theory intersects with individual psychology as the individual functions in and reflects a relationship system. Following a loss, a family system is likely to operate conservatively, maintaining the system as it was before the loss (Rosenblatt, 1983, chapter 10). For example, individuals who previously sought emotional support from a family member whose death they are grieving would be likely to continue to turn to family members for emotional support. Even in the best of times others in the system might not be able to meet the intense needs that arise in bereavement. They will be less able to do so when they are bereaved. Moreover, family members will have differed in their relationship with the deceased and as a consequence will differ in what they grieve (Lofland, 1985). This too may inhibit their ability to support one another. As a result, grief for the missing family member may be compounded by grieving for the system that now seems inadequate to meet the survivors' needs.

Family systems have implicit and explicit rules (Ford, 1983), including rules that deal with emotional expression. These rules may enable the achievement of some system and personal goals – for example, maintenance of equanimity or freedom from having to deal with the overt distress of others – while preventing the achievement of other personal goals, such as obtaining emotional support. Thus, because of the functioning of family rules, a family may or may not be helpful in dealing with grief.

Family systems are in constant flux, however, and the rules are always open to challenge, revision, and reinterpretation. A family bereavement may result in the negotiation of new rules and the change or reinterpretation of existing rules. Any radical challenge to the status quo, change in who the family players are, new problem, or new demand for public performance (e.g., at a funeral) is likely to lead to family interaction regarding family rules. These interactions may include family discussion of what is appropriate to do, feel, and believe. The needs of bereavement thus include the need of individuals to process family rules with other family members. This does not mean that grief is disrupted or overlaid by family matters, but rather that grief in a family context involves disagreement, negotiation, and expressions of feelings directed at other family members.

Family rules may inevitably add to what is grieved. For example, a decision to invest family resources of time and energy in one area means that other areas will be slighted. People cannot simultaneously maintain calmness and be emotive, talk a great deal about a loss and keep quiet about it, honor the deceased and act like nothing has happened, or get on with life without the deceased while trying to bring the deceased back. The rules that govern a family's dealing with a loss may, therefore, be frustrating and costly at times to some family members. This is another reason why at a time of loss families struggle with rules.

It is also important to note that family members are not equal players in the family system. Some family members will occupy more central positions in the system than others (in terms of communication with other family members, knowledge of family members and family events, influence over family members, and perceived responsibility for meeting the needs of other family members). Also, some family members may be linked to others in coalitions, either in specific situations or in general. Understanding these structures is important in understanding the impact of a loss on family relationships and on individual family members. For example, if the deceased was a communication link for other family members, that loss may complicate efforts to communicate about matters relating to grief and the shared loss. Similarly, a person who has lost a coalition partner may feel comparatively alone or powerless.

This last point about coalitions and bereavement is related to a more general matter. It is that family systems must deal with the differentiation of experience in many areas of life, including bereavement. Family members will have had different kinds of relations with the deceased, will have different kinds of support and involvements inside and outside the family, and will experience different feelings. Family systems may tolerate expressions of this differentiation or suppress them. Thus, when family members appear to speak or grieve as one, it may be useful to question whether their apparent unity masks a diversity of feelings and needs.

Social relationships in grieving and support

Grieving is not a constant, even in the first days of bereavement. People have to attend to other matters, may feel too exhausted or numb to grieve, or may withdraw from grieving in order to feel less pain (Rosenblatt, 1983, chapter 9). Grieving comes in surges or in what Parkes (1972a/1987, p. 57) has called "pangs." Following the earliest phase of intense grieving, however, renewed surges do not occur randomly, but are set off by reminders of the loss that have not yet been dealt with (Rosenblatt, 1983, pp. 21–29). Contact with others is a common cause of these surges of grieving. Interaction with others may thus be experienced as painful and disruptive. Yet working through grief and coming to terms with it require dealing with human and other reminders of the loss. People who are more isolated seem to make slower progress in grief work (Clayton, 1975), in part because of the role others can play both in defining a loss and in drawing a person into activities other than grieving. The isolation effect may also reflect a lack of social reminders that call forth the memories and hopes that are the raw material of grief work.

Other people often provide social input that is necessary in defining and coming to terms with a loss (Rosenblatt & Burns, 1986; Wright & Rosenblatt, 1987). Social support phenomena are complicated enough to make generalizations risky (Chesler & Barbarin, 1984; Shinn, Lehmann, & Wong, 1984; Shumaker & Brownell, 1984), but even brief interactions with people outside the immediate family may provide very important social support in grieving. For example, in a study of the long-term effects of miscarriage, stillbirth, and infant death, the crucial interactions perceived as most supportive were often very brief – for example, a 5-minute inter-action in which a co-worker heard a woman's story of a miscarriage and talked about her own miscarriage (Rosenblatt & Burns, 1986). Similarly, people forced out of farming by economic circumstances reported that brief, even indirect, comments from others about their loss could be experienced as quite supportive (Rosenblatt, 1990; Wright & Rosenblatt, 1987).

It may be that even brief interactions can be supportive in the sense that a "single moment can retroactively flood an entire life with meaning" (Frankl, 1973, p. 44). Symbolic interaction theory suggests that with a small number of words an enormous number of memories and a sense of reality can change. Consider, for example, a farmer who has defined past and current events (e.g., losing the family farm) as proof of personal failure. Hearing a neighbor say, "I know you were a fine farmer, and you were smarter than we were to get out when you did" may redefine much that has been painful, shameful, and troublesome. Similarly, a woman who has had a miscarriage and has been feeling like a failure or a medical oddity may transform her sense of self when a co-worker says, "I had a miscarriage, too, and I felt awful for years. Nobody talks about it, but people all around us have had them." If, in the perspective of symbolic interaction theory, grief work involves the development of a story dealing with the loss (cf. Cochran & Claspell, 1987), the role of such brief interactions may be in helping the bereaved to create, organize, or invest more fully in a personal story.

Instances of brief social support may also make a difference because families experiencing a loss may isolate themselves or become isolated from potential community supports. The dynamics of family isolation (Wright & Rosenblatt, 1987) may involve shared efforts to distance pain by avoiding reminders of the loss (e.g., the good fortune of others who are still in farming). Grieving family members may also become isolated because they are unclear about how to define the situation and thus lack a foundation for interaction with others. Family isolation may also occur because individual family members devote their time and energy to coping with the loss (e.g., a farm family putting extra hours into farming and taking off-farm jobs in order to try to save the farm).

The community may isolate the bereaved family – because people fear saying or doing the wrong thing (e.g., fearing that a casual remark could cause a person who is losing a farm to feel pain, become angry enough to shoot a loan officer, or commit suicide). Also, people may distance the bereaved family because they do not understand what has happened, because they lack an appropriate ritual or etiquette for dealing with them, or because they blame the family itself for what has happened. Further, they may fear that the loss is contagious, because another's loss reminds them of their own vulnerability or the neediness of the bereaved family is burdensome to deal with.

To the extent that community is based on mutual exchange, bereaved individuals may be distanced by others if their bereavement constrains their willingness or ability to maintain exchange relationships. People may also draw away because they believe their distance is polite and respectful and helps to minimize the discomfort of the bereaved (Rosenblatt et al., 1991). People may also be aware that well-meaning help can be a burden (Rosenblatt, 1983, pp. 145–149). Finally, people may hold back because they think it is helpful not to acknowledge the loss, in effect to indicate that "nothing has changed and we still see you as okay."

Some encounters intended to be helpful may burden bereaved people with the needs of the person trying to help or remind them that, compared to the person who is offering help, they are not well off (Rosenblatt, 1983, pp. 145–149). However, social support that is burdensome may also be helpful – for example, in distracting the bereaved from the depths of depression, pushing them to deal with the grief in order to escape the "help," or giving them the good feelings that can come from helping another.

Troublesome social prescriptions

In trying to help bereaved people, psychological practitioners, clergy, physicians, and other professionals generally operate with a sense of what normal bereavement is. In some cases it may not matter whether those standards are culturally appropriate or statistically normal. Bereaved people may benefit from a wide range of structurings to their experience (Rosenblatt et al., 1976, p. 34). But the professional's perspective might also seriously violate the norms of a bereaved person's culture, be out of touch with what is common in the grief process, or be insensitive to the feelings and needs of the person. The bereaved may be pushed toward meanings that do not make sense, to difficulty with people whose support is important, or to intolerable levels of pain.

For example, a common prescription is that grieving should be virtually complete at some definite point after a significant loss. Yet grieving may recur with intensity throughout one's lifetime (Johnson & Rosenblatt, 1981; Lehman, Wortman, & Williams, 1987; Rosenblatt, 1983; Rosenblatt & Burns, 1986). In some cultures, a person bereaved for a spouse, a grown child, or some other significant person will be expected to mourn for a lifetime. When a therapeutic prescription for normal grieving is so discordant with common human experience or with cultural norms, bereaved people may reject potentially valuable aspects of the therapy or inappropriately question their own mental health.

Other common therapeutic prescriptions concern the "sane" expression of grief. Therapeutic norms for the expression of grief may conflict with common human experience and the norms of many cultures. For example, people commonly sense the presence of deceased individuals who have been important in their lives (Rosenblatt, 1983, pp. 123–126; Rosenblatt et al., 1976, pp. 57–58). They may feel the spiritual nearness of the person who has died, have a sense that the deceased person is aware of them, or have clear sensory experiences of the deceased, lasting over a considerable amount of time. In many cultures, such experiences are culturally legitimate; they are neither normatively nor statistically abnormal. Indeed, it is not uncommon for Americans to believe that they have contact with a deceased relative and that they will reunite with that relative in heaven (Rosenblatt & Elde, 1990). However, if psychological professionals fail to legitimate such experiences or label them hallucinatory, bereaved people may fear for their sanity and may become more isolated from family members and others as they work at keeping their experiences secret.

It is crucial, therefore, that professionals working with the bereaved understand the ethnic and cultural circumstances of a bereaved person. It also is crucial that professionals working with the bereaved know the literature on the time course of grief, "sense of presence" experiences, and other aspects of bereavement. A great deal has been learned in the past decade, and some of that is in direct contradiction to what can still be read in the professional literature (Lehman et al., 1987; Rosenblatt, 1983, p. 31).

The limits of social knowledge of others' feelings

This chapter incorporates two contradictory perspectives that recur in psychology and the social sciences. One perspective holds that humans are basically the same. The other holds that there are enormous differences among people. In the case of bereavement, the competing perspectives suggest that grieving processes are rather similar across people and across losses, and that each person has a unique constellation of culture, social context, and connections to the object of grief so that everyone is limited in how much he or she can understand what another person is feeling. Both positions should be treated as true.

To the extent that individuals are unique, it is probably always wrong, although not necessarily always a mistake, to say to another, "I know exactly how you feel." Yet basic human similarity, life experience, and knowledge of another person's situation can help us understand what another person feels and allow empathy and an appreciation of the person's feelings. Imperfect knowledge may still permit effective listening and supportive action. Communication may enhance the extent to which one knows what another feels, but communication also involves constructing feelings, not just reporting them. As a result, farther along in interaction, feelings may be better understood in part because they have been constructed in a shared interaction process.

American culture views the individual as a freestanding agent of personal control and mastery (Sampson, 1985). By contrast, this chapter argues that we must turn to others in order to understand ourselves and our grief. However, because of our uniqueness and the limits of words to communicate, the reality we construct with others is unlikely to encompass all that we feel or experience. There is always more to know. Nonetheless, the sense that there is a core grieving process across the species justifies applying one's personal experiences and cultural knowledge of reactions to understanding and dealing with the loss of others. Thus, it is appropriate to look for expressions of grief even in cultures where open expressions of grief are condemned (Kracke, 1981). It is similarly appropriate to look in western European culture for the experience of something like ghosts, for hidden rituals of mourning even months or years after a death, and for other forms of grief and mourning commonly out of sight in western European culture but common in the experiences of people in other cultures. Indeed, it is at times of crisis that what is common in the human species is most likely to be evident (Jackson, 1989, p. 67).

8

Bereavement from the perspective of cognitive-experiential self-theory

SEYMOUR EPSTEIN

Cognitive-experiential self-theory (CEST) is a broad, integrative theory of personality that is compatible with major aspects of a wide variety of other theories, including classical and neopsychoanalytic theory, Jungian psychology, Adlerian psychology, reinforcement theory, existentialism, phenomenology, and modern cognitive psychology. Unlike other cognitive theories, it assumes the existence of not one but three conceptual systems, each operating by its own rules of inference, and each capable of influencing the others. It also differs from other cognitive theories in assuming that the systems are not simply a collection of discrete cognitions or even of isolated networks of cognitions, but function as organized wholes.

CEST shares with psychoanalysis an emphasis on the importance of the unconscious determination of human thought and behavior. However, without denying the importance of the Freudian unconscious for certain kinds of behavior, it introduces another level of unconscious processing of information that it considers to have a far more general influence on everyday thought and behavior. Because this other level of the unconscious is more accessible to consciousness than the Freudian unconscious, it is useful to refer to it as *preconscious*. Whether one wishes to understand individual personality or the more general effects of significant life events, such as bereavement, on people, it is necessary to understand how this system operates, for it is this system, not the rational system, or the one that operates at a deeper unconscious level, that primarily determines people's cognitive, emotional, and behavioral reactions.

It is beyond the scope of this chapter to present a thorough review of CEST. It will suffice here to emphasize those aspects of the theory that are most relevant to bereavement. These include (1) the assumption that everyone has an implicit theory of reality that determines the subjective meanings that people derive from experience, (2) the importance of a preconscious level of processing information that operates according to its

Preparation of this chapter was supported by NIMH Research Grant MH01293 and NIMH Research Scientist Award K05MH00363.

own rules of inference, (3) the delineation of four basic needs and four related basic beliefs, (4) the importance of sensitivities and compulsions, broadly defined, and (5) the concept of constructive thinking. The interested reader can consult more general summaries of the theory, which also provide references to articles that discuss selected aspects of the theory in greater depth (e.g., Epstein, 1973, 1980, 1990a, 1991).

The experiential system: Principles of operation and the subjective construction of reality

Principles of operation of the experiential system

According to CEST, people operate not by the use of a single conceptual system but by the use of three: a rational system, an experiential system, and an associationistic system. The rational system operates by linear logic and socially prescribed rules for drawing inferences and citing evidence. CEST has nothing new to say about the rational system, other than to note that it is far less important in determining everyday behavior and emotions, and it is far more influenced by subconscious processes than most people, including psychologists, realize. The associationistic system as conceived by CEST is a combination of Freud's and Jung's views of unconscious processes. Its rules of inference correspond to those of Freud's primary process thinking (e.g., loose association, displacement, condensation, symbolic representation; see Epstein, 1983a, for a more complete description of the associationistic system). The conceptual system that will be of most use in understanding people's reactions to bereavement is the experiential system, as it is the system that is most intimately associated with emotions. Accordingly, it is this system that is the focus of the remainder of this article.

Unlike the rational system, the experiential system has evolved over millions of years. As nature does not give up its hard-won gains easily, it is unthinkable that the experiential system was simply abandoned once humans developed more abstract, conscious ways of apprehending reality. Rather, it can be assumed that the experiential system is still in everyday use and that it is highly adaptive, for, if it were not, we would not be here today.

Table 8.1 presents the rules of inference of the experiential system as contrasted with those of the rational system. The list was derived from an analysis of people's thinking when they discuss highly charged emotional issues in comparison to their thinking when they discuss impersonal issues. It was also influenced by an analysis of the nature of the appeals made in advertising and in politics and by research on constructive thinking (Epstein, 1983a, 1991; Epstein & Meier, 1989) and on social cognition

Table 8.1. *Comparison of the experiential and rational systems*

Experiential system	Rational system
1. Holistic	Analytic
2. Emotional: pleasure–pain–oriented (what feels good)	Logical: reason-oriented (what is sensible)
3. Associationistic connections	Cause-and-effect connections
4. Outcome-oriented	Process-oriented
5. Behavior mediated by "VIBES" from past experiences	Behavior mediated by conscious appraisal of events
6. Encodes reality in concrete images, metaphors, and narratives	Encodes reality in abstract symbols: words and numbers
7. Rapid processing: oriented toward immediate action	Slower processing: oriented toward delayed action
8. Slow to change: changes with repetitive or intense experience	Changes rapidly: changes with speed of thought
9. Crudely differentiated: broad generalization gradient; categorical thinking	More highly differentiated; dimensional thinking
10. Crudely integrated: dissociative, organized into emotional complexes (cognitive–affective modules)	More highly integrated
11. Experienced passively and preconsciously: We are seized by our emotions	Experienced actively and consciously: We are in control of our thoughts
12. Self-evidently valid: "Experiencing is believing"	Requires justification via logic and evidence

Source: Adapted from Epstein, 1991; reprinted with permission.

(e.g., Epstein, Lipson, Holstein, & Huh, 1992; Kahneman & Miller, 1986; Nisbett & Ross, 1980).

There are a few particularly important principles that can be derived from Table 8.1 that warrant special comment. First, several of the features of the experiential system, such as its being holistic, imagery-oriented, categorical, and self-evidently valid, make it eminently well suited for assimilating information and directing behavior automatically, rapidly, and effortlessly. Second, it is important to consider the implications of the assumption that the experiential system is outcome- rather than process-oriented. It operates, therefore, in a manner that encompasses conditioning but is not restricted to it. According to the experiential system, all is well that ends well. It is the experiential system that provides us with the impulse to reward the messenger who bears good tidings and to punish the one who brings bad news, despite our rational system informing us that they are simply doing their job.

Unlike the rational system, which attempts to assess situations without being influenced by emotions, the operation of the experiential system is mediated by "vibes," subtle feelings of which individuals are usually unaware as well as full-blown emotions of which they usually are aware. The experiential system is assumed to operate in the following manner. When an individual is confronted with a situation that requires a response, the experiential system scans the person's memory banks for related experiences. Depending on the memories accessed, the person experiences feelings, or vibes. The vibes then motivate behavior that it is anticipated will produce pleasant and avoid unpleasant further vibes. The whole process occurs automatically and with such rapidity that to all appearances the behavior that is elicited is an immediate reaction to the eliciting event.

This same process also guides the behavior of nonhuman higher order animals. In the case of humans, however, the vibes not only mediate tendencies to act in certain ways but also to think in certain ways. The result is that people are less in control of their conscious thinking than they normally realize. According to CEST, Freud was right when he emphasized the influence of unconscious processes on conscious thinking. However, he emphasized the wrong unconscious. It is the experiential, and not the associationistic, system that exerts the most widespread influence on conscious thought and behavior.

With this information as background, we are now ready to apply the concepts of CEST to bereavement.

Implications of the subjective determination of reality for bereavement

CEST reminds us of the importance of distinguishing between consciously held rational beliefs and preconsciously held experiential beliefs. Of primary importance with respect to adjustment is the meaning of an event in the experiential system. A person in his or her conscious, rational system may believe that he or she should be deeply distressed following the death of a sibling. In the experiential system, however, the death may be perceived as the defeat of a rival and evoke feelings of victory along with those of regret. In such a case, the person is apt to be surprised by the inappropriate feelings that he or she experiences.

Loss of a spouse is widely recognized as one of the most distressing experiences a person is likely to have. Nevertheless, 2 years after the death of a spouse, no clear picture emerges of a widespread decline in emotional and physical well-being of the bereaved. How is this to be explained? According to McCrae and Costa (this volume), it is a testimony to people's resilience. An alternative explanation is that not all marriages are unmitigated blessings, and for more than a negligible number of people the net effect of the death of a spouse may be an experiential gain rather than a loss in ultimate quality of life (Parkes, this volume; Hansson, Stroebe, & Stroebe, 1988).

If this is so, what does it tell us about research in which all individuals who have had a similar experience are treated alike, without consideration of the experiential meaning of the event? It is not surprising that McCrae and Costa (this volume) find that 10 years after bereavement, widows and widowers report themselves to be in as good physical and mental health as those in a control group. Very likely, a more fine-grained analysis would reveal that some are better adjusted and others worse adjusted, and the two groups cancel each other out. In any event, to learn more about the effect of bereavement following the loss of a spouse it is important to obtain information about the quality of the relationship and what it has experientially meant to the individual. Equally important is the person's general coping ability, which will be discussed in detail later.

Remaining to be explained is why, in the face of a lack of a mean difference later, there is a widely observed decline in mental and physical well-being during the first 6 months to a year. This can be explained by the consideration that no matter what the overall quality of the relationship, bereavement is likely to be followed by a destabilization of a person's habitual ways of making sense of and operating in the world (Parkes, this volume). As will be seen shortly, maintaining a belief system for assimilating the data of reality is one of four basic needs postulated by CEST.

Basic needs and basic beliefs

The four basic needs

According to CEST, there are four basic needs that are sources of motivation in a personal theory of reality and four related beliefs. The basic needs are to maximize pleasure and minimize pain, to assimilate the data of reality (and, by inference, to maintain the belief system that does the assimilating), to maintain relatedness to others, and to maximize self-esteem. One or more of these basic needs is postulated by every major theory of personality; but, unlike other theories, which emphasize one or at most two of them, CEST emphasizes all four and considers them equally important.

The consideration of four basic needs interacting with each other has important implications for understanding human behavior, for their influence becomes more than the sum of their parts. Behavior, according to CEST, is motivated by a compromise among the four basic needs. The result is that the four basic needs act as checks and balances against each other, which helps keep behavior within adaptive limits. For example, the need to maximize self-esteem is moderated by the need to assimilate realistically the data of reality, and vice versa. This keeps most people from developing delusions of grandeur, and it also causes people to interpret events, within limits, according to a self-enhancing bias. The finding that there is a widespread tendency for people to exhibit a self-enhancing bias has led some researchers to conclude that reality awareness is not an important aspect of normal adjustment (see review in Taylor & Brown, 1988). From the perspective of CEST, all that is indicated by such research is that reality awareness is not the only important factor, and that its influence is moderated by other factors, including the need to enhance self-esteem.

According to CEST, a breakdown in the balance of the four basic needs in influencing behavior is an important source of psychopathology. This tends to occur when a threat to one of the needs results in defensive overcompensation, such as when a person develops delusions of grandeur following a significant failure or rejection. Depending on the degree to which a person's self-esteem, relationships with others, pleasure in living, and sense of reality are influenced by the loss of a significant other, bereavement can be a source of maladaptive overcompensation for the need that was affected, and for the neglect of other needs. For example, in order for a person to hold onto his or her sense of reality, the person may have to withdraw from excessive stimulation, which may be more than the person can assimilate at the time. In doing so, the person may also temporarily or permanently sacrifice everyday pleasures in living and rewarding relationships with others, a syndrome that is commonly observed in bereavement.

The four basic beliefs

In order to fulfill the four basic needs, the experiential system must assess relevant aspects of the self and the environment. These intuitive assessments amount to basic beliefs about the nature of the self and the world. The basic beliefs, which are derivatives of the basic needs, vary along the following dimensions: the degree to which the world is viewed as benevolent and a source of pleasure versus the opposite; the degree to which the world is viewed as meaningful, including predictable, controllable, and just, versus the opposite; the degree to which other people are considered to be a source of affection and support versus a source of rejection and betrayal; and the degree to which the self is viewed as worthy, including competent, lovable, and good, versus the opposite. Trait terms associated with these needs, in the order in which they are listed, are optimistic versus pessimistic, integrated and centered versus disorganized, trusting versus suspicious, and high versus low self-esteem.

Because the basic beliefs are at the top of the hierarchy of constructs in an implicit theory of reality, changing any of these beliefs will result in a reorganization of the overall theory and therefore of the person's personality. Moreover, because the beliefs are interrelated, changing any one of them will change the others. Because of the disorganizing consequences of sudden changes in basic beliefs, such changes are strongly resisted. As a result, people will go to great lengths to produce experiences that validate their basic beliefs, even when it is apparent that the behavior is self-destructive. It was the observation of just such repetitive self-destructive behavior that led Freud (1959) to revise his theory of personality by introducing the repetition compulsion and the death instinct.

When a basic belief is threatened with invalidation, the person experiences acute anxiety, and, if the threat cannot be adequately defended against, disorganization occurs (Epstein, 1973). Because of the resistance to disorganization of the conceptual system, only events of extreme potency, such as traumatic events (including bereavement), and highly favorable events, such as love relationships, are capable of producing relatively rapid changes in basic beliefs.

Coping with bereavement

Coping with trauma. Elsewhere (Epstein, 1990b), I have presented a theory of trauma that is applicable to bereavement. The normal sequence of reactions following a traumatic experience is that there is an initial destabilization of the personality, as the traumatic event cannot be assimilated into the person's extant theory of reality. Following the initial destabilization, several courses may be followed. One is that the destabilization will endure. If so, the person will be unable to fulfill the four basic needs of a personal theory of reality and will consequently experience an enduring state of dysphoric affect, will lack direction and involvement with the world, will be prone to disorganization, will experience little joy in living, will have low self-esteem, and will be unable to relate to others. More often, resolution of one kind or another will occur. In the case of a successful resolution, the person will assimilate the experience by differentiating and integrating his or her implicit theory of reality so that the experience can be accepted in a manner that will allow for the four basic needs to be satisfactorily fulfilled. The person will, accordingly, become a sadder but wiser human being.

It is important to recognize that it is not sufficient for the differentiation and integration to occur in the person's rational thinking. It is critically important that the differentiation and integration occur in the experiential system. To accomplish this, the traumatic event must be worked through in an emotionally meaningful way, which is not to say that emotional ventilation is the only route through which this can be accomplished. The essence of successful resolution is assimilation of the experience, not ventilation of stored-up emotions. The reason that ventilation is often helpful is that avoidance of experiencing distressing emotions often prevents people from confronting what must be integrated (see Epstein, 1984, for a more complete discussion of this issue).

Maladaptive resolutions take place in two general ways. One is by dissociating the threatening event from the main conceptual system. Such a resolution succeeds in preserving the integrity of the person's implicit theory of reality, but does so at a considerable cost, for the person remains vulnerable to a breakdown in the dissociation, either because inhibition is weakened or stimulation is excessive. Moreover, the person is forced to maintain a high degree of vigilance in order to avoid the occurrence of experiences and thoughts that can activate the dissociated complex. When, for reasons beyond the individual's control, avoidance is impossible, and disinhibition occurs, the person will experience overwhelming distress and disorganization, much as if the original trauma were reinstated.

The other basic maladaptive resolution occurs when coherence and assimilation of the data of reality are achieved at the cost of satisfying the other three basic needs. A coherent theory of reality is constructed, but at the sacrifice of the ability to enjoy living, to maintain a favorable level of self-esteem, and/or to establish satisfactory relationships with others. Frequently, the resolution occurs around the basic emotions of fear, anger, and depression, which, according to CEST, provide conceptual–affective modules for the integration of behavior (Epstein, 1990b).

Coping with bereavement. As coping with bereavement, at least in its more extreme, symptomatic forms, can be viewed as a special case of coping with trauma, what has been said about trauma can be directly applied to bereavement.

In addition, an understanding of basic needs and beliefs can help us understand why bereavement under certain circumstances is more distressing than under others and why different individuals adjust differently to bereavement. For example, given the belief that the world is meaningful (including predictable, controllable, and just), it follows that the death of children, stigmatized deaths such as suicide, violent deaths, and unexpected deaths will be particularly distressing. Such deaths are not supposed to happen in an orderly, predictable, and just world. Given the need to assimilate the data of reality and the recognition that assimilation takes time and must proceed in an orderly way if the individual is not to be overwhelmed with anxiety (Epstein, 1976, 1983b, 1990b), it can be anticipated that unexpected deaths will be more distressing than those that are expected.

The four basic needs and beliefs can also account for why bereavement is often accompanied by mental and physical symptoms in the first year following the loss, but the picture is much more mixed after 2 years, with symptoms of both kinds returning to normal levels, on average, but with some individuals remaining symptomatic and with all individuals retaining sensitivities associated with the loss (Rubin, 1990a). It takes time for people to assimilate and adjust to a vastly changed personal world and to develop new ways of fulfilling the four fundamental needs. Depending on the person's success in learning to fulfill the needs, the final level of adjustment may be better, worse, or the same as the level of adjustment before bereavement.

It is beyond the scope of this chapter to consider all the ways in which basic beliefs can affect and be affected by reactions to bereavement. Suffice it to note that, to the extent that bereavement is associated with threats to making sense of the world, to the maintenance of a person's pleasure–pain balance, to self-esteem, and to relatedness, it can be expected to have negative consequences on mental and physical well-being. It is evident that bereavement can readily affect all of these. Making sense of the world has already been discussed. The pleasure–pain balance will be affected to the extent that the loss of the spouse is viewed as the source of increased versus reduced pleasurable and unpleasurable experiences, whether because of the nature of the relationship with the spouse or because of the influence of the spouse on the availability of social and other activities. Self-esteem will be affected, for better or worse, by the role that the spouse played in supporting versus denigrating the partner and in encouraging versus dis-couraging his or her self-development, as well as by reflected glory from the spouse (or its opposite) on the self in the eyes of the self and others. Related-ness with others will be affected to the extent that the spouse was a source of increased versus reduced social contact with others and to the extent that the relationship with the spouse was a rewarding or distressing one.

Events do not operate in a vacuum but in interaction with the attributes of the person who experiences them. Thus, individual differences in basic beliefs will influence how the kinds of events described earlier are likely to affect different individuals. Those with unfavorable basic beliefs or basic beliefs that are insufficiently differentiated (overgeneralized, rigid, and/or Pollyannaish) can be expected to be particularly prone to have maladaptive reactions following bereavement under such conditions.

Sensitivities and compulsions

General aspects of sensitivities and compulsions

According to CEST, the primary sources of beliefs, or schemas, in a personal theory of reality are emotionally significant experiences. To a considerable extent, the schemas are generalizations from experience. A person who has been raised in a rejecting, destructive family environment is likely to develop the beliefs that people are rejecting and the world is destructive. A person raised under more benevolent circumstances is more likely to develop a feeling of trust toward people and an optimistic view of the world. Most beliefs are flexible and change as a function of cumulative experience. Sensitivities and compulsions are beliefs that are resistant to change and are therefore major sources of maladjustment.

Sensitivities refer to unrealistic beliefs in the experiential system that certain kinds of situations or events are dangerous. An example of a sensitivity is a person reacting to a situation in which he or she must depend on another person as if it were a life-threatening circumstance. Compulsions refer to rigid beliefs in the experiential system that certain kinds of behavior are necessary to reduce threat. An example of a compulsion is the need to avoid depending on anyone at all costs. Sensitivities and compulsions are highly resistant to modification and extinction because they were learned under conditions of high emotional arousal and have, over time, become nuclei of cognitive–affective networks. As defined in CEST, compulsions are much broader constructs than as defined in clinical psychology, where they refer to highly specific, abnormal reactions, as in a hand-washing compulsion.

From the viewpoint of CEST, sensitivities and compulsions, not unconscious conflict and repression, are the most fundamental sources of maladaptive behavior. Unconscious conflict and repression are complications that make the sources and sometimes the nature of the sensitivities and compulsions unavailable to awareness. Accordingly, in many cases, removing repression, that is, making the unconscious conscious, is not enough to correct maladaptive behavior, as the initial sensitivities and compulsions remain. All that may be accomplished by such a procedure is to transform a neurotic without insight into one with insight.

Implications of sensitivities and compulsions for reactions to bereavement

The emotional effect of bereavement on an individual will depend on the individual's previous sensitization to events associated in some way or other with the loss of a significant other. A child who, as a result of past experiences, has been sensitized to abandonment, rejection, or disapproval will automatically interpret new experiences in light of this sensitivity. In effect, the person has encoded in his or her experiential system representations of a wide variety of situations as indicative of abandonment, rejection, or disapproval. The experience of the death of a significant other for such an individual is therefore likely to be interpreted as abandonment, rejection, or disapproval. It matters not that the individual interprets the event differently at the rational level, for what affects the person's emotions, and therefore his or her mental and physical well-being, is what occurs at the experiential level.

Further complications in the interpretation of bereavement at the experiential level can occur because of the limited cognitive capacity of children. A child who was angry at a parent shortly before the parent's death may believe the anger was responsible for the death. Similarly, a child who misbehaved before a parent's death may view the death as punishment for his or her behavior. Because such beliefs are held in the experiential system, they do not necessarily become modified as the person's intellectual understanding matures. As a result, the beliefs in the experiential system can be a source of maladaptive reactions to bereavement in adulthood.

An important area for research on bereavement is the interpretations children of different ages make of the loss of significant others under various conditions. The research need not be restricted to children who have experienced significant losses. Much can be learned from what children who have not experienced losses say when asked to describe what a hypothetical child would think following the death of a significant other under certain circumstances, such as the death of a parent after a child had been disobedient or expressed intense anger at a parent.

Given sensitivities, it is likely that compulsions exist, as the main reason compulsions develop is to cope with sensitivities. Compulsions can consist of any driven way of responding that is insensitive to situational requirements. Examples of compulsions that are likely to be associated with bereavement are extended withdrawal reactions, hyperactivity, promiscuity, dependency, and an excessive need for control.

Withdrawal serves to reduce stimulation, and is therefore likely to be resorted to in situations where the person's capacity to assimilate new information is under strain. Hyperactivity can serve the same purpose, by distracting the person from the data that are difficult to assimilate. Promiscuity can be a way of establishing relationships with others without the threat of rejection or loss following deep involvement. It can be viewed therefore as a compromise between relating and not relating, or, relatedly, as the manifestation of an approach–avoidance conflict with respect to relating.

Dependency is apt to result if the person has lost a significant source of support that he or she wishes to reestablish. The more the person has been sensitized to a loss of support from significant others, the greater the likelihood that a compulsion for establishing dependent relationships with others will be activated in some individuals by a significant loss. An alternative way of dealing with the same sensitivity is to avoid compulsively the possibility of establishing dependent relationships, which can result in withdrawal or in an inability to relate to others. Because death is beyond human control, concern about control is likely to be aroused in those who have previously been threatened (sensitized) by an absence of control. It follows that a compulsion will develop in some to demonstrate that events can be controlled.

These interpretations, viewed as psychodynamic within a psychoanalytic framework, are regarded as cognitive strategies for managing anxiety from the perspective of CEST. In other words, the concept of psychodynamics as employed in psychoanalytic theory is compatible with the formulations of CEST, with the exception that CEST regards the process in terms of the employment of cognitive strategies rather than as energy transformations.

The construct of constructive thinking

Constructive thinking is defined as the ability to solve problems in living at a minimal cost in stress. According to CEST, constructive thinking is more of a function of a person's automatic thinking at the preconscious, experiential level than of his or her abstract thinking ability or intelligence within the rational system. Constructive thinking is measured by the Constructive Thinking Inventory (CTI). The CTI is a broad, differentiated measure of coping ability. It contains a global scale plus the following six subscales: emotional coping, behavioral coping, categorical thinking, esoteric thinking, personal superstitious thinking, and naive optimism. Typical items in the CTI are the following. "I think about how I will deal with threatening events ahead of time, but I don't worry needlessly." "I worry a great deal about what other people think of me." "There are basically two kinds of people in this world, good and bad." "When something bad happens to me, I feel that more bad things are likely to follow." Subjects respond to these items on a 5-point true–false scale.

It has been found in research with the CTI that it is much more strongly associated with a wide variety of criteria of success in living, such as success in the workplace, success in social relations, and success in establishing satisfactory intimate relationships, and with mental and physical well-being than other tests of coping style, including the Rotter Locus of Control Scale, the Attribution Style Questionnaire, and the Hardiness Questionnaire, as well as intelligence tests (Epstein, 1990a, in press; Epstein & Katz, 1992; Epstein & Meier, 1989).

It is important to recognize that constructive thinking is not the same as positive thinking. Although it contains an element of positive thinking, global constructive thinking is characterized more by flexible thinking and realistic optimism than by unmodulated positive thinking. It is noteworthy, in this respect, that the subscale of naive optimism contributes no items to the global scale.

The concept of constructive thinking can provide a useful perspective for interpreting relations that have been reported between other measures of coping style and coping with stress, including bereavement. Measures of specific coping styles, such as internal versus external control and self-blame versus situational blame, can readily produce anomalous results because what is effective coping in one situation may not be effective in another. There is a time to attempt to control events and a time to accept what cannot be controlled, and there is a time to blame oneself and a time to consider the situation responsible. This can account for why the results on specific coping styles are often inconsistent across studies. The advantage of constructive thinking over other coping styles is that a good constructive thinker flexibly alters his or her behavior to adaptively meet the requirements of situations in the context of his or her own current needs. Thus, sometimes good constructive thinkers are internal and sometimes external controllers, sometimes they are optimistic and sometimes pessimistic, and sometimes they blame themselves and sometimes the situation.

An interesting example of how the construct of constructive thinking can provide a useful perspective for interpreting findings on coping with stress is provided by a study by W. Stroebe and Stroebe (this volume). In a study in which they compared adjustment to unexpected versus expected deaths in individuals with low and high levels of belief that they can control events, they found a significant interaction between expectedness and belief in control. Individuals with low levels of belief in internal control ("externals") reported more depression and physical symptoms than individuals with high levels of belief in internal control ("internals") and showed less improvement over a 2-year period following the unexpected death of a loved one.

At first glance, the results appear paradoxical, as one would expect that an unexpected event would be more assimilable to externals than to internals, as the event is more in accord with their belief that events cannot be controlled. The investigators explained their results by speculating that the externals had a more difficult task in reestablishing a measure of reasonable control. An alternative, not incompatible, explanation is that externals are poorer constructive thinkers than internals, which is supported by research findings (Epstein & Meier, 1989).

It may well be that in many studies that find a relation between a measure of a specific coping style and reactions to a stressful event, such as bereavement, the mediating variable is global constructive thinking. The person who thinks constructively in a particular situation is likely to be a good constructive thinker in general, and it therefore may be the person's general level of constructive thinking, not his or her specific coping style, that is responsible for whatever relations are found between particular kinds of coping style and adjustment.

Some support for this hypothesis is provided by the finding that when a measure of constructive thinking has been added to regression equations in which significant relations were found between measures of specific coping styles, such as locus of control, attribution style, and hardiness, treated as independent variables, and emotional and physical symptoms, treated as dependent variables, in all cases constructive thinking completely displaced the other variables. Constructive thinking by itself accounted for as much variance as constructive thinking plus any of the other measures of coping style (Epstein, 1990a, 1991; Epstein & Katz, in press). If it is true that the relations with other measures of coping style are often mediated by constructive thinking, the CTI should provide a particularly valuable instrument for measuring individual differences in coping with a wide variety of adverse events, including bereavement.

Conclusions

Cognitive-experiential self-theory (CEST) provides a broad theoretical framework for understanding reactions to bereavement and for identifying significant variables for research. It emphasizes the personal theories of reality that people automatically construct, describes the rules of inference by which they operate, and draws attention to four fundamental functions, four fundamental beliefs, sensitivities and compulsions based on past experiences, and constructive thinking, all of which are relevant to bereavement research. The Constructive Thinking Inventory, the construction of which was influenced by assumptions in CEST, appears to be a particularly promising tool for investigating coping with stress, including bereavement.

PART IV

Physiological changes following bereavement

9

Biobehavioral consequences of loss in nonhuman primates: Individual differences

MARK L. LAUDENSLAGER, MARIA L. BOCCIA, AND MARTIN L. REITE

Psychoneuroimmunology contends that important relationships exist among behavior, the psychosocial environment, prior experience, and the immune system. These relationships are reflected, for example, in increased morbidity and mortality among the recently bereaved. The rapidly growing number of studies supporting psychosocial/immune relationships in the field of psychoneuroimmunology generally support the biopsychosocial model proposed by Engel (1977) many years ago. This model focused on the role of behavioral and psychosocial factors in the disease process. In spite of the many observations relating psychosocial factors to either disease processes or immunity (see Ader, Felten, & Cohen, 1991, for recent reviews of this rapidly progressing field), there remain questions and doubts regarding the role of these factors by many in the medical community (Angell, 1985). Much of the difficulty in drawing clear relationships between behavior and health outcome is related to the problems inherent in the study of human populations. Appropriate animal models can often resolve some of these dilemmas. This chapter focuses primarily on studies in nonhuman primates that have a particular relevance for loss and ensuing grief in humans. The reader is referred to chapter 11 in this volume by Irwin and Pike, which considers studies of immune function associated with loss in humans, and chapter 10, by Kim and Jacobs, which covers neuroendocrine function in humans during the bereavement process.

Although the relationship between bereavement and increased morbidity and mortality has been well documented (W. Stroebe & Stroebe, 1987; see also this volume), the biological mechanism(s) by which this experience leads to increased risk for medical illness is not clear. Yet if one is going to postulate a relationship among loss experiences, bereavement, and health,

Supported by USPHS Grants MH37373 (MLL), MH44131 (MLB), MH19514, and MH46335 (MLR)

it is important to provide biological links. In this review, we outline a basis for the correlation between bereavement and alterations in health status via a specific homeostatically regulated system, the immune system. The following is limited to a discussion of immunologic changes potentially relevant to autoimmunity, cancer, and infectious illness rather than a description of the numerous studies of noninfectious processes, such as cardiovascular disease, associated with loss. The immune system is described. Next, an animal model of grief is presented with an emphasis on the relevance of behavioral reactions to stressor experience in predicting the immunologic consequences of loss. Finally, the influences of social (e.g., the presence of social support) and heritable (e.g., often referred to as temperament) differences are presented as additional ways of accounting for variations in the response to the same psychosocial stressor.

The three R's of the immune system: Recognition, removal, and regulation

Information about the immune system is increasing at an extremely rapid pace, making it difficult to provide a simple survey. For a comprehensive overview of the immune system, the reader is directed to a text by Roitt, Brostoff, and Male (1989). There are, however, some general principles of its operation that deserve mention here. These principles might be referred to as the "three R's of immunity"; they include recognition of toxic or foreign substances, removal of these foreign substances, and regulation of the immune response. These processes are accomplished by several different types of white blood cells. Foreign substances, also called antigens, are anything considered not part of the organism ("not-self"). Antigens include bacteria, viruses, tumor cells, toxins, and so on. The recognition of antigens is primarily the responsibility of the lymphocytes and a group of accessory cells called macrophages. Macrophages break down or "process" antigen prior to its recognition by the lymphocytes.

There are two major classes of lymphocytes, the B lymphocytes and the T lymphocytes. The B lymphocytes produce antibody (immunoglobulin), a complex protein molecule capable of binding to foreign proteins such as bacteria or viruses with a high degree of specificity. The binding of immunoglobulin to antigen might be all that is required to inactivate the antigen, or binding might result in the attraction of destructive phagocytic accessory cells. The T lymphocytes also recognize foreign materials and may be ultimately involved in the destruction of these materials, as in the rejection of a tumor or an organ graft. There are several types of T lymphocytes, including helper cells (which enhance the production of antibody), suppressor cells (which suppress the activity of the helper cells), and killer cells (which selectively destroy specific targets such as tumors).

Thus, the T lymphocytes participate in all three processes: recognition, regulation, and removal.

The process of removal and/or destruction of foreign materials is accomplished primarily by two groups of lymphocytes. The first group includes phagocytic cells (neutrophils and macrophages). These cells surround (engulf) the foreign material and break it down with destructive substances (enzymes) that they produce. Macrophages are involved in the recognition of "not-self," working in association with the lymphocytes. The other group of destructive lymphocytes includes cytotoxic cells (natural killer cells and killer cells). These cells produce a number of substances that are toxic to the target cell and cause its destruction (lysis). The natural killer (NK) cell differs from the killer cell in that the destructive properties of the NK cell do not require prior exposure to the antigen to produce full activation of this cell type. Nonspecific processes such as this represent innate host defense, whereas a specific killer cell may destroy only a particular target, requiring prior exposure and specificity. The killer cell is, therefore, considered to represent an example of acquired immunity, as does the production of specific antibody by the B cells. The NK cell functions as a first line of defense until the killer cells and other immunologic defenses can be activated and amplified, a process taking as much as a week or longer. Unlike the killer cell, the response of the NK cell is immediate. The activity of the NK cell seems highly susceptible to a variety of psychosocial and behavioral factors, as we describe later.

Superimposed on these cells is a complex regulatory system consisting of soluble cellular secretions (cytokines) that are important in the initiation and continuation of the immune response. Some of these cytokines include interferon, the interleukins (seven of which have been identified to date), tumor necrosis factor, migration inhibition factor, and so on. In addition to the cytokines, there is a growing list of neuroregulatory substances that also participate in the regulation of immune response. These include classical neurotransmitters such as catecholamines, acetylcholine, and serotonin, not to mention steroids such as cortisol, testosterone, and numerous peptides such as ACTH, β-endorphin, growth hormone, and TSH (Blalock, 1989). It is particularly important to recognize that this is not a unidirectional flow of information from the brain to the immune system. A number of these cytokines appear to have important feedback effects on central nervous system function, affecting a number of regulatory processes. Cytokines such as interferon have been implicated in altered sleep patterns (Reite, Laudenslager, Jones, Crnic, & Kaemingk, 1986), normal feedback regulation of the hypothalamic–pituitary–adrenal axis (Dunn, 1990), and as sensory signals for the brain, providing afferent information regarding the activity of the immune system (Blalock, 1989).

There are two possible routes through which behavioral factors, via the central nervous system, might affect the functioning of the immune system: direct neural innervation by the sympathetic nervous system (Ader, Felten, & Cohen, 1990; D. L. Felten et al., 1987a) and circulating neuroendocrine factors such as glucocorticosteroids (Calabrese, Kling, & Gold, 1987; Munck, Guyre, & Holbrook, 1984). Abundant data support each of these systems in immunomodulation associated with behavioral factors (see Ader et al., 1991, for extensive reviews of these studies).

A few precautions with regard to the interpretation of studies investigating relationships between behavior and the various immune parameters: First, there is no single measure of immunity that completely characterizes host defense and immunity, any more than there is a single personality instrument that characterizes behavior. Second, and importantly, the fact that an immunologic parameter declines in association with an event or experimental manipulation does not imply that the immune system *as a whole* is suppressed or compromised. There are multiple backup systems that might potentially compensate for the change. It does suggest, however, that the system has been modified or modulated in an important manner, but the implication of suppression is often unfounded. For this reason the term *immunomodulation* will be used instead of such terms as *immunosuppression*, *immunoenhancement*, or *immunocompromised*. This is not to say that immunosuppression does not occur in association with stressful events, but at present, the measures currently available for monitoring the immune system do not always lend themselves to an evaluation of actual health risk for the organism. Finally, a finding of statistical significance may not necessarily imply clinical significance (Cohen, 1985). In other words, changes that have been noted in many studies, both human and animal, may not always reflect an increased risk for clinical illness.

An animal model relevant to bereavement

Maternal separation in nonhuman primates

Bereavement is an exceptionally complex phenomenon, as reflected in other contributions to this volume. Some of these complexities can be controlled in well-designed animal studies. For example, a brief 4- to 10-day separation of an infant monkey from its mother fulfills many of the criteria for an adequate animal model of grief and bereavement in both human children and adults (Bowlby, 1960; Reite & Capitanio, 1985). The behavioral reaction to separation in the infant monkey is similar to the reaction noted in human infants and children. In fact, Harlow, Gluck, and Suomi (1972) stated the reaction was "so much like childhood anaclitic depression that no thinking man has, and no thinking man ever will, question an enormous, near generality from monkey to man" (p. 714).

Reite and Capitanio (1985) carried the analogy further and suggested that nonhuman primate mother–infant separation might be an appropriate model for adult grief as well, as Bowlby (1960) has theorized that the behavioral responses of the young child to separation or loss were no different from those noted in an adult following a loss experience. One might ask, Are the immunologic alterations seen in association with a recent loss due to poor health maintenance behaviors (e.g., loss of sleep, altered nutrition, increased use of psychoactive substances, and so on), or does the biobehavioral process of grief have a direct impact on immune regulation?

Unlike human populations, health behaviors such as these can be monitored and use of psychoactive substances can be controlled when studying nonhuman primates. The behavioral response of a socially housed young pigtail monkey (*Macaca nemestrina*) follows a predictable species-specific pattern when the mother is removed and the infant remains with its natal group (Kaufman & Rosenblum, 1967; Laudenslager, Held, Boccia, Reite, & Cohen, 1990; Mineka & Suomi, 1978; Reite, Short, Seiler, & Pauley, 1981b). It is important to emphasize that in these studies the infant remains in its natal social group and only the mother is removed, thereby eliminating the possibility that the changes are due to changes in environmental stimuli or social isolation. The protest-despair response is characterized by an initial period of agitation lasting 24 to 48 hours, immediately following maternal separation. During this time the infant monkey is much more active, locomoting and giving distress vocalizations as it actively searches the environment, presumably for its mother. The second phase is one of withdrawal or behavioral depression. The pigtail infant's activity drops dramatically, play with peers ceases, motor activity is quite awkward, and oral behaviors such as eating increase.

Social support in nonhuman primates

A young bonnet macaque (*Macaca radiata*) also follows a species-specific response, which includes far less behavioral disturbance, following maternal separation. A part of this difference may be due to the presence of allomaternal care in the social group (Boccia, Reite, & Laudenslager, in press; Laudenslager et al., 1990). Allomaternal care is observed as a form of "aunting" behavior in which other females in the social group care for the separated infant.

The bonnet infant, remaining with its natal social group during maternal separation, demonstrates a typical protest response on the first day of separation. In contrast to pigtail social groups, members of the bonnet social group provide allomaternal care for the separated infant. After removal of the mother, allomaternal care is noted as a significant increase in contact with other group members. Allomaternal care includes social contact with the infant in the form of cradling and protection. As contact with individuals providing allomaternal care increases during maternal separation of bonnet infants, there is a parallel increase in play behavior, which had previously declined, and reduction in disturbance behaviors, which had initially increased. Allomaternal care generally declines on the return of the mother. If all individuals capable of providing allomaternal care are removed, the bonnet infant will demonstrate the same sequence of behavioral disturbance as the pigtail infant does, including prolonged behavioral disturbance, slouched, withdrawn postures, and altered autonomic regulation (Kaufman & Stynes, 1978; Laudenslager, Reite, & Harbeck, 1982; Reite & Snyder, 1982).

The mother–infant relationship in bonnet macaques can be altered when there are changes in environmental resources such as under conditions of clumped, monopolizable food resources or increased foraging demands (Boccia, Laudenslager, & Reite, 1988). These conditions are associated with more restrictive mothering behaviors. Restrictive mothering limits the number of individuals in the social group with which the infant might develop an allomaternal relationship, and the response to separation in the bonnet infant becomes quite profound even in the presence of conspecifics (Boccia et al., in press). This process of adoption by other group members in the bonnet macaque may serve as an animal model of social support. The number of individuals can be experimentally manipulated, as described earlier, by manipulating food resource availability, for example, or removing the alternative individuals from the group at the time the mother is removed, thus further enhancing the usefulness of the model.

Autonomic correlates of separation in nonhuman primates: Physiological, endocrinologic, and immunologic

Physiological correlates

The autonomic responses to separation in infant pigtail monkeys have been well studied in unrestrained infants implanted with telemetry devices that transmit biological signals reflecting heart rate (EKG), body temperature, and electroencephalogram (EEG). (See Reite et al., 1981a, for a comprehensive review of these studies.) Heart rate, although high during the agitation phase, declines during the second phase. Arrhythmias (missed heartbeats) also increase during separation. There are changes in the patterns of sleep (more frequent arousals, delayed sleep onset, and reduced rapid eye movement stage). Circadian rhythms of body temperature and heart rate also change during separation. The observed changes in circadian rhythms may be particularly relevant for immune parameters, which show circadian variations (Cohen & Crnic, 1982). Many of the autonomic parameters return to baseline values when the mother and the infant are reunited in the social group. However, for some infant monkeys, these parameters never return to baseline after reunion, at least within battery-life limitations of the biotelemetry devices. Similar autonomic changes occur in children briefly separated from their mother during the birth of a sibling (Field & Reite, 1984) or from both parents during barrier isolation in association with immunosuppressant drug therapy (Hollenbeck et al., 1980).

Endocrinologic correlates

The endocrine system of the young monkey is also affected by a separation experience. In a comprehensive series of studies in nonhuman primate infants, Levine and co-workers (Bayart, Hayashi, Faull, Barchas, & Levine, 1990; Coe, Weiner, Rosenberg, & Levine, 1985; Levine, Johnson, & Gonzales, 1985; Wiener, Bayart, Faull, & Levine, 1990) have evaluated the contributions of a number of important behavioral factors to the response of the hypothalamic–pituitary–adrenal (HPA) axis during mother–infant separation in both rhesus monkeys (*Macaca mulatta*) and squirrel monkeys (*Saimiri scuireus*). Squirrel monkeys, a New World species, have a more labile endocrine response to a stressor, whereas rhesus monkeys, like humans, are less reactive in their endocrine response under similar conditions. A prominent similarity between the two species is that the agitation phase of the separation response is marked by HPA activation, reflected in elevated blood levels of cortisol, which also covary with elevated biogenic amine metabolites in the cerebral spinal fluid (CSF), suggesting greater turnover in these neurotransmitter substances.

For the squirrel monkey infant, distress vocalizations were not related to the rise in circulating adrenal hormones, as cortisol levels continued to rise even as calling declined. One must entertain the notion that there may be a degree of independence of the behavioral and autonomic responses to mother–infant separation. The quality of the vocalizations is affected by the social situation. Separation (mother in the vicinity) and isolation (mother out of immediate vicinity) calls of squirrel monkey infants are quite different acoustically (Bayart et al., 1990). Indeed, Bowlby (1960) clearly described the vocalization at separation as an attachment behavior that serves to attract the mother back to location of the infant. The calling response may also reflect a coping behavior on the part of the infant, which serves to reduce the cortisol (stress) response (Bayart et al., 1990).

For the rhesus monkey, HPA activation declined during prolonged separation experiences (greater than 24 hours), which was not the case for the squirrel monkey. The presence of peers, duration of the separation, number of repeated separations, availability of the mother (i.e., visual, auditory, or olfactory cues), and novelty of the environment interact significantly with the magnitude and duration of the HPA response (Coe et al., 1985). In addition to adrenal cortical activation associated with elevations of plasma cortisol, it has also been shown that maternal separation is associated with increased levels of catecholamine synthesizing enzymes, suggesting increased peripheral sympathetic activity (Breese et al., 1973).

Immunologic correlates

A number of studies have demonstrated that maternal separation in non-human primates is associated with important immunologic consequences. These studies were initiated on the basis of both anecdotal and epidemiologic observations in human populations of increased morbidity and mortality in the recently bereaved (W. Stroebe & Stroebe, 1987) and altered immune function following recent loss (Bartrop, Luckhurst, Lazarus, Kiloh, & Penny, 1977; Schleifer, Keller, Camerino, Thornton, & Stein, 1983; see also Irwin & Pike, this volume). Studies of macaque monkeys have documented a number of immunologic changes associated with social separation, including lower total nonspecific plasma IgM and IgG levels (Scanlan, Coe, Latts, & Suomi, 1987) and reduced lymphocyte activation by mitogens (Laudenslager et al., 1982; Laudenslager et al., 1990; Boccia, Reite, Kaemingk, Held, & Laudenslager, 1989; Reite et al., 1981a). Mitogens are plant extracts that nonspecifically stimulate cellular division in lymphocytes and other cells. Reite et al. (1981a) noted changes in lymphocyte responsiveness during the separation of peer-reared monkeys, with the response returning to baseline at reunion with the peer mate. Peer separations are associated with a number of behavioral and physiological changes, including reduced lymphocyte activation by mitogens (Boccia et al., 1988), similar to those observed in infant monkeys separated from their mothers (Mineka & Suomi, 1978). That peer separation also affects the immunologic parameters suggests that nutritional loss due to deprivation of maternal milk does not account for these changes in immune parameters.

In the squirrel monkey, maternal separation has been associated with reduced complement (an inflammatory protein of immunologic origin that increases during infection) levels (Coe, Rosenberg, & Levine, 1988b), lower neutralizing antibody levels to bacteriophage following immunization during separation (Coe, Rosenberg, Fischer, & Levine, 1987; Coe, Cassayre, Levine, & Rosenberg, 1988a), and prolonged changes in macrophage function (Coe, Rosenberg, & Levine, 1988b). The use of in vivo probes of immune competence, such as immunization with a foreign protein, is particularly important in light of our recent comments regarding the need for in vivo assays of the intact immune system (see Maier & Laudenslager, 1988) rather than the more routine testing of aspects of the system under artificial in vitro culture conditions.

Recent work (Laudenslager, Held, Boccia, Gennaro, Reite, & Cohen, in press) from our group in the macaque infant has indicated that plasma levels of specific antibodies (IgM and IgG) following challenge with a foreign protein are directly related to the behaviors occurring during the separation experience. The appearance of specific antibodies in the plasma represents an integrated immunologic response, reflecting the process from the initial processing of the antigen by the macrophages to the cooperation of the B and T cells and the ultimate production of immunoglobulin molecules (antibody). Following immunization, plasma IgM levels rise first following immunization followed by an increase in plasma IgG in 5–7 days. It is our belief that lower plasma antibody levels reflect altered immune functioning and an impaired ability to recognize and remove a novel antigen. However, antibody levels alone fail to provide an indication of the site of the immunologic defect. Instead, they reflect an integrated response of the various accessory cells, such as macrophages, and the cooperation of the B and T cells.

We have found that IgM levels varied positively with social behaviors such as time spent in contact with other members of the social group during separation, and IgG was negatively related to distress behaviors such as vocalization on the first day of separation and the amount of time spent in slouched postures during the first week of separation. Together these behaviors accounted for more than 50% of the variance in specific IgM and IgG antibody levels in separated and control subjects. Knowledge of the behavioral response associated with maternal separation was also important in predicting the magnitude of the change in lymphocyte activation following separation (Laudenslager et al., 1990). The in vitro response of lymphocytes to mitogens during the second week of separation significantly covaried with the level of vocalization on the first day of separation and the amount of time spent in slouched withdrawn postures during the first week of separation. Thus, both in vitro (lymphocyte activation) and in vivo (specific antibody levels) immunologic parameters covary with the same behaviors. We will return to the unique relevance of these behaviors later.

Long-term immunologic correlates of early experiences

Little was known regarding long-term effects of early stressor exposure on immune regulation or developmental psychoneuroimmunology when reviewed several years ago (Ader, 1983). Less is known regarding the long-term consequences of early separation experiences in monkeys. Childhood losses have been associated with an increased risk for adult depression (Clayton, 1979; Lloyd, 1980) and increased somatic complaints (Rubenstein & Shaver, 1980). There is considerable controversy at present, however, with regard to the increased risk for adult depression (Crook & Eliot, 1980; Peris, Holmgren, von Knorring, & Peris, 1986; Tennant, Bebbington, & Hurry, 1980). It is possible that animal models might provide some clues as to the importance of the relationship of early events to adult functioning.

Studies of adult pigtail monkeys at 4 years of age indicated that separated monkeys, all of which were reunited with their mothers following a 10-day separation at 6 months of age, displayed smaller social networks (Capitanio & Reite, 1985), greater behavioral disturbance in a novel situation (Capitanio, Rasmussen, Snyder, Laudenslager, & Reite, 1985), and a reduced lymphocyte response to mitogenic stimulation (Laudenslager, Capitanio, & Reite, 1985).

We (Rager, Laudenslager, Held, & Boccia, 1989) have replicated these observations longitudinally in the pigtail monkey from 15 to 24 months of age. We found lower lymphocyte activation in previously separated monkeys compared to that in matched controls, in addition to lower natural cytotoxicity levels (a measure of natural killer activity). Furthermore, for the same age ranges, previously separated bonnet macaques appear to show higher lymphocyte activation and natural cytotoxicity levels when compared to matched controls. Eighteen-month-old pigtail monkeys, which experienced an early 2-week separation followed by a reunion, took a longer time to take a piece of preferred fruit in a novel environment compared to nonseparated matched controls. No differences were noted in bonnet infants with a similar history of maternal separation, in the same test situation. The observed species differences noted in lymphocyte activation and natural cytotoxicity and behavior in the novel environment may be related to the behavioral differences between the two species associated with separation. That is, both species show an initial period of agitation, but only the pigtail proceeds on to a depressive phase. In addition, the mother–infant relationship after reunion in the social group changes more for the pigtail mother–infant pairs than for the bonnet mother–infant pairs (unpublished observations).

Early weaning (Ackerman et al., 1988) or early handling experiences (Solomon, Levine, & Kraft, 1968) are important modulators of the immune response in laboratory rodents, albeit in apparently different directions. Early weaning was associated with increased infections due to opportunistic organisms, whereas early handling enhanced the antibody response to a novel antigen. Early weaning may have affected immunologic maturation associated with the absence of maternal milk, whereas early handling may have influenced behavioral coping responses, which may have been evoked during the immunization protocol in the adult subjects.

Rearing of rhesus macaque infants in social isolation is associated with an enhanced responsiveness of their lymphocytes to mitogens (Coe, Lubach, Ershler, & Klopp, 1989). The isolated infants in this study were fed a commercial formula developed for human infants, which might have contributed to differential development of the immune response in isolated infants compared to mother-reared infants. Although there are some suggestions that rearing experiences might affect immune regulation, there is very little known regarding how early experiences, stressful or otherwise, influence host defense in the adult organism. Developmental psychoneuroimmunology remains an important uncharted research area.

Some factors accounting for individual differences: Temperament and social support

It is quite clear that not all animals respond to the same stressor in the same way. If one is able to assess differences in behavioral responses associated with the stressor, one may also account for substantial immunologic variance as well (see, e.g., Fleshner, Laudenslager, Simons, & Maier, 1989; Laudenslager et al., 1990; Laudenslager et al., in press). Two factors, one biological and the other social, may account for a portion of the variability in immunologic responses following stressor exposure. These factors are temperament and social support.

Temperament

The concept of temperament, defined as a biological predisposition to respond in a particular fashion, has been of value in understanding a number of individual differences in normal development and as a risk factor for some childhood disorders in both human and nonhuman primates (Carey, 1990; Suomi, 1987). Both behavioral (shyness or lack of behavioral inhibition in new situations [Kagan, Reznick, & Snidman, 1988]) and biological (cardiac pattern as reflected in resting heart rate variability or vagal tone [Fox, 1989]) markers have been described for temperament. It may be possible to sort out individuals at high risk for immunomodulation by psychosocial factors on the basis of a biological dimension: autonomic reactivity. This is not a new idea (as indicated for developmental differences), but its application to psychoneuroimmunology is new. A temperamental trait like autonomic reactivity, as reflected in a measure such as vagal tone or heart rate variability, may represent a heritable trait that covaries with a susceptibility for behavioral factors to influence immunoregulation.

Temperament has also been observed to vary with health outcome in human subjects. College students rated behaviorally as gamma type (irregular and uneven) were found to have a much greater incidence of medical disorders (cardiovascular, cancer, and mental health) than individuals identified as either alpha (slow and solid) or beta (rapid/facile) type (Betz & Thomas, 1979). This study did not assess biological markers of either health or temperament. Behaviorally inhibited college students (shy and cautious in unfamiliar situations) were noted to report a greater incidence of allergies, particularly hay fever, than socially outgoing college students, suggesting a relationship between temperament as reflected in behavioral inhibition and immunity (Bell, Jasnoski, Kagan, & King, 1990). Recent observations by Manuck, Cohen, Rabin, Muldoon, and Bachen (1991) indicate that a composite measure of autonomic reactivity consisting of resting blood pressure, heart rate, and plasma catecholamines discriminated high reactors most likely to show immunologic perturbation (increased numbers of suppressor T cells and reduced lymphocyte activation by a mitogen) following a mild psychological challenge.

Heart rate variability, a presumed biological marker of temperament (as described earlier), is also a significant predictor of the endocrine and behavioral responses of macaque monkeys to novel situations (Rasmussen & Suomi, 1989; Rasmussen, Fellowes, & Suomi, 1990). Those monkeys with a low and variable heart rate showed a smaller cortisol response to acute stress and also emigrated into a new social group at a younger age. The researchers suggested that these patterns of reactivity may offer a simple marker of temperament in both humans and animals. The existence of strain-related behavioral differences in open field activity of mice, which vary closely with a number of immunologic characteristics in response to stressor exposure (see, e.g., Cohen & Crnic, 1984), may also indicate a potential role of heritable differences reflected in temperament. Finally, Mason (1991) has developed the thesis that genetic variation in the neuro-endocrine response to stress may have important implications for variation in susceptibility to disease.

Based on preliminary analysis of data collected over the past 2 decades in our laboratory, we have been encouraged to consider heart rate as an important marker for both behavioral and immunologic consequences of maternal separation. We looked at mean day heart rate in infant pigtail macaques implanted with telemetry devices that permitted the monitoring of heart rate in unrestrained subjects as previously described. In order to classify infants as having high or low heart rates, a median split was performed on heart rates observed during the baseline period prior to a maternal separation. Behavioral responses to separation, including vocalization, time spent in slouched postures, exploration, ingestive behaviors, and locomotion, were analyzed by ANOVA for heart rate (high/low) as a between-subjects variable and separation day as a within-subjects variable. We found that subjects classified as high heart rate were more likely to spend more time in a slouched posture during the first week of separation and emit more distress vocalizations on the first day of separation than subjects with low heart rates during the baseline period. An important unifying observation is that these are the same behaviors that covary with both in vitro and in vivo immune measures (Laudenslager et al., 1990; Laudenslager et al., in press). Thus, it may be that heart rate or its variability might also predict the infant monkey's immunologic response to maternal separation and, perhaps, other social stressors. This hypothesis is currently under evaluation in our laboratory.

One must be cautious in interpreting biological (genetic) origins of heart rate as a predictor because experiential factors can also modify heart rate. For example, a relationship between social status and heart rate has been noted in male macaque monkeys (Kaplan, Manuck, & Gatsonis, 1990) such that high social rank animals had consistently lower heart rates than subordinate animals. When rank shifts occurred, there was an associated alteration in heart rate. We recognize that heart rates, obtained at 5–6 months of age in our infants, was influenced by a number of experiential and social factors, but we remain encouraged about its potential usefulness as a risk marker.

Social support

A large literature in health psychology suggests that social support is associated with better health outcomes under a variety of stressful conditions (Cohen, 1988). It is possible that some features of social support can be modeled in nonhuman primates, as described earlier. Differences in patterns of maternal care noted in bonnet and pigtail macaques may permit the development of such an animal model. Maternal care in pigtail macaques is typically provided only by the natural mother of the infant, resulting in a restricted social network that permits few interactions with other females in the natal social group. In contrast, bonnet macaque infants are cared for by several adult females in the social group, resulting in a broader social network consisting of a number of adult "aunts."

Manipulation of the availability of social support during maternal separation significantly affects the response of bonnet infants to maternal separation (Boccia et al., in press; Boccia, Scanlan, Laudenslager, Broussard, & Reite, submitted; Scanlan, Boccia, Laudenslager, & Broussard, 1990). It was noted that infants that retained social partners (juvenile monkeys in the social group that showed affiliative interactions with the infant) during a maternal separation failed to show an alteration in lymphocyte activation by mitogens or in natural cytotoxicity during the 2-week maternal separation. In contrast, separated infants that had no affiliative partner showed a significant reduction in lymphocyte activation by mitogens and a reduction in natural cytotoxicity. The bonnet infants lacking a social support partner showed greater behavioral disturbance associated with separation than subjects permitted access to a social support partner. Studies of heart rate changes occurring during maternal separation in pigtail infants have noted that the magnitude of these changes was less when the infant was in contact with other members of the social group (Caine & Reite, 1981). Once again this suggests that the presence of social affiliations provides a buffering effect on the consequences of maternal separation in macaque infants.

Implications

There is compelling evidence from the discussed animal studies that brief maternal separation in nonhuman primates influences immune regulation and that these early experiences may also have consequences that are observable in the adult organism. Furthermore, there seem to be a number of factors that predict immunologic outcome following stressor exposure, such as the presence of social support or autonomic reactivity, that are common to both human and nonhuman primates. The task before us is to develop risk profiles that permit the identification of individuals most likely to be affected by psychosocial stressor experiences. Current animal studies have primarily assessed markers of immune status, but we know little regarding their relationship to disease risk for the organism. This is an important question that needs to be addressed in future studies, as does the long-term impact of early experiences on health in the adult. Needless to say, these are not simple tasks, but animal models have identified a few intrinsic and extrinsic variables, in the absence of confounding health behaviors such as diet or psychoactive drug use, that can be considered.

10

Neuroendocrine changes following bereavement

KATHLEEN KIM AND SELBY JACOBS

Normal grief is a process consisting of sadness, longing for the deceased person, somatic complaints, and subsequent recovery. Although the majority of people do not suffer adverse consequences following bereavement, a significant minority experience increased morbidity and mortality. These individuals may be more vulnerable to bereavement, and this vulnerability may be due to some unidentified psychological, neuroendocrine, or immunologic factor that places them at increased risk (Hirsch, Hofer, Holland, & Solomon, 1984).

This chapter focuses on the neuroendocrine changes associated with bereavement, with an emphasis on the psychiatric morbidity following bereavement. The chapter is divided into four sections. The first section briefly summarizes studies of the psychiatric complications of bereavement, and the second section reviews the basic concepts of the neuroendocrine system and stress research in order to facilitate interpretation of neuro-endocrine studies. The third section summarizes the neuroendocrine findings in depression and anxiety disorders; both disorders have been found to complicate bereavement. The neuroendocrine abnormalities in these disorders provide clues for neuroendocrine changes that may be associated with complicated bereavement. The fourth section reviews neuroendocrine studies of bereavement.

Psychiatric complications of bereavement

Pathological grief is distinguished from normal grief by the nature, duration, and severity of symptoms. Although the concept of pathological grief has been well described (cf. Middleton, Raphael, Martinek, & Misso, this volume), there is no consensus on the diagnostic criteria of the syndrome. Recent bereavement studies have adopted an atheoretical or nonetiologic model of psychiatric disorders, avoiding conceptual models of pathological grief and focusing on the descriptive quantification of symptoms. These studies have used diagnostic interview schedules or clinical interviews to assess psychiatric status in bereaved individuals.

143

The psychiatric complications of bereavement are syndromes diagnosed using standardized, descriptive criteria. The rate of complications is dependent on the type of adverse outcome. For pathological grief, the rate ranges from 4% to 34% (Parkes & Weiss, 1983; Zisook & DeVaul, 1983; Clayton, Desmarais, & Winokur, 1968; Maddison & Viola, 1968); for major depression, 17%–31% (Bornstein, Clayton, Halikas, Maurice, & Robins, 1973; Jacobs, Hansen, Beckman, Kasl, & Ostfeld, 1989; Bruce, Kim, Leaf, & Jacobs, 1990); for panic disorder, 13% (Jacobs et al., 1990); and for generalized anxiety disorder, 39% (Jacobs et al., 1990). The rate of comorbidity is significant, with more than half of the acutely bereaved spouses suffering from two disorders (Jacobs & Kim, 1990; Kim & Jacobs, 1991).

The psychiatric disorders found to complicate bereavement – that is, major depression, panic disorder, and generalized anxiety disorder – have been associated with neuroendocrine abnormalities. These abnormalities may provide clues to the pathophysiology of complicated bereavement and are described in the third section of the chapter.

Regardless of the psychiatric complications, bereavement is considered a stressful event with characteristic behavioral and physiological manifestations. Hofer (1984) and Bowlby (1963) considered the physiological changes as correlates of the emotional response to the loss. Neuroendocrine changes may be part of the normal adaptive response of bereavement. However, if the neuroendocrine changes persist, they may become maladaptive and increase the individual's risk for morbidity or mortality. Complicated bereavement may be analogous to Gold's concept of depression; he believes that depression arises when an individual's acute generalized stress response escapes the usual counterregulatory restraints (Gold, Goodwin, & Chrousos, 1988).

The neuroendocrine system and stress research: Basic concepts

The neuroendocrine system is not one system but several interdependent systems (Mason et al., 1976). The main components are the central nervous system (CNS), hypothalamus, pituitary, thyroid, adrenal medullary system, and gonads. The "vectors" of the neuroendocrine system are hormones and catecholamines that interact in a variety of ways – that is, the relationships can be antagonistic, synergistic, or additive. For example, corticotropin-releasing hormone (CRH) stimulates the release of adrenocorticotropin hormone (ACTH), which then stimulates the release of cortisol, and cortisol in turn has a negative feedback relationship with ACTH.

The neuroendocrine system performs several vital functions. The locus coeruleus (part of the CNS) produces norepinephrine, and the adrenal medullary system produces both norepinephrine and epinephrine. These catecholamines regulate blood pressure, heart rate and cardiac output and mobilize blood glucose. Norepinephrine and epinephrine have central and peripheral nervous system effects. The hypothalamus controls food intake, libido, and circadian rhythms, as well as the synthesis and release of hormones into the rest of the brain and the systemic circulation. The pituitary produces hormones that exert specific biological actions and influence the functional activity of brain neurotransmitter systems. The adrenal–medullary system produces hormones as well as catecholamines. The hypothalamic–pituitary–adrenal (HPA) axis is activated by physical or psychological stressors. The hormones CRH, ACTH, and cortisol are produced by the HPA axis.

Other vital functions of the neuroendocrine system include stimulating tissue growth, lactate production, and sexual and reproductive function. The hormones involved in these processes include growth hormone, prolactin, and gonadal hormones, including gonadal hormone releasing hormone (GHRH), testosterone, estrogen, and progesterone. These hormones, like the hormones of the HPA axis, are activated by physical or psychological stressors.

Stress research in the 1950s was characterized by studies of nonspecific adrenal–medullary responses to a wide variety of stimuli – heat, cold, exercise, and so on. Mason noted that all of these studies shared an important characteristic: exposure of the animal to a novel, strange, or unfamiliar environment (Mason, 1975). The common factor was not the stressor itself but the psychological relevance of the stressor. If the animal was not distressed or exposed to novelty, there was no activation of the adrenal system. This was an important concept that had been ignored in earlier stress research.

In his review of endocrine responses to stress, Rose (1980) emphasized the significance of individual differences in the responses of human subjects when confronted with potentially challenging or threatening stimuli. Individuals do not always respond in a similar manner to the same stressor. For example, in a combat unit awaiting a threatened enemy attack, the captain of the unit had an elevated urinary 17-hydroxycorticosteroid (a metabolic breakdown product of the hormone cortisol) excretion rate, but the soldiers did not. The individual's subjective experience of the stress was an important determinant of the endocrine response.

Lazarus described this as the cognitive appraisal of the significance of the stressor (Lazarus & Folkman, 1984). Furthermore, several other determinants are involved in the response to a stressor: the nature of the stressor (Lazarus & Folkman, 1984), gender differences (Vingerhoets & Van Heck, 1990; Folkman & Lazarus, 1980), and individual variation in personality function. Given the multiple determinants, the individual's coping style when exposed to threatening stimuli must be considered.

A final concept to emphasize is that of adaptation to chronic stress. Mason noted that endocrine responses may undergo rapid extinction upon exposure to the stimulus. He demonstrated this finding in a study of rhesus monkeys: After repeated shocks, they quickly adapted to the stressful nature of the stimulus and did not exhibit evidence of adrenocortical arousal (Mason, Brady, & Toliver, 1968). In other studies, humans have adapted to stressful events after repeated exposure. For example, novice parachute jumpers show a very large increase in cortisol levels on their first jump, but most fail to show an increase on subsequent jumps (Rose, 1980).

Bereavement is a novel and distressing situation that can stimulate neuroendocrine responses. However, the response of the bereaved person is highly subjective and dependent on individual characteristics, such as the significance of the loss, gender, and coping style, as well as factors related to the loss (sudden, traumatic, anticipated). Furthermore, bereavement is unlike other stressors in that it is a single event with multiple consequences. There is the acute distress of bereavement, and then there are chronic stresses, such as adapting to a new social role as a widow or widower, assuming the household tasks of the lost person, and in some cases, adjusting to reduced financial circumstances. The bereaved person will face many novel or distressing situations as he or she adapts to life after the loss. Because these novel or distressing situations could potentially stimulate neuroendocrine responses long after the death of the other person, the timing of a neuroendocrine study is an issue. If measures are collected shortly after the loss, they will presumably reflect acute changes in the system. If the neuroendocrine system may adapt to chronic stress, will neuroendocrine measures collected several months afterward reflect chronic adaptation to the loss or current perturbations of the system?

Neuroendocrine changes in depression and anxiety

The purpose of this section is to review the neuroendocrine findings in two psychiatric disorders: major depression and anxiety disorders. As discussed earlier in the chapter, these disorders are among the most frequent psychiatric complications of bereavement. The goal is to increase our understanding of the pathophysiology of the potential psychiatric complications of bereavement.

Neuroendocrine changes in major depression

Many neuroendocrine abnormalities have been associated with major depression. However, the findings are often conflicting. Instead of reviewing all of these abnormalities, we will focus primarily on evidence related to the catecholamines, cortisol, growth hormone, and prolactin.

Catecholamines. The norepinephrine abnormalities in major depression have been studied more frequently than any other catecholamine abnormalities, so we will focus on norepinephrine in this review. The principal CNS site of norepinephrine synthesis occurs in the locus coeruleus. In animal studies, electrical stimulation of the locus coeruleus produces intense anxiety, hypervigilance, and inhibition of exploratory behavior (Redmond & Huang, 1979; Aston-Jones, Foote, & Bloom, 1984). Spontaneous firing of the locus increases during threatening situations and diminishes sleep, grooming, and feeding (Redmond & Huang, 1979; Aston-Jones et al., 1984). Recent studies indicate that the locus coeruleus is activated during major depression. There are normal or increased levels of CSF norepinephrine, increased plasma norepinephrine, and increased CSF and urinary 3-methoxy-4-hydroxyphenylglycol (MHPG), a norepinephrine metabolite (Gold et al., 1988).

Cortisol. Some of the symptoms of major depression – disturbances in appetite, sleep, and libido – indicate a malfunction of the hypothalamic–pituitary–adrenal axis. Gold et al. have postulated that hypersecretion of CRH is the primary cause of the HPA malfunction (Gold et al., 1988; Altemus & Gold, 1990). CRH hypersecretion causes pathological arousal: anxiety, obsessive ruminations, early morning awakening, anorexia, decreased libido, and activation of the sympathetic nervous system and pituitary–adrenal axis.

Patients with major depression have attenuated ACTH responses to the administration of synthetic ovine CRH (Gold et al., 1984); this finding indicates that the elevated cortisol levels in depression provide negative feedback to the pituitary, so ACTH secretion is reduced. Normal controls given continuous infusions of CRH exhibit the pattern and extent of hypercortisolism seen in depressed patients (Schulte et al., 1985). Furthermore, CRH in the cerebrospinal fluid of depressed patients positively correlates with indices of pituitary–adrenal activation.

Gold postulates that CRH and the locus coeruleus/norepinephrine systems are the principal effectors of the normal adaptive stress response (Gold et al., 1988). When homeostasis is threatened, CRH and the locus coeruleus/norepinephrine systems act in concert to promote attention, arousal, and aggression, as well as to inhibit vegetative functions such as feeding, sexual behavior, and reproduction. In addition, CRH and the locus coeruleus/norepinephrine systems act through the catecholamines and glucocorticoids to redirect blood flow to the CNS. Glucocorticoid secretion is thought to restrain or counterregulate the effectors of the stress response, in order to prevent prolonged or excessive activation. Thus, glucocorticoids antagonize the CRH neuron and perhaps the locus coeruleus/norepine-phrine systems as well.

The dexamethasone suppression test (DST) is also used to evaluate the HPA axis. Dexamethasone is a synthetic steroid similar to the hormone cortisol. If the HPA axis is functioning normally, dexamethasone suppresses cortisol release. If the HPA axis has lost its normal regulatory mechanisms, dexamethasone does not suppress cortisol release. Dexamethasone does not suppress cortisol in approximately 43% of hospitalized, endogenously depressed patients (Carroll et al., 1981) and in 15% of endogenously depressed outpatients (Winokur, Amsterdam, & Caroff, 1982).

Growth hormone. Depressed patients hypersecrete growth hormone, particularly before sleep (Mendlewicz et al., 1985), and exhibit abnormal responses to stimuli that usually promote secretion. Growth hormone responses to insulin-induced hypoglycemia, amphetamine, clonidine, and growth hormone releasing hormone (GHRH) infusion are attenuated (Rupprecht & Lesch, 1989; Lesch, Laux, Erb, & Beckman, 1988). It is not clear why depressed patients hypersecrete growth hormone and have attenuated responses to these stimuli.

Prolactin. Prolactin has not been studied systematically in depressed patients. Anxious and depressed women secrete prolactin during a stressful task, but depressed men and controls do not (Miyabo, Asato, & Miyushima, 1977). Clinical observations of psychiatric patients suggest that changes in prolactin are associated with depressed mood and irritability (De La Fuente & Rosenbaum, 1981).

Neuroendocrine changes in anxiety disorders

Anxiety disorders are either episodic, such as panic disorder and phobia, or chronic, such as post-traumatic stress disorder and generalized anxiety disorder. The former disorders are intermittent and have specific symptoms associated with the discrete episodes of anxiety; the latter have more continuous symptoms. All of the anxiety disorders have symptoms that are suggestive of hypothalamic and sympathetic adrenal–medullary system dysfunction, that is, insomnia, hyperarousal, and appetite changes (Altemus & Gold, 1990).

Generalized anxiety disorder

Currently, there is little evidence of neuroendocrine abnormalities in patients with generalized anxiety disorder (GAD). Urinary free cortisol excretion in GAD patients is not different from normal controls (Rosenbaum et al., 1983). GAD patients have a rate of nonsuppression following the dexamethasone suppression test which is intermediate between normals and depressed outpatients. The rate of nonsuppression does not correlate with the severity of depressive symptoms (Avery et al., 1985).

Post-traumatic stress disorder

Post-traumatic stress disorder (PTSD) patients are chronically anxious, with symptoms of flashbacks, exaggerated startle response, nightmares, and sleep disturbance. They frequently have concurrent disorders, such as major depression, substance abuse, and other anxiety disorders. The majority of published neuroendocrine studies have focused on adrenocortical activity.

Cortisol. Mason found that PTSD patients had the lowest urinary free cortisol before and after treatment as compared to patients with depression or schizophrenia (Mason, Giller, Kosten, Ostroff, & Podd, 1986). PTSD patients without concurrent depression had normal cortisol suppression in response to the DST (Kundler, Davidson, Meador, Lipper, & Ely, 1987).

The CRH stimulation test demonstrated a blunted ACTH response in depressed and nondepressed PTSD patients (Smith et al., 1989). Altemus and Gold (1990) postulated that this reduced ACTH response might reflect a history of intermittent acute increases in CRH during episodes of severe anxiety. They questioned whether reduced ACTH secretion persists even after episodic CRH hypersecretion, which would result in a blunted ACTH response to exogenous CRH infusion. This hypothesis would explain the normal suppression of cortisol secretion in response to the DST because negative feedback to the hypothalamus and pituitary would still be intact.

Panic disorder

Patients with panic disorders suffer from episodes of intense anxiety and somatic symptoms (tachycardia, dyspnea, dizziness) that occur several times each day. Between the panic attacks, these patients often experience low-grade anxiety and tend to become easily aroused in unfamiliar or novel situations. Panic disorder patients often have concurrent major depression, and there is a high incidence of depression in families of panic disorder patients.

Catecholamines. During panic attacks, there is conflicting evidence regarding activation of the sympathetic nervous system and little evidence of pituitary–adrenal activation. In spontaneously occurring panic attacks, one study found small variable increases in norepinephrine but no changes in the epinephrine or norepinephrine metabolites (Cameron, Lee, Curtis, & McCann, 1987). Another study found no changes in norepinephrine or catecholamine metabolites (Woods, Charney, McPherson, Gradman, & Heninger, 1987). In sodium lactate–induced panic attacks, no evidence was found of pituitary or adrenal activation (Carr et al., 1986; Hollander et al., 1989). In yohimbine-induced panic attacks, increased plasma MHPG (norepinephrine metabolite) was found (Charney, Woods, Goodman, & Heninger, 1987).

Cortisol. During spontaneous panic attacks, small variable increases in plasma cortisol were found in one study (Cameron et al., 1987), but not in another (Woods et al., 1987). Similarly, there is conflicting evidence in experimentally induced panic attacks (Carr et al., 1986; Hollander et al., 1989; Charney et al., 1987). In general, panic disorder patients have elevated urinary free cortisol, as compared to controls. However, when patients with coexisting depression or agoraphobia are excluded, the remaining patients are not different from normals (Kathol, Noyes, Lopez, & Reich, 1988). Panic disorder patients have rates of non-suppression following the DST that are intermediate between controls and depressed patients (Carson, Halbreich, Yeh, & Goldstein, 1988). If panic patients with coexisting depressions are excluded, DST rates are the same as controls (Roy-Byrne Bierer, & Uhde, 1985). Two studies have shown a blunted ACTH response to CRH and lower ACTH/cortisol ratios (Holsboer, von Bardeleben, Buller, Heuser, & Steiger, 1987; Roy-Byrne et al., 1985).

Other findings. During spontaneous panic attacks, small variable increases in prolactin were found in one study (Cameron et al., 1987), but not in another (Woods et al., 1987). There were also decreased growth hormone responses to gonadal hormone releasing hormone (GHRH) and clonidine in patients with panic disorder (Rapaport, Risch, Gillin, Goshan, & Janowsky, 1989; Uhde, Vittone, Siever, Kaye, & Post, 1986).

The neuroendocrine findings in panic disorder patients are limited and confounded by comorbidity with major depression. If patients with concomitant depression are excluded from the analyses, panic disorder patients exhibit only a few abnormalities. These neuroendocrine abnormalities are small and variable (Cameron et al., 1987) or are exhibited in response to specific challenge tests, that is, CRH or GHRH infusions.

Neuroendocrine studies of bereavement

Given the practical problems of studying individuals following bereavement, it is not surprising that there are few studies of the neuroendocrine changes associated with bereavement. This section briefly summarizes the seminal studies of Wolff, Hofer, and co-investigators and then reviews the more recent studies of Jacobs and co-investigators.

Wolff, Hofer, and co-investigators

Wolff et al. (1964a,b) studied parents of fatally ill children. Based on a clinical assessment of the effectiveness of each parent's ego defenses in modulating "psychic tension," the researchers successfully predicted the parent's urinary 17-hydroxycorticosteroid (OHCS) excretion rate (17-OHCS is a cortisol metabolite and reflects adrenocortical activity). The more effectively a parent defended against the impact of the threatened loss, the lower his or her 17-OHCS rate. The predictions were more accurate for fathers than mothers. This was attributed to the methodological problem of evaluating affect expression in the mothers, and discrepancies between self-reports and observed behavior in two mothers. There was a significant sex difference in excretion rates, with men having higher rates than women.

In a follow-up study, Hofer et al. (1972a, 1972b) studied the same parents after the death of the children. The group-17 OHCS excretion rate means at 6 months and 2 years after the loss were virtually unchanged from the group mean during the illness. This was not due to individual stability of 17-OHCS excretion rates but to two opposing trends: Parents with high preloss excretion rates had decreased rates after the loss, and parents with low preloss excretion rates had increased rates after the loss. At 6 months, most parents were actively grieving, and the return visit either exacerbated grief or provoked it. In contrast to the findings prebereavement, ego defenses did not explain the variation in 17-OHCS excretion rates. High adrenocortical activity values were associated with the intensity of active mourning and the consequent disruption of psychic homeostasis. At 2 years, there was a reduction in the amount and intensity of mourning but no corresponding change in 17-OHCS excretion rates. The adrenocortical activity values did not reflect the diminished intensity of grief.

Jacobs and co-investigators

Jacobs and several co-investigators conducted a comprehensive study of bereaved spouses and spouses threatened with a loss due to a life-threatening illness (Jacobs, 1987b). The study examined the role of psychological defenses as mediating processes that would predict level of

Table 10.1. *Summary of demographic, psychological, and neuroendocrine variables for the study sample*

Variable	Bereaved (B)	Nonbereaved (NB)	Total
Age (±S.E.)	62 (±1)	61 (±1)	62
Sex (% F)	50	49	49
Separation anxiety (±S.E.)[a]	10.3 (±1.0)	6.8 (±1.5)	9.1
Depression (CES-D) (±S.E.)[b]	19.5 (±1.4)	18.6 (±2.0)	19.2
Urinary free cortisol μg/d (±S.E.)[c]	37.8 (±3.0)	33.9 (±3.0)	36.4
Serum cortisol change μg/dl (±S.E.)[c]	0.76 (±0.8)	0.80 (±1.3)	0.77
Urinary epinephrine μg/d (±S.E.)[d]	13.5 (±0.8)	12.0 (±0.9)	13.0
Urinary norepinephrine μg/d (±S.E.)[d]	53.8 (±3.2)	47.5 (±4.2)	51.6
Baseline serum prolactin ng/ml (±S.E.)[b]	8.9 (±0.8)	10.0 (±1.9)	9.2
Serum prolactin change ng/ml (±S.E.)[b]	0.19 (±0.5)	−0.99 (±0.6)	−0.16
Baseline serum growth hormone ng/ml (±S.E.)[c]	1.5 (±0.4)	1.2 (±0.4)	1.4
Serum growth hormone change ng/ml (±S.E.)[c]	0.06 (±0.3)	−0.9 (±0.4)	−0.01

[a] $n = 59$, $n(B) = 41$, $n(NB) = 18$.
[b] $n = 54$, $n(B) = 38$, $n(NB) = 16$.
[c] $n = 63$, $n(B) = 41$, $n(NB) = 22$.
[d] $n = 59$, $n(B) = 39$, $n(NB) = 20$.
[e] $n = 66$, $n(B) = 39$, $n(NB) = 27$.
Note: Total sample, $n = 67$ (B = 43, NB = 24).

neuroendocrine activity, the value of structured assessments of psychological distress (both specific and nonspecific for bereavement) in understanding the level of neuroendocrine activity, and the use of neuroendocrine measures as predictors of health status 1 and 2 years after the stressful event.

Sixty-seven people were studied 2 months after the death of their spouse ($n = 43$) or the life-threatening illness of their spouse ($n = 24$). The interview was conducted by a psychiatrist, and included structured clinical assessments of ego defenses (Jacobs, 1987b) and coping style (Jacobs et al., 1991), structured, multiple-item indices of separation anxiety (Jacobs et al., 1986), depression (Jacobs et al., 1986), and generalized anxiety (Kosten et al., 1984b). The neuroendocrine measures were collected in relation to the interview, and included urinary norepinephrine and epinephrine, serum and urinary cortisol, serum growth hormone, and serum prolactin. The actual number of subjects varied slightly due to the completeness of data collection (see Table 10.1). The urinary measures were based on the mean of three 24-hour collections. The serum measures were done pre-interview (or baseline) and postinterview; the postinterview level minus the preinterview level is the change level. Standard, commercially available radioenzymatic assays were used for 24-hour urinary catecholamines, and standard radioimmunoenzymatic assays were used for 24-hour urinary free cortisol and serum cortisol, growth hormone, and prolactin (Jacobs et al., 1986; Jacobs, 1987b; Kosten et al., 1984b).

In general, there were no significant differences between the bereaved and nonbereaved on psychological or neuroendocrine parameters (see Table 10.1). Therefore, in order to make the sample size optimal, the two groups were combined in the analyses of association between psychological and neuroendocrine variables and in the longitudinal analyses. The methodological details are described elsewhere (Kosten et al., 1984b; Jacobs et al., 1986; Jacobs, 1987b).

The subjects were re-interviewed 1 and 2 years following the stressful event. There was some attrition; 52 people completed the 2-year interview. The follow-up interviews included measures of health status, that is, number of visits to the doctor, number of days in the hospital, self-rated health, mortality, and the psychological measures of separation anxiety, depression, and the like. The findings are summarized in the following subsections.

Urinary catecholamines. The 24 urinary norepinephrine and epinephrine output values following bereavement were higher than normative values, but there were no differences between bereaved and nonbereaved (Jacobs et al., 1986). The values were not associated with depression scores or other psychological variables. These findings differ from the literature that documents higher secretion of norepinephrine in depressed patients. However, individuals metabolize norepinephrine at different rates, so urinary excretion rates must be viewed with caution. In addition, there are often significant individual differences in excretion rates during stressful situations.

Older age was associated with higher levels of urinary norepinephrine and epinephrine output among bereaved subjects. The positive correlation between age and catecholamines suggests that the adrenal−medullary system's adaptation to chronic stress may be slower among elderly persons who are bereaved than middle-aged persons. This has been shown in other research, where older subjects were shown to have higher arterial blood pressure and plasma norepinephrine response to stress and also slower recovery after even mild stress.

Cortisol. The 24 urinary free cortisol output and serum cortisol values following bereavement were similar to normative values, and again, there were no differences between bereaved and nonbereaved (Jacobs, 1987b). Serum cortisol response was not related to any cross-sectional measures of psychological distress. Urinary free cortisol, however, was associated with persistently high levels of separation anxiety or worsening separation distress. Jacobs noted that single measures of psychological distress may be less predictive of adrenocortical activity than the evolution of this distress over time. Thus, increased adrenocortical activity is associated with the persistence and potential chronicity of the distress of bereavement.

Unlike the urinary catecholamines, older age was not associated with higher levels of urinary free cortisol in all persons. Older age correlated with higher levels of urinary cortisol only in those with higher depression scores. This would be in keeping with findings of hypercortisolism in depressed patients.

Serum growth hormone. Serum growth hormone levels were drawn before and after the interview (Kosten et al., 1984b). There were no differences between bereaved and nonbereaved. The change in serum growth hormone levels was not related to any measures of psychological distress. However, for persons with worsening separation anxiety, the number of responders (postinterview growth hormone level was higher than preinterview level) was significantly higher when compared to persons reporting a diminution or leveling off of the distress. This was similar to the association of separation distress and urinary cortisol.

High scores on the Taylor Manifest Anxiety Scale and a high score on repressive defensiveness on the Crowne Marlowe Scale distinguished growth hormone responders from nonresponders (Kosten et al., 1984b). Discriminant function analysis identified 73% of nonresponders and 70% responders.

Prolactin. Serum prolactin levels were drawn before and after the interview at 2 months. There were no differences in prolactin levels between bereaved and nonbereaved (Jacobs, 1987b). Separation anxiety and depression were directly correlated with prolactin response (postinterview level of prolactin was higher than preinterview level), and each dimension correlated with the other. Further analyses revealed that depression and separation anxiety, each in conjunction with high levels of the other but not independently, were associated with prolactin response. This finding suggests that global distress above a certain threshold is associated with the degree of prolactin response. There was no association between age and prolactin response.

Ego defenses. Ego defenses were not associated with neuroendocrine activity (catecholamines, adrenocortical activity, prolactin, or growth hormone). These findings were similar to Hofer's results but contrary to studies of other stressed individuals such as breast cancer patients and soldiers. This discrepancy may be related to the concept that bereavement is a unique stress. Hence, the ego defenses may not have the same relationship to neuroendocrine function as they might in other stressful situations.

Coping style. The relationship between coping factors and neuroendocrine function was limited. The only findings were associations with cortisol measures when the sample was grouped into the highest and lowest quartiles of adrenocortical activity. Bereaved persons with high scores on coping by suppression had significantly lower serum cortisol levels on the assay of preinterview serum cortisol. Although this association is interesting, the preinterview cortisol may not be an accurate measure of baseline cortisol. The change in serum cortisol (postinterview level minus preinterview level) was not related to coping. Finally, bereaved persons with high scores on coping by making changes were in the highest quartile of urinary free cortisol output.

Longitudinal analyses. Because a significant minority of bereaved individuals suffer increased morbidity and mortality (Hirsch et al., 1984), Jacobs et al. examined whether neuroendocrine measures were predictive of health status and psychological measures at 1 and 2 years following bereavement. The subjects were followed longitudinally for 2 years, but only 52 completed the study.

Multiple linear regression analyses revealed the following results. At 1 year, urinary epinephrine was positively associated with a measure of hopelessness but no other psychological measures. Urinary free cortisol was inversely associated with self-rated health, and there was a trend for urinary cortisol to be inversely associated with the measure of hopelessness. At 2 years, urinary epinephrine was again positively associated with the measure of hopelessness and inversely associated with the number of visits to the doctor. Urinary free cortisol was inversely associated with the measure of hopelessness. The neuroendocrine measures were not predictive of persistent grief, depression, or mortality at 1 or 2 years following bereavement.

Summary. Jacobs et al. concluded that the stress of bereavement was not more severe in terms of neuroendocrine physiology than threatened loss or anticipatory grief, nor was the stress of bereavement more severe in terms of psychological measures. Because both the bereaved and non-bereaved groups were under significant stress, the groups were more similar in neuroendocrine and psychological parameters than would be expected.

Ego defenses were not associated with levels of neuroendocrine activity. However, certain psychological distress measures were associated with neuroendocrine activity. Worsening (or persistently high levels) separation distress was associated with higher urinary free cortisol excretion and positive growth hormone response to the interview. High anxiety scores and high repressive defensiveness scores were also associated with growth hormone response. High separation anxiety scores in conjunction with high depression scores were associated with prolactin response. Thus, some individuals did exhibit a state of high physiological arousal as a function of the type, degree, and course of psychological distress over time. Urinary free cortisol was inversely associated with self-rated health at 1 year, and urinary epinephrine was inversely associated with the number of visits to the doctor at 2 years. In general, though, the neuroendocrine parameters did not predict health status outcomes at 1 and 2 years after the stressful event.

Dexamethasone suppression test studies

Three studies have examined the cortisol response of bereaved persons following the administration of dexamethasone (Kosten, Jacobs, & Mason, 1984a; Das & Berrios, 1984; Shuchter, Zisook, Kirkorowicz, & Risch, 1986). As noted earlier, dexamethasone is a synthetic steroid that normally suppresses cortisol release. If the HPA axis is not functioning properly, the administration of dexamethasone will not suppress cortisol. The DST is unlike naturalistic studies that collect neuroendocrine measures. The administration of dexamethasone is an exogenous stressor, and there is an assumption that the response to the stressor is state dependent. However, the neuroendocrine response may be determined by multiple factors, so the response to challenge tests such as the DST may be more multifactorial than state dependent.

The rate of nonsuppression in bereaved samples varied from 0% to 15%, and this rate was related to the timing of the DST in relation to the loss. Bereaved persons who were tested within 1 month after a loss showed an incidence of nonsuppression of 10% (Das & Berrios, 1984) to 15% (Shuchter et al., 1986); those tested 6 months after the loss had normal suppression (Kosten et al., 1984a). The 10% to 15% rates of nonsuppression following the DST in bereaved persons are similar to the rates of nonsuppression in depressed patients seen in outpatient clinics (Winokur et al., 1982). Of interest, in the Shuchter study, nonsuppression was related to higher levels of anxiety rather than levels of depression. Unfortunately, the DST literature of bereavement is too limited to draw any definitive conclusions.

Summary of neuroendocrine studies

We have reviewed studies of the neuroendocrinology of bereavement. These studies revealed evidence of higher adrenocortical activity, higher catecholamine excretion, increased prolactin activity, and altered growth hormone dynamics in some bereaved subjects. There were several differences in findings among the bereavement studies, as well as differences between the findings in bereavement studies and psychiatric disorders. These differences are discussed next.

The relationship between ego defenses and adrenocortical activity from Wolff's study was not confirmed in the studies by Hofer and Jacobs. This discrepancy may be due to the difference between the stress of bereavement and the stress of having a fatally ill child. Alternatively, the stress literature is characterized by a confounding of the assessment of affect with the assessment of ego defenses. There is a tautology that equates low affective arousal with ego defensive effectiveness. However, low affective arousal may actually indicate denial of emotions or maladaptive ego defenses, not effective ego defenses. Wolff et al. (1964b) also noted that the assessment of affective arousal was more difficult in women than men, which highlights gender differences in expression of affect. These issues lead to skepticism about the conclusions that low affective arousal is synonymous with ego defensive effectiveness.

Hofer et al. (1972b) reported that high adrenocortical activity was associated with the intensity of active mourning at 6 months, but there was no specific painful affect associated with high 17-OHCS excretion rates. Jacobs et al. found that certain individuals with high levels of separation distress or generalized anxiety had higher levels of urinary free cortisol and exhibited growth hormone or prolactin responses to the interview. Although active mourning is probably similar to separation distress, it is surprising that Hofer did not find that anxiety was associated with high adrenocortical activity. This discrepancy may be due to the fact that Hofer's study did not use structured assessments of affect, which emphasizes the value of using structured assessments of psychological measures or diagnostic interview schedules to evaluate subjects.

There is a suggestion that type of coping style may be related to adrenocortical activity: Bereaved persons with high scores on coping by suppression had significantly lower preinterview serum cortisol levels, and bereaved persons with high scores on coping by making changes were in the highest quartile of urinary free cortisol output. The findings have an intuitive appeal: Individuals whose predominant coping style is suppression would have lower or suppressed serum cortisol levels, and individuals whose style is to acknowledge stress and make changes would have higher cortisol levels. However, these findings have not been replicated.

The bereavement findings correspond to some of the neuroendocrine abnormalities of psychiatric disorders that were reviewed earlier. Although there are some common findings, such as increased adrenocortical activity, similar rates of nonsuppression following the DST at 1 month, the abnormalities in the bereaved are not identical to abnormalities in either major depression or the anxiety disorders.

There are several possible reasons for the discrepant findings. First, there have been only a few studies of neuroendocrine changes associated with bereavement, and it is difficult to draw conclusions based on the small number of studies. Second, because 31% of the bereaved met criteria for major depression and 13% to 39% of the bereaved suffered from some type of anxiety disorder (Jacobs & Kim, 1990), the sample sizes of the neuroendocrine studies may not have been sufficient to include individuals with psychiatric complications and manifest neuroendocrine abnormalities. Third, the Hofer study measured a cortisol metabolite (17-OHCS) that is highly dependent on individual metabolic rates. Fourth, the timing of the collection of neuroendocrine measures in the Jacobs study may have been too early to capture the maladaptive changes associated with the psychiatric complications of bereavement. Fifth, challenge tests, such as CRH infusion, have not been conducted in the bereaved, and may not be simply state dependent. Finally, the psychiatric complications of bereavement may have different pathophysiological mechanisms than the corresponding psychiatric disorders.

Conclusions

Certain individuals are more vulnerable to bereavement, and it is essential to identify risk factors associated with this vulnerability. We have focused on neuroendocrine factors and their relationship to the psychiatric morbidity of bereavement. Because there have been few studies of the neuroendocrine changes associated with bereavement and the sample sizes of these studies have been small, it is difficult to draw definitive conclusions about the results. The studies have revealed abnormalities in levels of catecholamines, cortisol, growth hormone, and prolactin. However, these abnormalities did not predict health status or psychological outcomes 1 and 2 years after the loss.

The neuroendocrine measures may not have predicted long-term outcome because they were collected early in the course of bereavement. Although the measures reflected the subjects' neuroendocrine profile at the time of collection, the measures may not be related to the process of adaptation to bereavement. The DST studies of bereavement indicate that the rate of nonsuppression in bereaved samples varied, depending on the timing of the DST in relation to the loss. Thus, the neuroendocrine profile of an individual at 1 or 2 months may reflect acute changes associated with loss but not long-term adaptation. Because novel and distressing situations stimulate neuroendocrine responses, the chronic stressors of bereavement might lead to intermittent stimulation of neuroendocrine responses.

The PTSD hypothesis of abnormal adrenocortical activity can be used as a paradigm for bereavement. Altemus and Gold (1990) postulated that PTSD patients have a blunted ACTH response to the CRH stimulation test because of intermittent acute increases in CRH during episodes of severe anxiety. In a similar fashion, bereaved individuals might experience intermittent acute increases in CRH during episodes of separation distress or stressors related to bereavement. Thus, the maladaptive neuroendocrine changes would develop several months after the loss or after intermittent hypersecretion of CRH has led to HPA axis malfunction. The manifestations of HPA axis malfunction include anxiety, obsessive ruminations, and disturbances in appetite, sleep, and libido. Although this paradigm of abnormal adrenocortical activity is applicable to bereavement, it does not explain all the neuroendocrine abnormalities and has not been tested in bereaved individuals. Nonetheless, it illustrates a possible interaction between the neuroendocrine system and the stresses related to bereavement.

11

Bereavement, depressive symptoms, and immune function

MICHAEL IRWIN AND JENNIFER PIKE

This chapter reviews the clinical studies that have found alterations of immune function in spousal bereavement, suggesting that individual psychological responses such as depressive symptoms may mediate changes in cellular immunity. In addition, the role of activation of either the pituitary–adrenal axis or the sympathetic nervous system to produce changes in immunity during bereavement is discussed. To facilitate a clearer understanding of the work linking bereavement and changes in immune function, a brief overview of the immune system, including a discussion of the relevance of immune measures to changes in health, is presented.

Overview of the immune system

The immune system functions to discriminate "self" from "nonself" cells, protecting the organism from invasion by pathogens such as viruses and bacteria or from abnormal internal cells such as cancer cells (Hood, Weisman, Wood, & Wilson, 1985; Cohn, 1985). These functions are closely regulated and performed without damage to the host, although an over-responsive immune system is purported to lead to autoimmune disease in which the organism's own tissues are attacked (Cohn, 1985; Morimoto et al., 1987; Talal, 1980; Paul, 1984).

The organs of the mammalian immune system are the thymus, spleen, and lymph nodes (Hood et al., 1985; Paul, 1984). The working cells of the immune system are represented by three distinct populations: T cells, B cells, and natural killer, or NK, cells (Paul, 1984; Hood et al., 1985; Ritz, 1989). Immune responses can be divided into two important components: cellular immunity and humoral responses (Nossal, 1987; Gilliland, 1983; Paul, 1984). Although there is evidence that T cells and B cells interact and cooperate in many cellular immune responses and in most humoral immune responses, cellular immunity is thought to be mediated

Supported by the San Diego Veterans Affairs Medical Center Merit Review Grant (MI) and the NIMH Mental Health Clinical Research Center Grant (MH30914) to MI.

160

primarily by T lymphocytes, whereas the humoral responses are constituted by the proliferation of B lymphocytes and the formation of antibody-synthesizing plasma cells (Hood et al., 1985).

The T lymphocytes develop from stem cells in the bone marrow and migrate to the thymus, where they mature into several subsets, including the cytotoxic T cell, T-helper cell, and T-suppressor cell (Paul, 1984). These T cells circulate into the periphery and are found in the lymph nodes, blood vessels, and spleen. Briefly, the cytotoxic T cell is characterized by its ability to seek out and destroy cells infected with viruses and tumor cells that have acquired foreign, nonself antigens (Henney & Gillis, 1984; Zinkernagel & Doherty, 1979). In the development of the cytotoxic T-cell response, a foreign antigen is first encountered and incorporated onto the surface of an antigen-presenting cell such as a macrophage. After the antigen is presented to the T cell, recognized, and bound by a specific receptor on the T cell, then the T cell multiplies and becomes capable of attacking any cell that presents that specific foreign surface antigen (Zinkernagel & Doherty, 1979). Other types of T lymphocytes such as the T-helper or T-suppressor cell interact with the T-killer cell to regulate its proliferative response to antigenic stimulation (Henney & Gillis, 1984), mainly by the secretion of interleukin 2 (Kern, Gillis, Okada, & Henney, 1981; Gillis, Gillis, & Henney, 1981). Reexposure of the cytotoxic T cell to an antigen produces a more rapid and extensive reaction than that found upon initial presentation.

The B cell primarily mediates the humoral immune response. Like the T cell, the B cell arises from a precursor stem cell in the bone marrow; however, in humans, its site of maturation remains unknown (Hood et al., 1985). Following exposure to an immunogen, B lymphocytes are further activated by interleukin 1 (secreted by macrophages) and a B-cell growth factor. In turn, the B cell proliferates and differentiates into plasma cells that synthesize antigen-specific antibodies of which the five major classes of immunoglobulins (Ig) are IgG, IgM, IgA, IgE, and IgD (Spiegelberg, 1974). Soon after antigenic stimulation, IgM is produced, followed by IgG. IgA is found primarily in the secretions of the body: nasal mucus, saliva, and the like. IgE, in combination with specific antigen, binds to mast cells and mediates the immediate hypersensitivity response. The function of IgD is not well known.

In addition to the T and B cells, a distinct subpopulation of lymphocytes comprising natural killer cells has been described. The NK cell is immunologically nonspecific and does not require sensitization to specific antigens to perform its cytotoxic activity (Trinchieri, 1989; Lotzova & Herberman, 1986; Herberman, 1980). Thus, the NK cell responds to a variety of cell surface markers, as long as the markers differ from "self" markers and lyse a wide variety of cell types. Although the role of the NK cell in tumor surveillance remains controversial (Lotzova & Herberman, 1986; Ritz, 1989), substantial evidence has demonstrated its importance in the control of herpes and cytomegalovirus infections in humans (Padgett, Reiquam, Henson, & Gorham, 1968; Sullivan, Byron, Brewster, & Purtilo, 1980; Biron, Byron, & Sullivan, 1989) and animals (Habu, Akamatsu, Tamaoki, & Okumura, 1984; Bukowski, Warner, Dennert, & Welsh, 1985; Bancroft, Shellam, & Chalmer, 1981).

Measures of immune function

The immune system can be evaluated by measures that assess the number of different cell types, as well as the function of various components of cellular and humoral immunity. To quantitate the number of cells in various subpopulations, specific monoclonal antibodies are available that bind to unique surface markers on cell types such as T-helper, T-suppressor, and NK cells (Bernard & Boumsell, 1984).

Measurement of the function of the immune system can involve in vivo and in vitro techniques. One in vivo assay of immunity includes measurement of the delayed type hypersensitivity response following administration of skin tests; another involves measurement of the antibody response to a specific antigen. Although both of these techniques provide valuable data about the physiological response of the organism to an antigenic challenge, practical aspects have limited their use in clinical research. Both assays are expensive to perform, and, because subsequent immunologic evaluations are altered by the primary immunization, they cannot be utilized in longitudinally designed studies.

Two immunologic assays widely used to assess in vitro the function of the cell-mediated immune system are mitogen-induced lymphocyte proliferation and NK cell activity. Mitogen-induced lymphocyte stimulation evaluates the proliferative capacity of lymphocytes following activation in vitro with plant lectins such as concanavalin A (Con A) or phytohemagglutinin (PHA), both of which predominantly activate the T lymphocyte to divide (Keller, Weiss, Schleifer, Miller, & Stein, 1981; Schleifer, Scott, Stein, & Keller, 1986). The proliferative response is quantitated by the cellular incorporation of radioactively labeled thymidine or idoxuridine into the newly synthesized DNA. Assay of NK cell lytic activity is carried out by the co-incubation of isolated lymphocytes with radioactively labeled tumor cells, and the release of radioactivity by the lysed target cells is proportionate to the activity of the effector NK cells (Herberman & Ortaldo, 1981; Irwin, Daniels, Bloom, Smith, & Weiner, 1987a).

To determine humoral response, B-cell function is assessed by the measurement of plasma concentrations of immunoglobulins. Utilizing a simple precipitation reaction, these immunoglobulin levels provide an index of B-cell responses but do not assess mechanisms by which this response is regulated (Schleifer et al., 1986).

Although these various measures of immunity assess different components of the immune system and are typically not correlated, most immunologic activities involve complex interactions among a number of cell types and their products. Thus, the components are not really discrete and independent of one another. For example, NK cells have inherent activity, but their reactivity is subject to regulation by either interferons or interleukin 2, and assays of levels of lymphokines (interleukin 1, interleukin 2, and interferon) in the plasma or following lymphocyte stimulation have been employed to quantitate the role of biological response modifiers in the regulation of both humoral and cellular responses (Dinarello & Mier, 1987; Gillis et al., 1981).

Bereavement as a life stressor

Loss of a loved one through death is considered the most stressful of all life events (Holmes & Rahe, 1967), with significant readjustment necessary for adaptation following loss (Brown & Harris, 1989). In addition, clinical and epidemiological data indicate that persons suffering loss are at increased risk for the development of cancers, cardiovascular disease, and viral infections, showing excess morbidity and mortality (M. Stroebe & Stroebe, this volume).

Since these epidemiological data have suggested a link between bereavement and illness, subsequent investigations have focused on the possible pathways through which changes in health status might occur. Broadly, inquiries have fallen along two lines: behavioral and biological. The behavioral theorists have hypothesized that changes in the day-to-day conduct of individuals during the postbereavement period might account for the association between loss and changes in health status (cf. Jacobs & Ostfeld, 1977). For example, increased alcohol and tobacco consumption in the postbereavement period might lead to the increased rates of neoplastic and infectious diseases associated with bereavement. Alternatively, increased mortality rates among the bereaved might be explained by suicide following prolonged states of depression (see Osterweis, Solomon, & Green, 1984, for a review). However, no systematic investigation has shown that behavioral changes solely mediate the association between bereavement and health status, even though behavior is an important moderator of illness.

The biological theorists have focused on physiological changes that co-occur with bereavement. Hypothesizing that bereavement produces physiological arousal that disrupts normal functioning and, if prolonged, may compromise the person's ability to ward off diseases, clinical researchers have begun to evaluate physiological systems important in maintaining health and protecting the body against disease. Consequently, investigations of the bereaved are now focusing on whether changes in the immune system, the host's defense against viral and bacterial infections and neoplastic disease, occur during bereavement.

Bereavement and immune functioning

In the first study of its kind, Bartrop and colleagues (1977) sought to link bereavement stress with changes in immune functioning. Lymphocyte responses to mitogen stimulation in 26 men and women whose spouses had died were compared with responses in 26 ethnic-, age-, and sex-matched controls at 2 and 6 weeks' post-bereavement. In the bereaved group, T-cell responses to low doses of phytohemagglutinin (PHA) were reduced at both the 2- and 6-week points. Responses to concanavalin A (Con A) were reduced only at 6 weeks' postbereavement. These alterations in lymphocyte responses to the mitogen PHA and Con A indicated decrements in T-cell functioning, but neither T- and B-cell numbers, hormone levels (mean serum concentrations of thyroxine, triiodothyronine, cortisol, prolactin, and growth hormone), nor B-cell function differed between groups. Although these results suggested that bereavement might be related to impairments in immunologic functioning, causal relationships between bereavement and changes in immunity could not be determined in this cross-sectional analysis. Furthermore, the time course of immune change during bereavement was not evaluated.

To answer these questions, a second study was performed by Schleifer and colleagues (1983) that assessed prospectively T- and B-cell populations and responses to PHA, Con A, and pokeweed mitogen (PWM) in a group of 15 men whose wives died from metastatic breast cancer. Immune measures were taken at 6-week intervals during the course of the wives' illness, at 2 months after death, and again at various times in the 4–14-month follow-up period. The results indicated that lymphocyte function in the postbereavement period was reduced as compared to that during prebereavement, with reduced responses appearing as early as 1 month following the loss of the spouse in 8 of the 15 subjects. However, follow-up beyond 2 months did not demonstrate differences in measures of immune function as compared with either prebereavement or 2-month postbereavement levels, suggesting a recovery of function of the lymphocytes in these bereaved men. Neither T- nor B-cell absolute cell numbers differed from pre- to postbereavement periods.

These findings of Schleifer and colleagues (1983) extended the work of Bartrop and colleagues and suggested that suppression of lymphocyte responses to mitogen stimulation was a consequence of the bereavement event. However, in contrast to Bartrop's study, Schleifer and colleagues found that decrements in lymphocyte function were apparent as early as 1 month after the loss and persisted for at least 2 months' postbereavement. The lack of change in numbers of T- and B-cell populations during bereavement suggests that stress does not alter the number of the immune cells, so much as it reduces the lymphocyte's ability to proliferate. As a further implication of this study, it appears that exposure to the stress of caring for the terminally ill does not produce a desensitization to the immunologic effects of life stress; lymphocyte function showed a diminution immediately following loss as compared to prebereavement levels.

These studies demonstrated an association between bereavement and changes in measures of lymphocyte responses to mitogen stimulation, but a number of questions remained. For example, are the changes in lymphocyte function representative of changes in other measures of cellular immune functioning? Do individuals who vary in their psychological response to the loss also differ in the magnitude of change in their immune measures?

To begin to address these questions, Linn and colleagues (1984) studied the effects of bereavement on various measures of humoral and cell-mediated immunity, comparing the responses of bereaved and nonbereaved men and examining the effects of depressive symptoms on immune functioning during bereavement. Subjects were separated into four groups: bereaved and nonbereaved, which were further divided into high and low depression on the basis of their responses to the Hopkins Symptom Checklist. Bereaved subjects exhibited significantly lower titers of immunoglobulin G and immunoglobulin A as compared to levels in nonbereaved subjects. However, lymphocyte responses to stimulation with PHA were reduced only in those individuals from the bereaved and nonbereaved groups who had high depression scores. Thus, bereavement, per se, was not responsible for changes in lymphocyte function; rather, reductions in lymphocyte responses appeared to be related to depressive symptoms.

Extending these observations on the effect of psychological processes on immune function during bereavement, Irwin and colleagues (1987a) conducted a series of clinical studies that addressed the role of bereavement and depressive symptoms in altering T-cell subpopulations and NK cell activity. In a cross-sectional study, measures of total lymphocyte counts, T-helper and T-suppressor cell numbers, and NK cell cytotoxicity were compared among three groups of women: those whose husbands were dying of lung cancer, those whose husbands had recently died, and those whose husbands were in good health. The 37 women who made up this study population were free of chronic medical disorders associated with altered immune function and did not abuse drugs or alcohol. Current changes in the spousal relationship and other life experiences were assessed using the Social Readjustment Rating Scale (SRRS), and the severity of the depressive symptoms was rated using the Hamilton Depression Rating Scale (HDRS). Subjects and controls were studied at least three times over a 1- to 3-month period.

On the basis of their overall mean SRRS scores, subjects were divided into one of three groups: low, moderate, and high SRRS scores. Women whose husbands were healthy were more likely to be classified in the low SRRS group, whereas women who either were anticipating or had experienced the death of their husband were likely to be in the middle or high SRRS group, respectively. Mean depressive symptoms as measured by HDRS were significantly more severe in the moderate and high SRRS groups as compared to those in the low SRRS group. Natural killer cell activity was significantly different among the three groups: The groups with moderate and high SRRS scores were found to have reduced NK cell activity as compared to low SRRS control subjects. Neither the absolute number of lymphocytes nor T-cell subpopulations, including number of T-helper, T-suppressor/cytotoxic cells, and ratio of T-helper to T-suppressor/cytotoxic cells, was different among the groups.

In addition to the effects of life events, the contribution of psychological responses to changes in immunity during bereavement was also evaluated in this cross-sectional study (Irwin et al., 1987a). Natural killer cell activity was found to be negatively correlated with the HDRS total score and also with the subscales of depressed mood and insomnia. Furthermore, the severity of depressive symptoms as measured by total HDRS score was related to a loss of T-suppressor/cytotoxic cells and an increase in the ratio of T-helper to T-suppressor/cytotoxic cells.

These studies of immunity during bereavement have separately demonstrated that either cell-mediated immunity such as lymphocyte responses to mitogenic stimulation, NK cell activity, or distribution of T-cell subpopulations may be altered in men and women undergoing severe, acute psychological stress such as bereavement. Furthermore, severity of depressive symptoms in response to the loss appears to be an important correlate of changes in at least one of these immune measures, namely, NK cell activity.

Depressive symptoms and altered immunity in bereavement

Bereavement is a process in which widows differ in their psychological responses to the actual death of their husband: Some women are distressed whereas others are relieved of the distress of acute anticipation. To clarify further the effect of psychological responses on NK cell activity during bereavement, Irwin and colleagues (1987b) conducted a second study of bereaved women that evaluated the role of depressive symptoms in mediating changes in immune function. Natural killer cell activity and severity of depressive symptoms were compared between women whose spouses had recently died with metastatic lung cancer and women whose husbands were in good health. In a cross-sectional analysis, the bereaved group was again significantly more depressed and had a reduction in NK cell activity as compared to the matched controls. These results confirmed that NK cell activity is affected by the bereavement process.

In order to evaluate the role of depression in mediating the change in NK cell activity during bereavement, a longitudinal analysis of a sub-sample of six women evaluated NK cell activity and depression during anticipatory (1 month before death) and postbereavement (1 month after death) periods. No significant differences in the women's mean depression scores or in levels of NK cell activity were found between the two periods. However, greater variance in the depression scores and in levels of NK cell activity was found in postbereavement as compared to the anticipatory period, suggesting individual variation in response to a husband's death. Anecdotally, the women who were distressed prior to their husband's death and remained so afterward, had similar depression scores at pre- and postbereavement periods, whereas women who showed relief from antici-patory bereavement stress endorsed fewer depressive statements during postbereavement. Change in NK cell activity paralleled change in severity of depressive symptoms from pre- to postbereavement. Indeed, change in NK cell activity was negatively correlated with change in depressive symptoms (Spearman's $r = -.89$, $p < .009$), indicating that as depressive symptoms resolved during the postbereavement interval, NK cell activity increased and returned to values comparable to those found in normal controls (Irwin et al., 1987a, 1987b).

Taken together, the results of these studies suggest that the relationship between bereavement and immune functioning is correlated with depres-sion. To the degree that one becomes depressed over the loss of a loved one, alterations in various parameters of the immune system are likely to occur. Furthermore, bereavement appears to be a process rather than a discrete event. Individual variances in reaction to loss should be considered when evaluating bereavement-associated changes in health status.

Depression and immune functioning

Psychological response to distressing life events is an important correlate of immune dysfunction in persons undergoing severe life stress, and it has been hypothesized that psychological depression or anxiety itself may be associated with immune changes.

To understand how depression impairs cell-mediated immunity, several studies have compared immune responses between depressed patients and control subjects. Cappell and colleagues (1978) reported that lymphocyte proliferation responses to the mitogen PHA are lower in psychotically depressed patients during the first days of illness than following clinical remission. Kronfol and colleagues (1983) replicated these observations in 26 drug-free depressed patients and found blunted lymphocyte responses to mitogenic stimulation with Con A, PHA, and pokeweed during depression. Schleifer and colleagues (1984) also found suppressed lymphocyte reactivity in severely depressed patients and further described abnormalities of lymphocyte subpopulations in depression: Absolute and T- and B-lymphocyte cell counts were reduced, although relative percentages were unchanged. Because no differences in immune measures have been found in mildly depressed outpatients as compared to controls (Schleifer et al., 1985), severity of depressive symptoms may be an important factor in altered lymphocyte responses in depression.

Extending these observations of altered lymphocyte responses in depression, Irwin and colleagues (1987c) have measured the cytolytic activity of peripheral lymphocytes in two groups of subjects: medication-free, hospitalized, acutely depressed patients and age- and sex-matched control subjects studied on the same day as the patients. Natural killer cell activity was significantly lower in the depressed patients as compared to the control subjects, a finding that has been replicated by Urch et al. (1988) and by Mohl and colleagues (1987). In addition, severity of depressive symptoms was correlated with a reduction of NK cell activity.

In an attempt to understand why some, but apparently not all, patients with major depression show immune changes, the contribution of other factors that might affect immunity in depressed patients has been studied. Schleifer and colleagues (1989) have examined the role of age in the relationship between depression and altered immunity. Employing an extensive assessment of the immune system, including enumeration of T-lymphocyte subsets, assay of NK cell activity, and measurement of mitogen-induced lymphocyte stimulation, the researchers found significant age-related differences between the depressed patients and controls for numbers of T-helper lymphocytes and for mitogen responses. Age-related increases in T-helper cells and in mitogen responses were found in the controls, whereas advancing age was associated with no changes in T-helper number and decreased lymphocyte responses in depressed patients. These findings suggest that both age and severity of depression are important correlates of immune changes in depression; immune changes in major depressive disorder might be present mainly in elderly, severely depressed patients.

In addition to the independent contribution of age to depression-related changes in immunity, alcohol consumption is reported to play a role in further reducing cellular immunity in depressed patients. Alcohol use, even in moderate doses, is associated with alterations in cell-mediated immune function such as NK cell activity. Alcohol use as contributing to a decrement in immunity in depressives with histories of alcohol abuse as compared to depressed patients without such alcoholism was studied (Irwin et al., 1990a). Consistent with earlier reports, NK cell activity was found to be significantly lower in both depressed and alcoholic patients as compared to controls. Perhaps of more interest, patients with dual diagnoses of either alcohol abuse and secondary depression or depression with a history of alcohol abuse demonstrated a further decrease in NK cell activity as compared to that found in patients with either depression or alcoholism alone.

Alterations in T-cell subpopulations have been characterized in depressed patients as compared to control subjects. Consistent with the findings of Irwin and colleagues (1987a), who found a relationship between severity of depressive symptoms and an increase in the ratio of T-helper to T-suppressor/cytotoxic cells in bereaved women, Syvalahti and colleagues (1985) found that depressed patients have a lower percentage of T-suppressor/cytotoxic cells and a higher ratio of T-helper to T-suppressor/cytotoxic cells than control subjects do. However, other studies have found no depression-related differences in quantitative measures of lymphocytes, including number of T cells, B cells, and T-helper, T-suppressor, and NK cells (Darko et al., 1988; Wahlin, Von Knorring, & Roos, 1984).

Beyond the use of more sophisticated measures of immune cell function, future investigations need to test the clinical relevance and biological significance of depression-related changes in the immune system. Furthermore, preclinical and clinical studies of the mechanisms that underlie changes in such biological parameters as measures of immunity in depression will help identify the pathways of communication among the nervous, endocrine, and immune systems.

Mechanisms of immune alterations in bereavement

Pituitary–adrenal axis and cellular immunity

The neuroendocrine system might exert influence on immune responses. The secretion of corticosteroids has long been considered the mechanism of stress-induced and/or depression-related suppression of immune function (Munck, Guyre, & Holbrook, 1984; Riley, 1981; Parrillo & Fauci, 1978; Cupps & Fauci, 1982; Selye, 1946). In vitro studies have demonstrated that glucocorticoids can act to inhibit the production of cytokines such as interleukin 1, interleukin 2, tumor necrosis factor, and interferon. These actions of glucocorticoids on cytokine production may explain many of the immunosuppressive effects of glucocorticoids such as suppression of lymphocyte responses to mitogenic stimulation (Gillis, Crabtree, & Smith, 1979) and NK cell activity (antibody-dependent cytotoxicity is relatively refractory to glucocorticoids) (Parrillo & Fauci, 1978).

Despite pharmacological in vitro and in vivo studies that show a suppressive effect of corticosteroids on cell-mediated immune function, a dissociation between adrenocortical activity and immunity has been found in depressed patients and in stressed persons. In depressed patients, decreased lymphocyte responses to mitogens are not associated with dexamethasone nonsuppression (Kronfol & House, 1985) or with increased excretion rate of urinary free cortisol (Kronfol et al., 1986). Furthermore, in bereavement, in which a reduction of NK cell activity has been demonstrated, these immunologic changes occur even in subjects who have plasma cortisol levels comparable to those of control subjects (Irwin, Daniels, Risch, Bloom, & Weiner, 1988a). However, at variance with these findings is the work of Maes and colleagues (1989), who found that dexamethasone nonsuppression was associated with significantly lower lymphocyte stimulation by PHA, PWM, and Con A than responses found in dexamethasone suppressors.

Sympathetic nervous system modulation of immunity

The other pathway that may have a physiological role in the modulation of immunity in animals is the sympathetic nervous system (S. Y. Felten et al., 1988; Livnat, Felten, Carlton, Bellinger, & Felten, 1985). Noradrenergic nerve fibers extensively innervate lymphoid tissue (D. L. Felten et al., 1987a; Williams & Felten, 1981; D. L. Felten et al., 1987b; S. Y. Felten & Olschowka, 1987c) and form synapticlike contacts with lymphocytes. Numerous studies have demonstrated the presence of beta-adrenergic receptors on lymphocytes, mainly of the beta-2 subtype (Williams, Snyderman, & Lefkowitz, 1976; Galant, Underwood, Duriseti, & Insel, 1978), which are linked to second messenger systems such as cyclic AMP formation (Motulsky & Insel, 1982; Coffey & Hadden, 1985). Binding of catecholamines at these sites has been found to inhibit in vitro cellular immune responses such as lymphocyte proliferation (Strom, Lundin, & Carpenter, 1977) and natural cytotoxicity (Hellstrand, Hermodsson, & Strannegard, 1985). Finally, the sympathetic nervous system appears to have a role in the in vivo regulation of cellular immunity, as chemical sympathectomy of lymphoid tissue increases values of NK cell activity (Livnat et al., 1985; Reder, Checinski, & Chelmicka-Schorr, 1989) and activation of the sympathetic nervous system mediates a reduction in cellular immunity following the administration of either a stressor (Cunnick, Lysle, Kucinski, & Rabin, 1990) or neuropeptides such as corticotropin releasing hormone (Irwin et al., 1987d, 1988b, 1990b, 1990c; Jain et al., 1991) or interleukin 1 (Sundar, Cierpial, Kilts, Ritchie, & Weiss, 1990).

Despite these preclinical data, the role of sympathetic nervous activity in the modulation of immune function in depressed patients and in individuals undergoing life stress has not yet been found. However, preliminary data from studies in our laboratory indicate an association between immunity and the neurochemical indices of sympathetic activity such as plasma levels of epinephrine, norepinephrine, and neuropeptide Y. For example, negative correlations have been found between NK cell cytotoxicity and measures of sympathetic function in spousal caregivers of Alzheimer patients and in depressed patients (Irwin, Patterson, Grant, & Brown, 1991), suggesting that these neurotransmitters, which are involved in the regulation of blood pressure, might also have a role in the in vivo modulation of immune function.

Summary

This chapter has reviewed findings that indicate an association among bereavement, depressive symptoms, and a reduction of in vitro correlates of cellular immunity. Although the reduction in immune function might have health consequences, no study has yet identified whether such a relationship exists between stress-induced immune changes and increased morbidity in humans. In addition, few studies have investigated the mechanisms through which these immune changes might occur in humans. Nevertheless, preclinical data suggest that central nervous system release of neuropeptides coordinates a reduction of immunity through activation of the sympathetic nervous system. Clinical studies in humans are needed to identify whether such changes in autonomic activity underlie the reduction of cellular immunity in bereavement.

PART V

The psychological, social, and health impacts of conjugal bereavement

12

The mortality of bereavement: A review

MARGARET S. STROEBE AND
WOLFGANG STROEBE

Increasingly in recent years researchers have focused on positive aspects of the experience of bereavement, emphasizing that it is a "growth experience," that people are "resilient," and that the illness metaphor should be abandoned in describing the consequences of grief. The chapters in this volume by Silverman and Worden, McCrae and Costa, and Shuchter and Zisook, to name only a few, underline this message. Yet the reason that so much research has focused on bereavement is because the loss of a loved one is associated with extreme mental and physical suffering, not for everyone, and not always lastingly, but for a significant minority. Even more disturbing are the statistics for mortality. Not only do some bereaved individuals fall ill following the loss of a loved one, but they also die.

Given that fatal consequences occur for some bereaved, it is important to identify those who are vulnerable and to understand why they and not others succumb. A decade ago we reviewed the research on mortality (M. Stroebe, Stroebe, Gergen, & Gergen, 1981) and concluded that there was some evidence that bereavement results in excess mortality. However, the surveyed research suffered from many methodological shortcomings. In the meantime, much research has been done and much has been written about the bereavement–mortality relationship. The goals of this chapter, therefore, are to review the scientific evidence that is now available, examine subgroup differences that suggest high-risk categories, and review and evaluate theoretical explanations that could account for the bereavement–mortality relationship.

The bereavement–mortality relationship: Empirical evidence

Most studies of the bereavement–mortality relationship have focused on conjugal bereavement. Evidence comes from two types of studies, cross-sectional surveys and longitudinal investigations. In both types the mortality rate of the bereaved is compared with that of a baseline. In the case of widow(er)hood, the baseline is sometimes a group of matched, nonbereaved

175

married counterparts, but frequently comparisons are made with national mortality statistics for total populations. It is critical that control groups be matched precisely for age and sex in order to avoid systematic and confounding differences in mortality rates between these groups (see W. Stroebe & Stroebe, 1987).

To assess whether the mortality rates of the bereaved are excessive, mortality ratios are calculated. Mortality ratios show the relative rate of mortality among the widowed (the number of deaths among the widowed as a proportion of the total widowed population under investigation) to that of the control group (the number of deaths among the controls as a proportion of the total control population under investigation). A ratio greater than 1.00 indicates an excess of widowed mortality in comparison with the control group.

Evidence from cross-sectional surveys

Cross-sectional studies usually compute mortality rates from secondary data sources and are typically conducted on a large scale (e.g., using national statistics). Frequently, information is available for the various marital status groups (married, single, divorced, widowed) and for the major sociodemographic variables (age, sex, race, socioeconomic status). In addition, cause of death statistics are generally available. However, such analyses are vulnerable to two important concerns: the lack of information concerning the duration of bereavement at the time of death and the inability to rule out a number of alternative explanations that could also account for the statistical relationship between bereavement and increased death rate. For these reasons, such investigations are given only brief consideration here (see M. Stroebe et al., 1981, and W. Stroebe & Stroebe, 1987, for more details).

Figure 12.1 (compiled from Mergenhagen, Lee, & Gove, 1985) illustrates the type of data available in cross-sectional surveys. These data show, for example, excess death rates for widowed persons compared with married counterparts, relatively greater excesses in most cases for widowers compared with widows, declining excesses with increasing age, and variable sizes of ratios according to the cause of death (e.g., the ratios for accidents are relatively high, those for leukemia relatively low). It is important to note that, although extremely large ratios may be found for such causes as liver cirrhosis, suicide, and motor-vehicle accidents (particularly among the young), far fewer widowed persons actually die from such causes, compared with heart disease or cancer deaths, because the former are relatively rare causes of death compared with the latter.

Findings from cross-sectional surveys have produced a remarkably consistent pattern: (1) Death rates are lowest for the married, followed by

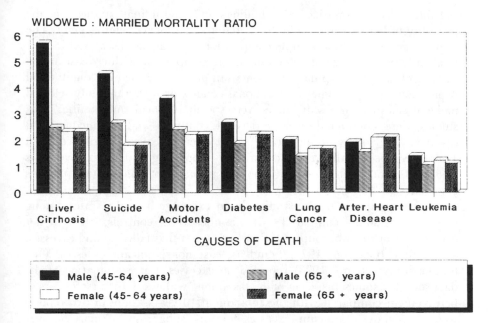

Figure 12.1. Widowed to married mortality ratios by sex, age, and cause of death (adapted from Mergenhagen et al., 1985). Data source: U.S. Bureau of the Census, 1984; data are for white citizens only, for the year 1979. Causes of death are selected. Ratios are calculated by dividing the mortality rate for each of the widowed groups (i.e., sex, age, and cause of death groups) by the rate of the corresponding married groups; for example, the ratio of 2.50 for liver cirrhosis for widowers over 65 years of age means that the mortality rate of this group is two-and-a-half times the rate for married men over 65 for this cause of death.

the single, widowed, and (the highest) divorced. This is true for both men and women. (2) The excess in mortality is highest for the younger age groups. (3) The excess for widowers (compared with married men) is greater than that for widows (compared with married women). Remarkably, this pattern has been replicated in many different countries of the world and across historical periods (W. Stroebe & Stroebe, 1987).

Evidence from longitudinal investigations

Longitudinal investigations of the bereavement–mortality relationship are conducted either prospectively or retrospectively. Such studies examine the incidence of mortality in a cohort of bereaved people (compared with nonbereaved controls) systematically over time, beginning with the date of bereavement.

Table 12.1 summarizes the findings of longitudinal studies on the mortality of bereavement. The list is remarkable for its heterogeneity. The studies varied greatly in sample composition (e.g., age and sex) and in size: some only in the range of 100 or so, others comparable with cross-sectional surveys of national populations. Some samples were based on longitudinal population surveys, some were national cohorts or were randomly selected national samples, and still others were specific to local communities. The studies were conducted in a variety of countries and spanned several decades. The follow-up period of study after bereavement ranged from 1 to 14 years. Finally, a wide variety of control group alternatives was evident. Despite such complexity, however, a number of interesting patterns emerged.

The vast majority of the studies found excessive mortality rates among bereaved persons, compared with nonbereaved controls, though not necessarily for all subgroups. Of the four studies that failed to find excesses, all but one (Clayton, 1974) found at least nonsignificant excesses. One further study (Niemi, 1978) reported no excesses, but examination of the data revealed some clustering of deaths among widows in the first 2 years of bereavement compared with the subsequent 10 years. Only in two reports were there any significant excesses for any subgroups of married over widowed mortality (McNeill, 1973; Smith, 1990), and in both of these it was concluded that there was, in general, evidence for a bereavement–mortality relationship. Moreover, most of the negative results may simply reflect a small sample size. Examination of Table 12.1 shows that all of the studies in question had samples of well under 1,000 bereaved persons. Less weight should probably be attached to the results of such small studies, as mortality occurs relatively rarely and differences in rates are unlikely to be detected in small samples (M. Stroebe et al., 1981).

It is noteworthy, also, that evidence for the bereavement–mortality relationship has been found in many different countries, although, to our knowledge, no longitudinal studies for undeveloped countries have been published. Cross-sectional surveys for non-Western countries are also hard to find, but similar excesses to those reported in the studies cited here have been found in Japan for widowed persons (Hu & Goldman, 1990; M. Stroebe et al., 1981). Furthermore, evidence of the relationship is available across time, from the early twentieth century (Cox & Ford, 1964) through recent decades.

The bereavement–mortality relationship may also generalize beyond spousal loss. A study by Rees and Lutkins (1967), for example, indicates excessive mortality also for bereaved parents, children, and siblings. A study by Levav, Friedlander, Kark, and Peritz (1988) received wide publicity for its negative findings on the mortality risk of bereaved parents (Levav, 1989). However, closer reading reveals that widowed parents'

Table 12.1. *Longitudinal studies of the mortality of bereavement*

Reference(s)	Country	Sample[a] (N; sex; age; relationship)	Controls	Follow-up period after bereavement (years)	Mortality excesses
Bowling (1988); Bowling & Benjamin (1985); Bowling & Charlton (1987)	United Kingdom	$N = 503$; M & F; mean age = 74 years (M), 70 years (F); spouses	Total population figures from English life tables	6	Significantly higher rates in first 6 months for widowers aged 75+; younger widowers and older and younger widows, nonsignificant.
Clayton (1974)	United States	$N = 109$; M & F; mean age = 61 years; spouses	Matched married individuals	4	No excesses.
Cox & Ford (1964)	United Kingdom	$N = 60,000$; F; age groups from <40 to <70 years; spouses	Compared with rates of same widows taken over 5-year period as a whole	5 (commencing with pension application)	Excessive in second year, over the rates for the same widows in the other years of study.
Ekblom (1963)	Sweden	$N = 634$; M & F; age = 75 years; spouses	Age- and sex-specific death rates of married	3	No significant excesses; tendencies for widowers in first 6 months, widows in third year, toward excessive rates.
Helsing & Szklo (1981); Helsing, Comstock, & Szklo (1982); Helsing, Szklo, & Comstock (1981)	United States	$N = 4,032$; M & F; age groups = 18+ to 75+; spouses	Matched married spouses (paired with bereaved)	12	Significant excesses for widowers 55–64 and 65–74 years of age. Nonsignificant excesses for younger widowers and widows under age 65 in second year. Little evidence of duration effects.

179

Table 12.1. *(cont.)*

Reference(s)	Country	Sample[a] (*N*; sex; age; relationship)	Controls	Follow-up period after bereavement (years)	Mortality excesses
Jones (1987); Jones (1988); Jones & Goldblatt (1987); Jones, Goldblatt, & Leon (1984)	United Kingdom	*N* = 156,060; M & F; age groups from <65 to >75; spouses	Expected deaths based on total population rates	10	Excesses for widowers (all age groups), for widows only under 65. Peak for widows for first 6 months, for widowers less extreme but for at least 1 year.
Kaprio, Koskenvuo, & Rita (1987); Koskenvuo, Kaprio, Kesäniemi, & Sarna (1980)	Finland	*N* = 95,647; M & F; age groups from <65 to >64; spouses	Expected rates based on national annual age- and sex-specific mortality rates	4	Excesses (M & F) greatest in first week, 4 weeks, and 6 months; greater excesses for widowers than widows.
Levav, Friedlander, Kark, & Peritz (1988); Levav (1989)	Israel	*N* = 3,646; M & F; age groups from >34 to >75; parents	Sex-, age-, and calendar year–specific rates for Jewish-Israeli population	Approx. 10–12	No excesses for married parents; widowed excesses, significantly higher for bereaved mothers.
McNeill (1973)	United States	*N* = 9,247; M & F; age groups from >19 to >70; spouses	Mortality rates of general population of state of Connecticut	3.5	Excesses for younger (under 60) for widowers in first 6 months; for widows in second year. Some significant expected over observed differences.
Mellström, Nilsson, Oden, Rundgren, & Svanborg (1982)	Sweden	*N* = 360,000; M & F: age range = 50–90 years; spouses	Mortality rates for married persons from national records	11	Mortality excesses for recently bereaved widowers and widows (all ages) in first 12 months

					for widowers, first 3 months for widows. Thereafter, lower but still excessive rates over the 11-year period.
Niemi (1978, 1979)	Finland	N = 545; M & F; age = approximately 60 (F), retirement age (M); spouses	Still-married persons on Pension Security Institute records	12	Nonsignificant excesses for widowers in first 6 months. No reported excesses for widows (clustering observable in first 2 years; twice as many deaths as occurred on average over the 10 years).
Rees & Lutkins (1967)	United Kingdom	N = 903; M & F; all age groups; spouses, parents, children, siblings	Matched nonbereaved individuals with living relatives	6	Overall excessive rates for the bereaved; reportedly greater for male than for female relatives; more excessive risk for widowed than for other bereaved relatives.
Smith (1990)	United States	N = 3,264; M & F; age groups from >25 to >65; spouses	Matched married persons	Up to 14 (persons widowed within this total study period)	Excesses for widows and widowers under 65 years. Rates less excessive for over 64-year-old widows than married women. No information on duration effects.
Ward (1976)	United Kingdom	N = 366; M & F; mean age = 64 years; spouses	Age- and sex-specific rates for total population from national life tables	2	No significant excesses, but more widower deaths than expected within 6 months of loss than between 6 and 24 months.

Table 12.1. (cont.)

Reference(s)	Country	Sample[a] (N; sex; age; relationship)	Controls	Follow-up period after bereavement (years)	Mortality excesses
Young, Benjamin, & Wallis (1963); Parkes, Benjamin, & Fitzgerald (1969)	United Kingdom	N = 4,486; M; age groups from >54 to >90; spouses	Rates for married men (national figures) of same age groups	9	Widowers' rates excessive in first 6 months, declining thereafter to levels similar to married.

Note: Included are all known longitudinal studies of the bereavement–mortality relationship, excluded are those with insufficient information to enable ratios to be calculated or longitudinal comparisons to be made.

[a] Because there is no standardized notation across studies, details given in the table (e.g., age) follow original presentation style.

mortality rates were indeed higher than those for the control population, the difference reaching significance for widowed mothers. A brief report from Israel by Roskin (1984) even mentions excessive mortality among bereaved compared with nonbereaved grandparents over a 5-year period, which suggests that death of any loved person, not only spouses but parents, children, and even siblings or grandchildren, may have fatal consequences for those left behind. More data are needed to establish the risk of mortality following bereavement other than widow(er)hood, as losses such as that of a child have been identified as exceptionally devastating (see Rubin, this volume; Sanders, this volume).

Subgroup differences in mortality

Because a small proportion of bereaved persons does in fact die following the death of a loved one, it is important to identify those who might be at particularly high risk. A focus on patterns of such risk also might help in sorting out alternative interpretations of the bereavement–mortality relationship. We turn first to the major sociodemographic variables.

Gender. One of the most stable patterns is a gender difference (for a more detailed discussion, see M. Stroebe & Stroebe, 1983). Widowers appear to experience greater risk than widows. Mortality rates for widowers were frequently excessive and typically higher than those for widows, although rates for widows were often not significantly different from expected. However, those studies that failed to detect differences were frequently the ones with very small samples (e.g., Rees & Lutkins, 1967; Ward, 1976).

This gender difference is similar to that reported in cross-sectional surveys. Although the effects appear to be weaker, the striking consistency of cross-sectional surveys in identifying smaller but still excessive ratios for widows supports the conclusion that they, too, are at somewhat higher risk of mortality than married women (cf. Gove, 1973; Hu & Goldman, 1990; M. Stroebe & Stroebe, 1983).

Age. Somewhat less clear are age differences in the magnitude of the bereavement–mortality effect or in the interaction of gender with age. Again, it seems likely that the smaller numbers involved in the younger age groups, where mortality is an even rarer event, precluded attainment of statistical significance in many studies. Even without statistical significance, all of the large studies – Helsing and Szklo (1981), Mellström et al. (1982), Kaprio et al. (1987), and Jones and Goldblatt (1987) – show as large or even larger ratios for the younger compared to the older widowed. Thus, younger persons appear to be at as high, if not higher, risk than older persons, and this may interact with gender, making younger widowers at greatest risk. Consistent with the findings of Bowling (1988; see Table 12.1), it may be that the relationship between age and mortality among the bereaved is curvilinear. It remains to be seen whether other studies can replicate the finding that the "young–old" are relatively less at risk (compared with controls) than the "old–old."

Socioeconomic status. There is an inverse relationship in general between social class and mortality: Those of lower social class die, on average, at earlier ages (see W. Stroebe & Stroebe, 1987). It is far less clear whether, or in what direction, there are also social class differences in excess mortality risk among the widowed. Very few of the longitudinal studies include information on social class differences. Bowling (1988) reported those of higher social classes to be more at risk of mortality after bereavement than those of lower classes. Parkes et al. (1969) reported a similar pattern, but numbers in the extreme social class groups (where differences were found) were extremely small, so statistical significance was not attained.

There is some contradictory evidence, however, albeit not from longitudinal sources. Population data in England show that the lower the social class, the greater the excess risk of mortality among widowers (W. Stroebe & Stroebe, 1987). Furthermore, in one of the few publications that considered mortality rates simultaneously by marital status and social class, Koskenvuo, Kaprio, Kesäniemi, and Sarna (1980) found that widowed, unskilled workers were particularly vulnerable. We conclude, therefore, that for most populations, the effects of bereavement on mortality cut across social classes.

Duration of bereavement. When are the bereaved particularly vulnerable? Do they suffer a higher risk during the immediate postloss period of intense grief, or are the fatal consequences prolonged? With the exception of a study by Helsing and Szklo (1981), the pattern seems quite consistent. As Table 12.1 shows, the classic finding of a peak excess for widowers in the first 6 months of bereavement (Young, Benjamin, & Wallis 1963; Parkes et al., 1969) has been confirmed in subsequent studies.

For widows, however, the trend is not so clear, a reflection, perhaps, of the fact that excess mortality risk for widows is generally lower than for widowers. There does, however, seem to be some clustering of deaths within the first 2 or 3 years of bereavement. The study by Cox and Ford (1964) has been cited frequently as evidence for a delayed risk, this being elevated in the second year, but has also been criticized for methodological flaws (M. Stroebe et al., 1981). One of the flaws may have caused the apparent delay in high risk: The sample was drawn from pension applicants and thus excluded those widows who had died in the first year of bereavement. Mellström et al. (1982) and Jones and Goldblatt (1987) did not find such a delay for widows in most excessive mortality but reported, instead, patterns similar to those for widowers – that is, most excessive deaths in the period immediately following widowhood and persisting for a number of months. The data so far, then, suggest an overall peak in risk during the months following bereavement.

Other factors. Recent studies have examined variables that might mediate the bereavement–mortality relationship. For example, not surprisingly, *moving into a chronic care facility* is associated with higher mortality in the bereaved group (Helsing, Szklo, & Comstock, 1981). More important, however, is an analysis by the same investigators on *remarriage.* Mortality rates for widowers who remarried were very much lower than for widowers who did not, although among widows there was no difference between the remarried and those still of widowed status.

Some studies have focused on how *social interactions* in bereavement might mediate the bereavement–mortality relationship. Early surveys by Berkman and Syme (1979) and Kobrin and Hendershot (1977) showed that greater social and family ties were associated with lower mortality. Longtudinal studies by Bowling (1988) and Helsing et al. (1981) provided more specific information on the bereaveds' social contacts and risk of mortality. For example, Bowling (1988) found in a multivariate analysis that one of the most powerful discriminating variables independently associated with mortality was simply having no one to telephone. Similarly, Helsing et al. (1981) found that living alone was associated with higher mortality among the widowed than it was for those living with other persons in their households. In the absence of nonwidowed controls, however, such studies fail to show whether the protective effect of social support is greater for widowed than for nonwidowed individuals (i.e., main effect vs. interaction).

Further information on the protective effect of social support is available from the recent work of Gallagher-Thompson and her colleagues (Gallagher-Thompson, Futterman, Farberow, Thompson, & Peterson, this volume). In their study of the health consequences of bereavement among older spouses, widowers' mortality rates appeared to be highly excessive. Gallagher-Thompson et al. analyzed differences between these decedents and a similar group of widowers who survived the 30-month period after bereavement. They found that social isolation and interpersonal difficulties characterized decedents rather than survivors. By matching decedents with survivors on physical health ratings and for age, the problem of establishing direction of causality was overcome. That is, the alternative explanation that the frail elderly, due to their health status, were both less able to socialize and more likely to die, was – if they did manage to equate physical health in the two groups – ruled out.

An intriguing result was recently reported by Smith (1990), who examined the relative mortality risk of persons bereaved following *sudden versus expected deaths*. For widowers under 65 years, and even more so for widowers under 50 years, risk was greatest following a sudden bereavement. For very young widows (under 50 years) the pattern was similar: A sudden death of a husband had the most fatal consequences. However, for somewhat older widows (aged 50–64), highest risk of all the groups, male or female, occurred if their husbands had died from a chronic illness. By contrast, elderly widows (over 64 years) whose husbands had died either suddenly or expectedly had lower mortality rates than comparable married.

Causes of death

In general, longitudinal studies confirm the differential pattern of risk across causes illustrated in the cross-sectional survey in Figure 12.1. Bereaved persons are more likely to die from certain causes than from others. However, the longitudinal studies have not shown any consistent pattern with respect to order of magnitude of excesses by cause. Nor can one draw firm conclusions about age and sex subgroup differences in mortality risk for various causes.

Most but not all studies report an excess in heart diseases for the bereaved over controls. Thus, in one of the first longitudinal studies to examine causes of death in the bereaved, Parkes et al. (1969) found that the greatest increase in mortality during the first 6 months of bereavement was for widowers dying from coronary thrombosis and other arteriosclerotic and degenerative heart disease. Increases were found for other diseases, but these were not statistically significant, as numbers were small. Kaprio et al. (1987) also found excesses for heart diseases in all age groups and for both sexes. Furthermore, exceptionally high excesses occurred in the month immediately following bereavement, although excesses from heart disease were also observed in later years. Jones, Goldblatt, and Leon (1984) reported that the recently bereaved are at greater risk of cardiovascular disease than of cancer, although, as the authors pointed out, differences in the latencies of the diseases could be responsible for this. In Mellström et al.'s (1982) study, cancer and cardiovascular deaths were the main causes accounting for widowed excesses. In contrast to these findings, heart diseases were not significantly excessive in the study by Helsing, Comstock, and Szklo (1982), which is hard to reconcile with the consistent findings of the other studies.

More information is needed concerning excesses from cancer deaths, although indications are, as Mellström et al. (1982) and others found, that they are elevated. Jones (1988) concluded that there was weak support for an excess following a considerable "latent" period. Studies should, then, cover a long duration of bereavement to identify such consequences. Furthermore, it would seem important that future research distinguish among death risk from cancers of different sites (e.g., lung cancer, cancer of the digestive system).

Liver cirrhosis has consistently been identified as a highly excessive cause. Along with accidents and suicidal deaths, it may be a higher risk category than even heart or cancer deaths. Excessive risk of mortality also has been found from infectious diseases among widowers (Helsing et al., 1982), indicating not only a danger from violent acts but possibly also, as we discuss later, a lack of proper health care and resistance to infection.

Another fairly consistent finding is an excess for violent causes. Thus, Jones and Goldblatt (1987) reported the highest relative risk of mortality among the widowed for accidental, poisoning, and violent deaths. Similarly, in the Helsing et al. (1982) study, accidental deaths were significantly higher than expected among widowed males. Mellström et al. (1982) also reported excesses for accidents, though these were not as marked as those for cancer or heart disease. There is evidence, too, that excesses in deaths from violent causes occur particularly in the immediate postbereavement period (Jones & Goldblatt, 1987; Kaprio et al., 1987).

Perhaps most indicative of the devastating impact of bereavement are the findings for suicide. First shown by Durkheim (1897/1951) a century ago, more recent statistics have confirmed that the widowed are at particularly high risk of taking their own lives. This risk is relatively higher for widowers, particularly younger ones, compared with married men, than for widows compared with married women (although the latter ratios are also excessive). Longitudinal studies have shown that the risk of suicide is particularly high for the recently bereaved (Bojanovsky, 1980; Bunch, 1972; Kaprio et al., 1987; MacMahon & Pugh, 1965), and that this pertains worldwide. Not only spouses but also parents and sons have been found to have elevated rates (Bunch, 1972). Enormously high suicide rates during the first week strongly suggest bereavement as the cause: The excesses found in one study were 66-fold for men and 9.6-fold for women (Kaprio et al., 1987).

Do the bereaved die of the same causes as their predeceased spouses? Marked similarities across a variety of causes were reported in an early study by Ciocco (1940), but these have not been replicated in more recent times, although, tragically, this is likely to change with the spread of the AIDS virus (cf. Martin & Dean, this volume). Parkes et al. (1969) reported only a "tendency" for husbands and wives to die from the same causes, which could not account for more than a small part of the increased mortality. Other investigators (e.g., Helsing et al., 1982) found no evidence of any concordance between the causes of death of husbands and wives. However, a concordance for certain specific but rare causes of death may still occur. For example, Smith, Kinlen, White, Adelstein, and Fox (1980) found that wives of men who had died of cancer of the penis had significantly elevated rates of mortality from cancer of the cervix, suggesting a common etiology.

Summary

The review of cross-sectional and longitudinal studies of the mortality of bereavement provided considerable evidence of a loss effect: The bereaved are indeed at higher risk of dying than are nonbereaved persons. This seems to apply not only for the widowed but also for other bereaved relatives. Highest risk occurs in the weeks and months closest to loss, and men appear to be relatively more vulnerable than women. Although data for other risk factors are not so clear, indications are that younger bereaved (particularly males) are at higher risk, as may be the socially isolated. There is some evidence that type of death of the predeceased spouse may also differentially affect widowers and widows, the former being most vulnerable following sudden deaths, whereas this is the case only for younger widows, somewhat older ones being vulnerable following a death from a chronic illness. Finally, we have noted different patterns of relative excess across causes of death, with fairly well-established excesses from heart diseases, suicides, accidents, and liver cirrhosis. There is little evidence, though, that spouses die from the same causes.

In conclusion, although much is already known about the bereavement–mortality relationship, we still do not know enough about those bereaved who are likely to die subsequent to their loved ones. Longitudinal studies have not been completely consistent about risk factors, nor have they provided data on a wide enough range of variables to establish who is at greatest risk or to interpret why this should be the case. All too frequently, samples have been too small to detect significant differences between subgroups, and there are reasons to question the reliability of patterns found in the smaller investigations. Needed are large-scale longitudinal studies that enable multivariate analysis for identification of the most powerful discriminating variables.

The bereavement–mortality relationship: Theoretical explanations

There are three types of explanation of the bereavement–mortality relationship: that the relationship is in some way spurious (i.e., due to artifacts); that it is due to indirect changes associated with the status of being widowed (i.e., stress, role change); or that direct, psychological factors are responsible (i.e., broken heart). These explanations, and their physiological mediators, are discussed next.

Artifacts

Some explanations that fall into this category are artifacts of classification. Thus, certain statistical biases may occur. For example, the widowed within any specific age category are older than their married counterparts. Because higher age is associated with greater mortality, this could partly account for the bereavement–mortality relationship. Also well documented is a tendency for widowed persons to be underrepresented during the collection of census data and overrepresented in the collection of mortality statistics. This would exaggerate the true mortality associated with widow(er)hood. However, although these age biases and documentation errors might explain some of the excess mortality in the large cross-sectional surveys, they do not apply to carefully matched and controlled longitudinal studies, where excess ratios are still found.

Selection could increase the similarity in health status between marital partners and thereby the chances of them dying closer together. Because marriage is a selective, competitive process, it seems reasonable to suppose that healthy persons are more likely to be married and that they select similarly healthy partners. Selection could happen in remarriage, too, so that the healthiest widowed persons would be recategorized as married, leaving more of the unhealthy in the widowed category. Again, though this might explain some of the differences found in cross-sectional studies (notably the high excesses for the young and for widowers, as remarriage rates for these groups are the highest), longitudinal studies find excesses at times when there is practically no remarriage, that is, during the first few weeks and months of bereavement. The finding that remarried widowers have far lower mortality rates (Helsing et al., 1981) could be interpreted as supporting the selection hypothesis, but it could also be that marriage is protective (e.g., through social support). It is also noteworthy that although remarriage rates for the widowed have declined since 1965 (Bumpass, Sweet, & Martin, 1990), widowed to married mortality ratios have in fact increased (Mergenhagen et al., 1985). Taken together, these trends speak against a selection interpretation.

Homogamy could operate in a number of ways: Not only would the healthy marry the healthy, but they would most likely be of the same ethnicity, eat the same diet (and be similarly obese or undernourished), take the same amount of exercise, share the same risks (e.g., dangerous sports, smoking and drinking habits), and breathe the same clean or dirty air (e.g., carcinomic exposure). The last aspect has been considered under the label *joint unfavorable environment* (cf. Kraus & Lilienfeld, 1959), which refers to the possibility that a married couple may live under conditions that have mutual, detrimental health consequences. Along similar lines, *mutual infections and accidents* could increase the size of mortality ratios for the widowed. If both are infected or are in an accident together, they are more likely to die closer in time than those who are not. This explanation fits the data for the younger widowed, for among these groups accident rates are the highest.

If homogamy, joint unfavorable environment, and common disease etiology were valid explanations of the bereavement–mortality relationship, one would expect a high concordance between causes of deaths of spouses. As we reported earlier, this is not the case. On the other hand, testing these hypotheses by examining the occurrence of identical causes of death in spouses is not a perfect test. There is no direct one-to-one relationship between a pathogenic factor and a disease. The relationship is much more complex; for example, smoking can cause many different diseases (cf. Campbell, 1986). Also, there are limitations in the data available from death certifications. For example, important medical conditions present at death may not appear on the death certificate (cf. Comstock & Markush, 1986). These hypotheses have not yet been adequately tested, and their impact on the bereavement–mortality relationship may have been underestimated.

On the other hand, Helsing et al. (1982) controlled for most of these artifacts (e.g., joint accident victims were excluded from the analysis) and still found excesses. Other investigators (e.g., Mellström et al., 1982; Parkes et al., 1969) also have assessed the possible contribution of such artifacts to excess ratios, and none have argued that the relationship is spurious because of these factors.

Researchers have paid less attention to other, potentially confounding variables, for example, the possibility of undetected differences between study and control groups (despite matching), which one might label the *confounding factors hypothesis*. Socioeconomic status is one of these. For example, Helsing and Szklo (1981) found their widowed sample to be of lower socioeconomic status than their matched (by race, sex, age, and geography of residence) married controls. Because lower social class is associated with higher mortality, the higher rates of the widowed compared to the married could reflect in part social class differences. Helsing and Szklo did, however, use statistical techniques to make adjustments for this potential confound. Clearly, others need to do the same.

Another concern is *publication bias* (i.e., the "file-drawer problem"; see Begg & Berlin, 1988). In the present context this refers to the possibility that only studies finding a relationship between bereavement and mortality actually get published. However, this would not apply to the cross-sectional data, which are published by national agencies on a regular basis. Furthermore, negative results seem to have been newsworthy enough in this area to merit publication, as Table 12.1 shows.

In summary, it is quite possible that these various artifacts and biases account for a small portion of the excess risk of bereaved persons, but they are unlikely, even in combination, to provide an explanation of the total effect.

Secondary consequences of bereavement

Theories that fall into this category focus on concurrent changes in the lives of bereaved persons that might lead to heightened vulnerability. The two major theories of this type are stress theory and role theory (see M. Stroebe & Stroebe, 1983, and W. Stroebe & Stroebe, 1987, for more detailed accounts).

The basic assumption of *stress theory* is that stressful life events play an important role in the etiology of various somatic and psychiatric disorders. Stressful life events may precipitate the onset of physical or mental disease, particularly if a predisposition toward that disorder already exists. The negative impact of psychosocial stress on health appears to be mediated by two types of mechanisms. The first of these is a direct effect, through the brain's influence on physiological responses to psychosocial influences. For example, there is evidence that stressful life events can impair immune function and increase susceptibility to infectious diseases and increase cancer risk (see Kim & Jacobs, this volume; Laudenslager, Boccia, & Reite, this volume). Stress has also been shown to result in endocrine changes that contribute to coronary heart disease (cf. O'Leary, 1990; W. Stroebe & Stroebe, 1987). The second mechanism involves an indirect effect, whereby stressful life events result in health-impairing behavior patterns. There is some evidence, for example, that bereaved individuals tend to increase cigarette smoking, drink more alcoholic beverages, ingest more psychotropic drugs, and adopt irregular and unhealthy eating habits (cf. W. Stroebe & Stroebe, 1987).

Psychological conceptions of stress have emphasized its interactive nature. According to the definition offered by Lazarus and Folkman (1984), "Psychological stress is a particular relationship between the person and the environment that is appraised by the individual as taxing or exceeding his or her resources and endangering his or her well-being" (p. 19). Thus, cognitive models of stress (e.g., Lazarus & Folkman, 1984) and more narrowly focused approaches, such as the deficit model of partner loss (W. Stroebe & Stroebe, 1987), focus on the situational demands characteristic of widow(er)hood and of the coping resources needed to deal with these demands. The deficit model, for example, addresses the types of support (social, emotional, validational, and instrumental) that marital partners had provided for each other and that others in the postbereavement period would need to take over.

In contrast, *role theories* focus on the roles played by persons in different marital statuses that may differentially expose them to risk (see, e.g., Gove 1972, 1973; Lopata, 1973a). Thus, Gove (1972, 1973) attributed the lower mortality rates of married individuals to the fact that they have close interpersonal ties, which minimizes the strain of their roles. Gove argued that marriage benefits women less because they do not receive so much gratification from their one major role, that of being housewife, whereas men obtain gratification from being the head of the household and breadwinner. Although marital roles have changed in recent years, there is evidence that sex differences in role satisfaction still pertain (W. Stroebe & Stroebe, 1991).

Stress and role theories make similar predictions about the consequences of bereavement on life expectancy. Both account quite well for certain of the findings reported here, including most of the subgroup differences. Each can explain the gender differences in mortality among the widowed. Both types of theory hold that marriage is more protective for men, and that the effects of loss will therefore be greater for men. That remarriage lowers the mortality risk for widowers but not for widows is consistent with this argument. Also, we noted earlier the high vulnerability of widowers (particularly younger ones) who had lost their spouses suddenly. Undoubtedly, such an unanticipated death would be highly stressful and the possibility of adjusting to the new single role particularly difficult. Because loss of a young wife is relatively rare, there is less support from the environment, less knowledge of how to cope, more likelihood that one is the "odd man out," and so on.

However, role theory is less helpful in explaining the finding that middle-aged widows are especially vulnerable after an extended terminal illness of the spouse. Stress theory, on the other hand, would point to the strain of care giving, which is more typically carried out by female rather than male relatives.

These theories would also predict the peak in risk shortly after loss (although not, as we argue later, for the massive increase in suicides in the first week), for this is the time of greatest change and stress. Such theories also could explain why, in the loss of a child, widowed but not married parents have higher mortality. The former have lost the roles of both spouse and parent. Further, they are deprived of the potential support and companionship of a child for the rest of their lives. The married, on the other hand, appear to be protected by their marital partners from elevated risk of mortality following loss of their child, although, as Sanders (this volume) concludes, there are dire consequences of child loss on married parents, too, including excessive divorce and separation rates compared with nonbereaved parents.

What about the suggestion that grandparents die after the death of a grandchild? It might not seem that the role of grandparent would be close enough to have such severe consequences. However, grandchildren can become invested with tremendous symbolic importance. For example, Parkes (1984) described how in Israel, where the Roskin (1984) study was conducted, the death of a child and grandchild "strikes at basic assumptions which underlie the whole exodus" (p. 26). To ensure the future of generations is a major concern for all Jewish people.

All in all, role and stress theories do provide fairly adequate explanations of the bereavement–mortality relationship. Following the preceding analysis, it remains plausible that those bereaved who find life most stressful and/or the change in roles hardest to adjust to will be at high risk of mortality. Nevertheless, this does not rule out the possibility of other explanations, to which we turn next.

The direct consequences of loss

The final category of explanations, which we term the *broken heart hypothesis*, focuses on the loss of the beloved person, per se, not on other changes associated with the loss. Psychological theories explain the bereavement–mortality relationship in terms of emotion; it is grief for the loss of a loved person that is said to cause such a dire consequence as death. Hopelessness, loss of the will to live, and the desolation of grief are seen as mediators in this process. Clearly, depression theories belong within this framework. Yet they have rarely been used to explain the bereavement–mortality relationship, despite the fact that the major theoretical contributions to the area of bereavement, namely, Freud's (1917a) psychoanalytic and Bowlby's (1980/1981) attachment models, are both theories of depression (for detailed accounts, see W. Stroebe & Stroebe, 1987). These theories do, it must be added, undermine the romanticism of the broken heart hypothesis in that they incorporate constructs such as dependency, guilt, and insecure attachment as responsible for poor bereavement outcome rather than a close and loving relationship.

Just as role and stress theories seemed highly consistent with the pattern of results reported earlier in this chapter, so, too, does the broken heart hypothesis. That there is a peak risk soon after loss is understandable from this perspective. Similarly, excessive causes of death reflecting a lack of the will to live (e.g., suicide), failure to care for oneself (accidents), immune system depression (infectious diseases), or unhealthy living (liver cirrhosis) could all be seen as direct consequences of grief. The very high risk of suicide just after the loss (at a time when role changes have hardly had time to become evident) likewise supports a desolation explanation. Finally, that the effect is found in many different cultures and time periods, and for loved ones other than marital partners, despite differences in relationships and roles – all support a broken heart phenomenon.

Harder to explain from this perspective are the gender differences. Why (unless men love their wives more than their wives love them) should widowers be at relatively greater risk of dying than widows? An explanation in terms of the stress and role models seems more plausible. Similarly, if it is grief over the loss of a loved one alone that causes death, it would be hard to explain why social support in bereavement should affect longevity.

In support of the broken heart hypothesis, it could be argued that depression (which is a dominant symptom of grief) has well-established physiological consequences, for example, on the immune system (see Irwin & Pike, this volume). Thus, given that these physiological changes lead to physical health debilities, it seems reasonable to assume that a "broken heart" underlies many different causes of death in the bereaved. However, physical consequences of stress are equally well established, so the physiological changes could as well be interpreted in terms of stress and role theories.

Conclusions

In this section we have considered three types of explanation of the bereavement–mortality relationship. Artifacts and biases cannot explain more than a small part of the excesses. Explanations focusing on the secondary consequences of loss, as well as on direct effects, seem more plausible. Role and stress theories better explain the gender and social support differences. In contrast, the broken heart hypothesis seems a more viable explanation for certain other findings, notably the excess suicide rates immediately after death and the universality of the effect. Currently available data do not consistently support the one type of explanation over the others. In fact, the three explanations are neither completely contradictory nor mutually exclusive. It seems highly likely that both direct consequences, or a broken heart, and secondary effects, such as life-style changes, either alone or in combination (which will vary from one person to another), are responsible for the bereavement–mortality relationship.

Implications

We conclude from this review that mortality risk clearly increases for the bereaved. This effect has been shown across a wide range of cultures, historical periods, types of relationships, and even socioeconomic groups. We believe that the first few weeks and months are the most critical, but that substantial risk persists for longer than this period, particularly for causes of death with longer latencies. Widowers are at more excessive risk than widows (who are, however, also at greater risk than nonbereaved controls). The younger are relatively more affected than the older. These conclusions depart considerably from those of earlier reviews in the field. Furthermore, in contrast to earlier reviews (e.g., Jacobs & Ostfeld, 1977; Kraus & Lilienfeld, 1959), recent research has enabled us to identify further subgroup differences, permitting more detailed evaluations of the various theoretical interpretations. Such analyses suggest that the broken heart hypothesis alone cannot explain the bereavement–mortality relationship. Secondary changes associated with loss, as identified by stress and role theorists, are also, though not exclusively, responsible.

If this analysis is correct, it provides a note of optimism. That is, if the cause lies not only in the emotional grief response but also in the additional strains associated with the widowed or bereaved role, then others can do much to help compensate for the various deficits and buffer the bereaved against this most dire consequence of loss.

13

Psychological resilience among widowed men and women: A 10-year follow-up of a national sample

ROBERT R. McCRAE AND PAUL T. COSTA, JR.

Students of stress, illness, and adaptation have taken a particular interest in bereavement, and with good reason. Death of a spouse is consistently rated as the most stressful of normative events (Holmes & Rahe, 1967), requiring the maximal readjustment in life; it is also a common experience, which nearly half the population will eventually face. The intensity and frequency of this stressor make it of undeniable social importance. At the same time, there are powerful methodological advantages to the study of bereavement for an understanding of stress, coping, and adaptational processes. Because death of spouse is an objectively verifiable event generally beyond the control of the widowed individual, artifacts that plague the study of stress and illness (Schroeder & Costa, 1984) can be minimized.

The results of bereavement studies provide mixed support for the view that life stress causes subsequent mental and physical illness and mortality. Some studies show excess mortality, particularly for males, in the year or two following bereavement (Helsing, Szklo, & Comstock, 1981; Parkes, Benjamin, & Fitzgerald, 1969), but there are methodological difficulties with most studies of mortality (M. Stroebe, Stroebe, Gergen, & Gergen, 1981; Susser, 1981). Studies of health after bereavement are also complicated by the problems of disentangling subjective health perceptions from objective disease processes (Costa & McCrae, 1985a), and one of the few studies to use as control variables baseline measures taken before the loss event concluded that, "using a variety of health indicators, the effects of these [bereavement] events were either nonexistent or slight and brief. In fact, health improved over the long term following bereavement" (Murrell,

The NHANES I Epidemiologic Followup Study was jointly initiated by the National Institute on Aging and the National Center for Health Statistics, and has been developed and funded by the National Institute on Aging, National Center for Health Statistics, National Cancer Institute, National Heart, Lung, and Blood Institute, National Institute of Arthritis, Diabetes, and Digestive and Kidney Diseases, National Institute of Mental Health, National Institute of Alcohol Abuse and Alcoholism, National Institute of Allergy and Infectious Diseases, and National Institute of Neurological and Communicative Disorders and Stroke.

Himmelfarb, & Phifer, 1988, p. 104). However, most studies report a variety of adverse psychological effects (Gallagher, Thompson, & Peterson, 1981), at least at moderate levels (Feinson, 1986) and for a limited time, and a recent review of the effects of life crises (including bereavement) on psychopathology concluded that "a substantial minority of respondents – between 20% and 40% – do not recover fully from the crisis despite the passage of time" (Kessler, Price, & Wortman, 1985, p. 537).

Most research on the effects of bereavement and widowhood has concentrated on the period immediately after loss of the spouse, up to about 2 years. This focus is understandable given the dominant paradigm of stress research, which holds that adverse effects stem from the efforts needed to readjust to routine living after a disruptive event (Rahe, 1968). There is, however, another view, according to which daily hassles (Kanner, Coyne, Schaefer, & Lazarus, 1981) and continuing role-related strains (Pearlin, Lieberman, Menaghan, & Mullen, 1981) may have as much or more effect on well-being as do major life events. It seems clear that widowhood will lead to increased strains for many people: Death of a spouse means the loss of social, emotional, and physical support, and frequently entails a notable reduction in income. Because of the preponderance of widowed women, remarriage is not an option for most widows, and they must cope with these losses for the remainder of their lives. Will they – or a substantial minority of them – also continue to have lowered levels of well-being and impaired psychosocial functioning for the rest of their lives, or is adaptation primarily a matter of time? That is the question addressed in this chapter.

Follow-up of a national survey

The National Health and Nutritional Examination Survey (NHANES) I Epidemiologic Followup Study (Coroni-Huntley et al., 1983) provides an opportunity to examine the long-term consequences of bereavement and widowhood in a large national sample followed over a 10-year interval. Between 1971 and 1975, a total of 14,407 noninstitutionalized men and women between the ages of 25 and 74 were interviewed to obtain information on marital status, education, age, and a variety of medical and nutritional variables. The design for the NHANES I survey (National Center for Health Statistics, 1973, 1978) systematically oversampled certain groups, including women of childbearing age, elderly adults, and individuals below the poverty level. Seven to 12 years later, 13,380 respondents were located for follow-up or identified as deceased. Respondents lost to follow-up were about 11 years younger than those who were located and somewhat more likely to be women; they did not differ in initial levels of education or self-rated health. Because equal proportions of those initially married (94%) and widowed (93%) were traced, it seems unlikely that the results to be reported are seriously distorted by selective attrition among the widowed. Those who were willing and able to be reinterviewed (92% of the initially married and alive at follow-up and 90% of the initially widowed and alive at follow-up) gave information on household size, family income, social network size, self-rated health, activities of daily living, personality traits, and psychological well-being. (Note that Ns vary in different analyses due to missing data.) Sample frequencies for respondents initially widowed or married are given in Table 13.1.

Neither the original survey nor the follow-up provided information on the date or nature (e.g., accidental; following prolonged illness) of the spouse's death – variables of central importance in understanding the processes of coping and the timing of psychological recovery. However, the data do allow certain inferences. Individuals who were widowed at baseline can be compared to those who were married in terms of subsequent mortality in the 10-year follow-up period. Examination of follow-up data on individuals who were widowed at both surveys will give information on the long-term consequences of bereavement and continued widowhood. Do individuals adapt to their status and show no lasting psychological effects, or do the chronic strains of single status lead to changes in personality or deterioration of health, ability to function, or subjective well-being?

Two groups were compared with the long-term widowed: those who were married at first administration but were widowed at second, and those who were married at both surveys. It would also be reasonable to consider the group of individuals who were widowed at the first survey and subsequently remarried. However, among women in particular, this was so small a group that meaningful comparisons could not be made. The majority of analyses, therefore, are confined to a comparison of three groups: the long-term widowed (LTW), those widowed between surveys (WBS), and the long-term married (LTM). Again, the date of bereavement was not available at follow-up, so individuals in the second group might have been widowed shortly before follow-up or as much as 12 years earlier. It should also be noted that these categorizations are based only on a consideration of marital status at the times of the surveys; it is possible, therefore, that some respondents were widowed and remarried, or remarried and widowed again, in the interval between surveys. It is unlikely, however, that this happened often enough to distort results systematically.

Widowhood and mortality

The first question of interest concerns mortality: Are widowed men and women more likely to die in a 10-year interval than their married counterparts? To see if widowhood increased the risk of earlier mortality, a Cox

Table 13.1. *Summary of sample frequencies*

	Status at initial survey							
	Married				Widowed			
	Men		Women		Men		Women	
Status	Age 25–64	Age 65–74	Age 25–64	Age 65–74	Age 25–64	Age 65–74	Age 25–64	Age 65–74
Initial survey	3,333	1,463	5,006	949	65	171	382	870
Located at follow-up	3,131 (94%)	1,426 (97%)	4,624 (92%)	919 (97%)	55 (85%)	155 (91%)	350 (92%)	830 (95%)
Alive at follow-up	2,856	781	4,472	662	41	67	319	554
Marital status at follow-up								
Married	2,383[a]	578[a]	3,433[a]	290[a]	8	11	40	15
Widowed	65[b]	117[b]	344[b]	321[b]	26[c]	50[c]	253[c]	470[c]

[a] Long-term married (LTM) respondents.
[b] Widowed between surveys (WBS) respondents.
[c] Long-term widowed (LTW) respondents.

proportional hazards analysis was conducted examining length of survival after the initial survey for men and women initially age 65 and older and either married or widowed. Because the widowed were about 1 year older and somewhat less well educated even within the 65-and-over group, age and years of education (as well as sex) were also included in the model. Age, sex, and education were all significant predictors of survival, but initial marital status was not.

These analyses are admittedly approximate. Some of those classified as initially married may have been widowed before they died. Additionally, it might be argued that the long-term widowed were a select group, the more vulnerable individuals having died before the survey began; very recently widowed individuals may well have declined to participate in the initial survey. Within this group of respondents, however, widowhood itself was not consistently associated with significantly increased mortality.

Life-style changes

The failure to find differential mortality due to marital status does not gainsay the profound effects of widowhood on the individual's life. For example, within the group of individuals initially over age 65, 3.0% of those married at the time of the follow-up were living in sheltered housing, a nursing home, or other institution; by contrast, 10.8% of those who were widowed at the time of the follow-up were institutionalized. This association remained statistically significant when both age and education were controlled. Note that institutionalized respondents were included in the follow-up, so the disproportionate institutionalization of the widowed should not bias results.

Similarly, widowhood was associated with a reduction in family income for both sexes. Total family income from all sources was coded into 14 categories, from under $3,000 to over $100,000 in the past year. Among those initially 65 and older, both widows and widowers reported significantly lower income than did married women and men. Perhaps the most revealing statistic is that 12.2% of the widowed had incomes of less than $3,000 in the past year, whereas only 4.5% of the marrieds had so little income. Expenses are doubtless lower for a single person than for a couple; but with many fixed costs, it seems likely that the widowed, both men and women, bear more than their share of economic hardship.

Social and psychological outcomes

Analyses of covariance (ANCOVA) within sex were conducted to compare the three marital status groups on a number of variables relevant to social and psychological functioning; men and women initially over age 65 were included in these analyses. Social Network Size is a single-item variable that asks respondents to estimate the number of relatives and friends whom they feel close to, can talk to about private matters, and can call on for help; responses are coded on a 6-point scale from *none* to *twenty or more*. Activities of Daily Living is the sum of 26 items (e.g., "turn faucets on or off," "comb your hair") coded from (1), *no difficulty* to (4), *unable to do*. Self-Rated Health is coded on a 5-point scale from *excellent* to *poor*; higher scores indicate poorer perceived health. Extraversion and Openness to Experience are short versions of personality measures taken from the NEO Personality Inventory (Costa & McCrae, 1985b); validity data are given elsewhere (Costa & McCrae, 1986). The traits of Extraversion and Openness are generally stable in adulthood; however, it might be hypothesized that individuals would become more introverted or closed to experience as a result of significant life experience such as widowhood. The General Well-Being Scale (GWB; Dupuy, 1978) is a 10-item version of the original 18-item scale (see Costa et al., 1987b, for information on validity and age relations). The GWB measures subjective well-being in the areas of health, energy level, interest in life, cheerful mood, relaxation, and emotional and behavioral control; questions ask respondents how they have felt "during the past month." Finally, the CES Depression Scale (CES-D; Radloff, 1977) is a 20-item measure of depressive symptoms widely used in epidemiological research.

After correcting for the effects of age and education in the ANCOVA, none of these seven variables systematically distinguished the widowed from their married counterparts. Even the unadjusted means given in Table 13.2 show little difference. Indeed, the sole statistically significant finding was that the WBS women rated their health a bit better than long-term married or widowed women – a finding that runs counter to the usual expectation that bereavement will lead to lowered health and well-being (Thompson, Breckenridge, Gallagher, & Peterson, 1984).

Analyses were also conducted for women initially under the age of 65. Both LTW and WBS women reported more difficulty in performing activities of daily living and higher levels of CES-D than LTM women, and LTWs had smaller social networks, but these effects were quite small in magnitude. There were no effects on Self-Rated Health, Extraversion, Openness to Experience, or General Well-Being. These cross-sectional data suggest there may be some long-term effects of widowhood in younger women, although they appear quite modest in magnitude. (There were too few younger widowers to justify separate analyses of men.)

Longitudinal changes in self-rated health and well-being

All the analyses reported so far have considered only cross-sectional outcome data, essentially asking whether the widowed differ from the married

Table 13.2. *Mean levels of measures of psychosocial status and functioning for three marital status groups*

Follow-up variable	Men 65–74[a]				Women 65–74[a]				Women 25–64[a]			
	LTM	WBS	LTW	p	LTM	WBS	LTW	p	LTM	WBS	LTW	p
Social network	3.94	3.61	3.66	ns	3.82	3.82	3.61	ns	3.64	3.70	3.51	.05
Activities of daily living	30.97	33.18	33.78	ns	34.54	36.87	38.71	ns	27.80	30.83	30.49	.001
Self-rated health	3.12	3.05	3.28	ns	3.10	2.97	3.20	.05	2.37	2.85	2.98	ns
Extraversion	17.59	18.03	17.43	ns	16.99	17.25	17.18	ns	18.33	17.58	17.47	ns
Openness	10.52	10.41	10.53	ns	11.38	11.01	10.85	ns	12.24	11.81	11.63	ns
GWB	51.01	49.99	49.39	ns	45.91	47.73	46.40	ns	49.02	47.04	48.69	ns
CES depression	8.36	10.82	9.71	ns	10.43	10.80	10.63	ns	8.37	10.59	10.49	.01
Age	78.36	79.72	80.82	—	78.16	78.95	79.54	—	49.90	60.96	63.22	—
Education	9.32	8.74	7.59	—	10.28	9.10	9.19	—	11.87	10.40	9.83	—
Ns	483–572	93–117	35–49		235–290	253–320	368–465		3,220–3,432	311–341	230–251	

[a] Means are unadjusted; *p* values are given after covarying age and years of education; ns = not significant.

at a certain point in time. One potential problem with these analyses is that they do not take into account the baseline status of the three groups. Because individuals are not randomly assigned to the status of widowhood, it cannot be assumed the groups were necessarily equivalent before the event; unknown initial differences might obscure the effects of widowhood on adjustment. For example, widowed individuals (WBS) may have been higher in well-being than the married individuals at the beginning of the study and suffered a relative loss of well-being over the interval, so that at follow-up they showed the same level of well-being as the married individuals.

Another way of examining the long-term effects of widowhood – and one with more statistical power – employs both pre- and postevent assessments in a repeated-measures analysis that controls for any initial differences between the groups. Unfortunately, not all the variables of interest were measured in the original survey, and those that were measured were given only to randomly selected subsamples. It is, however, possible to examine three variables using a repeated-measures design: Self-Rated Health, the 10-item GWB scale, and the CES-D measure. The GWB and Self-Rated Health were gathered on a representative subsample of 6,913 respondents at the time of the initial survey. Of these individuals, 3,988 men and women could be classified as LTM, LTW, or WBS, and provided data on the GWB at follow-up; 4,066 provided data on Self-Rated Health. In the original survey the CES-D was given only to a further subsample; follow-up data were available from 1,676 respondents. For these three variables, respondents were classified by marital status but collapsed across age and sex to provide reasonably large cells, and repeated-measures analyses of variance were conducted.

The key term in these analyses is the Status × Time interaction, which shows the impact of differing widowhood statuses over time. (Note that in the analysis of Time and the Status × Time interaction, each subject serves as his or her own control, so it is unnecessary to use covariates.) Several hypotheses might be considered. For example, we might expect that the chronic strains of widowhood would result in lowered well-being in the long-term widows relative to the long-term married respondents. Conversely, we might expect that processes of adaptation would lead to an improvement in well-being among the long-term widowed, who may have been lowest in well-being at the time of the initial survey. Or we might hypothesize that the largest change in well-being would occur for those individuals who were married at the initial survey, but widowed at follow-up.

The results for Self-Rated Health showed a significant decline over time for the whole group ($p < .001$), and there was also a significant interaction effect: Both LTMs and LTWs reported a decline in health over the follow-up interval, whereas – somewhat unexpectedly – Self-Rated Health did not change for the WBSs. It is essential to keep in mind, however, the very limited magnitude of these effects: Omega-squared analyses showed that both effects accounted for less than one-half of 1 percent of the variance in Self-Rated Health. Mean health problems increased over the follow-up interval from 2.47 to 2.58 – about one-tenth of one standard deviation. The somewhat counterintuitive finding of sustained health levels among the more recently widowed is therefore perhaps best regarded as an anomaly.

Results from the longitudinal analyses of the GWB and CES-D were clearer, and in conformity with the outcome analyses reported earlier: Neither variable showed a mean change over the interval, and there were no significant interaction terms. These findings are consistent with other longitudinal analyses of well-being (Costa et al., 1987b) and with analyses of the influence of other major life statuses and changes on well-being (Costa et al., 1987a).

Discussion

The message these data seem to convey is clear: In the long run, although it affects life-style, widowhood does not appear to have any enduring effect on psychosocial functioning in older men or women, nor much effect in younger women. Although it seems counterintuitive, this result is consistent with much recent literature. Indeed, W. Stroebe and Stroebe conclude that, in general, "after twelve to eighteen months most bereaved begin to recover and ultimately show little sign of psychological or physical damage" (1987, p. 121). Nevertheless, the findings are striking enough to warrant a more detailed consideration.

Readers who expected to see more pronounced effects may suspect that artifacts are responsible for the largely null findings reported here. The adequacy of the dependent measures is not really in doubt, since most have been used repeatedly in epidemiological and clinical studies, and have shown more than acceptable levels of reliability and validity. Even the single-item Self-Rated Health measure had a 10-year retest reliability of .56 ($p < .001$) in this sample.

More difficult to assess is the possible effect of sampling. The NHANES I was a carefully drawn national probability sample, and probably came as close to a truly representative sample as social scientists ever attain. Still, some individuals could not be located, or declined to participate in the initial survey or follow-up, and it is possible that bereaved individuals (particularly quite recently bereaved individuals) were disproportionately represented in the group of non-participants. The data showed that widows and widowers are more likely than married persons to be institutionalized, and the original NHANES I Survey excluded institutionalized individuals (although institutionalized persons were included in the follow-up). It is possible that there is a subset of individuals for whom widowhood is a source of significant and lasting psychosocial disability, culminating perhaps in institutionalization and premature mortality. Long-term prospects for adaptation are clearly moot for those individuals who die shortly after bereavement. Also, recall that the date of bereavement was not asked in this study, so that the period of survival since bereavement is unknown.

One methodological consideration of importance in comparing the present study to others is that here neither respondents nor interviewers were aware that widowhood was to be a variable of interest. By contrast, Lehman, Wortman, and Williams (1987) recruited bereaved respondents with a letter explaining that their study "would focus on the consequences of serious motor vehicle accidents" (p. 220). Their procedure may have primed bereaved respondents to report more psychological impairment than they otherwise would have. (It is also possible that accidental deaths, which are unexpected, have more enduring consequences than deaths due to illness.)

Data from the present study show that for most people neither bereavement nor the subsequent burden of widowhood (Lopata, 1975c) has an appreciable long-term impact on psychosocial functioning. Older widowed men and women have as many friends and confidants, believe themselves to be as healthy, and are as able to perform daily activities as are older married individuals; they do not differ in the personality traits of Extraversion or Openness to Experience, nor in morale or the presence of depressive symptoms. Clearly, the great majority of individuals show considerable ability to adapt to a major life stress and continuing life strains – an ability we would call remarkable if it were not so nearly universal a process (cf. Brickman, Coates, & Janoff-Bulman, 1978).

These signs of psychological resilience are in fact remarkable only in comparison with our expectations. Grieving individuals may find it difficult to believe they will ever return to their previous level of happiness or interest in life, and may even continue throughout their lives to believe they were happier before bereavement by reconstruing their personal history (Lopata, 1981; Ross & Conway, 1986). Social scientists in general tend to attribute well-being to environmental rather than dispositional causes (Costa et al., 1987a), and they too may expect a more enduring impact of bereavement. In fact, however, individuals adapt to a great variety of stressors in a relatively short period (e.g., Cassileth et al., 1984; Ormel, 1983); they reconstruct social networks when these are disrupted (Costa, Zonderman, & McCrae, 1985), and they show enduring personality dispositions despite a variety of social and physiological changes and personal experiences (McCrae & Costa, 1984).

It should be emphasized that these findings do not mean the loved one has been forgotten or the sense of loss does not remain. Bereavement may be a central event in people's life histories, with a profound and enduring effect on their sense of identity. But individuals learn to accept their loss, and it appears widowhood ultimately ceases to have much effect on day-to-day mood and functioning.

The 2-point data of the NHANES I and its follow-up provide impressive evidence of the fact of psychological resilience, but frustratingly few clues to its course or nature. Indeed, terms like adjustment and resilience imply a return to normal following a disruption; however, for many of the variables examined here, such as Extraversion and Openness and Activities of Daily Living, we do not know whether bereavement ever had an impact. Lowered well-being shortly after bereavement is, of course, well documented, but the rate of recovery cannot be estimated from the NHANES data – except to put an upper bound of 10 years to the recovery process.

If a long-term effect of widowhood had been observed, we might have divided respondents into those who had shown recovery and those who had not, and might have sought variables that might moderate the response to bereavement. It appears, however, *among survivors*, nearly everyone ultimately adjusts psychologically (though more of the widowed above age 64 become institutionalized), and the key question may concern individual variation in the length of recovery. What features of social support; economic advantage, personality traits, or coping styles lead to an earlier return to baseline? This is a central question for future research on bereavement (cf. Kessler et al., 1985).

Note that we have posed the question in terms of "return to baseline" rather than "return to mental health" or some other absolute standard. Psychological well-being is deeply rooted in enduring personality dispositions (Costa & McCrae, 1980, 1984), and individuals have their own characteristic level of morale or satisfaction that, unfortunately, is not always high. Ignoring this fact can lead to misinterpretations of data. Depression following bereavement need not be due to bereavement: Prior dispositions, or an interaction of dispositions with the experience of bereavement, may be responsible. Characteristics of depressed widows and widowers, such as few social supports (Costa et al., 1985) or the use of ineffective coping strategies (McCrae & Costa, 1986), may instead be correlates of their personality traits, with no causal influence on the process of recovery from bereavement. Prospective longitudinal studies, in which individuals are used as their own controls, provide the best way to avoid these problems.

Some social implications

That the great majority of men and women show psychological recovery after widowhood does not mean that bereavement is not a major trauma, nor that society is doing enough to assist and speed the recovery. How many days of depression did the individual endure before returning to his or her usual level of well-being? How much time was lost from work, how many extra medical visits were made during the period of mourning? How much burden was placed on friends and family? How much creativity and altruism and humor was sacrificed? To see the results of the present study as support for nonintervention would be as erroneous as to discount the horrors of war on the basis of later economic recovery.

Limited as they are, the present data suggest two inferences: Interventions aimed at ameliorating psychological distress and psychosocial impairment should focus on recently widowed individuals, and interventions for the long-term widowed should emphasize objective sectors of life quality rather than subjective well-being (Lawton, 1983). The higher incidence of institutionalization and the lower level of income among the widowed point to clear problems that need to be remedied. That individuals can show high levels of subjective well-being despite poverty and poor housing does not mean these are desirable (or even tolerable) states. Needs assessment in the widowed, as in other groups, should address objective needs.

These data do, however, put the fact of bereavement and its consequences into perspective. They give the counselor an objective basis for reassuring the grieving client that life will improve, and they allow the social planner to estimate the well-being of the ever-increasing population of widowed individuals. In a generation that has been alerted to the dangers and ubiquity of stress, it may also be comforting to know that human beings are highly adaptable creatures, and that in the long run the great majority of us will be able to cope even with the most distressing and disruptive of events.

14

Determinants of adjustment to bereavement in younger widows and widowers

WOLFGANG STROEBE AND
MARGARET S. STROEBE

This chapter reviews the major findings of the Tübingen longitudinal study of bereavement, an in-depth study of younger widows and widowers that provides information about health deterioration following bereavement, the course of recovery and coping strategies over a 2-year period, and the risk factors that affect adjustment to the loss. The study employed methodological safeguards to avoid some of the pitfalls that typically threaten the validity of in-depth studies of bereavement.

Background

When we planned our longitudinal study, the decline in mental and physical health and general well-being following marital bereavement had already been well documented (for reviews, see Osterweis, Solomon, & Green, 1984, and W. Stroebe & Stroebe, 1987). A few earlier studies (e.g., Clayton, 1979) had tended to minimize the severity of these effects. However, epidemiological, clinical, and in-depth interview and questionnaire investigations strongly suggest otherwise. Although the majority of bereaved manage to adjust to their loss without professional help, a significant minority do succumb to a variety of ailments and ills, and the risk of this persists for a considerable time.

Therefore, instead of merely charting the health consequences of marital bereavement, it seemed important to identify the characteristics of people who were likely to suffer long-term health impairment, because they were the risk group that would need professional help. We investigated whether

The Tübingen longitudinal study of bereavement was funded by a grant from the Deutsche Forschungsgemeinschaft to W. Stroebe. The authors are grateful to Dr. Günther Domittner for his assistance in planning and conducting this study and to Georgios Abakoumkin, who assisted in analyzing the data.

bereaved individuals' adjustment to loss was influenced by sociodemographic (e.g., socioeconomic status, age, gender) and individual (e.g., personality traits, religiosity) characteristics, by antecedent situational factors such as the quality of the marital relationship, by mode of death (sudden vs. expected loss), or by circumstances after the loss, like the extent to which the bereaved received social support (cf. W. Stroebe & Stroebe, 1987).

Theoretical deficits of early research on risk factors

Our review of published evidence on risk factors for poor adjustment to loss revealed that much of the early research had been conducted without the guidance of a theoretical framework; and this lack appeared to reflect the limitations of the then dominant theories of grief. For example, Freud's psychoanalytic and Bowlby's attachment theories focus on the quality of the relationship with the deceased as the major cause of pathological developments in coping with loss (W. Stroebe & Stroebe, 1987). These theories do not permit predictions about other factors known to influence adjustment, such as the circumstances of the loss or the extent of social support following the loss. Therefore, we developed the Deficit Model of Partner Loss as a heuristic framework to guide our research (W. Stroebe & Stroebe, 1987; W. Stroebe, Stroebe, Gergen, & Gergen, 1980, 1982).

The Deficit Model is an adaptation of interactionist cognitive stress models to bereavement (e.g., French & Kahn, 1962; Lazarus, 1966; Lazarus & Folkman, 1984). According to these models, critical life events are stressful because they require major readjustment. The intensity of the stress created by a life event depends on the extent to which the perceived demands of the situation tax or exceed an individual's coping resources, given that failure to cope leads to important negative consequences. The Deficit Model assesses both the situational demands of spousal bereavement and the coping resources available to the grieving individual to predict the intensity of stress due to a loss (for an extensive description of the model, see W. Stroebe & Stroebe, 1987). As a stress theory, the Deficit Model allows a more detailed analysis of risk factors in bereavement than the depression theories of Freud and Bowlby. Risk is not seen only as a function of the relationship to the deceased; other intra- and interpersonal factors also may be relevant. In particular, the model emphasizes an interpersonal perspective, viewing social support as an important coping resource. Furthermore, outcome is not seen only in terms of normal and pathological grief (usually clinical depression). The model can also account for the range of physical health consequences that have been linked to bereavement.

Empirical deficits of early research on risk factors

Because large-scale epidemiological surveys do not permit detailed assessments of personality traits or coping processes, most research on risk factors has relied on the in-depth study of small samples. The advantage of this method is that it permits a more fine-grained analysis of predictors of health risk and processes of coping with bereavement. However, these in-depth studies also typically suffer from a number of weaknesses (cf. W. Stroebe & Stroebe, 1987), which the Tübingen study was designed to overcome.

Most studies concentrate on the elderly and on widows, who constitute the largest subgroups of widowed, despite indications that it is the younger widowed (Ball, 1977; Maddison & Walker, 1967), and particularly widowers (cf. M. Stroebe & Stroebe, 1983), who are at greatest risk (relative to comparison groups of the same age and sex). Few of these studies include nonbereaved control groups (producing frequent confusion of main effects with interactions). Also rare are longitudinal investigations following the same sample across the first few years of bereavement to examine patterns and rates of recovery and predictors of outcome. In the Tübingen study samples of widows and widowers were interviewed three times during the first 2 years following their loss, and measures of their health and well-being were compared to those of a matched sample of married individuals.

The Tübingen study was also designed to assess two biases inherent in the design of in-depth studies that threaten the validity of the conclusions drawn from previous research: selection and social desirability. First, understandably, the recently bereaved are often not very willing to participate in interviews regarding their loss. Because participation and health status are likely to be related in bereavement studies, low participation rates could therefore introduce a selection bias in findings about the health consequences of bereavement. To assess this bias, the health status was measured for some of the widowed who refused participation. Second, grief is a central part of the widowed role, and there may be normative pressures on the bereaved to report symptoms of depression. Social desirability biases are therefore particularly critical in bereavement studies. It is surprising that they have never been examined, as they are likely to increase the number of symptoms reported by the widowed. To assess this bias, the social desirability responses of the widowed in our study were related to their self-reported health status.

Method

Participants in the study were 60 widowed and 60 married individuals under the age of retirement. Names and addresses of all persons in this category who had been maritally bereaved for 4 to 7 months were supplied by the municipal registrars in five towns in southern Germany. The bereaved persons received a letter outlining the study and asking for their cooperation. Out of respect for their bereaved condition, no pressure was put on persons to participate, but individuals who refused interview participation by phone were asked whether they were willing to complete a short questionnaire.

Two hundred and seventeen persons had to be approached to achieve a sample size of 30 widows and 30 widowers (mean age: 53.05 years) for the interviews, but 24 of those who refused to participate in an interview filled out the mailed questionnaire. Although at 28% the acceptance rate for interviews was rather low, it is not atypical for research in this area (M. Stroebe & Stroebe, 1989).

The 30 married women and 30 married men (mean age: 53.75 years) who participated in the nonbereaved comparison group were individually matched to the widowed by sex, age, socioeconomic status, and number of children. They were recruited from addresses of a large number of matched individuals supplied by the registration offices of the same five towns. Letters were sent to these married individuals, explaining that we were interested in the relationship between marital status and the quality of life, and the same procedure was followed as with the bereaved. For the married sample, the acceptance rate was 34%.

Of the individuals who agreed to be interviewed, 82% of the widowed and 90% of the married participated in all three interviews. There was no significant health difference between those who participated in three sessions and those who dropped out. The participants were interviewed three times. For the bereaved, the first interview was conducted 4 to 7 months, and the second interview approximately 14 months after the loss. The third, and final, interview took place approximately 2 years after bereavement.

Structured interviews as well as self-report scales were used for data collection. The first two interviews were extensive sessions held at the homes of the participants. The third interview was a shorter one, conducted by telephone. At the end of each interview, participants were given (or at time 3 sent) a questionnaire containing personality and health measures. This questionnaire (with an additional page containing questions on socio-demographic status) was also mailed to widowed individuals who declined to participate in the study but were willing to answer some written questions.

Although a great number of self-report measures of psychological and physical health as well as of grief-specific symptoms were included in this study, this chapter is restricted to two of these health measures, a depression inventory and a measure of somatic complaints. However, the pattern of health findings was very consistent across measures. Depression was assessed by the German version of the Beck Depression Inventory, or BDI (Beck, 1967; Kammer, 1983), a self-report scale that assesses the major symptoms of depression (e.g., loss of interest in everyday activities, self-reproach, sleep and appetite problems). Somatic complaints (e.g., dizziness, difficulty in swallowing, indigestion, excessive sweating, restlessness) were assessed by a symptom checklist (*Beschwerdenliste*, BL), which is widely used in Germany and has high reliability (von Zerssen, 1976).

Whenever appropriate, data were analyzed using factorial analyses of variance, usually with gender and marital status as one of the factors. Sometimes hierarchical regressions were also employed. A detailed description of our methods of data analysis can be found elsewhere (M. Stroebe & Stroebe, 1989, 1991; W. Stroebe, Stroebe, & Domittner, 1988).

Assessing biases in bereavement research

For a recently bereaved individual, the decision to participate in interviews about his or her loss experience is likely to be influenced by current mental and physical state. Selection could operate in two quite different ways: (1) Participants might be more healthy than nonparticipants (the latter being too depressed or too physically ill to participate), or (2) participants might be less healthy than nonparticipants (the latter having no need to talk to bereavement experts and being able to cope well by themselves). If the first hypothesis were true, then conclusions from empirical studies about the well-being and health status of the bereaved would be overly optimistic; if the second were true, the consequences of bereavement would appear unduly negative.

To our surprise, neither hypothesis was supported for the total sample. Whereas the widows who refused to participate were less depressed than those who participated, the pattern was reversed for the widowers. However, this sex difference in selection was limited to depression (BDI). No such pattern was observed for somatic symptoms (BL).

Why should such differential selection have occurred? The second hypothesis implies that the more emotionally distressed widowed would be more interested in talking to a bereavement expert than those who felt better. Although this hypothesis was apparently correct for widows, the opposite hypothesis was supported for widowers. Due to the gender difference in norms governing self-control of emotion in our culture, it is more embarrassing for a man than for a woman to break down and cry during an interview. Fear of this happening could have led those widowers who felt most depressed, and thus most likely to break down during the interview, to refuse to participate. The selection effect that we found may thus reflect a more general gender difference in coping styles. That the differential selection only occurred for a test measuring depressive symptoms but not for the test of somatic complaints is consistent with this interpretation. Whether individuals suffered from a greater or smaller number of somatic complaints had little bearing on their decision to participate in an interview (for a more extensive discussion, see M. Stroebe & Stroebe, 1989).

To assess the impact of social desirability demands on health measures, the sample was divided into two groups on the basis of scores on the so-called lie scale of the Eysenck Personality Inventory, which was used as a measure of social desirability response tendencies. If social desirability affected self-reported health, the health differences between the married and the widowed should be greater for individuals with high scores on the lie scale than for low-scoring individuals. However, there was no evidence of such a difference for any of the health measures at any of the three points in time.

What are the implications of these findings for the interpretation of the data on health consequences of bereavement? Because there was no demonstrable effect of social desirability biases on the health measures employed, social desirability can be disregarded as a potential cause of differences in the health scores of the widowed and the married samples. Selection, on the other hand, did have a noteworthy relationship to depression. Although there were no overall differences in health between those who participated and those who refused, there was a gender by participation status interaction on the BDI. The implications of these findings are that interview studies overselect the better recovered widowers and the poorer recovered widows. Thus, although selection should have little impact on overall differences in the health of the bereaved and married samples, it is likely to bias interpretations of sex differences in health outcomes of bereavement (at least as far as depression is concerned).

Recovery from bereavement

The health impact of bereavement was examined by comparing the health differences between the bereaved and married participants at the three points in time. Table 14.1 presents the BDI and BL scores of the widowed and married samples. At 4 to 6 months after the loss, the widowed had higher levels of depressive and somatic symptoms than the married, but they showed considerable improvement during the 18-month period of the study. In addition, there were the usual gender differences (main effects) in depressive and somatic symptomatology: Across all marital status

Table 14.1. *Means and standard deviations of the BDI and BL by marital status, sex, and time for individuals who participated in all three interviews*

Variable and time	Measure	Married		Widowed	
		Female	Male	Female	Male
BDI[a]					
Time 1	M	6.0	3.6	11.4	8.4
	SD	5.8	4.2	7.7	7.3
Time 2	M	5.4	5.0	9.7	6.7
	SD	5.2	6.2	8.7	6.6
Time 3	M	6.0	3.8	9.4	4.3
	SD	5.8	4.6	7.8	5.7
	(N)	(25)	(28)	(26)	(22)
BL[b]					
Time 1	M	18.0	14.0	25.7	20.2
	SD	11.5	9.2	17.0	14.2
Time 2	M	18.6	13.6	20.6	18.3
	SD	12.0	9.7	16.2	12.9
Time 3	M	20.2	12.8	20.8	14.3
	SD	14.8	8.1	15.2	11.7
	(N)	(25)	(28)	(27)	(22)

[a] Higher means indicate more depression (maximum score: 60).
[b] Higher means indicate more psychosomatic symptoms (maximum score: 56).

categories and the three points in time women had higher symptom levels than men.

To evaluate the severity of the health consequences of bereavement, we used the cutoff points suggested by Beck (1967) to assess the percentages of married and widowed individuals who could be categorized as at least mildly depressed (a score of 11 and above). At 4 to 7 months after their loss, 42% of the widowed (as compared to 10% of the married) had scores on the BDI that indicated at least mild depression, a difference that was statistically significant (chi-square). Two years after the loss, the percentage of widowed with BDI scores that indicated at least mild depression had fallen considerably, but at 27% was still significantly higher than the 10% figure for the married.

Severity of symptoms on the BL was defined in terms of the distribution of the scores of the married controls. The cutoff point for severe symptoms was set at 2 standard deviations above the mean of the married controls for the BL. At the first interview 20% of the widowed (as compared to 3% of the married) had BL scores above the cutoff point, but the percentage was down to 12% after 2 years and was no longer significantly different from that of the married individuals.

Thus, the findings of this study support the expectation that the first 7 months following a loss are characterized by high levels of depressive symptoms and somatic complaints. Additional data indicate that during that period 13 of the 60 bereaved reported an increase in the use of psychotropic medication, whereas none of the married did. Similarly, 19 of the bereaved but only 4 of the married reported instances of new illnesses for the 4 to 7 months after bereavement (or a comparable time period in the case of the married controls).

Even though the health of the widowed showed significant improvement over the 2 years of our study and was finally no longer significantly different from that of the married when average scores were considered, nearly a third of the widowed were still mildly to moderately depressed 2 years after their loss. Thus, although the majority of the bereaved recovered over the 2-year period, a significant minority did not. In the next section an attempt is made to identify this subgroup of high-risk individuals.

Risk factors in bereavement outcome

Risk factors in bereavement are characteristics of bereaved individuals or features of their situation that increase their vulnerability to the loss experience (vulnerability factor) or slow down adjustment to widowhood (recovery factor). Because most potential risk factors in bereavement are also associated with poor health outcome in the general population, it is insufficient merely to show that their presence in a bereaved sample is related to health impairment. It has to be further demonstrated that the health deterioration observed in the bereaved is caused by difficulties in adjusting to widowhood that are due to the presence of the specific risk factor. For example, the finding that widows have higher levels of depressive symptomatology than widowers has frequently been interpreted as a gender difference in *adjustment* to loss (e.g., Carey, 1977). Because gender is also related to depression in the general population, this conclusion is unfounded, unless one can demonstrate that gender is more strongly or differently associated with depression in bereaved rather than nonbereaved populations (e.g., that loss results in a greater *increase* in depressive symptomatology in widows rather than widowers).

There are two strategies to establish that general risk factors also affect adjustment to widowhood: One can either include nonbereaved controls, so that between-group comparisons can be made, or one can rely on longitudinal comparisons, where relative recovery can be plotted. Thus, to demonstrate that a general risk factor is negatively associated with adjustment to loss, one has to show a statistical interaction of that risk factor with marital status on health in cross-sectional designs or an interaction with time on health in longitudinal designs.

Sociodemographic factors

Socioeconomic status. Although the association between low socio-economic status and ill health has been widely demonstrated for the general as well as for the bereaved population, studies that compare bereaved to nonbereaved control groups (e.g., Gallagher, Breckenridge, Thompson, & Peterson, 1983b; Morgan, 1976; Sanders, 1980) tend to show that the health differential due to social class is the same for bereaved as for nonbereaved. Consistent with these results, our study did not find inter-actions of sociodemographic status and marital status on any of our health measures.

Age. Because the negative health impact of bereavement is generally attributed to the fact that it aggravates existing health problems, one would expect older rather than younger bereaved individuals to be more vulner-able to the detrimental effects of such stressful life events as the loss of a spouse. Therefore, it is rather puzzling that it is the younger bereaved who seem to suffer more severe health deterioration (W. Stroebe & Stroebe, 1987). This pattern has typically been attributed to the greater expected-ness of loss in older age groups, but there is no empirical evidence to support this hypothesis.

Due to the focus of our study on younger widowed individuals, the age range of our sample was somewhat restricted and did not include indi-viduals who were elderly and retired. This may have been the reason why we did not find any association between age and well-being either in our bereaved or nonbereaved sample.

Gender. We have repeatedly argued (cf. M. Stroebe & Stroebe, 1983; W. Stroebe & Stroebe, 1987) that men have greater difficulties in adjusting to spousal bereavement than women. Our review of the literature on gender differences in bereavement outcome suggested that when widows and widowers were compared with same-sex, nonbereaved comparison persons (thus controlling for the main effects of sex on health), widowers were found to suffer greater health impairment compared to married men than widows compared to married women. We reasoned that this gender difference was due to the greater availability of alternative sources of support to women than to men.

Consistent with this assumption, the loss of a partner resulted in a decrease of social support for widowers but not for widows. However, there is no evidence of a gender difference in bereavement outcome (see Table 14.1). In fact, analyses of variance yielded neither significant marital status by gender interactions nor (considering only the bereaved) gender by time of measurement interactions on health measures. One obvious reason for our failure to find a gender difference in bereavement outcome is selection. Even though selection seemed to be mainly mediated by emotional stability, the fact that our interview study differentially attracted men who (compared to those who refused) were relatively well adjusted and women who were relatively poorly adjusted may have minimized gender differences in health outcome.

Individual characteristics

Personality. Intuitively, personality variables would seem to be among the most important determinants of adjustment to loss. And yet, the mediating role of personality traits in health impairment following bereavement has largely been neglected by researchers in this area (cf. Sanders, this volume; W. Stroebe & Stroebe, 1987).

In the Tübingen study, emotional stability and locus of control were assessed at Time 1 as two personality variables likely to affect bereavement outcome. In terms of the Deficit Model, emotional stability is an intrapersonal resource that buffers the individual against the impact of a loss experience. It was measured with the German version of the neuroticism scale of the Eysenck Personality Inventory, or EPI (Eggert, 1983). High scores on the EPI-N reflect low emotional stability. Repeated measures analyses of variance of the health measures over all three points in time resulted in interactions of neuroticism, marital status, and time on depression and somatic complaints.* Consistent with our predictions, emotionally stable individuals reacted with lower levels of depressive and somatic symptoms to bereavement than individuals who had high scores on the EPI-N, but this difference became less marked over time. This suggests that emotional stability decreased vulnerability but did not seem to affect adjustment to the loss experience.

Locus of control was measured because, according to the theory of learned helplessness (e.g., Abramson, Seligman, & Teasdale, 1978), control beliefs should play an important role as stress moderators. Surprisingly, there are conflicting hypotheses about the precise nature of this relationship. Some have argued that since the state of learned helplessness is characterized by a perceived lack of control, people who already believe that they have little control should be more likely to react with depression to loss (e.g., Ganellen & Blaney, 1984; Johnson & Sarason, 1978). In contrast, others have argued that individuals who expect control will be

---

* This conclusion is somewhat discrepant from that reported by W. Stroebe and M. Stroebe in 1987 because at the time we had only a preliminary analysis based on data collected for part of the sample at the first interview.

more severely stressed by situations that are truly uncontrollable (e.g., Mikulincer, 1988; Pittman & Pittman, 1979).

Locus of control was measured with the German version of the Interpersonal Control Scale, or IPC, of Levenson (Mielke, 1979). The IPC provides three scores indicating the extent to which individuals believe that what happens to them is under their own control (IPC-I) or is externally controlled by chance (IPC-C) or powerful others (IPC-P). The scores on these three dimensions are assumed to be independent of each other. As one would expect, individuals who had just experienced the death of their spouse showed an increased belief in chance control, but there was no marital status difference in scores on the other two scales.

To assess the potential role of control beliefs as moderators of the bereavement–health relationship, we divided our sample by a median split into groups with high or low beliefs in chance (IPC-C) and internal control (IPC-I). (The powerful other scale was considered less relevant in the context of bereavement.) Although individuals who had low beliefs in internal control or high beliefs in chance were more depressed than individuals who believed that they had control over their own outcomes (high IPC-I) and that their lives were not controlled by chance (low IPC-C), there was no evidence that control beliefs had a differential impact on the depression of bereaved and nonbereaved individuals. Thus, although the belief that one has control over one's life did not increase the vulnerability of the bereaved toward withstanding the stressful experience, it also did not appear to buffer them against the impact of their loss experience, as one would have expected on the basis of the findings of Ganellen and Blaney (1984) or Johnson and Sarason (1978). However, as we will see later, internal control beliefs do serve a buffering function for losses that are highly unexpected.

Religiosity. It would seem plausible that religiosity should help individuals to cope with stressful life events such as the death of a spouse. Religion not only offers systems of beliefs that may be comforting to the bereaved (e.g., the belief in life after death) but also usually offers a religious community and thus a social support network. Because our review of the literature had indicated very little empirical evidence on the supportive nature of religious beliefs (W. Stroebe & Stroebe, 1987), we took great care in constructing a religiosity scale for our study to assess the impact of religious beliefs and habits on coping with loss. We found no evidence for an association between religiosity and health for either of the two groups. Thus, even though nearly half of our sample were religious enough to believe in a life after death, these religious beliefs did not seem to help them cope with their loss experience.

Antecedent situational factors

The quality of the marital relationship that was disrupted by the death of a spouse is a major aspect of the situation before the loss and one that is likely to affect bereavement outcome. The romantic notion of the broken heart implies that the more intensely loved a partner was, the more that person will be grieved for after death. This prediction is in line with our Deficit Model, according to which deficits in the various support functions served by the partner are major determinants of the stress experience in bereavement.

A somewhat conflicting hypothesis can be derived from psychoanalytic and attachment theories. According to Freud (1917a), it is the existence of ambivalence in marital relationships that is likely to lead to poor bereavement outcome. Ambivalence refers to a relationship in which elements of love and hate coexist. Even though it does not mean that attachment is no longer present, it is most characteristic of marriages that are conflict-ridden and in which one or the other spouse may well have considered divorce (cf. Parkes & Weiss, 1983; W. Stroebe & Stroebe, 1987). Because this type of relationship is also likely to be characterized by insecure attachment, predictions from attachment theory would coincide here with those from the psychoanalytic perspective.

It is problematic to use a retrospective assessment of the marital relationship to study the impact of marital quality on bereavement outcome because the loss of a partner is likely to stimulate a need to idealize the relationship. In constructing our measure of marital quality, therefore, we not only asked for evaluations of the relationship but also encouraged reports about the extent to which time was spent together and friends, activities, and decisions were shared. Surprisingly, our findings supported both conflicting predictions. There was an interaction of marital quality, marital status, and gender on depression and somatic complaints. Whereas widows suffered higher levels of symptomatology after the loss of a happy rather than an unhappy relationship, the opposite was true for widowers. They seemed to suffer more if they had been less happy and close to their spouse. Although correlations between marital quality and level of symptomatology computed separately for each gender and marital status category tended to support this pattern, they also suggested that the relationship was somewhat weaker for men than for women. Thus, marital quality seemed to be a less important determinant of well-being for men than for women, and this was true for marriage as well as for bereavement.

How do we account for this pattern? The findings for widows are in line with predictions derived from our Deficit Model. It is also intuitively plausible that the loss of a spouse should be the harder to bear, the closer and happier the marital relationship had been. But why should men react differently? One could speculate that because marital quality seemed to be less important for the men in our sample while they were married, they might have suffered more guilt feelings after the loss. There is some evidence for a gender difference in guilt feelings that would be consistent with this interpretation. However, this gender difference certainly needs further replication and clarification.

Mode of death

The circumstances of the death of a spouse are likely to affect the course of bereavement. Thus, the situation of a person whose spouse dies in a car accident differs in important ways from that of an individual who loses his or her partner after an illness lasting for several years. The tremendous readjustment required by the loss of a spouse is always likely to be painful, but it should be the more stressful the less time had been available to the survivor to adjust to the change. Sudden, unexpected, untimely deaths are believed, therefore, to result in higher risk of mental and physical debilities during bereavement than losses that had been anticipated.

And yet, the empirical evidence for this hypothesis is not all that consistent (cf. W. Stroebe & Stroebe, 1987). Some studies found unexpectedness of the loss to have negative effects on health outcome (Ball, 1977; Lundin, 1984; Parkes, 1975a; Sanders, 1983), but other studies did not (Bornstein, Clayton, Halikas, Maurice, & Robins, 1973; Breckenridge, Gallagher, Thompson, & Peterson, 1986; Maddison & Walker, 1967). Although the failure of the studies of Breckenridge et al. and Bornstein et al. to find greater health deterioration following unexpected rather than expected losses could have been due to the fact that the widowed participants in these studies were elderly, and thus of an age when death of a partner could not have been completely unexpected, this explanation does not apply to the findings of Maddison and Walker.

It was, therefore, important to check whether an expectedness effect could be demonstrated for our sample of younger widowed. These widowed were divided into two groups, according to whether they had less than 1 day of warning of the death or more. Although unexpected loss was associated with higher levels of depressive symptoms (means: 13.6 vs. 9.1) and somatic complaints (means: 27.0 vs. 20.5) than expected losses at 4 to 7 months after the death, this difference was only marginally significant for the BDI and not significant for the BL. Furthermore, there were no significant effects of expectedness at any of the later interviews. Thus, expectedness seemed to increase the immediate vulnerability to the loss experience, but the effect weakened over time as the bereaved who had suffered a sudden loss had had a chance to adjust.

It is plausible that unexpected losses are more threatening to individuals' feelings of control over their lives than losses that follow a period of forewarning. After all, circumstances are different following an expected death, offering greater opportunities to exercise some control over the course of events before death. Therefore, we conducted further analyses to examine whether expectedness of loss had a differential impact on widowed, depending on their level of beliefs in internal control (IPC-I) and chance (IPC-C). Although there was no evidence for a moderator role of chance belief, the interaction of expectedness and internal control beliefs on BDI and BL was highly significant. This interaction was due to the high scores of one group only, the individuals who believed that they had little internal control over their outcomes and who experienced an unexpected loss. These persons suffered from high levels of depression and somatic complaints at 4 to 7 months after their loss and improved very little over the 2-year period of the study (Figures 14.1 and 14.2).

Why should the combination of unexpected loss and low internal control beliefs constitute such a powerful risk factor? The following explanation seems plausible: Those bereaved by sudden death have been exposed to a truly shattering life event. There are alternative strategies available for coping with and coming to terms with this circumstance. On the one hand, a person can try to retain a belief that he or she can turn life around again, even though the situation seems hopeless and desperate. This option is more likely to be followed by people who believe in internal control. They would feel that it is up to themselves to come to terms with the unexpected change in their lives. As a consequence, they are likely to make more of an effort to recover from depression. On the other hand, if individuals do not believe in internal control, and if the sudden death confirmed their belief that they have no control over their outcomes, they will more likely respond with resignation, make only feeble efforts to recover, and remain depressed.

Circumstances after the loss

There is general consensus that the extent to which the bereaved can rely on their families and friends to stand by them in their distress is one of the most important moderators of bereavement outcome (cf. W. Stroebe & Stroebe, 1987; Stylianos & Vachon, this volume). The availability of alternative sources of social support should help bereaved individuals to cope with the deficits created by the loss of a spouse and thus should reduce their vulnerability to the stress of bereavement. Because married individuals are much less likely to be in need of alternative sources of social support, the availability of social support should have less impact on psychological health and well-being of the married than the widowed. In line with other interactionist approaches to stress, the Deficit Model would, therefore,

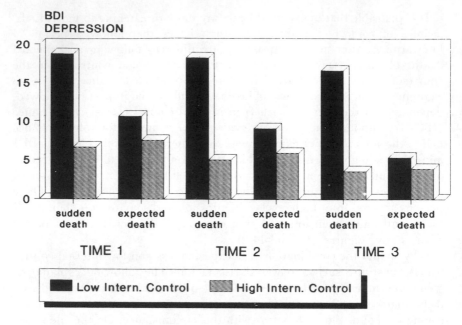

Figure 14.1. Mean BDI scores of widowed respondents by internal control beliefs and expectedness of loss, for individuals who participated in all three interviews.

predict an interaction of marital status and social support on health measures (i.e., buffering effect).

The Tübingen study included measures of perceived as well as received social support. *Perceived social support* was measured with a scale that assessed different functions of social support (emotional, instrumental, appraisal, contact support). Because the different subscales were highly correlated, we used the total support score in all our analyses. *Received social support* was assessed in the interview. Participants were asked about the number of social contacts they had experienced during the last month *and* the satisfaction with these contacts. Though there was no relationship between perceived social support and number of contacts, there was a moderate correlation ($r = .54$) when number of contacts was weighted by satisfaction.

To our surprise, there was no evidence of a buffering effect for either measure, even though there was a significant positive relationship between the availability of social support and health: Individuals who had a great number of supportive relationships suffered from fewer depressive symptoms and somatic complaints than those with less social support, but the availability of social support had similarly positive effects on married and widowed individuals (i.e., a social support main effect). This failure to

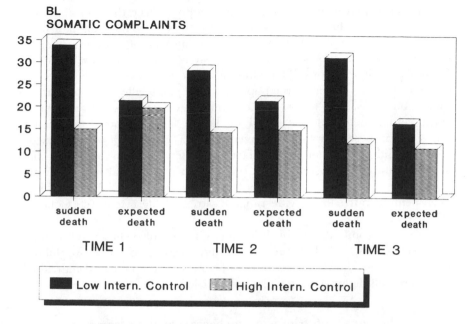

Figure 14.2. Mean BL scores of widowed respondents by internal control beliefs and expectedness of loss, for individuals who participated in all three interviews.

find a buffering effect of social support is not only inconsistent with our Deficit Model but is also discrepant with the conclusions of Cohen and Wills (1985). One potential explanation could be that, although there was a marked difference in perceived or received social support between our two groups, even the "low support group" enjoyed a level of social support that seemed quite adequate. This would imply, however, that buffering effects should mainly occur at the lower end of the social support continuum.

Conclusions

In view of the long list of risk factors commonly discussed in the literature, it was somewhat disconcerting that many of these did not seem to affect bereavement outcome in the Tübingen study. In some cases this may have been due to features of our study. Thus, the focus on younger widowed resulted in a restriction in the age range and lowered the chance to study the impact of age on bereavement outcome. Similarly, the unexpected gender bias due to selection bias procedure made it unlikely that the expected gender difference in adjustment to bereavement would be confirmed in our study.

For many of the other factors studied, the failure to find a differential impact on bereavement outcome may simply reflect the fact that their previous status in the literature as risk factors was based more on plausibility than on sound empirical data. We would also argue that much of the evidence on risk factors is derived from designs that do not allow one to test for statistical interactions. These findings may, therefore, merely reflect the general effect of a factor on the population (i.e., main effects) rather than its impact on adjustment to loss. By insisting on interactions between marital status and a potential risk factor on health for all general risk factors, our study imposed far more stringent criteria than much of the previous research did. Nevertheless, the fact that there was no buffering effect of social support on bereavement (even when hierarchical regression procedures were used) is puzzling, as buffering effects of social support have been demonstrated for a wide range of stressful life events (cf. Cohen & Wills, 1985).

With the combination of low internal control beliefs and sudden, unexpected loss, the Tübingen study did uncover a very powerful risk factor, one that allowed us to account for most of the bereaved individuals who were still depressed 2 years after their loss.

The impact of grief work on bereavement outcome

A further aim of the Tübingen study was to analyze the processes that mediate adjustment to loss. There is general consensus among theorists and practitioners in the area of bereavement that grief work plays a central role in adjustment to loss (e.g., Bowlby, 1980/1981; Freud, 1917a; Lindemann, 1944; Raphael & Nunn, 1988). The grief work hypothesis claims that bereaved individuals have to work through their loss in order to come to terms with it. Although the concept has never been clearly defined, grief work seems to imply a cognitive process of confronting the reality of loss, of going over events that occurred before and at the time, and of focusing on memories and working toward detachment from the deceased (M. Stroebe & Stroebe, 1991).

As the grief work hypothesis had never been tested, we had to develop our own measure of grief work (for a detailed description, see M. Stroebe & Stroebe, 1991). Based on the assumption that people who work through their grief confront their loss, whereas those who do not engage in grief work distract themselves and avoid anything to remind them of the deceased, our measures of grief work assessed the extent to which individuals avoid or confront their loss.

Hierarchical multiple regressions were used to test whether individuals who did grief work during the first 4 to 7 months following their loss (Time 1) suffered less depressive and somatic symptoms after 2 years (Time 3). By entering the health measure (BDI or BL), taken at the same time as the grief work measures, into the equation before entering the measure of grief work, we controlled for initial differences in levels of health.

Our results did not unequivocally support the grief work hypothesis. Widows who avoided confronting their loss did not differ in their depressive or somatic symptomatology from widows who worked through their grief. However, for widowers, performance of grief work was associated with better adjustment over the 2-year period of our study (M. Stroebe & Stroebe, 1991). We attributed this pattern to gender differences in the effectiveness with which avoidant strategies can be used. Widowers are often more successful in blocking confrontation with their loss than widows, because they are more likely to spend their working day outside their home environment and because their social environment does not encourage them to dwell on their grief (M. Stroebe & Stroebe, 1991).

General conclusions and implications

The results of the Tübingen study have far-reaching empirical and theoretical implications. On the empirical level, the study contributed to our knowledge about the course of recovery, risk factors in bereavement outcome, and grief work. Our findings showed that, even though the majority of our bereaved participants recovered from their grief to the extent that they no longer suffered from a raised level of depressive symptoms and somatic complaints, approximately one third showed few signs of recovery. They were exceedingly depressed at the beginning of our study and did not improve much over the 2-year period. We were able to identify a combination of personality and situational factors that characterized most of the individuals in our high-risk group. Finally, the findings of our study also challenged the long-standing belief in the necessity of grief work for adjustment to bereavement. Although for widowers, the performance of grief work was associated with better adjustment over the 2 years of our study, widows who avoided confronting their loss did not differ in depressive or somatic symptomatology from those who did not. The implications of this result are that working through grief may not be as essential for adjustment to loss as has been frequently assumed.

On a theoretical level, the results of the Tübingen study were only partly supportive of our Deficit Model of Partner Loss. Thus, the lack of support for the prediction that high socioeconomic status and social support would buffer individuals against the stress of bereavement is inconsistent with our theory. Even though the absence of these buffering effects could have been due to the fact that none of the participants in our study was really poverty-stricken or completely lacked social support, these inconsistencies do raise some doubt about the explanatory power of stress models as theories of bereavement. Furthermore, the fact that cognitive factors emerged as strong predictors of vulnerability and adjustment suggests the need for further theoretical reassessment of the cognitive processes that underlie the appraisal of loss.

15

The impact of spousal bereavement on older widows and widowers

DOLORES GALLAGHER-THOMPSON,
ANDREW FUTTERMAN,
NORMAN FARBEROW, LARRY W. THOMPSON,
AND JAMES PETERSON

The purpose of this chapter is twofold: to summarize basic results from two longitudinal studies of how elders adapt to death of their spouse, depending on whether the death was due to natural causes or to suicide; and to review what these studies have found regarding the possible correlates of good versus poor outcome. A final objective is to present some thoughts about unanswered questions and to suggest further research to shed light on these issues.

The University of Southern California (USC) spousal bereavement study

Although spousal loss occurs predominantly late in life (U.S. Bureau of Census, 1988), few studies have systematically assessed the response to this loss in older adults. The primary objective of the USC study was to assess longitudinally the impact of spousal loss on the mental and physical health of older widows and widowers. In addition, we also evaluated specific predictors of bereavement outcome in light of existing theory and previous research (e.g., Freud, 1917b; Parkes & Brown, 1972). Of particular interest in the USC study were the following factors, each of which alone, and in combination, was thought to be causally related to bereavement outcome: personality and ego strength, social support, religiosity, marital quality, anticipation of loss, and cumulative losses/stressors.

Sample characteristics and research design

Two samples of older adults were compared in the USC study. One sample comprised 212 recently widowed elders (99 males and 113 females) who

Preparation of this work was supported in part by grant RO1-AGO1959 from the National Institute on Aging and RO1-MH36834 from the National Institute of Mental Health.

had lost their spouse as a result of natural causes. These subjects are referred to as the Natural Death Survivors throughout the remainder of this chapter. The second sample comprised older individuals who had not lost a spouse within the last 5 years (84 males and 78 females). These individuals are referred to as the Comparison Group. The actual number of subjects in any one group available for different sets of analyses varies as a function of subject attrition and/or availability of complete data. To obtain Natural Death Survivors, death certificates at the Los Angeles County Health Department were searched periodically, and all spouses of persons over 55 who had died within the preceding 2 to 4 weeks were mailed a description of the project and a stamped postcard with which willingness to be interviewed could be indicated. Mailings were sent to 2,450 persons. Of the 735 who responded (30%), 212 met the age criteria and also resided within a reasonable distance from the research center to permit home interviews. The Comparison Group was recruited from senior centers, residential facilities for elders, and the Emeriti Center mailing list of the University of Southern California. These were adults over age 55 who either were currently married or, if single, had not lost a spouse through death within the previous 5 years. Most of these respondents had experienced the death of either another family member or a close friend within the past 5 years.

Both groups were composed of Caucasians who were well educated (80% had at least 1 year of high school) and of moderate socioeconomic status (SES) (most had income between $10,000 and $30,000). The age range of all subjects was 55–83 years. The Natural Death Survivors were slightly younger (mean = 68.20 years; SD = 7.84) than the Comparison Group (mean = 70.11 years; SD = 7.65). Subjects in both groups had been married for many years (mean = 38.68 and 37.43 years for the Natural Death Survivors and the Comparison Group, respectively). In general, higher socioeconomic status (income, education, occupation) was demonstrated for males than females regardless of bereavement status.

Because of some differences in these background variables between samples, a principal components analysis was completed on residuals of all sociodemographic variables after the effects of bereavement and gender had been removed. The resulting four components were used as covariates in all subsequent analyses. These were labeled as spouse SES, respondent SES, income, and longevity (including both number of years married and age of respondent). The general plan for data analysis was a three-factor design with group status (Natural Death Survivors vs. Comparison Subjects) and gender (male vs. female) as between-subject variables and time of measurement as the within-subject variable.

Dependent variables were obtained at 2, 6, 12, and 30 months following spousal loss. A structured interview designed by the investigators was administered at each time of measurement. This interview covered demographic characteristics, religious beliefs and practices, coping strategies, prior stressful events, utilization of social supports, upheaval in routines of daily living, judgments of the subject's marital relationship, and self-ratings of mental and physical health. A number of self-report measures were also completed because of theoretical interests; in the present chapter, though, we will focus on measures of mental health symptoms, including: Depression measured by the Beck Depression Inventory (BDI) (Beck, Ward, Mendelson, Mock, & Erbaugh, 1961); overall psychopathology measured by the Brief Symptom Inventory (BSI) (Derogatis & Spencer, 1982); and grief measured by the Texas Inventory of Grief–Revised (TRIG) (Faschingbauer, Devaul, & Zisook, 1977; Faschingbauer, 1981).

Comparable interviews and measures were completed by subjects in the comparison group at identical intervals. Note that in several of the analyses reported on here, we did not use data obtained at 6 months, because a number of interviews were missed at that time point. However, all intervals are used in some analyses, depending on the nature of the problem being addressed. These interviews and measures have been used successfully in several subsequent studies with older adults (Lund, Caserta, & Dimond, 1989a; Van Zandt, Mou, & Abbott, 1989).

Mental health

Distress and depression. At 2 months following the loss, the natural death survivors reported significantly higher levels of distress and depressed mood than the comparison group (Gallagher, Breckenridge, Thompson, & Peterson, 1983b). By 1 year, however, these differences had diminished to nonsignificant levels. The decline was linear on all measures of general distress for the bereaved, whereas the nonbereaved participants demonstrated nonsignificant change (Thompson, Gallagher-Thompson, Futterman, Gilewski, & Peterson, 1991).

With the customary BDI cutoff score of 11 for mild to severe depression (Beck, 1967; Gallagher, Breckenridge, Steinmetz, & Thompson, 1983a) as an indicator, more than 30% of the bereaved was experiencing mild depression or greater at 2 months following the loss. However, by 30 months this figure had dropped to about 18%. By contrast, little change was demonstrated in the frequency of comparison subjects meeting clinical levels of depression on the BDI, ranging from 17% at 2 months to 19% at 30 months (Futterman, Gallagher, Thompson, Lovett, & Gilewski, 1990).

In agreement with M. Stroebe and Stroebe (1983), older women reported greater distress than older men and higher frequency of meeting clinically significant levels of depression at all times of measurement regardless of bereavement status (Thompson et al., 1991). For example, 65% of respondents with BDI scores in the clinical range were women (Gallagher et al., 1983b). This was consistent with a gender-specific style of reporting depression (Nolen-Hoeksema, 1987).

Depression and grief. Although symptoms of general distress and depression diminish to "normal" levels within 30 months of loss, behaviors associated with grief (e.g., yearning for the spouse, missing the tenderness of the spouse) and distress specifically tied to the loss experience are maintained at high levels throughout this period (Thompson et al., 1991). Furthermore, levels on the TRIG were generally as high or higher than those demonstrated by younger bereaved (Faschingbauer, 1981). Thus, elders may grieve no less than their younger counterparts, and furthermore the psychological effects of bereavement may be felt longer than 30 months, at least with respect to loss-specific behaviors and grief. Gender differences present in depression and distress measures were also not found in measures of grief. Older men and women report comparable levels of grief at each time of measurement regardless of the type of loss event they experience.

Previous studies based on USC study data (e.g., Breckenridge, Gallagher, Thompson, & Peterson, 1986) suggest that bereaved elders report different depressive symptoms than older depressed patients. Whereas the patients report a wide range of depressive symptomatology on the BDI, including endorsement of self-deprecatory items, the bereaved report fewer items reflecting self-deprecation. The different courses of grief and depression following loss, and the presence of gender differences in depression but not in grief, further encourage efforts to differentiate grief from depression.

Physical health

In general, the Natural Death Survivors reported poorer physical health than the Comparison Group at 2 months following loss, even after controlling for sociodemographic and other factors known to influence health (Thompson, Breckenridge, Gallagher, & Peterson, 1984). With both gender and sociodemographic factors controlled, the odds of a new or worsened illness among the bereaved were estimated to be 1.40 times the risk for the nonbereaved. The odds of reporting a new or worsened illness were 1.43 times greater for women than for men; and there was a significant interaction between gender and reported income, indicating a greater likelihood of illness for women in lower income brackets. The odds of reporting new and/or increased medication use were 1.73 times greater for the bereaved. Gender could not account significantly for medication use, nor was there any indication of a sex by bereavement interaction. Perception of current physical health and health relative to others on single-item Likert self-ratings was significantly lower in bereaved than in controls, as was an empirically developed illness severity rating (Wyler, Masuda, & Holmes, 1968). There was no effect of gender or gender by bereavement interaction on these measures.

These results are consistent with other findings reporting health decrements following spousal loss (W. Stroebe & Stroebe, 1987). In general, older bereaved subjects reported their health to be poorer than it was prior to spousal loss, and they were at greater risk for new or worsened illnesses as well as increased medication use than comparison subjects. Visits to physicians and hospitalizations, however, were similar for both groups. The effect of gender independent of bereavement was consistent with the findings of large-scale population studies reporting poorer scores for women on indices of health irrespective of marital status (National Center for Health Statistics, 1976). Contrary to expectations based on prior studies (e.g., Berardo, 1970), self-report data did not provide evidence of greater morbidity for bereaved men than for bereaved women. However, data on mortality suggest that men are likely to underestimate their health difficulties during the early stages of bereavement.

Although the Natural Death Survivors reported worse health than the Comparison Group on virtually all measures of physical health at 2 months following the loss of a spouse, these differences were no longer apparent at 6 months following the loss, with one exception (current self-rating of health), and no differences were noted at 30 months (Futterman, Rodman, Thompson, & Gallagher, 1989). These results, together with the mental health findings described earlier, demonstrate clearly that the loss of one's spouse late in life may be followed by a period of considerable mental and physical distress. This general distress, unlike grief itself, diminishes to roughly "normal" levels by 30 months following the loss.

Subject attrition

As in any longitudinal study, differential subject attrition across groups may confound observed effects (Botwinick, 1984). Overall, 28% of the participants were dropped because of failure to be interviewed at appropriate times of measurement; 33% were from the bereaved and 22% from the nonbereaved group. (Note that if subjects who refused to complete all self-report scales at each time of measurement are included, the proportion of drops is nearly 40%.) This level of subject attrition compares favorably with the level obtained in other longitudinal studies of bereavement including both younger and older adults (e.g., Lund et al., 1989a). As expected, subjects who dropped from this study were slightly higher on self-report measures of mental and physical distress than those who continued to participate. However, there were no differences between the two groups in the effects of attrition on these measures.

Reasons for dropping were grouped into three categories: whether participants refused to continue as subjects; whether they had moved out of the catchment area and could not be located; or whether they were deceased. Refusal to continue participation was not related to group status, any sociodemographic characteristics or measures of social support. There was a suggestion that more male than female survivors dropped because they moved ($X^2 = 3.60$, $df = 1$, $p = 0.058$), whereas the comparison sample evidenced no gender effect ($X^2 = .355$, $df = 1$, $p = .551$). Thus, for dropout that was not due to mortality, these findings argue that the differential rate of change between the bereaved and comparison groups was not likely to be due solely to selective attrition.

The differential mortality rate, however, introduces an exception to this picture that deserves further attention. By the end of the first year, 12 deaths occurred among the bereaved men (12.1%) compared to only 1 male control (1.2%) and 1 female bereaved (0.8%). Half of these occurred in the first 6 months and the remaining half in the second. By the end of the 30-month period, 17 bereaved males (17.2%) had died compared to 3 male controls (3.6%) and 3 female bereaved (2.6%). Only one female control (1.3%) died within the 30-month period. While a formal survival analysis has not yet been completed, these data suggest that bereaved males are at greater risk for death than are bereaved females, particularly within the first year of bereavement ($X^2 = 11.69$, $df = 1$, $p = 0.001$). Although more males died than females in the nonbereaved group, this trend was not significant (Fisher's Exact Probability Test = .623).

Preliminary data analyses have been completed to ascertain what factors in our current data set might account for this differential mortality rate. In the first step, a sample of 17 male bereaved survivors was randomly selected, and differences between the deceased and survivors on all socio-demographic, physical, and psychosocial variables were tested using t-tests. The first survivor sample was then replaced, and the procedure was repeated with a second sample. Inspection of the pattern of results in both sets of analyses revealed that the deceased were slightly older than survivors by about three years and reported that they were in poorer health. Following this observation, a third sample of 17 survivors with age and health ratings comparable to the deceased were selected and t-tests were again obtained for differences on all demographic and psychosocial variables. Visual inspection of the pattern of the remaining variables across the three sets of data was then completed. The following criteria were used to determine which variables were significantly different: A significant difference between the survivors and deceased had to be obtained at the $p < 0.01$ level on at least two sets of analyses or at the $p < 0.05$ level on all three comparisons for the variable to be accepted as indicative of a genuine difference. Inspection of variables meeting these criteria revealed the following general picture: In addition to the age and health effects mentioned, deceased individuals had reported more often than survivors that their wife was their main confidante. They also reported less involvement in fewer socially oriented activities and had a much smaller social network. Of further interest was the observation that they generally reported positive feelings about socially oriented activities and would have been interested in increasing them. Thus, in addition to being somewhat sicker and slightly older, the decedents had more interpersonal difficulties and probably suffered loneliness to a significant degree. Although these findings suggest fairly specific interventions to assist elderly widowers during the bereavement process, they are in need of replication.

The Suicide Prevention Center (SPC) spousal bereavement project

Arguments have been made that reactions to suicidal deaths are more extreme and generally last longer than natural deaths (Cain, 1972; Demi, 1978). To our knowledge, few empirical studies involving older persons have addressed this issue. In collaboration with colleagues at the SPC in Los Angeles, we assessed a Suicide Survivor Group for comparison with the USC samples. Procedures used for recruiting subjects and collecting data were similar across both study sites. The same structured interview and self-report measures used in the USC study were employed, with some additions made that were relevant to issues surrounding a suicidal death.

Survivors of suicides of persons over the age of 55 were recruited for participation in this project (females = 88, males = 20). These made up about 35% of all potential respondents who fit the criterion for inclusion, which was comparable to the volunteer proportion in the USC sample. However, some differences in sociodemographic characteristics were noted. The suicide survivors were younger (mean age 62.4), had lower occupation levels, and included some Hispanics (7%) and blacks (5%). As was described earlier with regard to the USC study, the background variables were again used as covariates in all the comparisons to adjust for these differences.

Initial comparisons of the three groups at 2 months following spousal loss indicated that the nonbereaved Comparison Group had significantly less depression, general psychological distress, and, as expected, was experiencing lower levels of grief than both bereaved groups. Differences between the two survivor groups were not significant on any of the mental health or grief measures when sociodemographic differences were controlled (Farberow, Gallagher, Gilewski, & Thompson, 1987). A more detailed analysis of the BSI revealed that both bereaved groups were significantly higher than the nonbereaved group on the depression, anxiety, and psychoticism subscales. Overall, the hypothesis that survivors of suicide would report comparatively greater psychological distress compared to survivors of natural deaths was not supported. In fact, there were practically no significant differences between the two types of survivors within the first 8 weeks after death, after controlling for sociodemographic differences among the samples (Farberow et al., 1987).

These findings may be accounted for by the fact that within the first 2 months after death, the impact of the loss may be paramount, regardless of the way the loss occurred (cf. Parkes's description of the numbness and shock that typify early grief, 1972a/1987). Although these findings were contrary to prediction (cf. Ball, 1977), they suggest that mourning the death of a mate with whom one has spent an average of 30+ years is a highly significant and stressful event, regardless of how the loss occurred.

However, when viewing the course of bereavement over time, differences began to appear in measures of psychological distress for the two bereaved groups, both in degree and in the nature of the change experienced. After adjustments were made for sociodemographic differences in the two groups, it was evident that symptoms of depression in the Suicide Survivors persisted longer than in the Natural Death Survivors, as did other indices of psychopathology. Anxiety in particular remained significantly higher for the Suicide Survivors throughout the course of the study. Grief also showed little change during the first year for the Suicide Survivors with some improvement during the second, whereas the Natural Death Survivors showed a gradual but consistent decline on the grief measure throughout the course of the study. It is worth noting again that despite some slight improvement, the level of grief for both groups was still substantial 2.5 years following the loss. Finally, Suicide Survivors rated their overall mental health as improving much slower than the Natural Death Survivors, whose ratings eventually approximated those of the nonbereaved Comparison Groups (Farberow, Gallagher-Thompson, Gilewski, & Thompson, in press-a).

In summary, the results indicate that psychological distress experienced in bereavement by these two groups of older survivors does not differ so much in initial level, but in the course of change during the first 2.5 years following the death, general psychological distress remains at more intense levels and persists longer in the Suicide Survivor Group when compared with Natural Death Survivors. In common with the findings of Parkes (1972a/1987), Zisook and Shuchter (1986), and others, we found that both suicide survivors and natural death survivors reported high feelings of grief, depression, and generalized psychological distress immediately following a death. In the ensuing period of 2.5 years, all of these feelings subside, but not to the same level nor in the same way. Grief, for example, abated for both bereaved groups over the full period, but even so, continued to be experienced to a significant degree. This is consistent with the work of Osterweis, Solomon, and Green (1984) and Zisook and Shuchter (1986), who emphasized that bereavement is a long-term experience that does not necessarily end at a fixed point after 1, 2, or 3 years. These data also have clinical implications, as it is clear that suicide survivors have more of a variable pattern of change across time and thus may be more vulnerable to development of more severe psychopathology during the course of their adaptation.

Comparison of the three groups on measures of perceived physical health status over time has not yet been done, and so we do not know the extent to which that pattern will mirror the change in psychological distress.

Factors associated with bereavement outcome

A number of studies have been conducted to identify factors that predict or correlate with adaptation to spousal bereavement. These are discussed in detail elsewhere in this volume (see Sanders). Thus far, we have examined factors in three domains other than the mode of death that we felt might be correlated with successful bereavement outcome. These included the initial level of depression, use of general coping strategies, and extent of social supports.

To examine the first, we formed subgroups of respondents according to their initial level of depression. Depression status was determined by scores on the BDI: those scoring at 10 or below were classified as not depressed, those between 11 and 16 were classified as mildly depressed, and those scoring at 17 or greater were classified as moderately or severely depressed (Gilewski, Farberow, Gallagher, & Thompson, 1991). Individuals who were moderately to severely depressed at 2 months after the death of their spouse appeared to have higher scores on other indices of psychological distress, in particular the BSI overall severity index and its nine subscale scores, compared to bereaved individuals with mild or no depression at the outset. More importantly, their symptoms appeared to persist across time and they reported having more difficulty in adjusting to the loss. A significant interaction with mode of death was also found. Within the moderate to severe depression group, those whose spouses committed suicide were the most depressed initially of any subgroup (mean BDI = 29), had higher levels of distress on the other indices, in particular, the measures of interpersonal sensitivity, hostility, and phobic anxiety from the BSI, and showed no change in overall severity of psychopathology across time, whereas the Natural Death Survivors had slightly lower scores and showed some improvement over the 30-month period of the study. Thus, the interaction of surviving a spouse's suicide death and experiencing a clinical level of self-reported depression early on in the bereavement process may seriously complicate the subsequent course of bereavement.

The relationship between coping style and adjustment to bereavement was examined using only the USC data (similar studies including the SSG from the Suicide Prevention Center study are currently under way). While the cause–effect relationship of adaptive coping to level of psychological distress may be problematic, a number of researchers have hypothesized that adaptive coping strategies may be important mediating factors between stressful life events and successful psychological adjustment (see Billings & Moos, 1981, for an example). We explored the frequency of use and the helpfulness of 12 common cognitive, behavioral, emotional, and avoidance coping strategies used over the 2.5-year course of the bereavement period (Gallagher, Lovett, Hanley-Dunn, & Thompson, 1989). The strategies selected for consideration were logically derived from the coping literature at that time (e.g., Pearlin & Schooler, 1978). As might be expected, the use of expressing sadness declined substantially and was rated as less helpful as time passed. Second, the strategy of seeking to find a purpose in the death was more frequent earlier in the bereavement process than it was later on. Third, reflecting on past memories was used more frequently both early and late in the bereavement than it was around the anniversary of the death. Finally, respondents indicated that they found the use of self-talk significantly more helpful early on in the bereavement process than they did at 30 months. Generally consistent with the findings of Lund et al. (1986a), only minimal gender differences were observed in the reported frequency and helpfulness of use of these coping strategies. Contrary to our expectation, level of depression, as measured by BDI, was not significantly predicted by frequency of use or helpfulness of the cognitive or behavioral coping strategies at any time of measurement. We did find that intensity of grief was consistently correlated with the degree to which expression of sadness was done (and found useful) for both the men and women.

In summary, the data analyzed thus far do not reveal a relationship between less adaptive coping strategies at initial measurement and a subsequent poor adjustment, as was hypothesized. However it should be noted that since the time that the USC study was conducted (1981–1985) several reliable and valid coping indices have been published. It may be that use of a more standardized measure, such as the coping index developed by Folkman, Lazarus, and their associates, would be more informative in terms of sampling a wider array of coping strategies. Their own research has found differences based on both age and type of event being coped with when their measure was used in fairly large-scale studies of community older adults (Folkman, Lazarus, Pimley, & Novacek, 1987).

The final correlate examined in some depth is the adequacy of the social support network. The three available samples were directly compared on several indices of social support developed by the investigators and incorporated into the interviews. The Natural Death Survivors initially reported that they received significantly more emotional support than did the Suicide Survivors, but there was no difference between the two groups in the amount of practical help obtained. Furthermore, multivariate analyses of covariance with repeated measures indicated that this effect persisted across the 30-month period. Both sexes reported less satisfaction from emotional help received after the initial time of measurement, with the males reporting slightly less satisfaction than the females at every subsequent measurement point. However, the effect of gender on the reporting of emotional help received was not apparent within the Suicide Survivor Group (Farberow, Gallagher-Thompson, Gilewski, & Thompson, in press-b). In brief, it appears that there is an interaction between the mode of death and the nature of the social support network, with those who survived a natural death reporting overall a more adequate experience of social support compared to those whose spouses committed suicide. We have not yet analyzed the data in such a way that we can relate the adequacy of the social support network to the mental and physical health outcome measures.

Some unanswered questions and some suggestions for future research

Several conclusions seem apparent from our work thus far. First, adjustment to bereavement appears to be a multifactorial process, with indices of physical and mental health yielding somewhat different patterns; second, it seems that most persons who experience the loss of their spouse (whether it be from natural causes or from suicide) seem to adapt reasonably well over a 2.5-year period of time, whereas those who are more psychologically distressed at the outset have a more difficult adjustment over time, particularly if they have lost their spouse by suicide; third, most older adults are quite resilient in showing relatively good adaptation to what has been thought to be the most severe psychosocial stressor one can experience; and finally, there are fewer gender differences in adjustment than had been anticipated, with the most marked difference appearing in the mortality data in older males. Although these points are generally supported by our data, we are also reminded of the work of Wortman and Silver (1987), which reflected on how idiosyncratic the process of bereavement can be, making it very difficult to generalize about the likely course of bereavement, especially across various groups of people (e.g., suicide vs. natural death survivors). Along these lines, it seems to us that future research should be conducted to examine carefully whether or not the process of bereavement or active grieving ever ends or whether some residual effects, both psychological and physical, may be present for the remainder of the individual's life. This latter position is favored by Zisook and Shuchter (1985), who studied their bereaved group for 4 years and found that 25% of them rated their overall life adjustment at only fair or poor at that point in time. That study contained one of the longest follow-ups; yet it seems to us that follow-ups of 10 to 20 years are needed in order to answer this question more directly.

Another concern has to do with the clinical implications of our findings. Most of us are active clinicians in addition to being clinical researchers, and so have a strong interest in seeing our findings translated into the intervention arena. For example, the findings of Gilewski et al. (1991) regarding the negative impact of initial levels of clinical depression on subsequent adjustment, particularly for Suicide Survivors, suggests early intervention may be warranted. It should also be noted that in addition to high depression, Suicide Survivors were also experiencing several other distressing psychological symptoms, such as phobic anxiety and high levels of hostility. Thus it may be that a multifaceted treatment approach targeted primarily to treat the depression but also attending to these other indicators of stress would be in order. We would recommend some modifications to cognitive–behavioral therapy in order to facilitate both the reduction of depression and fuller engagement in the bereavement process (Gantz, Gallagher-Thompson, & Rodman, in press). Further, the suggestion that mortality in elderly bereaved males may somehow be linked to an impoverished social network argues strongly for intervention providing for network enrichment with older males, who are somewhat isolated very early in the bereavement process.

For others undergoing the stress of bereavement, it may be that self-help groups are extremely appropriate, although a number of authors have noted that it can be difficult to engage older individuals in widow-to-widow type programs (Lund, Redburn, Juretich, & Caserta, 1989d). It may be that providing interventions that are more prevention oriented would be a way around this resistance. For example, because a number of older adults are chronically ill and die after a period of relatively prolonged illness, it may be very feasible to offer grief counseling while they are in hospital or hospice-type settings, where the opportunity to anticipate future stress and strain would be readily available. Many older widowed men have a great deal of difficulty adapting to the emotional demands of being alone, whereas older widowed women frequently have the most problem with practical concerns such as getting their car serviced or balancing the checkbook. It may be that a prevention-oriented program that focused on teaching them some of these skills before they are actually experiencing the more severe throes of bereavement would be very appropriate and helpful in assisting the long-term adaptation process.

Another potentially viable approach would focus on enhancing both social supports and use of adaptive coping strategies to ensure later subsequent good adjustment. Psychoeducational programs that focus on these factors might be very acceptable to a wide variety of older bereaved individuals. We have found that such an approach is well received among family caregivers, for example, who frequently do not have severe mental health problems but who nevertheless are undergoing significant stress (Gallagher-Thompson, Lovett, & Rose, 1991).

Finally, we would hope that any clinical intervention programs that are designed and implemented are done so with careful attention to hypothesis testing and solid principles of empirical research, so that despite numerous methodological difficulties such as random assignment of persons to conditions, differential attrition, and the unexpected occurrence of other stressful life events and consequent treatments, the research will address the challenge of identifying the most appropriate kinds of interventions to use with both recent and long-term bereaved older adults.

16

The course of spousal bereavement in later life

DALE A. LUND, MICHAEL S. CASERTA, AND
MARGARET F. DIMOND

The overall purpose of this chapter is to provide an overview of the major findings from our research over the past 11 years on spousal bereavement among older adults in the United States. We began in 1980 with a longitudinal study funded by the National Institute on Aging (NIA) designed to describe, from a multidisciplinary perspective, the process of adjustment that follows the death of a spouse, examine factors that influence the observed outcomes, and identify potential focuses and strategies for intervention. A sample of 192 recently bereaved spouses and a control group of 104 currently married adults over the age of 50 participated in the study. Findings from this project were used to develop a second study, also funded by NIA, to examine the effectiveness of self-help groups in facilitating the bereavement adjustment process. Another sample of 339 recently bereaved spouses participated in this intervention study, with 241 assigned to self-help groups and 98 assigned to a control condition.

In the late 1970s, the National Institute on Aging recognized that little or no empirical research on bereavement had been completed that specifically focused on older adults. Although some studies had included older adults in their samples, there was no systematic attempt to learn more about their bereavement experiences until NIA established bereavement and aging as a priority for research funding. Our first study was one of three that the institute initially supported. Each project had its own unique focus, questions, and measures, but they were similar in their purpose and prospective longitudinal designs. Larry Thompson, Dolores Gallagher, and their colleagues (1989) began their study in Los Angeles in 1979; we followed in Salt Lake City in 1980; and Martin Faletti, Jeanne Gibbs, and colleagues began in Miami in 1981. Although the untimely deaths of Gibbs and Faletti limited the analysis and dissemination of their data, these three studies, and

The studies described in this chapter were funded by the National Institute on Aging (R01 AG02193 and R01 AG06244).

others that followed, have helped to fill the void in our knowledge about late life spousal bereavement. Selected findings from these three studies and six other research projects in the United States have been compiled in the book *Older Bereaved Spouses: Research with Practical Applications* (Lund, 1989a).

These studies were important because they not only provided information specific to the bereavement experiences of older adults but used improved research designs and more representative samples. For example, these studies were among the first to use prospective longitudinal designs with early assessments and nonbereaved control groups. Bereaved spouses in these studies were interviewed between four and six times over a period of 2 to 2.5 years. In the study by Faletti and his associates (1989), participants were interviewed as early as 14 days following the death. The use of nonbereaved controls allowed estimations of how much impact bereavement had on the well-being of the survivors in the absence of making the ideal pre- and postbereavement comparisons for each person. Also, the community-based sampling procedures provided for the inclusion of both men and women in the same sample and allowed for greater heterogeneity. Although each study had its own sampling limitations, collectively they covered a relatively broad cross section of bereaved elders in the United States. The Miami sample included a sizable portion of Jews (57%), the Salt Lake City sample was unique in the high percentage of Mormons (72%), and the Los Angeles sample had considerable religious and ethnic diversity.

We were particularly pleased that the Salt Lake City study was similar to and conducted concurrently with the other two projects because we were concerned about the generalizability of our findings. Although we did not find Mormons to differ from others in our study sample (Lund, Caserta, & Dimond, 1988), it is quite valuable to know that most of our findings are strikingly similar to those from Miami and Los Angeles, as well as from subsequent studies in Riverside, California (Schuster & Butler, 1989), rural Nebraska (Van Zandt, Mou, & Abbot, 1989), several midwestern cities (Gass, 1989), and Cleveland, Ohio (Kitson & Roach, 1989).

Understanding this broader context within which our research has occurred is critical to the value and usefulness of our findings. Although our samples were unique in the proportion of those who were of the Mormon religion, we have concluded that older Mormons experience spousal bereavement in much the same manner as older adults across the United States (Lund, 1989b). Their difficulties, needs, and likelihood of making successful adjustments are similar to others who are adjusting to the death of a spouse after many years of marriage. The highlights of our research findings presented here should be interpreted in the context of this broader base of recent research.

Methods

Because we summarize findings from two separate studies, it is necessary to provide a brief description of the sampling and data collection procedures for each project. The following descriptions contain only the most essential features because detailed accounts already have been published elsewhere. For example, the most complete description of the methodology used in our first longitudinal study (Lund, Caserta, & Dimond, 1989a) and the second self-help group project (Lund, Caserta, Dimond, & Shaffer, 1989c; Lund, Redburn, Juretich, & Caserta, 1989d) can be found in *Older Bereaved Spouses* (Lund, 1989a). Many of the same measures were used in both studies, so we combined the brief descriptions of them into a single section.

Longitudinal descriptive study

Recently bereaved spouses aged 50 and over were identified through the use of local newspaper obituaries in order to complete the first interview or questionnaire as early as three weeks following the spouse's death. Official mortality data obtained later from the Utah State Department of Health Statistics revealed that this procedure missed only 9% of the actual deaths for those in the same age category. No significant gender, age, or socio-economic differences were found between those who had a published obituary and those who did not.

All potential bereaved participants were randomly assigned to either a home interview group ($N = 104$) or a mailed questionnaire group ($N = 88$) in order to test for an interview effect. No major interviewer effect was observed (Caserta, Lund, & Dimond, 1985), so the two samples were combined into one sample for most of the statistical analyses. A total of 192 bereaved people participated in the study.

Nonbereaved older adults were identified through the use of public voter registry data and were selected on the basis of sex, age, and socioeconomic area of residence. In order to reduce the number of matching procedures, a matched nonbereaved person was selected only for each of the 104 bereaved respondents in the interview group. The refusal rate for this sample was 50 percent and the major reasons for refusal were busyness and lack of interest. The first two questionnaires for each of the nonbereaved partici-pants were delivered by a research assistant according to the same pro-cedures as those used for the mailed questionnaire group of bereaved participants. In both samples, the respondents completed them without the assistance of an interviewer and returned them by mail.

All of the 192 bereaved persons were asked to complete questionnaires at six times during the first 2 years of bereavement: 3 to 4 weeks, 2 months, 6 months, 1 year, 18 months, and 2 years after the death. With the exception of the demographic variables, all six questionnaires were essentially the same. The 104 nonbereaved controls completed similar questionnaires at the same six times.

The mean age for the sample of bereaved elders at the beginning of the study was 67.6 years (SD = 8.2), with a range of 50 to 93 years, and they had been married an average of 39 years. The majority were female (74%), white (97%), had graduated from high school (78%), and were Mormon (73%). The mean age of the nonbereaved participants was 66.3 years (SD = 7.8), with a range of 50 to 88 years, and they had been married an average of 38 years. The majority were female (73%), white (98%), had graduated from high school (77%), and were Mormon (70%).

Self-help group study

This study was designed to investigate the effectiveness of self-help groups in facilitating bereavement adjustments and more specifically the roles of group leadership and duration by comparing self-help groups led by widows versus professionals and short- versus long-term formats. All groups met weekly for 2 months, but the long-term groups continued to meet once a month for an additional 10 months. Because we are still in the process of analyzing the data regarding the effects of the intervention, we summarize in this chapter the findings about predictors of adjustment.

Recently bereaved spouses over the age of 50 were identified through newspaper obituaries and were randomly assigned into one of the four intervention condition groups or the control group. Questionnaires were hand-delivered 2 months after the death event to those who agreed to participate. Three hundred and thirty-nine (241 assigned to intervention condition groups and 98 to the control group) returned the first question-naires. The second measures were obtained immediately after the com-pletion of the eight weekly self-help meetings (roughly 4–8 months' bereaved) and the third questionnaires followed the completion of the long-term groups (roughly 14–17 months' bereaved). The fourth and final questionnaire was obtained at 2 years following the death. The control group also was assessed at the same four time periods but received no intervention.

The sample consisted of 242 women (71.4%) and 97 men who ranged in age from 50 to 89 years (M = 67.5, SD = 8.5), were fairly well educated (85% high school graduates), were primarily Caucasian (98.8%), and were generally not employed outside the home (76.3%).

Measurement instruments used in the two studies

In addition to the typical sociodemographic characteristics of age, gender, education, number of years married, employment status, religious membership, race, and income, we included several already existing standardized scales, several inventories and single-item indicators that we developed specifically for the studies, and open-ended questions to generate qualitative data about bereavement adjustments. Again, we only present a brief review of these instruments because more detailed descriptions are available elsewhere.

The major measures that we refer to as the indicators of bereavement adjustments, outcomes, and well-being included a standarized scale of life satisfaction (Neugarten, Havighurst, & Tobin, 1961), two depression scales (Yesavage et al., 1983; Zung, 1965), and the Revised Texas Inventory of Grief (Faschingbauer, 1981). Also, we developed an inventory of bereavement – related feelings and behaviors with subscales measuring emotional shock, helplessness/avoidance, psychological strength, anger/guilt/confusion, and grief resolution behaviors (Caserta et al., 1985) – and used several single-item measures of health, coping, stress, and loneliness (Caserta, Lund, & Dimond, 1990; Johnson, Lund, & Dimond, 1986). Numerous open-ended questions were asked concerning their greatest difficulties, advice to others, prospects about remarriage, experiences with support networks, health functioning, and social activities.

Some measures were used as both predictor and outcome variables, depending on the research questions and appropriate analyses. The following measures, however, primarily served as predictor variables. These included the Twenty Statements Test, which assesses various dimensions of a person's self-concept (Kuhn & McPartland, 1954; Spitzer, Couch, & Stratton, 1971); Rosenberg's self-esteem scale (1965); a single-item rating of self-esteem (Johnson et al., 1986); a scale of social support that we developed to assess both structural and qualitative dimensions (Dimond, Lund, & Caserta, 1987; Lund, Caserta, Van Pelt, & Gass, 1990); a detailed skill survey of 94 tasks of daily living; and a competencies scale we adapted to assess social, instrumental, and resource identification skills (Lund et al., 1989c).

Results

Highlights of our findings from these two research projects, with an emphasis on the first longitudinal study, are presented in two parts. First are the findings that describe what we believe are the most essential features about the course of spousal bereavement over time. This information helps to describe the process of adjustment. Second is a summary of what we have learned about the factors that influence the course of adjustment. We learned that some variables were far more important than we expected in predicting bereavement outcomes, and conversely, some factors were less influential than anticipated. Also, we believe that it is as important to know what was not significant as it is to know what was significant. This is particularly important when we expect a particular finding and learn that the data do not support the expectation.

Descriptive findings

First, our data indicate that there was considerable diversity in the adjustment process both among and within bereaved spouses. Nearly every outcome measure that we used revealed a broad range of responses at each time period among the research participants. Some individuals appeared to manage the stressful situation very well even experiencing personal growth and learning new skills (Lund et al., 1989c). Others, however, were quite devastated by their loss and had great difficulty managing their personal lives for several years (Lund et al., 1985). Some described themselves as being socially active, independent, helpful to others, involved with hobbies, and motivated to make the best of a very difficult situation, whereas others reported being despondent, angry, miserable, and sick of living (Lund, Caserta, Dimond, & Gray, 1986b).

This diversity in bereavement reactions also was found within the individual. It was common to find a person simultaneously experiencing a full range of feelings and behaviors. For example, it was not unusual for the bereaved to feel angry, guilty, and lonely, yet at the same time feel personal strength and pride in how he or she was coping (Lund, Caserta, & Dimond, 1986a). A 70-year-old woman described herself at length as being busy, enjoying many different activities, and doing things with other people, but her final self-descriptive comment was that she still feels lonely.

Second, our findings are clear in identifying loneliness as the single greatest difficulty for older bereaved spouses (Lund, 1989b). Although other researchers have reported on the problem of loneliness (Barrett & Schneweis, 1980; Lopata, 1973a; Parkes, 1972a/1987; Carey, 1979), we learned that in the opinions of the bereaved spouses, it was the most common difficulty and it persisted through the first 2 years of adjustment. Unfortunately, loneliness can be very painful and difficult to resolve. Loneliness cannot be managed simply by surrounding oneself with others, as indicated by the statement of a 69-year-old woman who said, "I am lonely but not alone."

In addition to the pervasive problem of loneliness is the lack of skill among older bereaved spouses to deal effectively with a relatively unique set of problems of daily living. Older men were found to be deficient in a predictable set of skills, including cooking, shopping, and housecleaning, and older women lacked skills in doing home repairs and managing legal affairs and financial records (Lund et al., 1986a). These deficiencies were sources of difficulty because the tasks were performed primarily by the deceased spouses. Nearly 73% indicated that these deficiencies had made their coping more difficult. Similarly, those who had learned some of these new skills during bereavement reported feeling better about themselves, more independent, and better able to get along with others, and over 30% said that they benefited directly by being better able to deal with their grief (Lund et al., 1989c).

Other common problems of bereavement included difficulties with depression (Lund et al., 1986a), family relationships and friendships (Lund et al., 1990), emotions of grief (Lund et al., 1985), physical health (Caserta et al., 1990), personal identity (Lund et al., 1986b), and living according to one's own expectations versus those of others. Although we have not yet reported on the numerous examples of older bereaved spouses who struggled with living their lives according to the expectations of others, this is a problem of considerable importance. This problem usually manifests itself during decision-making times wherein the bereaved spouse must choose between what they want to do and what they believe others would want them to do, or even what they imagine their deceased spouse would expect. We found this dilemma in a variety of situations, including decisions about forming new relationships, dating, sexual practices, traveling, making major purchases, selling homes and personal belongings, and establishing new patterns of social activities. We discovered that some bereaved spouses agonized over the decision to keep or give away a pet that they had never liked. They felt anxious and guilty for wanting to get rid of a dog or cat that was so important to their deceased spouse. They were troubled over what others might think about them, and in some instances this meant that their deceased spouse would be so upset that they decided to keep the pet (Lund, Johnson, Baraki, & Dimond, 1984). Without adding more detail, we believe that it is essential to report that, for many, there is great difficulty in making bereavement adjustments while trying to live according to the expectations of others, including the expectations of the deceased.

A third general conclusion about the bereavement process of older spouses is the high degree of resiliency, resourcefulness, and adaptability that they exhibited. Although 72% of our research participants reported the death of their spouses to be the most stressful event they had ever experienced, and the self-reported levels of stress were quite high for the entire sample, we found that there were numerous indicators of personal strength, social support, and resourcefulness that helped them cope quite well with the many difficulties they faced. We estimated that 18% of our sample was having major difficulties 2 years after the death (Lund et al., 1985). The positive aspect of this finding is that about 82% of the bereaved spouses were managing with a good degree of success. Life satisfaction, perceived health, self-esteem, and social support remained relatively high (Lund et al., 1989a; Lund et al., 1985; Lund et al., 1990). Also, our findings that Wortman and Silver (1989) used in their publication on the myths of coping with loss were consistent with data from other studies in confirming that resiliency and even immunity are more common patterns of adjustment than previously reported. In other words, many bereaved persons were resourceful enough to find effective ways of managing their grief and making satisfying adjustments. Further documenting this personal resourcefulness were the findings that only 12% of the participants in our second study reported seeking professional help for bereavement difficulties (Caserta & Lund, 1992) and about 72% had learned new skills during the first 2 years of bereavement (Lund et al., 1989c). Although bereavement after many years of marriage is a highly stressful situation, we also need to acknowledge the considerable capability of older adults in meeting many of the demands of a markedly changed life-style.

Fourth, because we could not find support for stages of bereavement adjustment, we believe it is more accurate to describe the process like a roller coaster of many ups and downs with gradual improvement over time. We were unable to identify specific times, events, or markers that would parallel stages of adjustment (Lund et al., 1986a). In support of the notion of gradual improvement, our data consistently revealed that the early months following the loss were the most difficult (Lund et al., 1989a, 1989b) and that these early indicators were relatively good predictors of longer term adjustment (Lund et al., 1985; Johnson, Lund, & Dimond, 1986). In both our studies most of the outcome measures showed gradual improvement over the 2-year period. An additional brief telephone survey at 4 to 5 years after the death confirmed that the bereaved spouses in our first study were still improving in terms of their self-reports of stress, coping, and health (Burks, Lund, Gregg, & Bluhm, 1988).

With 2- to 6-month intervals between interviews it was difficult to observe the many ups and downs of the bereavement process, particularly with the use of standardized quantitative scales. Fortunately, we included questions that allowed the respondents opportunities to describe in their own words their feelings, difficulties, successes, and advice to others. Transcripts from these parts of the interviews revealed the transitory nature of the process. Typical is a comment by a 70-year-old male who said, "It comes on gradual and reaches a peak until you break down and cry. You get a little better for awhile and it goes up again." Similarly, a 68-year-old woman replied, "These periods of grief come and go. It might strike at any time and it might leave at any time. But they come and go." The ups and downs of the roller coaster can easily be precipitated by mistakenly seeing the face of the deceased in a crowd, hearing an old familiar song on the radio, driving by the hospital where the spouse was treated, or conversely, feeling proud for successfully balancing a checkbook for the first time, meeting a new friend at a club, or simply mastering the use of a microwave oven.

The roller-coaster metaphor is far from ideal to describe the complexities of the bereavement process, but it does help to emphasize both the ups and downs and gradual improvement that we have found in our research. For some, the ride may never end, but they learn to "live with it" or "adjust to it." Others are more active in meeting the challenges and find ways to manage the ups and downs of the process. The next set of findings examines the factors that influence the degree of success in managing the unfavorable consequences and producing more favorable outcomes.

Findings about the predictors of bereavement adjustments

Two of our findings that describe features about the process of bereavement are particularly relevant to conducting research on the predictors of adjustment. Because of the many relatively spontaneous ups and downs during the course of bereavement, it is imperative to use longitudinal designs. Using repeated measures over time enables more accurate assessments, consideration of the transitory nature of bereavement, and specification of cause-and-effect relationships. Also, because of the great diversity in how bereavement can affect each individual and the variability among different people, it is critical that investigators include multiple indicators of adjustment. Using only one or two mesures will not reflect the complexity or multidimensional effects of bereavement.

As we described in the Methods section of this chapter, we used an array of quantitative and qualitative indicators of physical, emotional, psychological, and social well-being. Although some of our findings about predictors of adjustment were specific to only certain indicators, the following summary avoids some of the lesser details in order to highlight the more important and practical findings. For those who wish to examine more closely some of the specifics, we have included citations for further reading.

Our research findings could be characterized as much by what we have found not to be important as what we found to be predictive of bereavement adjustments. In other words, we have been surprised by the lack of significant effects for some variables we expected to influence the course of adjustment. We have, therefore, organized this section of findings into three parts. First is a summary of the factors we found to be relatively unimportant as predictors of adjustment, followed by variables that were moderately influential, and then we review and discuss the five best predictors.

Relatively unimportant predictors. We begin with a cautious reminder that although the factors presented in this category were found to have little or no direct influence on the course of bereavement adjustments, we do not recommend that they be dismissed from future consideration for research or practice. Our samples included only bereaved spouses and those age 50 years and over. We suspect that in other bereavement contexts they might be more influential than what we found.

In this category of nonpredictive variables were nearly all of the socio-demographic characteristics, including age, gender, education, income, religious membership and religiosity, and other factors such as perceived health status, marital happiness, and pet ownership. Because our samples were relatively homogeneous in terms of race and ethnicity, we are unable to address the degree of influence they might have on the course of bereavement.

Participants in our studies ranged in age from 50 to 93 years. Although we found those over the age of 75 years to be at the greatest risk for experiencing declines in the size and perceived closeness of their social support networks (Lund et al., 1990), age did not predict any of the major indicators of adjustment (Lund et al., 1986a; Dimond et al., 1987). Surprisingly, years of education, income, and income adequacy did not exert a clear influence on bereavement. The only exception was that women in the higher income categories showed slightly better early adjustments (Caserta, Lund, & Dimond, 1989). The number of years of formal education may not be the best way to measure the broad range of potential benefits from education because it ignores the specifics of curriculum, effort, performance, and other issues of quality and practicality. The measures of income and income adequacy are similarly limited because they do not account for how they were used and whether or not they were shared with others.

We carefully examined the influence of both gender and several aspects of religion and concluded that they were not very predictive of our global indicators of adjustment. With respect to gender, we learned that older males and females differed in their lack of specific skills of daily living, but they were similar in their emotional, psychological, social, and health adjustments (Lund et al., 1986a). Also, contrary to our expectations, males were as likely as females to participate in both of our studies – even the second project, which required participation in self-help group meetings (Lund et al., 1989b; Lund et al., 1989d).

Our focus on religion was necessitated by the high proportion of Mormons who lived in our study area. Our samples included about 70% to

73% who were Mormon. Without elaborating on all of the unique features of Mormonism, it was possible that their large family size, emphasis on family life (Ericksen, 1975), and belief in an afterlife (Backman, 1970) could affect the course of bereavement. As expected, the Mormons in our samples were found to have more people in their support networks and more frequent contact with them, were more active in their religion, and more religious (Lund et al., 1988). These features, however, did not result in any major differences in the well-being of the study participants during the 2 years of bereavement. Religious activity did have a positive association with more favorable outcomes, but there was evidence in other analyses that led us to conclude that it was not necessarily the religious nature of the activity but the fact that social activity in general has a positive influence on bereavement adjustments.

The remaining three variables that we found not to be predictive of adjustment were pet ownership, marital happiness, and health status. We included pet ownership as a study variable after learning about a variety of benefits from animal–human interactions (Fogle, 1981). Because some pets were actually owned more by the deceased spouse rather than the surviving spouse and pets require care during periods of time when the bereaved were already occupied by legal, emotional, and social demands on their time, pets were not very helpful during the first year of bereavement (Lund et al., 1984).

Also unexpected was the finding that the degree of reported marital happiness with the deceased was unrelated to the course of adjustment. One could argue that the loss of a happy marital relationship would be a greater loss than an unhappy relationship or, conversely, that a long happy relationship would provide a valuable set of memories that could sustain one during the difficult times of bereavement. The complexities of the marital relationship merit closer examination in future studies, but our analyses revealed that the degree of happiness in the marriage did not affect the course of bereavement. Some bereaved respondents reported that they missed the arguments with their deceased spouses even though they rated their marriages as being unhappy.

We examined self-reported health status as both an independent and dependent variable and found considerable stability in the measure over time (Lund et al., 1989a) and that it did not have much effect on overall coping and adjustment during bereavement (Lund et al., 1985). We should caution, however, that the bereavement context influences the factors that older adults take into account in making their perceived health ratings and that these self-reports should be understood within the specific context.

Moderately important predictors. All three of the factors we found to be moderately related to the well-being of the older adults during bereavement underscore the importance of social relationships with others. Positive associations revealed advantages to those who remarried, had supportive relationships with others, and were active in their religious participation. Self-reports of religious activity remained quite stable through the first 2 years of bereavement for both Mormons and non-Mormons (Lund et al., 1988). Although the statistical associations of religious activity on grief resolution behaviors were modest, we found additional support for the benefits of keeping busy during bereavement when we analyzed more of the qualitative data through content analyses. Many of the respondents recommended keeping busy and socially active when asked what specific advice they would give to others in similar circumstances. Those who gave this advice showed greater gains in their perceived coping ability (Caserta, Van Pelt, & Lund, 1989).

Only 10% of the respondents in our first study had remarried within 4 to 5 years after the death of their spouses (80% men). We concluded that those who eventually remarried were more positive in the early interviews about their consideration of remarriage and likely viewed remarriage as a way to help them adjust to the loss and maintain their well-being (Burks et al., 1988). We would certainly not suggest remarriage as a coping strategy for those who express considerable reluctance or opposition, but we did find the remarried persons to have greater reduction in their stress levels and greater improvement in the measures of life satisfaction and resolution of grief.

We expected features of the social support networks to be among the strongest predictors of adjustment and were surprised to learn that only a few characteristics had a moderate impact. Generally, social supports were quite positive and stable over time, with slight increases in the reliance on friends as opposed to relatives and decreases in the ease of contacting persons in the support network (Lund et al., 1990). When we closely examined the role of social support on bereavement outcomes, we found that stable support was a buffer of stress 2 years later (Duran, Turner, & Lund, 1989). More important, however, were the qualitative aspects of a support network (e.g., perceived closeness, self-expression, contact, shared confidence, and mutual helping) in leading to lower depression and more positive ratings of coping, health, and life satisfaction (Dimond et al., 1987).

These findings about the benefits of social support networks need to be tempered with numerous qualitative examples about negative effects of support persons. Our interviewers heard detailed accounts of disappointment, frustration, anger, and sadness expressed by the bereaved because some friends and family members were judgmental, avoidant, inconsiderate, pushy, and demanding. A common complaint of the bereaved was that they wished they could tell others what they had expressed to the interviewers.

We concluded that there is considerable room for improvement in the way support persons can be of help to the bereaved.

The best predictors. Contrary to the moderate predictors of bereavement adjustment primarily consisting of factors related to social relationships and support received from others, the strongest predictors were personal resources unique to each person. Experiencing the death of a spouse in later life requires a wide range of adjustments to meet the demands of a radically different social environment and lifestyle. We have seen repeated evidence that supports the need for bereaved adults to take charge of their life-styles and situations if they are to preserve and sometimes enhance their well-being. Taking control requires motivation, pride, skill, flexibility, some help from others, and the passage of time. The five best predictors of spousal bereavement that have emerged from our studies emphasize these requirements.

First, as we discussed earlier, a common pattern of adjustment is one with many spontaneous ups and downs but with subtle and gradual improvement. When we entered *amount of time* since the death event as a variable in a variety of statistical procedures, it was consistently one of the most influential factors. With only few exceptions, the bereaved spouses had more positive well-being scores at each subsequent data collection period. This gradual improvement was evident in both of our studies (Lund et al., 1986a, 1989a, 1989b). We do not believe that simply the passage of time by itself brings about successful adjustments. Time is important because the many difficulties require time to emerge, be identified, develop strategies, and achieve some degree of successful adjustment or resolution. A passive strategy of waiting for time to heal a wound will not lead to satisfactory bereavement adjustments.

Second, also related to time, is the finding that *initial or early bereavement adjustments* were good predictors of longer term well-being. Early success or extreme difficulty appears to set the direction for future growth and development or an unhappy and dissatisfying life-style. In one of our most important publications we reported that difficulties in the first month of bereavement as evidenced by intense negative emotions (e.g., desire to die, frequent crying) were associated with poor coping after 2 years (Lund et al., 1985). These findings and others from our research document the possibility and value of identifying early in the course of bereavement those who are most likely to have long-term difficulties and need greater assistance from others. Our limited resources should be appropriately targeted to those who are at greatest risk and implemented early.

In simple terms, good use of time and getting off to a good start will lead to more satisfying adjustments, but more is required to ensure positive well-being. Another good predictor of adjustment was a variable that deals with both a personal trait and the existence of a relationship with another person(s). Bereaved individuals who were *communicative with others* about their thoughts and feelings were more likely to have positive adjustments later (Lund et al., 1985). Again, self-expression that occurs early in the process was most advantageous. The willingness and ability to express oneself about very sensitive, emotional, and personal issues is not equally shared. Also, not all bereaved persons have available to them a confidant who will actually listen to these expressions.

The final two predictors had the strongest impact on the course of adjustment and affected nearly every aspect of well-being that we measured. *Positive self-esteem* and *personal competencies* in managing the tasks of daily life resulted in the most favorable long-term bereavement outcomes (Lund et al., 1989c; Lund, 1989b). We believe that those who had high regard for themselves were more likely to be dissatisfied with not coping well, feel that they deserve better, be motivated and skilled to take control of the situation, and persist until they have more favorable outcomes. Conversely, those who had little regard for themselves were more likely to believe that they deserved feeling depressed and being overwhelmed by their grief. With low self-esteem there is little motivation, confidence, and skill to change the circumstances. During the course of the interviews in our research projects, many of the bereaved made statements about the need "to find your own way through the mess," and that "others cannot do it for you." These statements, although somewhat simplistic, are meaningful because they call attention to the importance of not being passive but taking charge and doing something active about the situation. Self-esteem provides part of the foundation by motivating action necessary for more successful and satisfying adjustments.

Positive self-esteem coupled with the ability to use one's personal resources and skills can help bring about successful adjustments to the demands of the new environment. Particularly for those who have been married for many years and were socialized into accepting very narrow gender roles, spousal bereavement clearly revealed the lack of specific skills. As we reported earlier, the lack of skills in managing one's daily life further complicates the bereavement process. We discovered that being competent in social, interpersonal, instrumental, and resource identification skills lead to more favorable bereavement adjustments (Lund et al., 1989c).

Competencies and self-esteem are also interrelated and have mutually complementary effects. We found those who had high levels of competency had similar high levels of self-esteem and, conversely, those with low self-esteem had low levels of competency. In terms of the course of bereavement we suggest that one of the best ways to enhance self-esteem is to learn new skills. Fifty-eight percent of our respondents reported feeling better about themselves as a result of learning new skills (Lund et al., 1989c). With improved self-images the bereaved were often further motivated to work at making other adjustments. We highly recommend that the reciprocal relationship between self-esteem and personal competencies be acknowledged and integrated into intervention efforts.

After 11 years of research, perhaps our most important findings are those regarding the critical roles of internal coping resources, self-esteem and competencies, in making successful adjustments to the death of a spouse in later life. Future research is needed to delineate more clearly the cause-and-effect relationships among these internal coping resources and bereavement outcomes. We highly recommend intervention studies with longitudinal designs because they offer the most appropriate tests of these relationships.

17

Risk factors in bereavement outcome

CATHERINE M. SANDERS

It has been estimated that a third of all major bereavements result in problems where professional help may be required (Raphael, 1983). For example, conjugal bereavement, when there is intense loneliness, appears to increase health risk, often resulting in the death of the surviving spouse (M. Stroebe & Stroebe, this volume; Maddison & Viola, 1968; Parkes & Brown, 1972). Similarly, the death of a child is associated with high morbidity in surviving parents (Fish, 1986; Rando, 1983; Sanders, 1986). Other factors, such as sudden death, lack of perceived support, or reduced material resources, have also been implicated as associated with high health risk. This chapter focuses on high-risk factors for poor outcome of bereavement, separating them into four general categories: biographical/ demographic factors, individual factors, type and mode of death, and cir cumstances following the loss. It pays particular attention to the interaction and overlapping of these factors, which can cause greatly increased health risk.

It must be noted from the outset that a variety of methodological concerns cloud the interpretation of available data on bereavement research. For example, generalizability must be questioned when samples are composed of women primarily. Too, because of the private nature of grief in our culture and the inaccessibility of subjects, only those individuals who "volunteer" to participate can be included. This bias in subject selection introduces the possibility that a significant section of the population might evidence differing forms of grief than the ones described in the current literature. Studies have not always included a nonbereaved, matched control group of the same age to rule out nonbereavement-related explanations for changes in health or psychological status (which become more prevalent with increasing age). Finally, there are few reliable measures or criteria for assessing and classifying either symptoms or outcomes of bereavement. For the most part, researchers use different methodology, different time frames, and different measures (see Hansson, Carpenter, & Fairchild, this volume). The reader should understand, therefore, that this review attempts to present the knowledge available from research studies of varying validity and, where appropriate, also to reflect the consensus of clinical observation.

Biographical/demographic factors

Age

Age differences have been studied primarily within the context of conjugal bereavement. It might be expected that, in general, the older one is at the time of loss, the more serious the health consequences. This, however, is not necessarily the case. Ball (1977), in comparing three groups of widows – young, middle-aged, and old-age – found the youngest group to be more symptomatic than either of the other two. For the younger widows, the sudden death of a husband, with no warning, produced an additional negative effect on bereavement outcome.

In a study by Sanders (1981), it was shown that, initially, younger spouses had higher intensities of grief, yet 2 years later there was a significant improvement. Being younger, they could look ahead to a better future with new feelings of hope. Older widows showed the opposite reaction. Initially, there was a lowered intensity of grief, but after 2 years, a great deal of anxiety as well as loneliness was displayed. Feelings of helplessness were expressed. Health was more tenuous. The future did not look so bright as it did for younger widows. The results of this study suggest that being older does not contribute directly to grief symptoms, per se, but rather to the constellation of debilitating variables that commonly plague the elderly.

Gender: Widows vs. widowers

There is a lack of agreement regarding the effects of gender on bereavement outcome. Some researchers have concluded that widows suffer more health consequences than do widowers (Carey, 1979; Lopata, 1973a). On the other hand, considerably more writers find that widowers sustain greater problems (Helsing, Szklo, & Comstock, 1981; M. Stroebe & Stroebe, 1983; Siegel & Kuykendall, 1990). Still other investigators have noted no significant differences (Clayton, 1974; Heyman & Gianturco, 1973). These comparisons included such outcome measures as mortality, physical symptoms, and depression and other emotional sequelae, as well as positive events such as remarriage.

Examining the health aspects, Parkes and Brown (1972) found that men complained of fewer symptoms than did women in *both* the bereaved and control groups. These differences were so large that, in several cases, the control women indicated nearly as many symptoms as the bereaved men. A likely explanation is that men and women report symptoms differently. Men typically report fewer symptoms and less affective distress, compared to women, making widows appear more severely distressed than widowers. Too, men appear less prone to developing "neurotic" symptoms during a bereavement and consequently suffer less overt psychological symptoms than do women. However, although widows had higher depression scores than widowers 1 year after bereavement, on follow-up, 2 to 4 years later, the widows were no more depressed than married women of the same age; yet widowers remained significantly more depressed than married men. Parkes and Brown suggest this depressed state may reflect what Cumming and Henry (1961) described as "disengagement," in that widowers often showed signs of withdrawing from others and feeling more remote and apart from friends.

Another explanation for widowers doing less well than widows involves sex differences in social support. Men are more likely to depend on their spouse for emotional support, nurturance, and entrée to social interaction. When these resources are no longer available, widowers may have little practice or inclination to develop these new skills, and may simply bury themselves in work or isolation. Women, on the other hand, are more likely to cope by searching for social support, which in turn facilitates the bereavement process (W. Stroebe & Stroebe, 1987). Siegel and Kuykendall (1990) support this conclusion, but also show that widowed men who were active in their church or temple were less depressed than those without these social/religious connections. Their data show that "the connection with the church/temple served a stress-reducing function for men." They conclude that outreach programs for elderly men could initiate healthy interventions that may reduce health risks. Yet this is not always feasible. Stroebe, Hansson, and Stroebe (chapter 29, this volume) point out the greatest difficulty, noting that, ironically, the group for whom intervention is most needed displays the greatest propensity to withdraw and cope alone.

Parental bereavement: Mothers vs. fathers

Mothers appear to grieve more deeply than do fathers, and this could be attributed to the bonding of mothers to their infants early in life (Fish, 1986). However, Fish also noted that when a child died at an older age, mothers still reported higher grief responses than did fathers, so apparently the bonding is deeply ingrained. Isolation may also become a contributing factor to this outcome following the death of a child. Mothers feel more isolated than do fathers, primarily because work outside the home envelops fathers and keeps them occupied through a greater part of the day, thus offering them a respite from their sorrow. As newer studies are done with working mothers matching working fathers in numbers, this difference may equal out.

Reduced material resources

Economic difficulties often plague the bereaved, complicating their already painful existence. Because the majority of widows are aged, their economic circumstances are usually below average. The financial plight of widow-hood led Harvey and Bahr (1974) to state that "the negative impact sometimes attributed to widowhood derives not from widowhood status, but rather from socioeconomic status" (p. 106). They concluded that lowered morale and decreased affiliation are more directly correlated with change in income than change in marital status. In a Canadian study (Sheldon et al., 1981), it was found that low socioeconomic status contributed to poor adjustment and negatively influenced health among widows. These observations were supported by Atchley (1975) in a working-class group of older widows, where inadequate income led to reduced social participation, and consequently, "to greater loneliness and anxiety."

Marris (1958), in studying London widows, described the deprivation encountered by these women as they endeavored to maintain households, care for dependent children, and hold outside jobs, many working for the first time. Similar findings by Glick, Weiss, and Parkes (1974) led them to conclude that poor adjustment following bereavement is a consequence of an insecure economic position. Sanders (1980) found that low income did not contribute directly to poor bereavement outcome but, instead, was a preexisting factor that would contribute negatively to any stressful situation. This hypothesis was supported in a study by Morgan (1976), who statistically partialled out the effects of income and found that lowered morale was not attributable to bereavement in and of itself but was related primarily to the deprivation caused by lack of income. In a similar study (Jacobs, Hansen, Berkman, Kasl, & Ostfeld, 1989), examining depression following spousal bereavement, it was reported that unemployment was a major determining risk for depression. Thus, positive adjustment to bereavement is likely to be strongly associated with the firm financial situation of the widowed person.

Individual factors

Personality

Personality factors do contribute to the manner in which an individual reacts to stress. Yet the impact of personality characteristics of the bereaved on health risk has been largely neglected as studies instead have focused on demographic data and symptom assessment. For the most part, researchers conducting longitudinal studies have focused on the grief reactions producing poor outcome rather than examining premorbid personality characteristics for poor coping styles. Parkes (1985) identified the "grief-prone personality" as one involving excessive grief and depression, intense clinging behavior, or inordinate pining for the deceased. Individuals who are insecure, anxious, or fearful have also been identified as those being at high risk following a major bereavement (Parkes & Weiss 1983).

Vachon and her group (1982a), approaching from a different perspective, examined positive personality variables that might facilitate grief resolution. Using the General Health Questionnaire (GHQ) (Goldberg, 1972), they identified individuals who showed low distress after a bereavement and ones who indicated high distress; they were then followed for a period of 2 years. By pairing the GHQ scores with the 16 Personality Factor Questionnaire (16 PFQ) (Cattell, Eber, & Tatsuoka, 1970), they noted personality styles of those individuals who coped well and those who did not. Of 72 widows, the 23 (32%) in the "low-distress" group scored as emotionally stable, mature, conscientious, conservative, and socially precise. The 14 persons (19%) in the "high-distress" group described themselves as apprehensive, worried, and highly anxious, indicative of low emotional stability. The authors cautioned that the causal relationship is unclear: Were these individuals isolated because they were ordinarily unable to maintain relationships, or because the grief situation had caused their isolation? As M. Stroebe and Stroebe (1983) point out, GHQ scores may typically correlate highly with the 16 PFQ, suggesting a personality main effect rather than a specific reaction to bereavement.

W. Stroebe and Stroebe (1987; chapter 14, this volume) related health outcomes to two personality variables, emotional stability and locus of control, measured by the Eysenck Personality Inventory (Eggert, 1983) and the Interpersonal Control Scale (Levenson, 1973). The authors reasoned that emotionally stable persons would be better able to cope with the stress of bereavement and that people who believe they have little control would react to loss in a depressed manner. A bereaved group and a matched control group of married persons were given the same measures. Results showed that individuals high on neuroticism were more depressed than those low on neuroticism and that this effect was stronger for the widowed than the married. Thus, consistent with predictions, the widowed who were less emotionally stable appeared to have greater difficulties in adjusting to their loss. Although the comparable effect was not significant for internal control beliefs, there was a significant interaction between expectedness of loss and internal control beliefs: Individuals with low internal control beliefs reacted with greater depression to a sudden loss than did individuals with high internal control beliefs. This difference may have been due to a differential effort in regaining control following the shattering experience of sudden loss.

In a longitudinal study using the Grief Experience Inventory (Sanders, Mauger, & Strong, 1991) to assess grief reactions and the MMPI to examine personality characteristics, Sanders (1980) studied the effects of personality on bereavement outcome soon after the deaths and again 18 months to 2 years later when grief intensities had subsided. Matched controls also completed the inventories in order that relationships between bereavement and various types of personality coping patterns could be identified.

Four types of reaction to bereavement emerged from this study: a "disturbed" group, a "depressed" high-grief group, a "denial" group, and a "normal grief-contained" group. Individuals in the disturbed group reported feelings of inadequacy, inferiority, and insecurity, which seemed of a chronic nature. These individuals had few defenses, and when they suffered a severe loss, the result was long-lasting desolation.

The depressed group complained of depression and tension, as well as inordinate sensitivity. They almost always had a history of multiple family losses, so they were dealing not only with the present loss but with former losses as well. Because their anxiety was a trait phenomenon, when inordinate stress occurred, the depressed group was subject to intense emotionality. Two years later, although grief symptoms had abated, they still felt deeply saddened and remained withdrawn from others.

The denial group showed a psychological state nearly opposite to depression: compulsive optimism. They employed strong defense mechanisms in order to deal with crises, often using physical symptoms as a means of solving conflicts or avoiding responsibilities. However, this characteristic was so ingrained that they were not aware such a defense was being used. At follow-up, their emotional reactions were still suppressed. However, there were more psychosomatic symptoms evidenced than either of the other two groups.

M. Stroebe and Stroebe (1991) reported a similar pattern. When bereaved spouses were followed through their first two years of bereavement, they found that widowers who seek distraction from grief work or who control their emotions closely do not make as good an adjustment as widowers who were less controlled. Yet suppression of emotions has been shown to offer relief when confronting becomes too painful (Epstein, 1967; Horowitz, 1983). Furthermore, M. Stroebe and Stroebe (1991) found that for widows grief work was unrelated to adjustment to bereavement. Because of the many confounding and overlapping variables in this area, much careful research will be required in order to understand the effects of personality alone.

The findings of these studies suggest that there is no one intervention strategy that meets the needs of all bereaved people, pointing to the need for interveners to take accurate and complete histories when dealing with bereaved people. On the basis of past coping behavior, one can begin to see how the present stress situation will most likely be dealt with. If non-functional defenses are typically used, the caregiver can begin to work to modify those responses toward more adaptive ones.

Ambivalence

It is easy to understand how ambivalence, when present in a relationship before death, would cause problems for the bereaved after the death. There would be unfinished business to complete, as well as anger and self-reproach with which to deal. Fenichel (1945) believes that the greater the love–hate relationship and the greater the self-reproach, the greater the grief. Freud (1917b) felt that if there were ambivalent feelings, grief resulted in a pathological form that he called "obsessive reproaches," a constant form of self-denigration caused by the conflict of ambivalence. In cases where the relationship was one of passive/aggressive acting out, the bereaved may be trapped in an intrapunitive form of grief indefinitely. Parkes and Weiss (1983) noted that those who reported lower levels of conflict with their spouses had less anxiety, depression, guilt, and yearning for the dead spouse.

Dependency

Parkes and Weiss (1983) found that dependent widows and widowers needed to cling to the lost relationship in order to maintain their accustomed role of helplessness and inability to cope. Consequently, dependency was strengthened as their way of life.

Dependency needs are so closely correlated with safety needs that individuals who lose the one on whom they depend are vulnerable to excessive anxiety and worry simply because they are deprived of the strong, reliable support they once had. Parkes describes "clinging," dependent relationships as those leading to excessive yearning and chronic grief, consequently placing them in a high-risk category. Typically, those who have had significant losses in childhood will be more grief prone than others who have had a more secure early life (Parkes, 1972a/1987; Sanders, 1979). Sable (1989), in her study of 81 widows, supported this conclusion. She described an "anxious attachment" that formed from the intense fear of being alone and that tended to deepen and prolong sadness and grief. Raphael (1983) argued: "These (ambivalence and dependency) may lead to greater risks of inhibited or disturbed grief, chronic grief, and depression, as well as other possible outcomes" (p. 221).

These two areas of ambivalence and dependency have presented methodological difficulties in bereavement research in that hostility and guilt are usually repressed and are not easily dealt with after the death. The bereaved typically deny any problems with the relationship. Raphael (1983) suggests that when denial is profound, it probably indicates that exaggerated idealization is being used to cover up the ambivalence. Yet, because ambivalence and dependency have been noted as retardants in bereavement resolution, it is important that further work be done in these areas.

Health before bereavement

It is likely that, if an individual's mental or physical health is tenuous before the loss, the stress of grief will exaggerate that condition during bereavement. Early studies showed an exacerbation of congestive heart failure and essential hypertension when individuals were faced with the threat of grief and loss (Chambers & Reiser, 1953; Weiner, Thaler, Reiser, & Mirsky, 1957). Parkes (1985) pointed out, "The effects of emotion on coronary arteries are, of course, well known, and it is not unreasonable to suppose that people with severe heart disease may be vulnerable to the physiological accompaniments of severe grief" (p. 13). Parkes (1975) also reported a link between poor bereavement outcome and premorbid mental illness. Bunch (1972), in his study of suicide in bereaved persons, reported that 60% of those who succeeded in committing suicide had undergone psychiatric treatment prior to bereavement. Tracing premorbid physical symptoms and diagnoses is easier than tracing the severity of previous psychiatric problems. Individuals are far more apt to volunteer information regarding their physical problems than their emotional ones, especially if they have remained in outpatient treatment only. There is evidence that persons who used health services before the loss of a loved one were most susceptible to poor bereavement outcomes (Mor, McHorney, & Sherwood, 1986).

Still, the evidence connecting prior poor health to bereavement outcome derives primarily from clinical or anecdotal sources. With current emphasis being placed upon epidemiological studies of bereavement consequences, it is important for more studies to include prior health status among their variables.

Mode of death

Sudden unexpected death

Sudden unexpected death has been shown to have a debilitating effect on the bereaved in that shock acts to prolong grief as well as to produce excessive physical and emotional trauma (Lundin, 1984; Parkes & Weiss, 1983; Rando, 1983; Raphael, 1983; Sanders, 1989). In the Harvard study (Glick et al., 1974), sudden death was such a shock that the bereaveds' capacity to cope was greatly diminished and full functioning was not recovered by some even 4 years following the death.

Parkes (1975b) noted that mode of death was one of the primary predictive factors involved in spouses' bereavement outcome. Variables that contributed to a poor outcome of exacerbated grief were a short duration of terminal illness, cause of death not being cancer, and no opportunity to discuss impending death with the spouse. From these findings Parkes described a condition he termed "unexpected loss syndrome," characterized by social withdrawal, continued bewilderment, and protest. He concluded that this syndrome impaired functioning so severely that uncomplicated recovery could no longer be expected.

Lundin (1984) found that respondents who experienced a sudden death had significantly more somatic and psychiatric illnesses, when compared to persons who had experienced an anticipated death. When the bereaved who had anticipated loss were in poorer health before bereavement, however, they suffered no increase in health consequences after the loss. At the end of 8 years, there were no differences between the groups in good versus poor outcome.

These recovery effects, however, were not found in a study done by Lehman, Wortman, and Williams (1987). Examining the long-term effects of losing a spouse or child in an auto accident, they found that at 4 to 7 years after the crash, bereaved participants showed significantly greater distress than did matched controls. Both spouses and parents indicated severe depression (poor social functioning, future worries and concerns), as well as lack of resolution at the time of interview. Sanders (1989) noted that survivors of sudden-death situations showed more anger and suffered more physical symptoms than those whose family member had died of a chronic illness. The unexpected deaths left survivors with feelings of loss of control and loss of trust in a world in which they had previously placed their faith.

Death of a child

Parental bereavement is an overwhelmingly painful and long-lasting form of grief, and parents may be at risk for poor outcome solely due to this type of loss (Fish & Whitty, 1983; Osterweis, Solomon, & Green, 1984; Rando, 1983; Sanders, 1980). The improbability of surviving their child means that parents are unequipped to deal with the reality of the event. The question of why is an obsessive rumination. Because of the strong identification involved in the parent–child bond, when the child dies, the parents feel a part of themselves has also died. They then find grief doubly intense, for not only do they mourn the child but a part of themselves as well.

In a study comparing the grief of spouses, parents of children, and adult children of older parents (Sanders, 1980), significant intensities of grief were noted in parental bereavement. These parents suffered more somatic reactions, greater depression, and more anger and guilt with accompanying feelings of despair than did those bereaved who had lost either a spouse or an older parent. They felt a loss of control over their lives and the world; the untimeliness of the death of their child left them unsure of anything.

Fish (1986), studying the grief of parents, found that mothers experience greater levels of guilt and anger than do fathers, even 2 years after the loss. Mothers also experienced greater social isolation, feeling they were the only persons still actively mourning the lost child. Rando (1983) noted that parental grief actually escalated in the third year of bereavement, making the mourning period a long, drawn-out ordeal and further exhausting the resources of the parents. The support that marriage partners had counted on in the past is often lost in the bereavement situation as spouses find it hard to share their feelings with one another. Divorce and separation among bereaved parents is estimated to range anywhere from 50% to 90% as compared with couples who have not lost a child. Too, extreme isolation is felt by the parents when others avoid talking with them about their loss (Helmrath & Steinitz, 1978).

There is, therefore, much evidence that the death of a child frequently results in serious somatic problems, threat of marriage dissolution, and diminution of physical and emotional resources, so that resolution cannot be achieved for several years following the loss. The family structure might be so undermined that resolution or stability may never be fully attained by its members. Siblings and parents alike are left with severe survivor guilt that erodes ego strength and diminished feelings of worthiness. Because of these grave consequences, much research is needed regarding how and when to intervene in cases of parental bereavement.

Stigmatized deaths

Suicide. There is little question that the stigma of suicide puts a social strain on survivors (Osterweis et al., 1984). In their study of suicide survivors, Wrobliski and McIntosh (1987) noted three unique problems:

separation and isolation within and outside the family, rumination of the death scene, and difficulty in reconstructing events before the death. Although the problems appeared severe and debilitating, because there were no control groups employed, caution must be used in the interpretation of results.

Perhaps surprisingly, not all researchers consider suicide survivors to be at high risk during bereavement. Shepherd and Barraclough (1974) concluded that the results of their study of suicide bereaved was equally divided between "better off" and "worse off." However, W. Stroebe and Stroebe (1987) questioned the validity of this interpretation, noting that of the 44 spouses approached for an interview, 10 had died during bereavement. Although the sample size was small, this excessive number of deaths suggests a significant risk for the suicide survivors.

Investigations into these deaths are difficult. The paucity of systematic research is silent testimony that this type of bereavement represents a personal disaster that most people would prefer not to discuss. Based on the meager data available, suicide may constitute a high risk of illness and death for the survivors.

AIDS. Another stigmatized bereavement of growing concern involves the surviving family members or lover of someone who died of acquired immunodeficiency syndrome (AIDS). Batchelor (1984) has described AIDS as having the emotional impact of a modern-day black plague. As of August 1990, more than 89,000 known deaths had been reported in the United States (Centers for Disease Control, 1990a). Klein and Fletcher (1986) described a grief recovery group, continuing over an 18-month period, in which 32 men participated (ages 22–64). Most of the deaths had been AIDS related. These writers noted several important problems typical of this non-traditional grief situation, including no societal approval, frequent exclusion from intensive care units and funeral plans, and even being shunned as likely carriers of the AIDS virus.

Because AIDS has been stereotyped as a gay disease, homosexual males are treated by many as if they alone are responsible for the epidemic. Yet more heterosexual individuals will be affected, and families from all walks of life will be afflicted with this stigmatized grief as the epidemic grows. As yet, however, the literature is devoted primarily to understanding the illness rather than to supporting the bereaved (see Martin & Dean, this volume).

Circumstances following the loss

Lack of social support

Loneliness and lack of social support in the elderly have long been seen as major problems of adaptation to loss (see Lopata, this volume). Thus, Gallagher (1986) states that bereaved elders who are lonely and without adequate social support tend to be at risk for developing serious adjustment problems. If a grieving person can have available at least one confidant who will listen empathically and not turn away from tears or displays of frustration, that person will avoid one of the major risk factors of bereavement. The reader is referred to Stylianos and Vachon (this volume) for a detailed analysis of the social support issues in adjusting to bereavement.

Concurrent crises

During bereavement, the existence of additional debilitating stressors may result in an overwhelming situation. Parkes (1964a,b) and Raphael (1983), for example, noted the serious implications of multiple death situations, particularly when several members of a family are lost in the same disaster. Lifton (1968), in describing survivors of Hiroshima, described a "death guilt" as part of the survivor syndrome – survivors felt themselves saved at the cost of others' lives. Surviving individuals experienced what he called the "imprint of death" and grieved not only for family members but also for all who died in the disaster. Kaminer and Lavie (this volume) drew attention to these same guilt feelings among survivors of the Holocaust.

Concurrent stressors may also include other losses that the bereaved may be experiencing, such as loss of employment, divorce, loss of physical health, financial setbacks, and the like. The adaptive resources of the bereaved may already be at a minimum when a major bereavement occurs, leaving them even more vulnerable and helpless. Studies have shown that individuals involved in these multiple crises are at greater risk than others who are not so assailed (Parkes, 1975b; Raphael & Maddison, 1976).

Conclusions

The evidence presented in this chapter suggests several conclusions. Bereavement is a complex, multidimensional process involving physical, psychological, and sociological domains. These dimensions often cannot be separated for purposes of research and analysis. Thus, even well-designed studies may be at risk of confounding factors. There are also vast differences among individuals, making broad generalizations difficult. Research designs must, therefore, become more sensitive to this potential for confounding bias and to confusing interactions among variables. Similarly, clinicians treating bereaved individuals need to take more complete histories regarding early losses and concurrent stresses, as both appear to weigh heavily on the grieving process.

Certain risk factors appear to have been identified as seriously debilitating. They include the following:

- Sudden unexpected deaths, including suicide, murder, catastrophic circumstances, and stigmatized deaths
- Ambivalence and dependency
- Parental bereavement
- Health before bereavement
- Concurrent crises
- Perceived lack of social support
- Age and gender
- Reduced material resources

Although the majority of people do not become seriously ill or die immediately following a significant loss, it is difficult to know what long-term health risks exist. Sudden or untimely death creates such systemic shock that, for some, the impact does indeed cause immediate consequences. Early identification and treatment of these individuals may be a sustaining factor reducing their risk. Parental bereavement with its extreme levels of guilt and anger also falls into this category. Because bereaved parents are generally younger people, the physical consequences may not be seen for many years. However, the impact of this loss on family functioning may be more immediate and devastating.

Gender differences do appear to exist in bereavement. The question is what those differences suggest about better ways to treat and support bereaved men and women. It may be that a dependent personality, perceived lack of social support, and other concurrent losses all combine in the situation of many widowers, causing their higher mortality rates. In parental bereavement, what factors cause one marriage relationship to break down and others to remain stable? And would greater support from the partner reduce the dire consequences of that type of loss?

Grief affects everyone, but unequally. Some people are severely affected and die; others seemingly take it in stride, painfully acknowledging the loss but somehow managing to go on with their lives. A major goal for those conducting research, or offering care, is to learn how to make that disparity smaller.

PART VI

Grief reactions to different types of loss

18

Loss and recovery

ROBERT S. WEISS

Grief results when individuals lose certain "primary" relationships, but not when they lose others. Individuals who have lost emotional partners or children exhibit intense and prolonged grief (Glick, Weiss, & Parkes, 1974; Wortman & Silver, 1987). So do individuals who have lost parents to whom they were unusually close (Horowitz et al., 1984b). Grief, although to a lesser degree, is also exhibited by some who lose therapists, teachers, or other guides (Weiss, 1973b). In contrast, intense or prolonged grief is only rarely exhibited in response to the loss of friends, family members who live in different households, or colleagues or co-workers.

Relationships with spouses, children, siblings, friends, and colleagues are all "primary" in that they are close, face-to-face, emotionally important, and formed with a specific relational partner. Yet they divide into two distinct classes of relationships: those whose loss triggers grief and those whose loss does not.

The first class of relationships, those whose loss triggers grief, I will call *relationships of attachment*. The second class I will call *relationships of community*. Severe and persisting distress follows loss of any single relationship of the first class but not the loss of any single relationship of the second class. The death of a spouse or a child tends to be followed by years of grief; the death of a friend, a colleague, or an adult sibling living in a different household tends to be followed by distress and sadness but not by severe and persisting grief.

Severe and persisting distress does sometimes follow the loss of *all* of one type of relationship of community – all friendships, all work relationships, all family ties – even though it does not follow the loss of any single such relationship. The total loss of access to a community of work, as a consequence of layoff or retirement, or the total loss of access to a community of friends, as a consequence of geographic mobility or stigmatization, may give rise to persisting distress, whereas the loss of a single work colleague or friend would not (Benny, Weiss, Meyersohn, & Riesman, 1959; Weiss, 1974).

In relationships of attachment it is loss (or absence) of specific individ-

271

uals that triggers distress; in relationships of community it is loss (or absence) of a group or network. Furthermore, in relationships of attachment, distress is not to be assuaged by the substitution of another figure in the same relationship (another spouse, another child); in relationships of community it appears likely not only that new friends and work colleagues can be substituted, but also that membership in any meaningful community will limit the distress produced by loss of membership in another community (Gore, 1978; Henderson, Byrne, & Duncan-Jones, 1981).

This chapter takes as its underlying theoretical perspective the ideas of attachment theory as developed by John Bowlby (1969, 1973, 1980/1981) and extended to the functioning of adults by C. Murray Parkes (1972a/ 1987) and the author (Weiss, 1974, 1982). There seems a developing consensus that there is an attachment system in children that accounts for phenomena associated with their relationships to parents, including proximity seeking under conditions of threat and separation distress if the parents prove inaccessible. Although there seems no such developing consensus regarding the idea that the attachment system of children gives rise to derivative emotional systems in adults, I argue in this chapter that there is support for this view. (For descriptions of children's relationships of attachment, see Bowlby, 1969, 1973, and 1980/1981. For argument that "attachment" relationships of adults resemble those of children, see Parkes, 1972a/1987, and Weiss, 1982.)

Loss

I will use the term *loss* to refer to an event that produces persisting inaccessibility of an emotionally important figure. The experience of loss may be produced by such different events as the death of the emotionally important figure, estrangement from that figure, or even geographic distancing from the figure, although in the latter case letters, telephone calls, and anticipation of future reunion may reduce the impact of the separation. In all these instances there is likely to be distress; where the loss is viewed as permanent there is likely to be pain and disorientation. (For further discussion of disorientation as a consequence of loss, see Marris, 1974, and Parkes, 1971a.)

One common element of relationships of attachment is their linkage to feelings of security. A variety of investments, symbolic and real, can also have security-fostering implications. They may to this extent have the same emotional investment as an emotionally important figure. The security blanket of the child and the revered political leader of the adult are two examples. The loss of these security-fostering investments may produce the focusing of attention, search behavior, and distress that are associated with losses of attachment; some elements of attachment may be involved in the individual's linkage to these figures.

The quality of the separation distress that follows loss of a total community appears different from that which follows the loss of emotionally important figures. There appears more sense of marginality, more feelings of being intentionally misused or ostracized, less of a sense of having been abandoned. Fried (1963) suggests a similarity between the emotional states resulting from loss of community and those resulting from loss of emotionally important figures. I implicitly argue that the states are different in Weiss (1973a).

Even within the category of attachment relationships, experiences of loss can be significantly different. The death of a husband or wife produces great pain, but less disorientation (Glick et al., 1974); in marital separation, pain may be modified by other feelings, but disorientation and confusion are marked (Weiss, 1975). (Kitson & Zyzanski, 1987, contrast the self-blame associated with marital separation and the feelings of having suffered unjustly associated with bereavement.) The grief of parents of murdered children contains feelings of injury and rage much less evident in the grief of parents of children who died of leukemia, and markedly different from the quiet despair of a husband or wife whose spouse died in the fullness of age. (Members of Compassionate Friends, an organization of bereaved parents, often insist that the pain of a child's death – especially if it was caused by someone – cannot be imagined by those to whom it has not happened. See also Weiss, 1987.)

Relationships of attachment

As noted earlier, grief does not ordinarily follow the loss of a friend, a work colleague, or an adult relative, even when these figures were close and cared for. There may be sadness, a sense of a diminished community, and a feeling that a valued figure has been lost. There will not, ordinarily, be pain, pining, search, protracted distress, and the other elements of grief. A first reaction to loss of the community of work through retirement tends to be a mild elation, although there may later be a downturn in mood (Ekerdt, Boss, & Levkoff, 1985).

I characterize relationships whose loss produces grief as "attachments" because in the following significant respects they are identical to the relationships of attachment that bond children to their parents:

1. *They are security fostering*. The presence of the attachment figure or confidence in the accessibility of the attachment figure fosters feelings of security.

2. *They are displayed under conditions of threat.* Given absence of external threat, together with confidence in the attachment relationship, behaviors associated with the attachment system are in abeyance. Energy and attention are instead given to play or work, and there may be no indication of the special importance of the attachment figure. Under conditions of threat to the self or to the reliability of the attachment relationship, attachment feelings and behaviors are expressed.

3. *Attachment behavior (the behavior expressed in attachment relationships under conditions of threat) has the aims of establishing proximity to and gaining the attention and investment of the attachment figure.* Reassurance of security seems gained by seeing, hearing, or touching the attachment figure. In the absence of the attachment figure, some reassurance of security can sometimes be achieved through belief that proximity to the attachment figure will be established in the near future.

4. *Attachment relationships involve particular figures.* Separation distress follows loss of particular figures. Attempts to substitute other figures fail, no matter how ideally the other figures behave.

5. *The attachment system is not under conscious control.* In circumstances that elicit attachment feelings and behavior it is not possible for insecurities to be set aside and attention given to play or work.

6. *Attachments to particular figures are persistent over time.* They do not wane through habituation (as, among adults, sexual desire may), nor do they seem responsive to the absence of reinforcement. Continuing separation from an attachment figure produces pining, and often, anger and distrust, but only slowly and incompletely leads to diminution of attachment.

7. *The persistence of attachment is unaffected by the quality of experience with the attachment figure.* Attachment seems to persist even when the attachment figure is neglecting, disparaging, or abusive.

8. *Inability to achieve reassuring contact with the attachment figure under conditions of threat gives rise to the syndrome of separation distress.* This syndrome includes as elements a compulsion to search for the attachment figure, a sense of apprehension and fearfulness, a vigilant attentiveness to places where the attachment figure may be found, and a vigilant and tense anxiety regarding threat. Expressions of separation distress include focusing of attention on the search for the attachment figure, an inability to give attention to other matters, tension, and sleep difficulties.

In adults there are four relational bonds that display these eight characteristics. These four bonds are a pair bond, most obviously seen in the relationship of a married couple or a committed cohabiting couple; parental investment, most clearly evident in the relationship of parents to their children; transference, such as bonds that clients and patients form to professionals from whom they seek help; and persistence of childhood attachment into adulthood, with early relationships remaining as attachment figures. This last is an unusual development and, when it does occur, seems most common in mother–daughter pairs (Horowitz et al., 1984b). It is more usual for individuals to relinquish parents as attachment figures during their adolescent years, after which time their parents are treated as especially significant members of their kin group. The relinquishing of parents as attachment figures produces many of the tensions of adolescence.

Attachment behavior is elicited by threat. In the child, energy and attention are given to play, exploration, or the work of chores and schooling as long as the child is secure, but threat fosters a single-minded urgent need to regain access to a parent. In the four kinds of attachment relationships of adult life, attachment feelings and behavior are evoked by different kinds of threat:

1. In the pair-bond relationship, although threat external to the relationship (such as trouble on the job) may elicit attachment feelings, the full attachment syndrome, including separation distress, is most likely to be elicited by threat to the relationship itself. Thus, the death of the partner, the experience of marital separation, intense quarreling in which threats of abandonment are made, and the discovery of a partner's infidelity are all apt to elicit attachment feelings and behavior. That a threat to the relationship elicits attachment feelings is most evident when there is discovery of a partner's infidelity. Both self and partner may be managing well; nevertheless, threat to the relationship triggers separation distress with attendant panic and rage. It is a peculiarity of the pair bond that a threat to the *relationship*, irrespective of the well-being of the self or the other, regularly elicits a very high level of attachment feelings and behaviors.

2. In parental attachment to children, the threat most likely to elicit attachment feelings and behavior is a threat to the well-being of the child. Such a threat ordinarily evokes extremely high levels of protective energies and behavior, often accompanied by anxiety. Security is achieved when the parent is assured not of his or her own well-being, but rather of the child's. An example is the behavior of parents when they fear a child remains in a burning house: Firefighters report that it is all they can do to prevent parents from dashing into the house, oblivious to their own safety. Thus, parental relationships aim at the *protection of the other*, whereas pair-bond relationships aim at protection of the relationship.

3. In transference relationships to helpers, and also in persisting childlike attachment relationships to parents, threats to the individual from sources external to the relationship seem especially likely to elicit attachment feelings and behavior. When such threats occur, individuals may view attachment figures of this sort as sources of strength who can augment their own capabilities. This is, of course, the view of their parents maintained by small children. These relationships of attachment are called "transference" relationships to suggest a reinvoking of feeling originally experienced elsewhere – a sense of linkage to a strong and potentially protective figure like that found in children's relationships with their parents. The events that make transference relationships salient are almost always *threats to the self.*

4. The term *persisting childlike attachment* to parents means a continued view of the parents as attachment figures whose proximity provides assurance of security. This view of parents is ordinarily disrupted during adolescence and ultimately relinquished during early adulthood. It does not usually disappear entirely, as can be seen when a parent dies – then individuals often report that they briefly experience a feeling of being utterly bereft.

But ordinarily, adults supplant their parents as attachment figures with age-mates. However, some individuals seem not to relinquish parents as attachment figures. Although they are adult and may even be married, they feel insecure if they cannot contact their parents whenever they need to. The death of a parent produces for them the same grief reaction that for others is produced by the death of a husband or wife.

The source of adult attachment

Does the attachment system of adult life, as it displays itself in the four relationships named above (pair bonds, parental relationships, childlike attachment to parents, and transference relationships), derive from the attachment relationship in childhood? Transference relationships and child-like attachments to parents quite clearly are extensions into adulthood of children's attachments to parents; but pair-bond attachments and the nurturing investment of parents, though they closely resemble the attachment relationships of children, would require a modification of the earlier emotional system. Pair-bond attachment is directed toward a coeval, rather than the older and stronger attachment figure of childhood. Parental attachment is directed toward a younger and weaker figure.

My own belief is that, despite their differences, all the emotional systems underlying the attachment relationships of adult life will eventually be shown to be derived from the emotional system underlying attachment in children. At this time this is a theory consistent with observations of relational characteristics, but not demonstrated by observation of the processes by which a single childhood attachment system is supplanted by three distinct adult attachment systems. Nevertheless, assumption that the pair-bond relationship of adult life is a development of the attachment relationship of childhood has proven indispensable to the understanding of the phenomena of marital separation and conjugal bereavement (Parkes, 1972a/1987; Parkes & Weiss, 1983; Weiss, 1975).

Loss of attachment relationships

When individuals feel the objects of their attachment relationships to be secure, attachment feelings and behavior are in abeyance. Threat to the self, the attachment relationship, or the attachment figure produces, with different likelihoods in the different attachment relationships, an upsurge of attachment feelings and behavior.

Under appropriate conditions of threat, the individual's emotional system is dominated by attachment behavior and feelings. For example, if at two in the morning, a teenaged child has not yet returned from an evening with friends, parents may be awash with fear that something has happened to the child. They may be unable to restrain themselves from calling the state police and friends of the child in a compulsion to search. They desire nothing more than that the child should appear. When the child eventually does appear, attachment feelings subside, and in their place arise feelings of irritation, exasperation, or anger. The parents may also now crave sleep, although tension and vigilance had earlier made sleep impossible.

In a similar fashion, attachment feelings and behaviors are elicited when a marital quarrel culminates in abandonment threats, even if quietly voiced ("I think we should separate"). Individuals who have a transference relationship to a helper or a childlike attachment to a parent similarly experience an upsurge of attachment feelings, which they identify as a strong need to see the attachment figure, when they believe themselves threatened by events in their lives.

The arousal of attachment feelings together with their frustration results in the phenomena of grief. However, the different attachment bonds produce different emotional elements in grieving. For instance, the grieving of parents for a lost child is complicated by a sense of permanent commitment to the child's protection. The grieving of individuals for stronger and wiser helpers is especially intense when they find themselves overwhelmed.

What does it mean to recover from loss?

We should not suppose that people who have suffered a severe loss will return to the identity and emotional organization they maintained before the loss. As widows and widowers sometimes say, "You don't get over it. You get used to it." Severe grief, no matter how fully individuals emerge from it, should be expected to produce character change. In what sense, then, can we use the concept of "recovery"? A relationship of critical significance has been lost; the individual is likely to have been changed. Is "recovery" an appropriate term? Or would "adaptation," "accommodation," or even "degree of damage" be more appropriate?

I believe there is one query for which the term *recovery* is indispensable – namely, the extent to which there is a return of ordinary functioning. Recovery from grieving can be understood as a return to previous levels of functioning. With this definition in mind, the assessment of extent of recovery is a meaningful question.

We have, however, no universally accepted criteria for ordinary levels of effective functioning. One listing of reasonable expectations follows, together with the likely expressions of failure to recover in that particular respect.

1. *Ability to give energy to everyday life.* Effective functioning requires investment in the present, with adequate energy to meet current challenges. Failure to

recover in this respect might occur if the individual's energies remained bound by the experience of loss, with thought and effort still absorbed by that experience, or alternatively, absorbed by the effort to repress memories and feelings associated with the experience. Insofar as this is the case, current life would be seen as empty and meaningless.

2. *Psychological comfort, as demonstrated by freedom from pain and distress.* Effective functioning requires freedom from disturbing thoughts and feelings. Failure to recover would be exhibited by vulnerability to intrusions, which may have the character of flashbacks or of memories with associated pain and distress. Failure to recover could also be exhibited by an identification with the state of grieving, so that freedom from grieving would feel like a foreign and anxiety-provoking state.

3. *Ability to experience gratification – to feel pleasure when desirable, hoped-for, or enriching events occur.* Effective functioning requires the ability to experience pleasure as well as to anticipate pleasure should hoped-for events occur. Failure to recover would be demonstrated by an anhedonic state in which potentially pleasurable events are responded to as meaningless. Individuals may even feel regret or remorse when potentially pleasurable events occur because the events feel to them incomplete without the attachment figure or cruelly ironic in the light of their loss of that figure.

4. *Hopefulness regarding the future; being able to plan and care about plans.* Effective functioning requires being able to give meaning to activity, and such meaning requires a sense of a future that may bring with it something desirable. Failure to recover would be exhibited by a belief that the future is hopeless, pointless, or empty, and that life is already over. Alternatively, the individual's conceptual field may narrow so that memories of the past and thoughts of the future are avoided.

5. *Ability to function with reasonable adequacy in social roles as spouse, parent, and member of the community.* Effective functioning requires meeting social expectations well enough to maintain emotionally significant relationships. Failure to recover might be displayed, for example, by unpredictable behavior in attachment relationships because of distrust of their reliability or by so great a preoccupation with the possibility of new loss that energy cannot be invested in new relationships of attachment.

The return of ordinary capacity to function as an adult and as a member of the society seems to require that each of these five abilities return in at least some degree. Identifying them as aspects of recovery is based on the idea that recovery means the return of various aspects of personal and social functioning, and it also implies that recovery may be partial or incomplete.

Movement to recovery

The process of recovering from grief seems to involve phases in which different ways of relating to loss are dominant, although there is much intermeshing of these phases. The phases seem to follow a sequence: the loss is first emotionally denied, even though it may be consciously accepted;

then accepted but not viewed as permanent, with attempts made to end it; then accepted as permanent, with hopelessness marked by depression; and finally, accepted as permanent, but with hope of satisfactory life nevertheless.

Phases of grieving have been reported to occur with some reliability in all grieving that eventually moves to recovery, although the phases are best documented in connection with the loss of pair bonds (Bowlby & Parkes, 1970; Glick et al., 1974). Recent survey studies of individuals who have suffered losses have led some investigators to suggest that there may be a substantial proportion of such individuals who do not experience deep grief and so do not move through phases of recovery(Wortman & Silver, 1989). However, insofar as individuals move from grief to recovery, a sequence of phases seems likely. The phases of recovery that have regularly been identified may be named, following Bowlby (1980/1981), as shock, protest, despair, and then a long interval of adaptation.

The phase of *shock* is a numbed refusal to believe the reality of the loss event, and it precedes actual grief. Shock is especially apt to be seen where loss is not forewarned. It may also be more likely when the attachment figure undergoes the mysterious transition to death than when the attachment figure behaves in a hostile, rejecting, fashion yet remains alive. Shock does not seem a part of grief proper in that it is more nearly a defensive, and perhaps emotionally useful, temporary refusal to accept that loss has occurred.

The first phase of grief itself, Bowlby's phase of *protest*, is one in which effort is devoted to undoing the loss, even though there may be awareness that this is impossible. In this phase, the individual is agitated and fearful, oppressed by intense pain, and subject to bouts of anxiety mounting to panic. There is a vigilant scanning of the environment for sights or sounds that would indicate the return of the attachment figure. Pain and panic are heightened by awareness that the search is in vain. These phenomena can be understood as resulting from a massive upsurge of attachment feelings and behaviors, resulting in a compulsion to search for the lost object.

With continuing frustration of the search for the attachment figure, emotional conviction develops that further search is hopeless. Then the individual withdraws into despairing lethargic depression: Bowlby's phase of *despair*.

The two phases of grief proper, the phase of search and protest, and the phase of depressive withdrawal, may overlap, or intervals of one may occur before or after periods of the other. But, by and large, protest and search characterize an earlier phase of grieving, and depressive withdrawal a later phase.

A final phase of recovery may be identified – that of *adaptation*, in which the individual gives energy to establishing a new way of life with new potentials for satisfaction and goal attainment. It may require, according to one estimate, as long as 4 years or more for adaptation to occur (Glick et al., 1974).

At least three processes appear involved in movement to recovery. These may be characterized as cognitive acceptance, emotional acceptance, and identity change.

1. *Cognitive acceptance.* Individuals moving well toward recovery appear to develop a satisfactory account of the causes of the loss event. The objective validity of the account is less important than its subjectively felt validity. There seem to be some individuals for whom the formulas of religion – "It was God's mysterious way" – are a satisfactory account, although, it appears, fewer than are apt to be encouraged by relatives or friends to accept such explanations.

Ordinarily, it seems, satisfactory accounts can be developed rather quickly, if they can be developed at all. The absence of a satisfactory account seems to leave individuals anxiously perplexed, searching their cognitive field for contributions to the loss they may have made themselves, or that may have been made by third parties, such as physicians or ill-wishers.

2. *Emotional acceptance.* Recovery seems to require individuals to achieve a neutralization of memories and associations so that recall does not paralyze functioning. This process of neutralization requires the confrontation of emotion-laden memories and associations one by one, and with each, the reduction of associated pain until tolerance for the memory is developed. One process by which emotional acceptance is achieved is through an almost compulsive review of alternative scenarios that would have avoided the loss. These "if only's," must also be worked through and neutralized, along with painful memories and associations.

The process of neutralization requires variable amounts of time, depending on the nature of the loss, but may require several months for progress to be observable. In response to the death of a spouse or a marital estrangement, if the process is going well, much may be accomplished in 6 months or so, but anniversaries will ordinarily demonstrate that freedom from pain is by no means complete. Indeed, full emotional acceptance of significant loss seems to occur rarely. Most individuals who have lost marital relationships are vulnerable indefinitely to pangs of distress or remorse, although ordinarily of brief duration.

3. *Identity change.* Finally, it seems necessary for individuals to develop a new image of themselves, in which their connection to the attachment figure is seen as part of a past self rather than a present self. For this to be fully accomplished, the individual must make new commitments to new relationships. This appears much more possible after the loss of a spouse than after the death of a child.

Recovery and failures to recover

We are the walking dead, rotting inside with pain and anger. [Quotation in the *Boston Globe*, attributed to the mother of a murdered child, a member of the organization Parents of Murdered Children.]

When the processes of recovery are blocked, the result is a failure to recover. Since, in any event, recovery is apt to be less than total, the term *failure to recover* refers to one end of a continuum rather than a qualitatively distinct category.

Among the ways in which the processes of recovery can be impeded, the following may be noted:

1. The loss may make no sense. This is particularly likely to occur when the loss is entirely without forewarning. No satisfactory account can be developed, and it is absolutely reasonable to wonder, "Why did this happen to me?" There can, for a time, be a constant nagging search for explanation, which gives way to a blank, though painful, perplexity. Perhaps even more difficult for cognitive acceptance are those losses in which the self is felt to have been the primary cause. The repudiation of self that this "explanation" tends to foster must then be reacted against if the individual is to continue to function. Widows and widowers of a suicide may, for this reason, find it important to develop an account in which it is the suicide's own pathology that produced the death.
2. Ambivalence toward the attachment figure can impede emotional acceptance, partly because there will be confusion regarding the nature of feelings, and partly because self-blame, guilt, and remorse may complicate the pain of loss.
3. Low self-esteem, together with a feeling of having been dependent on the attachment figure, may make for hopelessness regarding the future. There may thus be a sense that security can only be found through continued maintenance of the attachment relationship, despite the attachment figure's permanent absence. In an older widow, for example, relinquishing a sense of the self based in the marital relationship – despite the relationship no longer existing – might produce unbearable anxiety. Without the marriage, the future is bleak, the present meaningless.
4. Feelings of responsibility to the attachment figure, of protectiveness and commitment to his or her well-being, may make a return to adequate functioning appear to be disloyalty. The pledge never to desert, never to forget, can become a pledge not to recover. Moreover, this commitment can be reinforced in cultural situations in which persistent grieving is expected.

The grief that follows the death of a child seems peculiarly resistant to recovery (Lehman, Wortman, & Williams, 1987; Weiss, 1987). When it is a child that has died, the parents' protective feelings, which make for a near-permanent need to save the child from hurt, produce a protracted phase of protest and search. Associated with this is almost unbearable pain produced at least in part by helplessness to save the child. The persistence of failure to recover from the death of a child is illustrated by an 88-year-old widow, interviewed in our pilot research, who no longer felt deep grief for her dead husband, but who continued to grieve for her first child, dead some 60 years. She reported that the child was always in her thoughts and that she still sometimes awakened in the middle of the night to sorrow over the child's death.

The forms of failures to recover

Most frequently, failure to recover is marked by *chronicity*. This is the unmoving persistence of one or both of the phases of grief proper: search and protest, or depressed withdrawal. There continues to be identification of the self with the relationship to the lost attachment figure; there may be refusal to acknowledge the reality or the permanence of loss. Anhedonia is marked, as is estrangement from others, in part a consequence of a picture of reality discordant with that of others (Parkes & Weiss, 1983).

Failure to recover may also be marked by *compartmentalization*. Here the feelings associated with the loss are fended off, and energy is given to weakening the stimulus value of any observation or memory that might trigger awareness of the loss. At the same time there may be heightening of the stimulus value of other emotional commitments. Compartmentalization is not the same as repression or denial; there is no refusal to recognize reality, only a refusal to attend to it. The loss is "put out of one's mind" or "walled away," to use terms offered by respondents. Compartmentalization is easily interrupted; for example, an uninformed friend asking "How is your husband?" will be enough to dispel the defense and leave a widow overwhelmed with distress.

It is difficult to judge the cost of compartmentalization. It may make for guardedness in interaction, as though a part of the self is being withheld. It certainly will make it difficult for the individual to neutralize painful memories, in that such neutralization depends on the acceptance of loss. The most apparent cost is that the vigilance necessary to prevent compartmentalization from being breached may overgeneralize and cause the exclusion from awareness of much of emotional significance. Insofar as there is defensive inattention, the result seems likely to be impoverishment of the individual's emotional life. Also, in new relationships that in some way duplicate the lost relationship, selective inattention may result in a failure to recognize the individuality of this new other. This would permit replacement relationships, but at a cost in relational sensitivity.

Observation suggests that compartmentalization as a form of failure to recover is not necessarily energy consuming. There can, indeed, be a great deal of energy expended in pursuit of goals distant from the loss (e.g., a new dedication to some task) despite any energy being devoted to vigilant refusal to attend to the loss. Whether there is anhedonia is difficult to say (Lindemann, 1944, seems to believe there is). The ability to function in new emotional relationships may be the area where those who have dealt with loss by compartmentalization will experience the greatest cost. Vigilance against reexperiencing the pain of their loss may make for the avoidance of new experiences that could elicit memories.

In most failures to recover, a mix of chronicity and compartmentalization can be observed. Horowitz et al. (1979) report that post-traumatic stress disorder gives rise to two classes of symptoms: "intrusion" symptoms, such as thinking about the traumatic event despite wishing not to, and "avoidance" symptoms, such as trying to remove the event from memory. It seems reasonable that failure to recover from a traumatic event and failure to recover from bereavement may give rise to similar symptom pictures; indeed, bereavement is among the traumatic events considered by Horowitz and his colleagues.

The mix of chronicity and compartmentalization may take many forms. There may be partial withdrawal from social life and relinquishing of hopes for the future, both suggestive of chronicity, together with a blank absence of interest in the past, suggestive of compartmentalization. There may be constant awareness that a crucial figure has died, suggestive of chronicity, together with refusal to talk about the death, suggestive of compartmentalization. There may be immersion in exciting activity, suggestive of compartmentalization, together with regular episodes of alcohol-facilitated sorrow, suggestive of chronicity. Failure to recover will not give rise to a single symptom complex. Rather, failure to recover from loss can be demonstrated only by tracing impaired functioning back to the individual's reaction to the loss.

Implications

Loss is inescapable. Deaths, estrangements, and separations are part of life. Recoveries tend to be either more or less adequate; only rarely can they be said to be either complete or entirely absent. Most of us have character structures influenced by partial recovery from loss.

Some among us, however, have suffered losses that have produced massive damage. Researchers know enough now to be able to anticipate the kind of losses that will subject anyone to such risk. They are losses that make the processes of recovery difficult: unanticipated losses, losses where the relationship was ambivalent, losses where the bereaved individual is under obligation to remain invested in the lost figure. We also know something about the kinds of people who are at special risk. They are people who lack the self-provided permission to relinquish the lost figure, or people who lack the hopefulness or the self-confidence to imagine a desirable future. For those who are at special risk, whether because of the experiences they have had or because of the nature of their personalities, special attention and special services are justified.

Services are already in place for those exposed to certain kinds of regularly disabling experiences. These especially include self-help groups for parents of children who have died and professionally led groups for those whose marriages have ended through death or discord (Weiss, 1975, 1987). Still, there seem more needs than there are groups available. In the professional provision of counseling, techniques for fostering recovery among those suffering from loss are being developed, and the need for trained "grief counselors" is increasingly recognized.

Whether enough is being done is difficult to say. As always, the allocation of social resources is a matter of priorities, and this is something about which honest people may disagree. Yet surely the development of further models for helping and fuller specification of effective elements in current helping models would be socially beneficial.

Loss and pain are inescapable, but permanent damage should not be. Our practical aim in this area of work should be to facilitate support for those undergoing loss and pain, so as to reduce the likelihood of permanent damage.

19

The death of a child is forever: The life course impact of child loss

SIMON SHIMSHON RUBIN

With few exceptions, parents are able to love and care deeply for all their children, whether these be few or many in number. In times of life crisis, parents may become temporarily unable to find the resources within themselves to actively manage their relationships with their children, but this situation is generally time limited. The capacity for parents to care deeply for each child and to find different but balanced ways of involvement with each of their children is the norm. That is, unless a child in the family dies. In that situation, the capacity for parents to undergo a normal mourning process in which they will grieve for the deceased child and emerge able to continue meaningful and balanced interaction with the surviving children is far from assured. In all too many cases, the parents maintain a continuing preoccupation with and heightened investment in the relationship to the lost one and the loss itself.

The book of Genesis is rich in the description of family themes that would prove taxing for even the most resourceful of family therapists. Of all the stories of loss, the one of Jacob mourning for his beloved favorite son Joseph, presumed dead, is prototypical for one complication of parent loss of children. Although favored in life, it is Joseph's sudden "death" that cripples the father emotionally so that he is a mere shell of himself.

And Jacob rent his garments, and put sackcloth upon his loins, and mourned for his son many days. And all his sons and all his daughters rose up to comfort him; but he refused to be comforted; and he said, "Nay, but I will go down to the grave to my son mourning." And his father wept for him. [Genesis 37: 34–35]

Jacob became a changed man, dominated by fear, who was a broken shard of the resourceful character described earlier in the Bible. Despite the fact that he was surrounded by his 11 other sons, his daughters, and their families, Jacob was dominated by the loss of the one son and was unable to resume his life. This is underscored in the narrative later on. When Jacob

The author wishes to thank the editors of this volume for their valuable comments and suggestions.

285

is finally convinced that Joseph is alive, he undergoes a transformation wherein his life force is restored many years after the loss.

Parents' reactions to the loss of a child take many forms, but the overwhelming picture is of a major blow and major organizing force in how life will be lived thereafter. Consider the following examples:

Mrs. D. lost her infant son to SIDS some 5 years earlier. She has had additional children whom she cares about a great deal. As the years pass, she follows children the same age as her son would have been and imagines what her son would have been like had he lived. (Rubin, 1984b)

Mrs. J. had lost her 17-year-old son 9 years before. To her, the relationship with her son was the most important and sensitive relationship she had ever had. At the confirmation of her younger son, she was preoccupied with images of his deceased brother, his confirmation, and covertly focused on these while pretending to be involved with the current celebration. (Rubin, 1985)

Mr. Z. was a retired handyman who had been bereaved of his grown son 13 years earlier in Israel's 1973 Yom Kippur War. Despite the passage of time, Mr. Z. was determined not to enjoy himself or allow himself pleasures of life. Although he went through the motions of playing cards with his old cronies, he rarely felt anything while doing so. Once the life of the party, he now felt guilty if he told or enjoyed a joke. Despite occasional lapses, he managed to live his life bereft of joy and health. Neither his other children, grandchildren, family, or friends were allowed to impinge upon his experience of himself as a bereaved and wounded old man.

Each of the responses described is typically present to some degree and for some time following the death of a child. The three vignettes illustrate long-term responses of parents to child loss over time and at differing stages in life. The dividing lines between ongoing grief and mourning as normative versus maladaptive or pathological mourning are difficult to draw. The constellation of individual, familial, biological, and social factors differs as parents mature, and these no less than the age and special identity of the child lost influence the nature and experience of parental response to loss.

The parents' responses quoted here share one important feature: They are indicative of the continuing relationship to the memories and internal psychological representations of the deceased. At any age, the loss of a child is exceedingly difficult to experience and assimilate into one's life structure (Levinson, 1978). The paths that parents follow as they respond to their losses change them in some ways temporarily and in others permanently. Delineating and measuring the multivariate nature of response to child loss, particularly with regard to the cognitive representations of the deceased, is a task that clinicians and researchers are gradually coming to terms with. It is this central feature in the understanding of response to loss that has significant theoretical, clinical, and research applications that will be explored later.

What is it that parents experience in child loss? Why is it so difficult for bereaved parents to continue to divide their emotional involvement among their children and their lives in a balanced manner in the event of child death? Although not all individuals or families respond the same way, the consensus among clinicians and researchers in Western societies is that this type of loss is particularly difficult to bear. The research literature on the impact of child loss has generally confirmed the exceedingly difficult nature of response to this type of loss (Gorer, 1965; Rando, 1986; Sanders, 1980).

In order to understand what is involved in the parental response to child loss, a number of aspects require consideration: the parent–child attachment bond and its meanings for parents, the psychological goals of the mourning process following child loss, and a conceptual framework for determining outcome to loss. The next sections address the parent–child attachment bond, the impact of child loss, and relevant research. These are followed by the presentation of an alternative conceptual and research paradigm, the Two-Track Model of Bereavement. Two studies stemming from this paradigm and their implications for parental response to child loss are described in detail. A section on select clinical and research implications completes the chapter.

The parent–child attachment bond

The parent attachment bond to children is both a stimulus and result of the human variation on the theme of the propagation of life. In addition to the powerful biological drives operating to ensure the continuation of life, equally powerful psychological and social drives operate for the production and caring of children (Bowlby, 1969, 1973). The biopsychosocial domains converge to shape family units that function for survival, kinship and caretaking purposes.

In order to survive, the individual must regard the self and those things dear to him or her as important. The formation of kinship and attachment bonds is related to the extension of self or narcissistic investment in the other so that the other's welfare becomes as important to one as the self. In general, this is an adaptive state of affairs for all involved. Whereas the formation of attachment bonds between spousal partners is one case of this, the children produced are a significant attachment variation (see Weiss, this volume). Parents conceive, nurture, and educate their children and regard the experience of the relationship as valuable. This process has periods of intense emotional involvement alternating with relative quiescence (Mahler, Pine, & Bergmann, 1975). Children have multiple meanings for their parents. At one level, children are a physical extension of their parents. Genetically, socially, and· psychologically, children are the repositories of their parent's beings. They represent a reworked variation of the past as they move dynamically toward the future (Cohler &

Grunebaum, 1981). The multiple meanings of children tend to coexist and amplify each other. Children are all of these: They are extensions of one's self; they are those who will rectify the errors of their elders; they are narcissistic adornments meant to reflect back well on the parents; they are those who are to care about and for their parents; they are mirror images of their parents' negative and positive sides; they are the opportunities for parents to exert themselves and to make a difference in the world; and they are a second chance to replay and reexperience aspects of the parents' own childhoods (Anthony & Benedek, 1970).

The confluence of the overwhelming body of literature on parent–child relationships places into theoretical and social scientific formulations that which is central to the functioning of the family: the care and investment placed in child rearing and the parent–child relationship from the perspective of both sides.

The emotion-laden parent–child bond evolves and changes as the partners grow and mature. Affection, aggression, sexuality, competition, jealousy, and the most basic emotions are stimulated and bound up in these relationships. Despite the complexity and depth of the parent–child tie, it is generally a dynamic and shifting relationship with a balance of closeness and distance manifest over time. This balance is deeply upset in the event of child death. To grasp why this should be so, we turn to the nature of the loss process.

Response to child loss: Overview and research

What is so striking to those who have experienced loss is the severity, depth, and sweep of the loss experience for significant others, and how little room is left in the meantime for living life in its usual fashion (Freud 1917b/1957). The pervasiveness of the loss experience, especially if it involves the untimely death of a close relative, proceeds to disrupt the daily patterns of living (Lindemann, 1944). Even when this overt distress begins to subside, there is still a great deal of work to be done in the mourning process.

In child death, parents experience the loss of a uniquely significant relationship. The effects of the loss are pervasive in the initial loss period. These effects are broad and effect a depletion of energy and the refocusing of emotional investment on the deceased. If successful, the need to shift the relationship to the deceased triumphs and an adaptation to the new state of life asserts itself. Among the emotions experienced, some are direct by-products of the feelings toward the deceased. There may be anger and depression at the abandonment by the deceased, as well as a sense of vulnerability as a parent experiences the sense of being bereft and exposed following loss. At conscious and unconscious levels, the parent is likely to feel partly responsible for the abandonment. These combine with the guilt, helplessness, and frustration that loss forces on one to a state of confusion and flux. The devaluation of the self that is now without the beloved child evokes the need to process and reorganize the self in relation to the deceased child, the self, and the general world.

During the first months and years of the response to loss, the couple and family relationships bear much of the individual parent's emotional reaction to loss. Some couple relationships founder under the stress while others protect and assist the bereaved. An understanding of the parental response can give valuable insights into the major interpreters, containers, and buffers of the nuclear family experiencing loss. These coexist within the context of couple and family responses to loss (Rubin, 1986; Rubin & Nassar, unpublished data; Walsh & McGoldrick, 1988).

The systematic study of the effects of child loss on adults has received significant attention, but much remains to be learned (Osterweis, Solomon, & Green, 1984). As a distinct category within the field of adult loss, the effects of this tragedy both overlap and diverge from that of spouse loss or parent loss.

Early clinical reports on the deleterious effects of incomplete mourning of a child tended to focus on the psychopathological effects and emerged from clinically based work. For example, Cain and Cain (1964) identified a replacement child syndrome that reflected incomplete mourning on the part of the parents. In this maladaptive response to child loss, a later child served as both a replacement for the deceased and a truncation of the painful mourning process.

A range of studies have emerged investigating numerous aspects of the parental experience of loss. Several reviews of the major studies have sought to organize the data accumulated to date. Bowlby (1980/1981) examined in some detail studies that emphasized parents' anticipatory and coping responses to child death. The National Institute of Mental Health report (Osterweis et al., 1984) referred to the need for more and better designed studies to expand our knowledge of this category of bereavement. Raphael's (1983) review of child loss emphasized a developmental perspective while surveying types of child loss from conception to adulthood. She concluded that child loss commonly evoked patterns of chronic grief and irrational guilt, and that the deceased child is never forgotten. Rando (1986) organized her review of child loss along both a developmental perspective and a selection of specific causes of death in her volume on the subject. This reflects a view that child loss is a multivariate event where unique features of types of loss deserve singular attention.

In the last decade, additional studies have considered the impact of child loss in the period shortly following the death and thereafter. These studies continue to add to our knowledge, but also demonstrate how much is yet to be learned. In a study of early outcome to child loss, 391 bereaved participants answered 2 sets of mail-administered questionnaires at 1-year intervals. Despite the passage of time, numerous indications of continuing distress were present. Neither involvement in psychotherapy nor the Compassionate Friends self-help group limited the preponderance of loss-related distress. At both time intervals, women were more distressed than men, but the rate of improvement was similar for both. Seventy-four percent of the sample reported mental health–related problems, and 44% indicated marital problems (Videka-Sherman, 1982a; Videka-Sherman & Lieberman, 1985). Rando (1983) studied 54 bereaved parents (27 married couples) following the loss of a child to cancer. The investigation studied the effect of variables such as the influence of previous losses, support, anticipatory grief, and time elapsed since loss (up to 3 years) on coping and a number of areas of functioning. She reported a trend for mothers to report more intense reactions to bereavement and poorer subsequent adjustment postloss than fathers, but these differences did not reach statistical significance. An interesting pattern emerged in her data that suggested that the bereavement response might be curvilinear, easing in the second year and becoming more pronounced again in the third year.

In several reports of research examining the long-term effects of spouse and child loss as a result of motor-vehicle accidents, a differential pattern of response to loss emerged (Lehman, Wortman, & Williams, 1987; Lehman, Lang, Wortman, & Sorenson, 1989). Four to 7 years after the loss, bereaved spouses tended to be more different from their matched controls than were bereaved parents from their controls. A continuing involvement with thoughts and feelings concerning the deceased with accompanying pain characterized both groups. The more pronounced reaction of bereaved spouses compared to bereaved parents is at odds with a number of the studies in the area (Sanders, 1980).

Outcome to loss and the Two-Track Model of Bereavement

At the conceptual level, a great deal of the research on bereavement has addressed the changes in symptomatology, psychopathology, and self-perception that follow bereavement in much the same manner they could be assessed with any other class of traumatic stressor (Clayton & Darvish, 1979; Parkes, 1965; Pitts, Meyer, Brooks, & Winokur, 1965; W. Stroebe & Stroebe, 1987). Conceptually and empirically, the outcome to child bereavement has often been considered without reference to the fact that loss is a double process event. At one level, it is the attack on the relational bond to a particular individual that requires the bereaved to make major modifications in the internal relationship to the deceased (Bowlby, 1980/1981; Klass, 1988; Freud 1917b/1957; Parkes, 1972a/1987). At another level, loss and its aftermath are a major traumatic stressor capable of affecting the bereaved at all levels of biopsychosocial functioning. Although the research adds incrementally to our understanding of the outcome of bereavement, I have elsewhere proposed that a dual axes paradigm, along the lines of the Two-Track Model of Bereavement, would clarify and sharpen the study of two related but not identical dimensions of loss: relationship and functioning (Rubin, 1981, 1982, 1984a).

On the one hand, bereavement in general, and child bereavement in particular, are responses to the loss of a highly charged and valued relationship whose specifically interpersonal and relational aspects are central to loss and outcome (Volkan, 1981). Both research and intervention programs must ultimately recognize this fact. Yet, on the other hand, loss is one of a broad range of stressful and traumatic events that precipitate crisis, disorganization, and reorganization of psychological, biological, and social functioning of those affected (Parkes & Weiss, 1983). As a subcategory of the stress and trauma field, we recognize that it will upset equilibrium and functioning in the bereaved across a broad range of areas. The specifically interpersonal nature of loss may exert its effects as the precipitant of varied changes in functioning. However, the extent to which the interpersonal aspects continue to influence long-term bereavement outcomes remains open to empirical examination (Wortman & Silver, 1987).

The parents' intense preoccupation with the deceased child and the relationship to that child following loss set in motion the bereavement response. Major somatic and psychological distress is encountered. While the bereaved has lost equilibrium, the process of grieving for the deceased is under way. Too painful and too disruptive to experience at once, over time the realization that the deceased is forever unavailable can be assimilated (Freud, 1917b/1957). There is a staccato fluctuation in the nature of the attachment and detachment from the deceased that proceeds over many years.

The effects of the loss can be considered at any time following loss. In light of the turmoil accompanying loss, it is logical to look for evidence of the lessening or disappearance of this turmoil. Outcome to child loss should consider changes in the attitudinal, behavioral, cognitive, interpersonal and social, personality, somatic, and self-system that are an outgrowth of how the parent has reintegrated following loss (Lehman et al., 1987). The extent to which a resumption of adequate functioning is present postloss is of significance. Adequate functioning, however, may be accompanied by a shift in any number of attitudes, behaviors, and affects that may have implications for adaptation and dysfunction in quite complex ways and at different points in the life cycle (Brown & Harris, 1978).

The continuing significance of the relationship to the child, and how this relationship is transformed and organized following loss, remain a distinct area equally central to the study of child bereavement outcome. Outcome on this variable is related to the current state of the bereaved parents' relationship and preoccupation with the deceased child (Klass, 1988).

Two studies of response to child death

In this section, two studies are presented that utilize the Two-Track Model of Bereavement to study the effects of child loss over time. A cross-sectional study design was adopted, comparing groups of bereaved parents at different times following the sudden death of their children.

Study 1

The loss of a young child today is a rare occurrence in Western society. The impact of such a loss on the mothers of these children was examined in the Chicago sudden infant death syndrome (SIDS) study. SIDS is a medical diagnosis in response to "the death of a child who was thought to be in good health or whose terminal illness appeared to be so mild that the possibility of a fatal outcome was not anticipated" (Valdes-Dapena, 1967, p. 123). The basic questions addressed were how did SIDS loss affect mothers behaviorally, cognitively, and emotionally, and for how long? Forty-five women, divided equally among recently bereaved, nonrecently bereaved, and nonbereaved, participated in this study. All participants were married, with an average age of about 30. Research participation was obtained with the assistance of the Greater Chicago SIDS Regional Center. The recently bereaved had suffered the loss between 3 and 10 months previously (average of 7.5); the nonrecently bereaved had suffered the loss between 2 and 6 years earlier (average of 4.5). The control group mothers were recruited via a local parent organization.

The study measures assessed a range of responses, including anxiety (Spielberger, Gorsuch, & Lushene, 1970), perception of the environment and the self, and the degree to which functioning was free from symptoms (Cox, 1970). The measures, described fully elsewhere, were based primarily on written protocols and an extensive semistructured interview (Rubin, 1977, 1981).

The research findings yielded a consistent pattern. The recently bereaved mothers showed heightened anxiety and lowered general functioning in such areas as the ability to invest in life goals, self-confidence, inhibition, and somatic complaints. The recently bereaved SIDS mothers were actively mourning their losses and thus emerged as a distinct group vis-à-vis the other women. Despite the indications of lowered general functioning, overall attitudes to life were not generally affected. This suggested a return to basic attitudes and life views held earlier. Although only the recent SIDS were showing impairment on measures of general functioning, there were indications that the nonrecent SIDS mothers were also sensitive to issues around the loss.

Had the research been confined to symptomatic and general change, a fairly consistent picture of recovery from loss would have been a parsimonious explanation of the data. However, by extending the assessment into the domain of affective involvement and preoccupation with the deceased, changes in how the self and family were viewed and other circumscribed features of response to loss, persisting mourning for the child was identified for all the bereaved. Only the degree of these effects varied. On the track of relationship to the deceased, the recently bereaved were more preoccupied with thoughts of the deceased, more depressed, and more guilty than their nonrecently bereaved counterparts. On the track of changes in bio-psychosocial functioning following loss, the bereaved groups did not differ on the measures of circumscribed attitude/personality change. On these indices, both bereaved groups indicated that there had been pronounced, albeit circumscribed, shifts in their attitudes. Continuity with the earlier worldview and attitudes predominated, but clearly recognizable changes in value structure and family perception were much in evidence.

Overall, the data suggested that strong involvement with the loss lessened with the passage of time, but continued over the years. The changes experienced by women who had lost infants were not centered in the areas of general functioning associated with either somatic or psychological sequelae. The moderate degree of change in how the mothers related to themselves, their children, and their spouses is consistent with the understanding of child loss as a major organizing event in an individual parent's life. For both bereaved groups, continuing sadness, guilt, and preoccupation with the loss remained permanent sequelae to the loss. These findings reflected the continuing significance of the bereaveds' relationship to the loss and the representation of the deceased for years following death. The outcome to loss was indicative of shifts in attitudes and behavior regarding relationships to the deceased, the self, and close family. These were shifts in both the meaning and management of the parents' significant relationships.

The bereaved parent's response to loss is an amalgam of change and of continuity with the person he or she was prior to the loss. In this study, the results pointed to circumscribed changes that did not extend to gross impairment of function.

In retrospect, having studied and worked with a spectrum of bereaved parents, the resilience of these relatively youthful mothers was heartening. They were, for the most part, able to rejoin the mainstream of family life and the outside world. The place of the deceased child in their lives is indicated by their preoccupation with thoughts of the child and the loss and by their continuing guilt and feelings of sadness that wax and wane. The loss of the child to SIDS and the relationship to the child's memory remained a major life organizer without being overbearing.

As in any odyssey into uncharted waters, much of what was learned from the study was not anticipated. In particular, the extent of fathers' needs to participate in the research and to share thoughts and feelings emerged from numerous informal contacts with them over the course of the research. Other findings include the persistent guilt that follows the loss of a child to SIDS (despite the fact that SIDS itself is a diagnosis partly intended to mitigate blame); the sensitivity of bereaved parents to the social and extended family messages that suggest that grief be set aside (which encourages the adoption of a facade of functioning but engenders resentment and isolation); and the bewildering multitude of ways that individuals cope and deal with their grief and loss at both manifest and covert levels.

For some of the bereaved women studied, continuing attachment to the representations of the deceased child as he or she was and might have been was a dominant feature of the outcome to loss in the years following. A second prominent theme was the changed sense of self that bereaved women constructed for themselves in the aftermath of their loss (Silverman, 1988b). The associations, memories, and reveries relating to the deceased child continued the relationship to the deceased. These phenomena underscore the importance of the object representation as an axis for understanding outcome to loss (Rubin, 1984a).

Prior to planning additional empirical research into the experience of child loss, additional clarification was required. How to conceptualize better the bereaved individual, the deceased, and the continuing attachment and preoccupation with the deceased needed further consideration. A series of articles followed on the continuing attachment bond to the deceased. The Chicago SIDS study was an early application of the Two-Track Model of Bereavement. Later articles stressed the understanding of bereavement from the standpoint of the bereaved's ongoing relationship to the memories and internal representation of the deceased for many years following loss (Rubin, 1984a,b, 1985). To emphasize the time period involved, and to underscore its distinctness from mourning as a process of response to loss, the term *epilogue to bereavement* was selected. It is during the epilogue to bereavement that one can assess the ultimate *resolution* of bereavement as an outgrowth of relationship and function (Rubin, 1985).

Study 2

Building on the Chicago SIDS study, a larger in-depth study was conducted to learn more about the nature of child loss. Smaller studies examining outcome to loss among parents of younger and older children pointed to

Table 19.1. *Bereaved Israeli parent sample characteristics*

| | Bereaved | | |
	1973	1982	Control
n	56	46	73
Sex			
M	23	22	27
F	33	24	46
Age			
M	62.9	56.1	52.5
SD	6.0	7.0	8.8
Education[a]			
M	11.9	12.5	15.9
SD	3.1	3.0	8.9
Age of son			
M	22.2	23.1	23.1
SD	4.1	4.7	11.0

[a] For differences between bereaved and control groups, $p < .05$.

greater resilience within the sample of younger parents bereaved of younger children (Rubin, 1990a). In contrast to the loss of an infant, the loss of a young adult son to war was a strikingly different type of child loss. How this type of loss would affect parents in the domains of functioning, attitude, affect, and relationship to the representation of the deceased as much as 13 years postloss was the focus of this second study (Rubin, 1987; in press).

One hundred and two bereaved parents and 73 nonbereaved parents participated in the research. The random sample of bereaved Israeli urban parents from the 1973 Yom Kippur and 1982 Sheleg (Lebanon) wars was obtained with the assistance of the Department of Rehabilitation of the Ministry of Defence. A comparison group was composed of parents who had an adult child who had left or was leaving home. The demographic characteristics of the sample are shown in Table 19.1.

Objective measures assessed anxiety (Spielberger et al., 1970) and multivariate functioning of the individual parent (Rubin, 1990a; Sanders, Mauger, & Strong, 1979). Structured and semistructured measures assessed the relationship to the deceased (Blatt, Chevron, Quinlan, & Wein, 1981; Osgood, Suci, & Tannenbaum, 1957; Sadeh, 1987). In addition, a series of supplemental measures, including a detailed semistructured interview, were administered to obtain a comprehensive view of the loss experience.

Bereaved parents in the study differed from the nonbereaved on anxiety without regard to the passage of time since loss. Parents bereaved 4 years earlier were functioning more poorly on affective, somatic, and cognitive scales than the nonbereaved. At the same time, parents bereaved 13 years functioned at levels between the other groups. In some areas, gender differences rather than time since loss were the more significant factor in response to child loss (M. Stroebe & Stroebe, 1983).

The research supported the existence of continuing and powerful responses to loss for a period extending as much as 13 years following death. The bereaved as a group functioned with greater impairment than their nonbereaved parental counterparts. Similarly, the bereaved group were the more anxious. Thus, demonstrable effects in the realm of behavior, affect, cognitive attitude, and somatic function characterized these bereaved parents for many years following loss. Overall, the women showed greater anxiety and difficulties in functioning following bereavement as a main effect.

The highly significant differences in anxiety between the bereaved and nonbereaved groups suggested a permanent shift in the homeostasis of tension regulation postloss. This may indicate that the impact of loss of a son for older parents affects basic personality resilience. At the phenomenological level, it is another indication that bereaved parents continue to experience emotional tension and concern for many years. What is the anxiety in relation to? It would appear to reflect a continuing unease about the loss, a greater awareness of the loved son no longer alive accompanied by sadness and pain, and the troubling emotions and thoughts that have receded but not disappeared. The despair, anger/ hostility, and so many other cognitive and affective responses following loss manifested themselves in the interviews as well as on the measures of functioning.

Data concerning the nature of the relationship to the deceased son conveyed the impact of the bereavement process in a different manner. There were consistent quantitative and qualitative differences between the nature of the attachment to living versus deceased sons. For example, parents viewed the deceased son as unique and reported having had a very special relationship with him. Their cognitive representations of the deceased reflected altered associations, memories, and affects linked with the deceased son. There were differences between bereaved and non-bereaved groups on the degree of enmeshment versus distinctness of self and son representations. The nonbereaved presented themselves more independently from their children and rated those children in less than idealized terms. The bereaved were very much involved with their sons and stressed an idealized picture of them.

These response characteristics are consistent with a tendency to over-identify with the deceased son. The son is viewed more positively than other children and other relationships among the living. The son's image is intensely bound up with the covert emotional life of the parents. As the son's representation becomes more central to the parent's internal psychological world, it becomes more difficult for the parent to move away from intense involvement with this private relationship.

The bereaved parents' covert internal relationship to the deceased remained striking both 4 and 13 years after loss. Findings suggest that the bulk of the adjustment and shifting in postloss reorganization had stabilized within the first 4 years postloss. The way the son was viewed did not support a picture of bereavement as a self-limiting response with a clear terminus. Numerous indications of strong involvement with the deceased were present. For example, on many of the parents' written characterizations of the deceased, vivid features of shock, searching, and disorganization were present. The singular difference between the bereaved groups was in the degree of reorganization that coexisted with the involvement with the loss and the lost. As might be expected, the parents bereaved in the Yom Kippur War had 13 years later achieved a greater degree of reorganization than parents bereaved in the 1982 Sheleg War. Reorganization following loss did not, however, replace the vivid elements of grief and mourning still experienced by the 1973 Yom Kippur group. Instead, it appeared to frame and organize the other elements of the relationship to the deceased. It provided perspective, but not necessarily other structural changes, in the extent to which the loss was central and "alive" for the bereaved. Succinctly, in the years following adult child loss, the phenomena of loss do not continue to recede. It is only that perspective on the loss continues to accrue.

As has been consistently reported in the literature, the tendency to idealize the deceased following loss is pronounced and characteristic of many cultures and age groups (Bowlby, 1980/1981; Lopata, 1981). Its origins have been attributed to various sources, including intrapsychic guilt and anthropologically recognized magical fear of the deceased. An equally important aspect may be the tendency to idealize those who are too far removed to confound our idealized view. They are thus unable to provide contradictory behaviors that might balance the idealized picture (Rubin, 1990b). Differences were related to how the living and deceased sons were perceived. They were not the product of differences in how the parental self-image, per se, was valued.

It is clinically useful to emphasize this phenomenon, as it can delay resolution of bereavement (Rubin, 1985). It appears rooted in the nature of the covert representation of the deceased and the relationship with him. These are sufficiently different from the exchanges of life between the living so that the absence of ongoing interpersonal feedback mechanisms can be powerfully self-perpetuating. The excessive valuation of the deceased child over living children is recognized as a major source of tension in bereaved families. The absence of negative feedback from the idealized deceased would appear to contribute to this (Rubin, 1990b).

Parents' continuing attachment to their deceased sons was apparent in other ways as well. At one end of the behavioral continuum, 46% of the sample visited their son's grave at least once a week. At the opposite end, 40% visited the grave less than once a month. Participation in memorial services for sons was high, with 76% attending all services and 18% attending some. At a more covert level of what parents reported they thought about, 87% of the parents indicated they thought about their sons very frequently. Many stimuli triggered thoughts, memories, and reveries of the deceased, but at family events, 97% of the parents thought about their sons a great deal. At holidays, the figure was 92%. Only on the anniversary of the death did thoughts of the sons attain greater dominance, when 99% reported they thought about the deceased a great deal. There were no differences between the bereaved groups on any of these variables.

The affective tone that accompanied these thoughts illustrates how dysphoric the experience of child loss continued to be. Sadness and yearning were the predominant emotions of the bereaved parents at 4 and at 13 years following the death. The emergence of some pleasant feelings associated with memories and reveries of the son was acknowledged by half of the respondents and vigorously denied by the other half. These findings suggest that demonstrable effects characterize bereaved parents for many years following loss. In addition, they underscore that responses to adult child loss have permanent effects on functioning and the inner lives of parents.

Clinical and empirical summary

The pattern of response to child loss may be conceptualized as follows. At the outset, the loss involves a global reaction encompassing virtually every area of functioning, as well as relationship to the deceased (Lindemann, 1944; Rubin, 1982). With the passage of time, the pronounced effect on functioning tends to subside, whereas the covert relationship to the deceased remains a major focus of adaptation. Despite the reduction in the dramatic impact of loss on functioning and overt areas of behavior, the impact of loss continues. It is the continuing interaction between function and relationship that students of bereavement can valuably address.

As to the question of where to focus interventions, a case can be made for a comprehensive intervention program to address both the relationship and the functioning of the bereaved. The research described here supports clinical wisdom in the need to focus both on functioning and on the relationship to the deceased in assessment and intervention with individuals who have suffered bereavement.

The emerging picture from the body of research investigations to date underscores a number of features of parental bereavement. The multiyear perspective for examining effects of loss showed that for many years following bereavement the extent of symptomatic and relational investment in the deceased remain elevated. Sex and age seem to be significant mediators of loss. Women often respond more dramatically than men, but exactly what this means is not yet clear (W. Stroebe & Stroebe, 1987). All things being equal, younger parents seem better able to adapt to the loss and better able to emerge from the loss of a child. All parents are changed by the experience, but it is the younger parents who appear less overwhelmed and better able to integrate the loss into a still flexible life structure. Developmentally, older parents appear less resilient and less able to emerge from the severe dislocation of loss of a child. Physiologically and psychologically, consciously and unconsciously, older parents often experience the death of an adult child as one of the most dominant themes and preoccupations of their later life (Caspi-Yavin, 1988; Dichterman, 1989; Rubin, 1987; Tamir, 1987).

Resuming a level of preloss functioning and regaining the necessary equilibrium to invest fully in life, spouse, and other children are difficult challenges. These are typically met with only partial success. For most parents, it is generally an amalgam of positive and negative effects that follow loss. Loss may spur some parents to experience their lives in sharp new ways, which bring them new levels of meaning and new valued behaviors. For other parents, loss wounds the ability to negotiate and live life adequately. Their focus on the unattainable past relationship with the deceased child skews and excludes much of the richness of the present.

The complexity and range of responses to loss call for multidimensional approaches to the understanding of bereavement. The advantages of the multidimensional perspective are many. Yet perhaps the most important is that such an approach allows us to retain an appreciation for the complexity of the response to the loss of an irreplaceable son or daughter.

20

Children's reactions to the death of a parent

PHYLLIS R. SILVERMAN AND
J. WILLIAM WORDEN

There is general agreement that the death of a parent for school-age children is a very stressful experience (Antonovsky, 1979; Garmezy, 1987). Some researchers have shown that such a loss can lead to depression or other behavior problems in children and also later on as adults (Furman, 1974; Birtchnell, 1980; Bowlby, 1980; Brown, Harris, & Bifulco, 1986). In contrast, other studies have not been able to point to any consistent findings supporting the hypothesis that the death of a parent in childhood leads to an increase in problem behaviors or to an increased risk of subsequently developing psychological problems (Van Eerdewegh, Bieri, Parilla, & Clayton, 1982; Osterweis, Solomon, & Green, 1984). Berlinsky and Biller (1982), in an extensive review of the research literature, observed that this lack of consistent findings may be due to an oversimplification of outcome measures, such as the presence or absence of psychiatric symptoms or other problem behaviors. Also contributing to the confusion is the use of a single-event model, which obscures the complexity of the situation.

The death of a parent cannot be viewed as a single stressful event but as a series of events that occur before and after the death (Berlinsky & Biller, 1982; Norris & Murrell, 1987). Brown et al. (1986), in their study of depressed women who, as children, lost their mother, and Elizur and Kaffman (1983), who studied Israeli children who lost fathers in war, suggest that factors other than the loss need to be in place before a bereaved child can be considered at risk. The way the surviving parent responds to the child, the availability of social support, and subsequent life circumstances (such as a poor parental remarriage) can all make a difference in whether children develop emotional problems.

Reese (1982) observed that the increased risk for developing emotional problems was associated with the lack of continuity in the child's daily life after the death, including the surviving parent's inability to provide a stable

This research was supported by grants from the National Institute of Mental Health (MH-41971), the National Funeral Directors Association, and the Hillenbrand Corporation.

home for the child. Brown et al. (1986) used the concept of "increased vulnerability" to describe the impact of childhood loss on the adult women studied. They posited that it was not the death alone that led to increased risk but a multitude of intervening variables played out over time that increased a person's vulnerability for developing social or emotional problems.

We need, then, to understand the context in which the stress is experienced. From the stress literature we learn that it is not simply that a death occurred but, rather, how people view the loss, the availability of personal and social resources, and how these resources are used that differentiate adaptive from maladaptive responses (Lazarus & Folkman, 1984; Antonovsky, 1979, 1987).

Silverman (1987a), in a retrospective study of college-age women who had a parent die years previously, found that most of these young women felt their lives were changed by the loss but were not necessarily filled with problems. Bereavement outcomes need to be conceptualized in more dynamic terms that emphasize change and adaptation rather than merely the presence or absence of symptoms or signs of psychological disturbance. The death of a loved one does lead to psychological and social stress, and the bereaved are faced with the need to adapt to many changes in their lives. However, one needs to ask what it is that influences one's ability to deal with these changes. The answer to this question lies in understanding the interaction among the social context, the family system, and the personal characteristics of those involved. We are dealing with a sociological as well as a psychological phenomenon (Shamgar-Handleman, 1986).

It is also important to be cautious when using psychiatric nomenclature to describe grieving behavior. Fifty-six percent of the surviving parents in the Harvard child bereavement study reported depressionlike symptoms that led to their being scored as depressed on the CES-D measure of depression (Radloff, 1977). On closer scrutiny, only 31% of the parents who scored as depressed selected low self-esteem items, such as feeling unloved or that their life was a failure. One must distinguish between the dysphoria of typical grieving behavior, such as feeling sad, and low self-esteem responses associated with clinical depression. If we use the diagnostic language of psychiatry to describe typical bereavement behavior, this will influence the findings on the side of pathology. We need to look at the broad range of responses from the bereaved so as to identify what is normative for them and only then impose statistical and clinical models of abnormality.

Cichetti (1984) noted that children are growing and developing, so that their situation is never static. Garmezy (1983) observed that while a specific stressor such as the death of a parent may put a child at risk, this risk is not necessarily sustained over time. We are looking at a dynamic interactive process to which time must be added as a factor.

Using data available from the Harvard child bereavement study based at the Massachusetts General Hospital, we will describe the normative responses of 125 bereaved school-age children and the family context that frames their reactions shortly after the death of one parent.

The child bereavement study

The Harvard child bereavement study is a prospective study of children between the ages of 6 and 17 who lost a parent to death. The study was designed to respond to deficits in other studies of childhood bereavement that involved clinical populations, interviewed only the surviving parent, measured outcome too soon after the death, looked at outcome primarily in terms of psychological problems, and did not have a control population. The study involved a nonclinical representative community sample, interviewed both the surviving parent and all school-age children in the family, followed the family for 2 years after the death, and assessed a matched nonbereaved sample of children.

Semistructured interviews with these children and their surviving parent were conducted in the family home at 4 months after the death and at the first and second anniversaries. The children were asked questions regarding their predeath status, experience with the death, mourning behavior, life changes since the death, school functioning, current health status, peer relationships, and attitudes and behaviors with other members of the family related to the loss. The parent interview covered family demography, predeath status, circumstances of the death, mourning behavior, current support, an appraisal of stress and coping, concerns about the children, family activities, and responses to the death. In addition to the interviews, standardized assessments of locus of control (Nowicki & Strickland, 1973), of self-esteem (Harter, 1985), and of the child's understanding of death (Smilansky, 1987) were completed by the children. The surviving parent completed standardized instruments measuring family structure and coping (FACES III, F-COPES) (Olson et al., 1983), family changes (FILE) (McCubbin, Larson, & Olson, 1987), depression (Radloff, 1977), impact of events (Horowitz et al., 1981), and for each child a Child Behavior Checklist (Achenbach & Edelbrock, 1983).

Families were recruited from communities in the greater Boston area that represented a range of socioeconomic, religious, and ethnic backgrounds. During the recruiting period funeral directors invited all the families they served that met the criteria for inclusion in the study to participate: parents living together at the time of the death with children in the family between the ages of 6 and 17. We were able to identify, with few exceptions, every bereaved family in the selected target communities. Of those who received invitations to participate, 70 families (51%) accepted. There were no significant differences between the families who accepted and those who refused based on gender and age of the deceased, suddenness of the death, family religion, and number of children. From a demographic point of view, the study population was a representative sample of bereaved families in these communities. We recognize that other than demographic factors may influence people's decision to participate (M. Stroebe & Stroebe, 1989). We must assume that there may be some bias in favor of people who see value in talking about their situation.

We interviewed 70 families having among them 125 children between the ages of 6 and 17. There were an almost equal number of boys ($n = 65$) and girls ($n = 60$) in the sample, with an average age of 11.8 years. Seventy-two percent ($n = 90$) lost their father and 28% ($n = 35$) their mother. Sixty percent ($N = 48$) of these parents had been ill for some time before the death, and the rest were sudden deaths.

The average age of the surviving parent was 42 years, with a range of 30 to 57 years of age for the surviving mothers and 33 to 50 for the surviving fathers. For most of these couples (91%) this was their only marriage, and the length of marriage ranged from 2 to 36 years, with a mean of 17 years. The modal number of children was two. In nine families the child who participated in this study was an only child. The religious affiliation of this population reflected the large concentration of Roman Catholics in the greater Boston area. Seventy percent of the families were Catholic, 23% Protestant, 6% Jewish, and 1% other. The families were all Caucasian with one exception.

Family incomes after the death ranged from less than $10,000 a year to more than $50,000, with a median income range of $20,000 to $29,000. Thirty-three percent ($n = 23$) of the surviving parents thought their income was inadequate or barely adequate, and 67% ($n = 46$) thought that their income was adequate or more than adequate. As might be expected, the amount of income correlated with the parent's sense of its adequacy ($r = .58$, $p < .01$). The assessment of income adequacy was related to employment status. People who were working saw their income as more adequate ($r = .25$, $p < .03$) than those not holding jobs.

Before the death men were the primary breadwinners for the family. There were significant differences between men's and women's employment status at the time of the first interview. Men were more likely to be working full time and women more likely to be working part time outside the home or to be full-time homemakers [$\chi^2(4, N = 70) = 12.68$, $p < .001$]. Women were more likely to have changed their employment status just before or right after the death. Women were also more likely than men to receive income from life insurance ($r = .51$, $p < .01$) and social security benefits

($r = .48$, $p < .01$). Such imcome made it possible for some of these women to stop working outside the home. A few women began work after the death so as to get health insurance coverage. Four men were not working outside the home. One was psychologically unable to find regular work after his wife died, and he supported his children by doing odd jobs. The other three men were receiving Disability Assistance or Aid for Dependent Children prior to the death. When the surviving parent was a mother, there was more continuity for the child, as she was more likely to be at home when children returned from school and available as the primary caregiver.

Most of the deaths (89%, $n = 62$) were from natural causes. Forty percent ($n = 28$) died either instantly or within a day. Five (7%) children went to bed with an intact family and woke up orphaned. Of the 60% ($N = 42$) who had expected deaths, 65% were men ($n = 13$), and 59% ($n = 29$) women. The proportion of men and women who had cared for a spouse during a long illness was similar and not significantly different. Of the 42 parents who died from a prolonged illness, 43% ($n = 18$) had been ill for more than a year. In families where the father died, mothers were more likely to plan financially with their husbands before the death than in families where mothers died [$\chi^2(2, N = 44) = 5.98$, $p < .05$].

Ninety-four percent of the children ($n = 118$) attended the funeral. Age was a factor in deciding whether to include the child in the funeral. Younger children were less likely to attend as were those whose mother died. Seventy-eight percent ($n = 97$) of the children saw their parent's body, most often at a wake or in the funeral home. Most (85%, $n = 106$) of the children went to the cemetery, and 73% ($n = 78$) have visited the cemetery since the funeral.

Children's reactions and experiences

Three conceptual domains best describe the experiences and reactions of these children in the early months after the death. Each cluster of information reflects an aspect of the child's reactions to the death and reflects our current understanding of the grief process (Silverman, 1986; Worden, 1991) and points to the complexity of the grief experience. These domains are the child's affective responses, the child's efforts at maintaining a connection to the deceased, and the impact on the child's behavior of the social network and support system. These data are taken from the children's responses to interviewers' questions at 4 months and 1 year after the death. Where indicated, data from the parent interview were used as well. Although some children came from the same family, we are treating them as 125 individuals in this analysis. We recognize that these observations of the children may not be totally independent. However, recent research has suggested that there is wide variance among children raised in the same family (Dunn & Plomin, 1990). Studies of identical twins raised apart or together show that the overlap in personality traits between them is not more than 25% (Scarr, 1987). These findings support our treatment of these children as individuals, each experiencing the death in his or her own way.

This chapter is intended to be descriptive, and the statistics used were so chosen. The analysis focuses on the impact of the gender and age of the children, the suddenness of the death, and the gender of the parent who died to see how these variables impact on the child's responses. Gender and age of the child are key factors in understanding a child's behavior (Selman, 1980; Youniss, 1980; Hartup, 1989; Jacklin, 1989). Gender differences have been identified in the way men and women mobilize social support (Belle, 1988) and in the roles family members play (Lynn, 1974; Carter, Scott, & Martyna, 1976), as well as in their response to bereavement (M. Stroebe & Stroebe, 1983; Silverman, 1988b). The suddenness of the death can impact on the nature of the stress a family experiences (Antonovsky, 1987).

Affective responses

These behaviors reflected a child's inner feeling about the death, such as crying, inability to sleep, learn, concentrate at school, and early health problems related to the somatization of feelings. We hypothesized that these feelings would diminish in intensity and frequency in the weeks or months following the death.

Children's reactions to the immediate news of the loss were more contained than one might have expected. Very few children expressed any immediate anger and a few expressed relief. Most children talked of feeling sad or confused upon hearing the news and of not being sure how to respond. Many talked of feeling dazed or shocked. Some turned to other family members for comfort, and others withdrew. A few children reported needing to be alone – retreating to their room or going out for a walk or to ride their bicycles. Others went in search of a friend. When the death was sudden (no warning), many children were stunned by the news. Some thought it was a cruel joke and were not sure how to react. Within the day, 91% ($n = 112$) of the children broke down in tears. There was no significant difference between the way boys and girls responded upon hearing the news, nor were there any differences in early responses based on the gender of the dead parent. As one might expect, children reported more immediate crying when there was a sudden death than when the death was expected. (See Table 20.1.)

Four months after the death, 67% ($n = 77$) of these children were no longer crying at frequent intervals or with any regularity. Those who were

Table 20.1. *Affective responses 4 months and 1 year after the death*

	Time 1 (N = 125)	Time 2 (N = 120)
Current crying		
Every day	10 (8.8%)	2 (1.7%)
Several times a week	27 (23.7%)	13 (11%)
Not too often	54 (47.3%)	59 (50%)
Never	23 (20.2%)	44 (37.3%)
	χ^2 (9, N = 109) = 32.38, $p < .001$	
Sleep problems		
None	87 (70.2%)	94 (80.3%)
	χ^2 (1, N = 120) = 4.24 $p < .05$	
Headaches		
None	33 (26.4%)	30 (25%)
Occasionally	66 (52.8%)	67 (55.8%)
Frequently	26 (20.8%)	23 (19.2%)
	n.s.[a]	
Accidents		
None	94 (75.2%)	79 (65.8%)
Yes, no medical	22 (17.6%)	29 (24.2%)
Yes, with medical	9 (7.2%)	12 (10%)
	$t = 2.07$, $df = 119$, $p < .05$	
Health status		
No problems	44 (35.2%)	23 (19.3%)
Mild problems	76 (60.8%)	84 (70.6%)
Serious illness	1 (.8%)	8 (6.7%)
Hospitalization	4 (3.2%)	4 (3.4%)
	$t = -3.29$, $df = 118$, $p < .001$	
Difficult concentration (school)		
Rarely	53 (43.1%)	78 (65%)
Occasionally	46 (37.3%)	23 (19.2%)
Frequently	18 (14.6%)	14 (11.7%)
Always	6 (4.9%)	5 (4.2%)
	χ^2 (9, N = 118) = 21.30, $p < .01$	

[a] n.s. = not significant.

crying frequently were more likely to be younger ($r = .17$, $p < .05$). There were no significant gender differences in their crying behavior, nor were there differences depending on which parent died. By the first anniversary fewer children were crying with any regularity ($\chi^2(9, N = 109) = 32.38$, $p < .001$).

Only 22% ($n = 27$) of the children felt that their school performance had changed for the worse 4 months after the death. In 18% ($n = 22$) of the cases, the children felt that their work improved. Thirty-seven percent ($n = 46$) said they occasionally had some difficulty concentrating in school, and

Table 20.2. *Child Behavior Checklist scores: Percentage of children with scores over 70 at 1 year after the death*

Clinical scale	Bereaved children ($N = 120$)	Nonbereaved children ($N = 73$)
Aggressive	6%	0%
Delinquent	4	2
Withdrawn	7	3
Somatic	8	3
Hyperactive	7	2
Schizoid	6	2

another 20% ($n = 24$) said this occurred frequently or very frequently. Inability to concentrate was one area where the impact of the death could be seen immediately, but it diminished significantly by the end of the first year [$\chi^2(9, N = 118) = 21.30, p < .01$]. Somatic symptoms were more frequent for the bereaved children than their matched nonbereaved controls (see Table 20.2). Nine children had had serious illnesses several months after the death and by the second interview this number had increased to twelve. Although most children (70%, $n = 87$) slept well, the one-third ($n = 37$) who had some sleep problems had difficulty either in falling asleep or waking early and attributed this to their parent's death. These were likely to be children who dreamed of the deceased ($r = .24, p < .01$), were still crying a great deal at 4 months ($r = -.19, p < .05$), and had difficulty concentrating in school ($r = .28, p < .01$). By the end of the first year fewer children were having sleep disturbance, and the difference was significant [$\chi^2(1, N = 120) = 4.24, p < .04$].

Neither the suddenness of the death nor the gender of the deceased made major differences in children's affective responses. Although younger children were better able than older ones to express feelings, many children did not have words for what they were experiencing. Interviewers observed this difficulty in articulating feelings when the children hesitated or were unable to answer questions.

The information described so far reflects the children's responses. To identify emotional and behavioral problems as seen by the surviving parent, each child was assessed on the Child Behavior Checklist (Achenbach & Edelbrock, 1983) at each interview. The 118 identified behaviors can be scored as a series of narrow band clinical scales that note the seriousness of problem behaviors. Elevated scores on the narrow band scales, that is, those exceeding a T score of 70, ranged in frequency from a low for 2% of the children on Delinquent Behaviors to a high for 13% on Somatic

Table 20.3. *Achenbach scores, by age and gender*

	Time 1	Time 2	Significance[a]
Younger boys ($N = 30$)			
Mean	53.13	51.67	n.s.
SD	10.97	12.13	
Older boys ($N = 34$)			
Mean	53.94	50.35	$t = 300$, df 30
SD	11.25	11.20	$p. < .005$
Younger girls ($N = 31$)			
Mean	55.26	50.90	$t = 351$, df 30
SD	11.18	10.89	$p. < .001$
Older girls ($N = 28$)			
Mean	53.34	53.08	n.s.
SD	9.93	13.04	

[a] n.s. = not significant.

Behaviors. The remaining clinical scales were high for 6% to 7% of the children, depending on the scale. Control children with high scores on the various clinical scales were in the 2% to 3% range. (See Table 20.2.)

In addition to the narrow band clinical scales normed for subgroups by age and gender, there are three broad band Child Behavior Checklist scales that enable one to compare behavioral profiles across age–gender quadrants (boys, girls, younger, older). These broad band scales measure total behavior problems, internalized behaviors such as anxiety and depression, and externalized behaviors such as delinquency and acting-out behavior. Highest Achenbach total scores were found in the group of younger girls; Scores for younger boys, older boys, and older girls were slightly lower. We used a T score of 65 or greater (above 1.5 standard deviations) to identify the group of children who were most distressed at 4 months. Twenty-seven children had scores exceeding 65 on one or more of these three broad band scales, representing 24% of the children. By the first anniversary of the loss, the percentage of children with high scores had dropped to 19%. (See Table 20.3.)

Children with the highest Achenbach total scores were those who had the poorest peer support ($r = .19$, $p < .05$) and who felt that they had less control over things happening to them. A high score on the Child Behavior Checklist correlated with more external locus of control ($r = .29$, $p < .01$) (Nowicki & Strickland, 1973) and with lower self-esteem ($r = .26$, $p < .01$) (Harter, 1985). The children with the most disturbed behavior had lower self-esteem and felt less in control of their lives regardless of their age.

Gender of the child and suddenness of the death were not significantly related to the broad band scales on the checklist. Gender of the deceased parent was correlated with high scores in two instances: Four month after the death, younger boys whose father died had significantly higher scores ($p < .01$); and, at the end of the first year, adolescent girls who lost their mothers had significantly higher scores ($p < .03$).

Maintaining a connection to the deceased

Most studies of bereavement have focused on affective responses expressed in typical grieving behavior such as crying and sadness. Worden (1982/1991) has identified four tasks of mourning, one of which is accepting the finality of the death. This involves acknowledging that the deceased is indeed gone, but it may not mean that the sense of the deceased in the child's life is obliterated as well. Silverman and Silverman (1979) have suggested that it is easier to accept the finality of the loss if the bereaved have an appropriate way to maintain a sense of the deceased in their current life. Klass (1988) observed that some bereaved parents actively sought ways of carrying a memory of the child with them.

We found that these bereaved children devoted considerable energy to connect with the deceased in some way. They did this through dreams, by talking to the deceased, by feeling that the dead parent was watching them, by keeping things that belonged to the dead parent, by visiting the grave, and by frequently thinking about him or her. (See Table 20.4.)

When asked what they believed happened after the death, most children said that their parent had gone to a specific place, and they usually talked about heaven. Fifty-seven percent ($n = 71$) spoke to the deceased parent, and 43% ($n = 29$) of these children, mostly younger, felt they received an answer. By the end of the first year children were speaking less frequently to their deceased parent [$\chi^2(1, N = 120) = 10.08, p < .001$]. Eighty-one percent ($n = 101$) felt that their parent was watching them, and of those who felt watched, 57% ($n = 71$) were frightened by this. For the frightened children their uneasiness was related to a fear that their parent might not approve of what they were doing. Those who felt watched but were not scared were more likely to see the parent watching over them in a protective way. For whatever reason, the deceased was a real presence in most children's lives and carried on a continuation of the relationship they had before the death such as protector or disciplinarian. Differences between the boys and girls on these variables were not statistically significant. By the end of the first year most children still had a sense of being watched by the deceased; however, they reported feeling less scared by this.

Most children (56%, $n = 69$) also dreamed about their parent, and for 63 of these children, the parent was alive in the dreams. Some children were

Table 20.4. *Connection with the deceased: Responses 4 months and 1 year after the death*

	Time 1 (N = 125)	Time 2 (N = 120)
Deceased parent watches child		
No	13 (10.4%)	24 (20%)
Not sure	11 (8.8%)	7 (5.9%)
Yes	91 (80.8%)	89 (73.7%)
	$t = 2.22$, $df = 119$, $p > .03$	
Speaks to deceased parent		
Yes	71 (56.8%)	46 (39%)
	χ^2 (1, $N = 120$) = 10.02, $p < .01$	
Thinks of deceased parent		
Everyday	69 (63.3%)	51 (43.2%)
Several times a week	30 (27.5%)	33 (28%)
Not too often	9 (8.3%)	32 (27.1%)
Never	1 (.9%)	2 (1.7%)
	$t = -4.92$, $df = 103$, $p < .001$	
Dreams of deceased parent		
Yes	69 (55.2%)	59 (50%)
	n.s.[a]	
Kept object		
Yes	95 (76.6%)	87 (74.4%)
	n.s.	

[a] n.s. = not significant.

frightened by these dreams, others felt saddened by them, and a few found the dreams very reassuring. The age and gender of the child seemed to make little difference in dreaming behavior or in how the child felt about the dreams.

At the 4-month interview, 90% ($n = 99$) of the children reported still thinking about their parent at least several times a week. When asked what they thought about, most children remembered in literal and concrete terms what they did with their parent. A few children reported that they still couldn't believe the death was real, and some reported forgetting at times that their parent was dead. Others wished for the parent back or thought about how hard it was to get along without their parent. The children whose mother had died were likely to be thinking about her more frequently than those whose father had died ($r = -.19$, $p < .05$). At the end of the first year, the time spent thinking about their deceased parent decreased significantly ($t = -4.92$, df 103, $p < .001$).

Seventy-seven percent ($n = 95$) of the children kept something personal that belonged to their dead parent, for the most part, either on their person or in their room.

Most children were involved with the deceased through their dreams, their waking thoughts, and keeping things close to them that belonged to the deceased. The deceased parent's presence was strongly felt. One way of looking at these behaviors is to see them as the struggle to make the loss real and a way to understand what had happened. For most children this struggle did not diminish during the first year after loss.

Social network and social context

The child's social context provided a frame for the experience of mourning and determined how the child expressed this grief and made meaning out of the loss. Belle (1988), in a review of the social support literature, observed that a clear relationship existed between the functioning of a given support network and its impact on the way stress is experienced. These contextual variables can increase the child's vulnerability or can act as a buffer or protective force in helping the child cope and adapt (Garmezy, 1987; Rutter, 1987). The social network can provide the child with a feeling of being supported and cared about and can make available resources that facilitate coping. These resources also included funeral and mourning rituals. Children's participation in the funeral ritual and other ceremonies surrounding the death did have important repercussions for how they understood death and how they saw themselves as participants in the family drama. The way grief was expressed by the surviving parent and the way loss was understood impact on how the family maintains itself as a functioning system that was able to deal with the many changes it was experiencing and able to adapt to a single-parent household.

Changes in the child's daily life, available support, and parental coping styles were all part of the context that frames the lives of these bereaved children.

Changes in daily life. Most children's lives continued as before, with few changes in their bedtime, the chores they had to do around the house, or in their allowance. Some children (19%, $n = 23$) were uneasy about coming to the dinner table now that one parent was absent. When there were younger children (under 12) at home and the mother died, children were more likely to experience a change in care giving when they were sick. They either took care of themselves or were cared for by a relative. Children whose mother died had more responsibility for household chores. Clear differences were noted at mealtimes after a mother died ($r = .29, p < .001$). Meals were served at a less regular time and may not have been as well prepared when the father was the surviving parent. We found that the death of the mother caused the greatest discontinuity in the lives of these children at 4 months after the death. These changes can be seen as concomitant losses for these children. Children with the greatest number of changes in their daily routines following the death also suffered more health problems, kept an object from the deceased parent close at hand, and felt very uneasy about coming to the dinner table.

Sharing and support. Around the time of the death and funeral, 42% ($n = 53$) of the children felt that they had to act a certain way for their surviving parent's sake and 45 of these children complied. Those who felt compelled believed that they had to be restrained and not create problems for the parent by their actions. This was especially true in families in which the death had been expected. Children over the age of 12 were more likely to be told specifically they had to be more grown up now [$\chi^2(1, N = 125) = 4.28, p < .02$], and this message was more likely to be sent to older boys [$\chi^2(1, N = 63) = 3.54, p < .05$]. Some children felt pressured by the surviving parent to express their feelings more openly, and some experienced this expectation as criticism rather than as help.

When asked to identify the person to whom they felt closest in their family, half the children chose their surviving parent. Equal numbers felt closest to a sibling or a relative such as a grandparent. Twelve children (11%) said they were not close to anyone. Three of these children were in one study family and two in another. They tended to be children whose mother died and who did not talk to the deceased parent. Most children reported that they could talk about the dead parent and their feelings about the death with this identified close person. Even when they weren't close to their surviving parent, half these children felt that they could, nonetheless, talk with this parent if they needed to. This included some children who felt that they weren't close to anyone. By the end of the first year all children had found someone in the family to whom they felt close and in whom they could confide.

Girls were much more likely than boys to share their feelings with an identified family member ($r = .26, p < .01$). Fathers who were left as the primary caregiver reported less communication about the death between themselves and their children [$\chi^2(1, N = 125) = 5.82, p < .01$]. The children themselves did not feel family communication was any more or less hampered when the mother died but did report more reluctance in sharing dreams of the deceased with a surviving father.

There were gender differences in the ways boys and girls related to their social network and in the way their network related to them. Girls were more likely than boys to talk with their surviving parent about the impending death when the death was expected ($r = .27, p < .01$). Girls were also more likely to talk about their feelings after the death ($r = .26$,

$p < .01$), and they were less likely to be told to be grown up, a message most often given to teenage boys.

When the mother died after a long illness, children were more likely to be sent back to school the day after the funeral ($r = -.24$, $p < .05$). Teachers uniformly knew about the death, but in only half the cases did they share this awareness with the child's classmates. Sharing information with the class was more likely to have occurred in the lower grades where children had one teacher for the entire school day. Children appreciated expressions of condolence and notes they received from their classmates.

Socially, most children (70%, $n = 84$) felt that after the death there was little change in the time they spent outside their home with their friends. All children reported having at least one close friend, with half of them reporting four or more friends. Seventy-three percent ($n = 82$) of these children saw their friends at least every day, as they usually went to school with them. Only 54% ($n = 67$) of the children reported that they talked with their friends about their dead parent. Those who did not talk with their friends wanted it that way. Most of them thought that at least one friend would listen if they wanted to talk. Boys were less likely than girls to talk to their friends about the death. Fourteen percent ($n = 18$) of the children felt that there were children in their neighborhood or in school who gave them a hard time because they only had one parent. This occurred more frequently to younger children, especially younger girls.

Parental coping. The focus thus far has been on the children's coping behavior. It is equally important to understand the parent's responses, as children's responses are intimately involved with those of their parents. Coping, as defined by McCubbin, Larson, and Olson (1987), is behavior that involves the management of various aspects of family life – that is, maintaining satisfactory internal conditions for communication and family organization; promoting member independence, self-esteem, coherence, and unity; and maintaining and developing social support transactions in the community. Differences between the way men and women perceived family coping styles, as measured by the F-Cope scale (McCubbin et al., 1987), indicated that the surviving mothers displayed greater competence in overall coping ability in contrast to fathers ($r = .31$, $p < .01$). Mothers were more able to help their families in acquiring support from the wider community ($r = .26$, $p < .05$). Full-time employment status was negatively correlated with accepting support from family and friends ($r = -.22$, $p < .04$) and total overall coping ($r = -.21$, $p < .05$) as measured by F-Copes. Working full time and taking care of their children while they were dealing with their own sorrow may have caused these families to pull into themselves and not reach out to others.

The meaning a family attaches to a stressful situation influences the family's appraisal of the situation and its coping behavior (McCubbin et al., 1987). We asked each parent to rank the degree of stress they were experiencing at the time of the interview on an 8-point Likert scale. A similar Likert scale was used to assess their current coping. Not surprisingly, parents who experienced the most stress also felt that they were coping the least adequately ($r = -.24$, $p < .05$). There was no correlation between the gender of the parents and their assessment of the stress they were experiencing or the success of their coping. Mothers were more likely than fathers to report that they had found unexpected sources of support [$\chi^2(1, N = 70)$ = 4.95, $p < .05$] since the death. The fact that fathers were more likely to be working outside the home may account for some of these differences. How prepared parents were to assume the role of single parent had a major impact on their performance as well. Fathers reported having the most to learn when they assumed the role of single parent and took responsibility for their children's daily care.

Conclusions

Understanding the children's responses to the death of a parent requires focusing on a number of interacting variables. By itself, the event is stressful, and its impact pervades most aspects of the child's life, affecting the way in which his or her world is structured. These stresses, however, did not seem to overwhelm most of the children. In the first months after the death, 22% of the children showed some indications of dysfunctional behavior, using their parent's assessment on the Achenbach as the barometer. From the children's view, we saw sadness and some confusion. We also saw children who were carrying on by going to school and by maintaining relationships with their friends and in their family. Clearly, these children were grieving, but the majority did not express their grief in prolonged crying periods, aggression, or withdrawal behavior, as has been traditionally thought. There was some sleep disturbance, some restlessness, but not to an excessive degree. Somatic symptoms, on the other hand, were high and confirm the notion that grief is often somaticized, especially in preadolescent children.

Among the more interesting findings were those pointing to the child's maintaining a connection to the deceased. These behaviors have frequently been labeled as "preoccupation with the deceased." This term implies symptomatic behavior that should end. Most of the descriptions of this phenomenon have been based on clinical observations (Miller, 1971; Volkan, 1981; Dietrich & Shabad, 1989), and this may have influenced the conclusion that in grief work it is necessary to disengage from the deceased. This conclusion did not seem consistent with the reality we observed. College-age women who lost a parent to death reported that as they got older they were constantly renegotiating their relationship with their dead parent (Silverman, 1987a). The parent may be dead, but the relationship did not die (Anderson, 1974). In the long run, accepting the reality of the death may mean finding a way for the dead parent to live in some way within the child's life (Silverman & Silverman, 1979; Rubin, 1985; Worden, 1982/1991). We saw similar behaviors in the surviving parent, who reported talking to the deceased and findings other ways of remaining connected.

These children understood the concept of death in the abstract, but many had very little way of talking about this experience. Based on these findings, we suggest that one of the tasks of the early stages of the bereavement is to develop a language that gives children the tools to talk about death and their dead parent and then to find a way of maintaining an appropriate place for the dead parent in their lives. Many surviving parents expressed concern that their children were not showing their feelings. They saw the exhibiting of feelings as the primary way for their children to express their grief. Parents did not sufficiently appreciate that conversations about the dead parent were also a part of grief work. Both the surviving parent and the children need to learn that this kind of reflection and remembering is also a critical part of the bereavement process. How well they learn to do this may hold the key to the kind of accommodation these families make to the loss over time.

These children were not only dealing with the death of a person but with the death of a way of life. Most were included in the mourning rituals and treated with respect as a mourner. However, many did not feel that it was acceptable to display uncontrolled feelings, and this was especially true for older boys. We found that by adolescence boys were being socialized to control their feelings. In so doing, families reflected the values of the larger society that teaches men not to express their feelings openly (Miller, 1986).

There were clear differences in how surviving fathers and mothers described the way they coped with their new situation. With one or two exceptions, mothers were the parent who dealt with the affective life of the family and on whom the stability in daily routines was dependent. Fathers were, for the most part, not as comfortable as the primary nurturer of the family, although with time they become more comfortable in this role. We need to see if these differences, based on gender, are sustained or blurred as these families learn to live in their new situation. Longitudinal data from this study will help answer some of these questions.

In these early data from the Harvard child bereavement study, we see the importance of looking at the child in his or her social and family system and the need to expand measures of outcome to include measures of good adaptation as well as poor adaptation. The majority of children were not functioning poorly either at 4 months or at 1 year after the death. We will add to our analysis an examination of specific coping behaviors related to the "resilience" that we find in some of these children.

White (1974) has written that all behavior is an attempt at adaptation, at solving both the small and large problems that people face in daily living. Adaptation, he observed, does not mean a total triumph over the environment or total surrender to it, but a striving toward acceptable compromise. White observed that we have become so absorbed by an image of people with compromised egos that we overlook the ways in which common sense, realism, inventiveness, and courage enable people to manage. Most existing models used to understand bereavement grow out of such an orientation that focuses on "compromised egos" rather than on accommodation. The very language that is usually associated with grief implies sickness – people "get over it," they "recover," they "heal." In this model, grief becomes a foreign object that inhabits the bereaved individual and that with the proper treatment will be expunged (Silverman, 1987).

We are suggesting that we move away from this model to one that sees death as a normative life-cycle event and grief a response to loss to which all people must learn to adapt. For some, this adaptation may reflect greater competency, whereas others may not cope as well but, in White's words, "they manage." Studies of children's responses to stresses other than death have made similar observations (Garmezy, 1987; Hetherington, 1989; Werner, 1989). Many children respond with a resiliency that is often overlooked when studies focus on dysfunction rather than accommodation. In identifying the issues with which children are dealing following the death of a parent and describing how they cope, we will have developed a pool of data about what actually happens in bereaved families, and then we will be better able to understand what adaptation looks like in these children and their families.

21

Bereavement following death from AIDS: Unique problems, reactions, and special needs

JOHN L. MARTIN AND LAURA DEAN

Being sick with acquired immunodeficiency syndrome (AIDS) is a difficult, and at times crushing, experience. The physical, emotional, and social hardships brought on by AIDS can be extraordinary and taxing. Though advances are being made in early and aggressive treatment of opportunistic illnesses that result from infection with human immunodeficiency virus (HIV), the cause of AIDS, the disease is nearly universally fatal. As with death from any cause, each person who dies of AIDS leaves a social network of individuals who are affected by the loss and experience some type of bereavement reaction. Although deaths from AIDS began to increase rapidly in 1980, little is known about the type and intensity of bereavement reactions associated with AIDS. Even less is known about bereavement reactions in the most heavily affected population in the United States: homosexual, gay, and bisexual men.

Bereavement and AIDS in gay communities

The epidemiology of AIDS in the United States is changing, with rates of the disease increasing more rapidly among the socially disadvantaged, compared with rates of increase among gay men (Miller, Turner, & Moses, 1990). Nevertheless, gay men have been the group most severely affected by AIDS and AIDS-related deaths since the epidemic began in 1980. By the end of 1990, more than 150,000 cases of AIDS had been reported to the Centers for Disease Control (1990b), and more than 90,000 of these *reported*

This research was supported by grant R01 MH39557 from the National Institute of Mental Health and by the New York City Department of Public Health. A portion of this chapter was prepared while the first author was a Fellow at the Center for Advanced Study in the Behavioral Sciences. We are grateful for financial support for this fellowship provided by the John D. and Catherine T. MacArthur Foundation. This work would not have been possible without the cooperation and trust of the gay community of New York City and the patience and generosity of the study participants over many years. This chapter is dedicated to the memory of Dan Alan Hirsch.

317

cases have been gay men. Within this group, 80%, or more than 65,000, have died.

This chapter focuses specifically on the urban, gay male community of New York City and the experience of these men as a result of the AIDS epidemic. The information provided here is primarily descriptive as so little is known, systematically, about the circumstances surrounding AIDS-related bereavement among gay men and the effects these losses can be expected to have on those who survive. The aims of this chapter are to specify the characteristics of AIDS illness that make this cause of death both similar to and different from other illnesses, describe the epidemiology of AIDS-related losses in the gay community, and examine the psychological consequences of AIDS-related bereavement. However, before moving into a discussion of these points, several issues related to methods and definitions must be addressed.

The interview and the sample

We will use data collected in the Longitudinal AIDS Impact Project, which began in 1984 and is currently ongoing at the Columbia University AIDS Research Unit in New York City. Analytic and descriptive summaries of this project may be found in Martin (1986, 1987, 1988) and Martin and colleagues (Martin, Dean, Garcia, & Hall, 1989). A major aim of the study has been to describe and analyze the psychological adaptation processes utilized by individuals and groups in the gay community as they cope with the AIDS epidemic. With the use of retrospective and prospective study designs and structured face-to-face interviews for data collection, a wide range of physical and mental health information has been gathered. Included in this information are responses to extensive probes on AIDS-related deaths in social networks and grief reactions surrounding these deaths.

The sample employed here was recruited in early 1985 using several methods. A complete description of these sampling methods may be found in Martin and Dean (1990). For the present discussion it is important to note that the approaches we used resulted in a broad cross section of the male homosexual community living throughout New York City in 1985. A total of 746 individuals were recruited and interviewed. The only exclusion criterion was having received a diagnosis of AIDS from a physician at the time of recruitment. It should be emphasized that a *diagnosis* of being sick with AIDS was required for exclusion, not simply being infected with HIV, that is, being HIV antibody positive.

A question arose with respect to how to define the presence or absence of a primary partner in a way that corresponds to married status in heterosexual population studies. At the same time, we did not want to impose a direct analog of this key social status variable on members of a minority group that are, by definition, nontraditional and atypical of the majority of the adult population. In keeping with standard language used by most gay men, we refer to men in this sample as persons who either have a lover or who do not have a lover. A respondent was classified as having a lover if he met all of the following criteria: he said he had a lover; his lover viewed him as his lover (reciprocity); friends viewed the two as a couple (public recognition); and the relationship was extant for 6 months or more (duration). This definition does not require that lovers live together or have an active mutual sexual relationship. On the basis of this definition, 37% of the sample had a lover at the baseline interview in 1985.

In summary, the group described here was primarily white (87%), was college educated (82%), and had a median income of $25,000 in 1984. The age of the sample ranged from 20 to 72 (M = 35.7, SD = 8.5). Just over one-third of the respondents had a lover, and none had been diagnosed with AIDS at the start of the study. Although this is a longitudinal study, most of the data provided here are confined to information collected at the first interview conducted in 1985. We draw on data collected in subsequent years in our brief exposition of the epidemiology of AIDS-related bereavement.

Defining bereavement

An additional problem of definition arose early in the research concerning how best to define "bereavement" among gay men. Considerable thought was given to this problem. The gay population lacks the right to form legal unions with chosen mates. Many gay men function principally within a primary group that can be described as a "family of choice," rather than a biological family. Our initial approach was simply to designate as bereaved men in the sample who had lost a lover. However, in extensive pilot interviews we often found that individuals considered to be close friends were former lovers or primary group members who were relied on by respondents for a variety of emotional and concrete resources. These close friends functioned much as a traditional family for many gay men. Thus, to have limited the definition of bereavement to include only men who had lost a lover would have classified as nonbereaved many men who experienced the loss of significant others to AIDS.

We were also induced to broaden our definition of bereavement by the fact that, during validation work, it became clear that probes within the interview regarding bereavement sequelae (e.g., financial hardship, social isolation) were appropriate and comfortable to answer when asked of men who lost a lover or close friend. In fact, when we omitted questions about close friends lost to AIDS many respondents questioned our apparent lack of interest in these losses. These probes, however, were found to be inappropriate for the loss of someone more emotionally distant than a close friend, such as a person classified as a "friend" or an "acquaintance" (Martin, 1988). Although we do not wish to imply that losing a lover to AIDS is equivalent to losing a close friend, these considerations have led us to use a more inclusive definition of bereavement at this early stage in our analyses.

We turn now to a description of some of the most distinctive features of being ill of AIDS, as there is some evidence suggesting that the nature of a death may influence subsequent adjustment among close survivors (see W. Stroebe & Stroebe, 1987, pp. 204–215). Whereas death due to AIDS shares a number of similarities with other illnesses, it is also unique in important ways.

The nature of AIDS-related illness and death

AIDS is an illness that shares a number of central characteristics with other fatal illnesses, both infectious and noninfectious, such as certain forms of cancer, Alzheimer's disease, and Huntington's chorea. The illness develops over a long period of time, becoming progressively more debilitating. With this disability come increasing demands for emotional and concrete support among members of the close social network. In addition, the illness results in lost role functioning at home and work, the diminution of sensory pleasures that come with eating and sexual relations, and a reduction or elimination of social involvement. There is frequently material hardship due to lost income and enormous medical costs. Two characteristics of AIDS may be especially important in understanding grief reactions following AIDS bereavement: One is the long period of anticipation of death and the other, the harsh and unpredictable course of the disease.

Bereavement due to a progressive illness with an extended time course is recognized as distinct from bereavement that occurs suddenly and without warning. The ability to anticipate a loss and prepare for both the emotional and practical consequences of the loss is generally considered protective with respect to the development of pathological grief reactions (Ball, 1977; Parkes & Weiss, 1983). AIDS may be considered one of the most extended illnesses among infectious diseases. Based on current knowledge, the time between initial infection with HIV and clinical illness onset is highly variable. A quiescent state of asymptomatic infection with HIV may exist for 10 years or more accompanied only by characteristic changes in immunologic laboratory test values.

For the first 5 years of the AIDS epidemic, this period of asymptomatic infection was not considered part of the disease, as the cause of AIDS was unknown and the ability to detect silent infection was unavailable.

However, with the discovery of HIV, the availability of a reliable HIV screening test, and the establishment of publicly funded blood-screening facilities available throughout the United States, any individual wishing to know his infection status may now avail himself of that information. The period of asymptomatic HIV infection may be an important time not only for anticipating death but also for engaging in hopefulness and adaptive denial (Lazarus, 1981), for both the infected individual and those close to him who know of the infection.

Once symptoms begin to develop, however, the disease takes on new meaning and urgency. Although the period of being clinically ill with AIDS frequently lasts from 2 to 5 years, this anticipatory period may not ease the impact of the ultimate loss. Death due to AIDS is rarely a quiet or peaceful process. People with AIDS and their caregivers engage in active and intensive fights for life in an ongoing battle frequently described as an emotional roller coaster. The natural course of the illness is characterized by alterations between relatively normal daily functioning and serious disability, until finally a critical failure due to iatrogenic or natural causes leads to death. The opportunistic infections and cancers associated with advancing AIDS are frequently intensely painful and at times disfiguring. Diagnostic procedures and treatments, as well as the illnesses themselves, often result in unrelenting nausea, fever, incontinence, and wasting. Thus, the lengthy time of anticipating death during the later stages of AIDS may be so traumatic that any buffering or adaptive function of the anticipatory period may be lost.

Not only are the material realities of coping with AIDS harsh and unpredictable, but the emotions aroused during the period of caring for a loved one with AIDS can be intensely distressing. We have found that it is not uncommon for those suffering with AIDS, as well as those close to a person in advanced stages of AIDS, to feel that death would be the preferred alternative to life with AIDS. Wishing for the death of a close loved one, no matter how humane, can be the source of serious pain or guilt, particularly after the death occurs. The need for social support of AIDS caregivers is a particularly significant problem within the gay community. We have shown that in the absence of adequate help with both practical and emotional problems arising in the course of caring for a person with AIDS, gay men are at significantly increased risk of prolonged and intense grief reactions (Lennon, Martin, & Dean, 1990).

Although death due to AIDS shares important similarities with death due to other illnesses, AIDS is also special, even unique, in a number of ways. Unlike most adult degenerative diseases, AIDS primarily strikes young to middle-aged adults in the prime of life, many of whom are at or nearing their peak of productivity. The occurrence of premature death can lead to greater intensity of grief reactions and increase the risk of prolonged or pathological grief outcomes (Lopata, 1979; Parkes & Weiss, 1983; Sanders, this volume).

More than any other disease, AIDS can be deeply stigmatizing, for both the person who is sick and for those close to him. For many gay men AIDS forces into the open one's identity as a homosexual to previously uninformed family members, friends, and co-workers, as well as a cadre of strangers encountered in the course of obtaining necessary health care. Not only is this "forced coming out" stressful to the individual with AIDS, but it also frequently strains individuals and relationships in the social network. It is not unusual, for example, for a gay man to be rejected by his bio-logical family because of the stigma surrounding AIDS and homosexuality. Irrational fears about contagion and the lack of understanding of AIDS, prevalent even among health care workers, add additional strain in the attempt to maintain dignity through the course of illness and death.

In addition to these unique characteristics of the disease, the community context in which AIDS has flourished makes AIDS-related bereavement among gay men special when compared with bereavement arising from other causes in other groups. The epidemic occurred in an organized community possessing a great deal of human potential, skill, and material resources. Unlike other diseases, the people involved most intensely in trying to control the epidemic and care for the sick constitute the group at risk. This situation represents a double-edged sword, because the very individuals who serve as sources of strength and support frequently become sources of sorrow and grief.

It is possible to document the extent to which the bereaved subsequently overlap with (i.e., become) the sick by examining the way in which AIDS bereavements are distributed in the community. Thus, we turn now to a description of the epidemiology of AIDS-related bereavement among gay men. As we shall see, understanding the psychological consequences of bereavement requires an appreciation for the fact that AIDS-related losses are not randomly distributed among gay men.

The epidemiology of AIDS-related bereavement

Based on our definition of bereavement, we have found that the non-cumulative annual incidence of bereavement in this sample ranged from less than 1% in 1981 to an initial peak of 23% in 1987; a second peak of 30% occurred in 1990. The cumulative prevalence of AIDS-related bereavement over a 10-year period is also informative. As of the end of 1989, half of the sample (52%) had experienced an AIDS-related bereave-ment within their gay male social networks. The fact that after 10 years of the epidemic, nearly half of the sample had *not* lost a lover or close friend to AIDS suggests that bereavement is not a random event in the gay community but rather that losses are clustered within a specific subgroup of the gay population.

This is in fact the conclusion we came to as of 1985 in our study of risk factors for bereavement in this population (Martin & Dean, 1989). That is, 5 years into the epidemic AIDS-related bereavements were heavily concentrated among men aged 35 to 45, with the probability of bereavement declining sharply among both older and younger age cohorts. In addition, bereaved gay men were one-third more likely to report early clinical symptoms of AIDS-related complex (ARC) – early symptoms of AIDS, such as chronic diarrhea, unexplained fevers, lymphadenopathy, oral candidiasis – and almost twice as likely to be infected with HIV compared with men who were not bereaved. Further study revealed that the underlying reason for these associations was the fact that bereaved gay men were much more sexually active in the year prior to the outbreak of the AIDS epidemic (1980–1981) compared to gay men who were not bereaved.

The experience of bereavement has continued to disseminate within this population and has clearly affected those who are not themselves at high risk for AIDS or HIV infection. However, the fact that half of the sample has not experienced a close loss suggests that AIDS-related bereavement continues to be concentrated among gay men at elevated risk for AIDS even 10 years into the epidemic.

Multiple and chronic bereavement

Two important aspects of the epidemiology of AIDS-related bereavement are the occurrence of multiple bereavements and the occurrence of chronic bereavement. Multiple bereavement and chronic bereavement are two characteristics of the AIDS epidemic that make it similar to previously studied stressors, such as the experiences of concentration camp survivors and soldiers in combat. Like the AIDS epidemic, concentration camps and war combat are lethal enough to kill many individuals in a brief time and are extended in time so that survivors experience unremitting death of fellow companions. Given the extreme situations required to produce multiple and chronic bereavement in a population, in the 1980s surprisingly large numbers of gay men experienced these patterns of loss due to AIDS.

For example, we have found that 7% of the total sample, or nearly 30% of the bereaved, had experienced two or more bereavements within the 12 months of 1987. Nearly half of these men experienced three or more bereavements in that year. In addition, as of 1989, 7% of the sample had experienced chronic bereavement, that is, at least one close loss in three consecutive years (Dean, Hall, & Martin, 1988). If we broaden our definition of "chronic" to 2 or more consecutive years of bereavement, this figure increases to more than 27% of the total sample. It is important to note that these figures do not reflect deaths of social network members classified as friends, acquaintances, or friends of friends, losses that may not represent bereavements but that we have found seriously erode one's sense of coherence and control.

The implications of the experience of multiple and chronic bereavement for this population are unknown. It is likely that such experiences make it difficult to grieve adequately for a particular loss and thus increase the risk of symptoms of pathological grief reaction. We turn now to an examination of the psychological consequences of bereavement in our sample, and the possible role of multiple and chronic loss in amplifying these reactions.

Psychological consequences of AIDS-related bereavement

Prior evidence suggests that numerous health outcomes are affected by bereavement (Osterweis, Solomon, & Green, 1984; see also the chapters in part V of this volume). These outcomes include not only mortality (Kraus & Lilienfeld, 1959; W. Stroebe, Stroebe, Gergen, & Gergen, 1981; M. Stroebe & Stroebe, chapter 12, this volume) and physical morbidity rates (Maddison & Viola, 1968) but also such psychological symptoms as depression and anxiety (Clayton, 1979; Clayton & Darvish, 1979; Parkes & Brown, 1972; Parkes & Weiss, 1983), use of substances such as tobacco, alcohol, sleeping pills, and tranquilizers (Clayton & Darvish, 1979; Maddison & Viola, 1968; Parkes, 1964a; Parkes & Brown, 1972; Gallagher-Thompson, Futterman, Farberow, Thompson, & Peterson, this volume), and help seeking and initiation of professional medical and psychiatric care (Clayton, 1974, 1979; Stein & Susser, 1969).

We examined a number of variables in each of these three domains of functioning in order to explore ways in which AIDS-related bereavement among gay men differs from previously studied bereavement experiences. These outcome variables were assessed in 1985 and inquired about for the 12-month period prior to the interview. Our main comparison was designed to examine the effects of any bereavement due to AIDS in the first 5 years of the epidemic, compared with no bereavement during that time. Thus, the sample was divided into the bereaved ($N = 200$) and the nonbereaved ($N = 546$) and compared on each outcome. Table 21.1 shows standardized means ($M = 0.0$, $SD = 1.0$) for eight continuous measures and percentages for six dichotomous measures for each of the two groups.

Before discussing the comparisons shown in Table 21.1, it is important to note that statistical adjustments for age and number of ARC symptoms were made prior to testing differences between the two groups. As noted earlier, we have shown that both of these variables are significantly related to the experience of bereavement (Martin & Dean, 1989). Because age and ARC are also related to psychological distress, substance use, and help

Table 21.1. *Standardized means (M = 0, SD = 1.0) and percentages comparing
bereaved and nonbereaved groups on 14 outcome measures*

Outcome	Nonbereaved (N = 546)	Bereaved (N = 200)
Psychological distress		
Depression	−0.14	0.39***
Suicidal ideation	−0.05	0.15*
Traumatic stress	−0.17	0.47***
Subjective threat	−0.13	0.34***
Substance use		
Alcohol consumption	0.01	−0.02
Sedative consumption	−0.05	0.15
Marijuana consumption	−0.04	0.10
Other drug consumption	−0.12	0.33***
Cigarette smoker	26%	29%
Professional help seeking		
MD visits, 10+	11%	21%**
Psychiatric visits, weekly	20%	20%
Spiritual counselor, 10+	2%	9%***
Increased MD visits	30%	45%***
Increased psychiatric visits	4%	15%***

Note: Statistical tests were conducted after adjusting for age and ARC symptoms using
multiple regression or multiple logistic regression techniques.
*$p < 0.05$; **$p < 0.01$; ***$p < 0.001$

seeking, it is possible that any differences found on these measures could be
due to age or the experience of symptoms rather than the experience of
bereavement.

The results shown in the table indicate that AIDS-related bereavement is
associated with higher levels of symptoms of severe psychological distress.
As a group, the bereaved score approximately one-half a standard deviation higher than the nonbereaved on three of the four distress measures.
More specifically, these results indicate that the bereaved men experienced
elevated levels of the following kind of symptoms: depression, including
feelings of hopelessness, helplessness, sadness, cognitive impairment,
somatic complaints, and problems falling asleep, staying asleep, and
waking early; suicidal ideation, including thoughts about taking one's life,
plans for doing so, and actual attempts; traumatic stress response, including alterations between intrusive and avoidant thoughts and emotions
about AIDS, inability to be comforted by others, numbing, nightmares
about AIDS, panic attacks involving fear of developing AIDS, and acute
episodes of sweats and diarrhea; and subjective threat, including pre-

occupation with one's body for signs of AIDS, subjective probability of developing AIDS in the future, and frequency of occurrence of fears about developing AIDS.

These findings for psychological distress are consistent with those reported by other investigators (e.g., Clayton, 1974; Glick, Weiss, & Parkes, 1974; Maddison & Viola, 1968; Parkes & Brown, 1972), particularly with respect to the elevated levels of depression and suicidal ideation. It should be noted, however, that the measures of anxiety included here are not measures of generalized anxiety but rather tap anxiety and threat tied specifically to the AIDS epidemic as a stressor and one's future likelihood of developing AIDS. Thus, findings based on these measures cannot be compared directly to prior work on bereavement. Instead, these types of anxiety symptoms should be viewed as being unique to gay men in the 1980s as a result of the rapid growth of AIDS in this population at this time in history.

Turning now to the measures of substance use in Table 21.1, the findings are more ambiguous. On the one hand, the results provide little evidence of elevated levels of alcohol use, sedative use, marijuana use, or likelihood of cigarette smoking among the bereaved. These findings contrast with previous results reported by others (e.g., Blankfield, 1983; Clayton, 1974), which would lead us to expect differences between the bereaved and non-bereaved on these measures. The lack of association between alcohol use and bereavement is further corroborated by findings reported elsewhere (Martin, 1988) showing that the bereaved and nonbereaved do not differ with respect to problems associated with excessive drinking.

On the other hand, the results in Table 21.1 indicate that the use of "other drugs" is significantly elevated among the bereaved. This category involves drugs taken for recreational, nonmedical, purposes and includes barbiturates, amphetamines, cocaine, and hallucinogens. Unfortunately, we know of no comparative data available from other bereaved samples regarding the use of these types of illicit drugs. Thus, it is unclear whether this effect is unique to urban homosexual men or whether use of these substances would be elevated in any (appropriately matched) group of bereaved heterosexual persons.

There is further ambiguity with respect to substance use and bereavement in this sample due to the fact that the difference in sedative use between the bereaved and nonbereaved is marginally significant ($p < .10$) and in the expected direction. Indeed, in prior work (Martin, 1988) we reported that a quantitative index of bereavement was significantly related to sedative use. That is, the correlation between sedative use and *number* of bereavements was positive and significant. Thus, it may be that in this population more than a single bereavement experience is required to lead to anxiety and distress at levels requiring a high level of sedative use.

For the area of help seeking, the results in Table 21.1 indicate a consistent tendency among the bereaved to seek professional help more frequently compared with the nonbereaved. Nearly twice as many bereaved men, compared with nonbereaved men, consulted a physician at least 10 times or more during the year. Over three times as many bereaved men, compared with nonbereaved men, consulted a member of the clergy or other spiritual counselor at least 10 times or more during the year. On the other hand, we found no difference associated with bereavement for the proportion of men attending weekly psychotherapy sessions with a psychiatrist or psychologist; 20% of both the bereaved and nonbereaved reported these regular consultations.

In addition to looking at indicators of the frequency of visits to physicians, psychotherapists, and spiritual counselors, we also examined the number of individuals who initiated or increased visits to physicians or psychotherapists due to concern or worry over developing AIDS. The results in Table 21.1 suggest that the bereaved are more likely, compared with nonbereaved men, to seek help from both of these professional sources in response to their personal anxiety over AIDS. Fifty percent more bereaved men increased visits to physicians in response to concern over AIDS, and nearly four times as many bereaved men increased or initiated visits to psychologists or psychiatrists in an effort to cope with fears about AIDS. Taken together, these findings are consistent with prior reports indicating that bereavement leads to increased use of professional medical help (Clayton, 1974; Glick et al., 1974; Parkes, 1964b), as well as psychiatric or psychological help (Stein & Susser, 1969).

Multiple and chronic bereavement. Up to this point we have demonstrated that the experience of AIDS-related bereavement among gay men is associated with higher levels of psychological symptoms, help seeking, and, less consistently, substance use. We turn now to a closer examination of the bereaved group of respondents in order to explore the role of multiple and chronic bereavement in determining the level of reactions to loss.

It is difficult to examine the independent effects of multiple and chronic loss because these factors are confounded, both conceptually and empirically: An individual who has experienced chronic loss has also experienced multiple loss. However, by dividing the time period during which the losses occurred into "recent" (i.e., within the past 12 months) and "past" (i.e., from 12 to 48 months), and determining whether an individual experienced a single loss or multiple loss within each period, we can begin to examine each of these aspects of the bereavement experience.

The groups of adequate size that we were able to form by cross-classifying time of loss with number of losses are as follows:

Table 21.2. *Standardized means (M = 0, SD = 1.0) and percentages comparing four bereaved groups on 14 outcome measures*

		Recent only		
Outcome	Past only (N = 33)	Single (N = 104)	Multiple (N = 31)	Chronic (N = 32)
Psychological distress				
Depression	−0.01	−0.03	−0.11	0.22[a]
Suicidal ideation	−0.21	0.05	0.08	−0.03
Traumatic stress	−0.13	−0.17	0.22	0.45**
Subjective threat	−0.10	−0.09	0.12	0.29*
Substance use				
Alcohol consumption	0.11	0.04	−0.02	−0.22
Sedative consumption	−0.09	−0.01	−0.13	0.25[a]
Marijuana consumption	0.19	−0.06	0.19	0.19
Other drug consumption	0.18	−0.09	−0.01	0.12
Cigarette smoker	30%	35%	16%	22%[a]
Professional help seeking				
MD visits, 10+	27%	17%	29%	16%
Psychiatric visits, weekly	21%	18%	13%	28%
Spiritual counselor, 10+	6%	9%	6%	13%
Increased MD visits	52%	41%	55%	41%
Increased psychiatric visits	24%	10%	19%	19%

Note: Statistical tests were conducted after adjusting for age and ARC symptoms.
[a]$p < 0.10$; *$p < 0.05$; **$p < 0.001$

> *Past loss only.* This group ($n = 33$) included respondents who reported one or more past bereavements and no recent bereavements. Only six respondents in this category reported two or more bereavements, making it impractical to subdivide this group further into single versus multiple loss.
> *Single loss, recent only.* This group ($n = 104$) included respondents who reported one recent bereavement only and no past bereavements.
> *Multiple losses, recent only.* This group ($n = 31$) included respondents who reported two or more recent bereavements and no past bereavements.
> *Chronic loss.* This group ($n = 32$) included respondents who reported at least one past bereavement and at least one recent bereavement.

The standardized means and percentages for each of these four groups on 14 outcome variables are shown in Table 21.2. Of the entire set of 14 outcome variables, only two appear to be significantly influenced by either chronic loss or multiple loss: traumatic stress symptoms and subjective threat. In both cases the chronically bereaved and the (recently) multiply bereaved have elevated scores, compared with those who reported a single loss or those whose losses occurred more than 1 year prior to assessment.

Other notable trends in Table 21.2 suggesting that chronic bereavement is particularly stressful involve the elevated scores for this group on depression and sedative use. Although these differences are statistically significant at only a marginal level ($p < .10$), the chronically bereaved seem to be clearly different on these measures, compared with the other three groups.

There is no evidence in Table 21.2 indicating that chronic or multiple bereavement lead to systematic differences in help-seeking behavior. The chronically bereaved group contains the largest proportion of respondents who attended weekly psychotherapy and who have consulted a spiritual counselor 10 times or more during the prior year. These proportional differences, however, are nonsignificant and are not consistent with the other figures shown in Table 21.2 for physician consultations or initiating or increasing visits to physicians or psychotherapists for help in coping with personal concerns over developing AIDS.

Summary and conclusions

In this chapter we have tried to provide a descriptive analysis of the experience and effects of the AIDS epidemic in an urban sample of gay men, making comparisons when possible to prior findings on bereavement in other samples. In many ways AIDS-related bereavement appears to lead to similar types of distress among homosexual men as has been reported for heterosexual individuals: Bereaved gay men are more depressed, they consider suicide more frequently, and they tend to use or initiate more frequent help from medical, psychological, and spiritual professionals.

On the other hand, evidence presented here suggests that gay men also respond to AIDS-related bereavement in ways that can be considered unique. Although they certainly experience elevated levels of anxiety, as demonstrated in other samples, anxiety among bereaved gay men is highly specific to the AIDS epidemic as a stressful event and to their personal vulnerability to developing the disease, rather than being a generalized anxiety reaction or phobia. As in other samples, bereaved gay men also appear vulnerable to increased substance use. But, again, the particular types of substances, that is, illicit drugs, are different drugs from those reported to be used excessively in other bereaved groups (e.g., alcohol and tobacco).

The evidence presented here with respect to chronic and multiple bereavement must be considered preliminary and suggestive. At this point, we can safely conclude that multiple loss and chronic loss are associated with levels of AIDS-specific anxiety (i.e., traumatic stress response symptoms and a sense of subjective threat) that go beyond levels experienced by those with a single loss or whose loss was confined to a remote time period. Although the findings suggest that depressive symptoms and sedative use might also be outcomes that are sensitive to chronic loss in the bereaved population, further work is clearly needed to establish the presence or absence of these effects.

The epidemiology of AIDS-related bereavement reveals a further unique characteristic of the disease: AIDS struck a definable community of individuals and was transmitted throughout segments of this population along sexual and social pathways. Thus, individuals at highest risk for bereavement tend to be not only those who were most integrated into the gay community in the beginning of the 1980s, but also those at increased risk of developing AIDS. The experience of multiple and chronic bereavement, two characteristics of the AIDS epidemic that are rarely found outside of extremely stressful situations of an ongoing nature, are also heavily concentrated in the subset of gay men most intensively involved in and connected with the gay community.

An additional point about the AIDS epidemic should be raised because it may affect the methods and interpretation of future work on this problem. The changes that occurred in the mid-1980s in the ability to detect HIV infection and observe its progression prior to clinical symptoms were pivotal events, not only for the medical research community but for the gay community. Simply put, during the first 5 years of the epidemic the cause of AIDS was unknown, its next targets were unknown, and there was a sense of undifferentiated vulnerability that blanketed urban gay communities. This ambiguity heightened public stigma surrounding AIDS, leading to an increased sense (and experience) of social isolation among those with afflicted loved ones.

With the exception of the fatality rate of HIV infection, the situation has changed dramatically in recent years: The cause of AIDS is known, who will get AIDS can be known with near certainty, and ways to avoid becoming infected with HIV are well documented and have been extensively publicized. Although there is no question that stigma toward AIDS and prejudice toward homosexuals continue at a high level in the United States (Dean, Wu, & Martin, 1992; Herek, 1988; Herek & Glunt, 1988), supportive resources for those with loved ones with AIDS have grown enormously. Thus, the changing historical context produced by biomedical progress and social enlightenment may very well have influenced the meaning and experience of AIDS-related bereavement in gay communities. Such contextual factors must be considered in future work on AIDS among gay men.

22

Sleep and dreams in well-adjusted and less adjusted Holocaust survivors

HANNA KAMINER AND PERETZ LAVIE

The Holocaust as an extreme trauma

The Holocaust constituted an extreme trauma that produced long-term effects on the lives of the survivors. The systematic extermination of Jews in the concentration camps created situations previously unknown in history. The horrors and inhumanity that the inmates experienced daily in those camps are difficult to describe. The endless threat to life was faced each and every day, constituting a never-ending struggle to survive.

In addition, there were physical pressures, such as intense hunger, crowded quarters without even minimal hygienic conditions, gruelling work, exposure to bodily torture, and resulting diseases. Mental pressures included painful separation from one's family, often accompanied by the knowledge that dear ones had perished or were in a similar situation, and uncertainty about one's existence, how long the imprisonment would last, and what the future would hold. The camp prisoners endured methodical humiliation at the hands of the wardens. The inmates lost their identities: Their names were replaced by a serial number; their professions and social standing were also lost. All the values and the moral and social norms by which they had led their lives were destroyed.

Even after the Holocaust, the feeling of loss did not subside. Most survivors wandered from their homeland to other countries. As immigrants, they were forced to adjust to a new place, a new language, and new leadership, while distancing themselves or cutting themselves off altogether from their origins. Thus, both during the Holocaust and for a long period afterward, survivors experienced losses in every aspect of life.

The study described in this chapter was supported by a grant from the Deutsch-Ledler Foundation. The help of the Technion Sleep Laboratory staff is greatly appreciated.

331

Characteristics of the survivors' coping and adaptation

Coping during the Holocaust

The results of incarceration in the concentration camps can be divided into several stages (Bettelheim, 1943; Krystal, 1968; Chodoff, 1970; Eitinger, 1974). The first stage was primary shock, characterized by serious agitation and a feeling of severe repulsion by the surroundings. This generally led to a period of apathy, emotional isolation, and alienation, with a major concern to remain alive in the hope of returning to the outside world. Emotional numbness constituted a defense mechanism for preserving one's personality. This emotional alienation consequently led to feelings of depersonalization and denial of reality and of what was happening. Eitinger (1974) said that use of this mechanism for an extended period led to an eventual surrender to death.

Later, the mechanism of ego automatism was added. The prisoner began to act like a robot. At this stage, the prisoners perceived their incarceration as realistic and concrete. However, they experienced a general regression and massive limitation of personality functions. The perspective of time shrank, and the individual related primarily to the present. The central purpose was to preserve existence, and the main impulse was to get food. Other impulses disappeared; for example, the sexual impulse became virtually nonexistent (Frankl, 1962).

The automatism stage, characterized emotionally by apathy and emotional isolation, protected the prisoners from aggression and depression. According to Krystal (1968), this defense mechanism was the most accepted and adaptive one in the camp. Individuals who could not sustain themselves at the level of regression reached the destructive stage of Mussulman. Prisoners in this stage no longer tried to help themselves in any way. They were apathetic, allowed the surroundings to control them absolutely, and, in effect, let themselves die.

Maintaining certain human values within the inhuman conditions of the camp, such as preserving a close interpersonal relationship with a relative or friend, constituted a very adaptive mechanism that helped some prisoners preserve their humanity and emotional health. Another characteristic of prisoners' coping was the strong will to survive in order to bear testimony about the events in commemoration of those who did not survive (Eitinger, 1974; Dimsdale, 1974; Matussek, 1975).

A survey of the coping strategies during the incarceration period for extermination camp prisoners showed that the most common effective defense mechanisms were denial and emotional isolation (Kahana, Kahana, Harel, & Rosner, 1988a).

Coping after the war

After World War II, it became apparent that signs of the trauma continued for many years, expressing themselves in different psychological and somatic problems (Krystal, 1968; Eitinger, 1974; Niederland, 1968). Yet reports in the literature show that these signs did not appear immediately. There was a transitional period between the end of the war and the appearance of signs of difficulties. Called the latency period, it was characterized by the absence of symptoms, evidently either out of hope of reunification with one's family and a return to one's previous life or out of a need for rapid rehabilitation in the difficult conditions of the immediate postwar period.

Many survivors had to rebuild their lives while adjusting to a new environment, a new language, and so on. The transition period was characterized by the hope of a new life in the adopted homeland, but there were many new pressures stemming from the difficulties of reorganizing in strange places. This period saw an attempt at coping using massive defenses like denial, repression, and suppression of memories and living in the present only. We can assume that this attempt did not always succeed, and the symptoms burst forth only after a brutal confrontation with loss and the perception of the scope of the Holocaust in general (Krystal, 1968; Berger, 1977).

Psychiatric and psychological treatment of survivors during the years following the war showed evidence of traumatization so severe that the literature speaks of the creation of a personality syndrome that developed unrelated to age, sex, personal background, or socioeconomic status (Haefner, 1968; Niederland, 1968; Hoppe, 1971; Eitinger, 1974; Lederer, 1965; Furst, 1967; Krystal, 1968). The major characteristics of the syndrome, called "concentration camp syndrome" (Chodoff, 1970), include chronic depression, which sometimes expressed itself externally as psychosomatic pains, neurological phenomena, rheumatic pain, and the like. An in-depth study of this syndrome uncovered anxiety, regression, a tendency toward isolation, apathy, extreme tiredness, and lack of self-confidence. There was a display of anhedonia – the absence of any pleasure and the inability to enjoy life – which was related to unprocessed mourning, and wordless grief. Anxiety was a common symptom, especially related to the fear of renewed persecution and various phobic fears. The survivors' emotional sensitivity was extremely high, and was connected to the tension and the difficult physical and emotional reactions to stimuli that reminded them of their past. Their reactions frequently led to sleep problems, nightmares, and anxiety dreams related to their experiences of persecution. Some of the survivors displayed hyperamnesia, with a tendency to dwell on past events. These events endlessly hounded them, because they were bound up with sharp, extremely painful memories. Psychosomatic states also appeared, such as asthma, ulcers, thyroid gland disorders, hypertension, and other disturbances.

Holocaust survivors also displayed unique symptoms related to the duration of the experience and to the degree of their humiliation and dehumanization at the hands of the Nazis. These symptoms include loss of childhood memories and unique changes in their perception of personal identity and object relations. Some have claimed that the Holocaust's impact led to personality changes affecting their interpersonal relations, including parenthood (Danieli, 1982). Some of these same symptoms are also present in post-traumatic stress disorder (PTSD), as defined by DSM III (1980).

Over the years, Holocaust survivors were forced to cope with many life events and with pressures unrelated to their past trauma. They had to face the regular developmental hurdles of the aging process and of new losses such as retirement or widowhood, which constituted additional pressures. Among the phenomena revealed was an exaggeration of responses that were appropriate to the original trauma. Such symptoms recurred in times of additional stress. Furthermore, the motivational states, the cognitive and perceptual styles, and the coping behavior that was appropriate during the trauma period often repeated themselves during relatively minor stress situations. Thus, responses to the old trauma that were inappropriately applied to new stress situations led to maladaptive behavior.

Adjusting after the war

Relatively few studies have examined the Holocaust survivors' adjustment in major life spheres such as work and family. Although there are some contradictory results, a significant number of research investigations relating to daily life functioning have shown a positive and encouraging picture in comparison with the clinical description of "survivors' syndrome" (Eaton, Sigal, & Weinfield, 1982; Levav & Abramson, 1984; Carmil & Carel, 1986). Following the psychology of the ego, approach researchers have tended to perceive the survivors' control over previous extreme trauma as a coping resource that enhanced their sense of adapting and led to the perception of potential pressures as less threatening (Moos & Billing, 1982). In fact, there is evidence that most Holocaust survivors coped with problematic daily situations in an effective manner, especially those that did not constitute a threat to health or existence.

Furthermore, study results have shown that the survivors are not a homogeneous group, and that the heterogeneity is indicative of differences in post-traumatic adjustment. Despite the evidence that a large percentage of the survivors retained scars of various degrees from their experiences during the Holocaust, it has been found that an equally large percentage of the survivors adjusted well as individuals and became effective and contributing citizens in their new community. The literature mentions that as part of their adjustment, survivors tried to compensate for their losses and inner emptiness by material achievement, or "climbing the ladder of success." Psychiatric literature frequently describes survivors as "very successful business people, persecuted by extermination camp memories and fantasies of destruction" (Niederland, 1968). They have been described elsewhere as people who, despite their "dark memories," became very successful and functioned well as members of society. For the survivor, the traditional criteria of status, such as education, occupation, or socioeconomic standing, were considered a consequence of adjustment. Thus, researchers are justified in seeing these parameters as valid measures of adjustment, alongside the indicators of physical and emotional health (Kahana et al., 1988a, 1988b).

A number of socioeconomic studies have shown that the adjustment of Holocaust survivors is comparable to that of the general population in Israel (Winnik, 1967). In a longitudinal study of survivors, Davidson (1981) pointed out their remarkable adjustment – their ability to reorganize, to raise healthy families, and to attain significant social achievements. He also noted that existing traumatic symptoms did not preclude good social and familial functioning.

In light of this, there are still unresolved questions regarding the link between survivors' coping mechanisms and later social adjustment. The question has been raised: What enabled some of the survivors, who lived through such destructive experiences, to lead normal lives and adjust well, and even to feel satisfaction from their lives?

In summary, it can be seen that in spite of the post-traumatic symptoms, and the vestiges of suffering from the Holocaust period that apparently accompany the survivors all their lives, most of them achieved successful adjustment and rehabilitation within various social frameworks.

Sleep and dreams among Holocaust survivors

The majority of the studies and articles dealing with the medical and psychological states of Holocaust survivors concur that their stay in concentration camps had a large influence not only on the survivors' waking hours but also on their sleep behavior. Sleep difficulties and disturbed dreams are of particular interest because they are considered hallmarks of the long-term effects of traumatic events (Ross, Ball, Sullivan, & Caroff, 1989). Research has shown that 85% of the survivors still suffer from some type of sleep disorder (mostly insomnia), nightmares, and night terrors many years after the war. In their dreams, the victims saw themselves being persecuted, escaping, hiding, and the like. In their dreams, some were captured by uniformed pursuers; others managed to escape at the last moment. The dreamers' waking-up was often accompanied by screams and fear and a tendency to remain fearful until reality took over (Paul, 1963; Dimsdale, 1974; Dor-Shav, 1978).

Although there is no doubt that the Holocaust had an impact on sleep and dreaming, until now no controlled study had been performed on sleep patterns, sleep disturbances, or dreaming in Holocaust survivors. In the present study, we have tried to examine the assumption that a connection exists between disturbances in sleep patterns and nightmares, on the one hand, and variables of coping of trauma survivors, on the other. We have tried to examine the mechanisms that enabled some of the survivors to cope well even though they had undergone severe trauma. These survivors stand in contrast to others who even today, so many years afterward, have not freed themselves from the effects of the trauma, but continue to have adjustment difficulties in various areas of daily life.

Design of the study

Thirty-three subjects (23 survivors and 10 controls) participated in the study, recruited from the local community of Holocaust survivors. None was under psychiatric or psychological treatment, and all were informed that the study would investigate dreaming in Holocaust survivors. The survivors were selected following a clinical interview. All of them had lived in Nazi-occupied Europe during World War II. Eleven of the survivors had been in concentration camps, and 12 had spent most of the war in hiding or constantly on the run. All were free from major physical or mental illnesses and were able to abstain from taking drugs during the course of the study. The sampling included an approximately equal number of men and women, and an attempt was made to match the ages of the subjects between the groups, particularly the control group.

The subjects' average age was 60.2 years, ranging from 49 (a female survivor of the Bergen-Belsen concentration camp) to 69 (a female survivor from Holland who spent 2 years in hiding). The survivors came from both Eastern and Western Europe, and the concentration camps in which they had been incarcerated were Auschwitz, Birkenau, Bergen-Belsen, and Majdanek.

A control group was formed by randomly selecting Israelis who had passed the Holocaust period in Israel, which was then Palestine under British control. The control group was matched with the subjects according to age, sex, country of origin, and socioeconomic status. The control subjects had suffered no trauma during this period and were all emotionally and physically healthy.

The survivor population that was interviewed exhibited normal functioning and met most of the criteria of a socially adjusted citizen. Most of them had tried to create a supportive network, and, with the exception of one female subject in the well-adjusted group, had raised families. They had worked until becoming pensioners; or were still working in relatively steady jobs. In their daily lives, they functioned at an adjustment level within the normal range.

Despite this profile, the survivors could be categorized into those whose behavior and adjustment to daily life were completely normal, without any apparent distress, and those who complained of difficulties in various areas of daily life. This division was based on clinical interviews regarding the following areas of life: problems at work, marital and familial problems, social relations, somatic complaints, mental problems, and a general feeling of dissatisfaction and distress.

All subjects were interviewed by an experienced clinical psychologist. All those who during the course of the clinical interview raised complaints in three or more of the six areas of daily life were included in the less adjusted group, and those who raised complaints in fewer than two areas were included in the well-adjusted group. The control group was selected according to the same criteria.

The less adjusted group of survivors, both from the extermination camps and from the hideouts, included 11 subjects: 5 male and 6 female. They had a mean number of 3.8 (±0.98) complaints. The well-adjusted group of survivors, both from the extermination camps and from the hideouts, included 12 subjects: 5 male and 7 female. They had a mean number of 0.9 (±1) complaints. The control group included 10 subjects: 5 male and 5 female. They had a mean number of 1.1 (±0.8) complaints. There were no differences between the groups with respect to personal losses they had suffered during the Holocaust. In the well-adjusted group, four survivors had lost their entire family in the Holocaust; six had lost either a mother, father, or both parents; one had lost her husband and parents; and only one did not suffer any losses. In the less adjusted group, four had lost their entire family, six had lost either one or both parents, and one had lost both a father and brothers.

Because a preliminary data analysis did not distinguish significant differences between survivors from the concentration camps and survivors who were in hideouts or on the run, the two groups were combined and the samples were divided according to the adjustment variable.

This division was validated by the Symptom Checklist Questionnaire SCL-90 (Derogatis, 1977b) and the SSIAM Adjustment Questionnaire (Gurland, Yorkston, Stone, & Frank, 1964). During the course of the research, a battery of psychiatric and psychological tests was used to characterize the three groups. These included the Impact Event Scale

(IES) Questionnaire (Horowitz, Wilner, & Alvarez, 1979) and a modified version of the DSM III Questionnaire for the diagnosis of PTSD post-trauma, the MMPI Scale for manifest anxiety, Byrne's R-S Scale (1961), and Barron's Ego Strength Scale (1977).

The subjects were requested to spend four whole nights in the lab, during which polysomnographic recordings were taken and dreams were recorded. On the first, third, and fourth nights the subjects were awakened from all REM stages, starting from the second REM, for dream recall. REM, or dreaming, sleep is that stage of sleep characterized by rapid eye movements and low-voltage high-frequency EEG. On the second night, the subjects were not awakened at all. The subjects were awakened approximately 15–20 minutes after the beginning of each REM stage, and were questioned regarding their dreams. They were asked to report what had passed through their heads prior to awakening. The dreams were tape-recorded and then written down word-for-word for analysis. If the subject claimed not to recall any dream, the experimenter waited a little while and then repeated the question. In cases where the subjects did recall dreams, additional questions were asked concerning recognition of people or places appearing in the dream, the emotions accompanying the dream, and so on.

Across the nights, there was a total of 256 awakenings from REM sleep for the purpose of dream recall. The analysis of the dreams was based on Winget and Kramer (1979) and Gottschalk and Gleser (1969). More details of the experimental design and results can be found in Lavie and Kaminer (1991) and in Kaminer and Lavie (1991).

Results

Clinical characteristics

A study of the characteristics of the less adjusted group revealed that members of this group, in wakefulness and in sleep, showed symptoms related to trauma, despite the fact that almost 50 years have passed since the war. The post-trauma questionnaires significantly distinguished between the less adjusted group and the well-adjusted group. The less adjusted group was more disturbed by contents related to the Holocaust. This disturbance expressed itself in thinking about the events of the Holocaust and recurring dreams and images from the trauma arising without conscious intent. Memories returned, relentlessly flooding the less adjusted survivors day and night. At the same time, members of this group invested greater efforts in avoiding activities or associations reminding them of the war and its events. Their repeated efforts to overcome the trauma by avoiding traumatic contents were ineffective.

Results showed that, as the years passed, the gap between the two groups widened, and the difference in the manifestation of the symptoms became more significant, especially in the last 10 years. In contrast, members of the better adjusted group exhibited more effective coming to terms with the post-trauma syndrome. They reached a balance between the mechanisms of avoidance and intrusion such that the memories did not constitute obsession or disturbance. Recollection of the Holocaust contents occurred infrequently and was under their control.

Anxiety and depressive moods were revealed as the most dominant characteristic among the less adjusted Holocaust survivors. In addition, medical problems were prominent. A review of complaints showed that the less adjusted survivors suffered from greater medical problems, which manifested themselves primarily as pains throughout the body.

Coping style

Examination of the coping style during wakefulness with the Repression-Sensitization (R-S) Questionnaire, and the Ego Strength Questionnaire showed the existence of coping mechanisms corresponding to the above results. Members of the better adjusted group showed a clear tendency to be more repressive, with stronger ego forces. In other words, they were characterized by being free of strong emotions or the need to defend themselves if they existed. They refrained from giving expression to their feelings and repressed their traumatic experiences. To the extent that feelings arose, they were generally positive ones.

In contrast, the less adjusted group clearly showed a tendency to higher sensitization, a fact that manifested itself in the expression of emotional contents, with primarily negative feelings being raised. The less adjusted subjects revealed a prominent tendency to express anxiety and tension and to admit to weakness and traumas from the past. Hence, if a certain stimulus connected directly or indirectly with the trauma confronted the less adjusted survivor, he perceived it as more threatening, in contrast to the better adjusted survivor, who tended to distance himself and to smooth over the threat inherent in the stimulus.

Sleep patterns

An examination of the subjective sleep questionnaires and the poly-somnographic data showed that the less adjusted survivors suffered both subjectively and objectively from more sleep difficulties characterizing insomnia. In subjective reporting, they expressed more frequent complaints of difficulties in falling asleep, interrupted and unquiet sleep due to awakenings, awakening in the early morning hours and being unable to fall asleep again, fatigue and headaches in the morning, and prolonged fatigue throughout the day. Members of both the better adjusted group and the control group reported normative sleep patterns for their age population.

Examination of the physiological correlates in the lab showed that although the total time spent in bed was similar for the three groups, the actual sleep time was different (Table 22.1). The less adjusted group slept significantly less than the other two groups ($p < .001$). Sleep efficiency, which is the proportion of time in bed spent asleep, was found to be significantly lower in the less adjusted group ($p < .01$). Sleep efficiency suffered for several reasons. First, sleep latency was longer, that is, the individuals had difficulty falling asleep ($p < .0001$). Second, this group was characterized by a much larger number of awakenings during the night ($p < .001$). In the various sleep stages – during both the light sleep (stage 2) and the deep sleep stages (stages 3 and 4) – no clear-cut differences were found among the groups in the percentage of time that each stage took up within the total sleep. In most of the physiological parameters of REM sleep, no differences were found among the groups. REM latency and the percentage of the REM stage of the total sleep were similar in all three groups. Similarly, at this stage no differences were found in the physiological parameters of REM sleep: eye movement density, heart rate, respiration, and body movements.

Dreaming

Although virtually no differences in the physiological indices of the REM were found among the groups, a distinct difference in the rate of dream recall was found. The well-adjusted survivors displayed almost total denial during most of the REM sleep awakenings when asked what passed through their minds and if they remembered any dreams. Only in 33.7% of all the awakenings did the subjects recall their dreams. During the rest of the awakenings they denied the fact that they had dreamed at all.

The control group, on the other hand, reported a normal percentage (80%) of dream contents when awakened from REM sleep. The percentage of reporting by the less adjusted survivor group was between the other two groups, 50.7% recall from the total awakenings. The differences between the three groups were highly significant ($\chi^2 = 38.1$, $df = 2$, $p < .00001$). It should be noted that all the subjects were motivated to recall dreams, and each time the subjects were awakened and did not recall their dreams, they were very disappointed and even apologized to the experimenter.

Concerning the dream structure, the survivor groups differed significantly from the control group in the complexity and salience of their dreams. Whereas dreams of the control subjects were complex, lucid, detailed, and unrestrained, the survivors' dreams, particularly those of the well adjusted,

Table 22.1. *Sleep data (means of all nights) for the three groups*

	Well adjusted		Less adjusted		Control		
	Mean	SD	Mean	SD	Mean	SD	P
Total sleep (min.)	378	22.1	341	27.2	352	29.7	0.001
SE(%)[a]	77	5.2	70	12.7	79	2.9	0.001
Sleep latency[b]	20	7.6	33	25.4	12.3	6.8	0.001
REM latency	71	16.7	81	29.4	78	21.1	n.s.
% Sleep stages							
O + MT[c]	13	6	15	10	9	6	0.001
1	5	4	7	4	6	4	n.d.[d]
2 (light sleep)	43	8	45	10	46	11	n.s.
3–4 (deep sleep)	17	7	17	11	21	11	n.s.
REM	16	5	15	6	16	6	n.s.

[a] SE = sleep efficiency (% of time, in bed asleep).
[b] Sleep latency = time (in minutes) it takes to fall asleep.
[c] O = awake; MT = movement time.
[d] n.s. = not significant.

were characterized by their limitations; their complexity and salience were inferior.

For example, a surviving "Mengele twin"* from Auschwitz, in the well-adjusted group, was awakened 13 times from REM sleep during the four nights that he slept in the lab. From the total awakenings it was found that he had succeeded in recalling only two short dreams of conflictual content and totally unrelated to the Holocaust. When he was questioned regarding his feelings, he claimed "none," "nothing," "the dream has no influence over me." Analysis of variance applied to the scores of dream complexity ($p < .004$) and dream salience ($p < .01$) revealed significant differences among the groups. Post hoc Duncan tests revealed that the control group had significantly more complex and more salient dreams than the well adjusted, whereas the less adjusted held an intermediate position that was not significantly different from either group.

Regarding dream content it was clearly apparent that the survivor groups tended to express more negative contents and emotions in comparison to the control group. The less adjusted group reported more anxiety dreams and dreams in which negative contents appeared. For all the anxiety scores the control group had lower scores than the survivor groups.

---

*Joseph Menegele, one of Hitler's henchmen, was involved in constant experimenting on Jewish twins confined within the ghettos during World War II.

Significant differences were found for general anxiety ($p < .02$) and for three of the subscales: death anxiety ($p < .06$), guilt anxiety ($p < .002$), and diffused anxiety ($p < .04$). An examination of the percentage of anxiety dreams showed that the survivor groups experienced far more than the control group. In the less adjusted group there were 49% such dreams; in the well-adjusted group, 32%. In contrast, the control group showed only 6% nightmarish dreams. In a number of cases they reduced the sleep quality, but only in extreme cases did they cause the dreamer to awaken without the ability to fall asleep again. Only the less adjusted survivors experienced nightmares resulting in spontaneous awakening. For example, one survivor reported that sometimes half the night he dreamed about the camps and what happened there. A "bad" dream of this type would arouse great fear and terror; he would feel that although he wanted to scream, he was unable to do so, and he would become very agitated when he felt as though paralyzed and, sometimes, as though suffocating. Among the contents that arose in these dreams were shots fired, killing, transport to the ovens, selections, and so on. It should be noted that these contents were actually part of his everyday life in the camps.

Various types of anxieties appeared in the dream contents of the less adjusted group, including anxiety about death, anxiety about injury, anxiety related to helplessness, and feelings of guilt, shame, and diffused anxiety. Similarly, dreams related to aggressive experiences stood out. For example, there were dreams related to the Holocaust such as selection, chases, and threats of execution. In addition, many dreams included danger of injury not directly linked to the Holocaust, such as illness or threat of traffic accidents. Contents related directly to the Holocaust, generally of a nightmarish quality, appeared relatively infrequently. Holocaust contents did not appear at all in the control group, whose dreams were related to everyday life, such as family, work, and social gatherings.

Manifestations of aggression and hostility that appeared in the survivors' dreams were significantly greater than in the dreams of the control group. Furthermore, in the less adjusted group aggressive dreams occurred more frequently and the aggression expressed itself as hostility directed primarily at themselves. In other words, the survivors themselves were usually the victims. For example, one female survivor wanted, in her dream, to throw out the garbage while other people blocked her way and prevented her from doing so, an act that caused her great distress. In the well-adjusted group, on the other hand, the prominent characteristic was hidden hostility that was expressed by different factors and in which the survivors were not directly involved. They tended to distance from themselves the manifestation of aggression. For example, in one of these dreams the survivor witnessed others quarreling, while he himself was a spectator from the side.

In the less adjusted group, other persons were perceived as unreliable, dangerous, and bad. For example, in one survivor's dream there arose the image of a Jew from the Holocaust period who was known to be cruel to his fellow Jews. In the dream, he harassed both the dreamer and his wife. In sharp contrast, the control group perceived social interactions as more beneficial. Their dreams were characterized by the tendency toward helping others and sociability.

An interesting finding concerning interpersonal interaction in dreams showed that the less adjusted survivors' dreams that left an impression, and that recurred frequently, were primarily related to their childhood. In these dreams the feeling of longing for parents lost in the Holocaust was dominant, probably indicating loss processing in the course of sleep, a process not possible during wakefulness. For example, in one dream, repeated almost nightly, the survivor was united with his father from whom he had been separated when he was 3 years old. According to him, these dreams recurred all his life until he actually met his father many years hence.

In summary, sleep recordings show that the less adjusted group suffered both from sleep disturbances and from more threatening sleep contents, accompanied by more negative feelings (nightmares and anxiety dreams). In contrast, sleep disturbances were almost entirely absent in the well-adjusted group, whose dream characteristics indicated a different coping method. In the next section we try to understand these findings within the context of coping methods of the survivors.

Model of coping among Holocaust survivors

The parallelism found so far in processes in both wakefulness and in sleep leads to the assumption that the difficulties arising from trauma are integrated into the entire personality, during both states of existence, in both psychological and physiological dimensions. Significant correlations were found between coping mechanisms during wakefulness and sleep. The higher the sensitization among the survivors, the penetration of Holocaust-related memories, the psychopathology, the medical complaints, and the distress in daily life, the more disturbed was the sleep and the higher was the rate of dream recall.

The well-adjusted group of survivors is characterized by the absence of post-trauma symptoms, with strong ego forces and a repressive coping style. The style during wakefulness expressed itself in low penetration of traumatic memories, avoidance and distancing from the threatening stimulus, and repression of emotions. In sleep, high sleep efficiency was revealed, characterized by nonrecall of any dream contents.

In contrast, the less adjusted group was characterized by post-trauma symptoms both in wakefulness and in sleep, sensitivity in relating to others, and weak ego forces. They also showed high sensitivity to the environment in general and to threatening stimuli in particular. This style was related in wakefulness to a high penetration of trauma, adjustment difficulties, distress, and higher psychopathology. In sleep, this style was related to many sleep disturbances accompanied by nightmares. Table 22.1 shows that the well-adjusted group was very similar to the control group, with the exception that the latter had a coping style more balanced between repression and sensitization and a higher percentage of dream recall.

An examination of coping styles showed that better adjustment was characterized by the following repression mechanisms: in sleep, nonrecall of dream contents, interpreted as repression of the nightmares and anxiety dreams; and in wakefulness, in the repression of memories and the restraining of troubling thoughts related to the trauma.

From the dramatically low rate of dream recall in survivors, we raise the hypothesis that the dream-repression mechanism plays a significant role in their adjustment. During sleep it acts as a filter, preventing the penetration of traumatic contents into consciousness and enabling effective sleep. Moreover, an examination of the dream contents reinforces this supposition. The supposition that recall of nightmarish contents disturbs sleep is raised by the fact that among the survivors' dreams there were contents related to the Holocaust threatening existence, as well as to aggression, and especially contents expressing self-directed aggression.

We believe that penetration of the contents caused a degradation in sleep efficiency, as manifested among the less adjusted. Thus, the repression mechanism is the safeguard of sleep. Evidently there is an unconscious use of the coping mechanism, whose function is to prevent traumatic dreams from occurring. This mechanism is responsible for both the "forgetting" and the minimal recollection of the dream content, as well as for the dream characteristics themselves.

The dominance of the repression mechanism as found in the well-adjusted group both in wakefulness and in sleep opened the door to a better understanding of the efficient methods for coping with a trauma as major as the Holocaust. The repression mechanism significantly distinguished the well-adjusted group from the control group, which had not experienced a massive trauma, whereas in the other indices for both wakefulness and sleep the groups were very similar. Were it not for the dream recall rate, one could claim that the well-adjusted group had efficiently overcome the trauma while achieving a balance between the processes of penetration and avoidance in wakefulness and sleep without the need for unique mechanisms. However, it was the repression mechanism in sleep that clearly distinguished this group from the control group. Thanks to the development of this unique mechanism during sleep, the survivors apparently achieved normal adjustment.

As stated, the well-adjusted survivors also displayed a repressive tendency in their daily life-style. Most of them had not talked all these years about the Holocaust. In some cases, the avoidance was so dominant that even their close relatives barely knew anything about their experiences during that period, if they even knew at all that the survivors had actually lived through the Holocaust. By their own testimony, this does not mean that they have forgotten what happened to them during the Holocaust; they have just avoided, both in wakefulness and in sleep, the recurrent penetration of the feelings (pain, helplessness, anxiety, and depression) that they had felt during their confinement.

The development of these mechanisms actually contradicts previously held beliefs about the concept of repression. Repression has been understood as a pathological phenomenon, and the treatment for it was based on the fundamental view that one needed to bring reality into one's awareness and consciousness as much as possible. Treatment methods were structured accordingly. The analytic approaches consider repression a primitive, reality-distorting process. Repressive individuals might feel temporary relief, but in the long run they will suffer more severe emotional difficulties with which they will be unable to cope.

Our findings contradict this assumption. We see that in cases of massive trauma, repression does help in the long range. The survivors' ability to close off, repress, and prevent memories of past atrocities from reentering their consciousness has adaptive value and suggests that the treatment approach should be different. A method should be used that helps survivors to seal off the atrocities that they experienced and prevent them from being voluntarily or involuntarily remembered. Instead of allowing the traumatic experience to penetrate awareness, the treatment method should strive to remove the atrocities from consciousness. This approach helps the individual cope in the long run. Indeed, over the past decade more evidence and research have shown that repression mechanisms are coping mechanisms that promote better adjustment (Breznitz, 1983).

PART VII

Coping, counseling, and therapy

23

The meaning of loss and adjustment to bereavement

CAMILLE B. WORTMAN,
ROXANE COHEN SILVER,
AND RONALD C. KESSLER

In this chapter we provide an overview of our program of research on how people cope with loss. Most of this research has focused on bereavement (see Wortman & Silver, 1987, 1989, 1990, for reviews), although we have studied other types of loss as well, including physical disability (Bulman & Wortman, 1977; Silver, 1982), criminal victimization (Coates, Wortman, & Abbey, 1979), and incest (Silver, Boon, & Stones, 1983). We have had a special interest in understanding the impact of sudden, irrevocable losses – that is, events that involve permanent change and over which one has little, if any, control. Such losses can challenge people's beliefs and assumptions about themselves and their world (Janoff-Bulman & Frieze, 1983; Wortman, 1983) and disrupt their hopes and dreams for the future (Silver & Wortman, 1980). Our goals in this work are to clarify the processes through which people try to come to terms with the inexplicable events in their lives (Tait & Silver, 1989) and to understand the theoretical mechanisms through which such events can have deleterious effects on subsequent health and functioning (Kessler, Price, & Wortman, 1985).

We begin this chapter by tracing the development of theoretical ideas that we have employed in studying these events. In developing a conceptual framework for this research, we drew from two very different theoretical approaches: (1) the so-called stage models of grief, which represent the most influential theoretical approaches to the study of grief and loss (e.g., Bowlby, 1961, 1973, 1980/1981), and (2) the stress and coping approach, which has been influential in the study of life events more generally (e.g., Kessler et al., 1985). We then provide a brief overview of our initial studies conducted during the late 1970s and early 1980s on coping with sudden, traumatic losses. These losses included permanent paralysis as a result of a traumatic injury to the spinal cord, loss of an infant to sudden infant death syndrome (SIDS), and loss of a spouse or child in a motor-vehicle crash.

The data obtained from these studies appeared to be inconsistent with predictions from both of the predominant theoretical approaches and

349

from our common cultural understanding of how people cope with loss (cf. Wortman & Silver, 1989). Contrary to our expectations, many of the respondents did not seem to be devastated by the loss initially, as we might have expected. In addition to the negative emotions that would be expected from the stage models, we found positive emotions to be surprisingly prevalent in the first weeks and months following a major loss. Moreover, in the SIDS and motor-vehicle studies, many individuals were unable to resolve the loss and continued to remain distressed much longer than expected. There was also evidence to suggest that if individuals are going to be able to achieve a state of resolution regarding the loss (i.e., come up with a satisfactory account for why the loss occurred), they do so soon afterward.

Our findings led us to question the value of the theoretical approaches that we had been applying previously. Drawing from these initial studies, we began to reformulate our theoretical orientation. Because our data suggested that major losses do not always seem to bring about a period of initial distress, we were led to speculate that some people may have something in place beforehand – perhaps a religious or philosophical orientation, or a certain view of the world – that enables them to incorporate the event in question. In this chapter, we elaborate how we believe that life events are especially likely to result in intense distress and subsequent problems in mental and physical health when they shatter a person's assumptions about the world. In our judgment, the impact of a major loss is also likely to depend on the meaning of the loss to the individual. For a variety of reasons, including people's views of the world, a given loss can mean different things to different people. Only by disaggregating, or "unpacking," the loss into those stressors that it evokes for a particular person can the impact of the loss be understood (cf. Kessler, House, & Turner, 1987).

For the past decade, we have been involved in a comprehensive, multi-disciplinary program of research on conjugal bereavement that includes two prospective studies (see Wortman & Silver, 1990, for a review). Because these studies include an assessment of respondents prior to the loss of their spouse, they afford a unique opportunity to test the theoretical notions we have been developing. Moreover, because they involve large-scale representative samples of people who have lost a spouse in various ways, the new studies allow us to test the generalizability of findings obtained in our earlier work. In the pages to follow, we describe the new studies and discuss the theoretical significance of the data we have recently obtained. We conclude the chapter by identifying research directions we intend to pursue.

Original theoretical perspective

Stage models

Before initiating our research, we reviewed the predominant theoretical models in the area of grief and loss. The most influential theories are the so-called stage models of grief. According to such models, individuals go through several stages of emotional response as they attempt to come to terms with the loss of a loved one (see Shuchter & Zisook, this volume, for a review). Representative of such approaches is the stage model offered by Bowlby (1961, 1973, 1980/1981). He proposed that, following a major loss, individuals will pass through four stages or phases of mourning, including shock, searching, depression, and reorganization and recovery. Given the popularity of the notion that people go through stages of response following loss, we were interested in whether there was any empirical evidence to support it. Over the years, we reviewed dozens of studies on coping with stressful life events (Silver & Wortman, 1980; Wortman & Silver, 1989). Surprisingly, we were able to locate only a few studies that systematically assessed a variety of emotional responses longitudinally following a major loss. Moreover, the available data from these studies did not support, and sometimes contradicted, the stage approach. A close examination of the data suggests that there is considerable variability in the specific kinds of emotions that are experienced, as well as in their sequence and intensity (see Silver & Wortman, 1980, for a more detailed discussion). Nonetheless, as we detail elsewhere (Wortman & Silver, 1987, 1989), there is a pervasive belief among caregivers and helping professionals that such stages exist, and they are often used as a yardstick by which to assess a client's progress.

It should be noted that stage models are particularly difficult to test or disconfirm empirically; since some theorists have contended that people may experience more than one stage simultaneously, may move back and forth among the stages, and may skip certain stages completely (see, e.g., Klinger, 1977; Kubler-Ross, 1969). Because of the problems in subjecting such models to a rigorous empirical test, and because of the lack of evidence in support of them, there is growing speculation that these models may not be as useful as previously believed. In fact, the authoritative review of bereavement research issued by the Institute of Medicine cautioned against the use of the term "stages" of response. It noted that this term "might lead people to expect the bereaved to proceed from one clearly identifiable reaction to another in a more orderly fashion than usually occurs. It might also result in . . . hasty assessments of where individuals are or ought to be in the grieving process" (Osterweis, Solomon, & Green, 1984, p. 48).

Despite these shortcomings, we have found the work of the major stage theorists, particularly Bowlby (1980/1981) and Horowitz (1976/1986,

1985), to be extremely useful in a descriptive sense. The stage models devote considerable attention to the specific processes through which individuals move from emotional distress to adaptation or recovery. In our view, the major weakness of this theoretical approach is that it proposes no specific mechanisms through which loss may exert an influence on subsequent mental or physical health. For this reason, general stage models cannot account for the diversity of outcomes that occur in response to loss events and cannot explain, for example, why one person is devastated by a particular loss and another emerges relatively unscathed.

Stressful life events

In order to account for this variability of response, we turned to the literature on the effect of life events, which had its origins in the pioneering work of Cannon (1939) and Selye (1956). According to these theorists, life change creates disequilibrium, which imposes a period of readjustment and which can leave the person more vulnerable to stress and its deleterious consequences. Most of the research that has examined the physical and mental health problems following stress exposure has documented a relationship between stressful life events and subsequent health. However, the relations that have been documented are extremely small. For example, Rabkin and Struening (1976) estimated that no more than 9% of the variance in health outcomes is explained by life events. The same predictive power is found when mental health outcomes are the focus of analysis (Thoits, 1983). Subsequently, researchers have attempted to conduct a more careful analysis of the specific sorts of events that are associated with particular kinds of disorders. Some improvement results from considering events in terms of their desirability, controllability, predictability, seriousness, and time clustering (Thoits, 1983). Nonetheless, even with these improvements, the relationship between life changes and physical or mental health problems is modest.

In attempting to clarify the reasons for this weak association, work on the impact of life events progressed in two directions, both of which have important implications for research on bereavement. First, investigators have recognized that it is important to obtain information about the context in which the event occurred, and hence clarify the meaning of the particular event to the respondent. For example, the loss of a parent may have more impact on one person than on another because the parent was also the major child-care provider. There is controversy about the best way to obtain contextual information, however. A number of different approaches have been developed, each with advantages and disadvantages (see Kessler et al., 1985, for a more detailed discussion). For example, in a study of unemployment, Kessler et al. (1987) attempted to resolve this matter by examining specifically what a person lost when he or she lost a job – money, social contacts, self-esteem, and so on. For the most part, bereavement researchers have not concerned themselves with this issue. However, a focus on contextual factors that elucidate the meaning of the loss to a particular person may help to account for the variability in response to that loss.

A second major thrust of current research in the stress and coping area involves the identification of variables – or vulnerability or resistance factors – that can account for the variability of response. It is generally assumed that once a stressful life event is encountered, the appraisal of that stressor, as well as mental and physical health consequences, will depend on these vulnerability or resistance factors. Several different types of factors have been examined in the literature, including various personality predispositions, such as neuroticism (e.g., Depue & Monroe, 1986) and dispositional optimism (e.g., Scheier & Carver, 1985); resources, such as intellectual capacity, cognitive flexibility, and financial assets (Menaghen, 1983); coping strategies, such as reinterpretation of the situation as positive or denial that a problem exists (e.g., Lazarus & Folkman, 1984); and social support (see Cohen & Wills, 1985, for a review).

Thus, unlike the stage models, a major advantage of the stress and coping approach is that it can account for variability in response. Also, an implicit assumption underlying the stage approach is that virtually everyone will recover from a stressful life experience. However, according to the stress and coping model, those with more coping resources, such as social support, are likely to recover more quickly and completely than those with fewer resources.

Early empirical work

In the late 1970s, using the aforementioned theoretical approaches as a guide, we initiated a program of research designed to clarify the process of coping with an irrevocable loss. Over the next decade, we completed three studies that were designed to test theoretical notions concerning people's emotional reactions to a major loss and their ability to resolve the loss over time. In these studies, we combined rigorous sampling procedures and the use of carefully validated measures with open-ended questions designed to elucidate respondents' feelings about what the event meant to them and how they attempted to come to terms with it. The first of these studies focused on how people cope with physical disability following a sudden, traumatic injury to their spinal-cord (Silver, 1982; Wortman & Silver, 1987). In this study, interviews were completed with three groups of spinal-cord–injured persons: quadriplegics, paraplegics, and a control group of neurologically intact individuals who had been in an accident, but who had suffered no spinal cord damage. More than 100 individuals were interviewed at 1, 3, and 8 weeks following their injury. In the second study, interviews were conducted with parents who lost an infant to sudden infant death syndrome (SIDS; Downey, Silver, & Wortman, 1990; Wortman & Silver, 1987). Unlike the spinal-cord study, whose sample comprised primarily young white males, the SIDS sample was 50 percent black, and included mothers and fathers of varying socioeconomic backgrounds. The SIDS study also encompassed a wider time frame: 124 respondents were interviewed at 3 to 4 weeks, 3 months, and 18 months following the death of their baby. Our third study, designed to clarify the long-term impact of a major traumatic loss, focused on people who lost a spouse or child in a motor-vehicle crash (Lehman, Wortman, & Williams, 1987). This sample was restricted to people whose loved ones were not responsible for causing the accident. Eighty bereaved individuals were interviewed 4 to 7 years following the death of their loved ones, and their responses were compared to those of matched controls, who had not experienced a death of their spouse or child.

Findings emerged from these studies that were inconsistent with what would be expected on the basis of previous theories, as well as from our common cultural understanding of how people react to loss (cf. Silver & Wortman, 1980; Wortman & Silver, 1989). First, many respondents did not react to the loss initially with intense distress, and positive emotions were far more prevalent than expected. In fact, results revealed great variability in response, with some respondents experiencing anxiety, depression, and anger quite frequently and others reporting that they experienced these emotions much more rarely. Surprisingly, in the spinal cord–injury study, there was little relation between the severity of the stressor and the frequency of negative emotions: Quadriplegics were no more likely to report negative affect than were control respondents, who had suffered no permanent damage to their spinal cord. Moreover, at 3 weeks following the loss, subjects reported experiencing happiness significantly more frequently than depression or anger. By 8 weeks, respondents reported experiencing happiness significantly more frequently than any of the negative emotions. In the SIDS study, data on the frequency of emotions were highly similar to the findings from the spinal-cord study. By the second interview, conducted 3 months after the infant's death, positive affect was more prevalent than negative affect. This was also the case at the third interview, which was conducted 18 months after the death.

Second, we found little evidence to support the widespread assumption that intense distress or depression is inevitable following a major loss, and that failure to experience such distress will lead to subsequent difficulties (see Wortman & Silver, 1989). It is widely assumed among practitioners in the field of grief and loss (see, e.g., Rando, 1984), as well as among investigators in the stress and coping field, that when a major loss is experienced, individuals will react with intense distress or depression. In the study of SIDS parents, however, nearly 30% of respondents failed to show significant depression shortly after the death of their infant (Wortman & Silver, 1987), a pattern of results that has been reported by a number of investigators (e.g., Lund, Caserta, & Dimond, 1986a; Vachon et al., 1982a; and see Wortman & Silver, 1990, for a review). Moreover, we did not find those people who experienced a period of depression to adapt to their losses more successfully than did those who did not become depressed. In fact, those who had gone through a period of depression were significantly less likely to have emotionally resolved the loss and reported experiencing more symptoms and more emotional distress at the 18-month interview than did those who did not experience an earlier period of distress (see Wortman & Silver, 1987). Similar findings have also been obtained by other investigators in the area of bereavement (e.g., Bornstein, Clayton, Halikas, Maurice, & Robins, 1973; Lund et al., 1986a; Parkes & Weiss, 1983; Vachon et al., 1982a).

Third, many of the respondents in our studies were unable to resolve their loss or make sense of what had happened, even after a considerable period of time. Results of all our studies suggest that, contrary to clinical lore (see Craig, 1977; Miles & Crandall, 1983), only a small percentage of respondents searched for meaning in what happened to them, found meaning, and put the issue of meaning aside. In the motor-vehicle accident study, a significant majority of respondents had not achieved a state of resolution of their loss many years later. Despite the fact that 4 to 7 years had elapsed since the death had occurred, 72% of the respondents in this study reported that they were unable to make any sense or find any meaning in their loss.

Finally, a substantial percentage of respondents from our studies showed distress for longer than might have been expected (see Wortman & Silver, 1989). In particular, data from the motor-vehicle accident study provided compelling evidence that the traumatic loss of one's spouse or child poses substantial long-term emotional and social difficulties (see Lehman et al., 1987).

Taken together, the early studies have pointed our attention to three distinct findings, each of which is inconsistent with prevailing views from theorists and researchers in the field of grief and loss. First, it is clear from our own data (Wortman & Silver, 1987), as well as the data of others (see Wortman & Silver, 1990, for a review), that a substantial percentage of people do not appear to experience intense distress following a major loss. Instead, by as early as 1 month following the loss, there is marked variability in response. Moreover, initial reactions appear to be highly predictive of long-term adjustment.

This pattern of findings raises numerous questions. Most of the studies we have reviewed have included a valid measure of depression, but have included very limited, if any, measures of grief. Do those individuals who fail to exhibit intense depression also fail to show indications of grief (i.e., yearning for the person who has died, or strong feelings of distress when confronted with reminders of the lost loved one)? Is it possible that such individuals have already grieved for their lost loved one? Some people may begin grieving before their spouse has died if they have forewarning (e.g., in those cases where the spouse was terminally ill). Moreover, even in those situations where there is no opportunity to grieve for the loved one before the death (i.e., loss of an infant through SIDS), a substantial minority exhibit low distress shortly after the loss. It is important to establish whether those who fail to grieve, or to show intense distress following the loss, will experience a delayed grief reaction, and/or whether their failure to grieve will result in subsequent health problems. As we noted earlier, several studies have suggested that if respondents fail to manifest significant depression shortly after their loss, they are unlikely to manifest depression in subsequent interviews. But depression is not necessarily synonymous with grief. Because the studies to date have included virtually no questions about feelings of grief at different points in time, they do not really address the question of delayed grief reactions. Moreover, we are aware of no long-term longitudinal studies of the bereaved that have included hard health outcomes. Hence, at this point, virtually nothing is known about the impact of failure to grieve, or to exhibit or express feelings of distress, on subsequent health.

Second, results from the SIDS and motor-vehicle studies suggest that the process of resolution from loss may operate differently than we might have expected. Like most clinicians who work in the area, we initially expected that when faced with a major loss, individuals would attempt to find meaning or come to an understanding of why the loss occurred and what it means in their lives. However, the majority of our respondents were unable to find any meaning even after a considerable amount of time had elapsed. Moreover, the SIDS study suggested that if people were going to be able to come up with a meaningful account for why the loss occurred, they did so right away (Wortman & Silver, 1987). In subsequent studies, it will be important to test the generalizability of these results in other samples of bereaved individuals, and to determine whether individuals are able to achieve a sense of resolution concerning the loss over a longer time span.

Finally, the results of the motor-vehicle study, as well as findings from other investigators who have explored the issue (see Wortman & Silver, 1987, for a review), suggest that it may take far longer than we have previously expected for people to recover from the loss of a spouse or child. Compared to controls, respondents in our motor-vehicle study were experiencing symptoms and problems in many areas of their lives. It will be important to replicate these findings on other populations of bereaved, as there may be something particularly difficult about coping with a loss caused by another's negligence. As in the case of resolution, we would also like to determine whether people who experience such losses are able to recover over a time span longer than 4 to 7 years.

The pattern of findings from our early studies fails to confirm assumptions implicit in the grief and loss approach or the stress and coping approach to loss. Both approaches assume an initial period of intense distress, and both assume that, ultimately, recovery will occur. However, our findings can be understood in terms of a theoretical perspective that focuses on views of the world as an explanatory mechanism (cf. Janoff-Bulman, 1992). Some individuals, with some types of losses, may be able to incorporate the loss in question into their prevailing view of the world and, hence, may not show initial distress. For other individuals, the event may shatter their view of the world, but they may be able to regain equilibrium and restore their worldview over time. For still others, the event may so profoundly shatter their worldview that no integration or resolution is possible. In these latter cases, we might expect a "giving up" on the world, and the consequent failure to initiate coping efforts in other areas of life.

For the past several years, we have attempted to design a program of research that would allow us to address the questions raised by our early work, as well as to further refine and elaborate our theoretical thinking. Next we describe our recent studies in some detail.

Current research on widowhood: The Americans' Changing Lives (ACL) and Changing Lives of Older Couples (CLOC) studies

For the past decade, we have been involved in a comprehensive, multidisciplinary study of conjugal bereavement. The study has three distinct parts. First, we developed what we believe is the first large, nationally representative data base on conjugal loss. Our widowhood study is part of a large-scale interdisciplinary study of health, stress, and productive activities across the life span known as Americans' Changing Lives (ACL). In 1986, personal interviews were conducted with a probability sample of 3,617 adults who were 25 years of age and older. Blacks and persons over 60 were oversampled to permit more detailed analyses by race and age, in addition to maximizing the number of widowed respondents to be included. All sample members who could be recontacted ($N = 2,867$) were reinterviewed in 1989. Our data base of widowed respondents includes 804 individuals widowed from 3 months to over 60 years prior to the ACL study, 616 of whom were reinterviewed in 1989.

We have also completed a national prospective study of widowhood, including 92 ACL respondents who lost their spouse bet·veen Waves 1 and 2 of the study. Information on relevant risk factors was assessed before and after the loss as part of the ACL survey. Finally, we have launched a separate prospective study of widowhood designed to focus on older bereaved persons. This study, in which baseline data were collected from 1,532 members of older couples from the Detroit, Michigan area, is known as the Changing Lives of Older Couples (CLOC) study. State death records are monitored to identify respondents who become bereaved; they are recruited into a four-wave study in which they are interviewed at 6 to 8 months following the loss and at regular intervals thereafter (18 months and 49 months following the death). Matched control respondents are interviewed at comparable time periods. This study includes a separate biomedical component, funded by the MacArthur Foundation, in which data on physical health and cognitive functioning, as well as blood and urine samples, and collected from a subsample of still-married respondents, from those who become widowed, and from matched controls. The CLOC baseline data collection was completed in 1988 and follow-up is well under-way, with an 84 percent response rate in recruiting widows and widowers into the study. We have completed approximately 175 Wave 1 and 80 Wave 2 interviews.

In these studies, an effort was made to minimize methodological prob-lems that have characterized much previous work in the area, including biased samples, failure to include a control group, and failure to include valid and reliable measures of key variables. The design of the ACL study, in which individuals were approached to participate in a general study of stress and productive activity across the life span, helps to minimize prob-lems with selection inherent in designs that approach respondents shortly after the loss of a spouse. The prospective CLOC study also includes a large, representative sample of older adults. Moreover, because we will have CLOC baseline data on both respondents who agree to participate in the widowhood follow-up interviews and those who refuse later interviews, we will be able to determine if the two groups differ on major demographic or psychological indicators (cf. M. Stroebe & Stroebe, 1989). All of the study designs will afford the opportunity to compare bereaved and control respondents, and each study includes a wide range of outcome variables, including grief, depression, physical health, cognitive functioning, and involvement in productive activities.

The CLOC and ACL prospective studies are ideally suited to clarify how coping resources, assessed prior to the crisis, such as respondents' world-views, influence subsequent reactions to the loss. These designs will also permit us to address the issue of how worldviews, as well as other coping resources, such as social support or personality, are affected by the loss of a spouse. For example, widowed respondents may become less trusting of other people following their loss. In assessing changes occurring as a result of the loss, we will give full consideration to the possibility that widowhood may also produce long-term positive changes, such as greater self-confidence, as well as negative ones (cf. Wortman & Silver, 1990).

A strength of the ACL prospective study is that it will permit a comparison between the impact of widowhood and additional life crises experienced by other respondents after the ACL Wave 1 interview, including loss of a child ($N = 64$), divorce ($N = 84$), job loss ($N = 163$), and the onset of a life-threatening illness ($N = 201$). Because it includes a state-of-the-art assessment of both psychosocial and biomedical variables, the CLOC study represents an invaluable opportunity to assess the relationship between psychosocial and biomedical indicators of functioning, as well as assess how various coping resources prevent or reverse declines in health.

Findings from the ACL Wave 1 national cross-sectional data

Sex, age, and race effects. In past research, there is some consensus that widowhood has a greater impact on men than it does on women (M. Stroebe & Stroebe, 1983; W. Stroebe & Stroebe, 1987). In particular, it appears that there are sex differences in depression following widowhood, with widowed men showing greater vulnerability. However, past studies have failed to clarify why such sex differences exist. In analyses from the ACL study, we drew from the "unpacking" approach described earlier to determine whether widowhood may have a different meaning for men and women. Drawing from the literature on stressful life events and gender differences in marital roles, we hypothesized that widowhood results in different types and amounts of strain for men and women – strains related to the loss of roles previously filled by the survivor's spouse. Our results support this notion (Umberson, Wortman, & Kessler, 1992). It appears that women's primary source of vulnerability following widowhood arises from an increase in financial strain. In contrast, men's greater vulnerability stems in part from their more limited social relationships and from the difficulty in assuming tasks previously handled by their wives. Interestingly, our results show that widowhood is associated with significantly more strained relationships, particularly with children, for men but not for women. Many men may have relied on their spouses to maintain relationships with children, and may find it difficult to assume this role in widowhood. Previous lack of closeness between fathers and children, combined with male difficulty in expressing the need for support, may underlie the strained relationships with children that we found among our widowers.

Taken together, these results suggest that there may be considerable merit in an "unpacking" approach. On the surface, past research might appear to suggest a sex difference in vulnerability to the same event, widowhood. Upon closer examination, however, we find that widowhood is not the same event for the two sexes. Gender differences in the experience of various strains created by the loss help to explain the differential vulnerability seen at a more highly aggregated analysis.

We have also completed some preliminary results on the effects of age and race, and the results thus far are intriguing. Analyses conducted revealed that younger respondents are initially more affected by the loss of their spouse, but that they recover more quickly than older respondents (Wortman & Bolger, 1988). We have also obtained information that whites are hit harder initially, and take longer to recover, than do black respondents. Various explanatory mechanisms for these findings are currently being pursued using the same "unpacking" strategy described earlier.

Long-term effects of the loss. Data from the national cross-sectional study also corroborated the findings from our earlier research that the effects of widowhood last much longer than was previously expected (see Wortman, Kessler, Bolger, & House, 1992). Respondents who lost a spouse were compared with nonbereaved controls who were similar on a number of dimensions but who had not lost a spouse. It took bereaved respondents in our study approximately one decade to approach control respondents' scores on life satisfaction, and nearly two decades to approach their scores on depressed mood. In addition, we asked respondents several questions about their current thoughts and memories regarding their spouse. Painful memories were found to decline over time, although it took several decades for such memories to reach their lowest level. Finally, several questions were included to assess cognitive resolution from the loss, such as whether the respondent had been able to find any meaning in the loss, or whether he or she regarded the loss as senseless and unfair. Interestingly, such questions showed no time effects whatsoever. Individuals who lost their spouse more than six decades earlier were no more likely to have generated a reason for what happened than individuals who lost their spouse during the past year.

Preliminary findings from the ACL national prospective study

As noted, 92 individuals lost their spouse between Waves 1 and 2 of the ACL survey, and we have completed some preliminary analyses of these data. Compared to controls who were married at Wave 1 and did not experience a loss, the bereaved showed significantly higher depression. Further analyses were conducted to identify respondents most likely to experience distress. One set of analyses focused on characteristics of the marriage. According to clinical lore, people with ambivalent and conflictual marriages are at greatest risk for mental health problems following the death of their spouse. However, people involved in such marriages may have more mental health problems before the loss. In our study, we had data available on respondents' depression, as well as their evaluation of the marriage, before the loss. Our analyses show unequivocally that when we control for depression at Wave 1 and look at changes in depression as a function of marital satisfaction and conflict assessed before the loss, those with troubled marriages actually show less depression after the loss. Those who experienced relatively low levels of conflict and high levels of satisfaction were particularly distressed after the loss, suggesting that those with the best marriages may be the most at risk following bereavement and most in need of intervention efforts.

A second set of analyses has focused on the impact of coping resources, including social support, self-esteem, and feelings of mastery on the impact of bereavement. The stress and coping model suggests that those with more resources might be more resilient after the loss. An analysis in terms of the impact of life events on worldviews, however, leads to a different prediction. Those with views of the world as controllable, predictable, and safe may be particularly vulnerable to an uncontrollable life event, such as the death of a spouse. We explored the impact of social support, of subjective perceptions that one is in control (feelings of self-esteem, mastery, and belief that the world is a safe and secure place), and of objective indications of personal control (intellectual resources, financial resources). Surprisingly, social support as assessed prior to the loss had no effect on changes in depression following the loss. In every case, the other resources we studied were found to have a deleterious impact. Those with the highest self-esteem, the highest feelings of mastery, the greatest intellectual resources, and the most financial resources, were hit hardest by the loss of their spouse. Interestingly, it was not their spouse's income at Wave 1 but their own income that predicted deleterious effects, suggesting that those with the highest objectively determined sense of control over their lives were the most severely affected by the loss. Taken together, these findings suggest that those who experience the world as most controllable may be especially vulnerable to the loss of their spouse.

Future research directions

To date, we have focused primarily on the impact of widowhood on depression. In all three research designs, we will expand these analyses to focus on other outcomes, including self-esteem, involvement in productive activities, and physical health. The CLOC study, with its biomedical outcomes, will be ideally suited to this latter endeavor.

Once we have demonstrated, across the different designs employed in this study, how widowhood affects mental and physical health, we will try to identify the processes underlying such changes. Widowhood may influence outcomes through its impact on coping resources, such as social support, which may be eroded by the crisis. Alternatively, widowhood may have pernicious effects primarily because it results in increased chronic strains. It will be possible to examine this question by comparing the level of chronic strains among the widowed and control respondents, by examining increases in chronic strains among widowed respondents in the prospective components of the study, and by examining the relationship between the number and type of chronic strains and adjustment among widowed respondents. Of course, we suspect that widowhood is particularly likely to be associated with deleterious health consequences when it shatters an individual's view of the world. Because the prospective components of the study include measures of worldviews prior to and following the crisis, they should permit us to examine the validity of the theoretical notions that we have been developing.

A major goal of our subsequent analyses will be to elucidate the finding that individuals do not always become distressed after the loss of a spouse. Clinical lore maintains that failure to experience distress is indicative of pathology (see Wortman & Silver, 1989, for a review), but we believe that there may be other reasons why distress may not always occur. We will attempt to identify the conditions under which distress does not occur, as we know that respondents' initial reactions are predictive of their long-term adjustment. For example, failure to exhibit intense distress at Wave 1 may be most likely to occur in cases involving forewarning. Perhaps some individuals exhibit low distress because they have grieved for their loved one before the death.

We will also attempt to extend analyses conducted on the ACL prospective data suggesting that the amount of distress experienced following the loss is related to characteristics of the marriage. Wheaton (1988) suggests that individuals may exhibit relief rather than distress following life events that signal the end of ongoing chronic stress. This might be the case for respondents involved in a conflictual marriage, and if so, this could explain why some respondents show little distress following the loss. Knowledge of what the marriage was like is critical in interpreting the significance of low initial distress, as such a response could indicate either the end of a bad marriage or resilience following the loss of a great love. We will not only have prospective data on the marriage from the respondent's perspective, but in a sizable number of cases we will also have the spouse's assessment of the marriage prior to his or her death.

To elucidate further the finding that some individuals fail to become distressed following the loss, we will attempt to determine if those who fail to become distressed show other indications of mourning (e.g., preoccupation with thoughts or avoidance of reminders of the spouse), and if they show few signs of positive emotion, as some have speculated (e.g., Deutsch, 1937). Such information should help to clarify whether such a reaction is indicative of denial or repression of emotional distress, or whether it is indicative of resilience.

Because health consequences will be monitored in the CLOC study, we will be able to ascertain whether initial failure to experience distress results in subsequent health problems. In addressing this question, it is important to move beyond a self-report methodology, as those minimizing their distress may also minimize their health problems on self-report scales. The availability of pre- and postwidowhood data, as well as data from controls on such outcomes as blood pressure, cognitive functioning, prescription medications, and changes in catecholamines, cortisol, and blood lipids, will be ideal for these purposes. Moreover, the self-report measures of health utilized in the CLOC study can be validated against the more objective outcome measures also assessed. Finally, we will attempt to determine whether there is any relationship between initial distress and long-term positive changes. Are respondents who show little initial distress following the loss of their spouse less likely to experience personal growth than those who have struggled with depression and anxiety?

Summary

For over a decade, we have been involved in a program of research designed to clarify how people come to terms with major losses in their lives. Our major goal has been to clarify the theoretical mechanisms through which such events can have deleterious consequences on subsequent mental or physical health. In developing a theoretical framework for our research, we drew from two different theoretical approaches – the so-called stage models of grief (cf. Bowlby, 1961, 1973, 1980/1981) and the stress and coping approach (cf. Kessler et al., 1985). Our early studies focused on specific populations who had endured sudden, irrevocable losses, including physical disability, loss of a child to SIDS, or loss of a spouse or child in a motor-vehicle crash. Findings across these studies failed to confirm, and in some cases contradicted, assumptions that could be derived from previous theories, as well as our common cultural understanding of how people cope with loss.

For this reason, we have been developing a new theoretical framework that provides a basis for understanding these findings and for predicting the conditions under which major losses may be particularly likely to cause enduring difficulties. Although a full statement of this theoretical approach is beyond the scope of this chapter, the approach suggests that the impact of life events may be determined by whether they can be incorporated into an individual's philosophical perspective, or view of the world. By world-view, we mean the interwoven system of beliefs, assumptions, or expectations related to oneself, others, and the world that provide a sense of coherence and meaning (Janoff-Bulman, 1992; Silver & Wortman, 1991). People's views of the world may be shaped by a variety of factors, including the culture in which they live, their early family experiences, their religious orientation, and their subsequent life experiences, which may include previously experienced stressful life events. As a result of the interplay of these factors, people develop conceptions of the world that strongly influence their day-to-day coping efforts.

These conceptions have to do with the extent to which the world, and the people and institutions in it, are seen as predictable and orderly versus random, safe versus dangerous, benevolent versus malevolent, controllable versus uncontrollable, fair versus unfair, and trustworthy versus un-trustworthy. Regarding why things happen when they do, people may be fatalistic, seeing all things as part of a larger plan; they may feel that people get what they earn or deserve, either on this earth or in the afterlife; or they may view the world as a random universe or a "jungle" where things happen without purpose. Whether an event is compatible with a person's worldview may depend not only on the worldview but also on the charac-teristics of the event. Some events, those that happen without purpose or meaning – such as a drunk driver killing one's spouse or child – may be difficult to incorporate into almost any worldview. We suspect that a number of factors, such as the suddenness of the event, whether it would be expected at the particular point in the life span, and how common it is, will influence whether the event can be incorporated into a person's worldview.

The kinds of events we have studied, which are sudden, uncontrollable, and generally random, may shatter people's assumptions that the world is a predictable and orderly place and may leave people feeling that they cannot control the outcomes of greatest importance to them. When basic world-views are violated, this is likely to cause a period of intense disequilibrium or distress. Over time, we believe that this can lead to a reinterpretation of the event as compatible with one's preexisting views, which will result in a quick reduction of distress, or an attempt to alter the worldview to accommodate the event. Some individuals may be able to make changes in their worldview that allow them to reestablish equilibrium, whereas others may gradually reformulate their view of the world to incorporate the event. Among these latter people, some may arrive at a new worldview that facilitates subsequent coping efforts, where others may come to see the world as such a negative place that initiation of new coping efforts is difficult. Finally, we suspect that some individuals, despite major attempts to integrate the event into their view of the world, will be unable to do so.

These people, we believe, will continue "processing" the loss, and will continue to experience distress.

We believe that a theoretical account of the process of coping with loss that considers the impact of such losses on one's worldview has a number of advantages over previous formulations. First, such a model can account for the paradoxical finding that a substantial minority of respondents in our and others' studies do not appear to become intensely distressed following a major loss. Second, such a model can account for the striking variability in response that is often seen in response to a single life crisis, such as cancer (see Silver & Wortman, 1980, for a more detailed discussion). For example, a person who viewed illness as preventable through diet and exercise, and who went to considerable lengths to eat the right foods and get regular exercise, may be far more likely to experience a challenge to his or her worldview than a person who sees the development of disease as a more random and multidetermined process. Third, this perspective can help to account for the paradoxical finding that sometimes relatively trivial events seem to perpetuate major distress. For example, Brown and Harris (1978) report that depressive episodes may frequently be brought about by relatively small events that challenge one's view of reality, such as learning that a close friend cannot be trusted. Fourth, our analysis suggests a new way of thinking about vulnerability to major losses. In the past, vulnerability has been assumed to be a function of the coping resources that one possesses – one's self-esteem, socioeconomic status, belief in the ability to control one's environment, social support. Our analysis suggests that people who appear to have considerable coping resources – successful, control-oriented people who have a history of accomplishment and who have generally been rewarded for their efforts – may be particularly vulnerable to certain kinds of sudden, undesirable life events. Such people may be more devastated by a loss that challenges the view that efforts are generally rewarded than those who possess considerably less coping resources.

Since completing our early studies, we have been involved in designing and conducting a large-scale, comprehensive, multidisciplinary study of conjugal bereavement with three distinct parts, including (1) a nationally representative cross-sectional study of bereaved individuals who lost a spouse from 3 months to over 60 years previously; (2) a national prospective study of individuals who lost their spouse; and (3) a larger, more comprehensive prospective study of older couples, which includes the collection of biomedical as well as psychosocial data. Analyses conducted to date corroborate our earlier findings. One of the most important findings to emerge from the new study is that those who would seem to be the most resilient to widowhood – men, whites, and younger people – are the most likely to be hurt by the crisis, at least initially. Similarly, our preliminary results suggest that those with the most coping resources – feelings of personal control, mastery, self-esteem, higher income, and higher intelligence – are hit harder by the loss of a spouse than those who lack these resources.

In future work, we plan to explore the long-term physical and mental health consequences of early failure to experience or express distress. We also plan to determine whether individuals with particular worldviews are especially vulnerable to certain kinds of losses. We will be interested to see whether worldviews and other coping resources are changed as a result of a major loss, and if so, how long such resources continue to be diminished. We want to understand more about how previous losses may influence our ability to cope with current losses, and plan to see whether people who have experienced certain kinds of prior losses differ in current views of the world from people who have not. Hopefully, this work will result in the elaboration and clarification of our ideas regarding worldviews as an explanatory concept, as well as in the identification of those bereaved who are at particular risk for subsequent problems and hence in need of intervention.

24

Old age and widowhood: Issues of personal control and independence

ROBERT O. HANSSON,
JACQUELINE H. REMONDET,
AND MARLENE GALUSHA

Research on bereavement and widowhood typically has focused on under-standing the nature of the phenomenon, short-term consequences, and processes underlying recovery. Few investigations have attended system-atically to the contexts in which widowhood is experienced or to the likely influence of age-related changes in a widow's coping resources. Yet a number of such themes broadly influence the experience of widowhood in Western society.

First, widowhood usually occurs in one's later years; in the United States the mean age at widowhood is 69 years for men and 66 years for women. Second, it is primarily a women's issue, because of sex differences in expected life span favoring females and because men tend to marry women younger than themselves and are more likely to remarry following the death of a spouse. Among people 65 years or over, 51% of women compared to 13% of men are widowed (U.S. Bureau of the Census, 1984). On this point, however, it is noteworthy that widowers, although a minority, also ex-perience serious adjustment problems, and much of the discussion to follow applies also to them (M. Stroebe & Stroebe, 1983). A third concern is that widowed individuals are more likely to live alone and on a reduced income. Finally, and perhaps most important for the purposes of this chapter, widowed persons, especially women, have much of their life still before them. The mean duration of widowed life is approximately 14 years for women and 7 years for men (U.S. Bureau of the Census, 1984). The fact that most widows go on to live long lives, into old age, then raises issues of tremendous importance. They must somehow establish a life independent of the deceased, deal with evolving family relationships and support net-works, and meet emotional, health, and practical needs over the long term.

In this chapter we explore the experience of widowhood after the intense grieving has passed, and the interaction between the circumstances of old age and the demands of adjusting to widowhood. The first section of the chapter focuses on threats to personal control encountered in old age, on the connection between cognitive–aging issues and control, and on the

367

implications of widowhood for each of these topics. The second section explores the course and "career" of widowhood, which may unfold over many years. The career perspective integrates ideas from life-span developmental psychology (cf. Baltes, Reese, & Lipsitt, 1980) and from occupational–vocational psychology (e.g., Sterns, 1986; Super & Hall, 1978). At its core are two suppositions: It assumes continued plasticity, functioning, and capacity for growth into the later years, but it also assumes the need for older individuals to negotiate actively and planfully their own course within the parameters of changing life circumstances.

The final section addresses the role of heterogeneity in old age. Individual differences in health, cognitive functioning, personality, and social competence appear to be associated with successful aging generally and with the capacity to assert personal control. They also suggest priorities for prevention, intervention and social support efforts, and models for encouraging independence.

Aging and widowhood

It is not the purpose of this discussion to focus on age as a risk factor for short-term bereavement outcome. However, considerable research has been conducted on the topic, and findings generally suggest that older widows are actually at less risk, compared to younger widows, for immediate health and psychological outcomes within the first year or two. This may reflect the likelihood that the death was less unexpected, not considered to be premature, or a relief from the intense burden of care giving for an ill spouse. That research is reviewed in some detail by Sanders (this volume) and by W. Stroebe and Stroebe (1987).

Instead, we explore the implications of widowhood for the remainder of the life course into old age. In this endeavor it is useful to consider first the tasks of adaptation to the declines of old age generally. Pfeiffer (1977), for example, has suggested that successful aging be construed as adapting to one's constantly changing status and/or decline without undue disruption or suffering. As former roles and sources of satisfaction are lost, this process requires constant effort to replace lost personal relationships with new ones, accept limitations, and find new ways to feel that life has purpose and meaning. It may be important also to learn to make do with less. Many of these tasks involve the need to retain or reassert one's personal control over the process (Rowe & Kahn, 1987). Much of the discussion to follow, therefore, will focus on personal control as an integrating theme in long-term adjustment in widowhood.

Personal control

A number of the transitions associated with aging – declining health and mobility, widowhood, the loss of social or occupational roles, declining income – can substantially restrict an individual's range of influence over personal outcomes. The experience of uncontrollable situations has been shown, generally, to be related to increased stress and anxiety, reactance (Wortman & Brehm, 1975), and helplessness (Abramson, Seligman, & Teasdale, 1978) and, among the elderly, to health-promoting behavior and negative health outcomes as well (cf. Rodin, 1986, 1987).

Control is salient in the initial period of bereavement and, as W. Stroebe and Stroebe (chapter 14, this volume) have shown, it interacts with other factors surrounding the death of a spouse (e.g., an unexpected death) to affect physical symptomatology and depression during the first 2 years of bereavement. However, a variety of factors may also threaten an older adult's sense of personal control during the extended course of widowhood; the dynamics may be in part practical and in part symbolic.

First, in addition to its emotional impact, widowhood can be a particularly disruptive experience. That is, in addition to emotional loss, it may involve the loss of status, economic independence, mobility, and opportunity for social interaction. Simultaneously, it tends to disrupt the established interpersonal and support networks on which one may have come to depend for guidance and support in such matters in old age.

Second, age-related vulnerabilities complicate the issues of independence and personal control. Old age, generally, is a time of life when stressful life events tend to cluster and physical illness and disability are more likely. Widowhood itself may contribute a degree of social isolation and engender financial or legal concerns (cf. Barrett, 1978; Lopata, this volume; McCrae & Costa, this volume). Yet individual variability in health and functioning also appears to increase in later years. Thus, the effect of widowhood on an older person's well-being and ability to function should be influenced by the particular changes it mandates in life-style and the individual's perception of its implications.

Third, the elderly are more likely to experience chronic health problems, such as arthritis, heart disease, diabetes, hypertension, and visual and hearing impairments (U.S. Bureau of the Census, 1984). All of these could contribute to reduced mobility, social isolation, lost activity or workdays, and thereby to perceptions of decreased functioning and control. Moreover, a number of related health issues among the elderly may reinforce perceptions of decreased control. Such factors include reduced access to costly medical care, less predictable effects of medication (along with the increased risk of side effects and unintentional effects of combined medications), and nutrition (Kane, Kane, & Arnold, 1985).

A fourth threat to personal control among older widowed adults involves the interaction among functional health status, access to a supportive social environment, and current living arrangements. Older adults who are less competent in terms of health, psychological, or social resources may experience a narrower range of adaptability to increasing environmental demands, and therefore may more quickly reach stress thresholds under conditions of "environmental press" (Lawton & Simon, 1968; Morgan et al., 1984). Thus, a married older adult of marginal competence might still enjoy a relatively independent life-style, even under somewhat stressful or substandard living conditions, because a spouse is able to provide necessary support. With the death of the spouse, however, a widow might be expected to fall below the threshold for independent survival in that particular environment and require alternative, more dependent housing arrangements. It is consistent, then, that in our own research on housing for the elderly, widows are those most interested in moving into more supportive, congregate housing but are also those least able to afford it.

Fifth, the symbolic implications of losing a spouse in later years might also be expected to affect perceived control and independence. Assuming the cumulative effects of old age, for example, retirement, restricted income, and diminished health status, widowhood signals a most significant and permanent loss; in a striking parallel to the onset of an age-related physical disability, it "marks the line between not being old and being old" (Kemp, 1985). Finally, Parkes and Weiss (1983) have noted the importance of a widow establishing a new, autonomous identity centered on the self rather than as a part of a couple. Presumably, a reduced psychological dependence on the sense or memory of the deceased spouse (who cannot be there when the bereaved turns to him or her to help in coping) will reduce occurrences of perceived helplessness and facilitate the development of successful individual coping strategies.

Cognitive–aging issues and control

For older widows, maintaining independence involves solving new problems across several domains. There are emotional reactions to be played out and practical problems to solve that one never may have faced before because of traditional division of tasks in an enduring marriage. However, there are also psychological tasks, such as reshaping identities and self-perceptions to fit current circumstances and reconstructing a life without the deceased spouse. These processes are likely to occur under circumstances involving time pressure and uncertainty. Research suggests a number of factors that could interfere with such problem-solving efforts.

First, the motivation to persist in coping quite simply could hinge on an awareness of the time perspective involved (i.e., 14+ years of remaining life) and the knowledge that one can still assert some control over how that life is to be lived. Second, many of the problems involved in adjusting to widowhood after a long marital relationship will require exploring unfamiliar ground and mastering new tasks. Yet lack of task familiarity appears to become more important in later years and to interfere more with performance in problem-solving situations (Sanders, Sterns, Smith, & Sanders, 1975). Third, older adults appear less able to attend selectively to task- or problem-relevant stimuli and to ignore task-irrelevant information (Hoyer, Rebok, & Sved, 1979). Yet, in widowhood, coping efforts may be distracted by such things as the well-meaning desires and advice of family members or friends, financial uncertainties, and immediate logistic or housing concerns.

Fourth, assuming control may involve for some older widows a degree of risk (emotional, social, or financial). Yet, in the experimental literature on aging and problem-solving, elderly persons have been found to approach ambiguous problems with increased caution (Okun, 1976). The good news, however, is that the use of less effective problem-solving strategies by older adults may not actually reflect lack of competence. Interventions to alter motivation, for example, feedback or models, training in problem-solving strategies, and simply having more time to practice or plan, all appear to enhance performance (Reese & Rodeheaver, 1985).

Finally, an older widow's ability to manage finances, maintain social networks, and live independently would likely reflect current level of intellectual functioning. However, a study by Gribbin, Schaie, and Parham (1980), which investigated the relationship of life-style to the stability or decline of intellectual functioning among older widowed and nonwidowed men and women, suggests a disruptive effect of the circumstances of widowhood on such functioning. Over a 7-year period, scores on a family dissolution index (primarily defined by widowhood) were negatively associated with measures of Reasoning, Educational Aptitude, and Psychomotor Speed. In addition, those respondents characterized by widowhood in combination with a somewhat socially disengaged life-style (e.g., low involvement in "people activities," little involvement in work activities, and more frequent passive and solitary activities) showed substantially greater cognitive declines in Word Fluency, on a summary score for Intellectual Ability, and in Psychomotor Speed. The authors concluded that current level of cognitive functioning may be influenced by the circumstances of an older adult's environment—life-style and that the greatest declines were among widowed persons whose life-styles more broadly reflected social disengagement. In response to such findings, it has been suggested that adult education programs may help older widowed individuals to acquire or reacquire skills necessary for independent living in two ways: directly through instruction and indirectly through social stimulation (cf. Willis, 1985).

Age-related cognitive factors in problem solving to date have been investigated primarily in the laboratory setting (Reese & Rodeheaver, 1985). Thus, we can only speculate regarding generalizability to the experience of coping with widowhood. Such findings are consistent, however, with the literature on coping with other difficult, yet common events in old age. The cognitive barriers to coping with one such event, unemployment in old age, are particularly instructive (cf. Sheppard, 1976).

Unemployment, like widowhood, can be a major life stressor at any age, and tends to be associated with helplessness, depression, stress-related illness, mental hospital admission, and suicide (Brenner, 1973). As with widowhood, the consequences of becoming unemployed also are related to what the person actually loses when he or she loses a job. That is, work and the occupational role provide more than economic security: They structure one's time and life-style, and they provide predictability and a degree of control over one's fate, social status, and a network for social and reciprocal care-giving interactions (Buss & Redburn, 1983; Hansson, Briggs, & Rule, 1990). These issues are especially important to older adults, as they are likely to have committed a greater portion of their lives to the work organization and hence are more likely to have developed a great deal of interdependency in the relationship. Enduring commitment and interdependency in a work relationship, as in a marriage, may become emotional, symbolic, and practical barriers to dissolution of the relationship and obstacles to recovery when the relationship ends (Levinger, 1976). Finally, older adults also face subtle cognitive interference in coping with unemployment (cf. Sheppard, 1976). Being more committed to the employing organization, they are more likely to expect a recall and wait longer before beginning the job hunt. They pursue more limited job search strategies, are more reluctant to consider extending the search to new industries or geographic locations in which they have no firsthand experience, and avoid companies they expect to age-discriminate.

Older unemployed adults, then, appear to emit a more restricted range of potential control responses as they try to cope with this threatening life event. Some of the restricting factors are practical (e.g., lack of mobility), but there appear also to be important cognitive and social constraints. We believe such constraints may also affect the range of available coping responses among elderly widows.

Rehearsal for widowhood

One solution, however, may be to begin the coping process before the death of a spouse and involvement in the emotionally consuming bereavement process. There is evidence that a majority of widows have some warning of the impending death, and that using that time to prepare, or rehearse, for widowhood is associated positively with long-term adjustment. One recent study found more positive long-term adjustment (e.g., perceived preparedness, resolution of grief, expectations for survival, and satisfaction with adjustment to the death of a spouse) and decreased emotional disruption (e.g., fear, despair, depression, anxiety, and loneliness) among women who prior to the death of their spouse had engaged in such activities. Rehearsal activities included social comparison with similar others (widows), beginning to plan and make decisions, and actually beginning to try to do things on their own, such as making new friends, becoming involved in the community, taking over family finances, learning to get around on their own, and the like (Remondet, Hansson, Rule, & Winfrey, 1987).

The career of widowhood

Gerontologists have often analyzed the experience of life events in old age with an eye on age-graded influences. We have done so ourselves, in the discussion so far. Now we introduce two concepts that help in thinking about issues of personal control during an individual's later years and about how society might facilitate well-being and independence among older widowed persons.

The *life-span developmental orientation* (cf. Baltes, Reese, & Lipsitt, 1980) holds that growth and adaptation are possible at any stage of life. More specifically, this orientation is founded on assumptions that could foster the opportunity for change and personal control at any time during the later years. This orientation posits no particular point of maturity or end state with regard to functional competence, psychological state, or ability to adapt, and therefore no predicted schedule for decline. The focus is on qualitative differentiation rather than on growth, maturity, and decline. Development is viewed as a lifelong process; behavioral change and development can occur at any point in the life course.

The orientation further assumes the role of complex, pluralistic determinants of individual development. Three primary influences are normative age-graded influences (e.g., physical maturation, family and occupational events associated with the life cycle), normative history-graded or cohort influences (e.g., reflecting the effects of common historical experiences like the Great Depression, or the civil rights movement), and non-normative influences (e.g., reflecting an individual's unique history, accomplishments, and traumas). The relevance of non-normative influences is assumed to increase throughout the life span and to predominate in old age.

Neither does the orientation assume a developmental path that is unidirectional, sequential, or cumulative. Any variety of life change processes may commence at any time, in response to discontinuous internal or environmental events, for better or for worse. Thus, older adults should be expected to exhibit immense heterogeneity, to participate actively in society rather than disengage, and to pursue goals, careers, and relationships normally available to other individuals (Sterns, 1986). The life-span developmental orientation then implies that older individuals can continue to learn and adapt to changing life circumstances and that they should be able to benefit from the facilitating educational and supportive efforts of society (Willis, 1985). They can learn to compensate for change, decline, and the consequences of difficult life events; cognitive and emotional growth and self-actualization remain realistic goals.

In this context, we believe it useful to conceptualize the course of widowhood in terms of a *career*. That is, for most persons, widowhood need not be considered the end to productive life but, rather, the beginning of a major segment of the life course, to be pursued vigorously if it is to be successful and fulfilling. In this sense, it is analogous to the circumstances of an individual having to begin a new occupational career in mid- to late life, recognizing the implications of one's new situation, assessing strengths and limitations, and finding a way to rise to the occasion.

The career orientation helps in several ways in thinking about the course of widowhood. First, it reminds us that for many widows there is a substantial "lifetime" still ahead, to be planned for and lived, rather than passively experienced as one's remaining, declining years. The career model also implies the need to assume personal control over the course of one's life; it is important to manage one's own career. In addition, the model suggests that we adopt a broad, temporal perspective and view the course of widowhood in its entirety. It helps to have thought about where one hopes to be at the various phases of one's life (Super, 1974).

It might also be useful to encourage individuals to conceptualize the potential stages in the course of their career as a widow. The stages in a typical widow's future might then include a time for emotional recovery; a time for taking stock, reestablishing or restructuring support relationships, and formulating personal directions for the future; a time for discovering a comfortable and satisfying independent life-style and for determining an approach to maintaining economic, psychological, and social functioning; perhaps a time for personal growth and change; and a time for reasoned consideration of one's last years and the assertion of a degree of control over the arrangements surrounding one's own decline and death. The specific details of such stages are of little importance here, as they are likely to reflect myriad individual differences and non-normative environmental constraints. We believe, however, that the successful assumption of personal control rests in the widow's ability to thus construe her own life course.

The value of career planning models of this sort has been amply demonstrated in the literature on occupational career development. For example, Hall (1976) has proposed a four-stage model. In the first stage, a person explores his or her potential, interests, opportunities, and the environment. The second stage is one of trial experiences, developing independence and identity. The third stage involves continuing growth, maintenance of current state, or stagnation and premature decline. The fourth stage assumes eventual decline and withdrawal.

Hall's model, then, is a global model; within each of the four stages (according to the life-span developmental perspective) we might expect to see occasional adjustments, refinements, or dramatic alterations to course in response to normative age-graded or non-normative events or influences. Nevertheless, theory and research on such stages (with respect to occupational development or one's career as a widow) can play an important role in identifying developmental or adaptational tasks characteristic of each stage and the factors that influence how people progress through such stages, make choices, become motivated, develop feelings and beliefs, and so on.

Finally, having first assumed that the rest of one's life (even in old age) is worth pursuing vigorously, the career orientation permits us to draw on a rich body of research on career planning and development (cf. Liebowitz, Farren, & Kaye, 1986). Counseling strategies to assist widows could follow well-defined occupational counseling models, focusing on occasional self-assessments of interests, abilities, and needs, identifying goals, gathering information, detail planning, providing feedback regarding progress, and so on. We would also assume, however, the need for a strong motivational component in the counseling strategy, as any depression associated with bereavement may suppress one's ability to imagine or plan for the future (Weiss, this volume), and because many individuals are simply not by nature planful or future-oriented in their approach to life. In widowhood, then, such counseling might help an individual at almost any point in the process to devise and carry out plans that are realistic, consistent with personal values, and within his or her areas of competency.

The question of heterogeneity

A broad range of individual difference factors may influence a person's vulnerability to the deleterious consequences of widowhood. In the short term, such risk factors may include a previous frail health status, concurrent multiple life changes, income, coping style, personality, available social support, the nature and success of the marital relationship, the meaning of the death (i.e., of what one felt was lost in losing the spouse), and so on. These risk factors for short-term bereavement outcome are discussed in detail by Sanders (this volume) and by W. Stroebe and Stroebe (1987).

It also seems critical, however, to understand the role of such variables in long-term adjustment among older widows. Moreover, it seems important to consider how they might influence the counseling process or provision of support services.

In this connection, Rowe and Kahn (1987) distinguish between *usual* aging (i.e., the broadly expected patterns of age-related decline) and *successful* aging (the many available examples of people who retain health and well-being into very old age). They argue that the substantial heterogeneity among older adults in health and well-being generally cannot all be attributed to genetic influences. They point to examples of successfully retained function (e.g., metabolic or cognitive function, emotional or health stability) and to systematic but unevenly distributed predicting factors (e.g., exercise, cardiac function, lack of stimulation, lack of autonomy or perceived personal control, lack of social support). They further note that a "revolutionary increase in lifespan has already occurred," and that a "corresponding increase in health span, the maintenance of full function as nearly as possible to the end of life, should be the next gerontological goal" (p. 149). The path to such a goal, they argue, involves the search for, and modification of, risk factors.

The capacity to assert personal control in widowhood would likely be influenced by a variety of external factors, including, for example, cultural norms regarding widows' reentry into social and economic life (Lopata, this volume; Rosenblatt, this volume). Personal coping resources, such as education, employability, health, and mobility, also appear critical (Lopata, this volume). In addition, a variety of personality traits (e.g., the hardy personality) have been associated with resistance to stress generally and might be expected to continue to influence adjustment in widowhood (Kobasa, Maddi, & Kahn, 1982), as would one's characteristic style of coping with stressful events (Lazarus & Folkman, 1984). A growing consensus among researchers suggests that personality is quite stable throughout the adult life span, and that personal traits or styles could serve or undermine coping efforts in old age much as they would in one's youth (cf. McCrae & Costa, 1984; see also McCrae & Costa, this volume). Such personality characteristics may be associated with substantial individual differences in preference for control and willingness to assume responsibility in old age (Rodin, 1986), as well as differences in ability to exert control. In the section that follows, we present an example of how what the individual brings to the situation could influence his or her control over the availability of needed social support.

Relational competence

Social support networks cannot always be taken for granted. At least three phenomena suggest why this is so. First, they are, by definition, anchored in personal relationships that are themselves often problematic. Second, across a lifetime, the personal and support relationships that constitute a person's "convoy of social support" change in form, membership, and function as one ages and needs change (Antonucci, 1985). As important members of the network drop out (often through death), and as an older adult's demands on the network change, the issue becomes one of managing transition. Third, any dependency on a support network in old age is more likely to involve a chronic health problem or disability than in earlier ages (Brody, 1985). Thus, the network may be called on to assume responsibility for extended periods of time for the health or emotional needs of an older person. The inherent risk in this sequence is that the older person's long-term needs will be served by a family network that is strained to the limits of its capacity and is itself at risk. Such risks have implications not only for the quality of care received but also for the increased likelihood of premature institutionalization.

The characteristic vulnerabilities of support networks in old age, then, suggest that it may be important for an individual to try to impose some degree of control over this social (coping) resource as well. We would expect one's relational competence to play an important role in that endeavor. The construct of relational competence includes those characteristics of the individual that facilitate the acquisition, development, and maintenance of the personal relationships necessary to social support (Hansson & Carpenter, 1990; Hansson, Jones, & Carpenter, 1984). Such characteristics may involve aspects of temperament, learned dispositions, and cognitive styles, operating individually or in combination.

Thus, the likelihood of *construing* one's opportunities for relationships optimistically might be inhibited by shyness, low self-esteem, and hostility. The ability to *construct* new networks might be enhanced by the characteristics of sociability, social skill, and a range of instrumental traits to include assertiveness, perseverance, internality, and so on. The ability to *access* the supportive potential of an already overburdened network might be facilitated by interpersonal skill and sensitivity, assertiveness, and low thresholds for embarrassment and self-consciousness. Finally, the task of nurturing and *maintaining* long-term, and perhaps strained, support relationships (in one's self-interest) would be expected to be easier for persons with traits like empathy, emotional stability, flexibility, and sociability and for persons able to take the other's perspective (Hansson, Jones, & Carpenter, 1984).

Conclusions

Three general points from the preceding discussion should be emphasized.

1. The course of widowhood can extend for many years, well into old age. It is, therefore, important to consider the interactions between the circumstances of old age and the coping demands of widowhood. The life-span—developmental and career perspectives have been useful in this regard, assuming continued plasticity, functioning, and capacity for growth into the later years, but also assuming the need for individuals to pursue actively and planfully their desired life course. In addition, both views imply the opportunity to adopt a long-term temporal perspective and the utility of self-assessment, planning, and preparation to impose a degree of predictability and control on one's future. Overshadowing such assumptions, however, is the acknowledgment that an individual's life course is multidetermined and that age-graded and non-normative influences particularly may largely determine one's capacity to exert such control.

We recently interviewed a panel of older widows (age 60–96 years, who had been widowed between 3 and 26 years) to obtain their reactions to the ideas discussed here and to ascertain the manner in which they had attempted to plan and assert some control over their remaining years. Understandably, most had not viewed the process within the abstraction of some prescriptive model for the life course. However, most had thought seriously about the years to come. Their plans and decisions reflected considerable foresight and personal diversity. For example, one widow had tried thinking about life in 5-year periods, taking on jobs and life tasks and then periodically reevaluating. She had also thought about what living she wanted to fit in during her remaining active years ("before age 70"), for example, traveling. Another widow started a business, "to accomplish something on her own for once," but also to provide income for the long term. Several women had learned new job skills to support themselves and had established relationships with professional financial advisers who could assist them in planning their financial futures. Some focused on consolidating their resources, for example, selling a home and investing the proceeds for the long term. For those who found a job, there was a feeling that it would help to establish a daily routine, provide structure, a place to belong, a sense of purpose and social contact. Others had relocated to a city closer to relatives, or had renewed church memberships, reinforcing a social support network to be drawn upon in later years. One had developed a system for nurturing and replacing social relationships, keeping up with friends at least twice a year and making one new friend each year. Another had begun to prepare for expected disabilities, saving for relocation to a retirement living center.

2. The perspective adopted in this discussion casts older widowed persons as functioning participants in society, with the capacity for growth into the later years and the responsibility to control their own destiny. This vision could require two important responses from our social institutions, including the family. It may be necessary to give older widowed persons the room to reconstruct their own lives (careers) and to encourage them to take control as they begin to compensate for change and negotiate their way. Both of these responses may at times contradict widely held assumptions about the elderly, or counter the reflexive, support response of the immediate family. Family members especially may find this difficult because the death of a spouse is a particularly emotional event and automatically elicits supportive responses. Yet the literature on old age and support suggests that families need to understand the implications of providing older persons with too comprehensive a level of care, even at times of greatest stress. Kahn (1975), for example, has shown that the elderly should be encouraged to develop their functional coping skills and expectations for self-help, and that total care can become a self-fulfilling prophecy, leading to premature decrements in cognitive and social performances and to premature dependency.

Widows, at least, will live another 14 years on average, long after the dissipation of intense short-term support during bereavement. Because that period of life will, typically, be lived alone, it may be important for families to learn to make needed support available while encouraging elderly persons to develop the skills to cope independently. In this connection, a recent study found that a majority of families appear to approach this issue with great caution and sensitivity to individual differences among their older parents (Hansson et al., 1990). In this study, 71% of adult children intended to become involved in an older parent's care and decision making when they perceived the need. However, intended involvement seemed to follow a "threshold" model and vulnerability criteria that conservatively reflected crises of physical or mental health, environmental press, or disrupted social support. In addition, the process of being drawn into a parent's affairs appeared to reflect a conservative, sequential progression of first thinking and learning about aging issues, increased monitoring of the parent's status, and then becoming involved as needed.

3. We have speculated in this chapter regarding the variety of factors that might influence adaptation and well-being in widowhood, adopting personal control as an integrating theme. We believe the control concept to have heuristic value, and there exists a rich literature on helplessness, self-efficacy, locus of control, reactance, the attribution of control, related health and psychological outcomes, and potential counseling strategies (cf. Brown & Heath, 1984). Our understanding of successful aging and the course of widowhood might now be substantially advanced in two ways. First, our knowledge of control needs to be contextualized; that is, we need to "bring time" into our analyses (Ables, 1987, p. 1). It would be useful, for example, to assess in field studies of older adults (widowed and nonwidowed) the domains in which control (helplessness, self-efficacy, reactance) is most salient, likely, and problematic. It would be useful also to focus on which coping resources are most critical to the successful assertion of control (cognitive, intellectual, personality, social competence, level of preference for control); on how these factors interact with the experience of stressful life events, physical health status, available social support, and economic status; and on the identification of reliable interventions with the elderly.

Second, we need integrative models regarding the assumption and assertion of personal control over the course of widowhood (and old age more generally). Such models might emulate current models of the changing nature of social support over the life course (e.g., "convoys of social support"; Antonucci, 1985) and attempt to account for non-normative influences, such as health, family, perceived self-efficacy, and personality, as well as age-graded influences, such as maturation and social and occupational role changes associated with the life cycle. Such models would need to integrate these factors, while addressing the levels, forms, patterns, and variability in control likely to be adopted or asserted at different points in the life course.

25

The support systems of American urban widows

HELENA ZNANIECKA LOPATA

Many characteristics of a society, a community, and a person influence the organization of that person's life at any stage, as well as the degree of its disorganization introduced by dramatic events. For example, American society tends to be voluntaristic, in that social involvement of adults is mainly dependent on their own initiative. This is particularly true when prior involvements, in the form of social roles, the social relationships they contain, and support systems, are broken by choice or through life events. The voluntaristic nature of the society can be a problem for persons who were not originally socialized into such initiating behavior or who do not have in their self-concept the self-confidence to enter new social relationships and social roles. The traditional American culture discouraged women from assertive social engagement outside the private sphere of the home and related interactions. They were often dependent on others as connecting links between themselves and the public sphere. This is now particularly true of older, less educated women. In contrast, younger women are likely to have greater knowledge of the urban world and its resources and also the self-confidence that enables voluntaristic building and reconstruction of support systems.

This chapter examines the support systems of American urban women whose lives have been disorganized by the death of their husband, in order to determine the extent to which they are dependent on traditional support networks versus broader societal resources. A *support* is defined as any object or action that the receiver and/or the giver sees as necessary or helpful in maintaining a life-style. A *support system* is a set of supports of a similar type. I will consider here the economic, service, social, and emotional support systems of widows. A *support network* consists of all those people and groups who provide supports or to whom an individual provides them. *Resources* can be people, such as relatives, friends, co-workers, organization co-members, or neighbors, or objects or conditions, such as money or health. The community or society at large can provide, with varying degrees of choice, other resources for the development of support systems. We need to examine the extent to which the same, or different,

381

resources are utilized by women after the death of the husband as were involved in the couple's joint support systems while he was living and well.

The analysis of support systems of widows is based on two studies conducted in the Chicago area (Lopata, 1973a, 1979). Additional insights come from examinations of widowhood in other parts of the world and of North America contained in a two-volume edited work (Lopata, 1987a,b). The second study, on support systems, involved a sample drawn by Social Security Administration statisticians from five groups of widows: recipients of old-age benefits, mothers of eligible father-orphans, women who received only the lump-sum benefits to help defray funeral costs, former social security beneficiaries who remarried, and former beneficiaries whose children became no longer eligible. The five subsamples were drawn in different ratios, and the weighted sample represented a total of 82,078 widows. The women were interviewed in their homes, and the questions focused on the four support systems (see Tables 25.1–25.4).

Disorganization of life

The degree of disorganization of life produced by the death of a husband depends on the degree to which he was an integral part of the wife's life and self-concept, as well as on the customary status of "widow" in the community. In many societies the husband does not provide major supports, and the widow can continue life immersed in interaction with her family or other persons and roles. However, if her status as a widow changes all her relationships, it can be devastating, as in traditional India for women without adult sons. In America, despite the idealization of marriage and the ease of divorce with which one can leave an unsatisfactory relationship, not all women are focused on the role of wife (Lopata, Barnewolt, & Miller, 1985). A woman can have other sources of important identifications and self-concept and can be devoted to other roles.

In general, the greater a woman's dependence on the husband, or their interdependence, the more every aspect of her life is disorganized when he dies. He is often the major contributor to support systems, so others may have to take over the supports he supplied in the past. In addition, relations with others are almost inevitably changed, making some supports impossible to duplicate, creating needs for new supports, or pushing the widow to provide new supports for others, such as children. Motherhood is different without a father, particularly when the children are young. Couple-companionate friendship can become impossible without a partner (Lopata, 1975b). In modern America, in-law relationships can wither, as there is no strong legal or cultural imperative to keep them alive, unlike the situation in many other societies (Lopata, 1973a, 1979, 1987a,b). Membership in voluntary associations may change if they require couple participation or if a drop in income makes it too expensive. Economic resources often diminish, as most American wives are still, at least partly, dependent on their husband's earnings or other sources of income provided by him. Financial problems may result in the need to sell the home or move into a less expensive dwelling, sometimes in a less desirable location, leaving behind neighbors and the children's school friends.

Thus, the resources that were the source of the support systems may vanish or change considerably. The husband is likely to have provided not only economic but also service supports, sharing work in and around the household and in other areas of their life. Much of middle-class social interaction is of a couple-companionate nature and other social supports, such as the sharing of meals, often involve the husband. Finally, mates provide all forms of emotional supports, ranging from sexual satisfaction to comforting to anger.

The loss of a husband can have quite traumatic effects on the self-concept. The woman can no longer be a wife, yet the role of widow is absent in this culture, and returning to being a single woman is impossible. Many of the widows we studied reached a point during their grief work of feeling "out in limbo," not knowing "what to do with the rest of my life" (see also Rubin, 1979). For those women who had built their identity around being a wife, and the wife of a particular man, shifting the core of the self-concept to alternative roles or other identities can be very painful. The events surrounding the death can lead to a loss of self-confidence, as well as to feelings of lack of control and incompetence in trying to create a new life (see Parkes, as well as Hansson, Remondet, & Galusha, this volume; see also Parkes & Weiss, 1983; Lopata, 1975a, 1986).

The strain of transition is usually accompanied by feelings of loneliness, especially in cases in which the husband—wife relationship involved a great deal of interaction. No other person can replace the deceased in such cases. The first study of metropolitan Chicago widows brought forth numerous forms and components of loneliness (Lopata 1969, 1973a). A widow can miss the late husband as a person – unique and irreplaceable, a love object, someone who loved her, a companion, an escort to public places, a partner in couple-companionate interaction, someone around whom time and work were organized, or just another presence in the home. One widow explained that her husband had been the only one who thought what she said was important enough to argue with, and they fought much of the time. Loneliness can be felt for the whole life-style a woman enjoyed while the husband was living.

Some women are involved in what Papanek (1973) calls a "two-person career" in which the wife is the backup person at home. Many occupations, in America and in some other societies, are "greedy," as Coser (1974) defines them, in that they demand so much commitment by the worker as to require also backup work. The husband's job can impinge on the wife's time, space, and energy and can require cooperative effort, making it impossible for her to have strong commitments in other roles (Finch, 1983). Although such work is often hard and personally demanding, and the rewards very indirect, widows can miss it. The rewards include not only social interaction and social events but also such direct benefits as access to housing or medical care, a comfortable income, and so forth. One widow I interviewed greatly missed the social life she had when her husband, an officer in a major business company, was alive. Because of the absence of a husband and the drop in income, one of the few things she still could do was play bridge with the wives of his former associates. The discomfort everyone felt when she tried evening activities with the married couples led to a withholding of invitations on both sides (Lopata, 1979).

Obviously, many aspects of loneliness cannot be solved by interaction with others, but many can, if the widow can become involved in new social relationships. In fact, some widows developed a much more satisfactory life-style after the heavy grief was over, having been restricted by the husband in the past (Lopata, forthcoming).

Resources for new support systems

In order to build new support systems the widow must modify old relationships and her life-style, unless her marriage and presence of a husband were not involved in them. Voluntarily or not, she must make changes necessitated by the death, and she may be able to introduce other changes to meet her new needs or desires. There are many resources she can use for the reconstruction of her support systems.

The society at large, through its various agencies, can be a resource, providing services and economic supports. The community often has numerous services available at times of crises or in daily life (see Stroebe, Hansson, & Stroebe; Raphael & Nunn; Vachon & Stylianos, this volume). Employers, co-members of voluntary associations, neighbors, and people met in a variety of situations can become resources for supports and participants in life-styles. Of course, the availability of many resources may depend on the ability and willingness of the widow to reach out to them.

One of the main resources can be the family, defined along any lines, fictive or through marriage, biology, or adoption. A family can be particularly supportive if easily reachable. Sharing a complex household inevitably weaves the widow's life in with others. However, most widows who are able to do so, economically and in terms of ability, prefer living alone to moving into a residence controlled by another woman. Modern societies no longer require that the eldest son or an unmarried daughter remain with the parents in the "ancestral home," so that sharing a household means moving in with an offspring and his or her nuclear family (Chevan & Korson, 1972; Lopata, 1971). However, having someone in the same residence is not the only source of day-by-day supports. Meals, child and health care, and many household tasks are exchanged with children or other relatives living nearby. In fact, the recent family and historical literature documenting the absence of multigenerational households usually fails to test for the actual location of "split" or separated households (Laslett, 1971; Shorter, 1975). The extended family located in a close geographic space can thus be easily available for daily interaction, although technically, and in terms of census definitions, people are living in separate households. In fact, there is a considerable amount of research on children, especially daughters, exchanging numerous supports with the widowed mother (see Brody, 1990, for a summary of this work). Neighborhoods may also contain other people who provide a variety of supports, and the same is true of numerous voluntary associations.

Central to a widow's resources are her personal abilities. In several studies I have found the amount of education to be the most important variable influencing a woman's whole life-style (Lopata, 1973a, 1973b, 1979). It provides her with the ability to define her problems or desires, to locate outside resources, and take action toward solutions. It gives her the self-confidence to tackle new situations and enter new social roles. The differences in life-styles in consequence of degree of education are especially evident among widows in urban America, which, as stated earlier, requires voluntaristic social engagement. Our society has an extensive set of resources, but not many automatically connecting links between them and the person. Traditional connecting links are often absent. With some exceptions, it is the individual who must reach out to obtain supports from these resources.

Support systems

Resources in the form of people and various other social units can be pulled into a network within which supports are exchanged. Our research on Chicago area widows led to the description of four support systems, including 65 different supports. The systems are economic, service, social, and emotional. Our findings have been largely reproduced in other locations (see Lopata, 1987a,b).

Economic supports

In many parts of the world, even now, people can sustain themselves economically without money. In fact, most of human history took place in that stage of social development. People belong to work groups, organized by age and sex, and produce goods for consumption and exchange or barter necessary items. In patriarchal, patrilineal, and patrilocal societies, the woman enters her husband's family upon marriage and together they maintain themselves and the children. She usually continues living with the late husband's family, in widowhood, working as part of its productive force. If she has sons, it is their responsibility to care for her in old age.

Recent interest in the influence of modernization or social development on the economic supports of women has led to analyses of the methods by which they earn their (and sometimes their children's) maintenance in cases lacking an automatically supportive social unit. In societies in which much of the work has not yet been converted into jobs in the organized sector, there are many ways women can obtain necessary objects, even money, in the informal sector. However, American cities have fewer opportunities for the informal sector to operate, and the main source of economic support is in the form of paying jobs. Because of industrialization and other, recent social developments, the division of the social world into private and public spheres has favored the employment of men but not of their wives, because employment would take women out of their home where they take care of their husbands and children.

The public sphere, containing the paid labor force, has been dominated by men with certain occupations favored for unmarried, or otherwise economically needful, women. The income earned by a husband is assumed to be sufficient to enable the wife to purchase necessary objects and services for family maintenance. A problem arises, then, if the husband or his earning power is removed from this unit. Modern societies try to solve this economic problem in a variety of ways. Family members and church parishes are no longer held responsible for the financial support of widows of any age and their young children. American society has included social security benefits for women who are widowed in old age or while they have dependent children of the deceased in their care. The system, however, leaves many women ineligible for these benefits, even if they had been full-time homemakers during the life of the husband and lack skills to do paid work outside the home (Lopata & Brehm, 1986). Some jobs are available even to unskilled widows, but they tend to pay minimum wages and lack other benefits. Some informal means of subsistence still exist but they, too, are inadequate for urban living. As a result, many wives experienced a drop in income with the death of the husband (Lopata, 1979; Lopata & Brehm, 1986). Best off were those who had multiple sources of income. On the other hand, some women became better off financially in widowhood because the husband was not a steady provider.

We (Lopata, 1979) asked the Chicago area widows about the in- and outflow of economic supports, including payment, or help with the payment, of food, clothing, housing, vacations, bills, or gifts of money, and found them quite uninvolved in such activity (see Table 25.1). The highest percentage of women who responded that they were involved in such exchanges was 12, the activity was the giving of gifts or money, and they were the givers. Children, grandchildren, and charitable organizations were the recipients. Of those few who gave or received supports in the form of rent or food, very few involved a sibling or any other relative. Of course, most did not have living parents.

Our research team, in fact, was surprised by the absence of economic supports, especially in view of the frequency with which these widows live alone. This residential arrangement was enabled by social security, for the most part, and was desired by the woman for several reasons. In the first place, she wanted to remain in her own place, cooking and eating when and what she desired, having free access to the facilities. In the second place, she anticipated problems living in the home of someone else, especially married children and their offspring. Finally, being independent, many American urban widows did not wish to do housework and help with the raising of children. They had done it once and they did not wish to do it again. This makes them very different from widows the world over, who often have no choice and whose adult children, especially sons, must either continue living in the parental home or bring the widowed mother to their dwelling. Much has been written about the conflicts or at least strain between mother-in-law and daughter-in-law who are living in the same dwelling.

Service supports

It is sometimes difficult to distinguish between economic and service supports. Cooking a meal is a service, but buying the food is an economic act. After much discussion with the various research teams who were to conduct the studies in other places than Chicago, we developed a set of in- and outflow services, including transportation, house repairs, housekeeping, shopping, yard work, car care, child and sick care, help with decisions, and legal aid (see Table 25.2).

The widows most frequently received help with transportation, but very few gave it and then only to parents. This one-way flow of service reflects how much the traditional American scene has been dependent on the automobile, and norms that define the car and everything connected with it, as in the male domain. Very few of the widows helped others with car care, but if they did, the recipients were parents. The reason so few received help with car care was that many did not own one, having sold or given away the family car after the death of the husband. The widows saw themselves as recipients of service supports much more often than as givers, but the numbers who claimed such help were relatively small, except with

Table 25.1. *Number of first listings and percentages of total listings of significant others contributing to the inflow and outflow of the economic support systems of Chicago area widows*[a]

Economic support	No. first listings[b]	No one, not receive or give (%)	Parents total	Children total	Siblings total	Other relatives total	Friends total	Other people, groups total	Present husband, boyfriend[c] total
Inflow									
Gifts, money	7,210	91	2	83	5	4	2	0	3
Rent	7,201	91	2	70	5	—	13	6	4
Food	9,193	98	1	77	7	2	0	8	4
Clothing	4,685	94	0	92	5	1	0	1	1
Bills	6,168	92	2	58	4	0	0	30	6
Outflow									
Gifts	10,844	87	2	43	4	29	1	20	2
Rent	4,380	84	5	81	10	3	1	—	—
Food	4,523	75	5	67	14	5	1	4	4
Clothing	2,811	97	1	60	9	17	2	11	—
Bills	3,554	96	3	68	8	10	8	4	0

[a] Percentages are computed from the universe of widows represented by our sample.
[b] First listings indicate the number of widows who receive or give this support out of 82,078.
[c] Most widows do not have a husband or boyfriend.

388

Table 25.2. *Number of first listings and percentages of total listings of significant others contributing to the inflow and outflow of service support systems of Chicago area widows*[a]

Services	No. first listings[b]	No one, not receive or give (%)	Parents total	Children total	Siblings total	Other relatives total	Friends total	Other people, groups total	Present husband, boyfriend[c] total
Inflow									
Transportation	44,771	45	0	57	8	6	18	7	5
House repairs	34,863	57	1	55	9	11	4	10	11
Housekeeping	18,702	77	3	69	2	7	5	11	4
Shopping	32,060	61	1	67	5	4	12	6	5
Yard work	25,836	69	2	55	4	13	2	14	11
Child care	2,806	96	21	28	4	9	12	10	17
Car care	10,787	87	2	50	4	6	5	17	17
Sick care	45,723	44	4	65	9	4	8	6	4
Decisions	33,663	59	2	70	10	5	2	2	9
Legal aid	15,670	81	0	19	8	10	5	55	2
Outflow									
Transportation	14,763	82	8	19	7	10	39	16	0
House repairs	1,320	98	25	34	3	9	20	3	4
Housekeeping	9,842	88	8	56	10	8	12	6	0
Shopping	10,727	87	20	13	9	8	34	16	0
Yard work	2,948	96	17	22	20	6	13	17	2
Child care	16,689	80	0	55	3	30	8	6	0
Car care	108	100	68	0	6	18	8	0	0
Sick care	29,302	64	10	44	10	10	14	16	2
Decisions	14,694	85	6	44	11	7	24	4	4
Legal aid	508	99	22	35	2	9	24	8	0

[a] Percentages are computed from the universe of widows represented by our sample.
[b] First listings indicate the number of widows who receive or give their support out of 82,078.
[c] Most widows do not have a husband or boyfriend.

transportation and during illness. Even sick care, which drew the most responses, was obtained by just over half of the respondents, which surprised us. Relatively few of these widows gave and almost none received help with child care, which can probably be accounted for by their ages: Many of their children were grown and without young children themselves.

It is interesting to note that the only time widows claimed to be giving or receiving service supports was when these were not part of the normal flow of work. A woman running her own home did not feel that she was providing help with housekeeping to those living in it. She also did not consider the regular work of household members to be a help to her unless there was a special arrangement concerning it.

In general, and reflecting the gender division of labor in American families, which is fully documented by many studies, the services given and received were gender-specific. Sons helped with house repairs, yard work, decisions, and car care if these were needed. Some widows explained that they moved from their home after the death of the husband, so no longer needed yard work. Daughters were much more frequent providers of service supports than were sons, partly because the work involved fell into the female province but mainly because they were more active in all support systems. When friends appeared, it was mainly as givers or, more frequently, as recipients of transportation and shopping. Such activity was shared with them more often than with children or other relatives.

Social supports

As with the other support systems, the social ones tended to be culture-bound. For example, in Chicago we could ask a widow if she went to public places, such as movies or restaurants, and if so, with whom, but the same question would be meaningless in many other parts of the world because such resources do not exist. The widows were asked if they went to public places or to church, engaged in visiting or entertaining, ate lunch, played games or sports, traveled out of town, celebrated holidays, or undertook any other social activity with anyone. If the responses were positive, we asked with whom they shared this activity (see Table 25.3).

Interestingly, half of the Chicago women claimed never to go to public entertainment establishments. Those who did were usually accompanied by friends or their children. Visiting drew many more responses than did entertaining, undoubtedly because the latter is a more class-biased concept, implying formal arrangements. Friends again appeared in this support. The women went alone to church but met people there. The most frequent social event, shared mainly with children and other relatives, was the celebration of holidays. On the other hand, there were relatively many Chicago area widows who were alone at these special events. About four in

Table 25.3. Number of first and total listings and percentages of total listings of significant others contributing to the social support systems of Chicago area widows[a]

Social activities	No. first listings[b]	No. total listings[c]	Does not engage in activity (%)	Parents total	Children total	Siblings total	Other relatives total	Friends total	Other people, groups total	Self total	Present husband, boyfriend[d] total
Public places	40,243	59,944	51	1	28	6	6	38	6	3	12
Visiting	64,869	110,063	21	2	29	11	10	40	5	2	2
Entertaining	48,964	88,970	40	1	23	6	19	43	5	0	2
Lunch	51,399	79,607	37	1	18	7	5	51	12	2	4
Church	62,078	79,318	24	1	35	6	5	15	3	33	3
Sports, cards, and games	34,337	56,709	58	0	12	5	10	58	8	2	4
Travel out of town	48,460	68,046	40	1	35	11	9	15	2	21	6
Celebrate holidays	73,853	142,108	8	2	52	10	25	7	2	0	2
Other activity	3,291	4,064	96	1	17	0	0	24	6	47	3

[a] Percentages are computed from the universe of widows represented by our sample.
[b] First listings indicate the number of widows who engage in this support out of 82,078.
[c] Total listings refers to all the people (up to three) the widows listed.
[d] Most widows do not have a husband or boyfriend.

ten of the respondents never traveled out of town and an even larger proportion did not play any kinds of games. Those who did were usually interacting with friends. In fact, it is in the social support system that friends finally appeared, not often being listed in the economic or service supports, with the exception noted earlier.

The concept of friendship is also culture-bound and, we suspect, class-bound (see the Lopata & Maines volumes on friendship, 1981, 1990). Americans appear to think that friendship is something of a luxury, that it should not interfere with the "important" social roles – occupation for the man, wife and mother for the woman. It is relegated to the young and the old. It often appears in descriptions of widows in retirement communities and we expected it to be very prominent in the lives of the widows, most of whom did not have small children and the vast majority of whom had not remarried and therefore were not engaged in an active role of wife. In fact, friends were more frequent than any other people as companions in ventures to public places, visiting and entertaining, sharing lunch, and playing games on the part of women who claimed such interaction. Thus, only 59 percent of the widows shared lunch with someone and 51 percent of these listed friends. Only 39 percent played games, and 58 of these women did so with friends. Holidays were spent with relatives, not with friends, which is a very interesting commentary on this type of event. The most friendless were widows who had either moved into a new neighborhood and lacked skills at friendship making, or were the remnants of their own ethnic group in a neighborhood now occupied by another group. Social interaction with friends also requires reciprocity, which is often hindered by health or financial problems. The most socially active were the middle- and upper-class widows in the Chicago area and the majority of rural widows all over the world (Lopata, 1987a).

Emotional supports

The emotional support system includes relational sentiments: To whom does she feel closest? Whom does she most enjoy being with, tells problems to and is comforted by? Who makes her angry most often, and to whom does she turn in times of crisis? Other emotional supports are feeling states or aspects of the self-concept. Who makes her feel important, respected, useful, independent, accepted, self-sufficient, and secure? The questions were distributed throughout the interview to avoid response set, and the answers proved highly indicative of social relationships in each society in which they were asked (see Table 25.4).

The importance of the son in highly patriarchal cultures is reflected in the study of widowhood in India, Korea, and Turkey (Lopata, 1987a; Ross, 1961). In America, it is the daughter who appeared most often in the

Table 25.4. *Number of first and total listings and percentages of total listings of significant others contributing to the emotional support systems of Chicago area widows at the present time*[a]

Emotional supports	No. first listings[b]	No. total listings[c]	Parents total	Children total	Siblings total	Other relatives total	Friends total	Others total	Self total	No one total	Present husband, boyfriend[a] total
Sentiments											
Closest	80,044	144,277	3	60	10	9	10	2	1	2	3
Enjoy	80,706	145,463	2	52	8	13	16	3	0	5	4
Problems	81,664	112,996	2	42	9	4	12	5	6	21	4
Comfort	81,304	117,671	2	45	9	4	11	5	4	21	5
Angry	80,320	89,275	0	22	3	4	2	9	1	63	2
Crisis	80,170	114,490	3	54	10	5	7	4	3	12	5
Feeling states											
Important	79,630	128,246	2	57	4	7	9	4	4	12	5
Respected	81,035	114,162	2	52	4	7	12	13	4	4	4
Useful	80,459	126,334	2	50	4	2	7	9	11	13	4
Independent	79,819	96,552	0	20	4	2	3	7	50	7	2
Accepted	77,698	128,472	1	40	4	7	19	14	7	10	4
Self-sufficient	78,953	100,140	1	21	4	3	6	5	49	10	3
Secure	79,883	111,801	1	36	4	7	4	9	30	10	5

[a] Percentages are computed from the universe of widows represented by our sample.
[b] First listings indicate the number of widows who receive or give this support out of 82,078.
[c] Total listings refers to all the people (up to three) the widows listed.
[d] Most widows do not have a husband or boyfriend.

emotional system, as she did in all the others (Lopata, 1979, 1991). There are several explanations for this divergence. In the first place, traditional patriarchal societies often forbid women from inheriting property, and the mother is highly dependent on her son. In the second place, the son is responsible for the welfare of the mother, and this usually means that they live together throughout the life course, whereas the daughter moves away upon marriage. In more industrialized societies the mother tends to be more independent economically and residentially. The son is also free to move away and concentrate on his family of procreation rather than being tied to his family of orientation. Mother–daughter relationships, on the other hand, can be close (Chodorow, 1978; Fisher, 1986). Their roles and lives are more similar than those of mother and son, and the younger woman no longer has to ignore the mother in favor of her husband's family. The studies of American widows indicate a strong involvement of at least one daughter in the support system of the mother (Lopata, 1979).

There were several surprises in the emotional support systems of the Chicago area widows. Each respondent was given the opportunity to list up to three persons in each of the 13 supports. Grandchildren did not contribute as often to the emotional supports as expected. Only if the interaction was frequent did the grandmother refer to grandchildren as people she most enjoyed being with. The geographic dispersal of the family can lead to rather infrequent contact. As mentioned earlier, relatively few of the widows were involved in helping others with the care of children. Only a tenth of the respondents listed a sibling as the person closest to them or someone to whom they turned in times of crisis. All other emotional supports drew even fewer listings of brothers and sisters (Lopata, 1978). The absence of siblings from the support systems of most widows contradicts the literature on the family, which stresses the importance of the extended unit (see Shanas & Streib, 1965; Litwak, 1965). A careful examination of the research on which this literature is based, however, points mainly to the parent–child, not to the collateral, line of supports. The failure of the siblings to enter most of the 195 supports of Chicago widows points also to the difference between them and the situation of widows in many other parts of the world (Lopata, 1978).

Another surprising finding of our study was the relative infrequency with which friends appeared in the emotional support system. The social supports or companionship did not necessarily translate into emotional supports. We expected greater use of friends as confidants and comforters, but here, again, it was mainly the children who provided such supports. Thus, the distribution for people to whom the widows felt closest was as follows: 60% children, 10% each siblings and friends, and 9% other relatives. A similar pattern emerges when we ask whom the women most enjoyed being with: 51% children, 8% siblings, 12% other relatives (usually grandchildren), and 16% friends. This certainly accentuates the importance of children. Finally, we had expected a more open admission of anger, but two-thirds of the Chicago widows claimed that no one made them angry.

Summary and conclusions

The modern urban world in which many American widows are living is considerably different from the traditional one in which women are embedded in networks of family and village. Some of the older Chicago area widows grew up within the traditional support networks, in other countries or in ethnic communities here. Social development, experienced particularly in America, expanded urbanization, industrialization, personal mobility, a money economy, and work organized into jobs: these changes introduced the need for voluntaristic engagement at all stages of life beyond childhood. However, they are not felt uniformly in all areas of a society; traditional and "modern" aspects of life often coexist. People socialized before the great changes are apt to have problems in social engagement and in reconstructing support systems that have become disorganized by such an event as the death of a spouse.

Generally speaking, older women appear to have typically been socialized into involvement in the private sphere of life while men operated in the public one. As a result, women were dependent on primary relations for their support systems, the husband, children, and others serving as the connecting links between them and the resources of a society. When such links are broken, and the society makes no effort to replace them, some widows can become socially isolated, economically destitute, and unable to create new support networks. Personal resources remain the main sources of support systems for the majority of widows. Some become heavily dependent on their children, usually a daughter, and live in a very restricted social life space. Such people need societally created links to existing resources for economic, service, social, and emotional support systems. Communities should be encouraged to develop neighborhood support networks. These could be composed of representatives of existing service organizations that would locate people going through disorganizing experiences such as the death of a significant other and to provide such connecting links. Like the "widow to widow" programs, such support providers could offer information about existing resources and contact with people and groups who can offer needed supports (Silverman, 1987b).

On the other hand, American society has provided mass education, a new view of women as competent to function outside the home, and resources for social engagement. Social security has created economic independence for many widows. In addition, there are many pockets of traditional social networks, extended families, neighborhoods, churches and other voluntary groups, and even communities purposefully created to ensure all forms of supports. As a result of social change existing side by side with the perseverance of many traditional life patterns, there is a great heterogeneity of life-styles and support systems among modern American widows.

26

The role of social support in bereavement

STANLEY K. STYLIANOS AND
MARY L. S. VACHON

Bereavement is a social network crisis. The vacuum created through the loss of a significant relationship, especially in a closed network, will draw the entire group into distress. The joint experience of suffering may render network members unable to support the individual for whom the loss is most immediate and profound.

The finding that the single best predictor of high distress 1 month after bereavement was a lack of contact with old friends who had often dropped away during a protracted period of illness (Vachon, 1979) underscores the importance of network support in the days following bereavement. Moreover, a deficit in social support has been associated with poor outcome in bereavement as measured by poor health in the first bereavement year (Maddison & Walker, 1967; Maddison, Viola, & Walker, 1969; Raphael, 1983), continued high distress 2 years after bereavement (Vachon et al., 1982b), an increased use of antianxiety medications (Mor, McHorney, & Sherwood, 1986), and for those who have lost a spouse, more strain in adjusting to the new role of being both single and a widowed person (Bankoff, 1986).

This chapter reviews the literature on social support as it applies to those bereaved through the death of a spouse, in order to examine the interaction of the bereaved with members of their social network and the perceived helpfulness of that network. Formal and informal support efforts that do and do not facilitate adaptation to bereavement are considered.

Social support: An overview

Support as a multidimensional process

Social support is a transactional process requiring, for its optimal provision, a fit among the donor, the recipient, and the particular circumstances (Heller & Swindle, 1983; Shinn, Lehmann, & Wong, 1984). Social support

The authors wish to express their appreciation to Darianna Paduchak for her assistance in the preparation of this manuscript.

includes four types: emotional support, appraisal support, informational support, and instrumental support (House, 1981). Emotional support involves actions that enhance self-esteem. Appraisal support provides feedback on one's views or behavior. Informational support entails giving advice or information that promotes problem solving. Finally, instrumental support is the provision of tangible assistance.

Social support is a process with multiple components. The "goodness of fit" between donor activities and the needs of recipients is governed by the amount, timing, source, structure, and function of social support. There must be an adequate balance between the amount of support offered and the perceived threat engendered by a particular situation. In addition, the type and amount of support most useful to distressed individuals may change over time.

Different sources of support may vary in effectiveness in different circumstances. Suggestions from family and friends may be perceived as criticism, whereas the same or similar suggestions made by professionals may be viewed as neutral expressions of helpful concern. The perception of disapproval from primary others can become a source of ongoing strain or conflict that may generate shame or guilt, anxiety, frustration, and/or despair (Thoits, 1985).

The structure and quality of a social network may facilitate or interfere with the provision of social support. One key variable is network density, the extent to which members of a social group know and contact one another (Walker, MacBride, & Vachon, 1977). In studies of the impact of divorce and widowhood, high- and low-density networks had differing effects (Hirsch, 1980; Wilcox, 1981). High-density networks, especially those in which families and their friends maintained close relationships, often promoted greater symptomatology, poorer mood, and lower self-esteem. For example, widows and widowers from large, long-standing support networks and making frequent contact experienced high levels of somatic symptoms and a loss of control (Warner, 1987). In contrast, in low-density networks, where group members were not necessarily well known to one another and did not have reciprocal relationships, women were able to develop new social roles consonant with their changed status. High-density networks also increase the possibility that in stressful life events involving loss, several group members may concurrently experience distress, a condition termed *network stress* (Eckenrode & Gore, 1981). In such situations network members may not have the emotional energy to deal with one another's needs.

Other structural and qualitative dimensions of social networks have been shown to be significantly associated with adjustment to bereavement. In a longitudinal study of bereaved spouses between the ages of 50 and 93, Dimond, Lund, and Caserta (1987) demonstrated that network size was negatively correlated with depression scores, while positively correlated with perceived coping and life satisfaction at 2 years' postbereavement. Qualitative network characteristics, such as having the opportunity to express oneself, sense of closeness to members, and quality of interaction, were significantly correlated with outcome at various intervals within the 2 years of loss. Similarly, Goldberg, Comstock, and Harlow (1988) found that total network size was related to widows' perceived need for help with an emotional problem 6 months following bereavement; in addition, friends were of greater importance in reducing the risk of developing emotional problems than family, and widows with four or more friends with whom they had regular contact were less likely to endorse the need for counseling.

Qualitative dimensions may be important to understand the different findings of Dimond et al. (1987) and Warner (1987) regarding the impact of network size and density on outcome; being a member of a large network does not guarantee that one will have adequate confidant relationships or opportunities for mutual support and caretaking.

Lund, Caserta, Van Pelt, and Gass (1990) examined the impact of bereavement on the social networks of bereaved men and women between the ages of 50 and 89 and found these networks to be relatively stable over the 2-year period following the death of a spouse. However, compared to younger study participants, those over 75 years of age had significant reductions in their primary networks of relatives and close friends and a diminished sense of closeness to primary network members. Such structural changes in the networks of elderly individuals may place them at increased risk for support deficits and negative adjustment outcomes.

Support functions

Social support serves a variety of functions. It may be important to have particular types of social support during certain life events. Cohen and McKay (1984) have hypothesized, for example, that bereavement and other disruptions of close interpersonal relationships create a need for the support mechanisms they call "belonging"; close, relatively intimate relationships will be most effective in meeting this need. Rook (1987) has found that those exposed to major life events require both help from others, or social support, and companionship, that is, social exchanges providing recreation, humor, and affection, which contribute to a sense of well-being. Whereas support may protect people from the debilitating effects of life stress, companionship protects them from the emptiness and despair associated with loneliness (Rook, 1987).

Social support also provides a mechanism for social comparison. In the absence of objective criteria or when confronted by new or ambiguous experiences, people tend to compare themselves with similar others, or individuals in similar situations, in order to evaluate their behavior or feelings (Festinger, 1954). Self-help groups can provide someone in a new and unaccustomed role with a group of peers for social comparison (Shinn et al., 1984). The possibility for social comparison is also enhanced by a heterogeneous social network, where there is increased likelihood that another network member will have had a similar experience (Walker et al., 1977).

Support system as stressor

Although social support systems are potentially helpful, they may also be a source of stress (Gottlieb, 1983; Lehman, Ellard, & Wortman, 1986; Wortman & Lehman, 1985; Wortman & Silver, 1989). The social support system may respond in a negative manner if the person undergoing a stressful life event is not adjusting as others would expect. Wortman and Silver (1989) have identified assumptions commonly held by researchers, clinicians, and laypersons regarding the grieving process: Intense distress or depression is inevitable; intense distress following loss is necessary and its absence is pathological; grief work is necessary; and recovery from loss is expected within a relatively short time. In reviewing recent, well-designed studies of irrevocable loss through the death of a spouse or a physical disability, Wortman and Silver (1989) failed to find support for these assumptions. In an earlier study, Lehman, Wortman, and Williams (1987) examined bereavement outcome following the sudden death of a spouse or child in a motor-vehicle accident. Compared with matched controls, bereaved spouses demonstrated significant differences on measures of social adjustment, psychiatric symptoms, and psychological well-being 4 to 7 years following their loss. These data, coupled with the finding that bereaved parents and spouses continued actively to think about and process the loss of their loved ones, challenge the belief that recovery will be rapid and complete. Shinn et al. (1984) have emphasized that negative inter-actions that derive from supportive efforts are actually additional stressors, not just indicators of a lack of social support. Such negative interactions may potentiate the effects of other stressors.

Positive social ties (relationships offering companionship, emotional and instrumental support) and negative social ties (relationships engendering feelings of anger and conflict and characterized by criticism, exploitation, and disappointment) appear to be distinct entities with differing impacts on distress and psychological well-being during major life transitions (Finch, Okun, Barrera, Zautra, & Reich, 1989). Factor analysis confirmed positive and negative social ties as independent and relatively invariant constructs across samples of elderly individuals experiencing the loss of a spouse, recently disabled through physical illness, and low-risk matched controls

(Finch et al., 1989). Positive social relationships were positively correlated with psychological well-being, and negative relationships were negatively correlated with psychological well-being and positively correlated with distress.

Perceived social support and adaptation to bereavement

There is no definitive way to measure the exact helpfulness of a specific support attempt. Therefore, social support may be construed as a property of the individual, as interventions must be seen as helpful by the recipient in order to be supportive (Shumaker & Brownell, 1984). The structural and functional characteristics of a social network influence the potential availability of support, but it is the individual's appraisal of actual network transactions that determines whether help has been provided in the face of threat (Heller, Swindle, & Dusenbury, 1986).

The appraisal of support

The findings of Antonucci and Israel (1986) emphasize the importance of individual appraisal in supportive exchanges. They showed that congruence of perception among network members (i.e., the extent to which a principal respondent and his or her network members agreed on the amount of support provided or received) was positively linked to the closeness of their relationship. There was typically a low degree of agreement between principal respondents' and network members' perceptions of specific supportive transactions. Importantly, however, congruence of perception was not predictive of life satisfaction, happiness, or negative affect, suggesting that the individual's perception of the support exchanged is of greater significance to outcome than the congruence of network members' perceptions.

Another theoretical perspective distinguishes between perceived support, defined as the belief that support is potentially available from one's social network, and received support, which refers to actual supportive exchanges between network members (Lakey & Heller, 1988; B. Sarason et al., 1991; I. Sarason, Sarason, & Pierce, 1990; Wethington & Kessler, 1986). Using a cross-sectional analysis, Wethington and Kessler (1986) examined the impact of perceived versus received support on psychological distress for 365 married participants undergoing a stressful life event. Perceived support appeared to mitigate distress independent of the support received in response to life crises and was not merely a reflection of supportive transactions, as suggested by others (Wethington & Kessler, 1986). Lakey and Heller (1988) studied the stress-attenuating effects of perceived versus received support by rating the responses of college students on social problem-solving tasks, finding that the tasks were experienced as less stressful by students with higher rather than lower perceived support scores. Perceived support was unrelated to the support efforts offered by students' companions who participated in the study.

Personality variables

There is growing evidence that personality attributes, either long-standing or temporal and mood-dependent, influence both the mobilization of support and the perception of its availability and provision (Heller et al., 1986; Hobfoll & Freedy, 1990; B. Sarason et al., 1991; I. Sarason et al., 1988; Wethington & Kessler, 1986). Hobfoll and Freedy (1990) posited that the traits of mastery and self-esteem are central to the effective mobilization and use of available support. In an experimental study of perceived social support, B. Sarason et al. (1991) demonstrated that beliefs about the availability of support and satisfaction with available support were strongly influenced by self-concepts and cognitive models that guide appraisals of social interactions. The data suggested that there was a linkage between self-esteem and perceptions of the coping abilities of self and others. Individuals with a greater sense of perceived support appeared to view others less defensively, probably as a consequence of greater self-esteem (B. Sarason et al., 1991). Moreover, individuals who believed that support was available should they need it, and who were satisfied with the level of support available to them, felt highly positive about themselves.

Although personality variables have been associated with social support and bereavement outcome, it is unclear whether people who were emotionally healthy to begin with were better able to elicit social support to meet their postbereavement needs (Osterweis, Solomon, & Green, 1984). For example, in a 2-year longitudinal study of bereaved spouses over age 50, Lund et al. (1985) found that low self-esteem, even prior to bereavement, was likely to predict coping difficulties 2 years following the death of a spouse. Therefore, the authors suggest, self-esteem appears to influence bereavement coping difficulties, rather than the reverse. In this study, personality factors were not directly associated with social support. Most of the study participants had fairly positive social support relationships, due in part to the fact that 76% were Mormon.

In a longitudinal study of 162 Toronto widows, Vachon and colleagues (1982b) demonstrated that personality factors were associated with 2-year bereavement outcomes. Widows with enduring high distress were more likely to have scored as being emotionally less stable, apprehensive and worrying, and highly anxious. Although those with high distress had lower social support, the limited number of high-distress women who completed the personality measure precluded finding a direct association between personality factors and social support.

A smaller study of 51 Israeli widows of soldiers (Malkinson, 1987) showed a more specific interaction between personality and social support. Widows with high self-esteem tended to perceive more emotionally helpful experiences as coming from their social support systems, whereas widows with low self-esteem perceived more instrumentally helpful ones.

An individual's personality may also determine the manner in which he or she attempts to elicit social support in bereavement. Bankoff (1986) found that widows with a low need for affiliation and strong prior dependency on their husband had less peer support than did those with the opposite characteristics. The finding may reflect a withdrawal of network members due to the closed and exclusive quality of these husband–wife dyads.

Perceived helpfulness of network members

Although findings are not consistent across studies, there are data indicating that widows receive support from a variety of sources. Vachon (1979) rank-ordered the perceived helpfulness of various network members of widows over the first 2 years of bereavement. Friends were most often endorsed as being helpful, followed by the widow's family of origin, and then by children over age 18. Children were most frequently listed as most helpful at 1 and 6 months after bereavement, but friends were important even that early, and their importance as the major source of social support increased over time. Friends were always seen as slightly more helpful than family of origin, and much more helpful than in-laws, whose supportive role dropped off quite quickly.

Bankoff (1986) studied young widows and also found that the role of friends became increasingly more important over the course of bereavement. Although parents initially were the most important source of social support, single friends and other widowed friends proved to be most helpful over time. Furthermore, peer social support was a key factor associated with an enhanced sense of psychological well-being. The widows with strong peer support were more apt to report that their close friends were widowed or otherwise single; though they continued to see their old friends, they reported that more of their closest friends were new friends who had been made since their bereavement.

In an earlier study of young widowed persons, Glick, Weiss, and Parkes (1974) found the role of family members to be more important. In a study by VandeCreek (1988), elderly surviving spouses who were satisfied with their adjustment found family members, friends, and neighbors equally helpful during the 8 to 9 months following bereavement. Parkes and Weiss (1983) have concluded that what seemed to matter most was not so much how many people were initially available to the bereaved spouse but whether their support was utilized over time. This persistence of support may, of course, be ultimately related to personality variables.

Ferraro, Mutran, and Barresi (1984) found that individuals widowed between 1 and 4 years were most likely to increase their involvement in friendship networks. Participation in formal associations often decreased, whereas relationships that offered intimacy and support were likely to be increased in order to compensate for the lost spousal relationship. Involvement with friends may be a function of social class, for middle-class widows have been found to be especially involved with friends as a major source of social support (Ferraro et al., 1984; Lopata, 1979).

It appears that, though family support is crucial in the initial stage of acute grief, as one adapts to the new role of widowed person, friends, and frequently new friends, become more important.

Support efforts that don't work

It has been hypothesized that part of the difficulty in the social interactions between the bereaved and their social networks may occur at the pre-conscious, physiological level. "The nonverbal signals, mannerisms, tones of voices, gestures, facial expressions, brief touches, and even timing of events and pauses between words may have physiologic consequences – often outside the awareness of the participants" (Hofer, 1984, p. 194). The individual's unconscious response to these variables may in part determine whether or not a given action is perceived as being helpful.

Wortman and Lehman (1985) classified situational factors that in-fluenced whether or not support attempts made to victims of life crises were seen to be beneficial. Lehman et al. (1986) compared helpful and unhelpful support attempts reported by 94 bereaved persons who had a spouse or child die in a motor-vehicle accident 4 to 7 years previously. The bereaveds' responses were compared with a matched control group of 100 subjects who were asked what they would do to support someone who had suffered such a loss. The most helpful supports mentioned by the bereaved were contacts with similar others and the opportunity to express feelings without having them dismissed or being given the message that one was coping poorly. The most unhelpful responses were giving advice and encouraging recovery.

When the control respondents were asked what they would do, they gave the right responses. Yet, within their own support networks, the bereaved did not feel they received as much help as they needed. Of course, it is possible that if the control group had actually been called on to help bereaved persons, they might have given more help than the bereaved reported receiving. Nevertheless, Lehman et al. (1986) suggest that part of the reason for difficulties that may occur in the interaction between the bereaved and help providers may be that people know hypothetically what to say to a person who is bereaved but "the tension inherent in face-to-face interactions with the bereaved impedes the delivery of those strategies that would be effective" (p. 443). This problem may be due to anxiety about interacting with victims of life crises, inexperience, or the fear of doing the wrong thing. In any case, the potential supporter may be so uncomfortable that natural expressions of concern are inhibited and the helper acts primarily to minimize his or her own anxiety (Wortman & Lehman, 1985).

It may be, as Hofer (1984) hypothesized, that there are nonconscious responses at a physiological level between the potential helper and the bereaved. Those closest to the bereaved may be least able to be helpful – the majority of the unhelpful responses in Lehman et al.'s (1986) study were from family and friends. These people may both feel most responsible for alleviating the distress of the bereaved and also have their lives most disrupted by the bereaved's ongoing distress. In addition, they may invest the most in attempting to alleviate the distress of the bereaved and feel very frustrated when the bereaved doesn't respond to their well-meaning interactions by soon becoming and staying less distressed. Dakof and Taylor (1990) noted that whether a specific support effort is viewed as helpful or unhelpful may depend on the nature of the relationship between support recipient and support provider.

Schilling (1987) observed that members of social networks who are frustrated in their support attempts may withdraw their support before the person in need can benefit from their approaches. Conversely, he warns, network members may become so invested in helping that the person is never encouraged or allowed to become self-reliant.

M. Stroebe and Stroebe (1985) note that in Maddison and Walker's study (1967), widows with bad outcome perceived deficits in areas involving emotional, validational, and instrumental roles. However, Malkinson (1987) found that both good-outcome and poor-outcome subjects were more bothered by inadequate emotional support than by a lack of practical assistance.

There is evidence that, if there are concurrent stressors in addition to bereavement, the social support network may be perceived as being less helpful. Both the Toronto bereavement study (Vachon et al., 1982b) and the Chicago study by Bankoff (1986) found an association between perceived low social support and health and financial problems. Both studies suggest that a recent drop in the status of one's health or finances might inhibit peer support, and that if within a friendship system one member experienced severe personal difficulties for a relatively long period of time, then the exchange could be seen as becoming too one-sided, thereby weakening the relationship and reducing support.

Facilitating adaptation to bereavement: Augmenting social support

Interventions to help the bereaved usually involve providing additional social support as well as helping the individual to access his or her pre-existing social network. Such intervention approaches may occur at various points along the continuum of adaptation to bereavement. Initially, family and friends might be most helpful, with possible assistance from professionals or one-to-one contact with members of a self-help support group. At a later point, friendships become crucial and a mutual self-help program might be helpful.

Naturally occurring intervention

Training for the family and friends of the bereaved, as well as for the professionals involved, has been advocated (Lehman et al., 1986; Wortman & Lehman, 1985). Family and friends should be encouraged to allow the bereaved to express his or her feelings rather than shutting them off in attempts to avoid the helper's own feelings of impotence or insecurity, which arise if the helper feels unable to act, help, or "do something" to make the bereaved person well or to alleviate suffering. Potential helpers might be assisted to gain insight into how their own grief, needs, and desires might cause them to become too invested in the victim's recovery. Finally, they might be advised to listen to the bereaved without feeling obliged to make comments or offer advice.

Helpfulness of professionals

Vachon (1979) found that at 1 month after bereavement 43% of the women had seen their physician at least once, and their physician visits increased over the first year of bereavement compared to the previous year. In a study on help seeking during life crises and transitions, Brown (1978) found that whereas bereavement was second only to unemployment in the percentage of people who reported being distressed by it, widows were less likely than many other groups to seek help with their crisis. When they did seek help, unlike those going through other life crises, widows were more likely to go to professionals than to members of their own informal network.

The utilization of physician services by the bereaved may be a search for legitimate social support, especially in the elderly (Mor et al., 1986). This is suggested by the fact that widows who sought counseling were found to have less social support and more concurrent stressors (Vachon, 1979). However, physicians and other health professionals are seldom endorsed as a major source of social support (Bankoff, 1986; Vachon, 1979; VandeCreek, 1988). This may be partly because the expectations and needs of the bereaved person are not clear to the professional, and in addition, there may be difficult relations between professionals and the bereaved. A physician may feel in part responsible for the death and the bereaved may fear they will be labeled as coping poorly with bereavement when in fact they are experiencing a normal reaction (Silverman, 1982). Research bearing on the physician's role in promoting the successful adaptation of the bereaved has been presented by Tolle, Bascom, Hickam, and Benson (1986). These authors examined the communication between primary care physicians and their patients' surviving spouses, and noted that of 105 surviving spouses who were interviewed, only 36% had some contact with hospital physicians. Moreover, 55% of the survivors had unanswered questions regarding the spouse's death. Although primary care physicians may provide important support to the bereaved at the outset of loss, effective communication with the surviving spouse is compromised by a lack of established follow-up procedure.

Individual intervention by professionals

The best example of the efficacy of professional intervention for the newly bereaved is Raphael's (1977) assessment of 200 Australian widows in the early weeks after their husband's death. The strongest predictors of morbidity were the bereaved's perception of nonsupport for her grief and mourning and an ambivalent relationship with the deceased. The most significant impact of intervention occurred with the subgroup of widows who perceived their social networks as being very nonsupportive during the bereavement period. Positive responses to individual professional intervention for individuals who perceived their social networks as inadequate were also reported by Gerber, Weiner, Battin, and Arkin (1975).

Williams and Polak (1979) reported negative results with interventions offered to families immediately following a sudden death. The unexpected availability of specially trained professionals, whose role it was to decrease the distress experienced in response to sudden death, may have interfered with naturally occurring help from the preexisting network. (See Raphael, Middleton, Martinek, & Misso, this volume, for a more complete review of this area.)

Individual intervention by trained volunteers

Individual intervention carried out by trained volunteers, who may or may not be bereaved, has been found to be effective in studies of survivors of suicide (Rogers, Sheldon, Barwick, Letofsky, & Lancee, 1982), as well as with high-risk bereaved survivors of hospice programs (Parkes, 1980). Negative results have been reported, however, in a large controlled study of bereavement intervention at the Royal Victoria Hospital in Montreal (Kiely, 1983). Bereavement intervention was provided for those whose family member had died on the Palliative Care Service and compared with bereavement intervention for those whose family member had died elsewhere in the hospital. The study also measured the impact of intervention by trained volunteers compared with nurses.

A small, earlier study of 20 cases (Cameron & Parkes, 1983) had shown that bereaved survivors from the Palliative Care Service who received 6-month follow-up by a nurse showed significantly fewer psychological symptoms and less lasting anger than a matched control group, but the larger study did not confirm these earlier findings. However, the larger study had a very substantial attrition rate, with complete data being available for only a small percentage of subjects, although it was not clear why there should have been such attrition in both the experimental and control groups. The data showed that the postbereavement intervention group from the Palliative Care Service reported twice as many symptoms as the other group and was worse off on several measures 2 years after the death. Those receiving intervention by nurses had more difficulty than those receiving intervention by trained volunteers (Kiely, 1983).

Group intervention by professionals

Group intervention by professionals is sometimes carried out by professionals alone and sometimes in conjunction with bereaved persons. Barrett (1978) examined three different group interventions for widows: a self-help group, a confidant group, and a consciousness-raising group. Two nonwidowed female doctoral students in clinical psychology conducted each group; their roles, based on distinct theoretical frameworks, varied for each group. The self-help group encouraged participants to assist each other in solving the problems posed by widowhood. In this group therapists facilitated discussion, rewarding members with praise when specific problem-solving suggestions were made. The confidant group had as its focus the development of close friendships. Widow dyads, paired for the duration of the group, were coached through intimacy tasks by the group leaders. The consciousness-raising group examined the relationship between a series of sex role topics and widowhood. Discussions were initiated by group leaders and then each group member commented on her own experience.

Participants in all conditions at posttest, including a waiting-list control group that would later receive intervention, had improved self-esteem, a significant increase in intensity of grief, and more negative attitudes toward remarriage (perhaps reflecting the fact that as they improved they did not see remarriage as being a panacea). It was hypothesized that even being assigned to a waiting-list group was therapeutic, and when the waiting-list subjects were seen after a 2-month wait, they were much happier in their initial meeting than the experimental group had been. Subjects in all experimental groups improved, and these gains were maintained at follow-up 14 weeks later, with the women in the consciousness-raising group having more positive life changes and rating their group higher. The waiting-list control group was not compared with the experimental groups in follow-up, so it is impossible to say whether the experimental group really had long-term effects or whether the changes observed represented the normal process of recovery from bereavement.

Self-help intervention

Mutual self-help groups have often been initiated by professionals, but in these groups the intervention is actually carried out by widowed persons. Most of these programs are based on the pioneering work of Silverman (1972, 1986), who views widowhood as a transition from one role to another: from wife to widow to woman on her own.

One of the earliest controlled studies of self-help bereavement intervention (Vachon et al., 1980a) found that those receiving the widow-to-widow individual intervention made faster progress along the pathway of adaptation to bereavement through intra- and interpersonal adaptation to the resolution of overall distress; those with low social support were most likely to benefit. (See Lieberman, this volume, for a more complete review of this area.)

A research agenda

There is much to be learned about basic mechanisms underlying support processes and adaptation to conjugal bereavement. Investigations in the area of perceived social support have renewed questions about the contribution of personality variables to the mobilization and use of network support. The relative contributions of perceived versus received support need to be elaborated in longitudinal studies of outcome in the loss of a spouse. The role of schema in guiding social transactions with network members during the crisis of bereavement should be explored further. More studies of the constructs of positive and negative social ties may provide a better understanding of stressful social exchanges and support attempts that are viewed as unhelpful. The relationship of changes in the structure and quality of social networks to bereavement adaptation merits further investigation.

The taxonomic analysis used by Dakof and Taylor (1990) in examining cancer patients' perceptions of support should be applied to studies of helpful and unhelpful transactions between bereaved spouses and network members. Supportive and nonsupportive network transactions should be examined from the standpoint of help providers and recipients at different stages of bereavement to examine how changing patterns of network interactions impact adaptation. The specific types of social support that are needed at various points in the bereavement process and the network members from which this assistance will be accepted need to be further delineated.

The recent work of Wortman and Silver (1989) calls into question fundamental beliefs regarding adjustment to bereavement. The linkages between clinical and social mythologies of coping with bereavement and unhelpful clinical and social interventions should be investigated. Further study of the grieving process across a variety of social and cultural contexts is needed to distinguish between normal and pathological grief.

Clinical interventions should be better informed by basic research and should also be tailored to meet the needs of those at greatest risk for support deficits. There is some evidence that support interventions might be least helpful for those most in need. For example, self-help programs represent a successful intervention strategy but are tailored to meet the needs of middle-income, white widows. More research is needed to ascertain the most appropriate forms of intervention for different ethnic groups, lower income groups, widowers, and individuals involved in nontraditional conjugal relationships.

Finally, the efficacy of naturally occurring interventions has not been adequately investigated. Negotiating the fit between needed and received support at the level of the social network may prove a valuable adjunct to interventions focusing on the bereaved individual. Although the concept of network stress is acknowledged, its impact on outcome is unknown. Altering the structural or qualitative dimensions of social networks could augment available support, reduce negative transactions, and attenuate the potentially harmful effects of negative social ties.

27

Bereavement self-help groups: A review of conceptual and methodological issues

MORTON A. LIEBERMAN

Exploring the benefits of self-help or mutual aid groups for the bereaved requires the prior examination of the bereaveds' social and psychological dilemmas and how these interact with the special characteristics of self-help groups (SHGs). This chapter addresses the following questions: What are SHGs? How do they work? What are the special problems of the bereaved? How do these interact with SHG processes to create a setting helpful to the bereaved? What is the empirical evidence that SHGs are useful in addressing problems of bereavement?

The designation self-help group is commonly applied to a wide variety of activities. SHGs are described as support systems, as social movements, as spiritual movements and secular religions, as systems of consumer participation, as alternative, care-giving systems adjunct to professional helping systems, as intentional communities, as supplementary communities, as expressive-social influence groups, and as organizations of the deviant and stigmatized (Killilea, 1976). Self-help, or mutual aid, groups are a poorly defined and unbounded area; arbitrary judgments rather than conceptual structure are the rule. In this chapter the working definition of SHG emphasizes (1) membership composition, people who share a common condition, situation, heritage, symptom, or experience; (2) self-governing and self-regulating; and (3) values, self-reliance and accessibility without charge.

SHGs are used extensively for a variety of problems. Mellinger and Balter (1983) and Lieberman (1986), using a national probability sample of more than 3,000 households, reported on 1 year's utilization rate. Five and one-half percent sought out mental health professionals, 5% used clergy or pastoral sources, and 5.8% utilized SHGs of varying kinds (groups directed toward behavioral change, such as AA, 2.3%; those whose goals were to provide support, such as widows' groups, 0.7%; and groups for personal development, 2.2%). SHGs are one major source of therapeutic treatment for a variety of physical and emotional difficulties; from 12 to 14 million

adult Americans utilize them. Accurate estimates of SHGs for the bereaved
are not available.

Empirical research on the effectiveness of SHGs in general and bereavement groups in particular is limited; the number and quality of studies
available for assessing their effects resemble the status of psychotherapy
research in the 1950s. SHGs, in contrast to psychotherapy, are not under
the control of the investigator. SHGs values and their community base
frequently make it difficult to design research using current standards of
psychotherapy evaluation. The methods that SHGs use to recruit their
members make the usual design requirements for random assignment,
alternative treatments, or delayed treatment controls logistically difficult.
The best quality research in this area uses quasi-experimental design,
contrast-groups designs, and occasionally alternative treatments. More
frequently, the research contrasts treated and untreated cohorts of the
similarly afflicted who have had access to self-help (the status of this
research is described in detail later in this chapter). Overall available
studies suggest that the spousally bereaved do show measurable benefit
in both mental health and social functioning when compared to both
untreated controls as well as psychotherapy. The beneficial effects of SHGs
for bereaved parents are less clear.

How they work

SHGs are complex entities. They create experiences that are thought to be
therapeutic, such as inculcation of hope, development of understanding,
and the experience of being loved. SHGs are also cognitive restructuring
systems, often possessing elaborate ideologies about the cause and source of
difficulty and the ways individuals need to think about their dilemmas in
order to be helped. They are also social linkage systems where important
supportive relationships are developed. Lieberman (1983) found that all
types of SHGs are unified by the simple fact that all are collections of fellow
sufferers in high states of personal need, and that all groups require some
aspect of the personal and often painful affliction to be shared in public.

Regardless of the type of group, participants uniformly indicated
that such groups provided an important source of "normalization" or
"universalization" (the problem they bring to the group is often experienced as shameful and abhorrent; finding others with the same problem
often produces considerable relief), as well as emotional and problem-
solving support. Despite these common elements (to be examined more
fully in the next section) findings from SHG research suggests considerable
variability in how they help participants. There are major differences
among groups in helping mechanisms (Lieberman & Borman, 1979).

Bereavement group processes

A good illustration of both process variability and specificity is provided by several studies of bereavement groups. Lieberman (1983) examined three types of SHGs to test whether specific "curative factors" were associated with benefit. All three involved significant personal losses, spousal bereavement (THEOS and NAIM), and child loss by parents (Compassionate Friends). A 31-item instrument indexing change mechanisms was administered after 1 year's participation. Members were asked how helpful, on a 3-point scale, each of the 31 items had been in their learning. The categories used to generate the items were universality, support, self-disclosure, catharsis, insight, social analysis, advice-information, perspective, feedback, comparative-vicarious learning, altruism, and existential experimentation (Lieberman & Borman, 1979).

Levels of perceived guilt and anger after 1 year's participation were used to index outcome. Studied were 491 THEOS members (a national SHG for the spousally bereaved), 187 NAIM members (Chicago Catholic Archdiocese–sponsored SHGs), and 197 members of Compassionate Friends (a national SHG for parents whose children have died). Low but significant correlations (.20 range) were found between guilt/anger and standard depression and self-esteem scales. Decreased guilt was defined by scores 1≥ SD below the group mean; scores ≥1 SD above the group mean were defined as increased guilt. Analyses of the 31-item checklist of change mechanisms revealed that the mechanism linked to decreases in guilt were unique for each type of bereavement SHG studied.

For the widows in NAIM the core experiences associated with guilt reduction were the sharing of troublesome feelings; normalization, not feeling out of place; the redirection of anger by externalizing it; seeing problems as being a product of an insensitive world; and the more socially acceptable mechanism of reaching out to others in need. Avoidance of hostile impulses by not venting anger, as well as avoiding the aggressive implications of social comparison, was characteristic of those who did not show guilt reduction.

For the widows in THEOS, in contrast, processes that emphasized expressivity, revelation, and externalization, cognitive mastery, and the use of the group context for experimentation, were associated with guilt reduction.

Among parents who had lost a child, change mechanisms different from either of the two widowhood groups were observed. Although normalization was common to all three, critical for guilt reduction in Compassionate Friends were existential considerations: the inculcation of hope and confrontation with the situation. Loss of a child, especially where the loss was unexpected, was uniformly accompanied by bitterness and fury at society.

Many experienced isolation from everyone; this appeared to represent a distinct psychological state different from what we have seen among our widows and widowers. Perhaps the dilemma facing those who have lost a child and the consequent experience of acute guilt and responsibility can best be resolved through confrontation with the ultimate meaning of their lives.

A framework for comparing helping systems

To understand further how SHGs function to address the problems of bereavement, comparisons of SHGs, peer support, and formal psychotherapy are examined. Differences among group settings that offer psychological help such as dynamic group therapy, SHGs, peer counseling, homogenous group therapy, and social supports can be usefully charted along five dimensions.

The helping group as a social microcosm. Most professionally directed groups view the group setting as a social microcosm: a small, complete social world reflecting in miniature all of the dimensions of real social environments. This aspect of the group – its reflection of the interpersonal issues confronting individuals in a larger society – is viewed as the group characteristic most closely linked to benefit. SHGs rarely rely on this group characteristic. The interaction among members as a vehicle for change is de-emphasized. The group is viewed as a supportive environment for developing new behavior, not within the group, but outside. The group may become a vehicle for cognitive restructuring, but analysis of the transaction among members is not the basic tool for this.

Technological complexity. This dimension captures the central characteristics of professional help: the theoretical model delineating the nature of the problem, methods for translating information provided by the client into a diagnosis, and principles guiding interventions used to bring about client change. In contrast, help provided within the client's informal network relies on the simplest of technologies: no formal definitions of problems, no diagnoses, and "interventions" rooted in everyday social interactions.

Nonprofessional helping systems, such as Goodman's (1972) companionship therapy, resemble normal social exchange. However, because peer counselors encounter more defined problems and have access to training and supervision, their interventions are somewhat more complex than those offered in ordinary social relationships.

SHGs offer more systematic codes of treatment than those provided by friends and relatives or peer counselors. Although SHG interventions appear simple, drawing on everyday skills, help methods follow a specific ideology that defines the problem and directs specific interventions. Through participation, members learn the ideology and incorporate principles into their thinking and interactions with others.

Psychological distance between helper and helpee. Located at one extreme, some professionals, through both special training and manipulation of symbols and settings, increase the psychological distance between themselves and the patient. Paraprofessional help begins with the premise that reducing psychological distance promotes identification and trust, conditions facilitating productive therapy. Of all help systems, SHGs achieve the greatest psychological parity between the helper and those being helped. Not only are helpers frequently similar in social background, but more importantly, they share the same affliction as those seeking help. Client control of the group also helps to lessen psychological distance between helper and helpee.

Specificity/generality of help methods. This dimension indexes how helping methods relate to the particular dilemma, distress, or affliction they address. High generality, in which methods do not vary with the particular psychological dilemma, characterizes the help offered by friends and family. People offer support, warmth, understanding, and instrumental help in much the same manner, whether the dilemma arose from widowhood, physical illness, or any one of the variety of problems and predicaments that plague the human condition. The help provided by peer counselors emphasizes general methods. Interventions rooted in normal social exchange resemble each other regardless of the nature of the particular problem. The help methods employed by professional therapists are more specific than the generalized support offered by peer counselors, but (with few important exceptions, e.g., behavioral modification regimes) less specific than the helping methods offered in SHGs. They are characteristically highly specific.

Antze's study (1979) of three types of SHGs demonstrates how each developed specific ideologies about the nature of the problem and tailor appropriate help methods to the specific affliction. For example, Antze found that drug abuse groups conducted by ex-addicts employed confrontative, often explosive, emotionally exhausting techniques in order to counteract the mounting anxieties and social withdrawal characteristics of certain types of drug abusers. Bond et al. (1979) report that Mended Hearts focuses on altruism in order to deal with the "survival" guilt found among such surgery patients.

Differentiation versus nondifferentiation among participants. Being neurotic, having psychological difficulty, or being a patient offers, at best, a vague basis for identification, compared to being a widow, a parent whose child has died, an alcoholic, or someone who has undergone open heart surgery. It is easier for SHGs to stress identity with a common core problem than it is in psychotherapy groups. The potency of SHGs appears to stem from their continued insistence on the possession of a common problem; the members believe themselves to derive support from their identification with a common core issue.

The intersection of these dimensions provides a definition of a SHG's uniqueness as a helping system. Most SHGs are low on complexity, use of the group context as a social microcosm, and differentiation. They are high on specificity and low on psychological distance. Traditional dynamic group psychotherapy, in contrast, is high on complexity and social microcosm, moderate on specificity, and high on psychological distance and differentiation. Social support from family and friends and peer counseling are low on complexity, low on specificity, and low on psychological distance. Paraprofessional help incorporating the training methods such as those used by Rioch, Elkes, and Flint (1963) is high on complexity, low on specificity, and moderate on psychological distance.

Basic processes in support groups: Fit or misfit for the bereaved

How do SHG procedures translate into particular psychological experiences for the bereaved? How good is the fit between the psychological issues facing the bereaved and SHG procedures?

Common processes

SHGs are small face-to-face interactive units. The fact that individuals enter such structures in a high state of personal need and are required to share with others topics and feelings that are often considered personal and private leads to important consequences for participants' experiences. They find themselves faced with a number of strangers frequently dissimilar to themselves except for one critical characteristic, the shared problem. Such groups share three basic elements: the intensity of need expressed by the individuals joining them; the requirements, no matter how banal, to share something personal; and the real or perceived similarity in their suffering. These conditions and the structure of a small face-to-face interactive system have profound consequences for what will occur.

Cohesiveness. Foremost is the capacity to generate a sense of belongingness, a shared sense of similar sufferers that creates high levels of cohesiveness. It provides the motivation to remain in and work with the group. Cohesive groups offer almost unconditional acceptance and provide a supportive atmosphere for taking risks: the sharing of personal material and the expression of emotions, which may, from the participants' perspective, be difficult to do among strangers. Another factor creating a high sense of belongingness is perception of their deviant status in society. The feeling of being stigmatized leads frequently to the creation of a feeling of "we-ness" and a sharp boundary line between them and us.

The high level of cohesiveness, perceived similarity, and the perception that they are "different" from others outside of the "refuge" influence the salience of being a participant. The group often takes on the characteristics of a primary group; it becomes "family-like" and does, in fact, serve as a new reference group. These interrelated properties of small groups are not a product of a particular group theory or ideology, type of problem, or style of leadership. Rather, they are intrinsic conditions of small groups, made all the more pronounced in groups of the similarly afflicted by the state of need in which they enter such groups and requirements for personal sharing and banding together against a perceived hostile external world. These group conditions provide for the individuals a sense of support, acceptance, and normalization of their perceived afflictions (Lieberman & Borman, 1979).

The felt isolation of widows and bereaved parents, their frequent references to being stigmatized, and their almost universal complaint that the considerable emotional support many received soon after the loss failed to last "long enough" suggest that those properties common to bereavement SHGs can provide a benign and potentially helpful setting.

Emotional intensity. The group's potential to stimulate emotionality bears directly on the experiences members have in small face-to-face groups. Most notable in the SHGs that I have studied are the emotional expressions of pain, anger, and profound sadness. Compassionate Friends' opening ritual requiring members to recite the loss of their child usually induces in new members strong affects that soon become shared by all. This process may be particularly helpful to men. They are stimulated, perhaps for the first time, to acknowledge their grief. We have found that when both the wife and the husband attend SHGs the likelihood of repairing the badly damaged marital relationship is enhanced. The ability of the husband to begin experiencing avoided emotions contributes to the ability of couples to rework their badly damaged relationship (Sherman, 1984; Videka-Sherman, 1982b).

The stimulation of intense affect is not, however, without its cost. Some of the bereaved in SHGs find the affective intensity alien and soon leave; others may become mired in a perpetual mourning.

Social comparison. SHG participants contrast their attitudes and feelings with things that matter, and such comparisons facilitate identity revisions through offering new possibilities in feeling, perceiving, and behaving. Compassionate Friends emphasizes the inculcation of hope through seeing others endure a similar loss. Because such groups focus on specific relevant issues in an emotionally charged setting, they can provide their members with a wide variety of information about how others who are perceived as similar feel, think, believe, and behave.

The dilemmas faced by the spousally bereaved – sanctioning for extending mourning, development of a new self-image that reflects current status of an "I" rather than a "we," renegotiating a viable social network – are all issues that appear to fit with the characteristic inherent in SHGs for widows and widowers. A simple example perhaps captures best the unique characteristic of SHGs for the spousally bereaved. One midlife widow, when asked what was important for her in the group, promptly responded, "It's the only place I can laugh." Social norms prescribe conventions for widows; many SHGs construct a set of group norms that may be better tailored to the common predicament (Lieberman, 1989).

For parents who have lost a child, feelings of guilt and anger and the need to repair a marriage that is under severe threat are central. The permission to find a comfortable equilibrium without the restrictive norms placed for grieving by society is among the most valued contributions of SHGs.

Taken together, these characteristics provide the communality among bereavement SHGs. They are conditions that have been found to prevail no matter what the ideology or the belief system of a particular SHG. These properties influence what members perceive as important and, in fact, influence the actual experiences people are likely to have in such groups.

Unique processes

Despite these critical common elements, SHG specificity is easy to demonstrate, as shown by two studies that examined bereaved parents and spouses (Lieberman & Videka-Sherman, 1986; Videka-Sherman & Lieberman, 1985). The methods in both studies were identical: Cohorts of bereaved in SHGs were compared to matched bereaved who had access to SHGs but chose not to join. All were followed for 1 year, and outcomes were measured by assessments of mental health, social functioning, and physical health. For the spousally bereaved, the development of linkages with others in which mutual exchange occurred was the necessary condition for significant change. Those participants who experienced a diversity of therapeutic mechanisms, including abreaction, advice, and inculcation of hope, but who did not form such new social exchange relationships, did not significantly improve. Among the bereaved parents, however, those who established such relationships were no more likely to improve than those who did not.

These findings suggest that detailed studies of processes are required. In these two outwardly similar problem areas, we found that the psychology of each is different and that the processes by which SHGs work are distinct. The all too common statement equating SHGs and social supportive relationships needs to be reexamined. Certainly, relationships are formed in all groups. People talk to one another, often about emotionally important and sensitive issues. Members frequently are exposed to information about coping strategies, and often they are provided acceptance and the enhancement of self-esteem by other group members. Thus, it is not an issue of whether certain socially supportive transactions occur both during formal meetings and in times between meetings. Their occurrence, however, does not translate directly into evidence that these are the necessary and sufficient conditions for the helpfulness of SHGs.

Empirical studies of effectiveness

The dilemmas created by some of the special characteristics of SHGs have already been mentioned. Crucial is the difficulty in creating random designs and in matching outcome measures to the values and beliefs about the "illness" held by SHG members. Beyond these are questions of how to address the classical issues confronting all intervention researchers – what to measure, when to measure, and whom to measure.

What to measure. Traditional criteria of mental health status are frequently employed. However, for many SHGs, the designations of illness and the criteria signifying the absence of illness are different from the traditional categories of mental health. Repeatedly found in our studies of bereavement groups was an emphasis on relatively lengthy extensions of the mourning process. The length of time for recovery was extended several times over that of the traditional mental health approach. We were unable to develop evidence that such extensions were, in and of themselves, pathological. Alternative perspectives, as well as a recognition of the relativity of the professional view of good functioning, are required for understanding SHGs.

Traditional measures used in bereavement research (symptoms, vicissitudes of grief, and social adjustment) represent a homeostatic model. The assumption is made that bereavement is a stressor and that the most appropriate way to assess its consequences is to examine whether or not the bereaved return to equilibrium. Commonly proposed is that after an "appropriate passage of time" following loss the optimal and only meaningful outcome is the resolution of depression and grief and a return to the previous adaptive pattern of social adjustment.

The homeostatic model has limitations; it is not sensitive to some important phenomena: that loss has such powerful and highly individualized meaning to the bereaved and that there is within each individual an unused, unrealized reservoir of personal potential. The spousally bereaved are faced with a number of significant challenges beyond a confrontation with loss. These involve a variety of areas of human functioning, but most importantly the bereaved are challenged with major and mortal questions about existence – about finitude, freedom and responsibility, isolation, and meaning in life.

The study of spousal bereavement must be broadened and individualized; it must go beyond loss and recovery. It must be sensitive to the fact that spousal loss in mid- and late life is highly complex; it impinges both on the inner life of the spousally bereaved as well as on external tasks and adjustments. Studies of bereavement have traditionally studied outcome by the presence or absence of physical and psychological symptoms, use of medication and drugs, crying, pining, insomnia, intrusiveness of thoughts of the lost person, and so on. Yet some of our research (Videka-Sherman, 1982, on bereaved parents; Yalom & Lieberman, in press, on widows) suggests that the presence of personal growth is uncorrelated to the more traditional measures of distress. Yalom and Lieberman (in press) found that within 1 year after the loss of a spouse about 25% showed patterns of growth.

When to measure. Traditional psychotherapy is usually time-limited. Evaluations are based on the expectation that patients will go through a set of therapeutic experiences and will leave when they show improvement. In contrast, most SHGs encourage long-term involvement. There are no "graduations" or clear-cut exit points; membership is indeterminate and may persist far beyond professionally defined recovery. Spousal bereavement groups often produce positive results in members within 6 months to 1 year; however, membership ordinarily lasts far longer. It is overly simplistic to see the extended membership as a pathological indicator. In part, the extension of membership is a reciprocation of help to others of similar status; more importantly long tenure expresses the primacy of affiliation needs.

Open-ended membership also serves the legitimate needs for the continued existence of SHGs. If the duration of membership were not indeterminate, SHGs could not endure, as there would be no one to carry on the group's work. The absence of clearly defined exit points makes the study of SHG outcomes less precise than comparable outcome research in psychotherapy.

Whom to measure. Psychotherapy researchers have adopted a shared perspective on whom to measure, as therapy is clearly defined and certain rules have been prescribed regarding participation in therapy. An investigator studying brief psychotherapy of 20 sessions, for example, often sets standards based on the number of sessions for which a patient is or is not considered to have been in therapy. For many SHG members, their participation patterns may be systematic but differ radically from the weekly or twice-weekly pattern of psychotherapy. They range from the not untypical behavior in AA of three to four times a week to Compassionate Friends' participants who use the group sporadically at points of particular stress. Another complication is the use of multiple helping resources by many SHG participants (Lieberman & Borman, 1979). Although multiple help use is not absent in psychotherapy research, its magnitude in SHGs precludes the simple isolation of particular intervention [psychotherapy participation: bereaved parents, 31% (Videka-Sherman & Lieberman, 1985); spousally bereaved, 22% (Lieberman & Videka-Sherman, 1986)].

These methodological and design problems do not negate the possibility of evaluating the impact of SHGs. Rather, these issues can alert us to the current state of knowledge and to the fact that good empirical research (by the very nature of the phenomena being studied) will have to be somewhat different from traditional psychotherapy outcome research. Evaluation models rather than outcome models may become the preferred direction.

Review of empirical studies

Beyond the methodological issues described, assessment of bereavement SHG outcomes is compromised by the range of SHG conditions studied. Three types of SHG research settings are apparent: *Type A*, the examination of existent SHGs that have a tradition or history, usually are characterized by a specific belief system about the cause and cure of the problem and above all are controlled and directed by the members, the bereaved, themselves. *Type B* are usually groups of brief duration set up and led by mental health professionals. (See Weiner, 1986, for an excellent discussion of homogeneously composed group therapy.) Although the group leader may not necessarily apply the technology associated with formal group therapy, research using this strategy does not present independent process data needed to make this distinction. *Type C* are experimenter-generated in which a formal experimental variation in type of groups including ones that are designated SHGs are examined. They differ from the type B studies

Table 27.1. *Evaluation of outcomes of self-help studies*

Author(s)	Sample characteristics	Study characteristics	Measures	Findings	Comments
Barrett (1978)	$N = 53$ (intervention); $N = 17$ (wait control); mean age = 55.7; widowhood: 4.9; 87% college.	Type C; retention = 29%; recruitment = newspaper ads; intervention: 2 hours per week for 7 weeks (3 types: women's issues, "self-help," and confidence groups).	Written self-reports (self-esteem, grief intensity, health, attitudes toward remarriage, social role engagement, other and self-orientation, attitudes toward women, frequency of social contact with other participants, life changes). Posttest and 2 weeks.	No significant main effects for treatment or treatment types. All improved over time.	Low retention rate and length of widowhood are serious threats to validity of study. No independent assessment of processes for three types of groups.
Marmar et al. (1988)	$N = 61$ (intervention); no control group; mean age = 58; mean weeks widowed = 54; 2 years' college.	Type B; recruitment = public notices (selected on DSM III criteria); intervention: 12 weekly group sessions (individual psychotherapy vs. SHG).	Patient self-report and clinicians' ratings of intrusive thoughts and avoidance. SCL 90, BDI, clinicians' ratings on Brief Psychiatric Rating Scale. Social adjustment scale, clinicians' ratings of social adjustment. Follow-up at 4 months and 1 year later.	No treatment differences. Both groups improved over time.	Well-designed study, using both self-report and ratings by experienced clinicians.

422

Study	Sample	Design/Method	Measures	Results	Comments
Vachon et al. (1980b)	N = 195, 88% participated (sampled seven area hospitals); N = 68 (intervention); N = 94 (controls); median age = 52; middle class, 29% employed.	Type B; random assignment; retention: 6 months N = 108, 12 months N = 76, 24 months N = 99; intervention: lay widowed people, a one-to-one contact plus group meetings.	Goldberg General Health Questionnaire. Categorical data derived ad hoc from the GHQ.	Based on 24 E & 38 C.[a] Authors suggest intervention enhanced rate of E's improvement.	Difficult to evaluate: Serious attrition, arbitrary division of GHQ into unreliable scales. Cf. other studies precluded: unspecified amount and length of group contact.
Constantino (1988)	N = 117; mean age = 58; widow length: 12, <1 year; 52, 1–5 years; 53, 6–20 years; 28% college.	Type B; recruitment: newspaper; random assignment to three conditions (control, social activity, intervention groups).	BDI, DAC, two self-report depression scales, and the social adjustment scale. Repeated measure analysis of variance. Assessed at four times prior to intervention, 3, 6, and 12 months' postintervention.	Main effects significant for groups, with the active treatment group lower in depression and higher in social adjustment. Most change at 3-month interval.	Sampling frame and pre-dominance of long-term widows make it difficult to isolate linkage of group to problems of widowhood vs. sample selection bias and other life problems.

Table 27.1. (Cont.)

Author(s)	Sample characteristics	Study characteristics	Measures	Findings	Comments
Lieberman & Videka-Sherman (1986)	$N = 502$ (394 E; 108 C[a]); 466 women, 36 men; age: 16% <40 years, 24% 40's, 40% 50's, 20% 60+; widowhood 43 months average; 39% college.	Type A; recruitment: national SHG roster; retention: 70% of T1 responders (T1 = 49% response rate).	Depression, anxiety, somatic symptoms, well-being, self-esteem, coping mastery, psychotropic medication use, life satisfaction, and ratings of target complaints improvement. Assessed at T1 & 1 yr later.	Significant differences E vs. C[a] (on MANCOVA). SHG members significantly decreased depression scores and decreased psychotropic medication use. Highly involved members became less anxious, had higher well-being, higher self-esteem, and more improvement on target problems.	Nonrandom assignment, reliance on large sample analyses and statistical controls with comparison to a random probability sample to provide "corrections" associated with absent randomization.
Videka-Sherman & Lieberman (1985)	$N = 391$ (294 E; 97 C); 75% women; bereavement <1 year = 41%, >2 years = 38%, >3 years = 21%, <3 years = 25%; 32% college degrees.	Type A, (1) SHG cf. psychotherapy; (2) SHG cf. never joined ($N = 97$), dropouts ($N = 43$), sporadic users ($N = 81$), former members ($N = 43$), active members	Mental health (depression, anxiety, somatic symptoms, self-esteem, life satisfaction, coping mastery). Marital role (reciprocity, strain and acceptance by spouse, strain and role	(1) No overall differences between SHG participants and psychotherapy. (2) No substantial changes over 1 year between SHG and other categories. Positive testimony based on	Complex study, nonrandom assignment to treatment modalities.

(N= 25), and active members with social exchange (N = 97).

expectations of spouse, marital distress/satisfaction, and comfort in communication). Parental role (parental distress, preoccupation with parental problems). Assessed at T1 & 1 year post.

questionnaire & intensive interviews noted. However (see Videka-Sherman, 1982), E Parents significantly higher than C on changes in values, belief systems, and worldview.

[a] E = SHG members; C = controls.

in that the leadership of such groups is provided by trained lay people. Similar to type B studies, the designation of different group types is rarely supported by independent process measures.

Table 27.1 summarizes outcome studies using contrast or control samples.

A perspective

The SHG for the bereaved is a vigorously growing and often used setting. Published reports from a number of different nations indicate that it is seen as a viable alternative to professional help. Its low cost, as well as its community base, provides a meaningful and valued alternative to many participants. The empirical research supporting their efficacy provides some bases for expecting that a large segment of the bereaved can meet their social and psychological needs in SHGs. The little evidence that is available does support the general proposition that they can be helpful. However, the variability of the research and the lack of consistency among studies about conditions or settings representing self-help make it well nigh impossible to develop precise statements about efficiency or efficacy, or about what kind of bereavement and at what points in their grief such groups would be helpful. In short, there is no critical mass of empirical evidence that would address these questions. Furthermore, SHG research is plagued by varying definitions of self-help and by a wide range of method problems – randomization, narrow and inconsistent range of measures, and wide diversity of bereaved clients (e.g., in the published literature widows who were studied in the various research projects cited in Table 27.1 range all the way from several months to two decades of widowhood). Required are studies that address the area of self-help research not as a black box but one in which characterizations of the treatment, as well as the outcome, are linked. Until such time, meaningful differences among the types of self-help studies cited in Table 27.1 make it impossible to provide even low-level generalization.

28

Counseling and therapy of the bereaved

BEVERLEY RAPHAEL, WARWICK MIDDLETON,
NADA MARTINEK, AND VIVIENNE MISSO

Caring for bereaved people involves a wide range of interventions, from the compassionate and empathic communication of a terminal illness diagnosis through the in-depth psychiatric management of bereaved people whose grief may or may not have contributed to their illness. There is also a powerful social movement of care that has evolved, particularly in the last three decades, recognizing the needs of, and supporting, bereaved people. Associated with this has been the development of self-help organizations that have contributed to the care and counseling of the bereaved. There are now many studies describing the effects of bereavement on health and well-being and the interventions that may be provided to prevent or deal with pathological outcomes. Still, there is much to be learned.

The models that have been used for counseling the bereaved have arisen for the most part from psychotherapeutic approaches and have traditionally applied to the one-to-one situation, with some extension to family and group treatments. Horowitz has been a significant contributor in defining the psychotherapeutic approach for grief (Horowitz et al., 1984a), dealing with bereavement in the context of stress response syndromes; other workers (Lindemann, 1944; Raphael, 1977, 1983) have utilized psychodynamic understanding for crisis intervention formats. Behavioral therapies have also been utilized, and descriptions have ranged from the broad model of Ramsay (1979), to the specifics of guided mourning (Mawson et al., 1981), to a more recent conceptualization that is cognitively oriented (Kavanagh, 1990).

Despite this breadth of therapies, as well as the differing conceptualizations of grief and bereavement, most approaches are relatively structured and often time-limited. This has fitted well with other current psychotherapies, especially brief therapies and cognitive behavioral approaches. Nevertheless, most clinicians in this field would agree that although there have been many patients for whom these grief therapies have been effective, there is still a small but significant number who do not respond, and who, despite extensive care, remain locked into their bereavement-related pathology. Furthermore, a number of studies indicate that there may be differential counseling needs in terms of disposition (Horowitz et al., 1984a), cognitive versus insight orientation frameworks at different times (Alexy, 1982), and facets of social support (Vachon & Stylianos, this volume). Thus, it is timely to examine bereavement counseling: to review the modes that have been utilized, to assess their success or otherwise, and to suggest issues of relevance for more in-depth consideration in view of current understanding of the bereavement field.

Contexts of bereavement counseling

Counseling for distress related to bereavement has now become a widely accepted practice. Yet, despite the studies outlined here, the purposes of such counseling, or indeed therapy, as it is often called, are not always defined. A key issue is whether or not counseling of any kind is needed by the majority of bereaved people. The need for counseling may range from support for specific distress and preventive counseling to reduce risk of pathological outcome to interventions aimed at treating bereavement pathologies.

Many studies and reports do not, in the model they propose, clearly define the need for counseling. Nor, in many instances, do they clearly specify goals. There seems to be general agreement that counseling is not necessary for "normal" grief, simply support and understanding. Yet, as indicated in chapter 3 of this volume, there is little agreement, even among experts, as to operational criteria that reliably discriminate normal and pathological bereavements. Conceptualizations separating grief counseling (e.g., for support and prevention) from grief therapy (for bereavement pathology; e.g., Worden, 1982/1991) are useful, but in practice such distinctions are difficult to make, and rarely made.

The whole issue of bereavement counseling should also be considered from the point of view of *health care provision*: Health systems or other interacting systems need to ensure that their policies are facilitatory and "healthy" for bereaved people and that they do not increase distress or add to the risk of disorder. This might be exemplified in areas such as viewing the body of the deceased, funeral arrangements that recognize the cultural prescriptions of the bereaved, registration of the birth and death of a stillborn child, compassionate leave from the workplace, to name a few.

Education is also a key issue. Community education has heightened awareness of normal grief and the acceptability of emotional expression. *Information* and education can be helpful at all levels for those affected and those who would offer their support. Similarly, with those who are bereaved, information may help in identifying the normality of reactions and feelings, the likely changes as time progresses, and sources of practical and other assistance.

Cross-cultural themes are also of great importance. Differing patterns of reaction to loss have not as yet been systematically studied scientifically, but there are many differing cultural prescriptions for the rituals surrounding loss, the definition of the bereaved, and the personal and public expressions of grief and mourning (Selby, 1991). Sensitive appraisal of these issues and their relevance to the cultural background of the bereaved is a vital aspect of all counseling and therapy, as is cultural bereavement (Eisenbruch, 1984a, 1984b). There is a need to develop and test culturally specific programs.

One further general area of enormous significance is that of the painfulness of *empathy* with the bereaved. For all those involved in providing care, so doing must inevitably reawaken aspects of their own separation and loss, involving actual or feared personal experiences. Empathy and identification may be more distressing than in other therapy or counseling situations, and as such may lead to distancing, defensiveness, excessive reliance on structural techniques, or alternatively enmeshed overinvolvement. Clearly, most workers in the field, whatever the model involved in their work, require a psychodynamic understanding of these themes and their possible impact. They also need opportunities for discussion and supervision to assist the therapeutic processes and to support the therapist.

The processes of counseling: A clinical model

Assessment and planning of care

With each bereaved person, it is important to explore the issues of the relationship, the loss, social support, other stressors, background, and family variables. Doing so sensitively may in itself constitute the first stage of therapy or counseling, and can be termed a therapeutic assessment. Several key questions are useful here and help further identify those who are vulnerable:

- *Can you tell me about him/her?* This evokes a history of the relationship, including its positive and negative aspects, its elements of ambivalence and dependence. It facilitates review and, by extension, may help the bereaved face the more negative aspects. For instance, "Can you tell me more about the times that were not so happy – difficulties such as we all have sometimes in relationships?"
- *Can you tell me about the death, how he/she died?* This enables an exploration of the circumstances surrounding the death. It indicates to the bereaved that

one accepts this issue as vitally important, and that all the fears and questions, all the horror or uncertainty that it evokes, are legitimate sources of distress that may need understanding and care. This topic can be expanded to cover the days leading up to the death, how the bereaved learned of it, and responses of the bereaved and significant others afterward.

- *Can you tell me about how others have responded to you since – what they said and did, what it meant to you?* This allows exploration of various aspects of social support and their perceived significance. It is useful to extend this into understanding whether "support" has helped the bereaved grieve or inhibited some aspect of the psychological mourning processes, if it has supported adaptation and self-esteem, if it has provided necessary practical assistance, and if it has done these things without demeaning or unduly obligating the bereaved in the process.
- *Can you tell me about the other things that have happened to you, or are happening now, that are making things harder for you as well?* This helps clarify the presence of other current losses or chronic stresses and to define their severity and effects.
- *Can you tell me about yourself, as a person, and your life before all this happened – how has it been, and what sorts of things have you had to face in the past?* This helps provide a framework that can be extended to explore specific issues such as earlier losses, previous illness and pathology, and long-term life circumstances, as well as personality. Sanders's (1988) review shows that different personality styles may also be important in outcome. The four reaction types (disturbed, depressed high grief, denial, and normal grief contained) may represent coping styles that require specific counseling or management approaches. It will be valuable for further research to delineate the most effective techniques for each type.
- *Can you tell me about the family – how this has affected the family as a whole, and what you feel it has meant for each person?* This topic may be assisted by giving general recognition to the problems families may face in fearing disintegration and struggling to comfort members, while each person is grieving in his or her own way and pace. Particularly helpful is at least one family interview or joint session, which can illuminate the dynamics and also allow therapeutic comments such as, "It is often hard to show your feelings at this time. Each person seems to feel afraid of affecting the others; yet it really helps if you can let go." Again, this contributes to the assessment and can show potential vulnerability, while at the same time it facilitates natural grieving processes.

All of this information can be combined to give a profile of bereavement coping and vulnerability, which provides the rationale to decide if counseling is necessary and for specific counseling goals to be set. The ultimate goal is to facilitate normal grief and mourning, and interim goals are relevant to particular vulnerabilities.

Key issues in counseling

Establishing a relationship with the bereaved person or family. This process will depend on a number of opposing forces, such as the bereaved's wish to talk, to share feelings and find meaning in this experience, or to be comforted. Or, on the other hand, there may be a wish to shut out, deny, and avoid facing the reality of counseling and the pain that discussion will bring. There may also be a feeling of resentment that the dead person is not there and available to offer comfort. However, the need to share feelings with a caring person usually predominates, particularly at the time of crisis. In more entrenched situations there may be more prolonged resistance to establishing a close and trusting relationship with the counselor, because to do so implies that the bereaved may have to face grief and to relinquish ties to the dead person.

In this process of negotiating the relationship the therapeutic contract also needs to be defined. This oral agreement should spell out the focus of the counseling, the role of each party, the expected duration, and so forth, including some mutual agreement about general goals and purposes.

Exploration of the loss. This includes the circumstances of the death, its reality to the bereaved, the psychological trauma associated with it, and personal and social responses to it. This can be expanded from the process of therapeutic assessment.

In most instances the spectrum of the bereaved's emotions – the separation anxiety, helplessness, and protest that appear early and the sadness, despair, anger, guilt, regret, and relief that may follow – are all likely to be intense. In others there are blocks and inhibitions. Then the counselor's role is to support and encourage the bereaved person in the "natural" release of affects related to the loss. However, it is important to recognize the vast range of individual responses – for instance, cases where affect is tied to the tasks of physical or emotional survival when injuries, illness, life threat, or overwhelming stress complicate the bereavement; or where cultural prescriptions powerfully dictate the "acceptable" responses. Emotion may also be difficult for those whose long-term personality styles inhibit expression of feeling. Although it is generally accepted that affective release and catharsis, as well as review of the issues surrounding the death, will be helpful to the bereaved, it is clear that these processes cannot be forced if the individual is too strongly defended against them or not yet ready for them. It is also clear that lack of emotional expression does not necessarily lead to unfavorable outcomes, at least for some individuals and in the short term (Singh & Raphael, 1981).

Another issue concerns the presence or absence of post-traumatic stress disorder (discussed later). If this has occurred due to the shocking circumstances surrounding the death or the psychological trauma suffered by the bereaved, it usually needs to be dealt with first so that the bereaved can grieve (Raphael, 1983, 1986). This is often relevant for individuals bereaved in a large-scale community disaster (Lindy et al., 1983).

Reviewing the lost relationship. This follows from assessment of the relationship of the deceased and issues of relevance in this. Its aim is to facilitate the internal and interpersonal processes of psychological mourning – the gradual undoing of the bonds to the lost person. The bereaved is encouraged to discuss the relationship: how it started, its course, its vicissitudes, its rewarding and its painful aspects. The patterns and nature of the interaction, the roles each fulfilled, areas of needs, and themes of gratification should all be reviewed. The idealization of the deceased that is often prominent needs gentle testing so that negative feelings underlying it can be faced and dealt with. Feelings of anger toward the dead person, who may be perceived as "abandoning" the bereaved, may need to be explored and are particularly likely to be a problem when the death is seen as "unnecessary" – the result of foolhardiness, accident, neglect, or self-destructive behavior, including suicide. Feelings of guilt may also need careful working through, especially if they are related to damaging, rejecting, or neglecting behavior in the past relationship. Ambivalence, often heightened by the circumstances of the death, as when sudden, unexpected death follows an argument, is important to resolve.

The ties to the dead person are profound and intricate, being in death as they were in life. The bereaved usually acknowledge only some of these. The aim of work in this sphere is to facilitate the undoing of some of these ties, so that the bereaved is not obsessed with and governed by bonds with the dead to the detriment of future life with the living. As Vaillant (1988) has so sensitively pointed out, the value that comes from loss lies in internalization that follows it, adding to the complexity and richness of our personalities and lives.

Exploring the background issues with the bereaved. Here important parameters include current life experiences (e.g., losses and stresses of an acute or chronic nature, sociodemographic factors, family and cultural issues) and the relevant past (family and personal history and especially responses to past stresses and losses). Following from this, elements contributing to difficulties in dealing with the loss can be addressed as far as possible to mitigate any negative influence that may interfere with the bereaved's capacity to adapt to this loss. It is important for the counseling process to focus on these elements specifically as they relate to the loss, and not to be drawn into the morass of long-term personality problems and chronic conflicts. If appropriate, therapy may be undertaken later to deal with these.

Providing support. The provision of support is, as noted earlier, a vital issue. Following on from assessment, counseling needs to facilitate and complement social interactive processes that will encourage grief and mourning processes and to assist the bereaved in dealing with any perceived unhelpfulness in his or her social network. This may be furthered by bringing the family together, or including in the counseling relevant others from the bereaved's social network. The counselor may also provide extra, skilled, social support. This merges with the benefits offered by self-help groups that have evolved to assist bereaved people.

Practical issues (finances, housekeeping) also need to be addressed, and they may provide a useful framework beside which the emotional support issues seem less threatening to those who find dealing with psychological feelings to be difficult.

Achieving goals. The goals of such counseling for the bereaved may be achieved in one or more sessions, depending on the situation, but six to ten are often needed. This allows time to deal with major issues and to set the bereaved on the path to recovery. This does *not* mean that the loss is totally resolved by the counseling, for achieving a resolution is by no means certain, and it is quite clear that nostalgic memories of the dead person and some ties to him or her continue for many years. But in adaptive outcomes, such ties and memories do not totally preoccupy and dominate the bereaved.

It is useful and important to provide for evaluation of the counseling, both in terms of individual outcomes and as part of a more general evaluation of service provision. Thus, it could be helpful to make measurements or ratings of counselees' recovery from distress, patterns of symptomatology, adjustment, and other relevant variables. Where major long-term problems exist or continue, the bereavement counseling model may have to give way to more traditional and long-term therapy.

Family intervention or counseling

The general principles described here may be applied with families, but are complex, whether in a crisis model or as part of longer term therapy. This therapeutic modality has not been widely utilized or tested, except for Polak et al.'s (1975) study of acute grief following traumatic loss and that of Black and Urbanowitz (1987) with children and surviving parents. Descriptions of longer term interventions are chiefly clinically based (Pincus, 1974; Paul & Grosser, 1965). Current work is attempting to assess grief from the family context and this may provide a more scientifically based framework for intervention with families (Bloch, 1991b).

Counseling for care, support, and prevention

As noted, bereavement counseling has become a popular movement as well as part of professional systems of care. This is reflected in the enormous growth of self-help movements for bereaved people, most of which provide some form of support and counseling for those who have lost a loved one. There are also now many carers who would formally identify themselves as bereavement counselors. These are usually people with a professional background in mental health, or sometimes in pastoral care, although there is really little formal definition of what is required for training in this sphere or what skills should be attained. Nor is there definition of minimum standards. Nevertheless, with a range of different counselors and counseling systems, there has developed a substantial body of evidence to suggest that there is a general benefit in what is done.

Polak et al. (1975) carried out one of the first reported clinical trials of counseling for bereaved people. This Denver-based group tested the effectiveness of two to six sessions over 1 to 10 weeks immediately following sudden deaths. The deaths they identified were traumatic and pathogenic in themselves, with suicide, violence, suddenness, and other complicating factors. The interventions focused on "increasing the effectiveness of the family in coping with feelings, decisions, and problems of adjustment related to the death" (p. 146) and began with the initial visit of the intervention group with the coroner within 1 to 6 hours of the death. These workers carried out independent examination of outcome 6 and 18 months later, and did not find any benefits for the bereaved who received intervention compared with the matched group who did not. Both bereaved groups showed significant impairment compared to the nonbereaved, and the complex interplay of traumatic environmental stressors of the particular death and way of dying, individual vulnerabilities, and family social system factors appeared to contribute to risk of morbidity.

They noted clinically that families with a high degree of effective communication, problem-solving capacity and flexibility tended to do better, as compared to those who were inflexible with fixed and often conflictual roles. Individuals who had high levels of hopelessness and despair, difficulties expressing these, and tendencies to somatization appeared to be more at risk. These clearly negative findings in a high-risk group should be viewed as understandable in light of subsequent research which indicates that such bereavements may indeed require more focused, prolonged, and in-depth psychotherapeutic interventions. It is also important to note that the effects were not totally negative. For instance, the nonintervention group showed a much greater increase in psychiatric ratings at follow-up than the control (30% vs. 12%).

An evaluation of a service provided to aged bereaved people in New York was carried out by Gerber et al. (1975). This was not a controlled intervention study, but evaluated the support provided by a psychiatric nurse or psychiatric social worker (supervised by a psychiatrist) over the 6 months following the death. The support aimed to encourage the bereaved to express feelings about the bereavement, to remember the lost relationship, to move toward relationships with others and the future, and to deal with practical problems. Follow-up showed significant benefits for the supported as compared to the comparison group 5–8 months after the loss with decrease in health care utilization and medication use.

The next reported trial of bereavement counseling was also oriented to prevention but with a defined high-risk population of bereaved widows. The therapeutic orientation in this instance was to the individual primarily, and in a focused psychotherapeutic framework. A large population of recently bereaved widows was independently screened for risk status in terms of risk factors defined in earlier prospective studies (Raphael, 1977; Maddison & Walker, 1967). High risk was defined by traumatic circumstances of the death, a previously ambivalent and/or dependent relationship with the deceased spouse, and perceived nonsupportiveness of the social network in facilitating grief and mourning. All these criteria were operationally defined. High-risk widows were then randomly allocated to intervention and control groups and a third non-high-risk control group generally matched for age and sociodemographic factors was also established. Intervention was provided from 3 to 12 weeks after the death and averaged six to eight sessions for each widow, the sessions being of 1.5 to 2 hours' duration in many instances. These focused on facilitating the widow's expression of grief, her mourning processes, her attempts to deal with and come to terms with traumatic circumstances surrounding the death where these existed, and promotion of supportive interactions with her social network.

Independent follow-up 13 months later showed significant benefits for the intervention group in terms of decreased risk to general health and psychological health. The risk status and levels of morbidity appeared to have been reduced to the levels of those of the low-risk group. Effects were most pronounced for those whose risk status had been defined in terms of perceived nonsupportiveness of their social networks and most effective in terms of reducing health care utilization. However, for those at risk through ambivalent relationships with the deceased, there were also beneficial effects with a lessening of the extent and severity of depression (Raphael, 1978). Effectiveness was also proportional to the degree to which the counseling goals of facilitating expression of grief and the mourning process had been rated as being achieved (i.e., if these goals were rated as significantly achieved at the end of the intervention, this correlated with better health outcome a year later). These psychotherapeutically based interventions utilized an understanding of dynamics, models of the grieving process, and transference phenomena. They were, however, focused on risk issues specific to the individual widow, carried out in the widow's own home in many instances, and at times incorporated sessions with significant others.

The next major study reported was Parkes's (1979) evaluation of a bereavement service provided through St. Christopher's Hospice in London for high-risk bereaved people. In a similar methodology to Raphael's (1978), he also used a validated predictive questionnaire to define a high-risk group: those who were clinging to the deceased before the death, showed angry or self-reproachful behaviors, lacked a supportive family, were of young age, and were of low socioeconomic status. Risk was also defined by a nursing staff rating of nurses' perceptions of the bereaved's likely coping ability. The high-risk group members were randomly assigned to intervention and control groups. The intervention group received support from a volunteer group (often professionals, but not mental health experts) whose skills increased as the program progressed and who were supported by psychiatrists and social workers. These bereaved people were independently followed up 20 months later, and there were positive benefits for those who had received support in terms of lower levels of adverse changes in health, both mental and physical. Like Raphael's group, the level of morbidity for the high-risk group who received intervention was significantly reduced, to the level of the low-risk group.

In Vachon's controlled group study of self-help intervention for widows (Vachon et al., 1980a), widows were provided with a widow-to-widow self-help intervention, whereas the control group had no intervention. The women in this study were not deemed to be at special risk, and all were contacted 1 month after their husband's death. Their average age was 52, and the majority of the deaths were anticipated. The initial assessment at 1 month was followed by the random assignment. Distress or disturbance was measured by the GHQ30 (General Health Questionnaire 30 Items). The intervention was from a widow deemed to have resolved her own bereavement. It could be initiated either by the widow or the support person, was not limited to a defined duration, and involved a wide range of activities as well as supportive counseling. The most interesting facet of this study was the "pathway of adaptation," which appeared to have been facilitated by the intervention. Here, too, the intervention helped the high distress widows, those who, in terms of current research, might have been most at risk. Their patterns of adaptation were shifted toward those of the low distress group, whereas the high distress women who had not received intervention had higher overall psychiatric disturbance at 24 months. This pathway of adaptation is probably an important concept, one that needs better understanding and further research, for it may indicate what other clinicians have suggested, that there are different psychological and social processes and different needs and patterns in the time course of adapting to the loss of a loved one.

Vachon's work suggests that the early phase involves intrapersonal adaptation. Widows receiving intervention felt better in themselves at 6 months, whereas at 12 months they were much better and were involved interpersonally and in new activities. The women receiving intervention clearly proceeded faster along this pathway of adaptation through the early inner turmoil, withdrawal, and preoccupation to resolution and renewal of social interactions. The intervention group resisted postbereavement deterioration in the emotional adjustment, with a significant decrease in overall disturbance and dysfunction. The long-term impact of this facilitated adaptation pathway showed its ultimate benefit 2 years later (Vachon et al., 1980a).

This research is interesting, for it fits with the clinical experience of needing to deal with the intense inner distress and meaning of the loss in the beginning and then, later, the need to learn new roles and socialization. Certainly self-help groups may offer valuable role models for identification and socialization in the latter phases, just as they provide supportive empathy of others who have been through, "know," and have survived the intrapsychic turmoil of acute grief.

Parkes's (1980) review of the effectiveness of bereavement counseling covers the studies outlined here, as well as his own work, and he concludes that "professional services and professionally supported voluntary and self-help services are capable of reducing the risk of psychiatric and psychosomatic disorders resulting from bereavement" (p. 6). He also notes from his own studies that it probably takes the volunteer counselor a year to become proficient. These findings are now a decade old and have resulted in a much wider acceptance of the appropriateness of counseling for bereaved people. However, despite such evidence of effectiveness, missing from many other psychotherapeutic and counseling programs, systematic service delivery programs are still lacking. This probably reflects the difficulties, as highlighted by Eisenberg (1989), of commitment to preventive and similar policies.

A number of other bereavement counseling programs have been described and evaluated. These include programs for parents after stillbirth (Forrest et al., 1982), sudden infant death syndrome (Lowman, 1979), self-help for parents who have lost a child (Lieberman & Videka-Sherman, 1986), the survivors of cancer deaths (Souter & Moore, 1989), the recently widowed (Sabatini, 1988), and bereaved children and their families (Black

& Urbanowitz, 1987). For the most part, there is some description of perceived benefits and helpfulness with these, but most do not present well-developed, controlled studies of longer term outcomes with measures of actual resolution of grief and lessening or prevention of pathology (although there are general improvements in many of these directions).

W. Stroebe and Stroebe (1987) provide a valuable overview of interventions postbereavement. They also differentiate prevention programs (e.g., Raphael, 1977; Vachon et al., 1980a) providing grief counseling from those providing grief therapy, which they see as being for those with complicated or pathological grief reactions. This distinction is not, however, utilized by many of the researchers and there appears to be a continuum of interventions from counseling to psychotherapy that are applied across the spectrum of normal to high risk to complicated/pathological grief reactions. Other reviews of the effectiveness of counseling have also been provided by Osterweis et al. (1984) and Windholz et al. (1985), and these support the conclusions drawn from Parkes's (1980) review and the studies outlined here: There is much to suggest that bereavement counseling does indeed work at least to lessen the risk of subsequent pathology for some at-risk bereaved people.

Counseling for support and prevention and the psychotherapeutic management of bereavement pathology

Psychotherapies

Where counseling becomes psychotherapy has never been well defined, and it is beyond the scope of this chapter to address this conceptual issue. However, several valuable in-depth studies of psychotherapeutic techniques for the bereaved have been presented and extend further the understanding of important ways to help bereaved people, especially those who are already demonstrating bereavement-related pathologies and problems. The Horowitz group (1984a) report an in-depth study of psychotherapeutic process and outcome in work with 52 bereaved adults (following the death of a husband or parent). These patients were diagnosed as suffering from *adjustment disorder* (evidenced by impairment of social or occupational functioning, low to moderate intrusive or denial symptoms, and depressive, anxious, and other symptomatology commonly seen in grief reactions, after an anticipated death) or *post-traumatic stress disorder* (with high levels of intrusive and denial symptomatology, as well as grief/depression, etc., and after an unanticipated death). A very careful independent pretherapy evaluation was performed. There were also detailed systematic evaluations of therapy process from recordings of sessions 4, 8, and 12. Outcome was measured by a battery of measures in domains of stress-specific symptoms, general psychiatric symptoms, and work and interpersonal functioning.

The intervention consisted of 12 sessions of time-limited, once-a-week *dynamic psychotherapy* aimed at establishing a trusting relationship. It used principles from Malan (1979) using triangles of insight and principles of Mann (1973) for dealing with separation and loss in time-limited therapy and dealing with termination issues. The further bereavement-specific issues included focus on the impact of the loss of the relationship on the self-concept of the bereaved person. Transference aspects were dealt with in those frameworks. Horowitz et al. (1984a) describe aims of relieving distress by facilitating normal rather than pathological grieving processes, realistic appraisal of the implications of the death, and exploration of the multiple self and other concepts activated during the mourning process. Techniques include abreaction, catharsis, and interpretation of defenses and affects.

The findings of this study were complex, with a number of interactions between dispositional, process, and outcome factors. However, symptomatic relief was substantial with a large effect size, whereas domains of work and relationship functioning showed less improvement. Patients with a more stable and mature self-concept before treatment tended to do better in work and interpersonal functioning posttreatment. There were also indications that supportive interactions were more likely to be helpful for poorer functioning or less motivated patients, whereas exploratory interpretations (including negative areas) were more likely to be of value to highly motivated or more mature and stable personalities. This also appeared to apply specifically to dealing with the termination. These findings fit well with other analyses of brief psychotherapy outcomes and processes and with clinical experience and descriptions of brief psychotherapy, and thus fit this type of bereavement counseling clearly into the field of brief psychotherapy models as they currently exist.

A further study of psychotherapy for bereaved women with difficulties adjusting to their husband's death and psychiatric diagnosis was carried out by Marmar et al. (1988) and by Horowitz et al. (1984b). They recruited 61 women after advertisement, screening, and pretreatment evaluation. Subjects were diagnosed as suffering from adjustment disorder, post-traumatic stress disorder, and major depression, and were between 4 months and 3 years after their husbands' deaths. They were randomly allocated to brief dynamic psychotherapy (12 sessions once per week) or mutual self-help groups (12 × 1½-hour sessions). There was considerable attrition in both groups, especially mutual help. Improvement occurred for both groups over time as measured at the end of therapy, 4 months and 1 year later by independent assessment and a battery of measures. Although there was significant improvement over time for both treatment conditions,

the overall decline in general symptoms was greater for the brief psychotherapy group, and significant differences in this direction occurred at
4 months and 1 year follow-up. The authors do not comment on the
matching between the groups on diagnosis or time following the loss, so
the implication of the results are unclear if these issues have not been
accounted for. The high attrition of the groups may support the aspect
noted earlier, that intrapsychic issues may still have predominated for these
women who saw their loss as unresolved and may have been better handled
in individual therapy.

Thus, these two studies, plus a comparative study by Kleber and Brom
(1987), discussed later, provide evidence of the value of brief psychotherapy
techniques for bereaved people with major adjustment difficulties and
diagnosable psychiatric disorder in association with their bereavement.
Clearly, other approaches, particularly those with support, do also help.

Behavioral therapies

Behavioral therapy models have also been described for the management of
bereavement pathologies. Ramsay's (1979) model is one of confronting the
loss and catharsis of feelings and then reintegration, not unlike the psychotherapeutic measures outlined in the previous section. This relies on
behavioral desensitization to the loss. Such processes are seen as being
unsuitable for normal bereavement, especially during the first year, but
rather as appropriate for "embedded" or phobic *pathological grief reactions*.

Mawson's group (1981) carried out a small controlled study of a systematic behavioral approach called *guided mourning*. It involved $1-1\frac{1}{2}$-hour
sessions given three times weekly for 2 weeks with subsequent follow-up
until 28 weeks. All the patients had had distress related to grief for more
than 1 year plus two or more other indications of pathological grieving. The
therapy involved confronting aspects of the loss repeatedly until affects
associated with them diminished, plus homework based on writing at least
a page daily about the deceased. This behavioral intervention involved
intense reliving of avoided painful memories and feelings associated with
the bereavement. In contrast, the control subjects had a similar framework
aimed at avoiding grief and dealing with the lost relationship. Substantial
improvement occurred in the intervention group on measures of approach
to bereavement, but less in terms of depressive mood. The guided mourning
patients ($n = 6$) overall improved significantly more than the controls on
three measures, with a supportive trend on four other measures, whereas
controls ($n = 6$) did not show any significant improvement or trends. The
improvement for those receiving this therapy was maintained 10–28 weeks
later. This small study is impressive and the results have recently been
replicated in a controlled study by Sireling et al. (1988). It is especially

important in that patients with such chronic grief are often notoriously difficult to treat, and their disability in personal and social terms and in suffering may be very significant. It would be helpful to extend this research and clinical work further.

Another report on behavioral treatments is that of Walls and Meyers (1985). They investigated four experimental groups each of which met for one 90-minute session per week for 10 weeks. The therapeutic modes for the groups were cognitive restructuring, behavioral skills, self-help, and a delayed treatment control group. However, these three group interventions appeared to have little effect on the adjustment to widowhood, although the cognitive restructuring was of some benefit to depressive phenomena. There is little to explain these outcomes, and there was considerable improvement in the control group while waiting. It may be that the inexperienced therapists (psychology students), or the group process, were not so suitable; but this was a small study and its significance is really unclear.

Kavanagh (1990) has suggested a basis for a cognitive–behavioral intervention for adult grief reactions. He sees such a cognitive paradigm as characterizing chronic grief as a negative feedback system. Nevertheless, many behavioral aspects of bereavement portend a relatively benign outcome for most sufferers. His intervention model postulates recognition of existing skills and supporting these. Intervention involves controlled exposure and cognitive stimuli associated with the bereavement. Graded involvement in roles and activities is also recommended (with encouragement of achievement and attention to positive aspects). Where excessive negativity occurs, as with depression or perhaps negative self-images, such as those described by Horowitz (1984a), then cognitive therapy following the model of Beck is suggested. In the bereaved, Kavanagh suggests, it is particularly important to focus on cognitions of hopelessness, guilt, or personal worthlessness. A similar cognitive approach in terms of examining the validity of cognitions seen as generating chronic anger is suggested. Reinforcement of social support and control of drug and alcohol use are additional general components of this therapeutic model. Kavanagh suggests that his behavioral model differs from earlier approaches of guided mourning by Mawson et al. (1981) and replicated by Sireling et al. (1988) in that it legitimizes controlled distraction, explicitly includes cognitive therapy and skills training, and can be used for a wider variety of grief problems. No studies reporting on the effectiveness or otherwise of this approach have yet appeared, however.

Comparing different interventions

A study of value in *comparing different therapeutic modalities* is that of Kleber and Brom (1987), who report on their work with 83 bereaved people who had experienced a major loss in the previous 5 years, had complaints of anxiety, sleeplessness, instability and guilt, and had post-traumatic phenomena of loss-related intrusions and denial. Seventy-five percent had suffered the loss of a child or spouse, and in 61% the deaths had been from accidents (traffic), homicide, suicide, and otherwise sudden and unexpected. Thus, this group of patients were a sample who had suffered traumatic bereavements and, apart from any symptom or disorder that was specifically related to their bereavements, also had much to suggest that they suffered from post-traumatic stress disorder. Although Horowitz's group has also defined bereavement within the stress response syndromes (e.g., Horowitz, 1976/1986), it seems likely that this is more the case with traumatic bereavements (i.e., particularly those with traumatic circumstances surrounding the death). Both Raphael (Raphael & Maddison, 1976; Raphael, 1977, 1983) and Lindy et al. (1983) highlight the fact that the two sets of phenomena are in many ways separate and that it may be necessary to treat, counsel, or work through the traumatic phenomena and related disorder before the bereaved person can grieve and mourn for the lost person. This is well exemplified when the bereaved person's preoccupation is with the scene or circumstances of the death. Traumatic intrusions of this memory or denying, numbing, and shutting out may be the predominant thoughts and feelings. The sadness, longing, and nostalgic reviewing of the lost relationship and the dead person do not occur or are overwhelmed by the traumatic anxiety or repression of the traumatic experience. Most clinical experience suggests that the trauma must be dealt with first, and it is with the lessening of the traumatic preoccupations, the intrusion and denial, that the nostalgic memories and mourning may follow.

Thus, the Kleber and Brom (1987) study, while dealing with pathological bereavements ($n = 83$), investigates and reports on outcome chiefly in terms of post-traumatic phenomena, although also symptomatic complaints. Three therapeutic modes were evaluated. *Trauma desensitization* involved the patient gradually confronting the relevant aspects of his or her loss and being desensitized to it in a learning theory model with relaxation techniques. *Hypnosis therapy* used hypnosis to assist the bereaved in confronting the loss. *Psychodynamic therapy* was based on Horowitz's model and aimed at working through conflicts related to the loss. The patients were seen an average of 23 months after the loss, so that they represented a group with entrenched problems, and had high scores on IES (Impact of Event Scale) and the SLC90 and State Trait Anger and Anxiety inventories. There was a matched waiting-list control group.

All therapeutic modes were effective, but their principal effects were on the symptoms of stress response syndromes – intrusion and denial – and substantially less on symptomatic somatic and psychoneurotic complaints.

This effect was less marked when pretest—posttest measures were also included and compared with the waiting-list control group, which showed some improvement. There was little difference between the different modes, although there was some trend for the psychodynamic therapy to be more effective and to have somewhat better results at follow-up. When intake variables were examined, the authors concluded that the psychodynamic therapy was equally effective for younger and older people and the behavioral treatments were better for those who were younger and of lower income. In terms of personality variables, those with an internal locus of control seemed to do better in therapy and the angry and distrustful did poorly. The average number of sessions was 15–20, not unlike Horowitz's original work, which strongly influenced this study, and other models of brief psychotherapy. As the authors conclude, it is a further validation of the effectiveness of psychotherapy – in this instance, for traumatic and pathological aspects of bereavement. But it did not completely remove symptom problems, and the data provided give little insight into the degree of resolution of the grief and loss that may have been achieved by these stressed people.

Other counseling techniques

A range of other models and techniques have been developed, utilized, and described by clinicians working with grieving people. All of them attempt to find formats and structures to deal with difficult therapeutic tasks. Many of these difficulties appear in relation to moving people on with their grieving process – particularly those who are often extremely difficult to help and who may suffer some form of inhibited, absent, or chronic grief or other pathological bereavement pattern. Even such distinctions about what is normal or pathological grief are difficult (see chapter 3, this volume). Nevertheless, taking the commonly accepted definitions (if not criterion-based), there is often a need to try new and flexible modes.

Most of these therapeutic models suggest specific structures or goals. In this context workers such as Shuchter have suggested that the *"therapeutic tasks of grief"* involve the following: Development of the capacity to experience, express, and integrate harmful affects; utilization of the most effective means of modulating harmful affects; integration of the continuing relationship with the dead spouse; maintenance of health and continued functioning; achievement of successful reconfiguration of altered relationships; and achievement of an integrated, healthy self-concept and stable worldview (adapted from Shuchter, 1986). These "tasks" are not dissimilar from Lindemann's original tasks of converting pathological to normal mourning (Lindemann, 1944) and reflect goals also suggested by other workers. Worden (1982/1991) also follows such a model.

Other techniques utilizing innovative methods have been reviewed in a volume by Stern (1985) and include *Gestalt therapy* (e.g., talking to the empty chair – what one would like to say to the deceased), imaging, and logotherapy. Another structured technique that has been widely used and is similar to those already mentioned is Volkan's (1971) *regrief work*, where emphasis is placed on symbolic *"linking objects"* (objects of the deceased utilized to facilitate therapy) and visits to the grave and reviews of photos and memorabilia. Similarly, "reliving, revisiting, and reviewing" is another somewhat ritualized and structured approach aimed at achieving a therapeutic resolution of the loss (Melges & DeMaso, 1980). Music therapy has also been suggested (Bright, 1986).

Rando (1984) has contributed a wealth of clinical and therapeutic descriptions of grief, its complications, and management. *"Therapeutic ritual"* and ritual leave-taking are important components of her therapeutic model (Rando, 1985). Rando describes general precepts such as the need to reach out to the bereaved, give them permission to grieve, and support their family systems. The therapist should determine the particular therapeutic tasks they still need to accomplish. This model encourages verbalization of feelings and recollection of the deceased, and helps the griever to identify and resolve secondary losses and unfinished business. Rituals, Rando states, have the value of facilitating emotional expression through the acting out of the ritual, legitimation of emotional and physical ventilation, and delineation of grief (p. 105).

More recently, Van der Hart and Goossens (1987) have described a set of therapeutic *leave-taking rituals* that they state are a "short term strategic form of mourning therapy" (p. 24). This process involves three phases. The first is preparatory – the therapist explains how the ritual may help to take leave of the deceased. The second is reorganization – the bereaved has to reorganize his or her life through the process of homework and other specified tasks. Third is the finalization phase, which may involve symbolic leave-taking, cleansing, and, finally, reunion rituals. These are fitted to the culture and beliefs of the bereaved and clearly represent symbolic and psychological processes deliberately set in motion to fulfill what has not happened internally and may or may not have occurred in social ritual. The authors specifically suggest that it is good for "conflicted grief," as described by Parkes and Weiss (1983), but no objective outcomes are provided. Reeves and Boersma (1990) are also proponents of the therapeutic use of ritual for maladaptive grieving and emphasize the cultural and cross-cultural importance of such understanding and facilitation.

Certain types of death may require particular attention and provide special difficulties for the bereaved. Violent deaths, suicide, murder deaths in which the bereaved played some part are prominent. Disaster deaths, deaths of wartime, deaths where no body can be found, or situations where death is uncertain are also extremely complex. AIDS-related bereavements have brought new levels of complexity and require sensitive therapeutic approaches to the grieving lover and family members. These aspects can usually be understood and explored in assessing circumstances of the death, and therapeutic work will need to deal with the various issues they involve, utilizing understanding from the various models and processes discussed here.

Pathological grief and its management

Bereavement counseling has been applied and tested in a wide variety of situations and with a wide variety of people. In some instances it has been with normal populations, with those at risk, and in others with long term and apparently chronically distressed/disturbed bereaved people, where the model used is more one of therapy. But the whole area of pathological grief and the suggestion of specific treatment programs is much more difficult to define. As noted in chapter 3, pathological grief has not been defined in operational terms, although commonly accepted categories include delayed, absent, inhibited, and chronic grief. These patterns may reflect the spectrum of phenomenology and be shaped by underlying personality or coping styles. There are no epidemiological studies defining these levels or patterns of pathological grief, although currently there are endeavors to provide operational criteria (Middleton & Raphael, current studies) Bearing in mind these provisos, the management of pathological grief follows Lindemann's (1944) original principles: that is, to convert pathological grief to normal grief (Raphael, 1975).

Delayed or absent grief. When grief is unduly delayed or absent, the therapeutic tasks involve assessment to identify any contributing factors, with particular note of current severe life stressors, past severe deprivation and loss, or personality patterns and coping that rely strongly on denial or repression of affect. It may also be that grief is absent because the relationship did not have a deep quality of attachment (if, for instance, the bereaved had an intensely narcissistic personality disorder). Another aspect is presence of a major psychiatric disorder, which may determine the main clinical picture. This should be treated alongside counseling.

The emphasis on counseling in this type of pathological grief is in exploring the reasons for such denial and absence, working psychotherapeutically to deal with these, and then helping the bereaved to confront and work through the realities of their loss, using counseling principles such as those outlined earlier. Regrief work and therapeutic rituals may also be helpful in these instances. The principle of progressing at a rate that the bereaved can encompass, with "doses" of affect that can be managed by the bereaved, is useful, as is the range of techniques identified previously.

Inhibited grief. Inhibited grief may be on a continuum with absent grief, and may also encompass distortion, such as excessive anger or guilt, with the absence of significant grieving. These may relate to experiences of dependency and/or ambivalence in the preexisting relationship with the deceased (Raphael & Maddison, 1976), and may result in syndromes such as conflicted grief or clinging grief (Parkes & Weiss, 1983). Therapeutic assessment should identify such parameters in the relationship, and the process of working through will involve psychotherapeutic work with the bereaved to deal with this ambivalence or dependence (and the latter may be the more difficult, especially if the bereaved brings excessive dependent needs into the therapy). It is useful to come back to a general structured model such as reviewing the loss and the lost relationship, as noted, or to Worden's (1982/1991) model of completion of the tasks of grieving. These include accepting the reality of the loss, experiencing the pain of grief, redefining the relationship with the deceased, adjusting to the environment from which the deceased is missing, and finally withdrawing emotional energy and reinvesting it in other relationships.

The psychotherapeutic processes of Horowitz et al. (1984a) may also be of use here, as may be such techniques as guided mourning and regrief work, and innovative techniques including gestalt. However, any method should be implemented only when there is a thorough dynamic understanding of the reasons why grief is inhibited and a recognition of the capacity or otherwise of the bereaved to deal with the grief at this time. This may be particularly relevant with children, where it may only be when there is a situation of stability in the home and security of current caring relationships that an earlier loss can be grieved.

Chronic grief. A picture of intense and prolonged grief may be presented with chronic grief, the bereaved appearing many years after the loss as though the grief were recent. Crying, intense preoccupation with, and idealization of the deceased are common. The bereaved's life may be a memorial to the dead person, with considerable cost to other family and personal relationships and functioning. A common pattern is of a woman who has lost her child, not infrequently a late adolescent who has died suddenly and unexpectedly. Parkes and Weiss (1983) also described this as common with clinging and dependent relationships. All clinicians agree that chronic grief is notoriously difficult to treat, for the bereaved is usually reluctant to relinquish the preoccupation with the deceased. Depression or other syndromes may coexist and should be treated appropriately, but a core syndrome of chronic grief is still likely to be resistant to therapeutic intervention.

General counseling principles, psychotherapy for bereaved as indicated in Horowitz's study, regrief work, and behavioral treatments may be tried, but behavioral interventions apply more usefully to the phobic and avoidant bereaved than to those with intense preoccupation with the loss, whose behavioral patterns are more like those of an obsessional disorder (Jacobs, 1991, personal communication). Practical interventions directing the grieving person to other roles and tasks may help in some instances, as may interpretations that deal with the reasons behind the bereaved's reluctance to give up the lost person. Perseverance, the use of innovative techniques, and advice to the bereaved may need to be part of the therapeutic regime.

Clearly, there is a need not only for operational criteria to define these syndromes (if they do indeed exist) but also therapeutic trials to determine optimal and effective therapy.

Unresolved grief: Past losses and deprivations. Some people who react severely or pathologically to a loss, or seem unable to do the necessary grief work, may be handicapped by vulnerabilities related to earlier severe losses (e.g., death of a parent in childhood) or severe deprivation (e.g., gross lack of parenting or absence of adequate attachment figures in childhood). A major loss opens into such issues of deprivation so that the bereaved may have difficulty tolerating the painful affects or may lack the ego strength to work through this and the current grief. These therapeutic issues must be fully understood. They may mean that the bereaved needs more skilled psychotherapeutic support, more in-depth psychotherapy, and gradual and appropriately modulated working through of the current loss. These and other issues highlight the importance of individually based assessments and treatment programs for the bereaved, and the great importance of avoiding simplistic formulas of "grief therapy" that are righteously applied.

Complementary therapeutic interventions for psychiatric disorders occurring in association with bereavement

Counseling the bereaved must also be considered alongside other therapeutic interventions. These may complement or indeed be essential in terms of symptomatology or syndromes or the relief of suffering.

Depressive disorder

Depressive disorder in the bereaved is important in this context. Although epidemiological studies have not yet fully defined the extent to which depressive disorder occurs in bereaved people, it is clear that for at least a percentage of the bereaved it is severe and disabling. Depressive phenomena are often difficult to distinguish from grief, with appetite, sleep, weight disturbance, and feelings of loss and despair. The picture is further complicated by the fact that many attempts to measure and define grief have been in terms of depressive symptomatology.

Jacobs et al. (1989) have carried out a systematic review and study of the depressions of bereavement. In the study, 29% of bereaved people met diagnostic criteria for depression in the year after their loss. This is a higher level than reported in some other studies (e.g., Clayton, 1979), which report 11% to 15% with lasting depression. These depressions in the bereaved are more likely to be transient and remit spontaneously. But many do not. Depressive disorder is more likely in those bereaved who show negative cognitions – low self-esteem, hopelessness, suicidal intentions, psychomotor retardation. If these symptoms are present, if a greater number of symptoms are present, or the depressive phenomena are severe and disabling, then specific treatment is required. There is also a high degree of overlap with anxiety disorders and pathological grief.

There are few systematic studies of the treatment of these bereavement-related depressions, and for the most part, psychotherapeutic interventions are suggested. These have been established to be effective in some instances in lessening the risk of depression and its severity in high-risk bereaved widows (Raphael, 1978). Such psychotherapeutic interventions have concentrated on helping the bereaved work through the ambivalent aspects of the lost relationship in line with Freud's (1917b) theoretical conceptualization in mourning and melancholia. They postulate that by dealing with the ambivalence, the depressive phenomena associated with the internalization of the lost object, the inward turning of aggression, and the fall of self-esteem are lessened.

There is clearly a need to define further, as has been done in the general area of depression treatment, the relative contributions of other treatments to these bereavement-related depressions – for instance, cognitive behavioral psychotherapies, physical treatments, and antidepressant medications. The findings on negative cognitions indicate the importance of trialing the effectiveness of cognitive therapies in such depressions.

Jacobs et al. (1987c) have reviewed the limited data available on other physical and pharmacological therapy modes and report on a pilot study of antidepressant treatment. These workers noted, in taking this therapeutic approach, that imipramine was effective in alleviating "depressive" behavior and social withdrawal in primates separated from mothers and siblings and in preventing the emergence of depressive behaviors in primates exposed to the stress of a loss (McKinney, 1986). Jacobs's group selected a community-based sample of 10 widowed people (8 widows and 2 widowers) who suffered depression as scored on the CESD depression scale and were verified as depressed by the depression segment of the SCID (DSM III) and by clinical interviews. These subjects participated in an open trial of imipramine 150 mg daily and were carefully monitored for depressive, grief, and other symptomatology throughout. After the 4 weeks their care was continued by their primary care physician. The authors report that seven (70%) reported a moderate to marked improvement of their depressive symptoms during this 4-week period, especially sleep and appetite, as well as mood and cognition. They believed that the biological, that is, pharmacological dimension, was significant in this improvement. Anxiety symptoms were also prominent in all but one of the subjects, and for the most part these also subsided. However, it was not possible to discern systematically a consistent effect of the antidepressants on the symptoms of grief nor the relationship between these and depressive phenomena in this small sample. This is a matter for further concern if the suggestions of correlations between unresolved grief and severe or ongoing depression are correct.

Clearly, this is a small pilot study, but it points the way to the importance of further systematic and controlled studies of treatment of psychiatric syndromes such as depression when these occur in relation to, and complicating, bereavement. Such studies must also, of necessity, address the interrelationships to grief and its course and the outcomes that are optimal for both depression and bereavement. This is particularly so in view of subjective accounts in some clinical settings where patients may report their grief being blocked or being in an "emotional straitjacket" because of psychotropic (including antidepressant) medication they have received.

Other earlier clinical reports suggest that electroconvulsive therapy may also be used with bereaved people who show evidence of severe depression, warranting such intervention in its own right. Nevertheless, as most workers suggest, it is still necessary to deal with the psychological issues of the bereavement, and in so doing to assist the grieving process alongside whatever other therapeutic measures are necessary.

Anxiety disorders

Further issues arise with regard to the concurrent treatment of other psychiatric disorders requiring medication, for example, the presence of anxiety disorders in bereaved people. Their relationship to the bereavement process has been discussed by Jacobs et al. (1990), who found that 10% of a bereaved sample met criteria for panic disorder and 30% for generalized anxiety disorder in the year following bereavement. With a personal history of heightened risk for this condition, there was a strong overlap with major depression and pathological grief. There is a need for further clinical understanding of the appropriate management of such anxiety disorders and how, in addition to counseling, appropriate pharmacological interventions with axiolytics can be utilized, when they are indicated.

The occurrence of post-traumatic stress disorder (PTSD) in relation to bereavement is not uncommon. The phenomena are often confused, however, mainly because bereavement was at one stage viewed in this model and because of the traumatic losses that have been described in crucial studies of the phenomena of grief (e.g., Lindemann, 1944). There are as yet few studies of the incidence of PTSD in the bereaved, but it may be more likely to occur in those whose loss is sudden, unexpected, and traumatic (e.g., violent). Therapy needs to involve both psychotherapeutic approaches aimed at working through the traumatic experience and specific intervention for grief and mourning. Whether or not pharmacological or other measures are required will depend principally on the phenomenology and severity of the PTSD. Both Raphael (1983, 1986) and Lindy et al. (1983) have noted the importance of dealing with the traumatic component and point out that it may block grief and may need to be worked through before grief work can be facilitated.

Severe and organic mental disorders

The grief suffered by patients who have a psychotic illness, those with organic brain syndromes, and those with intellectual handicap is of interest in this regard, but there is little systematic research or treatment trials in these circumstances. Physical health problems may coexist or be precipitated by the bereavement, or physical symptomatology may present either through the psychophysiological concomitants of grief, identificatory symptoms, or as a mechanism for entry into care. Such symptoms or conditions should be appropriately assessed, investigated as necessary, and included in the spectrum of care and treatment provided.

Substance abuse disorders

Bereavement may trigger substance abuse in those who are vulnerable, perhaps as they attempt to blot out the pain of grief and loneliness. Any such disorder should be carefully evaluated, but managed in the context of the bereavement, recognizing it may well represent maladaptive attempts to cope.

In the overall clinical care of bereaved people, it is critically important to ensure that the appropriate management of other concurrent conditions is skillfully interwoven with the counseling provided to help them deal with their loss. Of particular importance, and requiring further research understanding, is the impact of psychoactive medication on the grieving process. For, as noted earlier, it is often reported clinically that bereaved people suggest that some medication may interfere with their grief, though clearly for some it may help to settle distress to a degree where grieving becomes possible. For most people, however, medication is not an answer for the distress they experience. Rather, the support of empathic and concerned others and the understanding and skill of the counselor are more relevant variables.

Critical appraisal of the current status of bereavement counseling

As can be seen from this review, there are a number of systematic studies of both counseling, aimed chiefly at prevention, and grief therapies to deal with bereavement pathologies and/or related psychiatric disorders. Although many demonstrate positive effects, few of the studies have set clearly defined goals or identified how the therapeutic modality has attempted to achieve these. There is a lack of agreement over basic definitions of grief itself, let alone its pathologies, and none of the studies has clearly defined, in operational terms, specific bereavement outcomes. The lack of appropriate measures has been compounded by the lack of systematic trials, although a number have positively contributed to this field with controlled studies and independent outcome assessment.

As to which forms of counseling or therapy are applicable and produce optimal benefits, and with which group of bereaved people, it is clear that much further research is required. There are indications that some subjects may benefit more from insight-oriented measures, and that early in the course of bereavement addressing intrapsychic issues may be more relevant, whereas social/interpersonal issues are more relevant later. How these may be assessed in individuals and utilized in defining interventions and their desired goals needs further work. And the role of personality and coping styles and the possible influence of these on bereavement outcomes, as well as choice of counseling or therapy mode, require much further consideration.

There is a need for much more systematic and scientific evaluation of the models of counseling, the rationales for which they are applied, and their relationship to other psychologically based therapies. Of particular, and critical, importance is the need to be quite clear about if and when bereaved people need counseling, for there should be ethical concerns about providing a therapeutic framework for a natural human experience unless this is very clearly justified and indicated. Training of counselors, skills required, and quality assurance are further issues that have not yet been adequately addressed. Similarly, where counseling is indicated and effective, there must be ethical concerns about why counseling/therapy provisions are not available to those who might need them.

This chapter has reviewed some of the significant studies that have examined in detail different models of psychotherapeutic care and counseling for bereaved people. Much more could be said about the clinical work that is involved for the many different griefs that are experienced: the special problems for parents at the loss of a child, the death of a sibling, the needs for and difficulties of caring for bereaved children, grief in the elderly, disaster-related bereavements, and grief and bereavement counseling for the many other losses of life. Anticipatory grief should also be considered. Each of these bereavement situations needs to be evaluated to determine the specific needs of the individuals and families, whether or not counseling is required, and, if so, its goals and the form it should take.

It is clear that there is much supportive evidence indicating that bereavement counseling is effective, both as a preventive measure for bereaved people who are at high risk and as a therapeutic intervention. Yet, despite this, there is still neither adequate service development in many areas, with regard to provision of bereavement counseling services, nor evaluation of effectiveness where services do exist. Self-help and community support groups provide a very valuable resource in this context, but still many bereaved people who are in need of care do not receive it and may suffer unnecessarily as a consequence, both in the acute suffering of their loss and the pathology that arises subsequently.

For those who provide counseling, several themes must be borne in mind: Empathy, compassion, genuineness, and warmth are, as always, essential therapeutic components. Whatever model of counseling is applied, psychodynamic understandings are also vital, as are skill and a knowledge of loss and grief and their dynamics.

Transference themes that occur may reflect patterns of the bereaved's relationship with the deceased. There may be resentment that the counselor/therapist is there in place of the deceased, envy at his or her intact family, and attempts to use the therapist as a replacement figure to avoid the pain of loss or having to face other deprivations. All the aspects of grief are likely to appear, particularly with termination, where they may be used to facilitate further levels of the process of working through the grieving process.

Countertransference issues are likely to be particularly powerful, for all of us have experienced some loss, some separation pain, and are likely to reexperience it in our empathy and identification with those we care for. Some losses, perhaps those we particularly fear or dread, or have experienced, will evoke great pain and may lead to reactions of distancing or enmeshment as countertransference phenomena. It is particularly important that those involved in counseling bereaved people are sensitive to and knowledgeable about these issues, that they deal with their roles in terms that recognize their own as well as their patients' needs and vulnerabilities. It is critical that they carry out their work within professional support systems that can help them deal with such issues (e.g., supervision and case review).

It is also important that models do not become fixed: the only, the right, form of therapy. Most clinicians will acknowledge that their day-to-day work is eclectic and that there are at least some bereaved people who are not helped by the processes discussed here. More innovative approaches to the brief psychotherapy of bereavement – new and changing models with greater flexibility – may also need to be devised for those whose needs are not met by the existing frameworks (Hoey & Raphael, 1990).

Vaillant (1986) has pointed out how loss is not only associated with the painfulness of grief and yearning for our loved ones. There are also the richness of the internalizations of what we have lost, the memories, identifications, and other themes we take into ourselves that are part of human life and experience. The emotions of grief are often the most intensely painful and intolerable of our affective experiences. Yet we must all "know" loss at some time. The care others offer us, their comforting, consolation, and support, help us to tolerate the loss and to go on. Counseling should support these adaptive processes and their real and human outcomes and give courage to the bereaved for their present and their future.

PART VIII

Conclusions

29

Contemporary themes and controversies in bereavement research

MARGARET S. STROEBE,
ROBERT O. HANSSON,
AND WOLFGANG STROEBE

The *Handbook of Bereavement* has provided a comprehensive overview of current research on bereavement. The phenomenology of grief, distinctions between normal and pathological grief, and measurement and assessment techniques are described in considerable detail. The volume also brings into focus a wide variety of theoretical approaches that have been incorporated recently into bereavement research. It documents not only detrimental effects to mental and physical health but a much broader range of consequences associated with loss. It explores the relative vulnerability of different individuals and groups. Analyses also go beyond the consideration of marital bereavement to examine what is known about many different types of loss, including the special cases of AIDS survivors and of Holocaust survivors. Evaluations are provided regarding the availability and efficacy of many different types of support for bereaved persons, ranging from informal help to self-help groups to various counseling and therapy intervention programs.

Despite the length and scope of the volume, however, coverage still has been highly selective. We would have liked to have extended the discussion further to include, for example, comparisons with other types of loss or trauma, such as divorce. Also, as our authors have acknowledged throughout the volume, many questions remain unanswered. Finally, as the careful reader will have discerned, there are still disagreements and controversies between authors and some inconsistencies in results from one study to another.

In this concluding chapter we review theoretical, methodological, and empirical themes emerging from the contributions to this volume, identify continuing controversies and directions for future research, and highlight social and policy implications.

457

Theoretical developments

There have been significant advances from intra- to interpersonal and from clinical to biopsychosocial models of bereavement. There has also been some progress in using these theories to derive testable hypotheses, the results of which can, in turn, be integrated into the development of effective preventive and treatment strategies. We are still far from an integrative theory of grief and bereavement. However, as the contributions to this volume show, increased reference is now being made to theories from many disciplines, each of which contributes in unique ways to the understanding of bereavement phenomena.

To elaborate: Much research presented in the *Handbook* has been guided by theories, ranging from attachment theory, family systems theory, stress theory, life-span developmental theory, and personality theory to more reductionist physiological approaches. As a result of this advance, grief is now less likely to be treated as a purely intrapersonal phenomenon. Compare, for example, the classic formulation, based on psychoanalytic theory, of the symptomatology of grief by Lindemann (1944) with the much broader, multidimensional approaches presented in this volume. Throughout, interpersonal models are in evidence, taking into account the impact of such variables as social context, family context, and social support not only on affective but on many other cognitive and behavioral reactions.

Similarly, it seems evident now that a narrow interpretation of grief as a form of mental or physical illness or debility, or as a matter of clinical concern alone (which would fit into older conceptions within a medical or psychiatric framework), is no longer viable. Although Averill and Nunley (this volume) consider this possibility, it is apparent that the medical model of illness itself has changed. Medical science has increasingly incorporated psychosocial factors into models for the prevention and treatment of illness. This evolution is reflected in the growth of new areas of study, such as behavioral immunology and health psychology. Thus, it seems likely that the study of bereavement will be incorporated into an expanded biopsychosocial medical model (e.g., Engel, 1977; Averill & Nunley, this volume; Laudenslager, Boccia, & Reite, this volume).

An integration of knowledge into a grand theory of bereavement has not been achieved. Nevertheless, there are advantages to presenting the multiplicity of perspectives in this volume, rather than restricting scientific treatment to the viewpoint of a single discipline. Take, for example, the finding that widowers have higher mortality rates than widows, when compared with same-sex, nonbereaved controls. To explain this pattern, a psychologist would look for cognitive and behavioral response differences between the sexes, and would find them. A sociologist might analyze patterns of sex roles or male–female support systems, and find differences. A psychophysiologist might study sex hormones and identify their modulatory effect on immune effector cells. To limit explanations to those of a single discipline would preclude a full understanding of the phenomena of bereavement: As the *Handbook* chapters have shown, these are so complex that different levels of explanation are necessary for different phenomena (cf. Averill & Nunley, this volume).

The key question concerning theoretical developments, however, is whether they have increased our understanding of bereavement. In our judgment, the contributions to this volume have indeed advanced our understanding of a variety of phenomena. Theoretical formulations have been stated in ways that are empirically testable and results assessed. Thus, for example, empirical tests of the grief-work hypothesis, one of the oldest and most commonly accepted assumptions in the field, are reported (Kaminer & Lavie, this volume; W. Stroebe & Stroebe, this volume). The results of these investigations have implications for planning intervention, which the authors describe.

Encouraging though this development is, it is but a beginning. Although available theories account adequately for many observed phenomena of bereavement, explanations of other aspects are not so easy to derive. Thus, the chapters on AIDS survivors (Martin & Dean, this volume) and on Holocaust survivors (Kaminer & Lavie, this volume) raise a number of challenges to current understandings of bereavement. They demand that theoretical frameworks take into account the likelihood of chronic bereavement, multiple bereavement stresses, stigma and exclusion from supportive networks, the impact on a closed community system at increasing risk, the impact of personal life threat on bereavement reactions, and the inherent contradiction of a popular consensus (in both cases) regarding ameliorative effects of foreknowledge and the opportunity for emotional preparation. Similarly, Silverman and Worden's chapter (this volume) on childhood bereavement introduces special challenges, wherein a child loses not only a loved attachment figure but also a critical part of his or her heritage and developmental context.

Methodological issues

We have seen that there remain many concerns regarding the status of measurement and research design in the study of bereavement. This reflects, in part, a diversity of purpose across studies, as well as the methodological approaches characteristic of the various clinical and scientific disciplines conducting research. It also reflects a growing awareness of the complexity of the nature and experience of bereavement.

Measurement issues

Considerable effort has been devoted to conceptualizing and measuring the bereavement experience. Yet currently there is no standard approach to bereavement assessment, in either the clinical or research setting. It has been difficult, for example, to establish the validity of bereavement measures, as many levels of assessment (e.g., cognitive, affective, physiological, and social) appear to be involved and to change in relative importance over time. The discriminant validity of currently available instruments also remains in question, as the construct of grief itself overlaps considerably with related constructs, such as depression, physical health status, and mood state. In addition, there has been little effort to address the generalizability of measures across cultures or to extend the scope of bereavement assessments to the affected family system, whose stability and support functions may also be affected by the death of one of its members and whose grief reactions may be intricately interdependent.

Research design issues

Over the past decade, research designs also have become more rigorous and complex. The research represented in this volume reflects the wide variety of designs currently available. McCrae and Costa, for example, used a large probability sample, long-term, longitudinal data set to examine the course of recovery among the bereaved. They were able to measure the long-term effects of widowhood by comparing a pre- and postevent assessment on certain key variables, in a repeated measures analysis that controlled for initial differences between groups on key biographical variables. They were also able to avoid bereavement "priming," as respondents were not aware that widowhood was a variable of interest. A similar research strategy was available to Wortman, Silver, and Kessler (this volume), who were able to study large-scale representative samples as part of a multidisciplinary program. The large sample size, longitudinal design (including prebereavement), and variety of measures (including medical tests) should enable this latter study to answer many outstanding questions concerning coping and adjustment.

All of the longitudinal in-depth studies included in the volume used sophisticated, well-controlled designs and employed careful statistical analyses, thus improving on earlier methodology. Such designs permit control over biasing factors. For example, systematic, confounding differences between bereaved and nonbereaved samples can be controlled for by individual matching; sampling biases can be assessed and the social desirability bias of responses can be analyzed (cf. W. Stroebe & Stroebe, this volume).

Yet there remain concerns in the design of bereavement research (see W. Stroebe & Stroebe, 1987, for a more detailed discussion). Among the most critical of these are the problems of high subject attrition in longitudinal studies, varying degrees of appropriateness of control groups, and the difficulty of reconciling findings from large studies of probability samples (often involving only superficial measures of a limited number of variables) with findings of smaller studies (which may provide greater depth in assessment but risk using a non-representative sample).

A frequently overlooked concern is the failure to distinguish between main effects and interactions in the analysis of risk factors for poor outcome. For example, to make the statement that "social support helps buffer against the effects of bereavement," one has to have shown that bereaved people are relatively more helped by it than are nonbereaved. Similarly, to argue that "widows suffer greater depression after losing a spouse than widowers," one has to take into account the higher rates of depression for women in general.

Similarly, more care is needed in making inferences of causality. Again, to argue that social support helps the bereaved get over loss on the basis of the finding that the better adjusted have higher levels of social support than the worse off is not necessarily valid. Predisposing factors may jointly affect health outcome and the provision of support. Stylianos and Vachon (this volume) carefully consider the interaction of personality and social support; it is highly likely that certain personalities are not only better copers but also easier to provide with social support. Likewise, Gallagher and her colleagues (this volume), in their longitudinal design, were able to determine the direction of causality for the relationship that they found between mortality and social isolation (physical illness could lead to social isolation, or vice versa) by equating decedents and survivors on physical fitness.

Finally, an independent variable can easily be confounded with a measure of grief. Exemplary are coping variables and grief reactions; there is a very fine line between an adaptive coping strategy and low levels of grief symptomatology. To conclude that recovery is due to "positive coping strategies" when all that has been shown is that the more recovered dwell less on their loss or ruminate less is uninformative. Rumination is part and parcel of grieving. Similar cautions need to be made in drawing conclusions about self-esteem, which is closely related to depression, which, in turn, is part of grief.

Sophisticated designs and statistical techniques are now available that can overcome many of these problems. The empirical papers in this volume illustrate how these might be implemented.

Emerging themes, results, and controversies

In the process of editing this volume, it became evident that new issues of central concern are emerging in the bereavement field, that a number of controversies continue unabated, and that, although much has been learned, gaps in our knowledge remain. In the following pages, we select those issues that seem most critical.

The nature of grief

Individual and cultural heterogeneity. One of the major themes to emerge from this volume is that grief is not a simple, universal process, with a progression of fixed stages, each with its typical symptoms. It would do bereavement researchers an injustice to claim that grief is viewed in this way, for, beyond the search for "normal" or typical patterns of bereavement reactions (which must be an aim of any scientific endeavor), a major concern has been to understand individual differences in reactions to and coping with bereavement.

Indeed, many of the contributors to the volume have called for a greater understanding of the heterogeneity of individual responses to loss. As Weiss argues, there is much variability in the success with which individuals are ever able to come to terms with the painful memories, find ways to experience life again as enriching, and respond adequately to the demands of continuing social roles. Similarly, Wortman, Silver, and Kessler conclude that it is the meaning of loss to the individual that determines the nature and intensity of the grief response. Shuchter and Zisook point to individual differences in the effects of loss on diverse aspects concerning a person's future (identity change, knowledge of the self and world, insights into one's own coping, and so on). Middleton, Raphael, Martinek, and Misso, reviewing abnormal bereavement reactions, extend such reasoning to the complications of bereavement; the heterogenous nature of pathological grief is explored in great detail in their chapter. Finally, the papers that address the cultural context of bereavement (e.g., Averill & Nunley; Lopata; Raphael, Middleton, Martinek, & Misso; Rosenblatt) underline the diversity of "normal" grief reactions across cultures; what comprises normality (even "sanity") varies greatly across cultures. We need look no further than Averill and Nunley's example from Tahitian culture, in which bereavement responses are classified as symptoms of illness or fatigue, not as emotional signs.

The multidimensionality of bereavement reactions. A recurring theme throughout the *Handbook* concerns the multidimensional nature of responses to loss. Researchers have extended the study of grief beyond affective reactions to consider also a full range of behavioral and cognitive reactions, as exemplified in the chapters by Shuchter and Zisook and by Rubin. Also along these lines, Gallagher-Thompson and her colleagues argue that adjustment to bereavement is a multifactorial process, to the extent that indices of physical and mental health may yield different patterns. Lieberman indicates that these new extended perspectives need integration into our theoretical formulations, arguing that "traditional measures used in bereavement research (symptoms, vicissitudes of grief, and social adjustment) represent a homeostatic model in which the underlying assumption is that bereavement is a stressor that upsets the equilibrium of the person," a return to which is desirable. Such models are, in his view, not sensitive to important phenomena, that "loss has such powerful and highly individualized meaning to bereaved individuals that there is within each individual an unused, unrealized reservoir of personal potential." In our view, the contemporary perspectives included in this volume (e.g., those of Parkes and of Epstein) go far in the direction of specifying dynamic processes of change.

Other aspects of the concept of grief add to its complexity. Many contributors have argued that grief is not an emotion limited to negative affect, but that positive feelings and reactions are also present. Parkes, for example, spells this out in his theoretical analysis. It is also becoming well accepted, as Shuchter and Zisook put it succinctly, that "grief does not necessarily consume a person's whole existence . . . the bereaved can feel joy, peace, or happiness as oases amidst their sorrows." The work of Horowitz (e.g., 1976/1986) has extended understanding of such processes to the clinical field, examining the processes of denial and intrusion in reaction to traumatic loss.

"Stages" of grief. Much has been written on "stages" of grief. Most researchers would agree that these are to be taken only as general, flexible guidelines. However, Wortman, Silver, and Kessler argue that there are "stage theories" of grief, namely, those of Bowlby (e.g., 1980/1981) and Horowitz (1976/1986). Yet Bowlby's is a theory of attachment, Horowitz's one of stress, these concepts being the most central and critical for the prediction of outcome or adjustment. Reference to phasal changes in both theories are, as in earlier formulations, meant to be descriptive, not to be understood as set rules or prescriptions for where an individual ought to be in the "normal" grieving process (Shuchter & Zisook).

Bereavement and distress. Is intense emotional distress (grief) inevitable following a major loss? Wortman, Silver, and Kessler provocatively argue that it is not, and that this is one of a number of commonly held assumptions that bereavement researchers have claimed without adequate foundation. Most of the writers in the *Handbook*, however, would probably endorse the more moderate statement that distress is usual when there has been a bereavement (at least in Western cultures), rather than the extreme statement of inevitability. Empirical investigations are highly consistent in showing that distress is common in the weeks and months following bereavement, but that depression reaches levels of clinical magnitude in a much smaller proportion of bereaved persons. It is not necessarily considered pathological for people to show no (or low) distress in the early days of bereavement, and theoretical formulations included in the preceding chapters have suggested a variety of explanations, ranging from low attachment, early adjustment following an expected loss coupled, perhaps, with relief at the end of a long suffering, cultural norms guiding expression or precluding grief, initial shock, to the explanations of complicated, unresolved forms such as delayed or inhibited grief.

Because much focus in bereavement research in general, and in this volume in particular, has been on the maleffects of loss, it is important to remember that some people probably do not grieve intensely and that, as noted, loss of a close relationship can have positive consequences, which need not necessarily indicate pathology.

The universality of grief. A related question is whether grief is universal. Grief-like responses have been documented in very diverse societies (cf. the chapters by Averill & Nunley; Lopata; Rosenblatt) and across species (Laudenslager, Boccia, & Reite). On the other hand, manifestations of grief in different cultures (and from one primate group to another) have been shown to vary. Symptoms and phases of grief are shaped by cultural factors. Cultural factors have not yet been adequately accounted for, for example, in relation to pathological forms of grief. As Middleton, Raphael, Martinek, and Misso note, the cultural nature of relationships, bonds, and meaning influence patterns of response to loss.

We need, then, further systematic, scientific studies of differing patterns of reaction to loss, research that goes beyond the charting of mourning rites and rituals by anthropologists and ethnographers, on which so much of our knowledge has had to rely so far. Readers are referred to the recent work of the Norwegian anthropologist Unni Wikan (1988, 1990), whose insightful analysis of two Muslim societies explores in depth the experiences and expressions of grief in these cultures. Wikan's work is illustrative of a useful direction that research on this topic could follow.

The duration of grief and "recovery." How long does grief last? Is a calendar year sufficient, as the lay belief of many Western cultures specifies, to "get over" or "recover from" the loss of a loved one? Do researchers really believe that resolution of grief is achieved after a couple of years? Answers to these questions are likely to affect the perceived need for extended care for bereaved people.

At first glance, the contributors to this volume appear to disagree about the so-called duration of grief. Longitudinal studies (e.g., McCrae & Costa; W. Stroebe & Stroebe; Gallagher-Thompson et al.) and the review paper by Shuchter and Zisook document a course of gradual improvement toward recovery, and conclude that the majority, though not all, of bereaved persons adapt successfully after the first year or two. McCrae and Costa's data suggest a "resilience" among bereaved people. Silverman and Worden extend such conclusions to bereaved children, and argue that we should abandon the language of illness in association with bereavement. But this volume has also included, perhaps more extensively than ever before, research documenting the longer term adaptation of bereaved people, and these investigations (e.g., Hansson, Remondet, & Galusha; Kaminer & Lavie; Lopata) suggest the need for continued adjustments over a much longer period.

On closer inspection, these differences can be reconciled. First, a "return to baseline" reported for most of the bereaved by the majority of researchers after the first 2 years of bereavement does not mean a complete "resolution" of grief. The chapters by Rubin and by Weiss, for example, describe the well-nigh unbearable grief resulting from the violent death of a child and the whole lifetime of adjustment that may follow, even though, as Rubin notes, scores on mental and physical health measures may have declined to levels similar to those for the nonbereaved. In perhaps a mirror image of this phenomenon, Silverman and Worden, alongside their findings of good adjustment, point to a child's continuing need for a symbolic connection to a deceased parent.

It thus becomes evident that the concept of recovery needs careful specification. The contributors to this volume, notably Weiss and Shuchter and Zisook, cause us to reconsider what we mean by it: Recovery can no longer be understood simply as a return to baseline levels of functioning. Weiss, for example, asks whether bereaved persons ever "get over it," or whether we should substitute new terms, such as "adaptation," "accommodation," or even "degree of damage."

Second, different aspects of adjustment or recovery are in question. Ratings of health or well-being are more likely to return to baseline levels after the period of intense grief than are changes in life circumstances, such as financial concerns or shifts in the social network. The latter may continue to fluctuate or evolve, and may require adjustment and adaptation for many years to come. Or, as Kaminer and Lavie have shown, though a Holocaust survivor may appear to be functioning effectively to all outward appearances, inner scars left by the trauma and the multiple, chronic loss of loved ones may continue to influence coping in very subtle ways. Again, much depends on our definitions of recovery or resolution of grief.

Third, if the concern of the researcher is to identify persons at risk, then reports of continued depression and health problems are more likely than if one is studying the reaction of the "average" bereaved person (as in McCrae and Costa's large-scale investigation). Further, as McCrae and Costa acknowledge, selection factors may operate to exclude from study a "subset of individuals for whom widowhood is a source of significant and lasting psychosocial debility, culminating perhaps in institutionalization and premature mortality."

If these factors are taken into consideration, as they are in many of the chapters, the following conclusions can be reached: The majority of bereaved persons do cease to grieve intensely after a period of time, usually a year or two, but a minority continue to do so for longer. Some aspects of grief may never end for a proportion of otherwise normally adjusted bereaved individuals. Finally, if there has been strong attachment to a lost loved one, emotional involvement is likely to continue, even for a lifetime. Care programs and informal support need to understand these long-term consequences.

Grief reactions following different types of loss. One of the most fascinating controversies arising from this collection of chapters concerns what kinds of loss lead to grief. Is grief commonly and generally experienced following any type of loss, or is it unique to specific types of loss? Weiss argues that there are probably only four types of loss that lead adults to intense grief: loss of a pair bond, of a child, of a patient–professional transference bond, and of a persisting childhood attachment. On the other hand, both Parkes and Rosenblatt see close parallels in the grief reactions of those who have suffered the loss of a loved person with nondeath loss, such as loss of a limb or of a farm. Might the victims of the Holocaust or the Vietnamese boat people not experience a more generalized sense of grief that reflects the loss of countless individuals from family and community and the loss of homelands and heritage?

It is difficult to reconcile these positions. The disagreement seems to arise less from varying conceptions of grief than from differences in theoretical perspectives. Whereas Weiss draws his conclusions from assumptions of attachment theory, Parkes adopts a more cognitive approach, and Rosenblatt's interpretation follows from his symbolic interaction and family systems theory perspective. The question must remain open.

A related, and equally difficult, question concerns the intensity of grief reactions following different types of loss. Each of us probably has a subjective hierarchy about the relative effects of different types of bereavement:

Loss of a young spouse is "worse than" loss of an elderly partner, loss from a sudden, tragic accident harder to bear than one following a long and painful terminal illness. Research has helped identify subgroups of bereaved persons who are highly vulnerable to maleffects of loss, and we turn to this later. Here it should be noted that ranking types of bereavement according to relative grief reactions does not seem a useful exercise. Rather, it seems more profitable to identify particular reactions and special needs of the different types of bereavement, in order to increase the effectiveness of aid programs (cf. Lieberman). For example, the focus of Silverman and Worden on parental bereavement in childhood indicates reactions that may be particularly prominent in childhood loss: that children may have an accentuated feeling of being watched by the deceased, that they cling to and cherish his or her possessions but that, on the other hand, almost half would prefer not to talk about the deceased parent to their friends. Thus, in some important ways children's reactions may overlap with those of adults. In other important ways, though, they may diverge.

The consequences of bereavement

The impact of bereavement on health. Bereavement is associated, for most people, with intense suffering and increased risk for a variety of psychological and somatic complaints and illnesses. For a minority of the bereaved, there continues to be a high risk over longer periods, and there is evidence for an excess mortality rate among the bereaved.

There is considerable disagreement about the proportion of bereaved persons who suffer detrimental effects to their mental and/or physical health and about how many need professional help for psychological/physical ailments or illnesses. Middleton et al., for example, cite various percentages for depressive disorders from different empirical studies. Although it is not surprising that percentages vary according to specific measures, criteria used, individual sample characteristics, and so on, there is a further source of systematic bias that needs recognition: Estimates based on normal populations of the bereaved are likely to underestimate the frequency of health consequences; those of clinical populations are likely to overestimate them.

One of the most significant advances in the study of health consequences of bereavement is reflected in the contributions of Irwin and Pike, Kim and Jacobs, and Laudenslager, Boccia, and Reite. We are beginning to understand the physiological mechanisms that explain why and how an event external to the organism, such as bereavement, makes people ill. The connections are highly complex, and many aspects of the grief experience contribute to various and diverse physiological changes. Nevertheless, this work will lead to a better understanding of the types of illnesses to which bereaved people are particularly prone and enable medical intervention to be planned accordingly.

Outstanding research questions concern the relationship between mental and physical health consequences. Who, for example, becomes mentally and who physically debilitated by bereavement? Are those who suffer extreme grief the ones to become physically ill and even die? In general, the investigation of bereavement as stressor and the presence of somatic symptoms has been poorly researched (cf. Middleton, Raphael, Martinek, & Misso), although there is now sufficient evidence to show a connection. For example, almost a third of the widowed in the W. Stroebe and Stroebe study reported new illnesses in the 6-month period following loss, compared with only four out of sixty married persons for an equivalent period. Gallagher et al. also report poorer physical health in bereaved than in nonbereaved persons, after carefully controlling for factors known to influence health.

Differential vulnerability to health risks. Clinicians and researchers have made considerable progress in identifying those individuals most likely to suffer the extreme effects of bereavement (as Sanders's review shows). Grief does not affect all equally. Some persons and some classes of persons are at greater risk for poor outcomes. The factors involved range from internal characteristics or vulnerabilities that would be relatively complex to alter (e.g., a dependent personality, coping style, or poor prebereavement health status) to external influences that might be altered by societal efforts (e.g., social stigma surrounding the cause of death, as with AIDS deaths, ethnic barriers to social or formal support systems, the isolating effects of age or low socioeconomic status, or traditional sex roles that foster dependency on a husband and inhibit a widow's preparation and options for reintegration into occupational, social, or sexual relationships). Other factors fall between these two extremes, for instance, the nature of the relationship with the deceased and network strain. Those risk factors toward the external end of the dimension probably affect the most persons, and they are also the factors that society could do something about. They reflect the social issues, inequities, gaps, and oversights in the social system.

One of the most consistent patterns to emerge from the empirical studies (e.g., Gallagher-Thompson et al.; Lund et al.; W. Stroebe & Stroebe) is that a high level of distress early in bereavement is correlated with longer term complications. This result raises the question of the impact of predisposing factors – particularly personality factors – in outcome to bereavement. Middleton et al. provide one of the most detailed treatments of this issue. It is a critical one: Too little research has examined predispositional factors (with the notable exception of Parkes & Weiss, 1983), despite the fact that most bereavement theories predict personality-related differences in bereavement reactions. Preexisting risk factors do appear to be central to the development of pathological grief: Middleton et al. question the extent to which pathological reactions actually result from the loss event. The alternative hypothesis, a top priority for future research, is that in many instances the loss event may have exacerbated a preexisting disorder, adjustment problem, or personality structure.

Discrepancies are evident between empirical studies regarding the impact of various risk factors on outcome, although there seems considerable agreement regarding certain high-risk categories, for example, those following traumatic losses (including suicides, loss of a child, or multiple or disaster bereavements). Nevertheless, caution is needed in making generalizations about the impact of any one variable. For example, there has been a popular consensus regarding the ameliorative effects of foreknowledge and opportunity for emotional preparation before a death. Yet Martin and Dean's research with AIDS patients and their loved ones severely qualifies this claim.

A major discrepancy has appeared for the first time in this volume: Wortman et al. describe preliminary results which suggest that the bereaved of higher income, higher intelligence, and feelings of personal control and positive self-esteem are hit harder by the loss of a spouse. The studies of Hansson et al., Lopata, Lund, Caserta, and Dimond, and W. Stroebe and Stroebe contradict these patterns. Lopata, for example, describes educational level as one of the most important resources in adapting to widowhood. It remains to be seen whether Wortman et al. confirm their early results.

As indicated in the methodology section in this chapter, research on risk factors is particularly prone to a confusion of main effects with interactions. Future research needs to pay close attention to the question of whether results actually indicate that a particular variable is a high-risk factor specifically to bereaved persons, or whether it is not simply associated with poor health and well-being in the population at large.

The impact of coping variables on outcome. Another difficult question concerns coping styles or strategies that lead to good versus poor adjustment. There has been relatively little research on this topic thus far, but also it is very difficult to establish a cause–effect relationship of coping to intensity of symptomatology. For example, take the frequent result that highly distressed persons "cope" by ruminating and clinging to memories of the deceased, whereas low distress persons actively seek distraction. This tells us nothing about the impact of rumination on recovery from distress; the data are correlational.

Some contributors to this volume have begun to unravel such cause–effect sequences. In their ingenious study examining the dream content of

Holocaust survivors, for example, Kaminer and Lavie were able to show the impact of repression of memories as an adaptive coping mechanism. Longitudinal designs also enable one to control for initial differences in levels of distress, to establish the predictability of a coping strategy on subsequent levels (cf. W. Stroebe & Stroebe, this volume).

The examination of effective versus ineffective coping is a central research concern for the future. The empirical studies by Kaminer and Lavie and W. Stroebe and Stroebe have called into question one of the most fundamental beliefs about coping with bereavement, namely, the grief-work hypothesis. Is suppression of memories an alternative, effective strategy, as these investigations suggest, or is it essential, as Weiss argues, to try to develop a tolerance for memories of the deceased? Likewise, little is known about the use of defensive strategies in coping with the pain of grief. Shuchter and Zisook suggest that there is a need to "dose" or regulate the amount of feeling that is borne and divert the rest, perhaps through suppression. Rubin talks of the "staccato fluctuation between processes of attachment and detachment," which suggests a need for flexible coping strategies. Or how helpful is disclosure in coping with bereavement? Useful leads to follow here would be the work of Pennebaker (e.g., Pennebaker, Kiecolt-Glaser, & Glaser, 1988) on the disclosure of traumas and immune function.

Methodologically sophisticated techniques will be necessary to unravel these questions, but the examination of cognitive variables such as those suggested here promise breakthroughs in our understanding of the impact of bereavement.

Intervention

Many of the contributions to the volume address the question of intervention. Raphael, Middleton, Martinek, and Misso propose a model for counseling and therapy, appropriate for normal and pathological bereavement reactions. Stylianos and Vachon address the complexity of social support, its availability, and probable efficacy. Lieberman introduces and evaluates the more structured self-help groups that may be helpful to many bereaved persons. Parkes provides guidelines for how professionals and communities might develop interventions, and stresses the need for a sound knowledge of risk factors and methods of intervention.

Basic questions concern the effectiveness (do they work?) and the adequacy (has sufficient provision been made; do they reach those in need?) of social support and health service intervention. In answer to the first question, most of the contributors, including Middleton et al. in their general review, argue that there is much supportive evidence for the efficacy of support. Although this seems justified, more methodologically sound research is needed. Lieberman was able to find only a handful of empirical studies on the effectiveness of self-help groups, some of which reported negative results. Well-controlled studies of the effectiveness of professional intervention are also few, due in part to the ethical problem of assigning bereaved persons to "no-help" conditions. Such research can, though, be supplemented by investigations with animals. Laudenslager et al. provide remarkable insights from their studies on the role of social support, for example, on the impact of substitute attachment figures on the antibody levels of young primates.

Are support and intervention adequate in providing the needed relief of suffering? As the papers of Lopata and Rosenblatt suggest, informal social networks in the 1990s can no longer be assumed to provide adequate help. Family members, for instance, are no longer necessarily available when needed. Social networks cannot be taken for granted. Personal relationships may be problematic, they may change over the life span; and chronic health problems of old age may strain the family network to the limits of its capacity. Implications include a reduction in the quality of care and an increased likelihood of premature institutionalization (Hansson, Remondet, & Galusha, this volume).

More formal services must be provided to fulfill some of the former support functions of the family and close community. Such services are more available to the bereaved than was the case some years ago. Raphael et al. refer, for example, to the "powerful social movement of care" in recent years. For example, there has been a rapid growth of self-help groups (Lieberman, this volume). These supplement professional (and necessarily more bureaucratic) services and (economically) provide the opportunity for broader outreach opportunities and services (Raphael et al., this volume). Parkes emphasizes the usefulness of hospices and bereavement services in relieving suffering and reducing symptomatology for some, both before and after bereavement. Furthermore, increased public recognition of the problems of bereavement through the popular literature, nursing journals, and the like may help bereaved people to deal with their own grief and to show others how to help them. Not least, the publication *Omega: Journal of Death and Dying*, under the editorship of Robert Kastenbaum, has for years now been a source of information – for lay people and professionals alike – on a broad range of bereavement-related issues.

Many of the contributors identify specific reactions following different types of loss and a need for differential approaches to support. Consistent with this approach, specialized therapy and support programs have been founded in various countries to focus on particular subgroups, and more are needed. We have identified special needs of bereaved children, AIDS survivors, ethnic minorities, and those whose unique circumstances place them at particular risk. Very recently the voluntary agency in Britain,

Cruse-Bereavement Care, requested that the Department of Health form a Disasters Working Party to develop guidelines on meeting the social and psychological needs of those affected by disasters. This committee identified shortcomings in present support and detailed suggestions for planning care for survivors of disasters for the future, involving local government authorities and other professional bodies. Information is contained in the publication *Disasters: Planning for a Caring Response* (Government Printing Office Publication, 1991).

The model endorsed by contributors to this volume, and illustrated by the approach of the Disasters Working Party, is one of prevention. Apart from humanitarian reasons, carefully planned care reduces chronic and long-term demands on health and social services and the number of workdays lost through distress, anxiety, and sickness. Involved are all those in contact at the time of bereavement – physicians, clergy, nurses, social workers, and trained volunteers. Care needs to be based on knowledge of the bereavement experience, with attention paid to matching of deficits/needs/personal skills and resources with provision of various types of support (Hansson, Remondet, & Galusha, this volume).

Bereavement researchers have a role to play in contributing to the knowledge base, for example, in identifying why attempts to help may go wrong. Rosenblatt's work showed that a caregiver's perspective may violate the norms of the bereaved person's culture, be out of touch with what is common in the grief process, or be insensitive to the feelings and needs of the individual involved. He or she may be "pushed toward meanings that do not make sense, to difficulty with people whose support is important, or to intolerable levels of pain." Bereavement researchers also have the task of identifying and understanding the complexities of support during bereavement. To take a brief example, social support that is perceived as burdensome and responded to with anger and rejection may nevertheless be helpful.

Finally, to the question of whether we reach those in need. It has become evident from many of the chapters (e.g., Hansson, Remondet, & Galusha; Martin & Dean; Stylianos & Vachon) that those in most need may be among the least likely to seek, or even to be perceived as needing, help. For example, few would expect younger bereaved persons to be more vulnerable than older ones, who are already frail, yet much research, including studies of the mortality of bereavement (M. Stroebe & Stroebe, this volume), points to the former group as a high-risk one. Similarly, bereaved men who are severely grief-stricken are less likely than women to turn to others. As we saw, this was the subgroup of widowers who frequently refused to participate in the Tübingen study (W. Stroebe & Stroebe, this volume). Although they may prefer to cope alone and withdraw from others, the severity of their grief reaction indicates that intervention would be appropriate for this group. However, as this and other examples indicate, providing appropriate support for sufferers reluctant to accept it is no easy matter.

In diverse societies such as the United States, where there are many relatively unassimilated subpopulations, cultural barriers can impede social support or delivery of emergency or medical services to minority bereaved individuals; even members of cross-ethnic marriages may be constrained in their efforts to understand or support a partner's needs in grief (Rosenblatt, this volume). Social and bureaucratic resources need to develop aid programs for vulnerable, isolated, bereaved minority individuals (Lopata, this volume).

Social and policy change

We have already touched on a number of issues with implications for social and policy change, particularly in the last section in which gaps in intervention provision were identified. There are other critical areas where society fails to take sufficient care of the bereaved.

Great hardship is felt by bereaved people due to poverty. A number of chapters documented the reduced, and very low, incomes of widowed people and the social and health consequences of financial hardship, a fact that is borne out in a recent review of the economic consequences of widowhood (Holden & Smock, 1991). Despite changes over the past two decades in pension and social security policy in the United States that have sought specifically to improve the economic security of widows, the economic consequences of widowhood remain very high, as high for this subgroup as divorce. Hansson, Remondet, and Galusha (this volume) report secondary consequences of such financial hardship: that elderly widows were anxious to move into supportive, congregate housing, but that they were often also the ones least able to afford it. Instead, they are more likely to be institutionalized (McCrae & Costa, this volume). Holden and Smock (1991) suggest that insurance against potential earnings loss might be required. Furthermore, this should be effective at all ages, not just when survivors are elderly. Social policy intervention would be appropriate to implement such schemes.

By failing to ease financial burdens of bereaved persons, society escalates social and health problems. One of the hardest to bear, and the most frequent, is that of loneliness, which is brought forth in numerous forms and encompasses numerous components (Lopata, this volume). Financial problems hinder social interactions in many different ways. They force relocation and consequent loss of friends. They necessitate withdrawal from clubs and associations that would normally provide company and distraction. Again, humanitarian reasons apart, this ultimately places a greater burden on society, in that the natural resource of informal help is cut off.

We have argued for the provision of financial care. Throughout the volume, arguments have been made too for the provision of health care. The bereaved have elevated rates of mental and physical debilities and illnesses and should therefore be a target group for receiving medical aid, the objective being to prevent the occurrence of ailments by identifying high-risk subgroups and providing care and support. Yet, here, too, research knowledge needs application. Raphael et al. stress that health systems or other interacting systems need to ensure that their policies are facilitatory for bereaved people and do not increase distress or add to risk of disorder (e.g., recognition of the impact of viewing the body, compassionate leave from the workplace).

While endorsing the need for medical and financial aid programs, broader implications of provision of aid must also be considered. Averill and Nunley call attention not only to the positive but also some potentially negative consequences of incorporating grief into the health care system. Grief has increasingly been linked to adverse physiological and immunologic outcomes and to symptomatology associated with stress (Irwin & Pike, this volume; Kim & Jacobs, this volume; Laudenslager et al., this volume). If these findings cause grief to be seen as primarily a medical problem (within a medical treatment model), discounting the value of the "normal emotional process," the psychological benefits of the social process (including supportive social mourning practices, adaptive social roles assigned to the bereaved) might be diminished (Averill & Nunley, this volume). Along similar lines, Raphael et al. express ethical concerns about providing a therapeutic framework for what is, after all, a natural human experience.

Bereavement research implications

Concern for the bereaved extends beyond the boundaries of the clinical professions; at some point it touches every family, and it raises logistic and policy issues for the health and social service agencies of every community. Research on bereavement thus far has accomplished much, identifying and describing risk factors, physiological and psychological sequelae, patterns of societal response, and patterns of recovery. In addition, a variety of theoretical traditions have emerged relating the bereavement phenomenon to stress, emotions, and cognitive, social, and developmental-attachment processes. Progress has been made as well in developing educational and counseling strategies and in mobilizing professional and natural support systems to ease the transition through the grieving process. Yet, in each of these areas we have identified limits to our knowledge and shortcomings in the implementation of aid for the bereaved.

So what directions will bereavement research follow in the next decades? We can only pick up a few threads at this point in the volume, and we will select those that have been given little or no attention so far. We hope to see an expansion of research on the use and efficacy of pharmacological interventions for both the complications of bereavement (cf. Raphael et al., this volume) and for relieving the suffering of "normal" bereavement. Surprisingly, too little research on these topics has been done to merit a review chapter in this volume (Jacobs, personal communication). The topic is an important one, for opinions differ among bereavement researchers about the advisability of medication, and medical professionals frequently prescribe them (cf. W. Stroebe & Stroebe, 1987).

Bereavement research in "minority" groups is an emerging theme in many of the contributions to this volume. Such groups have special needs, as exemplified in the case of the handicapped. Handicapped people are strongly attached to and dependent on a smaller number of people than is the case in the general population. Bereavement for them is likely to be particularly harrowing if the relationship to the deceased was very close. Yet little is known about their reactions and support needs.

Bereavement research needs to keep abreast of change. For example, how do demographic changes affect the bereavement experience? The segment of the elderly population that is growing fastest is the "old-old," which will include the proportion of the elderly population that is widowed. These individuals are apt to be frailer than their counterparts of today, with lowered ability to manage finances, maintain social networks, and live independently. Gerontological research has much to offer the area of bereavement on these matters.

Contributions to the *Handbook* have shown the beginnings of an interest in the impact of bereavement not only on the individual most affected (spouse, parent, etc.) but on the small group, notably the family (Rosenblatt; Shuchter & Zisook). Family themes are a concern for the near future. Individual reactions are strongly molded by those of the family. Thus, the family may send messages to set aside grief following a SIDS death (Rubin, this volume) which "encourages the adoption of a facade of functioning but engenders resentment and isolation." Clearly, we need to understand the family context within which grief takes place, to extend counseling to the family (cf. Raphael et al., this volume), and to develop ways to measure and assess family reactions and their interplay (cf. Fairchild, Hansson, Vanzetti, & Howard, 1991).

Finally, the chapters in the *Handbook* have solved some controversies, while fueling or bringing others to light. Debate continues, for example, on the question of long-term debilities following childhood loss; on the necessity to retain ties with the deceased versus the need to disengage; on whether lowered self-esteem is symptomatic of normal or indicative of pathological grief. In contributing to debate on such topics, our hope is that the *Handbook* will be a significant contribution to the understanding of bereavement.

References

Ables, R. P. (Ed.). (1987). *Life-span perspectives and social psychology.* Hillsdale, NJ: Erlbaum.

Abraham, K. (1924). A short study of the development of the libido; viewed in the light of mental disorders. In K. Abraham, *Selected Papers on Psychoanalysis* (pp. 418–501). London: Hogarth Press.

Abramson, L. Y., Seligman, M. E. P., & Teasdale, J. D. (1978). Learned helplessness in humans: Critique and reformulation. *Journal of Abnormal Psychology, 87,* 49–74.

Achenbach, T. M., & Edelbrock, C. (1983). *Manual for the Child Behavior Checklist.* Burlington, VT: University of Vermont.

Ackerman, S. H., Keller, S. E., Schleifer, S. J., Shindledecker, R. D., Camerino, M., Hofer, M. A., Weiner, H., & Stein, M. (1988). Premature maternal separation and lymphocyte function. *Brain, Behavior, and Immunity, 2,* 161–165.

Acock, A. C., & Hurlbert, J. S. (1990). Social network analysis: A structural perspective for family studies. *Journal of Social and Personal Relationships, 7,* 245–264.

Ader, R. (1983). Developmental psychoneuroimmunology. *Developmental Psychobiology, 16,* 251–267.

Ader, R., Felten, D., & Cohen, N. (1990). Interactions between the brain and immune system. *Annual Review of Toxicology and Pharmacology, 30,* 561–602.

(1991). *Psychoneuroimmunology.* New York: Academic Press.

Ainsworth, M. D., & Eichberg, C. (1991). Effects on infant–mother attachments of mothers' unresolved loss of an attachment figure or other traumatic experience. In C. M. Parkes, J. Stevensen-Hinde, & P. Morris (Eds.), *Across the life cycle.* London: Tavistock.

Alarcon, R. D. (1984). Personality disorder as a pathogenic factor in bereavement. *Journal of Nervous and Mental Disease, 172,* 45–47.

Aldritch, C. K. (1963). The dying patient's grief. *Journal of the American Medical Association, 184,* 329–331.

Alexy W. D. (1982). Dimensions of psychological counselling that facilitate the grieving process of bereaved parents. *Journal of Consulting Psychology, 29*(5), 498–507.

Altemus, M., & Gold, P. W. (1990). Neuroendocrinology and psychiatric illness. *Frontiers of Neuroendocrinology, 11,* 238–265.

Anderson, R. (1974). Notes of a survivor. In S. B. Troop & W. A. Green (Eds.), *The patient, death and the family* (pp. 73–82). New York: Scribner.

Angell, M. (1985). Disease as a reflection of the psyche. *New England Journal of Medicine, 312,* 1570–1572.

Anthony, E. J., & Benedek, T. (Eds.). (1970). *Parenthood: Its psychology and psychopathology.* Boston: Little, Brown.

477

Antonovsky, A. (1979). *Health, stress, and coping.* San Francisco: Jossey-Bass.

(1987). *Unraveling the mystery of health: How people manage stress and stay well.* San Francisco: Jossey-Bass.

Antonucci, T. C. (1985). Personal characteristics, social support, and social behavior. In R. H. Binstock & E. Shanas (Eds.), *Handbook of aging and the social sciences* (2nd ed., pp. 94–128). New York: Van Nostrand Reinhold.

Antonucci, T. C., & Israel, B. A. (1986). Veridicality of social support: A comparison of principal and network members' responses. *Journal of Consulting and Clinical Psychology, 54*(4), 432–437.

Antze, P. (1976). The role of ideologies in peer psychotherapy organizations: Some theoretical considerations and three case studies. *Journal of Applied Behavioral Science, 12,* 323–346.

Aston-Jones, G., Foote, S. L., & Bloom, F. E. (1984). Anatomy and physiology of locus coeruleus neurons: functional implications. In M. G. Ziegler & C. R. Lake (Eds.), *Norepinephrine* (pp. 92–116). Baltimore: Williams & Wilkins.

Atchley, R. C. (1975). Dimensions of widowhood in later life. *The Gerontologist, 15,* 1976–1978.

Averill, J. R. (1968). Grief: Its nature and significance. *Psychological Bulletin, 70,* 721–748.

(1979). The functions of grief. In C. Izard (Ed.), *Emotions in personality and psychopathology* (pp. 339–368). New York: Plenum.

(1980). A constructivist view of emotion. In R. Plutchik & H. Kellerman (Eds.), *Emotion: Theory, research and experience. Vol. I. Theories of emotion* (pp. 305–339). New York: Academic Press.

(1990). Emotions as related to systems of behavior. In N. L. Stein, B. Leventhal, & T. Trabasso (Eds.), *Psychological and biological approaches to emotion* (pp. 385–404). Hillsdale, NJ: LEA.

(1991). Emotions as episodic dispositions, cognitive schemas, and transitory social roles: Steps toward an integrated theory of emotion. In D. Ozer, J. M. Healy, & A. J. Stewart (Eds.), *Perspectives in personality* (Vol. 3, pp. 139–167). London: Jessica Kingsley Publishers.

(1992). The structural bases of emotional behavior: A metatheoretical analysis. In M. S. Clark (Ed.), *Review of Personality and Social Psychology* (Vol. 13, pp. 1–24). Newbury Park, CA: Sage.

Averill, J. R., & Nunley, E. P. (1992). *Voyages of the heart: Living an emotionally creative life.* New York: The Free Press.

Averill, J. R., & Wisocki, P. A. (1981). Some observations on behavioral approaches to the treatment of grief among the elderly. In H. J. Sobel (Ed.), *Behavior theory and terminal care* (pp. 125–150). Cambridge, MA: Ballinger.

Avery, D. H., Osgood, T. B., Ishiki, D. M., Wilson, L. G., Kenny, M., & Dunner, D. L. (1985). The DST psychiatric outpatients with generalized anxiety disorder, panic disorder or primary affective disorder. *American Journal of Psychiatry, 142,* 844–848.

Backman, M. V. (1970). *American religions and the rise of Mormonism.* Salt Lake City, UT: Deseret Book Co.

Ball, J. F. (1977). Widow's grief: The impact of age and mode of death. *Omega, 7,* 307–333.

Baltes, P. B., Reese, H. W., & Lipsitt, L. P. (1980). Life-span developmental psychology. *Annual Review of Psychology, 31,* 65–110.

Bancroft, G. J., Shellam, G. R., & Chalmer J. E. (1981). Genetic influences on the augmentation of natural killer cells (NK) during murine cytomegalovirus infection: Correlation with patterns of resistance. *Journal of Immunology, 124,* 988–994.

Bankoff, E. A. (1986). Peer support for widows: Personal and structural characteristics related to its provision. In S. E. Hobfoll (Ed.), *Stress, social support and women* (pp. 207–222). Washington, DC: Hemisphere.

Barrett, C. J. (1978). Effectiveness of widows' groups in facilitating change. *Journal of Consulting and Clinical Psychology, 46,* 20–31.

Barrett, C. J., & Schneweis, K. M. (1980). An empirical search for stages of widowhood, *Omega, 11,* 97–105.

Barron, F. (1977). An ego strength scale which predicts response to psychotherapy. *Journal of Consulting Psycholology, 17,* 327–333.

Bartrop, R. W., Luckhurst, E., Lazarus, L., Kiloh, L. G., & Penny, R. (1977). Depressed lymphocyte function after bereavement. *Lancet, 97,* 834–836.

Batchelor, W. F. (1984). AIDS: A public health and psychological emergency. *American Psychologist, 39,* 1279–1283.

Bayart, F., Hayashi, K. T., Faull, K. F., Barchas, J. D., & Levine, S. (1990). Influence of maternal proximity on behavioral and physiological response to separation in infant rhesus monkeys (*Macaca mulatta*). *Behavioral Neuroscience, 104,* 98–107.

Beck, A. T. (1967). *Depression: Clinical, experimental and theoretical aspects.* New York: Hoeber.

Beck, A. T., Ward, C. H., Mendelson, M., Mock, J. E., & Erbaugh, J. (1961). An inventory for measuring depression. *Archives of General Psychiatry, 4,* 561–571.

Beckenridge, J., Gallagher, D., Thompson, L., & Peterson, J. (1986). Characteristic depressive symptoms of bereaved elders. *Journal of Gerontology, 41,* 163–168.

Begg, C. B., & Berlin, J. A. (1988). Publication bias: A problem in interpreting medical data. *Journal of the Royal Statistical Society, 151,* 419–463.

Bell, I. R., Jasnoski, M. L., Kagan, J., & King, D. S. (1990). Is allergic rhinitis more frequent in young adults with extreme shyness? A preliminary study. *Psychosomatic Medicine, 52,* 517–525.

Belle, D. (1988). Gender differences in the social moderators of stress. In R. C. Barnett, L. Beiner, & G. K. Baruch (Eds.), *Gender & stress* (pp. 257–277). New York: Free Press.

(Ed.). (1989). *Children's social networks and social supports.* New York: Wiley.

Benney, M., Weiss, R. S., Meyersohn, R., & Riesman, D. (1959). Christmas in an apartment hotel. *American Journal of Sociology, 65,* 233–340.

Berardo, F. M. (1970). Survivorship and social isolation: The case of the aged widower. *Family Coordinator, 19,* 11–25.

Berger, D. M. (1977). The survivor syndrome: A problem of nosology and treatment. *American Journal of Psychotherapy, 31,* 235–251.

Berger, P. L., & Kellner, H. (1964). Marriage and the construction of reality. *Diogenes, 46,* 1–24.

Berkman, L. F., & Syme, S. L. (1979). Social networks, host resistance, and mortality: A nine-year follow-up of Alameda County residents. *American Journal of Epidemiology, 109,* 186–204.

Berkowitz, D. A. (1977). On the reclaiming of denied affects in family therapy. *Family Process, 16,* 495–501.

Berlinsky, E. B., & Biller, H. B., (1982). *Parental death and psychological development.* Lexington, MA: D. C. Heath.

Bernard, A., & Boumsell, L. (1984). The clusters of differentiation (CD) defined by the First International Workshop on Human Leukocyte Differentiation Antigens. *Human Immunology, 11*, 1–10.

Bettelheim, B. (1943). Individual and mass behavior in extreme situations. *Journal of Abnormal and Social Psychology, 38*, 417–452.

Betz, B. J., & Thomas, C. B. (1979). Individual temperament as a predictor of health or premature disease. *Johns Hopkins Medical Journal, 144*, 81–89.

Billings A. G., & Moos, R. H. (1981). The role of coping responses and social resources in attenuating the stress of life events. *Journal of Behavioral Medicine, 4*, 139–157.

Biron, C. A., Byron, K. S., & Sullivan, J. L. (1989). Severe herpes virus infections in an adolescent without natural killer cells. *New England Journal of Medicine, 320*, 1732–1735.

Birtchnell, J. (1980). Women whose mothers died in childhood: An outcome study. *Psychological Medicine, 10*, 699–713.

Black, D., & Urbanowitz, M. (1987). Family intervention with bereaved children. *Journal of Clinical Psychology and Psychiatry, 28*, 467–476.

Blalock, E. (1989). A molecular basis for bidirectional communication between the immune and neuroendocrine systems. *Physiological Reviews, 69*, 1–32.

Blankfield, A. (1983). Grief and alcohol. *American Journal of Drug and Alcohol Abuse, 9*, 435–446.

Blatt, S., Chevron, E. S., Quinlan, D. M., & Wein, S. (1981). *The Assessment of qualitative and structural dimensions of object representations.* New Haven, CT: Yale University Press.

Bloch, S. (1991a). *Research studies into family grief.* Melbourne, Australia: University of Melbourne.

Bloch, S. (1991b). A systems approach to loss. *Australian and New Zealand Journal of Psychiatry, 25*(4), 471–480.

Boccia, M. L., Laudenslager, M. L., & Reite, M. L. (1988). Food distribution, dominance, and aggressive behaviors in bonnet macaques. *American Journal of Primatology, 16*, 123–130.

Boccia, M. L., Reite, M., Kaemingk, K., Held, P., & Laudenslager, M. L. (1989). Behavioral and autonomic responses to peer separation in pigtail macaque monkey infants. *Developmental Psychobiology, 22*, 447–461.

Boccia, M. L., Reite, M. L., & Laudenslager, M. L. (in press). Early social environment may alter the development of attachment and social support: Two case reports. *Infant Behavior and Development.*

Boccia, M. L., Scanlan, J. M., Laudenslager, M. L., Broussard, C. L., & Reite, M. L. (submitted). Presence of juvenile friends attenuate response to maternal separation in bonnet macaque infants. *Biological Psychiatry.*

Bojanovsky, J. (1980). Wann droht der Selbstmord bei Verwitweten? *Schweizer Archiv Neurologische Neurochirurgie und Psychiatrie, 127*, 99–103.

Bond, G. R., Borman, L. D., Bankoff, E., Lieberman, M. A., Daiter, S., & Videka, L. (1979, January/February). Mended Hearts: A self-help case study. *Social Policy*, 50–57.

Bornstein, P. E., Clayton, P. J., Halikas, J. A., Maurice, W. L., & Robins, E. (1973). The depression of widowhood after thirteen months. *British Journal Psychiatry, 122*, 561–566.

Botwinick, J. (1984). *Aging and behavior.* New York: Springer.

Bowlby, J. (1960). Grief and mourning in infancy and childhood. *Psychoanalytic Study of the Child, 15*, 9–52.

(1961). Processes of mourning. *International Journal of Psychoanalysis, 42,* 317–340.

(1963). Pathological mourning and childhood mourning. *Journal of American Psychoanalytic Association, 11,* 500–541.

(1969). *Attachment and loss. Vol. 1. Attachment.* London: Hogarth/New York: Basic Books.

(1973). *Attachment and loss. Vol. 2. Separation: Anxiety and anger.* New York: Basic Books/London: Hogarth.

(1980/1981). *Attachment and loss. Vol. 3. Loss: Sadness and depression.* London: Hogarth/New York: Basic Books/Harmondsworth: Penguin Books.

(1982). Attachment and loss: Retrospective and prospective. *American Journal of Orthopsychiatry, 52,* 664–678.

Bowlby, J., & Parkes, C. M. (1970). Separation and loss within the family. In E. J. Anthony & C. M. Koupernil (Eds.), *The child in his family.* New York: Wiley.

Bowling, A. (1988). Who dies after widow(er)hood? A discriminant analysis. *Omega, 19,* 135–153.

Bowling, A., & Benjamin, B. (1985). Mortality after bereavement: A follow-up study of a sample of elderly widowed people. *Biology and Society, 2,* 197–203.

Bowling, A., & Charlton, J. (1987). Risk factors for mortality after bereavement: A logistic regression analysis. *Journal of the Royal College of General Practitioners, 37,* 551–554.

Bradburn, N. M. (1969). *The structure of psychological well-being.* Chicago: Aldine.

Breckenridge, J. N., Gallagher, D., Thompson, L. W., & Peterson, J. (1986). Characteristic depressive symptoms of bereaved elders. *Journal of Gerontology, 41,* 163–168.

Breese, G. R., Smith, R. D., Mueller, R. A., Howard, J. L., Prange, A. J., & Lipton, M. A. (1973). Induction of adrenal catecholamine synthesizing enzymes following mother–infant separation. *Nature, 246,* 94–96.

Brenner, M. H. (1973). *Mental illness and the economy.* Cambridge, MA: Harvard University Press.

Breznitz, S. (Ed.). (1983). *The denial of stress.* New York: International Universities Press.

Brickman, P., Coates, D., & Janoff-Bulman, R. (1978). Lottery winners and accident victims: Is happinese relative? *Journal of Personality and Social Psychology, 36,* 917–927.

Bright, R. (1986). *Grieving: A handbook for those who care.* St. Louis, MO: Magna Music Batan Music Inc.

Brody, E. M. (1985). Parent care as a normative family stress. *Gerontologist, 25,* 19–29.

(1990). *Women in the middle: Their parent care years.* New York: Springer.

Brown, B. B. (1978). Social and psychological correlates of help-seeking behavior among urban adults. *American Journal of Community Psychology, 6,* 425–439.

Brown, G. W., & Harris, T. O. (1978). *Social origins of depression: A study of psychiatric disorder in women.* London: Tavistock.

(1989). *Life events and illness* (pp. 1–35). London: Guilford.

Brown, G. W., Harris, T. O., & Bifulco, A. (1986). Long term effects of early loss of parent. In M. Rutter, C. E. Izard, & P. Read (Eds.), *Depression in young people: Developmental and clinical perspectives* (pp. 251–297). New York: Guilford.

Brown, J. T., & Stoudemire, G. A. (1983). Normal and pathological grief. *Journal of the American Medical Association, 250,* 378–382.

Brown, S. D., & Heath, H. (1984). Coping with critical life events: An integrative cognitive–behavioral model for research and practice. In S. D. Brown & R. W.

Lent (Eds.), *Handbook of counseling psychology* (pp. 545–578). New York: Wiley.

Bruce, M., Kim, K., Leaf, P., & Jacobs, S. (1990). Depressive episodes and dysphoria resulting from conjugal bereavement in a prospective community sample. *American Journal of Psychiatry, 147,* 608–611.

Bukowski, J. F., Warner, J. F., Dennert, G., & Welsh, R. M. (1985). Adoptive transfer studies demonstrating the antiviral affect of natural killer cells in vivo. *Journal of Experimental Medicine, 131,* 1531–1538.

Bulman, R. J., & Wortman, C. B. (1977). Attributions of blame and coping in the "real world": Severe accident victims react to their lot. *Journal of Personality and Social Psychology, 35,* 351–363.

Bumpass, L., Sweet, J., & Martin, T. (1990). Changing patterns of remarriage. *Journal of Marriage and the Family, 52,* 747–756.

Bunch, J. (1972). Recent bereavement in relation to suicide. *Journal of Psychosomatic Research, 16,* 361–366.

Burks, V. K., Lund, D. A., Gregg, C. H., & Bluhm, H. P. (1988). Bereavement and remarriage for older adults. *Death Studies, 12,* 51–60.

Buss, T. F., & Redburn, F. S. (1983). *Mass unemployment: Plant closings and community mental health.* Beverly Hills, CA: Sage.

Byrne, D. (1961). The repression-sensitization scale: Rational reliability and validity. *Journal of Personality, 29,* 334–349.

Byrne, G., & Raphael, B. (1991, March). *A longitudinal study of bereavement in elderly men.* Proceedings of the 14th annual meeting of the American Psychiatric Association. New Orleans, LA.

Cain, A. C. (1972). *Survivors of suicide.* Springfield, IL: Charles C. Thomas.

Cain, A. C., & Cain, B. S. (1964). On replacing a child. *Journal of the American Academy of Child Psychiatry, 3,* 443–456.

Caine, N., & Reite, M. (1981). The influence of peer contact upon physiological response to separation. *American Journal of Primatology, 1,* 271–276.

Calabrese, J. R., Kling, A., & Gold, P. W. (1987). Alteration in immunocompetence during stress, bereavement, and depression: Focus on neuroendocrine regulation. *American Journal of Psychiatry, 144,* 1123–1134.

Cameron, J., & Parkes, C. M. (1983). Terminal care: Evaluation of effects on surviving family of care before and after bereavement. *Postgraduate Medical Journal, 59,* 73–78.

Cameron, O. F., Lee M. A., Curtis, G. C., & McCann, D. S. (1987). Endocrine and physiological changes during spontaneous panic attacks. *Psychoneuroendocrinology, 12,* 321–331.

Campbell, T. L. (1986). Family's impact on health: A critical review. *Family Systems Medicine, 4,* 135–328.

Cannon, W. B. (1939). *The wisdom of the body.* New York: Norton.

Capitanio, J. P., Rasmussen, K. L. R., Snyder, D. S., Laudenslager, M. L., & Reite, M. L. (1985). Long-term follow-up of previously separated pigtail macaques: Group and individual differences in response to novel situations. *Journal of Child Psychology and Psychiatry, 27,* 531–538.

Capitanio, J. P., & Reite, M. L. (1985). The roles of early separation experience and prior familiarity in the social relations of pigtail macaques: A descriptive multivariate study. *Primates, 25,* 475–484.

Caplan, G. (1961). *An approach to community mental health.* London: Tavistock.

Cappell, R., Gregoire, F., Thiry, L., & Sprecher, S. (1978). Antibody and cell mediated immunity to herpes simplex virus in psychotic depression. *Journal of Clinical Psychiatry, 39,* 266–268.

Carey, R. G. (1977). The widowed: A year later. *Journal of Counseling Psychology, 24,* 125–131.

(1979). Weathering widowhood: Problems and adjustment of the widowed during the first year. *Omega, 10,* 163–174.

Carey, W. B. (1990). Temperament risk factors in children: A conference report. *Developmental and Behavioral Pediatrics, 11,* 28–34.

Carmil, D., & Carel, R. S. (1986). Emotional distress and satisfaction in life among Holocaust survivors – A community study of survivors and controls. *Psychological Medicine, 16,* 1411–1419.

Carpenter, B. N. (in press). *Personal coping: Theory, research, and application.* New York: Praeger.

Carr, D. B., Sheehan, D. V., Surman, O. S., Coleman, J. H., Greenblatt, D. J., Heninger, G. R., Jones, K. J., Levine, P. H., & Watkins, W. D. (1986). Neuroendocrine correlates of lactate induced anxiety and their response to chronic alprazolam therapy. *American Journal of Psychiatry, 143,* 1087–1093.

Carroll, B. J., Feinberg, M., Greden, J., Tarika, J., Albala, A. A., Haskett, R. F., James, N. M., Kronfol, Z., Lohr, N., Steiner, M., de Vigne, J. P., & Young, E. (1981). A specific laboratory test for the diagnosis of melancholia. *Archives of General Psychiatry, 38,* 15–22.

Carson, S. W., Halbreich, U., Yeh, C. M., & Goldstein, S. (1988). Altered plasma dexamethasone and cortisol suppressibility in patients with panic disorders. *Biologic Psychiatry, 24,* 56–62.

Carter, L. A., Scott, A. F., & Martyna, W. (1976). *Women and men: Changing roles, relationships and perceptions.* New York: Aspen Institute for Humanistic Studies.

Caserta, M. S., & Lund, D. A. (1992). Bereaved older adults who seek early professional help. *Death Studies, 16,* 17–30.

Caserta, M. S., Lund, D. A., & Dimond, M. F. (1985). Assessing interviewer effects in a longitudinal study of bereaved elderly adults. *Journal of Gerontology, 40,* 637–640.

(1989). Older widows' early bereavement adjustments. *Journal of Women & Aging, 1*(4), 5–27.

(1990). Understanding the context of perceived health ratings: The case of spousal bereavement in later life. *Journal of Aging Studies, 4,* 231–243.

Caserta, M. S., Van Pelt, J., & Lund, D. A. (1989). Advice on the adjustment to loss from bereaved older adults: An examination of resources and outcomes. In D. A. Lund (Ed.), *Older bereaved spouses: Research with practical applications* (pp. 123–133). New York: Taylor & Francis/Hemisphere.

Caspi-Yavin, Y. (1988). *Coping and outcome in war bereaved Israeli parents.* Unpublished master's thesis, University of Haifa (Hebrew).

Cassileth, B. R., Lusk, E. J., Strouse, T. B., Miller, D. S., Brown, L. L., Cross, P. A., & Tenaglia, A. N. (1984). Psychosocial status in chronic illness: A comparative analysis of six diagnostic groups. *New England Journal of Medicine, 311,* 506–511.

Cattell, R. B., Eber, H. W., & Tatsuoka, M. M. (1970). *Handbook for the 16 Personality Factor Questionnaire.* Champaign, IL: Institute for Personality and Testing.

Centers for Disease Control (1990a, September). *HIV/AIDS surveillance report.* Atlanta.

(1990b, December). *HIV/AIDS surveillance report.* Atlanta.

Chambers, W. N., & Reiser, M. F. (1953). Emotional stress in the precipitation of congestive heart failure. *Psychosomatic Medicine, 15,* 38–60.

Charney, D. S., Woods, S. W., Goodman, W. K., & Heninger, G. R. (1987). Neurobiologic mechanisms of panic anxiety: Biochemical and behavioral correlates of yohimbine-induced panic attacks. *American Journal of Psychiatry, 144,* 1030–1036.

Chesler, M. A., & Barbarin, O. A. (1984). Difficulties of providing help in a crisis: Relationships between parents of children with cancer and their friends. *Journal of Social Issues, 40*(4), 113–134.

Chevan, A., & Korson, H. (1972). The widowed who live alone: An examination of social and demographic factors. *Social Forces, 51,* 5–53.

Chodoff, P. (1970). The German concentration camp as a psychological stress. *Archives of General Psychiatry, 22,* 78–87.

Chodorow, N. (1978). *The reproduction of mothering: Psychoanalysis and the sociology of gender.* Berkeley: University of California Press.

Cichetti, D. (1984). The emergence of developmental psychopathology. *Child Development, 55,* 1–7.

Ciocco, A. (1940). On mortality in husbands and wives. *Human Biology, 12,* 508–531.

Clayton, P. J. (1974). Mortality and morbidity in the first year of bereavement. *Archives of General Psychiatry, 30,* 747–750.

(1975). The effect of living alone on bereavement symptoms. *American Journal of Psychiatry, 132,* 133–137.

(1979). The sequelae and nonsequelae of conjugal bereavement. *American Journal of Psychiatry, 136,* 1530–1534.

(1982). Bereavement. In E. S. Paykel (Ed.), *Handbook of Affective Disorders* (pp. 403–415). London: Churchill Livingstone.

(1990). Bereavement and depression. *Journal of Clinical Psychiatry, 51,* 34–40.

Clayton, P. J., & Darvish, H. S. (1979). Course of depressive symptoms following the stress of bereavement. In J. E. Barrett, R. M. Rose, & G. L. Klerman (Eds.), *Stress and mental disorder* (pp. 121–136). New York: Raven Press.

Clayton, P., Desmarais, L., & Winokur, G. (1968). A study of normal bereavement. *American Journal of Psychiatry, 125,* 168–178.

Clayton, P. J., Halikas, J. A., & Maurice, W. L. (1972). The depression of widowhood. *British Journal of Psychiatry, 120,* 71–76.

Coates, D., Wortman, C. B., & Abbey, A. (1979). Reactions to victims. In I. H. Frieze, D. Bar-Tal, & J. S. Carroll (Eds.), *New approaches to social problems* (pp. 21–52). San Francisco: Jossey-Bass.

Cochran, L., & Claspell, M. (1987). *The meaning of grief: A dramaturgical approach to understanding emotion.* New York: Greenwood.

Coe, C. L., Cassayre, P., Levine, S., & Rosenberg, L. T. (1988a). Effects of age, sex, and psychological disturbance on immunoglobulin levels in the squirrel monkey. *Developmental Psychobiology, 21,* 161–175.

Coe, C. L., Lubach, G. R., Ershler, W. B., & Klopp, R. G. (1989). Influence of early rearing on lymphocyte proliferation in juvenile rhesus monkeys. *Brain, Behavior, and Immunity, 3,* 47–60.

Coe, C. L., Rosenberg, L. T., Fischer, M., & Levine, S. (1987). Psychological factors capable of preventing the inhibition of antibody responses in separated infant monkeys. *Child Development, 58,* 1420–1430.

Coe, C. L., Rosenberg, L. T., & Levine, S. (1988b). Effect of maternal separation on the complement system and antibody responses in infant primates. *International Journal of Neuroscience, 40,* 289–302.

(1988c). Prolonged effect of psychological disturbance on macrophage chemiluminescence in the squirrel monkey. *Brain, Behavior, and Immunity, 2,* 151–160.

Coe, C. L., Weiner, S. G., Rosenberg, L. T., & Levine, S. (1985). Endocrine and immune responses to separation and maternal loss in nonhuman primates. In M. L. Reite & T. Field (Eds.), *The psychobiology of attachment and separation* (pp. 163–200). New York: Academic Press.

Coffey, R. G., & Hadden, J. W. (1985). Neurotransmitters, hormones, and cyclic nucleotides in lymphocyte actions. *Federation Proceedings, 44,* 112–117.

Cohen, A. (Ed.). (1974). *The Soncino Chumash.* London: Soncino Press.

Cohen, J. J. (1985). Stress and the human immune response: A critical review. *Journal of Burn Care and Rehabilitation, 6,* 167–173.

Cohen, J. J., & Crnic, L. S. (1982). Glucocorticoids, stress and the immune response. In D. R. Webb (Ed.), *Immunopharmacology and the regulation of leukocyte function* (pp. 61–91). New York: Marcel Dekker.

(1984). Behavior, stress, and lymphocyte recirculation. In E. L. Cooper (Ed.), *Stress, aging, and immunity* (pp. 73–80). New York: Marcel Dekker.

Cohen, S. (1988). Psychosocial models of the role of social support in the etiology of physical disease. *Health Psychology, 7,* 269–297.

Cohen, S., & McKay, G. (1984). Interpersonal relationships as buffers of the impact of psychological stress on health. In A. Baum, J. E. Singer, & S. E. Taylor (Eds.), *Handbook of psychology and health* (pp. 253–267). Hillsdale, NJ: Erlbaum.

Cohen, S., & Wills, T. A. (1985). Stress, social support, and the buffering hypothesis. *Psychological Bulletin, 98,* 310–357.

Cohler, B. J., & Grunebaum, H. U. (1981). *Mothers, grandmothers and daughters: Personality and child-care in three generation families.* New York: Wiley.

Cohn, M. (1985). What are the "must" elements of immune responsiveness? In R. Guillemin, M. Cohn, & T. Melnechuk (Eds.), *Neural modulation of immunity* (pp. 3–25). New York: Raven Press.

Comstock, G., & Markush, R. L. (1986). Further comments on problems in death certification. *American Journal of Epidemiology, 124,* 180–181.

Constantino, R. E. (1988). Comparison of two group interventions for the bereaved. *Image, 20*(2), 83–87.

Cornoni-Huntley, J., Barbano, H. E., Brody, J. A., Cohen, B., Feldman, J. J., Kleinman, J. C., & Madans, J. (1983). National health and nutrition examination I – Epidemiologic followup survey, *Public Health Reports, 98,* 245–251.

Coser, L. (1974). *Greedy institutions.* New York: Free Press.

Costa, P. T., Jr., & McCrae, R. R. (1980). Influence of extraversion and neuroticism on subjective well-being: Happy and unhappy people. *Journal of Personality and Social Psychology, 38,* 668–678.

(1984). Personality as a lifelong determinant of well-being. In C. Malatesta & C. Izard (Eds.), *Affective processes in adult development and aging* (pp. 141–157). Beverly Hills, CA: Sage.

(1985a). Hypochondriasis, neuroticism, and aging: When are somatic complaints unfounded? *American Psychologist, 40,* 19–28.

(1985b). *The NEO Personality Inventory manual.* Odessa, FL: Psychological Assessment Resources.

(1986). Cross-sectional studies of personality in a national sample: 1. Development and validation of survey measures. *Psychology and Aging, 1,* 140–143.

Costa, P. T., Jr., McCare, R. R., & Zonderman, A. B. (1987a). Environmental and dispositional influences on well-being: Longitudinal followup of an American national sample. *British Journal of Psychology, 78,* 299–306.

Costa, P. T., Jr., Zonderman, A. B., & McCrae, R. R. (1985). Longitudinal course of social support among men in the Baltimore Longitudinal Study of Aging. In I. Sarason & B. R. Sarason (Eds.), *Social support: Theory, research, and applications* (pp. 187–154). The Hague, The Netherlands: Nijhoff.

Costa, P. T., Jr., Zonderman, A. B., McCrae, R. R., Cornoni-Huntley, J., Locke, B. Z., & Barbano, H. E. (1987b). Longitudinal analyses of psychological well-being in a national sample: Stability of mean levels. *Journal of Gerontology, 42,* 50–55.

Cox, P. R., & Ford, J. R. (1964). The mortality of widows shortly after widowhood. *Lancet, 1,* 163–164.

Cox, R. (1970). *Youth into maturity.* New York: Mental Health Materials Center.

Craig, Y. (1977). The bereavement of parents and their search for meaning. *British Journal of Social Work, 7*(1), 41–54.

Crook, T., & Eliot, J. (1980). Parental death during childhood and adult depression: A critical review of the literature. *Psychological Bulletin, 87,* 252–259.

Csikszentmihalyi, M., & Rochberg-Halton, E. (1981). *The meaning of things: Domestic symbols and the self.* San Francisco: Jossey-Bass.

Cumming, E., & Henry, W. E. (1961). *Growing old.* New York: Basic Books.

Cunnick, J. E., Lysle, D. T., Kucinski, B. J., & Rabin, B. S. (1990). Evidence that shock-induced immune suppression is mediated by adrenal hormones and peripheral B-adrenergic receptors. *Pharmacology Biochemistry and Behavior, 36,* 645–651.

Cupps, T. R., & Fauci, A. S. (1982). Corticosteroid-mediated immunoregulation in man. *Immunological Reviews, 65,* 133–155.

Dakof, G. A., & Taylor, S. E. (1990). Victims' perceptions of social support: What is helpful from whom? *Journal of Personality and Social Psychology, 58,* 80–89.

Danieli, Y. (1982). Confronting the unimaginable: Psychotherapists' reaction to victims of the Nazi Holocaust. In J. Wilson, Z. Harel, & B. Kahana (Eds.), *Human adaptation to extreme stress. From Holocaust to Vietnam* (pp. 219–237). New York: Plenum.

Darko, D. F., Gillin, J. C., Bulloch, S. C., Golshan, S., Tasevska, Z., & Hamburger, R. N. (1988). Immune cells and the hypothalamic–pituitary axis in major depression. *Psychiatry Research, 25,* 173–179.

Das, M., & Berrios, G. E. (1984). Dexamethasone suppression test in acute grief reaction. *Acta Psychiatrica Scandinavica, 70,* 278–281.

Davidson, S. (1981). Clinical and psychotherapeutic experience with survivors and their families. *Family Physician, 10,* 313–321.

Dean, L., Hall, W. E., & Martin, J. L. (1988). Chronic and intermittent AIDS-related bereavement in a panel of homosexual men in New York City. *Journal of Palliative Care, 4*(4), 54–57.

Dean, L., Wu, S., & Martin, J. L. (1992). Trends in violence and discrimination against gay men in New York City, 1984 to 1990. In G. M. Herek & K. T. Berrill (Eds.), *Hate crimes: Confronting violence against lesbians and gay men* (pp. 46–64). Newbury Park, CA: Sage.

De La Fuente, J., & Rosenbaum, A. (1981). Prolactin in psychiatry. *American Journal of Psychiatry, 138,* 1154–1160.

Demi, A. S. (1978). *Adjustment of widows after a sudden death: Suicide and non-suicide widows compared.* San Francisco: University of California Library, San Francisco Medical Center.

Depue, R. A., & Monroe, S. M. (1986). Conceptualization and measurement of human disorder in life stress research: The problem of chronic disturbance. *Psychological Bulletin, 99,* 36–51.

Derogatis, L. (1977a). *Brief symptom inventory: Administration, scoring, and procedures manual.* Baltimore: Johns Hopkins University, School of Medicine Clinical Psychometrics Unit.

——— (1977b). *The SCL-90 Manual F: Scoring, administration, and procedures for the SCL-90.* Baltimore: Johns Hopkins University, School of Medicine, Clinical Psychometrics Unit.

Derogatis, L. R., & Spencer, M. S. (1982). *Brief-symptom inventory: Administration, scoring, and procedures manual.* Baltimore: Clinical Psychometric Research.

Deutsch, H. (1937). Absence of grief. *Psychoanalytic Quarterly, 6,* 12–22.

DeVaul, R. A., Zisook, S., Faschingbauer, T. R. (1979). Clinical aspects of grief and bereavement. *Primary Care, 6,* 391–402.

Dewey, J. (1895). The theory of emotion. II. The significance of emotions. *Psychological Review, 2,* 13–32.

Diagnostic and statistical manual of mental disorders (3rd ed.). (1980). Washington, DC: American Psychiatric Association.

Dichterman, D. (1989). *Personality and interpersonal history and their relationship to long-term outcome to child loss in Israel.* Unpublished master's thesis. University of Haifa (Hebrew).

Dietrich, D. R., & Shabad, P. C. (1989). *The problem of loss and mourning.* Madison, CT: International Universities Press.

Dimond, M. F., Lund, D. A., & Caserta, M. S. (1987). The role of social support in the first two years of bereavement in an elderly sample. *The Gerontologist, 27,* 599–604.

Dimsdale, J. E. (1974). The coping behavior of Nazi concentration camp survivors. *American Journal of Psychiatry, 131,* 792–797.

Dinarello, C. A., & Mier, J. W. (1987). Medical intelligence: Current concepts: Lymphokines. *New England Journal of Medicine, 317*(15), 940–945.

Dohrenwend, B. P., Shrout, P. E., Egri, G., & Mendelsohn, F. S. (1980). Nonspecific psychological distress and other dimensions of psychopathology. *Archives of General Psychiatry, 37,* 1229–1236.

Dor-Shav, W. K. (1978). On the long term effect of concentration camp internment of Nazi victims: 25 years later. *Journal of Consulting and Clinical Psychology, 46,* 1–11.

Downey, G., Silver, R. C., & Wortman, C. B. (1990). Reconsidering the attribution-adjustment relation following a major negative event: Coping with the loss of a child. *Journal of Personality and Social Psychology, 59,* 925–940.

Dunkel-Schetter, C. (1984). Social support and cancer: Findings based on patient interviews and their implications. *Journal of Social Issues, 40*(4), 77–98.

Dunn, A. J. (1990). Interleukin-1 as a stimulator of hormone secretion. *Progress in Neuroendocrinimmunology, 3,* 26–34.

Dunn, J., & Plomin, R. (1990). *Separate lives: Why siblings are so different.* New York: Basic Books.

Dupuy, H. J. (1978, October). *Self-representations of general psychological well-being of American adults.* Paper presented at meeting of the American Public Health Association, Los Angeles.

Duran, A., Turner, C. W., & Lund, D. A. (1989). Social support, perceived stress, and depression following the death of a spouse in later life. In D. A. Lund (Ed.), *Older bereaved spouses: Research with practical applications* (pp. 69–78). New York: Taylor & Francis/Hemisphere.

Durkheim, E. (1897/1951). *Suicide: A study in sociology.* Glencoe, IL: Free Press.
 (1915). *The elementary forms of religious life.* New York: Macmillan.
Eaton, W., Sigal, J., & Weinfield, M. (1982). Impairment in Holocaust survivors after 33 years: Data from an unbiased community sample. *American Journal of Psychiatry, 139,* 773–777.
Eckenrode, J., & Gore, S. (1981). Stressful events and social supports: The significance of context. In B. Gottlieb (Ed.), *Social networks and social support* (pp. 43–68). New York: Sage.
Egbert, L. D., Battit, G. E., Welch, L. E., & Bartlett, M. K. (1964). Reduction of post-operative pain by encouragement and instruction of patients. *New England Journal of Medicine, 270,* 825–827.
Eggert, D. (1983). *Eysenck-Persönlichkeits-Inventar.* Göttingen, West Germany: Hogrefe.
Eisenberg, L. (1989). Public policy: Risk factor or remedy? American Academy of Child and Adolescent Psychiatry, P.S.A.P. Prevention Monograph, chapter 4, pp. 97–124.
Eisenbruch, M. (1984a, September). Cross-cultural aspects of bereavement. I. A conceptual framework for comparative analysis. *Culture, Medicine and Psychiatry, 8*(3), 283–309.
 (1984b, December). Cross-cultural aspects of bereavement. II. Ethnic and cultural variations in the development of bereavement practices. *Culture, Medicine and Psychiatry, 8*(4), 315–347.
Eitinger, L. (1974). Coping with aggression. *Mental Health and Society, 5,* 297–301.
Ekblom, B. (1963). Significance of psychosocial factors with regard to risk of death among elderly persons. *Acta Psychiatrica Scandinavica, 39,* 627–633.
Ekerdt, D. J., Boss, R., & Levkoff, S. (1985). An empirical test for phases of retirement: Findings from the normative aging study. *Journal of Gerontology, 40,* 95–105.
Elizur, E., & Kaffman, M. (1983). Factors influencing the severity of childhood bereavement reactions. *American Journal of Orthopsychiatry, 53,* 668–676.
Engel, G. L. (1961). Is grief a disease? *Psychosomatic Medicine, 23,* 18–22.
 (1977). The need for a new medical model: A challenge for biomedicine. *Science, 196,* 129–136.
Epstein, S. (1967). Toward a unified theory of anxiety. In B. A. Make (Ed.), *Progress in experimental personality research* (Vol. 4). New York: Academic Press.
 (1973). The self-concept revisited or a theory of a theory. *American Psychologist, 28,* 404–416.
 (1976). Anxiety, arousal, and the self-concept. In I. G. Sarason & C. D. Spielberger (Eds.), *Stress and anxiety* (Vol. 3, pp. 183–224). Washington, DC: Hemisphere.
 (1980). The self-concept: A review and the proposal of an integrated theory of personality. In E. Staub (Ed.), *Personality: Basic issues and current research* (pp. 82–132). Englewood Cliffs, NJ: Prentice Hall.
 (1983a). The unconscious, the preconscious, and the self-concept. In J. Suls & A. Greenwald (Eds.), *Psychological perspectives on the self* (Vol. 2, pp. 219–247). Hillsdale, NJ: Erlbaum, 1983.
 (1983b). Natural healing processes of the mind. II. Graded stress inoculation as an inherent coping mechanism. In D. Meichenbaum & M. Jaremko (Eds.), *Stress prevention and management: A cognitive behavioral approach* (pp. 39–66). New York: Plenum.
 (1984). Controversial issues in emotion theory. In P. Shaver (Ed.), *Annual review*

of research in personality and social psychology (pp. 64–88). Beverly Hills, CA: Sage.

(1990a). Cognitive experiential self-theory. In L. Pervin (Ed.), *Handbook of personality theory and research* (pp. 165–192). New York: Guilford.

(1990b). The self-concept, the traumatic neurosis, and the structure of personality. In D. Ozer, J. M. Healy, Jr., & A. J. Stewart (Eds.), *Perspectives on personality* (Vol. 3, pp. 63–98). Greenwich, CT: JAI Press.

(1991). Cognitive-experiential self-theory: An integrative theory of personality. In R. Curtis (Ed.), *The self with others: Convergences in psychoanalytic, social, and personality psychology* (pp. 111–139). New York: Guilford.

(in press). Constructive thinking and mental and physical well-being. In S. H. Filipp & L. Montada (Eds.), *Crises and loss experiences in the adult years*. Hillsdale, NJ: Erlbaum.

Epstein, S., & Katz, L. (1992). Coping ability, stress, productive load, and symptoms. *Journal of Personality and Social Psychology, 62*, 813–825.

Epstein, S., Lipson, A., Holstein, C., & Huh, E. (1992). Irrational reactions to negative outcomes: Evidence for two conceptual systems. *Journal of Personality and Social Psychology, 62*, 328–339.

Epstein, S., & Meier, P. (1989). Constructive thinking: A broad coping variable with specific components. *Journal of Personality and Social Psychology. 57*(2), 332–350.

Ericksen, E. E. (1975). *The psychological and ethical aspects of Mormon group life*. Salt Lake City: University of Utah Press.

Fairchild, S., Hansson, R., Vanzetti, N., & Howard, M. (1991). *Assessing the impact of bereavement on family systems: The family bereavement inventory*. Paper presented at the meeting of the Gerontological Society of America, San Francisco.

Faletti, M. V., Gibbs, J. M., Clark, C., Pruchno, R. A., & Berman, E. A. (1989). Longitudinal course of bereavement in older adults. In D. A. Lund (Ed.), *Older bereaved spouses: Research with practical applications* (pp. 37–51). New York: Taylor & Francis/Hemisphere.

Farberow, N. L., Gallagher, D. E., Gilewski, M. J., & Thompson, L. W. (1987). An examination of the early impact of bereavement on psychological distress in survivors of suicide. *The Gerontologist, 27*, 592–598.

(in press-a). Changes in grief and mental health of bereaved spouses of older suicides. *Journals of Gerontology: Psychological Sciences*.

(in press-b). The role of social supports and their vicissitudes in the bereavement of surviving spouses of suicide and natural deaths. *Suicide and Life Threatening Behavior*.

Faschingbauer, T. R. (1981). *Texas revised inventory of grief manual*. Houston: Honeycomb Publishing.

Faschingbauer, T. R., Devaul, R. D., & Zisook, S. (1977). Development of the Texas inventory of grief. *American Journal of Psychiatry, 134*, 696–698.

Faschingbauer, T. R., Zisook, S., & DeVaul, R. (1987). The Texas revised inventory of grief. In S. Zisook (Ed.), *Biopsychosocial aspects of bereavement* (pp. 111–124). Washington, DC: American Psychiatric Press.

Feeney, J., & Noller, P. (1990). Attachment styles as a predictor of adult romantic relationships. *Journal of Personality and Social Psychology, 58*, 281–291.

Feinson, M. C. (1986). Aging widows and widowers: Are there mental health differences? *International Journal of Aging and Human Development, 23*, 241–255.

Felten, D. L., Felten, S. Y., Bellinger, D. L., Carlson, S. L., Ackerman, K. D., Madden, K. S., Olschowka, J. A., & Livnat, S. (1987a). Noradrenergic sympathetic neural interactions with the immune system: Structure and function. *Immunological Reviews*, *100*, 225–260.

(1987b). Noradrenergic sympathetic neural interactions with the immune system: Structure and function. *Immunological Reviews*, *100*, 225–260.

Felten, S. Y., Felten, D. L., Bellinger, D. L., et al. (1988). Noradrenergic sympathetic innervation of lymphoid organs. *Progress in Allergy*, *43*, 14–36.

Felten, S. Y. & Olschowka, J. (1987). Noradrenergic sympathetic innervation of the spleen. II. Tyrosine hydroxylase (TH)-positive nerve terminals form synaptic-like contacts on lymphocytes in the splenic white pulp. *Journal of Neuroscience Research*, *18*, 37–48.

Fenichel, O. (1945). *The psychoanalytic theory of neurosis*. New York: Norton.

Ferraro, K. F., Mutran, E., & Barresi, C. M. (1984). Widowhood, health, and friendship support in later life. *Journal of Health and Social Behavior*, *25*, 245–259.

Festinger, L. (1954). A theory of social comparison processes. *Human Relations*, *7*, 117–140.

Field, T., & Reite, M. (1984). Children's responses to separation from mother during the birth of another child. *Child Development*, *55*, 1308–1316.

Finch, J. (1983). *Married to the job*: *Wives' incorporation in men's work*. Boston: Allen & Unwin.

Finch, J. F., Okun, M. A., Barrera, M., Zautra, A. J., & Reich, J. W. (1989). Positive and negative social ties among older adults: Measurement models and the prediction of psychological distress and well-being. *American Journal of Community Psychology*, *17*, 585–605.

Fish, W. C. (1986). Differences of grief intensity in bereaved parents. In T. A. Rando (Ed.), *Parental loss of a child* (pp. 415–428). Champaign, IL; Research Press.

Fish, W. C., & Whitty, S. M. (1983). Challenging conventional wisdom about parental bereavement. Forum Newsletter. *Forum for Death Education and Counseling*, *6*, 4.

Fisher, L. R. (1986). *Linked lives*: *Adult daughters and their mothers*. New York: Harper & Row.

Fleshner, M. R., Laudenslager, M. L., Simons, L., & Maier, S. F. (1989). Reduced serum antibodies associated with social defeat in rats. *Physiology and Behavior*, *45*, 1183–1187.

Fogle, B. (1981). *Interrelations between people and pets*. Apringfield, IL: Charles C. Thomas.

Folkman, S. & Lazarus, R. S. (1980). An analysis of coping in a middle-aged community sample. *Journal of Health and Social Behavior*, *21*, 219–239.

Folkman, S., Lazarus, R. S., Pimley, S., & Novacek, J. (1987). Age differences in stress and coping processes. *Psychology and Aging*, *2*, 171–184.

Ford, F. (1983). Rules: The invisible family. *Family Process*, *22*, 135–145.

Forrest, G. C., Standish, E., & Baum, J. D. (1982). Support after perinatal death: A study of support and counselling after perinatal bereavement. *British Medical Journal*, *285*, 1475–1479.

Fox, N. A. (1989). Heart-rate variability and behavioral reactivity: Individual differences in autonomic patterning and their relation to infant and child temperament. In J. S. Resnick (Ed.), *Perspectives on behavioral inhibition* (pp. 177–195). Chicago: University of Chicago Press.

Frankl, V. E. (1962). *Man's search for meaning*. New York: Touchstone Books.

(1946/1973). *The doctor and the soul*. R. Winston & C. Winston, Trans. New York: Knopf.

French, J. R. P., Jr., & Kahn, R. L. (1962). A programmatic approach to studying the industrial environment and mental health. *Journal of Social Issues, 18,* 1–47.

Freud, S. (1917a). Trauer und Melancholie. *Internationale Zeitschrift für ärztliche Psychoanalyse, 4,* 288–301.

(1917b). Mourning and melancholia. In J. Strachey (Ed. and Trans.) *Standard edition of the complete psychological works of Sigmund Freud.* London: Hogarth Press, 1957.

(1923). *The Ego and the Id.* Standard Edition (19, pp. 1–66). London: Hogarth Press.

(1920/1959). *Beyond the pleasure principle.* New York: Bantam.

Fried, M. (1963). Grieving for a lost home. In L. J. Duhl (Ed.), *The urban condition* (pp. 151–171). New York: Basic Books.

Fulton, R., & Owen, G. (1971, October). *Adjustment to loss through death: A sociological analysis.* Minneapolis: Center for Death Education and Research, University of Minnesota.

Furman, E. (1974). *A child's parent dies: Studies in childhood bereavement.* New Haven, CT: Yale University Press.

Furst, S. (1967). Psychic trauma: A survey. In S. Furst (Ed.), *Psychic trauma* (pp. 3–50). New York: Basic Books.

Futterman, A., Gallagher, D., Thompson, L. W., Lovett, S., & Gilewski, M. (1990). Retrospective assessment of marital adjustment and depression during the first two years of spousal bereavement. *Psychology and Aging, 5,* 277–283.

Futterman, A., Rodman, J. L., Thompson, L. W., & Gallagher, D. (1989). *The effects of spousal bereavement on indicators of physical health over a two-year period following loss.* Paper presented at the meeting of the Gerontology Society of America.

Gabriel, R. M., & Kirschling, J. M. (1989). Assessing grief among the bereaved elderly: A review of existing measures. *Hospice Journal, 5,* 29–54.

Galant, S. P., Underwood, S., Duriseti, L., & Insel, P. A. (1978). Characterization and high affinity of B2 adrenergic receptor binding by (−)(3H)-dihydropernolol binding to human polymorphonuclear particulates. *Journal of Laboratory and Clinical Medicine, 92,* 613.

Gallagher, D. (1986). Therapeutic issues in the treatment of spousal bereavement reactions in the elderly. In F. J. Pirozzato & G. J. Maletta (Eds.), *Assessment and treatment of the elderly neuropsychiatric patient* (pp. 215–240). New York: Praeger.

Gallagher, D., Breckenridge, J. N., Steinmetz, J., & Thompson, L. W. (1983a). The Beck Depression Inventory and the Research Diagnostic Criteria. *Journal of Consulting and Clinical Psychology, 51,* 945–946.

Gallagher, D., Breckenridge, J., Thompson, L. W., & Peterson, J. A. (1983b). Effects of bereavement on indicators of mental health in elderly widows and widowers. *Journal of Gerontology, 38,* 565–571.

Gallagher, D. E., Lovett, S., Hanley-Dunn, P., & Thompson, L. W. (1989). Use of select coping strategies during late-life spousal bereavement. In D. A. Lund (Ed.), *Older bereaved spouses: Research with practical applications* (pp. 111–122). New York: Hemisphere.

Gallagher, D., Thompson, L. W., & Levy, S. M. (1980). Clinical psychological assessment of older adults. In L. W. Poon (Ed.), *Aging in the 1980's: Psychological issues* (pp. 19–40). Washington, DC: American Psychological Association.

Gallagher, D. E., Thompson, L. W., & Peterson, J. A. (1981). Psychosocial factors affecting adaptation to bereavement in the elderly. *International Journal of Aging and Human Development, 14,* 79–95.

Gallagher-Thompson, D., Lovett, S., & Rose, J. (1991). In W. Myers (Ed.), *New techniques in the psychotherapy of older patients* (pp. 61–78). Washington, DC: American Psychiatric Association.

Ganellen, R. J., & Blaney, P. H. (1984). Stress, externality, and depression. *Journal of Personality and Social Psychology, 52,* 326–337.

Gantz, F. E., Gallagher-Thompson, D., & Rodman, J. (in press). Cognitive–behavioral facilitation of inhibited grief. In A. Freeman & F. Dattilio (Ed.), *Casebook of cognitive–behavior therapy.* New York: Plenum.

Garmezy, N. (1987). Stress, competence, and development: Continuities in the study of schizophrenic adults, children vulnerable to psychopathology, and the search for stress-resistant children. *American Journal of Orthopsychiatry, 57,* 159–185.

Garmezy, N. (1983). Stressors of childhood. In N. Garmezy & M. Rutter (Ed.). *Stress, coping, and development in children* (pp. 43–84). New York: McGraw-Hill.

Gass, K. A. (1989). Appraisal, coping, and resources: Markers associated with the health of aged widows and widowers. In D. A. Lund (Ed.), *Older bereaved spouses: Research with practical applications* (pp. 79–94). New York: Taylor & Francis/Hemisphere.

Gerber, I., Weiner, A., Battin, D., & Arkin, A. (1975). Brief therapy to the aged bereaved. In B. Schoenberg & I. Gerber (Ed.), *Bereavement: Its psychosocial aspects* (pp. 310–313). New York: Columbia University Press.

Gergen, K. J. (1985). The social constructionist movement in modern psychology. *American Psychologist, 40,* 266–275.

Gilewski, M. J., Farberow, N. L., Gallagher, D. E., & Thompson, L. W. (1991). Interaction of depression and bereavement on mental health in the elderly. *Psychology and Aging, 6,* 67–75.

Gilliland, B. C. (1983). Introduction to clinical immunology. In R. G. Petersdorf, R. D. Adams, E. Braunwald, K. J. Isselbacher, J. B. Martin, & J. D. Wilson (Eds.), *Principles of internal medicine* (pp. 344–354). New York: McGraw-Hill.

Gillis, S., Crabtree, G. R., & Smith, K. A. (1979) Glucocorticoid-induced inhibition of T cell growth factor production. I. The effect on mitogen-induced lymphocyte proliferation. *Journal of Immunology, 123,* 1624.

Gillis, S., Gillis, A. E., & Henney, C. S. (1981). Monoclonal antibody directed against interleukin-2. I. Inhibition of T-lymphocyte mitogenesis, and the in vitro differentiation of alloreactive cytolytic T-cells. *Journal of Experimental Medicine, 154,* 983.

Glick, I. O., Weiss, R. S., & Parkes, C. M. (1974). *The first year of bereavement.* New York: Wiley.

Goin, M. K., Burgoyne, R. W., & Goin, J. M. (1979). Timeless attachment to a dead relative. *American Journal of Psychiatry, 136,* 988–989.

Gold, P. W., Chrousos, G. P., Kellner, C., Post, R., Roy, A., Augerinos, P., Schulte, H., Oldfield, E., & Loriaux, D. L. (1984). Psychiatric implications of basic and clinical studies with corticotropin releasing factor. *American Journal of Psychiatry, 141,* 483–494.

Gold, P. W., Goodwin, F. K., & Chrousos, G. P. (1988). Clinical and biochemical manifestations of depression. Relation to the neurobiology of stress. *New England Journal of Medicine, 319,* 413–420.

Goldberg, D. P. (1972). *The detection of psychiatric illness by questionnaire.* Maudsley Monograph No. 21. London: Oxford University Press.

Goldberg, E. L., Comstock, G. W., & Harlow, S. D. (1988). Emotional problems and widowhood. *Journal of Gerontology, 43,* 5206–5208.

Good, B. J., Good, M. D., & Moradi, R. (1985). The interpretation of Iranian depressive illness and dysphoric affect. In A. Kleinman & B. Good (Eds.), *Culture and depression: Studies in the anthropology and cross-cultural psychiatry of affect and disorder* (pp. 369–428). Berkeley: University of California Press.

Goodman, J. (1972). *Companionship therapy.* San Francisco: Jossey-Bass.

Gore, S. (1978) The effect of social support in moderating the health consequences of unemployment. *Journal of Health and Social Behavior, 19,* 157–165.

Gorer, G. (1965). *Death, grief and mourning in contemporary Britain.* London: Tavistock.

Gottlieb, B. H. (1983). *Social support strategies: Guidelines for mental health practice.* Beverly Hills, CA: Sage.

Gottschalk, L. A., & Gleser, G. C. (1969). *The measurement of psychological states through the content analysis of verbal behavior.* Los Angeles: University of California Press.

Gove, W. R. (1972). The relationship between sex roles, marital roles, and mental illness. *Social Forces, 51,* 34–44.

(1973). Sex, marital status, and mortality. *American Journal of Sociology, 79,* 45–67.

Government Printing Office (1991). *Disasters: Planning for a caring response.* London: HMSO.

Gribbin, K., Schaie, K. W., & Parham, I. A. (1980). Complexity of lifestyle and maintenance of intellectual abilities. *Journal of Social Issues, 36,* 46–61.

Grossman, K. E., & Grossman, K. (1991). Attachment quality as an organizer of emotional and behavioral responses in a longitudinal perspective. In C. M., Parkes, J. Stevenson-Hinde, & P. Marris (Eds.), *Attachment across the life-cycle* (pp. 95–115). London/New York: Tavistock/Routledge.

Gurland, B. J., Yorkston, N. J., Stone, A. R., & Frank, J. D. (1974). *Structured and scaled interview to assess maladjustment.* New York: Springer

Habu, S., Akamatsu, K., Tamaoki, N., & Okumura, K. (1984). In vivo significance of NK cells on resistance against virus (HSV-1) infections in mice. *Journal of Immunology, 133,* 2743–2747.

Hackett, T. P. (1974). Recognizing and treating abnormal grief. *Hospital Physician, 1,* 49–54.

Haefner, H. (1968). Psychological disturbances following prolonged persecution. *Social Psychiatry, 3,* 79–88.

Hall, D. T. (1976). *Careers in organizations.* Santa Monica, CA: Goodyear.

Hansson, R. O., Briggs, S. R., & Rule, B. (1990). Old age and unemployment: Predictors of perceived control, depression and loneliness. *Journal of Applied Gerontology, 9,* 230–240.

Hansson, R. O., & Carpenter, B. N. (1990). Relational competence and adjustment in older adults: Implications for the demands of aging. In M. A. P. Stephens, J. H. Crowther, S. E. Hobfoll, & D. L. Tennenbaum (Eds.), *Stress and coping in later-life families* (pp. 131–151). New York: Hemisphere.

Hansson, R. O., Jones, W. J., & Carpenter, B. N. (1984). Relational competence and social support. In P. Shaver (Ed.), *Review of personality and social psychology* (Vol. 5, pp. 265–284). Beverly Hills, CA: Sage.

Hansson, R. O., Nelson, R. E., Carver, M. D., NeeSmith, D. H., Dowling, E. M., Fletcher, W. L., & Suhr, P. (1990). Adult children with frail elderly parents: When to intervene? *Family Relations, 39,* 153–158.

Harlow, H. F., Gluck, J. P., & Suomi, S. J. (1972). Generalization of behavioral data between nonhuman and human animals. *American Psychologist, 27,* 709–716.

Harter, S. (1985). Processes underlying the construction, maintenance, and enhancement of the self-concept in children. In J. Suls & A. Greenwald (Eds.), *Psychological perspectives on the self* (pp. 138–181). Hillsdale, NJ: Erlbaum.

Hartup, W. W. (1989). Social relations and their developmental significance. *American Psychologist* (special issue), *44*(2), 120–126.

Harvey, C. D., & Bahr, H. M. (1974) Widowhood, morale, and affiliation. *Journal of Marriage and the Family, 36,* 97–106.

Hatch, S., & Kickbusch, I. (1983). *Self-help and health in Europe: New approaches in health care.* Copenhagen: WHO/EURO/HEAD.

Heller, K., & Swindle, R. W., Jr. (1983). Social networks, perceived support and coping with stress. In R. D. Felner, L. A. Jason, J. Moritsugu, & S. S. Farber (Eds.), *Preventive psychology: Theory, research, and practice in community intervention* (pp. 87–103). New York: Pergamon.

Heller, K., Swindle, R. W., & Dusenbury, L. (1986). Component social support processes: Comments and integration. *Journal of Consulting and Clinical Psychology, 54,* 466–470.

Hellstrand, K., Hermodsson, S., & Strannegard, O. (1985). Evidence for a beta-adrenoceptor mediated regulation of human natural killer cells. *Journal of Immunology, 134,* 4095–4099.

Helmrath, T. A., & Steinitz, E. M. (1978). Death of an infant: Parental grieving and the failure of social support. *Journal of Family Practice, 6,* 785–790.

Helsing, K., Comstock, G., & Szklo, M. (1982). Causes of death in a widowed population. *American Journal of Epidemiology, 116,* 524–532.

Helsing, K. J., & Szklo, M. (1981). Mortality after bereavement. *American Journal of Epidemiology, 114,* 41–52.

Helsing, K. J., Szklo, M., & Comstock, G. W. (1981). Factors associated with mortality after widowhood. *American Journal of Public Health, 71,* 802–809.

Henderson, S., Byrne, D., & Duncan-Jones, P. (1981). *Neurosis and the social environment.* New York: Academic Press.

Henney, C. S., & Gillis, S. (1984). Cell-mediated cytotoxicity. In W. E. Paul (Ed.), *Fundamental immunology* (pp. 669–668). New York: Raven Press.

Herberman, R. B. (1980). *Natural cell mediated immunity against tumors.* New York: Academic Press.

Herberman, R. B., & Ortaldo, J. R. (1981). Natural killer cells: Their role in defenses against disease. *Science, 214,* 24–30.

Herek, G. M. (1988). Heterosexuals' attitudes toward lesbians and gay men: Correlates and gender differences. *Journal of Sex Research, 25,* 451–477.

Herek, G. M., & Glunt, E. K. (1988). An epidemic of stigma: Public reactions to AIDS. *American Psychologist, 43,* 886–891.

Hetherington, E. M. (1989). Coping with family transitions: Winners, losers, and survivors. *Child Development, 60,* 1–14.

Heyman, D. K., & Gianturco, D. T. (1973). Long term adaptation by the elderly in bereavement. *Journal of Gerontology, 28,* 359–362.

Hirsch, B. J. (1980). Natural support systems and coping with major life changes. *American Journal of Community Psychology, 8,* 159–172.

Hirsch, J., Hofer, M., Holland, J., & Solomon, F. (1984). Toward a biology of grieving. In M. Osterweis, F. Solomon, & M. Green (Eds.), *Bereavement reactions, consequences and care* (pp. 145–175). Washington, DC: National Academy Press.

Hobfoll, S. E., & Freedy, J. R. (1990). The availability and effective use of social support. *Journal of Social and Clinical Psychology, 9,* 91–103.

Hoey P., & Raphael, B. (1990, October). *New metaphors in the psychotherapy of grief.* Paper presented at the Australian and New Zealand Association of Psychotherapy.

Hofer, M. (1984). Relationships as regulators: A psychobiologic perspective on bereavement. *Psychosomatic Medicine, 46,* 183–197.

Hofer, M., Wolff, C. T., Friedman, S. B., & Mason, J. W. (1972a). A psycho-endocrine study of bereavement. I. 17-Hydroxycorticosteroid excretion rate of parents following the death of their children from leukemia. *Psychosomatic Medicine, 34,* 481–491.

(1972b). A psychoendocrine study of bereavement. II. Observations on the process of mourning in relation to adrenocortical function. *Psychosomatic Medicine, 34,* 492–504.

Holden, K. C., & Smock, P. J. (1991). The economic costs of marital dissolution: Why do women bear a disproportionate cost? *Annual Review of Sociology, 17,* 51–78.

Hollander, E., Leibowitz, M. R., Gorman, J. M., Cohen, B., Fyer, A., & Klein, D. (1989). Cortisol and sodium lactate–induced panic. *Archives of General Psychiatry, 46,* 135–140.

Hollenbeck, A. R., Susman, E. J., Nannis, E. D., Strope, B. E., Hersh, S. P., Levine, A. S., & Pizzo, P. A. (1980). Children with serious illness: Behavioral correlates of separation and isolation. *Child Psychiatry and Human Development, 11,* 3–11.

Holmes, T., & Rahe, R. (1967). The social readjustment rating scale. *Journal of Psychosomatic Research, 11,* 213–218.

Holsboer, F., von Bardeleben, U., Buller, R., Heuser, I., & Steiger, A. (1987). Stimulation response to corticotropin-releasing hormone (CRH) in patients with depression, alcoholism and panic disorder. *Hormone Metabolism Research, 16* (suppl.), 80–88.

Hood, L. E., Weisman, I. L., Wood, H. B., & Wilson, J. H. (1985). *Immunology.* Menlo Park, CA: Benjamin Cummings.

Hoppe, K. (1971). Re-somatization of effects in survivors of persecution. *International Journal of Psychoanalysis, 49,* 324–327.

Horowitz, M. (1976/1986). *Stress response syndromes.* Northvale, NJ: Aronson.

(1983). Psychological response to serious life events. In S. Breznitz (Ed.), *The denial of stress.* New York: International Universities Press.

(1985). Disasters and psychological responses to stress. *Psychiatric Annals, 15,* 161–167.

Horowitz, M. J., Krupnick, J., Kaltreider, N., Wilner, N., Leong, A., & Marmar, C. (1981). Initial psychological response to parental death. *Archives of General Psychiatry, 38,* 316–323.

Horowitz, M. J., Marmar, C., Weiss, D. S., DeWitt, K., & Rosenbaum, R. (1984a). Brief psychotherapy of bereavement reactions. *Archives of General Psychiatry, 41,* 438–448.

Horowitz, M. J., Weiss, D., Kaltreider, N., Krupnick, J., Wilner, N., Marmar, C., & DeWitt, K. (1984b). Reactions to the death of a parent: Results from patients and field subjects. *Journal of Nervous and Mental Diseases, 172,* 383–392.

Horowitz, M., Wilner, N., & Alvarez, W. (1979). Impact of event scale: A measure of subjective stress. *Psychosomatic Medicine, 41,* 209–218.

Horowitz, M. J., Wilner, N., Marmar, C., & Krupnick, J. (1980). Pathological grief and the activation of latent self images. *American Journal of Psychiatry, 137,* 1157–1160.

House, J. S. (1981). *Work, stress and social support.* Reading, MA: Addison-Wesley.

Hoyer, W. J., Rebok, G. W., & Sved, S. M. (1979). Effects of varying irrelevant information in adult age differences in problem solving. *Journal of Gerontology*, *34*, 553–560.

Hu, Y., & Goldman, N. (1990). Mortality differentials by mental status: An international comparison. *Demography*, *27*, 233–250.

Irwin, M. R., Britton, K. T., & Vale, W. (1987d). Central corticotropin releasing factor suppresses natural killer cell activity. *Brain, Behavior and Immunity*, *1*, 81–87.

Irwin, M., Caldwell, C., Smith, T. L., Brown, S., Schuckit, M. A., & Gillin, J. C. (1990a). Major depressive disorder, alcoholism and reduced natural killer cell cytotoxicity: Role of severity of depressive symptoms and alcohol consumption. *Archives of General Psychiatry*, *47*, 713–719.

Irwin, M., Daniels, M., Bloom, E., Smith, T. L., & Weiner, H. (1987a). Life events, depressive symptoms and immune function. *American Journal of Psychiatry*, *44*, 437–441.

Irwin, M., Daniels, M., Risch, S. C., Bloom, E., & Weiner, H. (1988a). Plasma cortisol and natural killer cell activity during bereavement. *Biological Psychiatry*, *24*, 173–178.

Irwin, M. R., Daniels, M., Smith, T. L., Bloom, E., & Weiner, H. (1987b). Impaired natural killer cell activity during bereavement. *Brain, Behavior and Immunity*, *1*, 98–104.

Irwin, M. R., Hauger, R. L., Brown, M. R., & Britton, K. T. (1988b). Corticotropin-releasing factor activates the autonomic nervous system and reduces natural cytotoxicity. *American Journal of Physiology*, *255*, 744–747.

Irwin, M., Hauger, R. L., Jones, L., Provencio, M., & Britton, K. T. (1990c). Sympathetic nervous system mediates central corticotropin-releasing factor induced suppression of natural killer cytotoxicity. *Journal of Pharmacology and Experimental Therapeutics*, *255*, 101–107.

Irwin, M., Patterson, T., Grant, I., & Brown, M. (1991). Elevated sympathetic activity and reduced immune function in Alzheimer caregiver stress and depression. *Psychosomatic Medicine*, *53*, 212.

Irwin, M., Smith, T. L., & Gillin, J. C. (1987c). Reduced natural killer cytotoxicity in depressed patients. *Life Sciences*, *41*, 2127–2133.

Irwin, M. R., Vale, W., & Rivier, C. (1990b). Central corticotropin-releasing factor mediates the suppressive effect of stress on natural killer cytotoxicity. *Endocrinology*, *126*, 2837–2844.

Jacklin, S. N. (1989). Female and male: Issues of gender. *American Psychologist* (special issue), *44*(2), 127–133.

Jackson, M. (1989). *Paths toward a clearing: Radical empiricism and ethnographic inquiry*. Bloomington: Indiana University Press.

Jacobs, S. C. (1987a). Measures of the psychological distress of bereavement. In S. Zisook (Ed.), *Biopsychosocial aspects of bereavement* (pp. 127–138). Washington, DC: American Psychiatric Association.

  (1987b). Psychoendocrine aspects of bereavement. In S. Zisook (Ed.), *Biopsychosocial aspects of bereavement* (pp. 139–155). Washington, DC: American Psychiatric Association.

Jacobs, S. C., & Douglas, L. (1979). Grief: A mediating process between a loss and illness. *Comprehensive Psychiatry*, *20*, 165–175.

Jacobs, S., Hansen, F., Berkman, L., Kasl, S., & Ostfeld, A. (1989 1, May/June). Depressions of bereavement. *Comprehensive Psychiatry*, *30*(3), 218–224.

Jacobs, S., Hansen, F., Kasl, S., Ostfeld, A., Berkman, L., & Kim, K. (1990).

Anxiety disorders in acute bereavement: Risk and risk factors. *Journal of Clinical Psychiatry, 51,* 269–274.

Jacobs, S., Kasl, S., Ostfeld, A., Berkman, L., & Charpentier, P. (1986). The measurement of grief: Age and sex variation. *British Journal of Medical Psychology, 59,* 305–310.

Jacobs, S. C., Kasl, S. V., Ostfeld, A. M., Berkman, L., Kosten, T. R., & Charpentier, P. (1987a). The measurement of grief: Bereaved versus non-bereaved. *Hospice Journal, 2,* 21–36.

Jacobs, S., & Kim, K. (1990). Psychiatric complications of bereavement. *Psychiatric Annals, 20,* 314–317.

Jacobs, S., Kim, K., Schaefer, C., Mason, J., Kasl, S., Berkman, L., & Ostfeld, A. (1991). *Conscious and unconscious coping under stress. I. Relationship to each other and neuroendocrine function.* Manuscript available from author.

Jacobs, S. C., Kosten, T. R., Kasl, S. V., Ostfeld, A. M., Berkman, L., & Charpentier, P. (1987b). Attachment theory and multiple dimensions of grief. *Omega, 18,* 41–52.

Jacobs, S., Mason, J. W., Kosten, T. R., Wahby, V., Kasl, S., & Ostfeld, A. M. (1986c). Bereavement and catecholamines. *Journal of Psychosomatic Research, 30,* 489–496.

Jacobs, S. C., Nelson, J. C., & Zisook, S. (1987c). Treating depression of bereavement with antidepressants: A pilot study. *Psychiatric Clinics of North America, 10,* 501–510.

Jacobs, S., & Ostfeld, A. (1977). An epidemiological review of the mortality of bereavement. *Psychosomatic Medicine, 39,* 344–357.

Jain, R., Zwickler D., Hollander, C. S., Brand, H., Saperstein, A., Hutchinson, B., Brown, C., & Audnya, T. (1991). Corticotropin-releasing factor modulates the immune response to stress in the rat. *Endocrinology, 128,* 1329–1336.

Janoff-Bulman, R. (1992). *Shattered assumptions: Towards a new psychology of trauma.* New York: The Free Press.

Janoff-Bulman, R., & Frieze, I. H. (1983). A theoretical perspective for understanding reactions to victimization. *Journal of Social Issues, 39*(2), 1–17.

Johnson, C. D., & Sarason, I. G. (1978). Life stress, depression and anxiety: Internal-external control as a moderator variable. *Psychosomatic Research, 22,* 205–208.

Johnson, P. A., & Rosenblatt, P. C. (1981). Grief following childhood loss of parent. *American Journal of Psychotherapy, 35,* 419–425.

Johnson, R. J., Lund, D. A., & Dimond, M. F. (1986). Stress, self-esteem and coping during bereavement among the elderly. *Social Psychology Quarterly, 49,* 273–279.

Jones, D. R. (1987). Heart disease mortality following widowhood: Some results from the OPCS longitudinal study. *Journal of Psychosomatic Research, 31,* 325–333.

(1988). Cancer mortality and widow(er)hood in the Office of Population Censuses and Surveys Longitudinal Study. In M. Watson, S. Green, & C. Thomas (Eds.), *Psychosocial oncology* (pp. 33–42). London: Pergamon.

Jones, D. R., & Goldblatt, P. O. (1987). Cause of death in widow(er)s and spouses. *Journal of Biosocial Science, 19,* 107–121.

Jones, D. R., Goldblatt, P. O., & Leon, D. A. (1984). Bereavement and cancer: Some results using data on deaths of spouses from the Longitudinal Study of Office of Population Censuses and Surveys. *British Medical Journal, 298,* 461–464.

Kagan, J., Reznick, J. S., & Snidman, N. (1988). Biological basis of childhood shyness. *Science, 240,* 167–171.

Kahana, B., Harel, Z., & Kahana, E. (1988b). Predictors of psychological well-being among survivors of the Holocaust. In J. Wilson, Z. Harel, & B. Kahana (Eds.), *Human adaptation to extreme stress. From Holocaust to Vietnam* (pp. 171–191). New York: Plenum.

Kahana, E., Kahana, B., Harel, Z., & Rosner, T. (1988a). Coping with extreme trauma. In J. Wilson, Z. Harel, & B. Kahana (Eds.), *Human adaptation to extreme stress. From Holocaust to Vietnam* (pp. 55–76). New York: Plenum.

Kahn, R. L. (1975). The mental health system and the future aged. *Gerontologist, 15,* 24–31.

Kahn, R., House, J., & Wortman, C. (1989, November). *Adaptation to widowhood: MacArthur Battery Physical and Physiological Function.* Paper delivered at the annual meeting of the Gerontological Society of America, Minneapolis.

Kahneman, D., & Miller, D. T. (1986). Norm theory: Comparing reality to its alternatives. *Psychological Review, 93,* 136–153.

Kaminer, H., & Lavie, P. (1991). Dream repression in adjusted Holocaust survivors. *Journal of Nervous and Mental Disease, 179,* 664–669.

Kammer, D. (1983). Eine Untersuchung der psychometrischen Eigenschaften des deutschen Beck-Derpessioninventars (BDI). *Diagnostica, 28,* 48–60.

Kane, R. A., & Kane, R. L. (1981). *Assessing the elderly: A practical guide to measurement.* Lexington, MA: Lexington Books.

Kane, R. L., Kane, R. A., & Arnold, S. B. (1985). Prevention and the elderly: Risk factors. *Health Services Research, 19*(6).

Kanner, A. D., Coyne, J. C., Schaefer, C., & Lazarus, R. S. (1981). Comparison of two modes of stress measurement: Daily hassles and uplifts versus major life events. *Journal of Behavioral Medicine, 4,* 1–39.

Kaplan, J. R., Manuck, S. B., & Gatsonis, C. (1990). Heart rate and social status among male cynomolgus monkeys (*Macaca fasicularis*) in disrupted social groupings. *American Journal of Primatology, 21,* 175–187.

Kaprio, J., Koskenvuo, M., & Rita, H. (1987). Mortality after bereavement: A prospective study of 95,647 widowed persons. *American Journal of Public Health, 77,* 283–287.

Kathol, R. G., Noyes, R., Lopez, A. L., & Reich, J. H. (1988). Relationship of urinary free cortisol levels in patients with panic disorder to symptoms of depression and agoraphobia. *Psychiatry Research, 24,* 211–221.

Kaufman, I. C., & Rosenblum, L. A. (1967). The reaction to separation in infant monkeys; anaclitic depression and conservation-withdrawal. *Psychosomatic Medicine, 29,* 648–675.

Kaufman, I. C., & Stynes, A. J. (1978). Depression can be produced in a bonnet macaque infant. *Psychosomatic Medicine, 40,* 71–75.

Kavanagh, D. G. (1990). Towards a cognitive-behavioral intervention for adult grief reactions. *British Journal of Psychiatry, 157,* 373–383.

Keller, S., Weiss, J. M., Schleifer, S. J., Miller, N. E., & Stein, M. (1981). Suppression of immunity by stress: Effects of a graded series of stressors on lymphocyte stimulation in the rat. *Science, 213,* 1397–1400.

Kemp, B. (1985). Rehabilitation and the older adult. In J. E. Birren & K. W. Schaie (Eds.), *Handbook of the psychology of aging* (2nd ed., pp. 647–663). New York: Van Nostrand Reinhold.

Kern, D. E., Gillis, S., Okada, M., & Henney, C. S. (1981). The role of interleukin-

2 (IL-2) in the differentiation of cytotoxic T cells: The effect of monoclonal anti-IL-2 antibody and absorption with IL-2 dependent T cell lines. *Journal of Immunology, 127,* 1323.

Kessler, R. C., House, J. S., & Turner, J. B. (1987). Unemployment and health in a community sample. *Journal of Health & Social Behavior, 28,* 51–59.

Kessler, R. C., Price, R. H., & Wortman, C. B. (1985). Social factors in psychopathology: Stress, social support, and coping processes. *Annual Review of Psychology, 36,* 531–572.

Kiely, M. C. (1983, September). *Royal Victoria Hospital bereavement study evaluation report.* Paper presented at Palliative Care Conference on Bereavement, Philadelphia.

Killilea, M. (1976). Mutual help organizations: Interpretations in the literature. In G. Caplan & M. Killilea (Eds.), *Support systems and mutual help.* New York: Grune & Stratton.

Kim, K., & Jacobs, S. (1991). Pathologic grief and its relationship to other psychiatric disorders. *Journal of Affective Disorders, 21,* 257–263.

Kitson, G. C., & Roach, M. J. (1989). Independence and social and psychological adjustment in widowhood and divorce. In D. A. Lund (Ed.), *Older bereaved spouses: Research with practical applications* (pp. 167–183). New York: Hemisphere.

Kitson, G. C., & Zyzanski, S. J. (1987). Grief in widowhood and divorce. *Psychiatric Clinics of North America, 10,* 369–385.

Klass, D. (1988). *Parental grief: Solace and resolution.* New York: Springer.

Kleber, R. J., & Brom, D. (1987). Psychotherapy and pathological grief: Controlled outcome study. *Israeli Journal of Psychiatry and Related Sciences, 24,* 99–109.

Klein, M. (1940). Mourning and its relation to manic-depressive states. In F. Jones (Ed.), *Contributions to psychoanalysis* (pp. 125–153). London: Hogarth Press.

Klein, S. J., & Fletcher, W. (1986). Gay grief: An examination of its uniqueness brought to light by the AIDS crises. *Journal of Psychological Oncology, 4,* 15–25.

Kleinman, A., & Kleinman, J. (1985). Somatization: The interconnections in Chinese society among culture, depressive experiences, and the meanings of pain. In A. Kleinman & B. Good (Eds.), *Culture and depression: Studies in the anthropology and cross-cultural psychiatry of affect and disorder* (pp. 429–490). Berkeley: University of California Press.

Klinger, E. (1977). *Meaning and void: Inner experience and the incentives in people's lives.* Minneapolis: University of Minnesota Press.

Kloeppel, D. A., & Hollins, S. (1989). Double handicap: Mental retardation and death in the family. *Death Studies, 13,* 31–38.

Kobasa, S. C., Maddi, S. R., & Kahn, S. (1982). Hardiness and health: A prospective study. *Journal of Personality and Social Psychology, 42,* 168–177.

Kobrin, F. E., & Hendershot, G. E. (1977). Do family ties reduce mortality? *Journal of Marriage and the Family, 39,* 737–745.

Kosberg, J. I., Cairl, R. E., & Keller, D. M. (1990). Components of burden: Interventive implications. *The Gerontologist, 30,* 236–242.

Koskenvuo, M., Kaprio, J., Kesäniemi, A., & Sarna, S. (1980). Differences in mortality from ischemic heart disease by marital status and social class. *Journal of Chronic Diseases, 33,* 95–106.

Kosten, T., Jacobs, S., & Mason, J. (1984a). The dexamethasone suppression test during bereavement. *Journal of Nervous & Mental Disease, 172,* 359–360.

Kosten, T., Jacobs, S., Mason, J., Brown, S., Atkins, S., Gardner, C., Schreiber, S.,

Wahby, V., & Ostfeld, A. (1984b). Psychological correlates of growth hormone response to stress. *Psychosomatic Medicine, 46*, 49–58.

Kracke, W. H. (1981). Kagwahiv mourning. I. Dreams of a bereaved father. *Ethos, 9*, 258–275.

Kraus, A. S., & Lilienfeld, A. M. (1959). Some epidemiological aspects of the high mortality rate in the young widowed group. *Journal of Chronic Diseases, 10*, 207–217.

Krell, R., & Rabkin, L. (1979). The effects of sibling death on the surviving child: A family perspective. *Family Process, 18*, 471–477.

Kronfol, Z., & House, J. D. (1985). Depression, hypothalamic–pituitary adrenocortical activity and lymphocyte function. *Psychopharmacology Bulletin, 21*, 476–478

Kronfol, Z., Hover, J. D., Silva, J., et al. (1986). Depression, urinary free cortisol excretion, and lymphocyte function. *British Journal of Psychiatry, 148*, 70–73.

Kronfol, Z., Silva, J., Greden, J., Dembinski, S., Gardener, R., & Carroll, B. (1983). Impaired lymphocyte function in depressive illness. *Life Sciences, 33*, 241–247.

Krystal, H. (1968). The problem of the survivor. In H. Krystal (Ed.), *Massive psychic trauma*. New York: International Universities Press.

Kubler-Ross, E. (1969). *On death and dying*. New York: Springer.

Kuhn, M., & McPartland, T. S. (1954). An empirical investigation of self attitudes. *American Sociological Review, 19*, 68–76.

Kundler, H., Davidson, J., Meador, K., Lipper, S., & Ely, T. (1987). The DST and posttraumatic stress disorder. *American Journal of Psychiatry, 144*, 1068–1071.

Lakey, B., & Heller, K. (1988). Social support from a friend, perceived support, and social problem solving. *American Journal of Community Psychology, 16*, 811–824.

Laslett, P. (1971). *The world we have lost* (2nd ed.). New York: Scribner.

Laudenslager, M. L., Capitanio, J. P., & Reite, M. L. (1985). Possible consequences of early separation experiences on subsequent immune function in adult macaque monkeys. *American Journal of Psychiatry, 142*, 862–864.

Laudenslager, M. L., Held, P. E., Boccia, M. L., Gennaro, M. M., Reite, M. L., & Cohen, J. J. (in press). Relationship of behavior to specific antibody levels in nonhuman primates. *Brain Behavior and Immunity*.

Laudenslager, M. L., Held, P. E., Boccia, M. L., Reite, M. L., & Cohen, J. J. (1990). Behavioral and immunological consequences of brief mother–infant separation: A species comparison. *Developmental Psychobiology, 23*, 265–283.

Laudenslager, M. L., Reite, M. L., & Harbeck, R. (1982). Suppressed immune response in infant monkeys associated with maternal separation. *Behavioral and Neural Biology, 36*, 40–48.

Lavie, P., & Kaminer, H. (1991). Dreams that poison sleep: Dreaming in Holocaust survivors. *Dreaming, 1*, 11–21.

Lawton, M. P. (1983). The varieties of well-being. *Experimental Aging Research, 9*, 65–72.

Lawton, M. P., & Simon, B. B. (1968). The ecology of social relationships in housing for the elderly. *The Gerontologist, 8*, 110–115.

Lazarus, R. S. (1966). *Psychological stress and the coping process*. New York: McGraw-Hill.

(1981). The costs and benefits of denial. In B. S. Dohrenwend & B. P. Dohrenwend (Eds.), *Stressful life events and their contexts*. New York: Prodist.

Lazarus, R. S., & Folkman, S. (1984). *Stress, appraisal, and coping*. New York: Springer.

Lederer, W. (1965). Persecution and compensation. Theoretical and practical implication of the "persecution syndrome." *Archives of General Psychiatry, 12,* 464–474.

Lehman, D., Ellard, J., & Wortman, C. (1986). Social support for the bereaved: Recipients' and providers' perspectives on what is helpful. *Journal of Consulting and Clinical Psychology, 54,* 438–446.

Lehman, D. R., Lang, E. L., Wortman, C. B., & Sorenson, S. B. (1989). Long-term effects of sudden bereavement: Marital and parent–child relationships and children's reactions. *Journal of Family Psychology, 2*(3), 344–367.

Lehman, D. R., Wortman, C. B., & Williams, A. F. (1987). Long-term effects of losing a spouse or child in a motor vehicle crash. *Journal of Personality and Social Psychology, 52,* 218–231.

Lennon, M. C., Martin, J. L., & Dean, L. (1990). The influence of social support on AIDS-related grief reaction among gay men. *Social Science and Medicine, 31*(4), 477–484.

Lesch, K, P., Laux, G., Erb, A., & Beckman, H. (1988). Growth hormone (GH) responses to GH-releasing hormone in depression: Correlation with GH release following clonidine. *Psychiatry Research, 25,* 301–310.

Levav, I. (1989). Second thoughts on the lethal aftermath of a loss. *Omega, 20,* 81–90.

Levav, I., & Abramson, J. H. (1984). Emotional distress among concentration camp survivors: A community study in Jerusalem. *Psychological Medicine, 14,* 215–218.

Levav, I., Friedlander, Y., Kark, J., & Peritz, E. (1988). An epidemiologic study of mortality among bereaved parents. *New England Journal of Medicine, 319,* 457–461.

Levenson, H. (1973). Multidimensional locus of control in psychiatric patients. *Journal of Consulting and Clinical Psychology, 41,* 397–404.

Levine, S. (1987). Psychobiological consequences of mother–infant relationships. In N. Krasnegor, E. Blass, M. Hofer, & W. P. Santherman (Eds.), *Perinatal development: A psychobiological perspective* (pp. 359–377). New York: Academic Press.

Levine, S., Johnson, D. F., & Gonzales, C. A. (1985). Behavioral and hormonal response to separation of infant rhesus monkeys and mothers. *Behavioral Neuroscience, 99,* 399–410.

Levinger, G. (1976). A social psychological perspective on marital dissolution. *Journal of Social Issues, 32,* 21–47.

Levinson, D. (1978). *Seasons of a man's life.* New York: Knopf.

Levy, R. I. (1984). The emotions in comparative perspective. In K. R. Scherer & P. Ekman (Eds.), *Approaches to emotion* (pp. 397–412). Hillsdale, NJ: Erlbaum.

Lewin, K. (1935). *A dynamic theory of personality.* New York: McGraw-Hill.

Lieberman, M. A. (1983). Comparative analysis of change mechanisms in groups. In H. H. Blumberg, A. P. Hare, V. Kent, & M. Davies (Eds.), *Small groups and social interaction* (Vol. 2, pp. 239–252). London: Wiley.

　(1986). Self-help groups and psychiatry. *American Psychiatric Association Annual Review, 5,* 744–760.

　(1989). Group properties and outcomes: A study of group norms in self-help groups for widows and widowers. *International Journal of Group Psychotherapy, 39*(2), 191–209.

　(1990). *Predictors of growth in widows. A seven year follow-up.* Unpublished manuscript.

Lieberman, M. A., & Borman, L. (1979). *Self-help groups for coping with crises*. San Francisco: Jossey-Bass.

Lieberman, M. A., & Videka-Sherman, L. (1986). The impact of self-help groups on the mental health of widows and widowers. *American Journal of Orthopsychiatry, 56*, 435–449.

Lieberman, M. A., & Yalom, I. (in press). Brief group psychotherapy for the spousally bereaved: A controlled study. *International Journal of Group Psychotherapy*.

Lieberman, P. B., & Jacobs, S. C. (1987). Bereavement and its complications in medical patients: A guide for consultation liaison psychiatrists. *International Journal of Psychiatry in Medicine, 17*, 23–29.

Liebowitz, Z. B., Farren, C., & Kaye, B. L. (1986). *Designing career development systems*. San Francisco: Jossey-Bass.

Lifton, R. J. (1968). *Death in life: Survivors of Hiroshima*. New York: Random House.

Lindemann, E. (1944). Symptomatology and management of acute grief. *American Journal of Psychiatry, 101*, 141–148.

Lindy, J. D., Green, B. L., Grace, M., & Titchener, J. (1983). Psychotherapy with survivors of the Beverley Hills Supper Club Fire. *American Journal of Psychotherapy, 37*, 593–610.

Lindzey, G., & Aronson, E. (Eds.). (1985). *The handbook of social psychology* (2 vols.). New York: Random House.

Linn, M. W., Linn, B. S., & Jensen, J. (1984). Stressful events, dysphoric mood, and immune responsiveness. *Psychological Reports, 54*, 219–222.

Litwak, E. (1965). Extended kin relations in an industrial democratic society. In E. Shanas & G. Streib (Eds.), *Social structure and the family: Generational relations* (pp. 290–323). Englewood Cliffs, NJ: Prentice Hall.

Livnat, S., Felten, S. Y., Carlton, S. L., Bellinger, D. L., & Felten, D. L. (1985). Involvement of peripheral and central catecholamine systems in neural-immune interactions. *Neuroimmunology, 10*, 5–30.

Lloyd, C. (1980). Life events and depressive disorder reviewed. *Archives of General Psychiatry, 37*, 529–548.

Lofland, L. H. (1985). The social shaping of emotion: The case of grief. *Symbolic Interaction, 8*, 171–190.

Lopata, H. Z. (1969). Loneliness: Forms and components. *Social Problems, 17*, 248–262.

(1971). Living arrangements of urban widows and their married children. *Sociological Focus, 5*, 41–61.

(1973a). *Widowhood in an American city*. Cambridge, MA: Schenkman.

(1973b). The effect of schooling on social contacts of urban women. *American Journal of Sociology, 79*, 604–619.

(1975a). Grief work and identity reconstruction. *Journal of Geriatric Psychiatry, 8*, 41–55.

(1975b). Couple-companionate relationships in marriage and widowhood. In N. Glazer-Halbin, (Ed.), *Old families/new families* (pp. 119–149). New York: D. Van Nostrand.

(1975c). On widowhood: Grief work and identity reconstruction. *Journal of Geriatric Psychiatry, 8*, 41–55.

(1978). Contributions of extended families to the support systems of metropolitan area widows: Limitations of the modified kin network. *Journal of Marriage and the Family, 40*, 355–364.

(1979). *Women as widows: Support systems*. New York: Elsevier.

(1981). Widowhood and husband sanctification. *Journal of Marriage and the Family*, *43*, 439–450.

(1986). Becoming and being a widow: Reconstruction of the self and support systems. *Geriatric Psychiatry*, *19*, 203–214.

(1991). Which child? The consequences of social development on the support systems of widows. In B. Hess & E. Markson (Eds.), *Growing old in America* (pp. 39–49). New Brunswick, NJ: Transaction Publishers.

(forthcoming). *Circles and settings: Role changes of American women.*

Lopata, H. Z. (Ed.). (1987a). *Widows: The Middle East, Asia and the Pacific* (Vol. 1). Durham, NC: Duke University Press.

(Ed.). (1987b). *Widows: North America* (Vol. 2). Durham, NC: Duke University Press.

Lopata, H. Z., Barnewolt, D., & Miller, C. A. (1985). *City women: Work, jobs, occupations, careers*. Vol. 2. *Chicago*. New York: Praeger.

Lopata, H. Z., & Brehm, H. (1986). *Widows and dependent wives: From social problem to federal policy*. New York: Praeger.

Lopata, H. Z., & Maines, D. (Eds.). (1981). *Research on the interweave of social roles: Friendship*. Greenwich, CT: JAI Press.

(Eds.). (1990). *Friendship in context*. Greenwich, CT: JAI Press.

Lotzova, E., & Herberman, R. B. (1986). *Immunobiology of NK cells II*. Boca Raton, FL: CRC Press.

Lowman, J. (1979) Grief intervention and sudden infant death syndrome. *American Journal of Community Psychology*, *7*, 665–677.

Luhmann, N. (1982). *The differentiation of society*. S. Holmes, Trans. New York: Columbia University Press.

Lund, D. A. (1989a). *Older bereaved spouses: Research with practical applications*. New York: Taylor & Francis/Hemisphere.

(1989b). Conclusions about bereavement in later life and implications for interventions and future research. In D. A. Lund (Ed.), *Older bereaved spouses: Research with practical applications* (pp. 215–231). New York: Taylor & Francis/ Hemisphere.

Lund, D. A., Caserta, M. S., & Dimond, M. F. (1986a). Gender differences through two years of bereavement among the elderly. *The Gerontologist*, *26*, 314–320.

(1988). A comparison of bereavement adjustments between Mormon and non-Mormon older adults. *Journal of Religion and Aging*, *5*, 75–92.

(1989a). Impact of spousal bereavement on the subjective well-being of older adults. In D. A. Lund (Ed.), *Older bereaved spouses: Research with practical applications* (pp. 3–15). New York: Taylor & Francis/Hemisphere.

(1989b, November). *Effectiveness of self-help groups for older bereaved spouses*. Paper presented at the 42nd annual meeting of the Gerontological Society of America, Minneapolis.

Lund, D. A., Caserta, M. S., Dimond, M. F., & Gray, R. M. (1986b). Impact of bereavement on self-conceptions of older surviving spouses. *Symbolic Interaction*, *9*, 235–244.

Lund, D. A., Caserta, M. S., Dimond, M. F., & Shaffer, S. K. (1989c). Competencies, tasks of daily living, and adjustments to spousal bereavement in later life. In D. A. Lund (Ed.), *Older bereaved spouses: Research with practical applications* (pp. 135–152). New York: Taylor & Francis/Hemisphere.

Lund, D. A., Caserta, M. S., Van Pelt, J., & Gass, K. A. (1990). Stability of social support networks after later-life spousal bereavement. *Death Studies*, *14*, 53–73.

Lund, D. A., Dimond, M. F., Caserta, M. S., Johnson, R. J., Poulton, J. L., &

Connelly, J. R. (1985). Identifying elderly with coping difficulties after two years of bereavement. *Omega, 16*, 213–223.

Lund, D. A., Johnson, R., Baraki, H. N., & Dimond, M. F. (1984). Can pets help the bereaved? *Journal of Gerontological Nursing, 10*(6), 8–12.

Lund, D. A., Redburn, D. E., Juretich, M. S., & Caserta, M. S. (1989d). Resolving problems implementing bereavement self-help groups. In D. A. Lund (Ed.), *Older bereaved spouses: Research with practical applications* (pp. 203–216). New York: Taylor & Francis/Hemisphere.

Lundin, T. (1984). Morbidity following sudden and unexpected bereavement. *British Journal of Psychiatry, 144*, 84–88.

Lynn, D. B. (1974). *The father: His role in child development.* Monterey, CA: Brooks/Cole.

MacMahon, B., & Pugh, T. F. (1965). Suicide in the widowed. *American Journal of Epidemiology, 81*, 23–31.

Maddison, D., & Viola, A. (1968). The health of widows in the year following bereavement. *Journal of Psychosomatic Research, 12*, 297–306.

Maddison, D. A., Viola, A., & Walker, W. L. (1969). Further studies in conjugal bereavement. *Australian and New Zealand Journal of Psychiatry, 3*, 63–66.

Maddison, D., & Walker, W. L. (1967). Factors affecting the outcome of conjugal bereavement. *International Journal of Psychiatry, 113*, 1057–1067.

Maes, M., Bosmans, E., Suy, E., Minner, B., & Raus, J. (1989). Impaired lymphocyte stimulation by mitogens in severely depressed patients: A complex interface with HPA-axis hyperfunction, noradrenergic activity and the aging process. *British Journal of Psychiatry, 155*, 793–798.

Mahler, M., Pine, F., & Bergman, A. (1975). *The psychological birth of the human infant.* New York: Basic Books.

Maier, S. F., & Laudenslager, M. L. (1988). Commentary: Inescapable shock, shock controllability, and mitogen stimulated lymphocyte proliferation. *Brain, Behavior, and Immunity, 2*, 87–91.

Malan, D. H. (1979). *Individual psychotherapy and the science of psychodynamics.* London: Butterworth.

Malkinson, R. (1987). Helping and being helped: The support paradox. *Death Studies, 11*, 205–219.

Mandler, G. (1984). *Mind and body: Psychology of emotion and stress.* New York: Norton.

Mann, J. (1973). *Time limited psychotherapy.* Cambridge, MA: Harvard University Press.

Manuck, S. B., Cohen, S., Rabin, B. S., Muldoon, M. F., & Bachen, E. A. (1991). Individual differences in the cellular immune response to stress. *Psychological Science, 2*, 111–115.

Marmar, C. R., Horowitz, M. J., Weiss, D. S., Wilner, N. R., & Kaltreider, N. B. (1988). A controlled trial of brief psychotherapy and mutual-help group treatment of conjugal bereavement. *American Journal of Psychiatry, 145*(2), 203–212.

Marris, P. (1958). *Widows and their families.* London: Routledge & Kegan Paul.

(1974). *Loss and change.* New York: Pantheon.

Martin, J. L. (1986). AIDS risk reduction recommendations and sexual behavior patterns among gay men: A multifactorial categorical approach to assessing change. *Health Education Quarterly, 13*(4), 347–358.

(1987). The impact of AIDS on gay male sexual behavior patterns in New York City. *American Journal of Public Health, 77*(5), 578–581.

(1988). Psychological consequences of AIDS-related bereavement among gay men. *Journal of Consulting and Clinical Psychology, 56,* 856–862.

Martin, J. L., & Dean, L. (1989). Risk factors for AIDS-related bereavement in a cohort of homosexual men in New York City. In B. Cooper & T. Helgason (Eds.), *Epidemiology and the prevention of mental disorders* (pp. 170–184). London: Routledge.

(1990). Development of a community sample of gay men for an epidemiologic study of AIDS. *American Behavioral Scientist, 33*(5), 546–561.

Martin, J. L., Dean, L., Garcia, M. A., & Hall, W. (1989). The impact of AIDS on a gay community: Changes in sexual behavior, substance use, and mental health. *American Journal of Community Psychology, 17,* 269–293.

Mason, D. (1991). Genetic variation in the stress response: Susceptibility to experimental allergic encephalomyelitis and implication for human inflammatory disease. *Immunology Today, 12,* 57–58.

Mason, J. W. (1975). A historical view of the stress field. I. *Journal of Human Stress, 1,* 6–12.

Mason, J. W., Brady, J. V., & Toliver, G. A. (1968). Plasma and urinary 17-hydroxycorticosteroid responses to 72 hour avoidance sessions in the monkey. *Psychosomatic Medicine, 30,* 608–630.

Mason, J. W., Giller, E. L., Kosten, T. R., Ostroff, R. B., & Podd, L. (1986). Urinary free-cortisol levels in posttraumatic stress disorder patients. *Journal of Nervous and Mental Diseases, 174,* 145–149.

Mason, J. W., Maher, J. T., Hartley, L. H., Mougey, E. H., Perlow, M. J., & Jones, L. G. (1976). Selectivity of corticosteroid and catecholamine responses to various natural stimuli. In G. Serban (Ed.), *Psychopathology of human adaptation* (pp. 147–171). New York: Plenum.

Matussek, P. (1975). *Internment in concentration camps and its consequences.* Berlin/Heidelberg/New York: Springer.

Mawson, D., Marks, I. M., Ramm, L., & Stern, R. S. (1981). Guided mourning for morbid grief: A controlled study. *British Journal of Psychiatry, 138,* 185–193.

McCrae, R. R., & Costa, P. T. (1984). *Emerging lives, enduring dispositions: Personality in adulthood.* Boston: Little, Brown.

(1986). Personality, coping, and coping effectiveness in an adult sample. *Journal of Personality, 54,* 385–405.

McCubbin, H. I., Larson, A., & Olson, D. H. (1987). F-Copes Family crisis oriented personal evaluation scales. In H. I. McCubbin & A. I. Thompson (Eds.), *Family assessment inventories for research and practice* (pp. 195–207). Madison: University of Wisconsin Press.

McGoldrick, M., & Gerson, R. (1985). *Genograms in family assessment.* New York: Norton.

McGoldrick, M., & Rohrbaugh, M. (1987). Researching ethnic family stereotypes. *Family Process, 26,* 89–99.

McKinney, W. T. (1986). Primate separation studies: Relevance to bereavement. *Psychiatric Annals, 16,* 281–287.

McNeill, D. N. (1973). *Mortality among the widowed in Connecticut.* Unpublished M. P. H. essay, Yale University.

Melges, F. T., & DeMaso, D. R. (1980). Grief resolution therapy: Reliving, revising and revisiting. *American Journal of Psychotherapy, 34,* 51–61.

Mellinger, G., & Balter, M. (1963). Collaborative Project, GMIRSB Report. Washington, DC: National Institute of Mental Health.

Mellström, D., Nilsson, A., Oden, A., Rundgren, A., & Svanborg, A. (1982). Mortality among the widowed in Sweden. *Scandinavian Journal of Social Medicine, 10,* 33–41.

Menaghen, E. G. (1983). Individual coping efforts: Moderators of the relationship between life stress and mental health outcomes. In H. B. Kaplan (Ed.), *Psychosocial stress: Trends in theory and research* (pp. 157–191). New York: Academic Press.

Mendlewicz, J., Linkowski, P., Kerhofs, M., Desmedt, D., Goldstein, J., Copinschi, G., & Van Clauter, E. (1985). Diurnal hypersecretion of growth hormone in depression. *Journal of Clinical Endocrinology and Metabolism, 60,* 505–512.

Mergenhagen, P. M., Lee, B. A., & Gove, W. R. (1985). Till death us do part: Recent changes in the relationship between marital status and mortality. *Sociology and Social Research, 70,* 53–56.

Middleton, W., Moylan, A., Burnett, P., & Martinek, N. (1991). *An international perspective on bereavement related concepts.* Paper presented to the Third International Conference on Grief and Bereavement in Contemporary Society, Sydney.

Mielke, R. (1979). Entwicklung einer deutschen Form des Fragebogens zur Erfassung interner vs. externer Kontrolle von Levenson (IPC). *Bielefelder Arbeiten zur Sozialpsychologie, 46.*

Mikulincer, M. (1988). Reactance and helplessness following exposure to unsolvable problems: The effects of attributional style. *Journal of Personality and Social Psychology, 54,* 679–686.

Miles, M. S., & Crandall, E. K. B. (1983). The search for meaning and its potential for affecting growth in bereaved parents. *Health Values: Achieving High Level Wellness, 7*(1), 19–23.

Miller, H. G., Turner, C. F., & Moses, L. E. (1990). *AIDS: The second decade.* Washington, DC: National Academy Press.

Miller, J. B. M. (1971). Children's reactions to the death of a parent: A review of the psychoanalytic literature. *Journal of the American Psychoanalytic Association, 19,* 697–719.

(1986). *Toward a new psychology of women* (2nd ed.). Boston: Beacon Press.

Mineka, S., & Suomi, S. J. (1978). Social separation in monkeys. *Psychological Bulletin, 85,* 1376–1400.

Mishler, E. G. (1981). The social construction of illness. In E. G. Mishler et al. *Social contexts of health, illness, and patient care* (pp. 141–168). Cambridge: Cambridge University Press.

Miyabo, S., Asato, T., & Miyushima, N. (1977). Prolactin and growth hormone responses to psychological stress in normal and neurotic subjects. *Journal of Clinical Endocrinology and Metabolism, 44,* 947–951.

Mohl, P. C., Huang, L., Bowden, C., Fischbach, M., Vogtsberer, K., & Talel, N. (1987). Natural killer cell activity in major depression (letter). *American Journal of Psychiatry, 144,* 1619.

Moitoza, E. (1982). Portuguese families. In M. McGoldrick, J. K. Pearce, & J. Giordano (Eds.), *Ethnicity and family therapy* (pp. 412–437). New York: Guilford.

Moos, R. H., & Billing, A. G. (1982). Conceptualization and measuring coping resources and processes. In L. Goldberger & S. Breznitz, *Handbook of stress, theoretical and clinical aspects.* New York: Free Press.

Moos, R. H., & Moos, B. S. (1986). *Family environment scale manual.* Palo Alto, CA: Consulting Psychologist Press.

Mor, V. (1987). *Hospice care systems: Structure, process, costs and outcome*. New York: Springer.

Mor, V., McHorney, C., & Sherwood, S. (1986). Secondary morbidity among the recently bereaved. *American Journal of Psychiatry, 143*, 158–163.

Morgan, L. A. (1976). A re-examination of widowhood and morale. *Journal of Gerontology, 31*, 687–695.

Morgan, T. J., Hansson, R. O., Indart, M. J., Austin, D. M., Crutcher, M., Hampton, P. W., Oppegard, K. M., & O'Daffer, V. E. (1984). Old age and environmental docility: The roles of health, support and personality. *Journal of Gerontology, 39*, 240–242.

Morimoto, C., Hafler, D. A., Weiner, H. L., Letvin, N. L., Hagan, M., Daley, J., & Schlossman, S. F. (1987). Selective loss of the suppressor-inducer T-cell subset in progressive multiple sclerosis: analysis with anti-2H4 monoclonal antibody. *New England Journal of Medicine, 316*, 67–72.

Motulsky, H. J. & Insel, P. A. (1982). Medical progress: Adrenergic receptors in man: Direct identification, physiologic regulation, and clinical alterations. *New England Journal of Medicine, 307*(1), 18–29.

Mullan, J. (1981, March). *Parental distress and marital happiness: The transition to the empty nest*. Unpublished dissertation, University of Chicago.

Munck, A., Guyre, P. M., & Holbrook, N. J. (1984). Physiological functions of glucocorticoids in stress and their relation to pharmacologic actions. *Endocrine Reviews, 5*, 25–44.

Murrell, S. A., Himmelfarb, S., & Phifer, J. F. (1988). Effects of bereavement/loss and pre-event status on subsequent physical health in older adults. *International Journal of Aging and Human Development, 27*, 87–107.

National Center for Health Statistics. (1973). *Plan and operation of the Health and Nutrition Examination Survey: United States, 1971–1973*. DHEW Publication No. (PHS) 79-1310. Washington, DC: U.S. Government Printing Office.

(1976). Differentials in health characteristics by marital status. United States, 1971–1972. *Vital and Health Statistics*, Series 10, No. 104.

(1978). *Plan and operation of the HANES I Augmentation Survey of Adults 25–74 Years: United States, 1974–1975*. DHEW Publication No. (PHS) 78-1314. Washington, DC: U.S. Government Printing Office.

Neugarten, B., Havighurst, R., & Tobin, S. (1961). The measurement of life satisfaction. *Journal of Gerontology, 16*, 134–143.

Niederland, W. (1968). The problems of survivors: Dynamics of posttraumatic symptomatology. In H. Krystal (Ed.), *Massive psychic trauma*. New York: International Universities Press.

Niemi, T. (1978). The mortality of women after the retirement and death of their husbands. *Psychiatria Fennica*, 113–115.

(1979). The mortality of male old-age pensioners following spouse's death. *Scandinavian Journal of Social Medicine, 7*, 115–117.

Nisbett, R. E., & Ross, L. (1980). *Human inference: Strategies and shortcomings of social judgment*. Englewood Cliffs, NJ: Prentice Hall.

Nolen-Hoeksema, S. (1987). Sex differences in unipolar depression: Evidence and theory. *Psychological Bulletin, 101*, 259–282.

Norris, F. H., & Murrell, S. A. (1987). Other adult family stress and adaptation before and after bereavement. *Journal of Gerontology, 42*, 606–612.

Nossal, G. J. V. (1987). Current concepts: Immunology: The basic components of the immune system. *New England Journal of Medicine, 316*(21), 1320–1325.

Nowicki, S., & Strickland, B. R. (1973). A locus of control scale for children. *Journal of Consulting Psychology, 40,* 148–154.

Nunley, E. P. (1986). *The impact of the empty-nest syndrome on females and the relationship between work status and the way the empty nest is perceived and experienced.* Unpublished doctoral dissertation, International Graduate School, St. Louis, MO.

Okun, M. A. (1976). Adult age and cautiousness in decision: A review of the literature. *Human Development, 19,* 220–233.

O'Leary, A. (1990). Stress, emotion, and human immune function. *Psychological Bulletin, 108,* 363–382.

Olson, D. H., McCubbin, H. I., Barnes, H., Larsen, A., Muxen, M., & Wilson, M. (1983). *Families: What makes them work.* Los Angeles: Sage.

Ormel, J. (1983). Neuroticism and well-being inventories: Measuring traits or states? *Psychological Medicine, 13,* 165–176.

Osgood, E. E., Suci, G., & Tannenbaum, P. (1957). *The measurement of meaning.* Urbana: University of Illinois Press.

Osterweis, M., Solomon, F., & Green, M. (Eds.). (1984). *Bereavement: Reactions, consequences, and care.* Washington, DC: National Academy Press.

Padgett, G. A., Reiquam, C. W., Henson, J. B., & Gorham, J. R. (1968). Comparative studies of susceptibility to infection in the Chediak-Higashi syndrome. *Journal of Pathology and Bacteriology, 95,* 509–522.

Papanek, H. (1973). Men, women and work: Reflections on the two-person career. *American Journal of Sociology, 78,* 852–872.

Parkes, C. M. (1964a). Recent bereavement as a cause of mental illness. *British Journal of Psychiatry, 110,* 198–204.

(1964b). The effects of bereavement on physical and mental health: A study of the medical records of widows. *British Medical Journal, 2,* 274–279.

(1965). Bereavement and mental illness. *British Journal of Medical Psychology, 38,* 388–397.

(1971a). Psycho-social transitions: A field for study. *Social Science and Medicine, 5,* 101–115.

(1971b). The first year of bereavement: A longitudinal study of the reaction of London widows to the death of their husbands. *Psychiatry, 33,* 444–466.

(1972a). *Bereavement: Studies of grief in adult life* (2nd ed.). New York: International Universities Press.

(1972b). Components of the reaction to loss of a limb, spouse or home. *Journal of Psychosomatic Research, 16,* 343–349.

(1975a). Unexpected and untimely bereavement: A statistical study of young Boston widows and widowers. In B. Schoenberg, I. Gerber, A. Wiener, D. Kutscher, D. Peretz, & A. Cam (Eds.), *Bereavement: Its psychological aspects* (pp. 119–138). New York: Columbia University Press.

(1975b). Determinants of outcome following bereavement. *Omega, 6,* 303–323.

(1978). Psychological aspects. In C. M. Saunders (Ed.), *The management of terminal disease.* London: Arnold.

(1979). Evaluation of a bereavement service. In A. DeVries & A. Carmichael (Eds.), *The dying human* (pp. 389–402). Ramat Gan, Israel: Turtledove.

(1980). Bereavement counselling: Does it work? *British Medical Journal, 281,* 3–10.

(1981). Evaluation of a bereavement service. *Journal of Preventive Psychiatry, 1,* 179.

(1984). Editorial comments. *Bereavement Care, 3,* 26.

(1985). Bereavement. *British Journal of Psychiatry, 146,* 11–17.

(1990). Risk factors in bereavement. Implications for the prevention and treatment of pathologic grief. *Psychiatric Annals, 20,* 308–313.

Parkes, C. M., Benjamin, B., & Fitzgerald, R. G. (1969). Broken heart: A statistical study of increased mortality among widowers. *British Medical Journal, 1,* 740–743.

Parkes, C. M., & Brown, R. J. (1972). Health after bereavement: A controlled study of young Boston widows and widowers. *Psychosomatic Medicine, 34,* 449–461.

Parkes, C. M., & Weiss, R. S. (1983). *Recovery from bereavement.* New York: Basic Books.

Parrillo, J. E., & Fauci, A. S. (1978). Comparison of the effector cells in human spontaneous cellular cytotoxicity and antibody-dependent cellular cytotoxicity: Differential sensitivity of effector cells to in vivo and in vitro corticosteroids. *Scandinavian Journal of Immunology, 8,* 99–107.

Pasnau, R. O., Fawney, F. I., & Fawney, N. (1987). Role of the physician in bereavement. *Psychiatric Clinics of North America, 10,* 109–120.

Paul, H. (1963). Psychologische Untersuchungen. In H. Paul & H. J. Herberg (Eds.), *Psychische Spaetschaden nach politischer Verfolgung* (pp. 207–243). New York: S. Karger.

Paul, N., & Grosser, G. (1965). Operational mourning and its role in conjoint family therapy. *Community Mental Health Journal, 1,* 339–345.

Paul, W. E. (1984). The immune system: An introduction. In W. E. Paul (Ed.), *Fundamental immunology* (pp. 3–22). New York: Raven Press.

Pearlin, L. I., Lieberman, M. A., Menaghan, E. G., & Mullen, J. T. (1981). The stress process. *Journal of Health and Social Behavior, 22,* 337–356.

Pearlin, L., & Schooler, C. (1978). The structure of coping. *Journal of Health and Social Behavior, 19,* 2–21.

Pennebaker, J., Kiecolt-Glaser, J. K., & Glaser, R. (1988). Disclosure of traumas and immune function: Health implications for psychotherapy. *Journal of Consulting and Clinical Psychology, 56,* 239–245.

Peris, C., Holmgren, S., von Knorring, L., & Peris, H. (1986). Parental loss by death in early childhood of depressed patients and their healthy siblings. *British Journal of Psychiatry, 148,* 165–169.

Pfeiffer, E. (1977). Psychopathology and social pathology. In J. E. Birren & K. W. Schaie (Eds.), *Handbook of the psychology of aging* (pp. 650–671). New York: Van Nostrand Reinhold.

Pincus, L. (1974). *Death in the family.* New York: Random Press.

Pine, V. R., et al. (1976). *Acute grief and the funeral.* Springfield, IL: Charles C Thomas.

Pittman, N. L., & Pittman, T. S. (1979). Effects of amount of helplessness training and internal-external locus of control on mood and performance. *Journal of Personality and Social Psychology, 37,* 39–47.

Pitts, F. N., Jr., Meyer, J., Brooks, M., & Winokur, G. (1965). Adult psychiatric illness assessed for childhood parental loss and psychiatric illness in family members. *American Journal of Psychiatry, 121,* i–x (suppl.).

Polak, P. R., Egan, D., Vandenburgh, R., & Vail Williams, W. (1975). Prevention in mental health: A controlled study. *American Journal of Psychiatry, 132,* 146–149.

Pollock, G. H. (1987). The mourning-liberation process in health and disease. *Psychiatric Clinics of North America, 10,* 345–354.

Pynoos, R. S., & Nader, K. (1990). Children's exposure to violence and traumatic death. *Psychiatric Annals, 20,* 334–344.

Rabkin, J. G., & Struening, E. L. (1976). Life events, stress and illness. *Science, 194,* 1013–1020.

Radloff, L. S. (1977). The CES-D Scale: A self-report depression scale for research in the general population. *Applied Psychological Measurement, 1,* 385–401.

Rager, D. R., Laudenslager, M. L., Held, P. E., & Boccia, M. L. (1989). Some long-term behavioral and immunological effects of brief, early maternal separation in nonhuman primates: Preliminary observations. *Society for Neuroscience Abstracts, 15,* 297.

Rahe, R. H. (1968) Life-change measurement as a predictor of illness. *Proceedings of the Royal Society of Medicine, 61,* 1124–1126.

(1979). Life events, mental illness: An overview. *Journal of Human Stress, 5*(3), 2–10.

Ramsay R. N. (1979). Bereavement: A behavioural treatment of pathological grief. In P. O. Sjodan, S. Bales, & W. S. Dochens (Eds.), *Trends in behavior therapy* (chapter 12, pp. 217–248). New York: Academic Press.

Rando, T. A. (1983). An investigation of grief and adaptation in parents whose children have died from cancer. *Journal of Pediatric Psychology, 8,* 3–20.

(1984). *Grief, dying and death: Clinical interventions for caregivers.* Champaign, IL: Research Press.

(1985). Creating therapeutic rituals in the psychotherapy of the bereaved. *Psychotherapy, 22,* 236–240.

(Ed.). (1986). Parental loss of a child. Champaign, IL: Research Press.

Rapaport, M. H., Risch, S. C., Gillin, J. C., Goshan, S., & Janowsky, D. S. (1989). Blunted growth hormone response to peripheral infusion of human growth hormone-releasing factor in patients with panic disorder. *American Journal of Psychiatry, 146,* 92–95.

Raphael, B. (1975). The management of pathological grief. *Australian and New Zealand Journal of Psychiatry, 9,* 173–180.

(1977). Preventive intervention with the recently bereaved. *Archives of General Psychiatry, 34,* 1450–1454.

(1978). Mourning and the prevention of melancholia. *British Journal of Medical Psychology, 41,* 303–310.

(1983). *The anatomy of bereavement.* New York: Basic Books.

(1986). *When disaster strikes.* New York: Basic Books.

Raphael, B., & Maddison, D. (1976). The care of bereaved adults. In O. W. Hill (Ed.), *Modern trends in psychosomatic medicine.* London: Butterworth.

Raphael, B., & Nunn, K. (1988). Counseling the bereaved. *Journal of Social Issues, 44,* 191–206.

Rasmussen, K. L. R., Fellowes, J. R., & Suomi, S. J. (1990). Physiological correlates of emigration behavior in adolescent male rhesus monkeys on Cayo Santiago. *American Journal of Primatology, 20,* 224.

Rasmussen, K. L. R., & Suomi, S. J. (1989). Heart rate and endocrine responses to stress in adolescent male rhesus monkeys in Cayo Santiago. *Puerto Rico Health Sciences Journal, 8,* 65–71.

Reder, A., Checinski, M., & Chelmicka-Schorr, E. (1989). The effect of chemical sympathectomy on natural killer cells in mice. *Brain, Behavior and Immunity, 3,* 110–118.

Redmond, D. E., Jr., & Huang, Y. H. (1979). Current Concepts. II. New evidence for a locus coeruleus-norepinephrine connection with anxiety. *Life Sciences, 25,* 2149–2162.

Rees, W., & Lutkins, S. (1967). Mortality of bereavement. *British Medical Journal, 4,* 13–16.

Reese, H. W., & Rodeheaver, D. (1985). Problem solving and complex decision making. In J. E. Birren & K. W. Schaie (Eds.), *Handbook of the psychology of aging* (2nd ed., pp. 474–499). New York: Van Nostrand Reinhold.

Reese, M. F. (1982). Growing up: The impact of loss and change. In D. Belle (Ed.), *Lives in stress: Women and depression* (pp. 65–88). Beverly Hills, CA: Sage.

Reeves, N. C., & Boersma, F. J. (1990). The therapeutic use of ritual in maladaptive grieving. *Omega, 20*, 281–291.

Reite, M. L., & Capitanio, J. P. (1985). On the nature of social separation and social attachment. In M. L. Reite & T. Field (Eds.), *The psychobiology of attachment and separation* (pp. 223–255). New York: Academic Press.

Reite, M. L., Harbeck, R. C., & Hoffman, A. (1981a). Altered cellular immune response following peer separation. *Life Sciences, 28*, 1133–1136.

Reite, M. L., Laudenslager, M. L., Jones, J., Crnic, L., & Kaemingk, K. (1986). Interferon decreases REM latency. *Biological Psychiatry, 22*, 104–107.

Reite, M. L., Short, R., Seiler, C., & Pauley, J. D. (1981b). Attachment, loss, and depression. *Journal of Child Psychology and Psychiatry, 22*, 141–169.

Reite, M. L., & Snyder, D. S. (1982). Physiology of maternal separation in a bonnet macaque infant. *American Journal of Primatology, 2*, 115–120.

Remondet, J. H., & Hansson, R. O. (1987). Assessing a widow's grief: A short index. *Journal of Gerontological Nursing, 13*, 31–34.

Remondet, J. H., Hansson, R. O., Rule, B., & Winfrey, G. (1987). Rehearsal for widowhood. *Journal of Social and Clinical Psychology, 5*, 285–297.

Riley, V. (1981). Psychoneuroendocrine influences on immunocompetence and neoplasia. *Science, 212*, 1100–1109.

Rioch, M., Elkes, D., & Flint, A. (1963). *A pilot project in training mental health counselors.* Publication No. 1254. Washington, DC: U.S. Government Printing Office.

Ritz, J. (1989). The role of natural killer cells in immune surveillance, *New England Journal of Medicine, 320*, 1748–1749.

Robinson, P. J., & Fleming, S. (1989). Differentiating grief and depression. *Hospice Journal, 5*, 77–88.

Rodin, J. (1985). The application of social psychology. In G. Lindzey & E. Aronson (Eds.), *Handbook of social psychology* (3rd ed.). (Vol. 2, pp. 805–881). New York: Random House.

— (1986). Aging and health: Effects of the sense of control. *Science, 233*, 1271–1276.

— (1987). Personal control through the life course. In R. P. Ables (Ed.), *Life-span perspectives and social psychology* (pp. 103–119). Hillsdale, NJ: Erlbaum.

Rogers, J., Sheldon, A., Barwick, C., Letofsky, K., & Lancee, W. (1982). Help for families of suicide: Survivors support program. *Canadian Journal of Psychiatry, 27*, 444–449.

Roitt, I., Brostoff, J., & Male, D. (1989). *Immunology* (2nd ed.). St. Louis, MO: C. W. Mosby.

Rook, K. S. (1987). Social support versus companionship: Effects on life stress, loneliness, and evaluations by others. *Journal of Personality and Social Psychology, 52*(6), 1132–1147.

Rose, R. (1980). Endocrine responses to stressful psychological events. *Psychiatric Clinics of North America, 3*, 251–276.

Rosenbaum, A. H., Schatzberg, A. F., Jost, F. A., Cross, P. D., Wells, L. A., Jiang, N. S., & Maruta, T. (1983). Urinary free cortisol levels in anxiety. *Psychosomatics, 24*, 835–837.

Rosenberg, M. (1965). *Society and the adolescent self-image.* Princeton, NJ: Princeton University Press.

Rosenblatt, P. C. (1983). *Bitter, bitter tears: Nineteenth century diarists and twentieth century grief theories.* Minneapolis: University of Minnesota Press.

(1990). *Farming is in our blood: Farm families in economic crisis.* Ames: Iowa State University Press.

Rosenblatt, P. C., & Burns, L. H. (1986). Long term effects of perinatal loss. *Journal of Family Issues, 7,* 237–253.

Rosenblatt, P. C., de Mik, L., Anderson, R. M., & Johnson, P. A. (1985). *The family in business,* San Francisco: Jossey-Bass.

Rosenblatt, P. C., & Elde, C. (1990). Shared reminiscence about a deceased parent: Implications for grief education and grief counseling. *Family Relations, 39,* 206–210.

Rosenblatt, P. C., Spoentgen, P., Karis, T. A., Dahl, C., Kaiser, T., & Elde, C. (1991). Difficulties in supporting the bereaved. *Omega, 23,* 119–128.

Rosenblatt, P. C., Walsh, R. P., & Jackson, D. A. (1976). *Grief and mourning in cross-cultural perspective.* New Haven, CT: Human Relations Area Files Press.

Rosenblatt, P. C., & Wright, S. E. (1984). Shadow realities in close relationships. *American Journal of Family Therapy, 12*(2), 45–54.

Roskin, M. (1984). A look at bereaved parents. *Bereavement Care, 3,* 26–29.

Ross, A. (1961). *The Hindu family in its urban setting.* Toronto: University of Toronto Press.

Ross, M., & Conway, M. (1986). Remembering one's own past: The construction of personal histories. In R. M. Sorrentino & E. T. Higgins (Eds.), *Handbook of motivation and cognition: Foundations of social behavior* (pp. 122–144). New York: Guilford.

Ross, R. J., Ball, W. A., Sullivan, K. A., & Caroff, S. N. (1989). Sleep disturbances as the hallmark of posttraumatic stress disorder. *American Journal of Psychiatry, 146,* 697–707.

Rowe, J. W., & Kahn, R. L. (1987). Human aging: Usual and successful. *Science, 237,* 143–149.

Roy-Byrne, P. P., Bierer, L. M., & Uhde, T. W. (1985). The dexamethasone suppression test in panic disorder: Comparison with normal controls. *Biologic Psychiatry, 20,* 1234–1237.

Rubenstein, C. M., & Shaver, P. (1980). Loneliness in two northern cities. In J. Hartog & R. Audy (Eds.), *The anatomy of loneliness* (pp. 319–337). New York: International Universities Press.

Rubin, L. (1979). *Women of a certain age: The mid-life search for self.* New York: Harper & Row.

Rubin, S. (1977). *Bereavement and vulnerability: A study of mothers of sudden infant death syndrome children.* Unpublished doctoral dissertation, Boston University.

(1981). A two-track model of bereavement: Theory and application in research. *American Journal of Orthopsychiatry, 51,* 101–109.

(1982). Persisting effects of loss: A model of mourning. In C. Spielberger & I. Sarason (Eds.), N. Milgram (guest ed.), *Stress and anxiety. Vol. 8* (pp. 275–282). Washington, DC: Hemisphere.

(1984a). Mourning distinct from melancholia. *British Journal of Medical Psychology, 57,* 339–345.

(1984b). Maternal attachment and child death: On adjustment, relationship and resolution. *Omega, 15*(4), 347–352.

(1985). The resolution of bereavement: A clinical focus on the relationship to the deceased. *Psychotherapy: Theory, research, training and practice, 22*(2), 231–235.

(1986). Child death and the family: Parents and children confronting loss.

International Journal of Family Therapy, 7, 377–388.

(1987). *The long-term adaptation of parents bereaved by war.* Unpublished research report submitted to the Department of Rehabilitation, Ministry of Defense, State of Israel (Hebrew).

(1990a). Death of the future: An outcome study of bereaved parents in Irsael. *Omega, 20*(4), 323–339.

(1990b). Treating the bereaved spouse: A focus on the loss process, the self and the other. *The Psychotherapy Patient, 6*(3/4), 189–205.

(in press). Adult child loss and the Two-Track Model of Bereavement. *Omega.*

Rupprecht, R., & Lesch, K. P. (1989). Psychoneuroendocrine research in depression. *Journal of Neural Transmission, 75*, 167–178.

Rutter, M. (1987). Psychosocial resilience and protective mechanisms. *American Journal of Orthopsychiatry, 57*, 316–331.

Rynearson, E. K. (1981). Suicide internalized: Existential sequestrum. *American Journal of Psychiatry, 138*, 84–87.

(1984). Bereavement after homicide: A descriptive study. *American Journal of Psychiatry, 141*, 1452–1454.

(1987). Psychotherapy of pathologic grief: Revisions and limitations. *Psychiatric Clinics of North America, 10*, 487–500.

Sabatini, L. (1988). Evaluating a treatment program for newly widowed people. *Omega, 19*, 229–236.

Sable, P. (1989, October). Attachment, anxiety, and loss of a husband. *American Journal of Orthopsychiatry, 59*(4).

Sadeh, A. (1987). *Object relationship, object representation and depression in Israeli college students.* Unpublished master's thesis, University of Haifa, Israel (Hebrew).

Sampson, E. E. (1985). The decentralization of identity: Toward a revised concept of personal and social order. *American Psychologist, 40*, 1203–1211.

Sanders, C. M. (1979). The use of the MMPI in assessing bereavement outcome. In C. S. Newmark (Ed.), *MMPI: Clinical and research trends* (pp. 223–247). New York: Praeger.

(1980). A comparison of adult bereavement in the death of a spouse, child, and parent. *Omega, 10*, 303–322.

(1981). Comparison of younger and older spouses in bereavement outcome. *Omega, 11*, 217–232.

(1983). Effects of sudden versus chronic illness death on bereavement outcome. *Omega, 11*, 227–241.

(1986). Accidental death of a child. In T. A. Rando (Ed.), *Parental loss of a child* (pp. 181–190). Champaign, IL: Research Press.

(1988). Risk factors in bereavement outcome. *Journal of Social Issues, 44*, 97–112.

(1989). *Grief: The mourning after.* New York: Wiley.

Sanders, C. M., Mauger, P. A., & Strong, P. A. (1985/1991). *A manual for the grief experience inventory.* Palo Alto, CA: Consulting Psychologists Press/Charlotte, NC: Center for the Study of Separation and Loss.

Sanders, J. A. C., Sterns, H. L., Smith, M., & Sanders, R. E. (1975). Modification of concept identification performance in older adults. *Developmental Psychology, 11*, 824–829.

Sarason, B. R., Pierce, G. R., Shearin, E. N., Sarason, I. G., Waltz, J. A., & Poppe, L. (1991). Perceived support and working models of self and actual others. *Journal of Personality and Social Psychology, 60*, 273–287.

Sarason, I. G., Sarason, B. R., & Pierce, G. R. (1990). Social support: The search for theory. *Journal of Social and Clinical Psychology, 9*, 133–147.

514   REFERENCES

Sarbin, T. R. (1989). Emotions as situated actions. In L. Cirillo, B. Kaplan, & S. Wapner (Eds.), *Emotions in ideal human development* (pp. 77–99). Hillsdale, NJ: Erlbaum.

Scanlan, J. M., Boccia, M. L., Laudenslager, M. L., & Broussard, C. (1990). Presence of social support affects behavioral and immunological response to maternal separation of infant bonnet macaques. *American Journal of Primatology*, 20, 230.

Scanlan, J. M., Coe, C. L., Latts, A., & Suomi, S. J. (1987). Effects of age, rearing, and separation stress on immunoglobulin levels in rhesus monkeys. *American Journal of Primatology*, 13, 11–22.

Scarr, S. (1987). Distinctive environments depend on genotypes. *Behavioral and Brain Sciences*, 10, 38–39.

Scheier, M. F., & Carver, C. S. (1985). Optimism, coping, and health: Assessment and implications of generalized outcome expectancies. *Health Psychology*, 4, 219–247.

Schieffelin, E. L. (1985). The cultural analysis of depressive affect: An example from New Guinea. In A. Kleinman & B. Good (Eds.), *Culture and depression: Studies in the anthropology and cross-cultural psychiatry of affect and disorder* (pp. 429–490). Berkeley: University of California Press.

Schilling, R. F. (1987). Limitations of social support. *Social Service Review*, 61, 19–31.

Schleifer, S. J., Keller, S. E., Bond, R. N., Cohen, J., & Stein, M. (1989). Major depressive disorder and immunity: Role of age, sex, severity, and hospitalization. *Archives of General Psychiatry*, 46, 81–87.

Schleifer, S. J., Keller, S. E., Camerino, M., Thornton, J. C., & Stein, M. (1983). Suppression of lymphocyte stimulation following bereavement. *Journal of the American Medical Association*, 250, 374–377.

Schleifer, S., Keller, S. E., Meyerson, A. T., Raskin, M. D., Davis, K. L., & Stein, M. (1984). Lymphocyte function in major depressive disorder. *Archives of General Psychiatry*, 41, 484–486.

Schleifer, S., Keller, S. E., Siris, S. G., Davis, K. L., & Stein, M. (1985). Depression and immunity: Lymphocyte stimulation in ambulatory depressed patients, hospitalized schizophrenic patients, and patients hospitalized for herniorrhaphy. *Archives of General Psychiatry*, 42, 129–133.

Schleifer, S. J., Scott, B., Stein, M., & Keller, S. E. (1986). Behavioral and developmental aspects of immunity. *Journal of the American Academy of Child and Adolescent Psychiatry*, 26(6), 751–763.

Schroeder, D. H., & Costa, P. T., Jr. (1984). Influence of life event stress on physical illness: Substantive effects or methodological flaws? *Journal of Personality and Social Psychology*, 46, 853–863.

Schulte, H. M., Chrousos, G. P., Gold, P. W., Booth, J. D., Oldfield, E. H., Cutler, G. B., & Loriaux, D. L. (1985). Continuous administration of synthetic ovine corticotropin releasing factor in man: Physiological and pathophysiological implications. *Journal of Clinical Investigation*, 75, 1781–1785.

Schuster, T. L., & Butler, E. W. (1989). Bereavement, social networks, social support, and mental health. In D. A. Lund (Ed.), *Older bereaved spouses: Research with practical applications* (pp. 55–68). New York: Taylor & Francis/Hemisphere.

Schut, H. A. W., de Keijser, J., & van den Bout, J., et al. (1991). *Incidence and prevalence of post traumatic stress symptomatology in the conjugally bereaved*. Paper presented to the Third International Conference on Grief and Bereavement in Contemporary Society, Sydney.

Schwartz, G. E. (1979). The brain as a health care system: A psychobiological framework for biofeedback and health psychology. In G. Stone, N. Adler, & F. Cohen (Eds.), *Health psychology* (pp. 549–571). San Francisco: Jossey-Bass.

Selby, J. (1991). *Cultural, ethic and religious prescriptions and practices with death, dying and bereavement in contemporary Australian society.* Ph.D. thesis, University of Queensland.

Selman, R. L. (1980). *The growth of interpersonal understanding.* New York: Academic Press.

Selye, H. (1946). *Stress in health and disease.* Boston: Butterworth.

—— (1956). *The stress of life.* New York: McGraw-Hill.

Shamgar-Handleman, L. (1986). *Israeli war widows: Beyond the glory of heroism.* South Hadley, MA: Bergin & Garvey.

Shanas, E., & Streib, G. R. (Eds.). (1965). *Social structure and the family: Generational relations.* Englewood Cliffs, NJ: Prentice Hall.

Shaver, P., & Hazan, C. (1987). Being lonely, falling in love. Perspectives from attachment theory. *Journal of Personality and Social Behavior, 2,* 105–124.

Shaw, M. J. (1974). *Social work in prison: An experiment in the use of extended contact with offenders.* London: HMSO.

Sheldon, A. R., Cochrane, J., Vachon, M. L. S., Lyall, W., Rogers, J., & Freeman, S. (1981). A psychosocial analysis of risk of psychological impairment following bereavement. *Journal of Nervous and Mental Disease, 169,* 253–255.

Shepherd, D. M., & Barraclough, B. M. (1974). The aftermath of parental suicide for children. *British Journal of Psychiatry, 129,* 267–276.

Sheppard, H. L. (1976). Work and retirement. In R. H. Benstock & E. Shanas (Eds.), *Handbook of aging and the social sciences* (pp. 286–309). New York: Van Nostrand Reinhold.

Sherman, B. (1984). *Impact on marriages among bereaved couples.* Unpublished dissertation, University of Chicago.

Sherman, R. R. (1980). *Parental bereavement and marriage: Coping by spouse after the death of their child,* unpublished dissertation, University of Chicago.

Shinn, M., Lehmann, S., & Wong, N. W. (1984). Social interaction and social support. *Journal of Social Issues, 40*(4), 55–76.

Shore, J. H., Tatum, E. L., & Vollmer, W. M. (1986). Evaluation of mental effects of disaster, Mount St. Helens eruption. *American Journal of Public Health, 76,* 76–83.

Shorter, E. (1975). *The making of the modern family.* New York: Basic Books.

Shuchter, S. R. (1986). *Dimensions of grief: Adjusting to the death of a spouse.* San Francisco: Jossey-Bass.

Shuchter, S. R., & Zisook, S. (1986). Multidimensional approach to widowhood. *Psychiatric Annals, 16,* 295–308.

Shuchter, S. R., Zisook, S., Kirkorowicz, C., & Risch, C. (1986). The dexamethasone test in acute grief. *American Journal of Psychiatry, 143,* 879–881.

Shumaker, S. A., & Brownell, A. (1984). Toward a theory of social support: Closing conceptual gaps. *Journal of Social Issues, 40*(4), 11–36.

Siegel, J. M., & Kuykendall, D. H. (1990). Loss, widowhood, and psychological distress among the elderly. *Journal of Consulting and Clinical Psychology, 58*(5), 519–524.

Silver, R. L. (1982). *Coping with an undesirable life event: A study of early reactions to physical disability.* Unpublished doctoral dissertation, Northwestern University.

Silver, R. L., Boon, C., & Stones, M. (1983). Searching for meaning in misfortune: Making sense of incest. *Journal of Social Issues, 39*(2), 81–102.

Silver, R. L., & Wortman, C. B. (1980). Coping with undesirable life events. In J. Garber & M. E. P. Seligman (Eds.), *Human helplessness: Theory and applications* (pp. 279–340). New York: Academic Press.

——— (1991). *A world view analysis of the impact of life events.* Manuscript in preparation.

Silverman, P. R. (1972). Widowhood and preventive intervention. *The Family Coordinator, 21*, 95–102.

——— (1982). Middle and late life transitions. *Annals of the American Academy of Political and Social Sciences, 464*, 174–187.

——— (1986). *Widow-to-widow.* New York: Springer.

——— (1987a). The impact of parental death on college-age women. *Psychiatric Clinics of North America, 10*, 387–404.

——— (1987b). Widowhood as the next stage in the life course. In H. Z. Lopata (Ed.), *Widows: North America* (Vol. 2, pp. 171–190). Durham, NC: Duke University Press.

——— (1988a). Research as process: Exploring the meaning of widowhood. In S. Reinharz & G. D. Rowles (Eds.), *Qualitative gerontology* (pp. 217–240). New York: Springer.

——— (1988b). In search of new selves: Accommodating to widowhood. In L. A. Bond & B. M. Wagner (Eds.), *Families in transition: Primary prevention programs that work* (pp. 200–220). Newbury Park, CA: Sage.

Silverman, S. M., & Silverman, P. R. (1979). Parent–child communication in widowed families. *American Journal of Psychotherapy, 33*, 428–441.

Sinclair, I. A. S., Shaw, M., & Troop, J. (1974). The relationship between introversion and response to care work in a prison setting. *British Journal of Social and Clinical Psychology, 13*, 51–60.

Singh, B., & Raphael, B. (1981). Post-disaster morbidity of the bereaved: A possible role for preventive psychiatry. *Journal of Nervous and Mental Disease, 169*, 203–212.

Sireling, L., Cohen, D., & Marks, I. (1988). Guided mourning for morbid grief: A replication. *Behaviour Therapy, 29*, 121–132.

Smilansky, S. (1987). *On death: Helping children understand and cope.* New York: Peter Lang.

Smith, K. R. (1990). *Risk of mortality following widowhood: Sex differences between sudden and expected widowhood.* Paper presented at the 1990 annual meeting of the Society for Epidemiological Research, Birmingham, AL.

Smith, M. A., Davidson, J., Ritchie, J. C., Kudler, H., Lipper, S., Chappell, P., & Nemeroff, C. B. (1989). The corticotropin-releasing hormone test in patients with post-traumatic stress disorder. *Biologic Psychiatry, 26*, 349–355.

Smith, P. G., Kinlen, L. J., White, G. C., Adelstein, A. M., & Fox, A. J. (1980). Mortality of wives of men dying of cancer of the penis. *British Journal of Cancer, 41*, 422–428.

Snowdon, J., Solomons, R., & Druce, H. (1978). Feigned bereavement: Twelve cases. *International Journal of Psychiatry, 133*, 15–19.

Solomon, G. F., Levine, S., & Kraft, J. K. (1968). Early experience and immunity. *Nature, 220*, 821–822.

Souter, S. J., & Moore, T. E. (1989). A bereavement support program for survivors of cancer deaths: A description and evaluation. *Omega, 20*, 31–43.

Spiegelberg, H. L. (1974). Biological activities of immunoglobulins of different classes and subclasses. *Advances in Immunology, 19*, 259–270.

Spielberger, C., Gorsuch, R., & Lushene, R. (1970). *State-Trait Anxiety Manual.* Palo Alto, CA: Consulting Psychologists Press.

Spitzer, S., Couch, C., & Stratton, J. (1971). *The assessment of self.* Iowa City, IA: Sernoll.

Stein, Z., & Susser, M. (1969). Widowhood and mental illness. *British Journal of Preventive and Social Medicine, 23,* 106–110.

Stern, E. M. (1985). *Psychotherapy and the grieving patient.* New York: Haworth.

Sterns, H. L. (1986). Training and retraining adult and older adult workers. In J. E. Birren, P. K. Robinson, & J. E. Livingston (Eds.), *Age, health, and employment* (pp. 93–113). Englewood Cliffs, NJ: Prentice Hall.

Stroebe, M., & Stroebe, W. (1983). Who suffers more? Sex differences in health risks of the widowed. *Psychological Bulletin, 93,* 297–301.

(1985). Social support and the alleviation of loss. In I. G. Sarason & B. R. Sarason (Eds.), *Social support: Theory, research and applications* (pp. 439–462). Dordrecht: Martinus Nijhoff.

(1989). Who participates in bereavement research? A review and empirical study. *Omega, 20*(1), 1–29.

(1991). Does "grief work" work? *Journal of Consulting and Clinical Psychology, 59,* 479–482.

Stroebe, M. S., Stroebe, W., Gergen, K. J., & Gergen, M. (1981). The broken heart: Reality or myth? *Omega, 12,* 87–105.

Stroebe, M., Stroebe, W., & Hansson, R. O. (1988). Bereavement research: An historical introduction. *Journal of Social Issues, 44,* 1–18.

Stroebe, W., & Stroebe, M. (1987). *Bereavement and health.* New York: Cambridge University Press.

(1991). Partnerschaft, Familie und Wohlbefinden. In A. Abele-Brehm & P. Becker (Eds.), *Wohlbefinden: Theorie-Empirie-Diagnostik* (pp. 155–174). Weinheim/Munich: Juventa.

Stroebe, W., Stroebe, M. S., & Domittner, G. (1988). Individual and situational differences in recovery from bereavement: A risk group identified. *Journal of Social Issues, 44,* 143–158.

Stroebe, W., Stroebe, M. S., Gergen, K., & Gergen, M. (1980). Der Kummer Effekt: Psychologische Aspekte der Sterblichkeit von Verwitweten. *Psychologische Beiträge, 22,* 1–26.

(1982). The effects of bereavement on mortality: A social psychological analysis. In J. R. Eiser (Ed.), *Social psychology and behavioral medicine* (pp. 527–560). Chichester: Wiley.

Strom, T. D., Lundin, A. P., & Carpenter, C. B. (1977). Role of cyclic nucleotides in lymphocyte activation and function. *Progress in Clinical Immunology, 3,* 115–153.

Sullivan, J. L., Byron, K. S., Brewster, F. E., & Purtilo, D. T. (1980). Deficient natural killer activity in X-linked lymphoproliferative syndrome. *Science, 210,* 535–535.

Sundar, S. K., Cierpial, M. A., Kilts, C., Ritchie, J. C., & Weiss, J. M. (1990). Brain IL-1-induced immunosuppression occurs through activation of both pituitary–adrenal axis and sympathetic nervous system by corticotropin-releasing factor. *Journal of Neuroscience, 10*(11), 3701–3706.

Suomi, S. (1987). Genetic and maternal contributions to individual differences in rhesus monkey biobehavioral development. In *Perinatal development: A psychobiological perspective* (pp. 397–419). New York: Academic Press.

Super, D. E. (Ed.). (1974). *Measuring vocational maturity for counseling and evaluation.* Washington, DC: National Vocational Guidance Association.

Super, D. E., & Hall, D. T. (1978). Career development: Exploration and planning. *Annual Review of Psychology, 29,* 333–372.

Susser, M. (1981). Editorial: Widowhood: A situational life stress or a stressful life event? *American Journal of Public Health, 71,* 793–795.

Swann, W. B., Jr. (1987). Identity negotiation: Where two roads meet. *Journal of Personality and Social Psychology, 53,* 1038–1051.

Syvalahti, E., Eskola, J., Ruuskanen, O., & Laine, T. (1985). Nonsuppression of cortisol in depression and immune function. *Progress in Neuro-Psychopharmacology and Biological Psychiatry, 9*(4), 413–422.

Szasz, T. (1986). The case against suicide prevention. *American Psychologist, 41,* 806–812.

Tait, R., & Silver, R. C. (1989). Coming to terms with major negative life events. In J. S. Uleman & J. A. Bargh (Eds.), *Unintended thought* (pp. 351–382). New York: Guilford.

Tajfel, H. (1981). *Human groups and social categories.* Cambridge: Cambridge University Press.

Talal, N. (1980). Autoimmunity. In H. H. Fudenberg et al. (Eds.), *Basic and clinical immunology* (pp. 220–235). Los Altos, CA: Lane.

Tamir, G. (1987). *Functioning and attachment in war bereaved Israeli parents.* Unpublished M. A. thesis, University of Haifa (Hebrew).

Taylor, S. E., & Brown, J. D. (1988). Illusion and well-being: A social psychological perspective on mental health. *Psychological Bulletin, 103,* 193–210.

Tennant, C., Bebbington, P., & Hurry, J. (1980). Parental death in childhood and risk of adult depressive disorders: A review. *Psychosomatic Medicine, 10,* 289–299.

Thoits, P. A. (1983). Dimensions of life events that influence psychological distress: An evaluation and synthesis of the literature. In H. B. Kaplan (Ed.), *Psychological stress: Trends in theory and research.* New York: Academic Press.

(1985). Social support and psychological well-being: Theoretical possibilities. In I. G. Sarason & B. R. Sarason (Eds.), *Social support: Theory, research and applications* (pp. 51–72). Dordrecht: Martinus Nijhoff.

Thompson, L. W., Breckenridge, J. N., Gallagher, D., & Peterson, J. A. (1984). Effects of bereavement on self-perceptions of physical health in elderly widows and widowers. *Journal of Gerontology, 39,* 309–314.

Thompson, L. W., Gallagher, D., Cover, H., Gilewski, M., & Peterson, J. (1989). Effects of bereavement on symptoms of psychopathology in older men and women. In D. A. Lund (Ed.), *Older bereaved spouses: Research with practical applications* (pp. 17–24). New York: Taylor & Francis/Hemisphere.

Thompson, L. W., Gallagher-Thompson, D., Futterman, A., Gilewski, M. J., & Peterson, J. (1991). The effects of late-life spousal bereavement over a 30-month interval. *Psychology and Aging, 6,* 434–441.

Titus, S. L., Rosenblatt, P. C., & Anderson, R. M. (1979). Family conflict over inheritance of property. *Family Coordinator, 28,* 337–346.

Tolle, S. W., Bascom, P. B., Hickam, D. H., & Benson, J. A. (1986). Communication between physicians and surviving spouses following patient death. *Journal of General Internal Medicine, 1,* 309–314.

Trinchieri, G. (1989). Biology of natural killer cells. *Advances in Immunology, 47,* 187–376.

Uhde, T. W., Vittone, B. J., Siever, L. J., Kaye, W. H., & Post, R. M. (1986). Blunted growth hormone response to clonidine in panic disorder patients. *Biological Psychiatry, 21,* 1077–1081.

Umberson, D., Wortman, C. B., & Kessler, R. C. (1992). Widowhood and depression: Explaining long-term gender differences in vulnerability. *Journal of Health and Social Behavior, 33*, 10–24.

Urch, A., Muller, C., Aschaver, H., Resch, F., & Zidinski, C. C. (1988). Lytic effector cell function in schizophrenia and depression. *Journal of Neuroimmunology, 18*, 291–301.

U.S. Bureau of the Census. (1984). Current Population Reports, Series P-23, No. 138, *Demographic and Socioeconomic Aspects of Aging in the United States*. Washington, DC: U.S. Government Printing Office.

(1988). *Statistical Abstract of the United States* (108th ed., p. 40). Washington, DC: U.S. Government Printing Office.

U.S. Department of Health and Human Services, Public Health Service. (1985). *Vital statistics of the United States, 1985* (Vol. II, Mortality, Part B). Washington, DC.

Vachon, M. L. S. (1979). *Identity change over the first two years of bereavement: Social relationships and social support in bereavement*. Unpublished doctoral dissertation, York University, Toronto.

Vachon, M. L., Lyall, W. A., Rogers, J., Freedman-Letofsky, K., & Freeman, S. J. (1980a). A controlled study of self-help intervention for widows. *American Journal of Psychiatry, 137*, 1380–1384.

Vachon, M. L. S., Rogers, J., Lyall, W. A. L., Lancee, W. J., Sheldon, A. R., & Freeman, S. J. J. (1982a). Predictors and correlates of adaptation to conjugal bereavement. *American Journal of Psychiatry, 139*, 998–1002.

Vachon, M. L. S., Sheldon, A. R., Lancee, W. J., Lyall, W. A. L., Rogers, J. & Freeman, S. J. J. (1980b). A controlled study of self-help intervention for widows. *American Journal of Psychiatry, 137*, 1380–1384.

(1982b). Correlates of enduring distress in bereavement: Social network, life situation and personality. *Psychological Medicine, 12*, 783–788.

Vachon, M. L. S., & Stylianos, K. L. (1988). The role of social support in bereavement. *Journal of Social Issues, 44*, 175–190.

Vaillant, G. E. (1988). Attachment, loss and rediscovery. *Hillside Journal of Clinical Psychiatry, 10*, 148–169.

Valdes-Dapena, M. (1967). Sudden and unexpected death in infancy: A review of the world literature. *Pediatrics, 39*, 123–128.

VandeCreek, L. (1988). Sources of support in conjugal bereavement. *Hospice Journal, 4*, 81–92.

Van der Hart, O., & Goossens, F. A. (1987). Leave taking rituals in mourning therapy. *Israeli Journal Psychiatry and Related Sciences, 24*, 87–98.

Van der Hart, O., Brown, P., & Turco, R. N. (1990). Hypnotherapy for traumatic grief: Janetian and modern approaches integrated. *American Journal of Clinical Hypnosis, 32*, 263–271.

Van Eerdewegh, M., Bieri, M. D., Parilla, R. H., & Clayton, P. J. (1982). The bereaved child. *British Journal of Psychiatry, 140*, 23–29.

Van Gennep, A. (1909). *Les rites de passage*. (1960). English translation, *The rites of passage*. London: Routledge & Kegan Paul.

Van Zandt, S., Mou, R., & Abbott, R. (1989). Mental and physical health of rural bereaved and nonbereaved elders: A longitudinal study. In D. A. Lund (Ed.), *Older bereaved spouses: Research with practical applications* (pp. 25–35). New York: Hemisphere.

Veit, C. T., & Ware, J. E., Jr. (1983). The structure of psychological distress and well-being in general populations. *Journal of Consulting and Clinical Psychology, 51*, 730–742.

Videka-Sherman, L. (1982a). Coping with the death of a child: A study over time. *American Journal of Orthopsychiatry, 52*(4), 688–699.

Videka-Sherman, L. (1982b). The effects of participation in a self-help group for bereaved parents. *Prevention in the Human Services, 1,* 69–77.

Videka-Sherman, L., & Lieberman, M. A. (1985). The effects of self-help and psychotherapeutic intervention on child loss: The limits of recovery. *American Journal of Orthopsychiatry, 55,* 70–81.

Vingerhoets, A., & Van Heck, G. (1990). Gender and coping: Their relationship to symptoms (abstract). *Psychosomatic Medicine, 52,* 239.

Volkan, V. D. (1971). "Regrief" therapy. In G. Schoenberg, I. E. Gerber, A. Wiener, A. H. Kutscher, D. Peretz, & A. C. Carr (Eds.), *Bereavement: Its psychosocial aspects* (pp. 334–350). New York: Columbia University Press.

(1972). The recognition and prevention of pathological grief. *Virginia Medical Monthly, 99,* 535–540.

(1981). *Linking objects and linking phenomena.* New York: International Universities Press.

von Zerssen, D. (1976). *Die Beschwerdenliste BL.* Weinheim, West Germany: Beltz.

Wahl, C. W. (1970). The differential diagnosis of normal and neurotic grief following bereavement. *Psychosomatics, 11,* 104–106.

Wahlin, A., von Knorring, L., & Roos, G. (1984). Altered distribution of T lymphocyte subsets in lithium-treated patients. *Neuropsychobiology, 11,* 243.

Walker, K. N., MacBride, A., & Vachon, M. L. S. (1977). Social support networks and the crisis of bereavement. *Social Science and Medicine, 11,* 35–41.

Walls, N., & Meyers, A. W. (1985). Outcome in group treatments for bereavement: Experimental results and recommendations for clinical practice. *International Journal of Mental Health, 13,* 126–147.

Wallston, B. S., Alagna, S. W., DeVellis, B., & DeVellis, R. F. (1983). Social support and physical health. *Health Psychology, 2,* 367–391.

Walsh, F., & McGoldrick, M. (1988). Loss and the family life cycle. In C. Falikov (Ed.), *Family transitions* (pp. 311–336). New York: Guilford.

Ward, A. W. (1976). Mortality of bereavement. *British Medical Journal, 1,* 700–702.

Warner, S. (1987). A comparative study of widows' and widowers' perceived social support during the first year of bereavement. *Archives of Psychiatric Nursing, 1,* 241–250.

Weiner, H., Thaler, M., Reiser, M., & Mirsky, I. A. (1957). Etiology of duodenal ulcer. Relation of specific psychological characteristics to rate of gastric secretion. *Psychosomatic Medicine, 19,* 1–10.

Weiner, M. F. (1986). Homogeneous groups. In A. Frances & R. E. Hales (Eds.), *Annual Review* Vol. 5, pp. 714–728. Washington, DC: American Psychiatric Press.

Weisaeth, L. (1983). *The study of a factory fire.* Doctoral thesis, University of Oslo.

Weiss, R. S. (1973a). *Loneliness: The experience of emotional and social isolation.* Cambridge, MA: MIT Press.

(1973b). Helping relationships: Relationships with physicians, social workers, priests and others. *Social Problems, 20,* 319–328.

(1974). The provisions of social relationships. In Z. Rubin (Ed.), *Doing unto others: Joining, molding, conforming, helping, loving* (pp. 17–26). Englewood Cliffs, NJ: Prentice Hall.

(1975). *Marital separation.* New York: Basic Books.

(1982). Attachment in adults. In C. M. Parkes & J. Stevenson-Hinde (Eds.), *The place of attachment in human behavior* (pp. 171–184). New York: Basic Books.

(1987). Principles underlying a manual for parents whose children were killed by a drunk driver. *American Journal of Orthopsychiatry, 57,* 431–440.

Werner, E. E. (1989). Children of the garden island. *Scientific American,* 106–111.

Wethington, E., & Kessler, R. C. (1986). Perceived support, received support, and adjustment to stressful life events. *Journal of Health and Social Behavior, 27,* 78–89.

Wheaton, B. (1988, August). *When more stress is stress relief: Life events as the resolution of ongoing stress.* Paper presented at the Society for the Study of Social Problems Meeting, Atlanta.

White, R. W. (1974). Strategies of adaptation: An attempt at systematic descriptions. In G. V. Coelb, D. A. Hamburg, & J. E. Adams (Eds.), *Coping and adaptation* (pp. 47–68). New York: Basic Books.

Widdison, H. A., & Salisbury, H. G. (1990). The delayed stress syndrome: A pathological delayed grief reaction? *Omega, 20,* 293–306.

Wiener, S. G., Bayart, F., Faull, K. F., & Levine, S. (1990). Behavioral and physiological responses to maternal separation in squirrel monkeys (*Saimiri scuireus*). *Behavioral Neuroscience, 104,* 108–115.

Wikan, U. (1988). Bereavement and loss in two Muslim communities: Egypt and Bali compared. *Social Science and Medicine, 27,* 451–460.

(1990). *Managing turbulent hearts.* Chicago: University of Chicago Press.

Wilcox, B. L. (1981). Social support, life stress and psychological adjustment: A test of the buffering hypothesis. *American Journal of Community Psychology, 9,* 371–386.

Williams, J. M., & Felten, D. L. (1981). Sympathetic innervation of murine thymus and spleen: A comparative histofluorescence study. *Anatomical Record, 199,* 531–542.

Williams, L. T., Snyderman, R., & Lefkowitz, R. J. (1976). Identification of beta-adrenergic receptors in human lymphocytes by (-)3H-alprenolol binding. *Journal of Clinical Investigation, 57,* 149–155.

Williams, W. V., & Polak, P. R. (1979). Follow-up research in primary prevention: A model of adjustment to acute grief. *Journal of Clinical Psychology, 35*(1), 35–45.

Willis, S. L. (1985). Towards an educational psychology of the older adult learner: Intellectual and cognitive bases. In J. E. Birren & K. W. Schaie (Eds.), *Handbook of the psychology of aging* (2nd ed. pp. 818–847). New York: Van Nostrand Reinhold.

Windholz, M. J., Marmar, C. R., & Horowitz, M. (1985). A review of the research on conjugal bereavement: Impact on health and efficacy of intervention. *Comprehensive Psychiatry, 26,* 433–437.

Winget, C., & Kramer, M. (1979). *Dimensions of dreams.* Gainesville: University Press of Florida.

Winnik, H. Z. (1967). Further comments concerning problems of late psychopathological effects of Nazi persecution and their therapy. *Israeli Annals of Psychiatry, 5,* 1–16.

Winokur, A., Amsterdam, J., & Caroff, S. (1982). Variability of hormonal responses to a series of neuroendocrine challenges in depressed patients. *American Journal of Psychiatry, 139,* 39–44.

Wolff, C. T., Friedman, S. B., Hofer, M. A., & Mason, J. W. (1964a). Relationship between psychological defenses and mean urinary 17-hydroxycorticosteroid excretion rates. I. A predictive study of parents of fatally ill children. *Psychosomatic Medicine, 26,* 576–591.

Wolff, C. T., Hofer, M. A., & Mason, J. W. (1964b). Relationship between psychological defenses and mean urinary 17-hydroxycorticosteroid excretion rates. II. Methodologic and theoretical considerations. *Psychosomatic Medicine*, *26*, 592–609.

Woods, S. W., Charney, D. S., McPherson, C. A., Gradman, A. H., & Heninger, G. R. (1987). Situational panic attacks. *Archives of General Psychiatry*, *44*, 365–375.

Worden, J. W. (1982/1991). *Grief counseling and grief therapy: A handbook for the mental health practitioner*. New York: Springer.

Wortman, C. B. (1983). Coping with victimization: Conclusions and implications for future research. *Journal of Social Issues*, *39*(2), 197–223.

Wortman, C. B., & Bolger, N. (1988). *Life course timing, degree of forewarning, and adjustment to widowhood*. Paper presented at the 41st annual meeting of the Gerontological Society of America, San Francisco.

Wortman, C., & Brehm, J. (1975). Responses to uncontrollable outcomes. In L. Berkowitz (Ed.), *Advances in experimental social psychology* (Vol. 8, pp. 277–336). New York: Academic Press.

Wortman, C. B., Kessler, R., Bolger, N., & House, J. (1992). *The time course of adjustment to widowhood: Evidence from a national probability sample*. Manuscript submitted for publication.

Wortman, C. B., & Lehman, D. R. (1985). Reactions to victims of life crisis: Support attempts that fail. In I. G. Sarason & B. R. Sarason (Eds.), *Social support: Theory, research and applications* (pp. 463–489). Dordrecht: Martinus Nijhoff.

Wortman, C. B., & Silver, R. C. (1987). Coping with irrevocable loss. In G. R. Vandenbos & B. K. Bryant (Eds.), *Cataclysms, crises, and catastrophes: Psychology in action* (pp. 189–235). Washington, DC: American Psychological Association.

(1989). The myths of coping with loss. *Journal of Consulting and Clinical Psychology*, *57*, 349–357.

(1990). Successful mastery of bereavement and widowhood: A life course perspective. In P. B. Baltes & M. M. Baltes (Eds.), *Successful aging: Perspectives from the behavioral sciences* (pp. 225–264). New York: Cambridge University Press.

Wright, S. E., & Rosenblatt, P. C. (1987). Isolation and farm loss: Why neighbors may not be supportive. *Family Relations*, *36*, 391–395.

Wrobliski, A., & McIntosh, J. L. (1987). Problems of suicide survivors: A survey report. *Israeli Journal of Psychiatry and Related Sciences*, *24*, 137–142.

Wyler, A. R., Masuda, M., & Holmes, T. H. (1968). Seriousness of illness rating scale. *Journal of Psychosomatic Research*, *11*, 363–374.

Yalom, I., & Lieberman, M. A. (in press). Spousal bereavement and heightened existential awareness. *Psychiatry*.

Yesavage, J. A., Brink, T. L., Rose, R. L., Lum, O., Huang, V., Adey, M., & Leirer, V. O. (1983). Development and validation of a geriatric depression screening scale: A preliminary report. *Journal of Psychiatric Research*, *17*, 37–49.

Young, M., Benjamin, B., & Wallis, C. (1963). Mortality of widowers. *Lancet*, *2*, 254–256.

Youniss, J. (1980). *Parents and peers in social development: A Piagetian–Sullivan perspective*. Chicago: University of Chicago Press.

Zautra, A. J., Guarnaccia, C. A., & Reich, J. W. (1988). Factor structure of mental health measures for older adults. *Journal of Consulting and Clinical Psychology*, *56*, 514–519.

Zilberg, N. J., Weiss, D. S., & Horowitz, M. J. (1982). Impact of event scale: A cross-validation study and some empirical evidence supporting a conceptual model of stress response syndromes. *Journal of Consulting and Clinical Psychology*, *50*, 407–414.

Zinkernagel, R. M., & Doherty, P. C. (1979). MHC-restricted cytotoxic T cells: Studies on the biological role of polymorphic major transplantation antigens determining T-cell restriction-specificity, function, and responsiveness. *Advances in Immunology* (pp. 51–177). New York: Academic Press.

Zisook, S. (Ed.). (1987). *Biopsychosocial aspects of bereavement*. Washington, DC: American Psychiatric Press.

Zisook, S., & DeVaul, R. A. (1977). Grief related facsimile illness. *International Journal of Psychiatry and Medicine*, *7*, 329–336.

(1983). Grief, unresolved grief, and depression. *Psychosomatics*, *24*, 247–256.

(1985). Unresolved grief. *American Journal of Psychoanalysis*, *45*, 370–379.

Zisook, S., DeVaul, R. A., & Click, M. A. (1982). Measuring symptoms of grief and bereavement. *American Journal of Psychiatry*, *139*, 1590–1593.

Zisook, S., & Lyons, L. (1990). Bereavement and unresolved grief in psychiatric outpatients. *Omega*, *20*, 307–322.

Zisook, S., Mulvihill, M., & Shuchter, S. R. (1990). Widowhood and anxiety. *Psychiatric Medicine*, *8*(4).

Zisook, S., & Shuchter, S. R. (1985). Time course of spousal bereavement. *General Hospital Psychiatry*, *7*, 95–100.

(1986). The first four years of widowhood. *Psychiatric Annals*, *15*, 288–294.

Zisook, S., Shuchter, S. R., & Lyons, L. E. (1987). Adjustment to widowhood. In S. Zisook (Ed.), *Biopsychosocial aspects of bereavement* (pp. 51–74). Washington, DC: American Psychiatric Press.

Zisook, S., Shuchter, S. R., & Schuckit, M. (1985). Factors in the persistence of unresolved grief among psychiatric outpatients. *Psychosomatics*, *26*, 497–503.

Zung, W. (1965). A self-rating depression scale. *Archives of General Psychiatry*, *12*, 63–70.

Author index

525

Subject index

accidental death, *see* causes of death;
    mortality of bereavement; risk factors in
    bereavement outcome; type of death/loss
age, *see* risk factors in bereavement outcome
AIDS (acquired immunodeficiency
    syndrome) and bereavement following
    death from AIDS, 14–15, 317–30, 459,
    471
    and AIDS-related complex (ARC), 323
    and anxiety, 326, 329
    denial of, 321
    epidemiology of, 322–3
    and Impact Project, 318
    and social support for caregivers, 321
    stigma of, 322, 330
    and survivor guilt, 321
alcohol consumption in bereavement, 37, 43,
    325–6
ambivalent relationships, *see* conjugal
    bereavement; relationship with/feelings
    toward deceased; risk factors in
    bereavement outcome
anger/aggression in bereavement, 27, 28,
    104, 307
animal studies of separation/loss, 9–10,
    129–42
anticipatory grief/loss, 220–1, 263, 320
anxiety in bereavement reactions, 27, 29, 37,
    326, 329
anxiety disorders, 148–50, 449–50
    in relation to pathological grief, 54, 449–50
assessment/measurement of grief reactions,
    5–6, 62–74, 244, 255, 460
    and aging/measurement issues, 70
    clinical, 6, 429–34
    and construct validity, 59–60, 62–3, 68
    cross-cultural issues in (*see also* cultural
    patterns/differences in bereavement
    reactions), 72
    family system, 73
    grief inventories/measures as (*see also entries
    for specific measures*), 63–5, 244, 255
    intervention efficacy of, *see* grief

intervention
    multidimensional, 26–42, 66–7, 290–2,
    299, 462–3
    of recovery (*see also* recovery), 68
    of symptomatology (*see also* grief), 62–74
attachment (*see also* health consequences of
    bereavement; risk factors in bereavement
    outcome; theories of/applied to grief),
    34–6, 271–84
    bond, 274–6, 287–8

bereavement (*see also* health consequences of
    bereavement; risk factors in bereavement
    outcome; type of death/loss)
    definition of, 5, 319–20
    and immunity, 164–71
    as life stressor, *see* stress/trauma of
    bereavement; stressful life events (SLEs)
    psychiatric complications of, 10, 143–4,
    445–51
    theory, *see* theories of/applied to grief
bereavement research overview, 3–19,
    457–75
    historical changes in, 5
biological mechanisms (*see also* physiological
    changes in bereavement), 9–10, 129–42,
    143–59, 160–71, 458
broken heart, 193–4, 219
buffering hypothesis, 222–3

cancer
    and care needs of terminally ill, 97
    as cause of death of bereaved, 177, 186–7
    and late-stage course of illness, 97
cardiovascular/coronary heart diseases
    as cause of death of bereaved, 177, 186
causes of death (*see also* mortality of
    bereavement; risk factors in bereavement
    outcome; *entries for specific causes*)
    of bereaved persons, 177, 186–8
    and relative excesses for widowed, by
    cause, 177